D1480548

Social Work in Mental Health

Social Work in Mental Health

An Evidence-Based Approach

Edited by
Bruce A. Thyer
and
John S. Wodarski

John Wiley & Sons, Inc.

This book is printed on acid-free paper. ♾

Copyright © 2007 by John Wiley & Sons, Inc. All rights reserved.

Published by John Wiley & Sons, Inc., Hoboken, New Jersey.

Published simultaneously in Canada.

No part of this publication may be reproduced, stored in a retrieval system, or transmitted in any form or by any means, electronic, mechanical, photocopying, recording, scanning, or otherwise, except as permitted under Section 107 or 108 of the 1976 United States Copyright Act, without either the prior written permission of the Publisher, or authorization through payment of the appropriate per-copy fee to the Copyright Clearance Center, Inc., 222 Rosewood Drive, Danvers, MA 01923, (978) 750-8400, fax (978) 646-8600, or on the web at www.copyright.com. Requests to the Publisher for permission should be addressed to the Permissions Department, John Wiley & Sons, Inc., 111 River Street, Hoboken, NJ 07030, (201) 748-6011, fax (201) 748-6008, or online at http://www.wiley.com/go/permissions.

Limit of Liability/Disclaimer of Warranty: While the publisher and author have used their best efforts in preparing this book, they make no representations or warranties with respect to the accuracy or completeness of the contents of this book and specifically disclaim any implied warranties of merchantability or fitness for a particular purpose. No warranty may be created or extended by sales representatives or written sales materials. The advice and strategies contained herein may not be suitable for your situation. You should consult with a professional where appropriate. Neither the publisher nor author shall be liable for any loss of profit or any other commercial damages, including but not limited to special, incidental, consequential, or other damages.

This publication is designed to provide accurate and authoritative information in regard to the subject matter covered. It is sold with the understanding that the publisher is not engaged in rendering professional services. If legal, accounting, medical, psychological or any other expert assistance is required, the services of a competent professional person should be sought.

Designations used by companies to distinguish their products are often claimed as trademarks. In all instances where John Wiley & Sons, Inc. is aware of a claim, the product names appear in initial capital or all capital letters. Readers, however, should contact the appropriate companies for more complete information regarding trademarks and registration.

For general information on our other products and services please contact our Customer Care Department within the United States at (800) 762-2974, outside the United States at (317) 572-3993 or fax (317) 572-4002.

Wiley also publishes its books in a variety of electronic formats. Some content that appears in print may not be available in electronic books. For more information about Wiley products, visit our web site at www.wiley.com.

Library of Congress Cataloging-in-Publication Data:

Social work and mental health : an evidence-based approach / Bruce A. Thyer and John S. Wodarski, editors
    p.   cm.
  Includes bibliographical references and index.
  ISBN-13: 978-0-471-69304-8 (cloth)
  ISBN-10: 0-471-69304-9 (cloth)
 1. Psychiatric social work. 2. Evidence-based social work. I. Thyer, Bruce A. II. Wodarski, John S.
  HV689.S638   2007
  362.2′ 0425—dc22

                                              2006009509

Printed in the United States of America.

10 9 8 7 6 5 4 3 2 1

The editors lovingly dedicate this book to our spouses,
Laura Lynn Myers and Lois Ann Wodarski.

Chapter 3

Autistic Disorder   53
Claire J. Calohan and Colin M. Peeler

Chapter 4

Attention-Deficit/Hyperactivity Disorder   75
David R. Dupper and Joy B. Musick

Chapter 5

Conduct Disorder   97
Carolyn Hilarski

PART II

Substance-Related Disorders   **155**

Chapter 8

PART IV
Mood Disorders   287

Chapter 13

Major Depressive Disorder   289
*Michael J. Holosko, Nansy Jean-Baptiste, Trang Le, Allison Eaton,
and Lisa Power*

Chapter 14

PART V

Chapter 15

Part VI

Sexual Disorders   **401**

Chapter 18

Sexual Desire and Arousal Disorders   **403**
*Sophia F. Dziegielewski, Barbara F. Turnage, Gary Dick, and
Cheryl Resnick-Cortes*

Chapter 19

Orgasmic Disorders   **427**
*Sophia F. Dziegielewski, George Jacinto, Gary Dick, and
Cheryl Resnick-Cortes*

Part VII

Eating Disorders   **457**

*Chapter 20*_____

**Anorexia Nervosa, Bulimia Nervosa, and Binge
Eating Disorder**   **459**
Laura L. Myers

Part VIII

Chapter 21

Kia J. Bentley
School of Social Work
Virginia Commonwealth University
Richmond, Virginia

Patrick S. Bordnick
School of Social Work
University of Georgia
Athens, Georgia

A. Suzanne Boyd
Department of Social Work
University of North Carolina at Charlotte
Charlotte, North Carolina

Claire J. Calohan
College of Social Work
Florida State University
Panama City, Florida

Hilary L. Copp
School of Social Work
University of Georgia
Athens, Georgia

Gary Dick
School of Social Work
University of Cincinnati
Cincinnati, Ohio

Catherine N. Dulmus
School of Social Work
State University of New York at Buffalo
Buffalo, New York

David R. Dupper
College of Social Work
University of Tennessee
Knoxville, Tennessee

Sophia F. Dziegielewski
School of Social Work
University of Cincinnati
Cincinnati, Ohio

Allison Eaton
Department of Social Work
University of Windsor
Windsor, Ontario, Canada

Daniel J. Fischer
Department of Psychiatry
University of Michigan Health Systems
Ann Arbor, Michigan

John Gerdtz
Special Education Program
  School of Education
St. Mary's College of California
Moraga, California

Susan Gerdtz
Early Intervention Program
Easter Seals of the Bay Area
Oakland, California

Carolyn Hilarski
Department of Social Work
State University of New York at Buffalo
Buffalo, New York

Joseph A. Himle
Department of Psychiatry
University of Michigan Medical Center
Ann Arbor, Michigan

Michael J. Holosko
School of Social Work
University of Georgia
Athens, Georgia

Lindsay Homesley
College of Social Work
University of Tennessee
Knoxville, Tennessee

Laura Hopson
School of Social Work
University of Texas
Austin, Texas

Bruce M. Hyman
The OCD Resource Center of Florida
Hollywood, Florida

André Ivanoff
Columbia University
School of Social Work
New York, New York
and
University of Washington
Department of Psychology
Seattle, Washington

George Jacinto
School of Social Work
University of Central Florida
Orlando, Florida

Nansy Jean-Baptiste
Department of Psychology
University of Windsor
Windsor, Ontario Canada

Trang Le
Department of Psychology
University of Windsor
Windsor, Ontario Canada

Laura M. Lokers
Department of Psychiatry
University of Michigan Medical Center
Ann Arbor, Michigan

Kimberly J. Long
College of Social Work
University of Tennessee
Knoxville, Tennessee

Jennifer Manuel
School of Social Work
Columbia University
New York, New York

Irma A. Molina
College of Social Work
University of Tennessee
Knoxville, Tennessee

Joy B. Musick
Middle Tennessee Mental Health
  Institute
Knoxville, Tennessee

Laura L. Myers
Department of Social Work
Thomas University
Thomasville, Georgia

Colin M. Peeler
Behavior Solutions, Inc.
O'Fallon, Missouri

Lisa Power
Department of Social Work
University of Windsor
Windsor, Ontario, Canada

Melissa Radey
College of Social Work
Florida State University
Tallahassee, Florida

Lisa A. Rapp-Paglicci
School of Social Work
University of South Florida at Lakeland
Lakeland, Florida

Cheryl Resnick-Cortes
School of Social Work
University of Central Florida
Orlando, Florida

Henry Schmidt III
Behavioral Affiliates, Inc.
Seattle, Washington
and
Washington State Juvenile Rehabilitation
Administration
Olympia, Washington

Nancy J. Smyth
School of Social Work
State University of New York at Buffalo
Buffalo, New York

Gail Steketee
School of Social Work
Boston University
Boston, Massachusetts

Charles D. Syms
School of Social Work
State University of New York at Buffalo
Buffalo, New York

Melissa Floyd Taylor
Department of Social Work
University of North Carolina at
   Greensboro
Greensboro, North Carolina

Matthew T. Theriot
College of Social Work
University of Tennessee
Knoxville, Tennessee

Bruce A. Thyer
College of Social Work
Florida State University
Tallahassee, Florida

Barbara F. Turnage
School of Social Work
University of Central Florida
Orlando, Florida

Barbara Van Noppen
Department of Psychiatry and Human
   Behavior
Brown University
Providence, Rhode Island

Joseph Walsh
School of Social Work
Virginia Commonwealth University
Richmond, Virginia

John S. Wodarski
College of Social Work
University of Tennessee
Knoxville, Tennessee

About a decade ago we edited the two-volume *Handbook of Empirical Social Work Practice* (Thyer & Wodarski, 1998; Wodarski & Thyer, 1998). These two volumes were explicitly dedicated to providing comprehensive reviews of the existing quality research that addressed empirically based approaches to the assessment and psychosocial treatment of a variety of mental disorders and other problems experienced by clients often seen by social workers. At that time (the late 1990s), the term *evidence-based practice* (EBP) had barely entered the social work lexicon, being apparently introduced to our field in a landmark paper by Eileen Gambrill (1999) and a less well-known but compelling article by social worker Geraldine Macdonald (1998). There have been remarkable developments since that time, leading us to prepare the present book more clearly aligned with this new perspective.

We recently conducted a literature search of the PsycINFO database, using the terms "social work" and "evidence-based practice" as keywords. We found only 3 hits in 1999, 3 in 2000, 14 in 2001, 22 in 2002, 20 in 2003, 46(!) in 2004, 32 in 2005, and 18 as of mid-July 2006. This indicates that the field of evidence-based social work has grown markedly in less than half a decade, so much so that in 2004 one of us (JSW) cofounded the *Journal of Evidence-Based Social Work* to help further promote the field. Moreover a number of social work books on the topic of EBP have appeared, for example, Corcoran (2000, 2003), Cournoyer (2004), Gibbs (2003), O'Hare (2005), Pritchard (2006), Roberts and Yeager (2004, 2006), Smith (2004), Sommerfeld and Herzog (2005), Springer, McNeece, and Arnold (2003), Thyer and Kazi (2004), and Wodarski and Dziegielewski (2002). The interest in EBP shows no signs of abating.

Although it would be incorrect to label EBP as old wine in new bottles, it clearly had several professional precursors both within and outside of the field of social work. For example, a number of authors have long argued that social workers could profitably integrate simple research methods into their practice to help in empirically evaluating their outcomes (e.g., Wodarski, 1981, 1997). Others have stressed the role of critical thinking skills and the systematic appraisal of research evidence to judge the credibility and validity of claims made relating to the effectiveness of social work treatments (e.g., Gambrill, 1990, 2005). Another predecessor was the assertion that social workers are ethically obliged to offer their clients social work interventions with the greatest degree of empirical support, as first-choice treatments, prior to offering treatments with weaker levels of support, assuming the intervention was otherwise a suitable match for the client and situation (e.g., Myers & Thyer, 1997; Thyer, 1995). The emergence of a sufficient body of scientific research to credibly support claims that a given intervention was helpful to clients with particular problems, and indeed that certain treatments were actually superior to others in this regard (see Hibbs & Jensen, 2005; Nathan & Gorman, 2002), was another essential foundation. A further supportive development was the rapid growth of empirically based practice guidelines for various disorders in the health care field, including mental health. This received attention in the field of social work through a special issue of the journal *Research on Social Work Practice* (Howard & Jensen, 1999) and a thorough book-length treatment by Rosen and Proctor (2003).

One prestigious program, the George Warren Brown School of Social Work at Washington University, has explicitly adopted evidence-based practice as the central framework of its didactic MSW curriculum and field instruction (Edmonds, Rochman, Megivern, Howard, & Williams, 2006; Howard, McMillen, & Pollio, 2003). Other programs appear to be moving in a similar direction. For example, the Department of Social Policy and Social Work at the University of Oxford in the United Kingdom now offers the MA and doctorate (DPhil) in evidence-based interventions. Of course, the soil of social work was well prepared to receive this confluence of developments, because from the very beginnings of our field we have prided ourselves on being more than friendly visitors with kind hearts and a handout. For example, social work was defined as

> *all voluntary efforts to extend benefits which are made in response to a need, are concerned with social relationships, and avail themselves of* scientific knowledge and methods. (*Cheney, 1926, p. 24*, emphasis added)

Further,

> *Employment of* scientifically approved and tested techniques *will ensure the profession the confidence and respect of clients and the public, for increasingly the social casework process will operate more certainly for known and desired ends in the area of social adjustment. (Strode, 1940, p. 142,* emphasis added)

As will be seen in the first chapter, these sentiments and many others like them are defining features of genuinely *professional* social work services.

We view this emergence of evidence-based practice with some gratification as it has the promise to create a more helpful and effective cadre of social workers providing services to clients in need. In the early part of the twentieth century, the Carnegie Foundation for the Advancement of Teaching commissioned Abraham Flexner to undertake a comprehensive review of medical education in the United States and Canada and to make recommendations regarding the improvement of these programs. He found that many medical schools had poorly qualified faculty, with substandard facilities and meager entrance requirements, and included teaching about many fringe or bogus treatments (e.g., homeopathy, naturopathy, chiropractic, magnetic healing). Flexner's (1910) report proved to be enormously influential; as a result of his analysis, marginal medical schools were closed down, academic standards tightened up, and fringe therapies excluded, accompanied by a dramatic increase in science-based instruction. The principles of evidence-based practice have the potential to exert a similar cleansing and leavening influence within social work education. We can but hope.

We are aware of some of the limitations of this model and share some of the concerns articulated by those honest voices truly seeking clarity amid some confusion, those legitimately interested in probing the applications and limits of EBP. We have little patience, however, with postmodernist pseudo-philosophers of science within social work who raise spurious arguments and specious objections based on a second- or third-hand misreading of the primary EBP literature, or the deliberate portrayal of EBP as evil incarnate, secondary to their objections to the better integration of science and social work (see Gibbs & Gambrill, 2002). To those who try to use philosophy and rhetoric to confuse and obfuscate, to further some postmodernist agenda that hinders the true intellectual and scientific development of our field, to those who cling to falsified theories and ineffective or harmful practices, we echo the words of Oliver Cromwell addressing the British Rump Parliament: "You have sat too long for any good you have been doing. Depart I say, and let us have done with you. In the name of God, go!"

We offer the present volume as a resource to social work professionals active in the field of mental health practice. Social workers are the largest group of providers of mental health services in the United States, and EBP is more fully developed in this area than in others. We both note and regret this temporary lacuna and look with anticipation to the continuing expansion of the principles of EBP to other, nonclinical areas of social work practice, up to and including community and policy-oriented practice (see Brownson, Baker, Leet, & Gillespie, 2003; Davies, 2004; Davies, Nutley, & Smith, 2000; Ohmer & Korr, 2006; Wodarski & Thyer, 1998). Organizations such as Social Programs that Work (www.evidencebasedprograms.org), the Coalition for

Evidence-Based Policy (http://coexgov.securesites.net/index.php
?keyword=a432fbc34d71c7), the California Evidence-Based Clearinghouse for Child Welfare (www.cachildwelfareclearinghouse
.org), the Juvenile Justice Evaluation Center's listing of evidence-
based programs (www.jrsa.org/jjec/resources/evidencebased
.html), and the British-based Social Care Institute for Excellence
(www.scie.org.uk) all represent not-so-embryonic efforts to ex-
trapolate EBP to the world of macrolevel practice and should
mute the plaintive objections that EBP has possible applications
only to clinical practice, or that social workers with larger-scale
interests have little to glean from this new model.

We also share the reservations of some of our colleagues regarding the appropriateness of structuring a book like this
around the conceptual framework of the *Diagnostic and Statistical
Manual of Mental Disorders,* a.k.a. the *DSM.* It is undeniable that
many social work clients display serious and problematic aberra-
tions in behavior and speech and report disturbing thoughts and
affective states, yet the legitimacy of construing the etiology of
these behaviors as residing in the *mind* of these individuals is
often open to question theoretically, philosophically, and empirically. We ourselves are more persuaded of the value of a genuine person-in-environment perspective, which avoids the
Cartesian dualism so rampant in contemporary psychiatry that
postulates that either a disordered biology or a disordered mind
causes folks to act in odd ways. We look forward to the time
when this simplistic perspective is done away with in favor of an
orientation more clearly related to natural science and absolved
of metaphysical elements (see Thyer, 2006; Wodarski, 1977).
Meanwhile, does the *DSM* possess serious problems in terms of
its reliability and construct validity? Yes, of course. But it nevertheless remains the major conceptual framework by which behavioral disorders are organized, and we believe that structuring
the present volume along this widely used nosological system
continues to be a useful approach.

We are also keenly aware that a very large number of
conditions found in the *DSM* could not be included in this
book. This reflects neither our disinterest nor dismissal of these
other disorders as trivial or unimportant. It is solely a function of
the page limitations inherent in any book, and we regret the
omissions.

We extend our sincere gratitude to the contributors to this
book, who devoted so much time and talent to the preparation of
their chapter. We hope that they, and you the reader, find the end
product to be worthwhile.

BRUCE A. THYER, MSW, PHD
JOHN S. WODARSKI, MSW, PHD

References

Brownson, R. C., Baker, E. A., Leet, T. L., & Gillespie, K. N. (2003). *Evidence-based public health.* New York: Oxford University Press.

Cheney, A. (1926). *The nature and scope of social work.* New York: D. C. Heath.

Corcoran, J. (2000). *Evidence-based social work practice with families.* New York: Springer.

Corcoran, J. (2003). *Clinical applications of evidence-based family interventions.* New York: Oxford University Press.

Cournoyer, B. R. (2004). *The evidence-based social work skills book.* Boston: Allyn & Bacon.

Davies, P. (2004, February 19). *Is evidence-based government possible?* Paper presented at the 4th annual Campbell Collaboration Colloquium, Washington, DC.

Davies, P., Nutley, S. M., & Smith, P. C. (2000). *What works? Evidence-based policy and practice in public services.* Bristol, England: Policy Press.

Edmonds, T., Rochman, E., Megivern, D., Howard, M., & Williams, C. (2006). Integrating evidence-based practice and social work field instruction. *Journal of Social Work Education, 42,* 377–396.

Flexner, A. (1910). *Medical education in the United States and Canada.* New York: Carnegie Foundation for the Advancement of Teaching.

Gambrill, E. (1990). *Critical thinking in clinical practice.* San Francisco: Jossey-Bass.

Gambrill, E. (1999). Evidence-based practice: An alternative to authority-based practice. *Families in Society, 80,* 341–350.

Gambrill, E. (2005). *Critical thinking in clinical practice* (2nd ed.). Hoboken, NJ: Wiley.

Gibbs, L. E. (2003). *Evidence-based practice for the helping professions.* Pacific Grove, CA: Brooks/Cole.

Gibbs, L. E., & Gambrill, E. (2002). Evidence-based practice: Counterarguments to objections. *Research on Social Work Practice, 12,* 452–476.

Hibbs, E. D., & Jensen, P. S. (Eds.). (2005). *Psychosocial treatments for child and adolescent disorders: Empirically based strategies for clinical practice* (2nd ed.). Washington, DC: American Psychological Association.

Howard, M. O., & Jensen, J. (Eds.). (1999). Practice guidelines and clinical social work [Special issue]. *Research on Social Work Practice, 9*(3).

Howard, M. O., McMillen, C. J., & Pollio, D. E. (2003). Teaching evidence-based practice: Toward a new paradigm for social work education. *Research on Social Work Practice, 13,* 234–259.

Macdonald, G. (1998). Promoting evidence-based practice in child protection. *Clinical Child Psychology and Psychiatry, 3*(1), 71–85.

Myers, L. L., & Thyer, B. A. (1997). Should social work clients have the right to effective treatment? *Social Work, 42,* 288–298.

Nathan, P. E., & Gorman, J. M. (Eds.). (2002). *A guide to treatments that work* (2nd ed.). New York: Oxford University Press.

O'Hare, T. (2005). *Evidence-based practices for social workers.* Chicago: Lyceum Books.

Ohmer, M. L., & Korr, W. S. (2006). The effectiveness of community practice interventions: A review of the literature. *Research on Social Work Practice, 16,* 132–145.

Pritchard, C. (2006). *Mental health social work: Evidence-based practice.* New York: Routledge.

Roberts, A. R., & Yeager, K. R. (Eds.). (2004). *Evidence-based practice manual.* New York: Oxford University Press.

Roberts, A. R., & Yeager, K. R. (Eds.). (2006). *Foundations of evidence-based social work practice.* New York: Oxford University Press.

Rosen, A., & Proctor, E. K. (Eds.). (2003). *Developing practice guidelines for social work interventions: Issues, methods, and research agenda.* New York: Columbia University Press.

Smith, D. (Ed.). (2004). *Social work and evidence-based practice.* Philadelphia: Jessica Kingsley.

Sommerfeld, P., & Herzog, P. (2005). *Evidence-based social work: Towards a new professionalism?* New York: Peter J. Lang.

Springer, D. W., McNeece, C. A., & Arnold, E. M. (2003). *Substance abuse treatment for criminal offenders: An evidence-based guide for practitioners.* Washington, DC: American Psychological Association.

Strode, J. (1940). *Introduction to social casework.* New York: Harper and Brothers.

Thyer, B. A. (1995). Promoting an empiricist agenda within the human services: An ethical and humanistic imperative. *Journal of Behavior Therapy and Experimental Psychiatry, 26,* 93–98.

Thyer, B. A. (2006). It is time to rename the *DSM. Ethical Human Psychology and Psychiatry, 8,* 61–67.

Thyer, B. A., & Kazi, M. A. F. (Eds.). (2004). *International perspectives on evidence-based practice in social work.* Birmingham, England: Venture Press.

Thyer, B. A., & Wodarski, J. S. (Eds.). (1998). *Handbook of empirical social work practice: Vol. I. Mental disorders.* New York: Wiley.

Wodarski, J. S. (1977). Anti-social children and labeling theory: A methodological critique. *Corrective and Social Psychiatry, 23*(4), 122–128.

Wodarski, J. S. (1981). *The role of research in clinical practice.* Baltimore: University Park Press.

Wodarski, J. S. (1997). *Research methods for clinical social workers: Empirical practice.* New York: Springer.

Wodarski, J. S., & Dziegielewski, S. (Eds.). (2002). *Human behavior and the social environment: Integrating theory and evidence-based practice.* New York: Springer.

Wodarski, J. S., & Thyer, B. A. (Eds.). (1998). *Handbook of empirical social work practice: Vol. 2. Psychosocial problems and practice issues.* New York: Wiley.

Evidence-Based Social Work: An Overview

Bruce A. Thyer

1

Chapter

Learning Objectives

After reading this chapter, the reader will be able to:

- Understand the philosophical foundations undergirding the approach called evidence-based practice.
- Be able to articulate the major steps involved in the process of conducting evidence-based practice.
- Be able to describe the strengths and limitations of a scientific orientation to social work practice.
- Be able to locate valid sources of information regarding the effectiveness of various psychosocial interventions and methods of assessment suitable for applications to social work.

Overview of the Problem

The focus of this book is empirical research that has direct applications to social work practice and informs evidence-based practice. It is always useful to begin by defining one's terms, and in turning to the *Social Work Dictionary* (Barker, 2003, p. 141), we find that the word *empirical* means "based on direct observation or experience" and that *empirically based practice* is defined as:

> *A type of* intervention *in which the professional social worker uses research as a practice and problem-solving tool; collects data*

systematically to monitor the intervention; specifies problems, techniques, and outcomes in measurable terms; and systematically evaluates the effectiveness of the intervention used.

On the face of it, this description seems quite reasonable. Indeed, should it not be characteristic of *all* of social work practice? Well, the issues are more complicated. For example, some areas of social work practice suffer from a lack of ways to measure the phenomena of interest (which makes data gathering problematic). Others are more value based, such as the advocacy of pro-choice laws pertaining to abortion rights or of the rights of gays and lesbians to legally marry. Empirical research is not a particularly salient argument in such discussions.

Even more fundamentally, the very term *empirical* has been subjected to differing interpretations. For some, it means something to the effect of "If I can see it, it is real." Hence, if I can see improvement in my clients, then I can be pretty sure they are indeed getting better, and you should take my word for this. A problem with this approach is that sometimes individuals (e.g., social work practitioners, and even clients) can be deceived. The history of quack medicine and the explanations for ghosts, crop circles, flying saucers, and extrasensory perception demonstrate how easy it is for well-educated, informed, and even skeptical persons to unintentionally deceive themselves or to be intentionally deceived by the unscrupulous. And, to be fair, so does the history of science: Witness the discovery in 1989 of so-called cold fusion, or the revelations of fraud in the publication of revolutionary advances in cloning research.

Additional safeguards are necessary, beyond the level of personal observation, for a finding to be considered to be empirical. For example, Arkava and Lane (1983, p. 11) claim, "Empiricism is the process of using evidence rooted in objective reality and gathered systematically as a basis for generating human knowledge." Here the key word is *systematic,* which implies a method of observation that can be reliably communicated to others, who, in turn, can undertake essentially the same method of observation.

Grinnell (1993, p. 442) adds another dimension to the definition of empirical as *"knowledge* derived from observation, experience, or experiment," as does a common dictionary (Berube, 1991, p. 449): "*Empirical* a: relying upon or derived from observation or experiment, b: capable of proof or verification by means of observation or experiment." These latter definitions indicate that there is more to empiricism than simply relying on the evidence of the senses. For an observation to be called empirical it should be *systematic,* capable of being *replicated* (i.e., verified) by other individuals, and subject to some evidentiary standards of *proof.*

Empirical methods are also founded on several other not unreasonable philosophical assumptions, such as *realism,* which maintains "that the world has an independent or objective existence apart from the perception of an observer" (Chapin, 1975, p. 443), and *naturalism*, "the point of view which regards mental processes, attitudes, and other psychological processes as part of the system of natural phenomena and therefore interpretable according to natural laws" (p. 335). Under empiricism, explanations for phenomena are first sought via material causes that do not rely on supernatural or metaphysical mechanisms. This perspective is also the point of view known as *positivism*, "a philosophical and scientific position which holds that knowledge is limited to experience and to observed facts and that metaphysical questions concerning the nature of ultimate reality are outside the scope of science or philosophy" (p. 397). The term *positivism* is also defined by Rubin and Babbie (2005, p. 753) as "a paradigm introduced by August Comte that held that social behavior could be studied and understood in a rational, scientific manner—in contrast to explanations based in religion or superstition."

To reiterate, empiricism implies more than data obtained by the senses. Some level of evidence in support of the validity of these perceptions is required:

> *If experience is a necessary ingredient of social work methods, then one must find means of discovering whether that experience is valid; whether the interaction with another did, in fact, lead to desired changes in that person's behavior, attitudes, and so forth; whether the methods are sound; and whether the theories that inform the methods are sound. (Williams, 1995, p. 881)*

A synopsis of the philosophical foundations undergirding the approach called evidence-based practice is depicted in Table 1.1. Now, what does all this philosophy have to do with social work? Very much, as so ably articulated by Reamer (1993, 1994). Certain philosophical positions are intimately linked with the profession's values and ethics. Among these are the valuing of the methods of science and of empirically based methods. More on this later.

Since the publication of an earlier version of this book in 1998 (Thyer & Wodarski, 1998) there have been significant developments in the maturation of the concept of *evidence-based practice* (EBP). Evidence-based practice originated in medicine in the 1990s, and its principles have since proliferated exponentially over the past decade. A recent Internet search of evidence-based practice yielded more than 1.2 million hits on 15 February 2006, and the newest recent edition of the *Social Work Dictionary* (Barker, 2003, p. 149) included this term for the first time, defining it as:

> *The use of the best available scientific knowledge derived from randomized controlled outcome studies, and meta-analyses of existing*

Table 1.1   Some Selected Philosophical Principles Related to Evidence-Based Practice

An Endorsement of:

Realism: The point of view that the world has an independent or objective existence apart from the perceptions of the viewer

Determinism: The assumption that all phenomena, including psychosocial ones, have physical causes (as opposed to metaphysical ones) that are potentially amenable to scientific investigation and discovery

Positivism: The belief that valid knowledge about the objective world can be arrived at through scientific research

Rationalism: The belief that reason and logic are useful tools for scientific inquiry and that, ultimately, truthful or valid accounts of human behavior will be rational or logically understandable

Empiricism: A preference to rely on evidence gathered systematically through observation or experiment and capable of being replicated (e.g., reproduced and verified) by others, using satisfactory standards of evidence

Operationism: The assertion that it is important to develop dependent (e.g., outcome measures) and independent (e.g., social work interventions) variables that can be reliably used and replicated by others

Parsimony: A preference to seriously consider the simpler of the available and adequate explanations of a phenomenon prior to accepting a more complex account

Scientific skepticism: The point of view that all scientific claims (e.g., the claim that Treatment X helps clients) should be considered of doubtful validity until substantiated by credible empirical data

A Rejection of:

Metaphysics: Explanations involving supernatural, incorporeal, or immaterial entities or factors

Nihilism: The doctrine that all values are baseless and that nothing is known or can be learned

Solipsism: The view that there is no proof that anything exists outside the mind

Dualism: The view that the world consists of the two fundamental entities of mind and matter

Reification: Attributing reality status to an abstract or hypothetical construct (e.g., the superego) in the absence of credible evidence supporting the existence of that construct

Circular reasoning: A supposed (but actually illogical) explanation for human behavior in which causes and effects cannot be distinguished from each other (e.g., Bruce is an alcoholic because he drinks too much; he drinks too much because he is an alcoholic)

Scientism: The position that the investigational methods used in the natural sciences should be uncritically applied to *all* areas of social work practice and decision making

Source: Portions of this table appear in "Introductory Principles of Social Work Research" (pp. 1–24), by B. A. Thyer, in *The Handbook of Social Work Research Methods*, B. A. Thyer (Ed.), 2001, Thousand Oaks, CA: Sage.

outcome studies, as one basis for guiding professional interventions and effective therapies, combined with professional ethical standards, clinical judgment, and practice wisdom.

This is reasonably accurate, but there is concern that much of the social work literature on EBP has relied on secondary sources, or even concepts completely at variance with its original formulations. Readers are encouraged to consult primary sources for learning about EBP, especially consulting the third edition of *Evidence-Based Medicine: How to Practice and Teach EBM* (Strauss, Richardson, Glasziou, & Haynes, 2005), which outlines this conceptual model in great detail. Strauss et al. define EBP as "the integration of the best research evidence with our clinical expertise and our patient's unique values and circumstance" (p. 1) and very clearly describe EBP as a *process of inquiry and practice,* and *not* as a set of practice techniques that have somehow passed a scientific litmus test as approved therapies. There is considerable conceptual confusion about this, perhaps engendered by a related initiative of the American Psychological Association, also undertaken during the 1990s, that was aimed at describing some research benchmarks by which psychosocial treatments could be evaluated (see Task Force on Promotion and Dissemination of Psychological Procedures, 1995); those that passed muster would be labeled as empirically supported treatments, or ESTs. Articles describing this process and actually listing interventions that met these minimal standards (roughly speaking, to pass an intervention must have been supported by the publication of at least two well-designed randomized controlled trials, or at least nine well-designed single-case evaluations). Reviewing the evidence and listing these ESTs was in some ways a good exercise (see Chambless et al., 1996,), albeit controversial (see Norcross, Beutler, & Levant, 2006), but one that did cause some people to conflate this initiative with the entirely separate but sympathetic EBP movement. According to Strauss et al. (2005), the process of EBP can be described by the following five steps to be undertaken by practitioners (regardless of discipline):

1. Convert one's need for information into an answerable question (e.g., What is helpful in the treatment of clients meeting the *Diagnostic and Statistical Manual of Mental Disorders* criteria for Panic Disorder?)

2. Track down the best evidence available to answer that question.

3. Critically appraise this evidence in terms of its validity.

4. Integrate this critical appraisal with one's clinical expertise and the client's circumstances, including biological variables and values and preferences.

5. Evaluate one's effectiveness in undertaking the prior four steps.

Strauss et al. (2005) devote chapter-length discussions to each of these steps. They explain how to formulate our information needs into answerable questions, usually including a client situation or problem, an intervention, and a clinical outcome. Considerable advances in computer and Internet technology have facilitated the finding of the best available evidence, with preference given to locating systematic reviews compiled by the Cochrane and Campbell Collaborations (www.cochrane.org and www.campbellcollaboration.org), international consortia dedicated to providing such comprehensive and systematic analyses, Cochrane in the general area of health care (including mental health) and Campbell in the areas of social welfare, criminal justice, and education. Other sources of information are examined, including recent issues of professional journals, and explicitly EBP-oriented journals, such as *Evidence-Based Mental Health* (see http://ebmh.bmjjournals.com).

One hierarchy of evidence to be considered in appraising the research literature related to the effectiveness of interventions, ranging from the most likely valid and credible to the least reliable (but still potentially valuable), follows:

- A systematic review of *all* available research, published and unpublished, written in English and in other languages, prepared by a group like the Cochrane or Campbell Collaborations (high end of reliable evidence)
- A meta-analysis
- Large-scale multisite randomized controlled trials
- An individual randomized controlled trial
- Quasi-experimental controlled trials
- Preexperimental trials
- Single-subject research designs
- Qualitative outcome studies
- Expert opinion or consensus standards (low end of reliable evidence, but still potentially informative)

Other factors are also relevant. For example, have results been replicated? Have they been replicated in independent investigations? Are the effects not only statistically reliable but also of sufficient magnitude (e.g., strong effect sizes) and clinical import (result in improved quality of life)? Is the intervention ethically acceptable (e.g., would castration for rapists be an acceptable intervention to reduce sex crimes)? Is the proposed intervention applicable to a particular client (e.g., is cognitive therapy for depression, an otherwise empirically supported treatment, appropriate for a person with an intellectual disability)? Is the proposed intervention acceptable to the client (e.g., is exposure therapy and response prevention, an otherwise empirically supported treatment for Obsessive-Compulsive Disorder, appropriate for a nonpsychotic client who honestly believes that her obsessions are the results of demonic influences)? Obviously the process of EBP involves far more than the rote application of empirically supported treatments, although the latter are an important aspect of this approach.

To reiterate, armed with the findings from a critical appraisal of the existing literature, the social worker then judges their applicability to the client, his or her circumstances, the social worker's own clinical expertise, and professional values. Evidence-based practice does *not* involve the blind adoption into practice of interventions supported by randomized controlled trials, meta-analyses, or systematic reviews. It *does* require that the evidence available from such sources be considered in making practice decisions.

The balance of this chapter offers an overview and positive presentation of the fundamental principles of evidence-based social work practice. Beginning with selected philosophical assumptions, initially touched on in the preceding section, this chapter shows how these apply to all areas of practice in the field of social work and inform the development of evidence-based practice. Along the way, certain misconceptions about evidence-based social work practice are addressed and corrected.

First Principles

1. There Is an Objective Reality

Apart from accepting this statement as a philosophical assumption (assumptions are accepted as true, by their very definition as assumptions), there are strong logical and practice grounds supporting this principle. Millions of years ago, sentient beings called dinosaurs roamed the earth. These animals were aware of their surroundings; they ate, slept, procreated, and hunted—in other words, they *lived*. Now dinosaurs are no more, but the world continues on unabated—a changed world, granted, lacking dinosaurs, but its essential nature continues. In the future, should human beings become extinct, perhaps as the victims of some lethal viral plague, it seems reasonable that the physical structure of the world would similarly not be changed. It would continue its existence, independent of the perceptions of human beings. The dark side of the moon was unobserved by humans until a few decades ago. Did we doubt its existence prior to that time? Of course not.

The opposite of realism is *constructivism*, which has been defined as "the view that 'reality' or what we 'know' about the world and our experience of it, is a product of our own mental processes rather than something that actually exists" (Gallant, 1994, p. 119). Constructivism itself is simply a reworking of the point of view known as *solipsism* (see Thyer, 1995a): "Whatever exists is a product of will" (Wolman, 1973, p. 352). And solipsism is itself derivative of a much earlier Greek philosophical school.

Although realism and constructivism are often seen as antithetical, they need not be. To accept realism is *not* to deny the possible merits of the solipsistic perspective. To state that the world has an independent or objective existence is not, on the face of it, to contend that subjective elements are irrelevant. Realism need not imply that the *only* reality is that which is objective and material, just that there *is* such a reality. Realism simply states that an objective and material reality is a very important piece of our universe. To claim, as do the constructivists, that the world is a social construction is certainly acceptable, as long as the position is that social constructivism may be *a part* of the universe, not the whole thing. To accept realism is not to deny the role of subjective elements as a part of the world. To accept constructivism need not be to deny the existence of an objective reality—witness the reaction of the constructivist who receives a speeding ticket while driving to the meeting of the Solipsism Society!

Those who label themselves empiricists, realists, or positivists delimit the scope of their inquiry to the material, the objective, to that which has an independent existence. To the extent that the problems addressed by social work practitioners contain a realistic, material, and objective reality, an empirical perspective is a useful one. Conversely, empirical research has little to say about those aspects of the world that are wholly subjective, immaterial, or supernatural. The study of these areas may form the subject matter of other disciplines, such as philosophy and religion.

2. Psychosocial Phenomena Are a Part of That Reality

As a practical matter, social workers accept this principle without too much debate. Few doubt that unemployment really exists out there in the world, that HIV disease is killing thousands, that spouses are being battered, and that children are being sexually assaulted. The phenomena labeled Bipolar Disorder are real (regardless of the current fad in diagnostic criteria) and exert their deleterious influences on the lives of clients and their families. Of course, there are gray areas: The validity of repressed memory syndrome, Multiple Personality Disorder, and Late Luteal Phase Dysphoric Disorder are a few examples. But the definition of Schizophrenia was similarly gray 100 years ago, and the widespread prevalence of child abuse and incest was barely guessed at then. Like the largely blank maps of Africa and Asia of 200 years ago, the gray areas of social work practice are slowly being pushed back. Preliminary work gives way to more detailed investigations; initial impressions are corroborated or disconfirmed, new questions arise, and more accurate answers slowly emerge.

While these gray areas are being sorted out, the profession of social work is hard at work on those that are fairly unambiguous: working to eliminate racial discrimination and poverty, to promote economic self-sufficiency, to reduce the deleterious effects of so-called mental illnesses, and to deter domestic and community violence. Indeed, the empirical social worker can reasonably contend that virtually the entire focus of our discipline is on the objective reality of deleterious psychosocial environments and of people's reactions to those circumstances. Our field is charged with discovering, not the meaning of homelessness or of being abused, but what can be done to *eliminate* homelessness and to prevent abuse.

One of the seminal figures in social work practice and education had this to say on the matter:

> *At first glance it seems unnecessary to state that, if we believe in a* noncapricious and objectively reliable universe, *such belief also includes social and economic forces with which we can cooperate. Actually, we constantly deny this reliance on objective reality in favor of subjective fantasies. (Reynolds, 1963/1991, p. 315;* emphasis added)

And:

> *A second characteristic of scientifically oriented social work is that* it accepts the objective reality of forces outside itself *with which it must cooperate. (Reynolds, 1942, p. 24;* emphasis added)

Here, Bertha Capen Reynolds is unambiguously asserting that the universe is noncapricious and does have its own existence apart from our social constructions of it. The implications of this position are not trivial. A lawful universe contains the potential for meaningful and effective social work intervention, whereas a capricious one contains little hope for the value of structured social work interventions at the micro or macro practice levels. If the objective realities of poverty are either denied or seen as unimportant, then the focus of social work is on changing the *perceptions* of clients about the world in which they live. If the material world is viewed as real and important, then the focus of intervention is most fruitfully seen as improving the *objective circumstances* of people's lives—for example, in housing, employment, and safety—as opposed to their perceptions of these matters. Gutheil (1992) provides a nice summary of the importance of the physical realities of life in social work assessment and intervention, one that does not discount the psychological ones.

3. Knowledge of Psychosocial Phenomena *Can* Be Arrived At

In support of this principle, we can again cite Reynolds's (1963/1991, p. 315) commonsense views: "I believe that it is possible to understand scientifically the movement of social and economic forces and to apply our strength in cooperation with them." And well before Reynolds's views, we can turn to the proceedings of the National Conference on Charities from more than 100 years ago:

> *Most of the leaders of the conference accepted the implications of a scientific approach to social work problems. They acted on the tacit assumption that human ills—sickness, insanity, crime, poverty— could be subjected to study and methods of treatment. . . . This attitude raised these problems out of the realm of mysticism into that of a science. . . . As a result of the adoption of this scientific attitude, conference speakers and programs looked forward toward progress. . . . They believed in the future; that it was possible by patient, careful study and experimentation to create a society much better than the one they lived in. (Bruno, 1964, pp. 26–27)*

However, the subject matter for the professional social worker is perhaps more complex than that for any other discipline. We envy the chemist who mixes uncontaminated chemicals in a flask and always finds the same result; the experimental physicist who turns on the apparatus and obtains replicable observations; and the rocket scientist charged with designing a spacecraft to fly to Mars, who, perhaps after some initial failures, finally lands a probe on the surface of an alien planet. Such problems, daunting though they may be, pale in comparison to the prospects of finding a sufficiency of families to adopt orphans, of eliminating drug abuse, or of making the inner cities safer places to live. Try developing an *effective* program to ensure that the maximum number of persons with chronic mental illness can live independent lives; to encourage single mothers to get off welfare when there are no jobs to be had; or even to do something simple, like prevent high school dropouts. Ours is far and away the more difficult challenge!

Nevertheless, the complexity of our field does not shake the calm, confident belief that the phenomena with which we deal are grounded in a physical reality, are potentially capable of being understood, and are based on natural laws governing human behavior and biology. Arthur Todd's (1920, p. 73) prescient book, *The Scientific Spirit and Social Work,* had this to say on the matter: "It [science] does not deny that a thing exists merely because it is not easily seen." The empiricist sees no need to invoke metaphysical variables in the face of our current lack of understanding. We recognize that it is better to withhold judgment than to seize upon spurious explanations. Outside of the laboratory, the physicist cannot predict where Forrest Gump's feather will fall, but this inability does not cause him or her to rush around invoking spirit entities or mental forces to explain what happens as the feather drifts down. Similarly, our present difficulties in explanation and prediction do not shake the faith (so to speak) that viable causal accounts are potentially achievable for even the most intractable personal and social problems our field deals with. Again, turning to Todd: "Science does not claim to have complete knowledge of the truth or to have established perfect order out of chaos in this world. It is less an accomplished fact than an attitude" (p. 71).

We can point to the considerable progress that has been made already. We now know much more than we did 50 years ago about the etiology of alcoholism, of the consequences of sexual trauma, and of the prevalence of domestic violence. And we know much more about effective psychosocial interventions (see the following chapters).

Mary Richmond (1917/1935, p. 53) asserted, "Thoughts and events are facts. The question whether a thing be fact or not is the question whether or not *it* can be affirmed with certainty." Richmond believed that some degree of certainty, and hence fact, *could* be arrived at. In fact, her entire text *Social Diagnosis* is an attempt to teach social workers a methodology to obtain as many facts in a case as possible and to make correct inferences from those facts. She lamented:

> No considerable group of social caseworkers . . . seem to have grasped that the reliability of the evidence on which they base their decisions should be no less rigidly scrutinized than is that of legal evidence by opposing counsel. (p. 39)

To rectify this, she devoted chapter after chapter to such relevant topics as the use of social evidence, bias in testimony, and making reasonable inferences, all operating on the assumption that objective knowledge of the psychosocial is possible.

The opposite of this principle is *nihilism*, "a doctrine that all values are baseless and that nothing is knowable or can be communicated" (Berube, 1991, p. 842). The very existence of the methods of science and of social work's application of these tools to make useful discoveries is a repudiation of nihilism.

It is often maintained that because research is conducted by human beings, who have their own set of values and beliefs, then by necessity the entire scientific enterprise is suspect (see Witkin, 1991, for one example of this position). This misses the point that science itself is intensely self-critical and has devoted extensive work to this very problem (e.g., Rudner, 1953). The answer lies in the ability of empirical findings to be effectively transmitted and replicated by others. As Gorenstein (1986, p. 589) noted:

It makes no sense to reject the potential scientific import of a construct simply because social values may have played some role in its formulation. The question of whether a construct has any scientific import is an empirical one. It has to do with whether the construct exhibits lawful properties.

In science, the culture, politics, religion, race, or gender of the investigator have little to do with the merits of what his or her research uncovers (although how the results are used is another matter). This is actually a great strength of the empiricist position. Entertain the opposite stance, and you have the Nazis burning the books of Einstein because he was Jewish, racists denigrating the agricultural research of George Washington Carver because he was Black, and chauvinists dismissing the findings of Marie Curie because she was a woman. Social work professor Leon Williams (1995, p. 881) summed this principle up well:

Social work must assume, for the sake of epistemology, that the field can attain certain, if not valid, knowledge about the human condition. To settle for something equal to or less than probable knowledge is to settle for knowledge dictated by dogma and naive belief, and that appears untenable in an applied discipline.

Does it (should it?) make any difference to you, the reader of this text, to learn that Mary Richmond was a White woman, or that Leon Williams is an African American man, in your appraising the views these scholars expressed or their research findings? Of course not.

4. Scientific Inquiry Is the Most Reliable Way to Arrive at Valid Knowledge

The previous sections have hinted at this principle, but it is worthy of being explicitly stated. Although the word *scientist* is barely 150 years old, the methodological tools of empirical science have proven to be an extremely valuable method for discovering facts about the world. Conventional scientific inquiry covers a multitude of methodologies, including both qualitative and quantitative approaches. Science is intensely self-critical and is constantly evolving, incorporating new methods and discarding outmoded ones. Again, there are historical precedents for this view within social work: "Science always moves on. The charitable methods of twenty years ago may be utterly obsolete now. Our methods, even the most scientific, may be the laughing stock of our descendants in the twenty-first century" (Todd, 1920, p. 85).

Field research, naturalistic observations, participant-observation studies, correlational investigations, surveys, longitudinal studies, quasi-experiments, single-system research designs, randomized controlled trials, and meta-analyses are all subsumed under the rubric of empirically based science. No subject or problem in social work is inherently excluded from scientific analysis, although some things are certainly more difficult to investigate than others. The edifice of conventional empirical science employs a multitude of methods, qualitative and quantitative—those that investigate linear, simple, causal phenomena, and those that are applicable to the analysis of complex, multiply determined, interactive psychosocial systems. As long as the phenomenon in question is seen as occurring (at least in part) in the material, physical world in which we live, then science can investigate it. As long as the methodology is systematic and replicable and possesses verifiable standards of proof, it is a welcome member of the community of scientific methods. It took Jane Goodall seeing only *one* chimpanzee eating meat in the wild to disconfirm the then current hypothesis that chimps are naturally exclusively vegetarian. Such field observational studies are a valuable tool in science. When others see the same thing in different settings, or when videotapes can be made of the event, naturalistic observational studies are granted even stronger credence. At the other end of the hierarchy (or rainbow, if you prefer) of scientific research methods is the multinational randomized controlled clinical trial, conducted by diverse investigators with disparate clients (e.g., with respect to such characteristics as race, gender, and age), which obtains replicated results.

All types of research methodologies are not given equal credence, however. Evidence obtained from a well-conducted randomized controlled clinical trial is seen as more persuasive than an individual case history presented narratively. Studies with long-term follow-up are seen as better tests of a treatment's efficacy than those that assess clients only immediately posttreatment. Correlational studies with thousands of respondents are seen as more credible than those using only 10 people, and replicated studies are seen as more reliable than unreplicated ones (see Thyer, 1989, 1991). Both qualitative and quantitative research methods have a valuable function in mainstream science. In general, qualitative methods are very useful for learning about a specific problem area or clientele and for generating hypotheses or meaningful questions. Quantitative methods are, in turn, most useful for developing *answers* to questions once they have been formulated, but they are not particularly strong for originating theory or generating hypotheses.

No research methodology is without its problems. In 1925, anthropology student Margaret Mead traveled to Samoa to learn something of the realities of adolescent life there. Using a qualitatively based participant-observation methodology and two key informants, teenage girls who served as her translators during her long-term stay, Mead came away with a view of Samoan adolescence characterized as being sexually uninhibited, anxiety-free, and generally without stress. Her work culminated in the popular book *Coming of Age in Samoa* (Mead, 1928). It was not until the 1980s that it emerged that Mead had been hoaxed by her informants, who had decided to play a trick on her and basically told her what they thought she wanted to know, and that quantitative data (e.g., statistics on juvenile crimes) failed to corroborate Mead's findings (see Gardner, 1993).

In 1989, chemists in Utah announced the discovery of cold fusion, a potential source of limitless energy. Within a few weeks, leading research laboratories across the world announced their replication of the cold fusion phenomenon. However, a few naysaying voices emerged, claiming alternative explanations for the chemical phenomenon in question, and over several months, it slowly became clear that the detractors were correct. The claims of cold fusion were erroneous (see Rothman, 1990).

One would have hoped that the length of Mead's stay in Samoa would have revealed the truth to her, and that their detailed knowledge of the laws of physics would have deterred the inventors of cold fusion (see Taubes, 1993) from making premature claims about their supposed energy source—but such are the vagaries of science, no matter what method is employed, whether the anthropologist's field study or the chemist's laboratory experiment. The process of scientific inquiry, though, tends to preclude errors from being perpetuated in the long run and allows the truth to emerge. This self-corrective feature is not characteristic of other ways of knowing, such as divine inspiration, reliance on prior authorities, intuition, or even practice wisdom. Science provides a manner—empirical research—to resolve conflicting views; revelation and other approaches to discovery do not. This is a distinctive strength of scientific inquiry.

The field of social work has long recognized this. So much so, that the Code of Ethics of the National Association of Social Workers (NASW; 1996 p. 20) clearly states, "Social workers should base practice on recognized knowledge, *including empirically based knowledge*, relevant to social work practice." Twenty-five years ago the Curriculum Policy Statement of the Council on Social Work Education (CSWE; 1982, p. 10) mandated, "Every part of the professional foundation curriculum should . . . help bring students to an understanding and appreciation of the scientific, analytic approach to knowledge building in practice. The ethical use of scientific inquiry should be emphasized throughout." The CSWE's statement has been superseded by its Educational Policy and Accreditation Standards, which reinforce this earlier standard: "The content prepares students to develop, use, and effectively communicate empirically based knowledge, including *evidence-based interventions*" (CSWE, 2001, p. 10; emphasis added).

One of the seven original organizations that formed the NASW was the Social Work Research Group (SWRG, established in 1949), which adopted the positivist philosophy of science as its guiding research paradigm (see Tyson, 1992, p. 542). When the NASW was founded in 1955 (incorporating the SWRG Research Section), the new organization's bylaws proclaimed that one of its major purposes was "to expand through research the knowledge necessary to define and attain these goals" (e.g., to improve conditions of life; NASW, 1955, p. 3). Numerous early articles and books in social work valued the methods of science and the potential that empirical research possessed to be of benefit to the field and to society (e.g., Gordon, 1956; Preston & Mudd, 1956; Todd, 1920; see Zimbalist, 1977, for a summary). In 1880, Charles D. Kellogg of the Philadelphia Charity Organization believed, "Charity is a science, the science of social therapeutics, and has laws like all other sciences" (quoted in Germain, 1970, p. 9). Though perhaps an overstatement, Kellogg's sentiment expresses the optimistic empiricist Zeitgeist surrounding the establishment of the social work profession.

To reiterate: To claim that empirical methods have much to contribute to developing advances in knowledge and practice in social work intervention is not automatically to deny the role of alternative ways of knowing. Rather, it is the responsibility of the advocates of methods of discovery that are outside of mainstream science to demonstrate the value of those other approaches. Neither does science inherently claim that issues that fall outside its purview are unimportant or meaningless to others. Love, altruism, faith, beauty, commitment, courage, and hope are all of vital significance to humanity. For science to say that it does not address such topics is not to say that they are insignificant. Thyer (1993, p. 6) stated it this way:

> *Many questions of great importance to our profession, such as the value base of social work, are simply outside the purview of scientific inquiry and other standards apply to the discussion of such topics apart from the conventional rules of scientific inference, standards such as those pertaining to religious beliefs, morality, and other philosophical convictions. Logical positivists are fully aware that many significant areas of our professional and personal lives should not be scrutinized through the lenses of science, but when the issues relate to social work theory and the evaluation of our practice methods, the role of controlled scientific investigations . . . becomes a relevant factor.*

5. There Are Some Good Methods to Measure Psychosocial Phenomena

Bloom, Fischer, and Orme (1995, p. xiii) have done us a service by uncovering an important quote from Dr. Richard Cabot, who addressed a national social work convention in 1931: "I appeal to you. . . . Measure, evaluate, estimate, appraise your results, in some form, in any terms, that rest on something beyond faith, assertion, and 'illustrative cases.' "

A major obstacle to the conduct of quality empirical research in social work was the lack of suitable measures. Preston and Mudd (1956, p. 36) asked (and answered): "What is preventing progress in the identification of factors contributing to positive [results] in social casework? First is the fact that movement indices, while reliable, have not yet been shown to be valid." This was a problem similarly noted by Gordon (1956, p. 82): "Social workers have . . . felt the lack of more systematic and objective means of making these observations . . . and with methods that make them more than individual impressions." Mary Richmond (1917/1935, p. 362) provided one partial solution to this problem when she claimed, "To state that we think our client is mentally deranged is futile; to state the observations that have created this impression is a possible help." In other words, be parsimonious in description, keep unwarranted inferences to a minimum, and report what actually occurs, as opposed to interpreting what is seen.

As it happens, considerable progress has been achieved in developing both reliable and valid measures of client progress. K. Corcoran and Fischer's (2000) sourcebook contains several hundred rapid assessment measures covering the panoply of fields of clinical practice: children, adults, families, and couples. Many of these reliable and valuable instruments are of great value in supplementing clinical judgment in social work assessment and in monitoring change during the course of intervention. An increasing number of similarly constructed sources is available to agencies and practitioners (e.g., National Institute on Drug Abuse, 1994; Nezu, Ronan, Meadows, & McClure, 2000; Sederer & Dickey, 1996; Wetzler, 1989). Apart from formal pencil-and-paper, client-reported, and rapid assessment instruments, corresponding advances have been made in systematizing the direct observation of behavior in its natural contexts (e.g., Baer, Harrison, Fradenburg, Petersen, & Milla, 2005; Polster & Collins, 1993).

Occasionally, one encounters a colleague who asserts, "Well, you just can't measure problem X." Smile on hearing remarks like this and gently inquire, "Well, do you mean that X can't *ever* be measured, by anyone? Or do you mean that *you* do not know how to measure X now?" Modesty usually compels the naysayer to back up a bit and acknowledge that the latter position is what was really meant. In point of fact, most of the psychosocial problems dealt with by social workers *have* had some form of reliable and valid method of assessment developed. Perhaps these methods do not cover every area, or are not evenly distributed across fields of practice. Depression, for example, enjoys a much richer assessment literature than does, say, Multiple Personality Disorder, and clinical social work practice has a more developed empirical assessment methodology than does community organization. But an operating assumption of the empirical social worker is that if a problem (or strength) exists in the real world, it is potentially measurable. And if it is measurable, we are in a better position to offer intervention services and to see if we are helping the client-in-situation. I once heard, "If you don't measure it, then you don't care!"

This does not disregard the unfortunate fact that our measures are often imperfect and require improvement. The national census undercounts illegal immigrants, racial minorities, and the homeless. Yet what alternatives are there to the census? What other database shall we rely on to estimate the numbers and characteristics of the citizenry? Clearly the answer is to improve the technology for taking the census, not to stop counting people. Similarly, ways to measure unemployment, the rate of inflation, the cost of living, and the quantity and quality of a client's Affective Disorder all suffer from varying degrees of imperfection. Like astronomers' calculations of the mass of the universe, the social work-related disciplines are getting better and better at assessing the psychosocial problems of clients. The measurement of clinical anxiety is considerably advanced over the techniques of 2 decades ago. Similar progress has been made in the analysis of social support, expressed emotion, caregiver burden, quality of life, and degree of independent living. Can these constructs be measured perfectly, in a manner completely isomorphic with nature's reality? Probably not. Are we coming progressively closer to capturing nature's reality? Most definitely!

6. There Are Some Empirically Supported Interventions

This is a really exciting area of social work practice—the ongoing development of psychosocial treatments that have been shown, through credible scientific evaluation studies, to *really* be of help to clients. Perhaps not for every client with a particular difficulty, and perhaps not to the point of complete resolution or cure, but for many problems we are in a position to offer professional social work services that are quite likely to benefit a significant proportion of our clients to a clinically meaningful extent. Indeed, the balance of this text provides summaries of this practice-research literature, so the point will not be belabored here. Rather, note that the American Psychiatric Association (1995), the American Psychological Association (Chambless et al., 1996; Task Force, 1995), and the NASW are at work developing practice guidelines as to what treatments are first indicated for particular problems (Ewalt, 1995). The American Psychological Association is making careful compilations of psychosocial interventions that work for particular disorders (see Sanderson & Woody, 1995), and this information will have an increasing influence on the conduct of practice.

In all the human services, it is becoming increasingly evident that some psychosocial treatments are effective for particular problems and some are not. A number of books summarize these findings, such as Giles (1993); Ammerman, Last, and Hersen (1993); the Institute of Medicine (1989); Nathan and Gorman (2002); Christophersen and Mortweet (2001); Drake, Merrens, and Lynde, 2005; Hibbs and Jensen (1997); and Hofmann and Tompson (2002), as do recent articles in social work, notably Gorey (1996); MacDonald, Sheldon, and Gillespie (1992); Rubin (1985); Thyer (1995b); Gorey, Thyer, and Pawluck (1998); and Reid and Hanrahan (1982). This is delightful news that should be shouted from the rooftops. Contrary to the nihilistic view that "virtually any intervention can be justified on the grounds that it has as much support as alternative methods" (Witkin, 1991, p. 158), numerous outcome studies comparing various forms of psychosocial treatment find that some types of interventions work better than others for particular problems. Consult any recent issue of *Research on Social Work Practice*, the *Journal of Consulting and Clinical Psychology, Evidence-Based Mental Health*, or the *Archives of General Psychiatry* for evidence of this contention.

7. We Have a Professional Obligation to Apply This Knowledge

Once the preceding principles have been established, it follows quite naturally that we should be obliged to apply this knowledge. Indeed, it would be premature to assert this, had the appropriate empirical foundations not been established. Now that our field has sufficiently progressed, the following position set forth over 25 years ago by two social workers is a reasonable one: "The clinician would first be interested in using an intervention strategy that has been successful in the past. . . . When established techniques are available, they should be used, but they should be based on objective evaluation rather than subjective feeling" (Jayaratne & Levy, 1979, p. 7).

Although, in K. J. Corcoran's (1998) analysis, jurisprudence has not yet established that social work clients have a legal right to effective treatment, Myers and Thyer (1997) argue that the ethical right certainly does already exist. Note that the principle is not that clients are guaranteed to benefit from social work intervention, but is rather the more limited concept that they have the right to *receive* treatment with some credible degree of support as a first-choice therapy, whenever such is available.

The right to receive effective treatment is being convincingly argued in a number of human service disciplines. In psychiatry, Klerman (1990, p. 417) states, "The psychiatrist has a responsibility to use effective treatment. The patient has a right to proper treatment. Proper treatment involves those treatments for which there is substantial evidence." This view came to be known as *evidence-based psychiatry* (see Goldner & Bilsker, 1995), itself morphing into evidence-based practice.

In behavior analysis it is asserted that "the individual has the right to the most effective treatment procedures available" (Van Houten et al., 1988, p. 113), and an organization called the International Association for the Right to Effective Treatment has been formed. Behavior analysts make an especially strong case in this regard, with their professional Code of Ethics asserting:

> *The behavior analyst always has the responsibility to recommend scientifically supported most effective treatment procedures. Effective treatment procedures have been validated as having both long-term and short-term benefits to clients and society.... Clients have a right to effective treatment (i.e., based on the research literature and adapted to the individual client). (Bailey & Burch, 2005, pp. 65–66)*

In clinical psychology, Chambless et al. (1996, p. 10) claim:

> *Whatever interventions that mysticism, authority, commercialism, politics, custom, convenience, or carelessness might dictate, clinical psychologists focus on what works. They bear a fundamental ethical responsibility to use where possible interventions that work and to subject any intervention they use to scientific scrutiny.*

And in social work, Tutty (1990, p. 13) suggests, "It is important to provide the most effective treatment available. This entails professionals keeping current on the research on treatment effectiveness for their particular client populations."

Whereas it would have been premature to assert this principle some 20 to 30 years ago, each new advance in clinical-research knowledge adds weight to the argument in favor of the right to effective treatment. This view is consistent with practice wisdom, with the NASW Code of Ethics, and with the accreditation standards of the CSWE. What are the merits of the alternative perspective?

8. We Have a Professional Obligation to Empirically Evaluate the Outcomes of Our Interventions

The need for social workers to regularly evaluate the outcomes of practice at all levels has long been recognized in the profession. This principle is codified in the NASW's (1996, p. 20, section 5.02(a)) Code of Ethics, which states, "Social workers should monitor and evaluate policies, the implementation of programs, and practice interventions."

In the furtherance of this principle, the CSWE's (1982, p. 11) Curriculum Policy Statement mandated:

> *The content on research should impart scientific methods of building knowledge and of evaluating service delivery in all areas of practice. It should include quantitative and qualitative research methodologies; designs for the systematic evaluation of the student's own practice; and the critical appreciation and use of research and of program evaluation.*

The CSWE's (2001) more recent governing document, the Educational Policy and Accreditation Standards, embodies the following standards that all BSW and MSW programs must adhere to:

- *Social work education combines* scientific inquiry *with the teaching of professional skills to provide* effective and ethical *social work services. (p. 3)*
- *[Social work education] prepar[es] social workers to* evaluate *the processes and* effectiveness *of practice. (p. 7)*
- *[Social workers] use theoretical frameworks supported by* empirical evidence *to understand individual development and behavior. (p. 9)*
- *[Social workers] evaluate research studies, apply research findings to practice, and* evaluate their own practice interventions. *(p. 9)*
- *Practice content also includes identifying, analyzing, and implementing* empirically based interventions *designed to achieve client goals; applying empirical knowledge and technological advances;* evaluating program outcomes and practice effectiveness. *(p. 12)*
- *Qualitative and quantitative research content provide[s] understanding of* scientific, analytic, and ethical approaches *to building knowledge for practice. The content prepares students to develop, use, and effectively communicate* empirically based knowledge, *including* evidence-based interventions. *(p. 12)*

The position on evidence-based practice articulated in this book is highly consistent with contemporary educational standards for the training of social workers.

The lack of research designs appropriate for clinical and program evaluations was keenly felt in our profession's early years. Preston and Mudd (1956, p. 36) noted in the inaugural issue of *Social Work* (NASW's flagship journal), "Much technical work remains to be done before even the most elementary of experimental designs can be applied." Field research on naturalistic social work services does not lend itself to the strictures of classical experimental research designs. It is almost always impossible to randomly *select* a sample of clients from the larger population of those with a particular psychosocial problem, and random *assignment* to treatment and no-treatment or placebo-control groups is equally problematic. Obtaining enough clients to allow for sufficient statistical power of inferential tests is also a difficulty.

To some extent, these problems have been dealt with pragmatically. For example, if we scale back our expectations and standards so that we limit initial investigations to answering the question "Did our clients get better after receiving social work services?" then nonexperimental designs such as pre- and posttest group studies on convenience samples of individuals are quite adequate to the task. Asking practitioners to provide credible answers to the question "Did social work intervention *cause* your clients to improve?" requires the imposition of rigorous experimental designs and may be an impractical endeavor. Asking the less rigorous but still important question "Did they get better?" is usually a far more feasible endeavor.

The development and application of single-system research designs (SSRDs) is another major positive development. About a dozen social work books have been published on the topic in the past 2 decades, as well as several hundred journal articles discussing and applying the approach (see Thyer & Thyer, 1992). Social work generalist research texts now regularly include one or more chapters on the conduct of SSRDs, and evaluation research making use of this methodology, representing a variety of practice and theoretical orientations, has appeared in all the major social work professional journals.

Concomitant advances have been made in the design and conduct of group research designs. The number of such published studies is growing exponentially. In Gorey's (1996) review, more than 85 outcome studies on social work practice appeared in print from 1990 to 1994. Contrast this to the *total* of 17 found by Fischer (1976) that appeared prior to 1972. More sophisticated statistical procedures such as meta-analysis permit the aggregation of group outcome studies, enhancing the power to detect changes in client functioning (see J. Corcoran & Dattalo, in press; Gorey, 1996; Gorey et al., 1998).

Conducting evaluation research in social work is perhaps our field's most challenging endeavor (Harrison & Thyer, 1988). However, students and practitioners are now being exposed to the practical tools necessary to undertake such evaluations (they weren't before), and the profession's Code of Ethics mandates such work (previously it did not). Outcome studies can be profitably undertaken by individual clinicians focused on individual clients, by administrators supporting program evaluations of the results of particular agency-based services, and by policy makers and legislators expecting some evidence of effectiveness. Soon, it is to be hoped, a stronger standard will be adopted by the profession, perchance one that reads something like this:

Clinicians should routinely gather empirical data on client's relevant behavior, affect, and reports of thoughts, using reliable and valid measures, where such measures have been developed. These measures should be repeated throughout the course of treatment and used in clinical decision-making to supplement professional judgments pertaining to the alteration or termination of treatment. (Thyer, 1995c, p. 95)

9. We Have a Professional Obligation to Promote Evidence-Based Practice

There are a number of points of leverage that social work professionals can utilize to promote empirical practices in the field (see Thyer, 1995c, 1996b). Practitioners can, of course, focus their continuing education training on acquiring skills in psychosocial treatments and methods of assessment that are well supported by sound research studies. Educators can commit themselves to transmitting the latest findings of empirical research in their classes and field supervision and can require their students to develop skills in applying such methods in practice. Supervisors can ask personnel to gather data on client functioning, graph it, and bring it to supervisory sessions, where it can be used to form a part of the supervisory process. On a macro level, we can all work within the NASW and our state regulatory boards toward the adoption of an ethical standard such as the following:

Clients should be offered as a first choice treatment, interventions with some significant degree of empirical support, where such knowledge exists, and only provided other treatments after such first choice treatments have been given a legitimate trial and shown not to be efficacious. (Thyer, 1995c, p. 95)

As social workers increasingly fall under the mandates of approved practice guidelines (see Ewalt, 1995) our profession should be at the forefront of ensuring that these standards are consistent with current clinical research findings.

Such ideas are not without some precedent. In 1992, the NASW's National Committee on Lesbian and Gay Issues (NCOLGI) developed a policy statement on therapies intended to convert gay men and lesbian women into heterosexuals. In part, this document reads as follows:

Proponents of reparative therapies claim—without documentation—many successes. They assert that their processes are supported by conclusive scientific data, which are in fact little more than anecdotal. NCOLGI protests these efforts to "convert" people through irresponsible therapies. . . . Empirical research does not demonstrate that . . . sexual orientation (heterosexual or homosexual) can be changed through these so-called reparative therapies. (p. 1; emphasis added*)*

Reparative therapies have been deemed unethical, in part because of the lack of appropriate empirical research. This is a remarkable position to take. Is it much of an extrapolation to infer that providing treatments that are not empirically supported for other problems—say, depression or anxiety—is also unethical? Particularly if effective treatments *have* been developed for those problems?

Once the profession has adopted on a wide scale the standard that the provision of treatments that are not empirically supported may be unethical (where such treatments are known to exist), and the legal right to effective treatment is also established, then a natural Darwinian process will result in the gradual elimination of the ineffective and unproven and the adoption of the efficacious. This will not be easy, and it will be slow, accompanied by the agonized lamentations of practitioners of spurious therapies and of those having to learn newer and more helpful psychosocial interventions that will perhaps be at variance with long-cherished practices.

In 1915, Abraham Flexner claimed that social work did not meet two requirements to be considered a profession: It lacked individual responsibility and educationally communicable techniques for practice (Syers, 1995). The movement toward empirical social work addresses these two deficiencies. The expectation for the ongoing evaluation of practice partly deals with the first, and the growing body of transmittable psychosocial interventions described in the balance of this book addresses the second. Flexner's 1910 report *Medical Education in the United States and Canada,* commissioned by the Carnegie Foundation for the Advancement of Teaching, sounded a clarion call for medicine to become a scientifically based field. Homeopathy, naturopathy, and other bogus health practices slowly were excluded from the medical school curriculum and from everyday practice. Today, the social work equivalents of homeopathy and naturopathy are routinely taught in schools of social work and are presented as credible treatment options in practice textbooks and in continuing education programs. As long as this continues, Flexner's mournful conclusion will remain valid. Fortunately, the tide seems to be turning.

Summary

It is almost superfluous to ask why social work should take on the character of science. It is hardly a question of "may or may not." Rather, should we say, it is a matter of the categorical *must* (Todd, 1920, p. 75).

It is clear that contemporary social work accepts the principles of conventional scientific inquiry. However, empirical clinical practice is not an uncritical embrace of the quantitative to the exclusion of the qualitative. We remain aware of the limitations of science and attempt to base our practices on a firm integration of the scientific *with* the art of social work. To the extent that empirical research yields information that is reliable, valid, and applicable, it is incumbent on social workers to make use of these advances in knowledge in a manner that remains consistent with those equally important foundations of practice that are not empirically justifiable: respect for the individual, a concomitant focus on individually based and societally directed interventions, and the promotion of self-determination and social justice (Thyer, 1996a).

One of the best tools to promote the values of the profession is evidence-based social work practice. Telling the truth is one of those values (Reamer, 1995, p. 897), and discovering the truth is something that empirical research is very good at. The balance of this book presents credible reviews of contemporary empirical literature pertaining to selected behavioral, affective, and intellectual disorders and their psychosocial assessment and treatment. That such a book is now possible is a striking affirmation of the merits of the approach to social work called evidence-based practice.

Study Questions

1. Describe any two philosophical principles that evidence-based practice accepts as givens.
2. Describe any two philosophical positions that evidence-based practice largely rejects.
3. What is meant by the term *positivism*?
4. Why does science place more reliance on certain forms of research evidence (e.g., controlled experiments), as opposed to other forms that are generally seen as less capable of yielding credible findings (e.g., a narrative case history)?
5. What does the Council on Social Work Education assert with respect to the place of scientific training for social work students?
6. Look up the web site of either the Campbell Collaboration or the Cochrane Collaboration. Locate a systematic review of some psychosocial intervention relevant to social work practice, and examine how this review was conducted and what the authors conclude.

References

American Psychiatric Association. (1995). *Practice guidelines for the treatment of patients with substance abuse disorders.* Washington, DC: Author.

Ammerman, R. T., Last, C. G., & Hersen, M. (Eds.). (1993). *Handbook of prescriptive treatments for children and adolescents.* Boston: Allyn & Bacon.

Arkava, M. I., & Lane, T. A. (1983). *Beginning social work research.* Boston: Allyn & Bacon.

Baer, D. M., Harrison, R., Fradenburg, L., Petersen, D., & Milla, S. (2005). Some pragmatics in the valid and reliable recording of directly observable behavior. *Research on Social Work Practice, 15,* 440–451.

Bailey, J. S., & Burch, M. R. (2005). *Ethics for behavior analysts.* Thousand Oaks, CA: Sage.

Barker, R. L. (Ed.). (2003). *The social work dictionary* (5th ed.). Washington, DC: NASW Press.

Berube, M. (Ed.). (1991). *The American heritage dictionary* (2nd college ed.). New York: Houghton Mifflin.

Bloom, M., Fischer, J., & Orme, J. (1995). *Evaluating practice.* Boston: Allyn & Bacon.

Bruno, F. J. (1964). *Trends in social work: 1874–1956.* New York: Columbia University Press.

Chambless, D., Sanderson, W., Shoham, V., Johnson, S., Pope, K., Crits-Christoph, P., et al. (1996). An update on empirically validated therapies. *Clinical Psychologist, 49*(2), 5–18.

Chapin, J. P. (1975). *Dictionary of psychology.* New York: Dell.

Christophersen, E. R., & Mortweet, S. L. (2001). *Treatments that work with children: Empirically supported strategies for managing childhood problems.* Washington, DC: American Psychological Association.

Corcoran, J., & Dattalo, P. (in press). Parent involvement in treatment for ADHD: A meta-analysis of the published studies. *Research on Social Work Practice.*

Corcoran, K. J. (1998). Clients without a cause: Is there a legal right to effective treatment in clinical social work? *Research on Social Work Practice, 8,* 589–596.

Corcoran, K., & Fischer, J. (2000). *Measures for clinical practice: A sourcebook.* New York: Free Press.

Council on Social Work Education. (1982). Curriculum policy for the master's degree and baccalaureate degree programs in social work education. *Social Work Education Reporter, 30*(3), 5–12.

Council on Social Work Education. (2001). *Educational policy and accreditation standards.* Alexandria, VA: Author.

Drake, R. E., Merrens, M. R., Lynde, D. W. (Eds.). (2005). *Evidence-based mental health practice: A textbook.* New York: Norton.

Ewalt, P. L. (1995). Clinical practice guidelines: Their impact on social work in health care. *Social Work, 40,* 293.

Fischer, J. (1976). *The effectiveness of social casework.* Springfield, IL: Charles C Thomas.

Flexner, A. (1910). *Medical Education in the United States and Canada.* New York: Carnegie Foundation for the Advancement of Teaching.

Gallant, J. P. (1994). New ideas for the school social worker in the counseling of children and families. *Social Work in Education, 15,* 119–128.

Gardner, M. (1993, Winter). The great Samoan hoax. *Skeptical Inquirer, 17,* 131–135.

Germain, C. (1970). Casework and science: A historical encounter. In R. Roberts & R. Nee (Eds.), *Theories of social casework* (pp. 3–32). Chicago: University of Chicago Press.

Giles, R. R. (Ed.). (1993). *Handbook of effective psychotherapy.* New York: Plenum Press.

Goldner, E. M., & Bilsker, D. (1995). Evidence-based psychiatry. *Canadian Journal of Psychiatry, 40,* 97–101.

Gordon, W. E. (1956). The challenge of research to today's medical social worker. *Social Work, 1*(1), 81–87.

Gorenstein, E. E. (1986). On the distinction between science and valuation in the mental health field [Letter]. *American Psychologist, 41,* 588–590.

Gorey, K. (1996). Effectiveness of social work intervention research: Internal versus external evaluations. *Social Work Research, 20,* 119–128.

Gorey, K., Thyer, B. A., & Pawluck, D. (1998). The differential effectiveness of social work interventions: A meta-analysis. *Social Work, 43*, 269–278.

Grinnell, R. M., Jr. (Ed.). (1993). *Social work research and evaluation* (4th ed.). Itasca, IL: F. E. Peacock.

Gutheil, I. A. (1992). Considering the physical environment: An essential component of good practice. *Social Work, 37*, 391–396.

Harrison, D. F., & Thyer, B. A. (1988). Doctoral research on social work practice: A proposed agenda. *Journal of Social Work Education, 24*, 107–114.

Hibbs, E. D., & Jensen, P. S. (1997). *Psychosocial treatments for child and adolescent disorders: Empirically-based strategies for clinical practice.* Washington, DC: American Psychological Association.

Hofmann, S. G., & Tompson, M. C. (2002). *Treating chronic and severe mental illness: A handbook of empirically supported interventions.* New York: Guilford Press.

Institute of Medicine. (1989). *Research on children with mental, behavioral, and developmental disorders.* Washington, DC: National Academy Press.

Jayaratne, S., & Levy, R. L. (1979). *Empirical clinical practice.* New York: Columbia University Press.

Klerman, G. (1990). The psychiatric patient's right to effective treatment: Implications of Osheroff v. Chestnut Lodge. *American Journal of Psychiatry, 147*, 409–418.

Macdonald, G., Sheldon, B., & Gillespie, J. (1992). Contemporary studies of the effectiveness of social work. *British Journal of Social Work, 22*, 615–643.

Mead, M. (1928). *Coming of age in Samoa: A psychological study of primitive youth for western civilization.* New York: Blue Ribbon.

Myers, L. L., & Thyer, B. A. (1997). Should social work clients have the right to effective treatment? *Social Work, 42*, 288–298.

Nathan, P., & Gorman, J. (2002) (Eds.) *A guide to treatments that work* (2nd ed.). New York: Oxford University Press.

National Association of Social Workers. (1955). *Bylaws of the National Association of Social Workers.* New York: Author.

National Association of Social Workers. (1996, November). The National Association of Social Workers Code of Ethics. *NASW News,* 17–20.

National Association of Social Workers' National Committee on Lesbian and Gay Issues. (1992). *Position statement: "Reparative" or "conversion" therapies for lesbians and gay men.* Washington, DC: NASW Press.

National Institute on Drug Abuse. (1994). *Mental health assessment and diagnosis of substance abusers* (NIH Publication No. 94-3846). Washington, DC: Author.

Nezu, A. M., Ronan, G. F., Meadows, E. A., & McClure, K. S. (2000). *Practitioner's guide to empirically based measures of depression.* New York: Kluwer Press.

Norcross, J. C., Beutler, L. E., & Levant, R. E. (Eds.). (2006). *Evidence-based practices in mental health: Debate and dialog on the fundamental questions.* Washington, DC: American Psychological Association.

Polster, R. A., & Collins, D. (1993). Structured observation. In R. M. Grinnell (Ed.), *Social work research and evaluation* (pp. 244–261). Itasca, IL: Peacock Press.

Preston, M. G., & Mudd, E. H. (1956). Research and service in social work: Conditions for a stable union. *Social Work, 1*(1), 34–40.

Reamer, F. G. (1993). *The philosophical foundations of social work.* New York: Columbia University Press.

Reamer, F. G. (1994). *The foundations of social work knowledge.* New York: Columbia University Press.

Reamer, F. G. (1995). Ethics and values. In R. L. Edwards (Ed.), *Encyclopedia of social work* (19th ed., pp. 893–902). Washington, DC: National Association of Social Workers.

Reid, W. J., & Hanrahan, P. (1982). Recent evaluations of social work: Grounds for optimism. *Social Work, 27*, 328–340.

Reynolds, B. C. (1942). *Learning and teaching in the practice of social work.* New York: Farrar & Reinhart.

Reynolds, B. C. (1991). *An uncharted journey.* Silver Spring, MD: NASW Press. (Original work published 1963)

Richmond, M. (1935). *Social diagnosis.* New York: Russell Sage. (Original work published 1917)

Rothman, M. A. (1990, Winter). Cold fusion: A case history in "wishful science"? *Skeptical Inquirer, 14,* 161–170.

Rubin, A. (1985). Practice effectiveness: More grounds for optimism. *Social Work, 30,* 469–476.

Rubin, A., & Babbie, E. R. (2005). *Research methods for social work* (5th ed.). Belmont, CA: Brooks/Cole.

Rudner, R. (1953). The scientist qua scientist makes value judgments. *Philosophy of Science, 20,* 1–6.

Sanderson, W. C., & Woody, S. (1995). Manual for empirically validated treatments: A project of the Task Force on Psychological Intervention, Division of Clinical Psychology, American Psychological Association. *Clinical Psychologist, 48*(4), 7–11.

Sederer, L. I., & Dickey, B. (1996). *Outcomes assessment in clinical practice.* Baltimore: Williams & Wilkins.

Strauss, S. E., Richardson, W. S., Glasziou, P., & Haynes, R. B. (2005). *Evidence-based medicine: How to practice and teach EBM.* New York: Elsevier.

Syers, M. (1995). Abraham Flexner. In R. L. Edwards (Ed.), *Encyclopedia of social work* (19th ed., pp. 2584–2585). Washington, DC: National Association of Social Workers.

Task Force on Promotion and Dissemination of Psychological Procedures. (1995). Training in and dissemination of empirically-validated psychological treatments: Report and recommendations. *Clinical Psychologist, 48*(1), 2–23.

Taubes, G. (1993). *Bad science: The short life and very hard times of cold fusion.* New York: Random House.

Thyer, B. A. (1989). First principles of practice research. *British Journal of Social Work, 19,* 309–323.

Thyer, B. A. (1991). Guidelines for evaluating outcome studies on social work practice. *Research on Social Work Practice, 1,* 76–91.

Thyer, B. A. (1993). Social work theory and practice research: The approach of logical positivism. *Social Work and Social Services Review, 4,* 5–26.

Thyer, B. A. (1995a). Constructivism and solipsism: Old wine in new bottles? *Social Work in Education, 17,* 63–64.

Thyer, B. A. (1995b). Effective psychosocial treatments for children and adolescents: A selected review. *Early Child Development and Care, 106,* 137–147.

Thyer, B. A. (1995c). Promoting an empiricist agenda in the human services: An ethical and humanistic imperative. *Journal of Behavior Therapy and Experimental Psychiatry, 26,* 93–98.

Thyer, B. A. (1996a). Forty years of progress toward empirical clinical practice? *Social Work Research, 20,* 77–81.

Thyer, B. A. (1996b). Guidelines for applying the empirical clinical practice model to social work. *Journal of Applied Social Sciences, 20,* 121–127.

Thyer, B. A. (2001). Introductory principles of social work research. In B. A. Thyer (Ed.), *The handbook of social work research methods* (pp. 1–24). Thousand Oaks, CA: Sage.

Thyer, B. A., & Thyer, K. B. (1992). Single-system research designs in social work practice: A bibliography from 1965–1990. *Research on Social Work Practice, 2,* 99–116.

Thyer, B. A., & Wodarski, J. S. (1998). (Eds.). *Handbook of empirical social work practice: Vol. 1. Mental disorders.* New York: Wiley.

Todd, A. J. (1920). *The scientific spirit and social work.* New York: Macmillan.

Tutty, L. (1990). The response of community mental health professionals to client's rights: A review and suggestions. *Canadian Journal of Community Mental Health, 9,* 1–24.

Tyson, K. B. (1992). A new approach to relevant scientific research for practitioners: The heuristic paradigm. *Social Work, 37,* 541–556.

Van Houten, R., Axelrod, S., Bailey, J., Favell, J. E., Fixx, R. M., Iwata, B. A., et al. (1988). The right to effective behavioral treatment. *Behavior Analyst, 11,* 111–114.

Wetzler, S. (Ed.). (1989). *Measuring mental illness: Psychometric assessment for clinicians.* Washington, DC: American Psychiatric Press.

Williams, L. F. (1995). Epistemology. In R. L. Edwards (Ed.), *Encyclopedia of social work* (19th ed., pp. 872–883). Washington, DC: National Association of Social Workers.

Witkin, S. (1991). Empirical clinical practice: A critical analysis. *Social Work, 36,* 158–163.

Wolman, B. B. (Ed.). (1973). *Dictionary of behavioral science.* New York: Van Nostrand Reinhold.

Zimbalist, S. E. (1977). *Historic themes and landmarks in social welfare research.* New York: Harper & Row.

Disorders Usually First Diagnosed in Infancy, Childhood, or Adolescence

Mental Retardation

John Gerdtz and Susan Gerdtz

2
Chapter

Learning Objectives

After reading this chapter, the reader will be able to:

- Describe the general characteristics of persons with mental retardation.
- Describe the process for arriving at an accurate diagnosis of mental retardation.
- Evaluate the role of social workers in the diagnosis of mental retardation.
- Describe the current service system for children and adults with mental retardation and evaluate strengths and weaknesses in the system, especially from the perspective of a social worker.
- Describe and evaluate future trends in services and the roles that social workers may have in a future service system for persons with mental retardation.

Overview of the Problem

A review of the professional social work literature (see Gerdtz & Bregman, 1998, pp. 25–26) indicated a curious lack of interest in providing services to children and adults with mental retardation, along with an almost complete absence of published evidenced-based interventions by social workers involving persons with mental retardation and other developmental disabilities. Since 1998 there has been additional discussion of the need for more social work involvement in services to persons with mental retardation and other disabilities and their families (e.g., Galambos, 2004), as well as an increase in the number of studies in the social work literature involving people with mental retardation and other disabilities. Unfortunately, there still does not appear to be significant interest in professional social work preparation programs in helping students develop the information and competencies needed to effectively serve persons with mental retardation or other developmental disabilities (Malone, McKinsey, Thyer, & Straka, 2000, pp. 174–177).

We argue that the continuing focus of providing individualized and community-based services and supports for persons with mental retardation and other developmental disabilities (for more information on these trends, see Bradley, 2000; Schalock, Baker, & Croser, 2002) provides many opportunities for evidenced-based social work services. As we see in this chapter, some social workers have already taken up the challenge and demonstrated the effectiveness of their interventions for children and adults with mental retardation and their families. This chapter reviews recent changes in the definition and assessment of mental retardation, important changes in terminology that may make the term mental retardation obsolete, and recently published evidence-based social interventions in the field of mental retardation.

Operational Definitions of the Problem

Mental retardation is a lifelong disability with three essential characteristics:

1. Mental retardation must be first diagnosed during the developmental period.
2. The disability must involve a significant impairment in cognitive or intellectual functioning.
3. The disability must involve a significant impairment or delay in adaptive behavior (or daily living skills).

It is important to note that all three criteria must be met for an accurate diagnosis of mental retardation (Editorial Board, 2000, p. 14).

Specific criteria for diagnosing mental retardation are listed in the *Diagnostic and Statistical Manual of Mental Disorders* (American Psychiatric Association, 1994); this manual is commonly known as the *DSM-IV.* The *DSM-IV* defined the developmental period for diagnosis as before age 18 years (p. 37). A manual developed by the American Psychological Association (Editorial Board, 2000, p. 13) defined the developmental period as before the age of 22 years. Basically, mental retardation is, in the words of *DSM-IV,* "A disorder usually diagnosed in infancy, childhood or adolescence" (American Psychiatric Association, 1994, p. 37).

The second important diagnostic criterion of significant impairment in intellectual functioning is generally defined by both the *DSM-IV* (American Psychiatric Association, 1994, p. 39) and the American Psychological Association (Editorial Board, 2000, p. 14) as an Intelligence Quotient (or IQ score) of 70 or less, or a score of at least 2 standard deviations below the mean on a standardized test of intelligence. Both the *DSM-IV* and the American Psychological Association list degrees of severity of mental retardation according to approximate IQ scores and impairments in adaptive behavior. The levels of severity are Mild Mental Retardation (with IQ scores of approximately 55 to 70); Moderate Mental Retardation (with IQ scores of approximately 35 to 54); Severe Mental Retardation (with scores of approximately 20 to 34); and Profound Mental Retardation (with IQ scores below 20). Each level of severity is also associated with increasing impairments in adaptive behavior (for more information and examples, see Editorial Board, 2000, pp. 39–41).

The third diagnostic criterion for mental retardation is significant impairment in adaptive behavior, those behaviors a person needs to function in daily life in society. There is evidence of a relationship between IQ scores and measures of adaptive behavior, although the strength of the relationship seems to vary at different levels of severity of mental retardation. Adaptive behavior is commonly assessed through the use of standardized measures (see the Assessment section for a discussion of these measures). In addition, a comprehensive psychosocial assessment, familiar to most social workers, is often very helpful in arriving at a diagnosis of mental retardation and for planning appropriate services for individuals and families, as discussed later in the chapter.

The American Association on Mental Retardation (AAMR) has been involved in definition and diagnosis of mental retardation for more than 100 years, and this organization has also developed diagnostic and classification criteria that differ somewhat from the *DSM-IV.* Founded in 1876, the AAMR is the oldest professional organization in the United States dedicated to providing services to children and adults with mental retardation and their families: there is a social work division of the AAMR.

The AAMR definition of mental retardation retains the basic concept of the *DSM-IV* definition in that mental retardation is understood as a significant impairment in both intellectual ability and adaptive behavior. The AAMR (2000) definition adds an assessment component involving the evaluation of the level and type of supports that an individual with mental retardation would need to function as independently as possible in society. In the AAMR diagnostic system, supports needed by an individual with mental retardation may include human development activities, teaching and education activities, home and community living activities, employment activities, health and safety activities, behavioral activities, social activities, and protection and advocacy activities; further specific information about each of these activity domains is discussed at length in AAMR (2002), and summarized in detail at AAMR (2002, pp. 157–159). The goal of the AAMR system is to move services and support systems from specialized programs largely based on level of disability (mild, moderate, severe, or profound) to an individualized, flexible, and community-based system of supports. The valued outcomes measured by the AAMR system are improvements in the areas of independence, personal relationships, community involvement and contributions, school and community participation, and personal well-being (p. 67). As part of the AAMR system, the family and members of the clinical team supporting the child or adult with mental retardation need to evaluate the individual's needs in the various domain areas in terms of no support, some support, or significant support. It is expected that these support needs will vary from individual to individual (even among individuals with the same severity of mental retardation), that these levels of support needs will change over time and over environments, and that support needs will be driven by the individual's preferences and desires (pp. 184–187). There is also an assumption that all supports will be provided in community settings rather than in specialized programs or institutions.

The AAMR system of diagnosis and evaluation was criticized for a number of reasons. Critics argued that the new system was driven more by an ideology of total community-based services rather than by the need to develop new diagnostic schema. Other critics claimed (with justification) that there were no acceptably reliable and valid instruments to measure support needs and systems of support for individuals, so that the assessments may be simply the subjective and time-limited impressions of individuals, family members, and team members, and that these perceptions could change on a daily basis. With no valid and reliable data there was no way to measure the effectiveness and outcomes of the assessment system or of service programs based on this support system. There was also a concern that individuals with mental retardation with no involved family members, or no active clinical teams to support them, may actually miss out on important services. Some thought that necessary supports may be prematurely withdrawn from people with mental retardation based on the possibly unreliable perceptions of family members or other caregivers (see AAMR, 2002, pp. 191–192).

The developers of the AAMR system admitted that some of these criticisms were justified. They (AAMR, 2002, pp. 183–194) admitted that their goal was to move services from large congregate facilities based on diagnostic labels to individualized community-based services, and that the problem facing many individuals with mental retardation was not the imposition of inappropriate services but that no support services of any kind were available. There was also an admission that there were no acceptably reliable and valid measures of adaptive behavior that assessed support needs and levels of support that were called for in the AAMR diagnostic system.

Another classification system relevant to persons with mental retardation and their families is the category first developed by the federal government in 1970 known as *developmental disabilities*. Developmental disabilities are lifelong disabilities that become apparent before the age of 22 and result in significant difficulties in three or more areas of adaptive behavior or major life activity (self-care, learning, use of language, mobility, etc.). Mental retardation, cerebral palsy, and epilepsy are the major disabilities included under the rubric of developmental disabilities, although any other disability that involves impairment in intellectual functioning and adaptive behavior similar to mental retardation would be included in the definition. The only disability specifically excluded is mental illness (AAMR, 2002, pp. 117–118).

In most parts of the United States, agencies that provide services for adults with disabilities generally use the criterion of developmental disabilities, rather than the diagnosis of mental retardation, as a basis for determining eligibility for services. This can be confusing for persons with disabilities and their families or caregivers because a diagnosis of mental retardation is usually sufficient to provide services such as special education for children with disabilities. To add to the confusion, a number of studies (see AAMR, 2002, pp. 116–117) found that some adults diagnosed with mental retardation (especially mild mental retardation) might not fit the criteria for developmental disabilities, and so be denied services. The U.S. Social Security Administration also uses an assessment system that takes into account impairment in major life activities to determine eligibility for funding and services (pp. 118–121).

At least in theory, social workers should have important roles to play in supporting individuals with disabilities and their families through the diagnostic process and in helping them understand the implications of the various systems of diagnosis. Also, again in theory, social work support, case management, and advocacy would seem to be valuable to individuals and families who are trying to negotiate the often confusing maze of the various service systems for persons with mental retardation. Finally, social worker advocacy would seem to be important given the reality that services for individuals with mental retardation (especially adults) in the United States have long waiting lists in virtually every area of the country (AAMR, 2002, pp. 187–188). In the United States at present there are about 80,000 persons with mental retardation and other developmental disabilities on waiting lists for residential and other services, and some have been on the list for more than 10 years. The poverty rate for families with a child or adult with mental retardation or other developmental disability living with them is twice the national average, according to one study (Ansberry, 2005, pp. A1, A5).

Future Terminology

There has been considerable discussion of the appropriateness and future use of the term "mental retardation." Advocates and others (see summary in Batshaw & Shapiro, 2002, p. 294) argue that the term is both obsolete and degrading. Alternative terminology, such as *intellectual disabilities* and *cognitive disabilities*, has been proposed, and in many other countries (e.g., the United Kingdom, Australia, New Zealand) mental retardation is not accepted as appropriate terminology, and intellectual or cognitive disabilities is the accepted term. In August 2006, members of the AAMR (2006) voted to change the name of the organization to the American Association on Intellectual and Developmental Disabilities.

General Characteristics of Persons with Mental Retardation

People with mental retardation have to be treated as individuals for purposes of diagnosis, assessment, and planning for support needs, but there are some common characteristics of this population. There has been controversy in the past about estimates of prevalence of mental retardation in the general population. It is generally accepted that the overall prevalence is about 2.5% of the general population, although estimates have ranged from 1% to 3%. Readers interested in more information on the incidence and prevalence of mental retardation in the general population should consult Batshaw and Shapiro (2002) and Gerdtz and Bregman (1998). The vast majority of persons with mental retardation (about 85%) fall into the mild mental retardation category. As with many disabilities, the number of males with mental retardation is higher than the number of females (the male-to-female ratio is about 2:1 overall). Children and adults with mental retardation are significantly more likely than the general population to have associated disabilities, including cerebral palsy, seizure disorders, speech and language difficulties, and feeding and eating disorders (Batshaw & Shapiro, 2002, pp. 296–297). A number of physical and dental health problems seem to be more common for people with mental retardation than for the general population. In addition, the prevalence of a number of mental health disorders (such as anxiety disorders and depression) seems to be higher among persons with mental retardation than in the general population (AAMR, 2002, pp. 171–175). Individuals with mental retardation and specific genetic syndromes such as Down syndrome may be vulnerable to particular behavioral and psychiatric disabilities; for example, persons with Down syndrome are especially vulnerable as adults to early onset of some types of dementia (p. 173). Readers interested in a brief but comprehensive survey of the various genetic syndromes associated with mental retardation and behavioral and psychiatric disabilities that are commonly found with each syndrome should consult AAMR (2002, especially pp. 138–139).

In the past, the etiology of mental retardation was generally separated into two major groups: familial/sociocultural (family poverty, maternal malnutrition, lack of stimulation, etc.) factors which were generally associated with mild mental retardation (by far the most common form of mental retardation), and biological factors (such as chromosomal disorders, metabolic disorders, injuries at birth), which were usually associated with the severe and profound levels of mental retardation. More recently, models have developed that look at the complex interaction of biological risk and environmental risk factors for mental retardation, not simply assuming that the etiology was either cultural-familial or biological. Some researchers maintain that the more complex multifactor model of the etiology of mental retardation is not necessarily an improvement over the old model (see AAMR, 2002, pp. 125–137, for a detailed discussion of these issues). In general, the major risk factors for the development of mental retardation are prenatal factors (including genetic disorders, maternal malnutrition, parental substance abuse), perinatal factors (including prematurity, birth injury, lack of access to birth care), and postnatal factors (including traumatic brain injury, malnutrition, seizure disorders, child abuse, and neglect). Readers seeking more information on etiology and risk factors for mental retardation should review AAMR (2002, especially pp. 125–137).

As noted previously, the prevailing model and philosophy of services for children and adults with mental retardation in the United States (and in most countries that have service systems) is in a transition from services determined by level of severity in specialized settings to individualized services in local and community settings. Recent data from the United States (Prouty, Coucouvanis, & Lakin, 2005) continues to indicate a slow and steady transition of adults with developmental disabilities (including mental retardation) from relatively large congregate settings to more individualized community settings. Similarly, services for infants and children with mental retardation are moving from specialized clinics and classrooms to general education classrooms and other natural settings in the community. Even with this change in philosophy and services, there remains, at least in the United States, a considerable unmet need for any kind of service for adults with mental retardation (AAMR, 2002). In addition, there is considerable variability in the availability of services in different regions and states of the United States (Prouty et al., 2005, pp. 150–151).

Although many advocates, family members, and individuals with mental retardation strongly support the move away from congregate settings to more independent community living for individuals with mental retardation, it should not be assumed that all individuals and families necessarily support this change in philosophy. For example, a study of a group of Latina mothers in Los Angeles (Rueda, Monzo, Shapiro, Gomez, & Blacher, 2005) found that these parents did not endorse independent community living as a goal for their teenagers with developmental disabilities.

Residential services for children and adults with mental retardation in the United States will probably never return to a model of intensive congregate programs based on level of severity of disability for many reasons, including the tremendous expense of the large centralized programs. The move to individualized community-based services has benefited many individuals with mental retardation and their families. Certainly, the community-based service model offers more opportunity for social workers, with their focus on person-in-environment, to provide services to persons with mental retardation and their families.

Evidence-Based Approaches to Assessment

The diagnosis of mental retardation involves three main criteria: the disability should be manifested during the developmental period; there must be a significant impairment in intellectual functioning (usually defined as a score of 2 or more standard deviations below the mean on a standardized test of intelligence); and there must be a significant impairment in adaptive functioning (i.e., the ability to function independently in daily life). Valid and reliable assessment of these factors can be difficult especially when the individuals being evaluated have significant limitations in expressive and receptive language (as do most people with mental retardation), along with, in many cases, problems with basic literacy. This impairment in language and literacy obviously limits the usefulness of interviews and many self-report pencil-and-paper measures in the diagnosis and assessment of persons with mental retardation.

Self-Report Methods

Standardized tests of intellectual functioning, sometimes known as intelligence tests or IQ tests, have traditionally been an important component in the assessment and diagnosis of persons with mental retardation. There are a number of well-known intelligence tests with acceptable reliability and validity, such as the Wechsler series for adults and children, Stanford-Binet IV, and the Slosson Intelligence Test. There are standardized intelligence tests designed to assess individuals with limited language and literacy skills, such as the Comprehensive Test of Nonverbal Intelligence and the Leiter International Performance Scale (see AAMR, 2002, pp. 51–71, for a discussion of the strengths and limitations of intelligence tests). In most circumstances in the United States, the administration and scoring of standardized intelligence tests are the responsibility of school and clinical psychologists, not social workers.

The standardized assessment of adaptive behavior, or the ability to successfully complete the tasks of everyday life, is done with instruments known as adaptive behavior scales. These scales usually involve interviewing family members or other caregivers who have direct experience living or working with the individual under assessment. Based on the caregivers' responses, a standardized score of adaptive behavior is generated. The AAMR (2002, p. 87) reported that there were more than 200 different scales of adaptive behavior available. All of the major adaptive behavior scales, including the Vineland Adaptive Behavior Scales, AAMR Adaptive Behavior Scales, Scales of Independent Behavior, and the Comprehensive Test of Adaptive Behavior, have acceptable to good psychometric properties (measures of reliability and validity) and can be administered by an appropriately trained social worker. The adaptive behavior scales are useful not only in diagnosis, but also in planning treatment and other interventions for children and adults with mental retardation. Readers interested in an overview of the strengths and weaknesses of the major adaptive behavior scales should consult AAMR (2002, pp. 73–91).

The AAMR also developed another form of adaptive behavior scale, the Supports Intensity Scale (SIS; AAMR, 2004). The SIS is a standardized measure of adaptive behavior and current support needs according to the AAMR diagnostic system. The SIS relies on information from the individual with mental retardation (if possible), family members, caregivers, and other members of the clinical team to develop a profile of individual preferences, needs, and levels of support. The scale has acceptable reliability and validity and would be appropriate for diagnostic and clinical use. Social workers will find that the SIS fits the person-in-environment assessment and intervention framework familiar to them. The SIS can be administered and scored by social workers and other trained professional and paraprofessional staff. Although there is a growing acceptance of the SIS, some agencies and school districts continue to insist on the familiar *DSM-IV* criteria to determine eligibility for services.

Another significant form of self-report assessment, and especially relevant for social workers, is the comprehensive psychosocial assessment or social history. Greenspan, Switzky, and Granfield (2000) argued that the core disability of mental retardation has always been an inability to function in everyday life, and that this problem is not well assessed through cutoff scores on standardized tests of intelligence. The authors argued that informed clinical judgment and social history were more important than test scores in the accurate diagnosis of mental retardation (see Greenspan et al., 2000, especially pp. 128–131). A comprehensive psychosocial assessment, familiar to most social workers, can be a crucial factor in the accurate diagnosis of mental retardation. Readers interested in more information should consult Gambrill (1997; especially chapters 14–20), for a comprehensive framework for developing and using psychosocial assessments relevant for social workers serving persons with mental retardation and their families. In addition, Schalock and Luckasson (2005) have useful evidence-based guidelines for using social histories and psychosocial assessments to assist in the diagnosis of mental retardation.

There are a number of self-report measures, including measures using reports of family members or caregivers, that may be useful in clinical planning for children and adults with mental retardation. For assessment of the nature and frequency of problem behaviors, the Aberrant Behavior Checklist and the Behavior Problem Inventory have acceptable to good psychometric properties and could constitute an important part of a social worker's comprehensive assessment (see Gerdtz & Bregman, 1998; Rojahn & Tasse, 2000). For those interested in general screening for psychiatric disorders in populations of persons with mental retardation, instruments such as the Reiss Screen for Maladaptive Behavior and the Psychopathology Instrument for Mentally Retarded Adults would be useful (Rojahn & Tasse, 2000). There has been progress in developing self-report instruments for adults with mild mental retardation who are seeking counseling for problems with interpersonal relationships. Kellett, Beail, and Newman (2005) reported on the Inventory of Interpersonal Problems 32, a self-report measure of interpersonal relationships that developed relatively good reliability and validity data when normed on a sample of adults with mild mental retardation.

There are self-report instruments (mainly based on family and other informant information) that may be useful in assessing the social skills of children and adults with mental retardation for purposes of planning clinical or educational interventions. Two scales for assessing the social skills of children, including children with mental retardation, are the Social Skills Questionnaire and the Matson Evaluation of Social Skills in Youth. The Matson Evaluation for Social Skills for Individuals with Severe Retardation is the only instrument available to assess the social skills of children and adults with severe and profound levels of mental retardation. All of these scales have generally acceptable psychometric properties. Readers interested in more discussion of these measures of social skills should consult Matson and Hammer (2000).

There have also been attempts to measure the quality of life of children and adults with mental retardation using a variety of self-report instruments. Quality of life is an important outcome measure (or dependent variable) in assessments of the effectiveness of community-based residential placements, supported employment, individual and family support, and other interventions. Although some instruments to measure quality of life (usually involving a combination of direct self-report and information from informants) have been developed, the psychometric properties of these instruments have been quite variable and generally not of an acceptable standard (see Heal, Borthwick-Duffy, & Saunders, 2000). Clearly, more research is needed in this area.

One area of particular interest to social workers is self-report assessments of family functioning for use as a basis of assessment and intervention with families. Although a number of family self-report assessment instruments are available (Floyd, Singer, Powers, & Costigan, 2000), in general these instruments fall short of acceptable standards of reliability and validity. For an overview of available family assessment instruments, the reader is directed to Floyd et al. (2000) and Gerdtz and Bregman (1998).

Behavioral Assessment

Behavioral assessment, usually involving the systematic and direct observation of behaviors, is an important component of clinical assessment and intervention with individuals with mental retardation. In cases of aggression, self-injury, or other disruptive behaviors, it is essential that the function of the behavior in the particular environment be determined. The function involves the antecedent conditions, environmental factors, rewards and punishments, and other factors in the environment that make it more likely that disruptive behaviors will be exhibited and less likely that positive behaviors will be exhibited by the individual. The goal of the functional analysis of the problem behavior is to develop interventions and manipulate the environment so that disruptive behaviors are less likely and positive behaviors are more likely to occur.

Available self-report instruments are the Motivation Assessment Scale (MAS), which uses information from family members and other informants to identify a function of problem behavior. Unfortunately, the MAS has proven unreliable in assessing behavioral functions (Linscheid, Iwata, & Foxx, 2000). Direct observations of problem behaviors seem necessary to conduct an accurate functional behavioral assessment. As part of this assessment, initial hypotheses, developed from information from informants provided by the MAS or informal interviews, are evaluated through direct controlled observations, so that hypotheses regarding behavioral function can be directly tested (see Linscheid et al., 2000, pp. 195–196). Social workers could certainly design and implement functional behavioral assessments and interventions, but considerable training and resources will be necessary to carry out these interventions effectively.

Services for school-age children with mental retardation are governed in the United States through the Individuals with Disabilities Education Act of 2004 (IDEA; Smith, Polloway, Patton, & Dowdy, 2006). IDEA 2004 requires that systematic functional behavioral assessments be used in assessing school-age children with severely disruptive behaviors (Smith et al., 2006). Readers interested in more information on conducting a functional behavioral assessment in a school setting, along with the direct observation data collection instruments, should consult McConnell, Hilvitz, and Cox (1998). More information on this topic is also included in Gerdtz and Bregman (1998).

Evidence-Based Approaches to Intervention

The purpose of this section is to review available social work interventions for children and adults with mental retardation and their families and communities. Where possible, the interventions reviewed have empirically verified evidence of effectiveness and usually have been published in peer-reviewed professional journals. This section follows the review of social work interventions in mental retardation published in Gerdtz and Bregman (1998); interventions discussed in 1998 will not be reviewed again here. A recent development in the social work literature is the presence of detailed treatment planners (see, e.g., Slaggert & Jongsma, 2000) for social workers involved in serving children and adults with mental retardation.

This section reviews interventions and potential interventions in the areas of individual therapies (infants, children, adults, and elderly persons with mental retardation), family-based interventions, and community advocacy for persons with mental retardation.

Individual Therapies

Early intervention
In the United States, early intervention refers to services provided to infants and young children with disabilities (including mental retardation) and children at risk of developmental delay. The services are authorized under Part C of IDEA updated in 2004, otherwise known as Public Law (PL) 108-446. The early intervention services include therapy, education, and family support services, provided in collaboration with the child's family (as much as pos-

sible) and in the infant's "natural environment" (usually the family home or child care program). After a transdisciplinary assessment to determine family and child needs is completed, an individualized family service plan is developed to guide interventions with the child and family (Smith et al., 2006, p. 104). The family-centered nature of services envisioned in the early intervention system has a clear role for social work intervention (Malone et al., 2000). Overall, early intervention legislation envisions a service system that is based on a transdisciplinary model of assessment and intervention, with a focus on the strengths, goals, and needs of the family. In addition, there is a requirement that every family involved in early intervention have a service coordinator or case manager to help the family coordinate services and negotiate the service system.

There is certainly evidence that appropriately designed and structured early intervention programs can benefit infants and toddlers with mental retardation or other disabilities and their families (Ramey, Mulvihill, & Ramey, 2000; Zeanah, Stafford, & Zeanah, 2005). At the same time, there is no evidence that social workers are uniquely qualified to provide the family support dimension of early intervention programs. Studies (e.g., Hallam, Rous, & Grove, 2005) have indicated that early intervention case managers from various professional backgrounds tend to favor the interventions from their particular profession. In general, social workers may have more expertise working with families, whereas educators have more expertise in direct interventions with infants and toddlers. It appears, however, that with the appropriate training and supervision, case managers can attain competencies in both family intervention and direct intervention with infants. In some agencies and situations, social workers (and other professionals) have a purely case management function and do not provide direct services to infants with disabilities. Some studies of families involved in early intervention (see Adams, 2003) suggest that many families prefer case managers who can also demonstrate competence at direct interventions with their infant or toddler along with case management.

Research-based guidelines for working with families that meet IDEA requirements for social workers and other professionals in early intervention programs can be found in Hanson and Lynch (2004). Dunst, Trivette, and Deal (1988) developed a series of assessment questionnaires and other instruments to help identify family goals and strengths in early intervention programs, and these instruments are still useful for assessment, planning, and evaluating early intervention programs.

Interventions with Children
The primary interventions for children with mental retardation who are of school age usually involve educators and/or special educators. Educational services for eligible students with mental

retardation and other disabilities in the United States are governed by the provisions of IDEA 2004 (Smith et al., 2006). IDEA offers potential roles for social workers to serve students with mental retardation in the areas of family support and advocacy and collaboration with teachers and other professionals and through positive behavior support, counseling, social skills training, and other psychosocial interventions that support the educational needs of the student. The recent social work literature describes collaborations between teachers and social workers to support student mental health needs (Lynn, McKay, & Atkins, 2003); implementation of a successful social skills training program for elementary students in a school setting (Anderson-Butcher, Newsome, & Nay, 2003); and a successful professional development program implemented by social workers to teach the principles of positive behavior support and reduce the number of disruptive behaviors in school and the number of referrals for special education (Gottlieb & Polirstok, 2005).

Although these social work interventions did not directly involve many students with mental retardation, they do illustrate potential social work services and roles in serving school-age children with mental retardation. Readers needing more information on social work interventions with children with mental retardation should review Gerdtz and Bregman (1998).

Interventions with Adolescents and Adults
As children with mental retardation progress through adolescence to adulthood they and their families are faced with a range of opportunities and challenges. One significant problem for this population in the United States is that adolescents with mental retardation leave the world of educational and other support services required by IDEA 2004 and face the world of adult services. In general, no agency or government body in the United States is legally required to provide services to adults with mental retardation, so individuals and families usually face adult service systems with long waiting lists or services that are unable to support an individual in the community (AAMR, 2002; Hayden & Goldman, 1996).

Individuals with mental retardation are also at increased risk for mental health problems (AAMR, 2002). Unfortunately, the community mental health systems are often overwhelmed and are unable to meet the needs of individuals with mental retardation. There have been innovative efforts to develop collaboration between mental health and developmental disabilities and mental retardation service systems to address these mental health needs (see Gerdtz & Bregman, 1998, for more information). Community mental health agencies frequently employ large numbers of social workers, and there is the potential for fruitful collaboration between social workers in the mental health and mental retardation and developmental disabilities service systems. There have been some interesting recent developments in providing mental health services to adolescents and adults with mental retardation. Some useful mental health assessment instruments, such as the Inventory of Interpersonal Problems 32, have been found to be both reliable and valid when used with adults with mild mental retardation (Kellett et al., 2005). There is also an increasing body of evidence (see Hurley, Pfadt, Tomasulo, & Gardner, 2000; Newman & Beail, 2005) that some adults with mild mental retardation can benefit from certain types of psychotherapy.

It appears that adolescents and adults with mental retardation may also have more difficulties with substance abuse than the general population (AAMR, 2002). The difficulty here is familiar: Just as the substance abuse treatment system appears to have little understanding of persons with mental retardation and other developmental disabilities, the mental retardation and developmental disabilities system seems to have little understanding of substance abuse treatment (Campbell, Essex, & Held, 1994). There have been calls for more social work involvement in substance abuse treatment and promotion of good health for adolescents with mental retardation and other developmental disabilities (e.g., Zacijek-Farber, 1998), but there are still few documented effective interventions in mental retardation and substance abuse by any profession.

As adults with mental retardation move to individually designed and supported community living options, these adults become more dependent on a network of paid caregivers. Studies of populations of adults with disabilities (including mental retardation) who receive personal attendant services to meet their daily needs indicate relatively high levels of abuse and mistreatment in these programs (Oktay & Tompkins, 2004). Obviously, this is not solely a concern of social workers. There is some evidence (Khemka, Hickson, & Reynolds, 2005) that adults with mental retardation can be trained to protect themselves from abuse or potentially abusive situations. Social work interventions with evidence of effectiveness would clearly be welcome in the areas of investigation of abuse (e.g., through the Adult Protective and Child Protective Service Systems) and through the effective prevention and treatment of the abuse of persons with mental retardation.

Family Interventions

The most common published social work interventions in the practice area of mental retardation continue to be studies of interventions with families. This is not surprising given the traditional focus of social workers on family-based interventions. Also, there is considerable evidence that the birth and diagnosis of a child with mental retardation can be a source of stress for many families. For example, a useful retrospective study of parents of young adults with Fragile X and Down syndrome (Poehlmann, Clements, Abbeduto, & Farsad, 2005) indicated the stresses experienced by many families at initial diagnosis, but also the coping strategies and positive experiences that many families had as they raised a child with a disability. A recent Spanish survey of mothers of newborns with Down syndrome (Skotko & Bedia, 2005) gave evidence of the ongoing need for information and support for many families and indicated that gaps in services for these families was not just confined to the United States.

Freedman and Capobianco-Boyer (2000) studied groups of families in Massachusetts with a child or adult family member diagnosed with mental retardation or other developmental disability. The families identified a variety of needs, but there was a consensus that flexible family support programs were extremely helpful. The families also felt that, at times, social workers and other case managers were unable to provide useful information on available community resources for their child or other family member. Hayden and Goldman's (1996) earlier study of family members and caregivers of adults with mental retardation also found a variety of needs and coping strategies reported. In this study, some families expressed concern at the lack of information provided by social workers and other case managers regarding available resources. A common theme from both these studies is that families have coping strategies as well as problems and crises, and that appropriate family support is based on the particular family's unique coping style, is flexible, and is able to provide useful information about community resources.

In many ways, families provide most of the support needed by people with mental retardation (see Freedman & Capobianco-Boyer, 2000). An often neglected area of the family support system is the contribution of the siblings of children and adults with mental retardation. A recent study of the brothers and sisters of children with mental retardation by Hannah and Midlarsky (2005) found that these siblings made a significant contribution to the family caregiving system. Support for siblings is another area of potential social work intervention with families.

Training parents in home-based educational and behavioral interventions so that children with mental retardation can be more independent has been found to be effective with some families (Baker, 2000). It appears that this type of parent training can be effective with low-income, non-English-speaking families; participating families reported improvements in the skills of their child with mental retardation and an improvement in their general family life (pp. 293–294). This is an obvious area for social work intervention, but this type of intervention is almost completely absent from the social work literature. Baker, who has conducted the most detailed research and evaluation of parent training in the area of mental retardation and developmental disabilities, is a psychologist. Those who are interested in the specific training programs used by Baker and his colleagues for application in the home or in parent training programs should consult Baker et al. (2004).

Aging, Mental Retardation, and Families
As the number of aging and elderly persons increases across the world (Ansello & Janicki, 2000), there has been a concurrent increase in the population of elderly adults with mental retardation and other lifelong disabilities (Janicki & Ansello, 2000). Over 75% of older adults with developmental disabilities in the United States live with their parents, who are themselves aging or elderly (Botsford & Rule, 2004). Many of these individuals and families may not be served by any agency or program (Ansello & Coogle, 2000). There is a clear need to develop collaborative relationships between the service systems for persons with mental retardation and developmental disabilities and the systems for aging adults. The development of these collaborations is possible (see Ansello & Coogle, 2000) and offers many opportunities for social work involvement.

Although surveys of families of persons with mental retardation provide useful information, social workers also need information on effective interventions with these families. Botsford and Rule's (2004) recent study of the outcomes of a group intervention to help aging mothers of adults with mental retardation plan for the future needs of their children is a welcome addition to the literature. The study used a true experimental design with random assignment and demonstrated the effectiveness of the social work group intervention for these parents.

A significant limitation to the family support literature discussed here is the almost complete focus of this literature, and the associated interventions, on mothers. As Baker (2000, p. 296) and other researchers noted, there is very little information or research on effective family support programs for fathers of children and adults with mental retardation and other developmental disabilities. This issue has been discussed in the literature for years, and more studies of fathers would be most welcome.

Community Interventions

Surveys of families and individuals with mental retardation consistently identified the need for advocacy services. Advocacy services could be at the individual or family level, to assist in protecting legal rights, obtaining services, or negotiating service systems. Advocacy can also involve policy development, analysis, and recommendations at the local and national levels.

Studies of social work advocacy at the individual and family level were described in Gerdtz and Bregman (1998). More recently, Pollack (2005) provided a useful legal analysis and recommendations for assisting individuals with mental retardation make appropriate decisions in the difficult areas of abortion and sterilization.

On a systems level of advocacy, Palley and Van Hollen (2000) analyzed the policy implications of long-term care for elderly individuals with mental retardation and other developmental disabilities. Hall's (1996) article was an interesting description of the role of social workers and other professionals in the movement toward integrated systems of community support for individuals with developmental disabilities in Colorado.

Summary

There has been some increase in both the quantity and quality of the social work literature devoted to the field of mental retardation since the review by Gerdtz and Bregman (1998). It would be helpful if future social work research could match the methodological rigor and clinical usefulness of Botsford and Rule's (2004) recent published study. Clearly the time has now come to move away from articles proclaiming social work competence in the field of mental retardation and developmental disabilities and toward actual research that demonstrates the effectiveness of social work interventions for this population.

Study Questions

1. What are the main characteristics of persons with mental retardation? Compare and contrast mental retardation with another disability.

2. How is mental retardation diagnosed? How might social workers participate in this diagnostic process? What challenges might social workers who participate in the diagnostic process face?

3. How have services for persons with mental retardation changed over the past 20 years? Do you think these changes have generally benefited children and adults with mental retardation and their families? Why or why not?

4. What kind of services do you think children and adults with mental retardation will need in 20 years? What role do you think social workers will have in providing these services? What challenges will face social workers in providing services to people with mental retardation and their families in the future?

5. If you were the parent of a child or adult with mental retardation at the present time, would you be afraid of the changes in the service system as discussed in this chapter, or supportive, or both? Discuss.

6. If you were a social worker in an agency providing services to persons with mental retardation and their families, what specific kinds of knowledge and information would you need to be effective? What other kinds of professionals and staff persons might you have to collaborate with? How might you build good collaborative relationships with other staff and professionals at your agency?

References

Adams, C. (2003). *Relationship of early intervention service coordination model to quality of transition and family empowerment.* Unpublished doctoral dissertation, University of Rhode Island.

American Association on Mental Retardation. (2002). *Mental retardation: Definition, classification, and systems of supports.* Washington, DC: Author.

American Association on Mental Retardation. (2004). *Supports Intensity Scale: User's manual.* Washington, DC: Author.

American Association on Mental Retardation (2006). *Results of the vote on the name.* Retrieved August 22, 2006, from the American Association on Mental Retardation web site: http://aamr.org/About_AAMR/name.shtml.

American Psychiatric Association. (1994). *Diagnostic and statistical manual of mental disorders* (4th ed.). Washington, DC: Author.

Anderson-Butcher, D., Newsome, W. S., & Nay, S. (2003). Social skills intervention during elementary school recess: A visual analysis. *Children and Schools, 25,* 135–146.

Ansberry, C. (2005, September 20). Needing assistance, parents of disabled resort to extremes. *Wall Street Journal,* pp. A1, A5.

Ansello, E. F., & Coogle, C. L. (2000). Building intersystem cooperation: Partners III integrated model. In M. P. Janicki & E. F. Ansello (Eds.), *Community supports for aging adults with lifelong disabilities* (pp. 457–476). Baltimore: Paul H. Brookes.

Ansello, E. F., & Janicki, M. P. (2000). The aging of nations: Impact on the community, the family, and the individual. In M. P. Janicki & E. F. Ansello (Eds.), *Community supports for aging adults with lifelong disabilities* (pp. 3–18). Baltimore: Paul H. Brookes.

Baker, B. L. (2000). Parent training. In J. W. Jacobson & J. A. Mulick (Eds.), *Manual of diagnosis and professional practice in mental retardation* (pp. 289–299). Washington, DC: American Psychological Association.

Baker, B. L., Brightman, A. J., Blacher, J. B., Heifetz, L. J., Hinshaw, S. R., & Murphy, D. M. (2004). *Steps to independence: Teaching everyday skills to children with disabilities* (4th ed.). Baltimore: Paul H. Brookes.

Batshaw, M. L., & Shapiro, B. (2002). Mental retardation. In M. L. Batshaw (Ed.), *Children with disabilities* (5th ed., pp. 287–305). Baltimore: Paul H. Brookes.

Botsford, A. L., & Rule, D. (2004). Evaluation of a group intervention to assist parents with permanency planning for an adult offspring with special needs. *Social Work, 49,* 423–429.

Bradley, V. J. (2000). Changes in services and supports for people with developmental disabilities: New challenges for established practice. *Health and Social Work, 25,* 191–200.

Campbell, J. A., Essex, E. L., & Held, G. (1994). Issues in chemical dependency treatment and aftercare for people with learning differences. *Health and Social Work, 19,* 63–68.

Dunst, C., Trivette, C., & Deal, A. (1988). *Enabling and empowering families: Principles and guidelines for practice.* Cambridge, MA: Brookline Books.

Editorial Board. (2000). Definition of mental retardation. In J. W. Jacobson & J. A. Mulick (Eds.), *Manual of diagnosis and professional practice in mental retardation* (pp. 13–53). Washington, DC: American Psychological Association.

Floyd, F. J., Singer, G. H. S., Powers, L. E., & Costigan, C. L. (2000). Families coping with mental retardation: Assessment and therapy. In J. W. Jacobson & J. A. Mulick (Eds.), *Manual of diagnosis and professional practice in mental retardation* (pp. 277–288). Washington, DC: American Psychological Association.

Freedman, R. I., & Capobianco-Boyer, N. (2000). The power to choose: Supports for families caring for individuals with developmental disabilities. *Health and Social Work, 25,* 59–68.

Galambos, C. M. (2004). Social work practice with people with disabilities: Are we doing enough? *Health and Social Work, 29,* 163–165.

Gambrill, E. (1997). *Social work practice: A critical thinker's guide.* New York: Oxford University Press.

Gerdtz, J., & Bregman, J. (1998). Mental retardation. In B. A. Thyer & J. S. Wodarski (Eds.), *Handbook of empirical social work practice: Vol. 1. Mental disorders* (pp. 25–54). New York: Wiley.

Gottlieb, J., & Polirstok, S. (2005). Program to reduce behavioral infractions and referrals to special education. *Children and Schools, 27,* 53–57.

Greenspan, S., Switzky, H. N., & Granfield, J. M. (2000). Everyday intelligence and adaptive behavior: A theoretical framework. In J. W. Jacobson & J. A. Mulick (Eds.), *Manual of diagnosis and professional practice in mental retardation* (pp. 127–135). Washington, DC: American Psychological Association.

Hall, S. R. (1996). The community-centered board model of managed care for people with developmental disabilities. *Health and Social Work, 21,* 225–229.

Hallam, R. A., Rous, B., & Grove, J. (2005). Professional background of service coordinators and collaboration with community agencies. *Journal of Early Intervention, 27,* 285–294.

Hannah, M. E., & Midlarsky, E. (2005). Helping by siblings of children with mental retardation. *American Journal on Mental Retardation, 110,* 87–99.

Hanson, M. J., & Lynch, E. W. (2004). *Understanding families: Approaches to diversity, disability and risk.* Baltimore: Paul H. Brookes.

Hayden, M. F., & Goldman, J. (1996). Families of adults with mental retardation: Stress levels and need for services. *Social Work, 41,* 657–667.

Heal, L. W., Borthwick-Duffy, S. A., & Saunders, R. R. (2000). Assessment of quality of life. In J. W. Jacobson & J. A. Mulick (Eds.), *Manual of diagnosis and professional practice in mental retardation* (pp. 199–209). Washington, DC: American Psychological Association.

Hurley, A. D., Pfadt, A., Tomasulo, D., & Gardner, W. I. (2000). Counseling and psychotherapy. In J. W. Jacobson & J. A. Mulick (Eds.), *Manual of diagnosis and professional practice in mental retardation* (pp. 371–380). Washington, DC: American Psychological Association.

Janicki, M. P., & Ansello, E. F. (2000). Supports for community living: Evolution of an aging with lifelong disabilities movement. In M. P. Janicki & E. F. Ansello (Eds.), *Community supports for aging adults with lifelong disabilities* (pp. 529–547). Baltimore: Paul H. Brookes.

Kellett, S., Beail, N., & Newman, D. W. (2005). Measuring interpersonal problems in people with mental retardation. *American Journal on Mental Retardation, 110,* 136–144.

Khemka, I., Hickson, L., & Reynolds, G. (2005). Evaluation of a decision-making curriculum designed to empower women with mental retardation to resist abuse. *American Journal on Mental Retardation, 110,* 193–204.

Linscheid, T. R., Iwata, B. A., & Foxx, R. M. (2000). Behavioral assessment. In J. W. Jacobson & J. A. Mulick (Eds.), *Manual of diagnosis and professional practice in mental retardation* (pp. 191–198). Washington, DC: American Psychological Association.

Lynn, C. J., McKay, M. M., & Atkins, M. S. (2003). School social work: Meeting the mental health needs of students through collaboration with teachers. *Children and Schools, 25,* 197–209.

Malone, D. M., McKinsey, P. D., Thyer, B. A., & Straka, E. (2000). Social work early intervention for young children with developmental disabilities. *Health and Social Work, 25,* 169–180.

Matson, J. L., & Hammer, D. (2000). Assessment of social functioning. In J. W. Jacobson & J. A. Mulick (Eds.), *Manual of diagnosis and professional practice in mental retardation* (pp. 157–163). Washington, DC: American Psychological Association.

McConnell, M. E., Hilvitz, P. B., & Cox, C. J. (1998). Functional assessment: A systematic process for assessment and intervention in general and special education classrooms. *Intervention in School and Clinic, 34,* 10–20.

Newman, D. W., & Beail, N. (2005). Analysis of assimilation during psychotherapy with people who have mental retardation. *American Journal on Mental Retardation, 110,* 359–365.

Oktay, J. S., & Tompkins, C. J. (2004). Personal assistance providers' mistreatment of disabled adults. *Health and Social Work, 29,* 177–188.

Palley, H. A., & Van Hollen, V. (2000). Long-term care for people with developmental disabilities: A critical analysis. *Health and Social Work, 25,* 181–189.

Poehlmann, J., Clements, M., Abbeduto, L., & Farsad, V. (2005). Family experiences associated with a child's diagnosis of Fragile X or Down syndrome: Evidence for disruption and resilience. *Mental Retardation, 43,* 255–267.

Pollack, D. (2005). The capacity of a mentally challenged person to consent to abortion and sterilization. *Health and Social Work, 30,* 253–257.

Prouty, R., Coucouvanis, K., & Lakin, K. C. (2005). Fiscal year 2004 institution populations, movement, and expenditures by state with national comparisons to earlier years. *Mental Retardation, 43,* 149–151.

Ramey, C. T., Mulvihill, B. A., & Ramey, S. L. (2000). Prevention: Social and educational factors and early intervention. In J. W. Jacobson & J. A. Mulick (Eds.), *Manual of diagnosis and professional practice in mental retardation* (pp. 215–227). Washington, DC: American Psychological Association.

Rojahn, J., & Tasse, M. J. (2000). Psychopathology in mental retardation. In J. W. Jacobson & J. A. Mulick (Eds.), *Manual of diagnosis and professional practice in mental retardation* (pp. 147–156). Washington, DC: American Psychological Association.

Rueda, R., Monzo, L., Shapiro, J., Gomez, J., & Blacher, J. (2005). Cultural models of transition: Latina mothers of young adults with developmental disabilities. *Exceptional Children, 71,* 415–430.

Schalock, R. L., Baker, P. C., & Croser, M. D. (2002). Trends and issues. In R. L. Schalock, P. C. Baker, & M. D. Croser (Eds.), *Embarking on a new century: Mental retardation at the end of the 20th century* (pp. 255–261). Washington, DC: American Association on Mental Retardation.

Schalock, R. L., & Luckasson, R. (2005). *Clinical judgment.* Washington, DC: American Association on Mental Retardation.

Skotko, B., & Bedia, R. C. (2005). Postnatal support for mothers of children with Down syndrome. *Mental Retardation, 43,* 196–212.

Slaggert, K. H., & Jongsma, Jr., A. E. (2000). *The mental retardation and developmental disability treatment planner.* New York: Wiley.

Smith, T. E. C., Polloway, E. A., Patton, J. R., & Dowdy, C. A. (2006). *Teaching children with special needs in inclusive settings* (4th ed.). Boston: Pearson.

Zacijek-Farber, M. L. (1998). Promoting good health in adolescents with disabilities. *Health and Social Work, 23,* 203–211.

Zeanah, P. D., Stafford, B., & Zeanah, C. H. (2005). *Clinical interventions to enhance infant mental health: A selective review.* Retrieved September 20, 2005, from National Center for Infant and Early Childhood Health Policy at UCLA web site: www .healthychild.ucla.edu.

Autistic Disorder

Claire J. Calohan and Colin M. Peeler

3
Chapter

Learning Objectives

After reading this chapter, the reader will be able to:

- Describe the prevalence and trends in the incidence of autism.
- Identify the diagnostic criteria for Autistic Disorder.
- Identify evidence-based assessment techniques and the necessary conditions and training requirements for using them.
- Identify evidence-based intervention techniques shown to be effective and select one most appropriate for a child and family.
- Describe the importance of early diagnosis and intervention in the treatment of Autistic Disorder.
- Describe the role of social workers in the assessment and treatment of autism.

Overview of the Problem

Social workers' contact with a child diagnosed with autism may occur in many practice settings. A social worker providing case management services in an early intervention program will be involved in the assessment phase, administering parent questionnaires and completing a biopsychosocial assessment; a social worker providing home-based intervention could

53

serve as a member of the treatment team. In their role as liaison between the school and the family, school social workers are involved in assessment and intervention. Social workers may also provide support to families as they deal with the reality of this diagnosis and the day-to-day stresses of living with a child with a disability. Rapport building, listening skills, and empathic responses are utilized in this situation. Hepworth, Rooney, and Larsen (2002) describe the roles of social workers as broker, case manager/coordinator, mediator/arbitrator, and client advocate. Each of these roles can play an important part in assisting families of children with Autistic Disorder. Parents can become overwhelmed due to the intricacies of navigating the service delivery system and may need assistance to obtain optimum service provision. Whether connecting families to resources, facilitating development of a community support group for parents, or organizing a letter-writing campaign to legislators in support of a bill to increase funding for a respite program, social workers provide essential services to families of children with autism.

Our understanding of Autistic Disorder and how to treat it has vastly improved since Leo Kanner first described it in 1943, but there is still a great deal that is unknown. Autism was once considered a rare disorder, with prevalence studies conducted prior to 1985 estimating 2 out of every 10,000 being affected with Autistic Disorder and 4 out of 10,000 for the more broadly defined Autism Spectrum Disorders (Lotter, 1966; Wing, 1993; Wing & Gould, 1979). More recent U.S.-based epidemiological studies estimate that Autistic Disorder affects as many as 3 to 4 of every 1,000 children (Bertrand et al., 2001; Bryson & Smith, 1998; Yeargin-Allsop et al., 2003). As many as 50 children are diagnosed each day, and males are affected more than females at a rate of 4:1 (Fombonne, 1998). With prevalence rates as high as 1 in 250, representing a greater than 500% increase in the past decade, autism is more common than spina bifida, Down syndrome, and all forms of childhood cancer combined (Muhle, Trentacoste, & Rapin, 2004).

In the absence of treatment, fewer than 5% of individuals with autism fully recover from the disorder and will require life-long educational or social services at an estimated expense of $4 million per person (Jacobson, Mulick, & Green, 1998). Although aggregate costs incurred by our society are difficult to obtain (Jarbrink, Fombonne, & Knapp, 2003), it has been estimated that the United States spends $90 billion per year to provide care for the country's 1.5 million autistic children and adults (Clark, 2004). Families appear to provide most of the care for children with disabilities (Fujiura, Roccoforte, & Braddock, 1994), which costs approximately three times as much as rearing a nondisabled child (Dobson & Middleton, 1998).

At this point there is insufficient data to explain why there has been such a dramatic increase in observed cases of autism in the past 10 years; however, changes in diagnostic criteria and classification, improved assessment techniques, increased availability of services, and the requirement of a diagnosis of autism to receive those services all likely play a role. A variety of environmental causes have been suggested as contributing to the rise in observed cases, although none has been confirmed through scientific evidence. One of the first proposed was by psychoanalysts (e.g., Bettelheim, 1967, cited in Smith, 1996) who believed that extremely cold mothering techniques led to the development of autism as a defense mechanism, allowing the child to withdraw from the situation. More recently, claims have been made that the measles-mumps-rubella vaccine and the preservative this and many other vaccines contain, thimerasol, is the cause of autism (Wakefield et al., 1998). However, extensive research using biological and population-based studies has failed to find a link between the vaccine and autism (Fombonne & Chakrabarti, 2001; Hviid, Stellfeld, Wohlfahrt, & Melbye, 2003). Although speculation and inquiry into the potential factors leading to autism is critical to the search for the cause and potentially a cure for autism, we must be cautious in evaluating claims and must evaluate them based on existing scientific evidence.

Autism is currently seen as a neurobiological disorder likely to be caused by a variety of factors. Recent research on twins, families, and recurrence of autism in siblings of affected children suggest that there are likely several genes involved (Korvatska, Van de Water, Anders, & Gershwin, 2002; Volkmar & Pauls, 2003). Other research indicates that families who have a child with autism are 8% to 10% more likely to have a second child with autism (Muhle et al., 2004). Another factor associated with autism is abnormal brain development. Advances in brain imaging and the greater availability of brain tissue from people with autism have led to the discovery that several areas of the brain may fail to normally develop during the first few months of life (Strock, 2004).

Operational Definitions of the Problem

Autism is a disorder characterized in the *Diagnostic and Statistical Manual of Mental Disorders* (*DSM;* American Psychiatric Association, 2000) by impaired functioning in (a) social interactions and (b) communication and demonstration of (c) repetitive and stereotyped patterns of behavior. For a diagnosis to be made, the child must experience abnormal functioning across all three areas and abnormal functioning in at least one of these areas before age 3. The severity of these symptoms varies from child to child and is often referred to as occurring across a spectrum or along a continuum (Autism Spectrum Disorder).

Children with autism have difficulty interacting with others, preferring to be alone, avoiding eye contact (even when prompted) and often interacting only to have needs met. In terms of play skills, children with autism engage in parallel play in which they play side by side with another child but fail to show reciprocal social interactions such as shared enjoyment in an activity, seeking the other person's attention, or pointing to objects of interest. For example, a child with autism may play with cars by lining them up or repeatedly moving them back and forth, with very little variation. If prompted to play cars with another child, the child with autism may tantrum to escape the demand or just walk away to avoid the social interaction altogether.

Communication problems are usually observed by 18 months to 2 years, as this is when normal children are typically developing language. Some children with autism remain nonverbal, some develop very basic receptive and expressive language skills, and some develop fairly good language. Those with advanced language often demonstrate difficulties with initiating or sustaining a conversation with others, understand language in a very literal sense (not understanding jokes, sarcasm, or voice intonations), and talk in repetitive and stereotyped ways, such as reciting lines from movies, songs, or books. Early signs of communication problems may include failure to babble, babbling in the first few months and then stopping, or delayed language development compared to age-typical peers. Because the range for what is considered normal language development varies, pediatricians, teachers, friends, and family often tell parents not to worry about it. Many nonautistic children's language does in fact catch up, yet the importance of early detection and treatment in autism requires that parents suspecting a problem be encouraged to seek out a specialist to have a more thorough assessment done.

Perhaps two of the most apparent features of autism are stereotyped behaviors and persistence with same. Stereotyped behavior has been defined as repetitive and persistent behavior that serves no apparent adaptive function (LaGrow & Repp, 1984). In more severe cases, children with autism will sit for hours rocking, flapping their hands, walking in circles on their toes, gazing at reflections and lights coming through windows, lining up toys or objects, or engaging in self-injurious behaviors such as hand biting, skin picking, and head banging. Other children with more advanced language will become preoccupied with certain topics such as dinosaurs, bugs, trucks, or planes and will talk about, write about, or draw them endlessly throughout the day and often communicate with others via these topics. Aside from the potential physical harm associated with many forms of stereotyped behavior (e.g., skin picking, head banging), these behaviors can also interfere with learning new skills and performing previously learned skills (Epstein, Doke, Sajwaj, Sorrel, & Rimmer, 1974;

Koegel & Covert, 1972; Morrison & Rosales-Ruiz, 1997). Stereo-typed behaviors can socially isolate children and set them apart from peers (Jones, Wint, & Ellis, 1990) and have been found to be a precursor to self-injurious behavior (Guess & Carr, 1991). Persistence varies from demanding the same food for every meal to wearing only certain types of clothing. Children will become agitated and tantrum if the daily routine or route taken home is changed. Even minor changes, such as the shirt picked for the day or the absence of a certain toy, can result in major tantrums.

Evidence-Based Approaches to Assessment

Due to the importance of early identification and intervention for children with autism, the challenge for researchers has been to develop screening instruments that can be used prior to 3 years of age. One such screening tool is the Checklist for Autism in Toddlers (CHAT). It is used to identify the early signs of autism at 18 months of age and assesses the child's attainment of developmental milestones (Baird et al., 2000; Noland & Gabriels, 2004). The CHAT is administered by the child's pediatrician and includes a parent questionnaire and an observation component. A modified version, the M-CHAT, which consists of 23 items, can be administered to all children during pediatric visits. It relies on parents' report of current skills and behaviors and is simple to administer; parents can complete it in the waiting room (Robins, Fein, Barton, & Green, 2001). Physicians should be encouraged to utilize one of these screening instruments and refer children for further evaluation if indicated. The Screening Tool for Autism in Two-Year-Olds was designed to use with children 24 through 35 months of age. It is made up of 12 activities that are assessed by direct observation. The areas assessed relate to children's early social-communicative behavior (Stone, Coonrod, Turner, & Pozdol, 2004).

Research confirming the reliability of these instruments should be provided to physicians and community agencies to encourage early assessment. Implementing early screening could result in an accurate diagnosis and the implementation of therapeutic interventions at a younger age (Goin & Myers, 2004). The ultimate goal of early intervention is the achievement of better outcomes (Lovaas, 1987). Children who are identified as having characteristics of autism will need a multidisciplinary assessment to confirm or rule out the diagnosis.

The diagnosis of Autistic Disorder should include medical, psychosocial, and cognitive assessments as well as an assessment of adaptive behavior. A complete medical history must be obtained and a lead screening obtained, especially if a child is still in the oral-motor stage (Noland & Gabriels, 2004). Hearing and visual impairments must be ruled out. Measures of cognitive assessment should be completed by clinical or school psychologists who are trained to administer standardized intelligence tests such as the Wechsler Preschool and Primary Scale of Intelligence, the Wechsler Intelligence Scale for Children, and the Stanford-Binet Intelligence Scale (Klin, Carter, & Sparrow, 1997). Several tests exist that can be used with children who have poor verbal skills, such as the Leiter International Performance Scale and the British Picture Vocabulary Scale (Klin, Carter, & Sparrow, 1997; Skuse et al., 2004). Because communication difficulties are commonly present with a diagnosis of autism, a comprehensive speech and language assessment should be completed as well.

Social workers typically complete a biopsychosocial assessment, including a thorough pregnancy and neonatal history, medical history, family history, and assessment of family strengths, resources, and coping mechanisms. Particular attention should be paid to the acquisition of developmental milestones (sitting, walking, talking, feeding, toileting). In addition, questions should be asked regarding early babbling, social interest, and motor development, as well as excessive echoing, peculiar interests, and repetitive patterns of behavior (Klin, Carter, Volkmar, et al., 1997). Information in the biopsychosocial assessment provides a very important piece of the puzzle when dealing with children with autism, as the family plays a vital role in the child's progress and prognosis.

The diagnosis of autism relies heavily on interviews with parents, teachers, and others who have direct contact with the child. There are several instruments available to obtain information from parents. One of these tools is the Childhood Autism Rating Scale (Schopler, Reichler, & Renner, 1988). This scale, known as the CARS, consists of 15 items with a 4-point scale for each item. Although designed to be used by a clinician after direct observation, the ratings can also be based on observations by parents or teachers (Schopler et al., 1988). The CARS does not require extensive training to administer and has been documented as a reliable diagnostic instrument for autism, especially when combined with other autism diagnostic assessments (Lord, 1997; Noland & Gabriels, 2004). One study found that, of 65 children evaluated, 54 met the *DSM-IV* criteria for Autistic Disorder. These 54 children also had a CARS score above the cutoff for autism. This agreement between *DSM-IV* and CARS indicates that the CARS is able to identify children with autism. Research has also shown that the scale can differentiate between autism and other disorders (Rellini, Tortolani, Trillo, Carbone, & Montecchi, 2004). The CARS classifies the child as not autistic, mild or moderately autistic, or severely autistic. The last portion of the scale asks the rater to give a general impression of the presence or absence of autism (Rellini et al., 2004). The CARS can be used in various settings, such as schools and day care facilities.

The Autism Behavior Checklist (ABC) is a self-administered checklist completed by parents and measures a variety of autistic symptoms, including sensory, relating, body and object use, language, and social and self-help (Walker et al., 2004). The ABC is one component of the Autism Screening Instrument for Educational Planning. It was developed to be used by teachers for educational planning, but has also been used by parents (Lord, 1997). In the Rellini et al. (2004) study mentioned previously, of the 54 children who met the *DSM-IV* criteria for Autistic Disorder, only 29 had a total ABC score above the cutoff for a diagnosis of autism, indicating that the ABC does not detect children with autism as well as the CARS.

Experience in interviewing and working with children with autism is necessary for clinicians who administer the Autism Diagnostic Interview-Revised (ADI-R), which is a semistructured, investigator-based interview for caregivers of children with autism (Lord, Rutter, & LeCouteur, 1994; Noland & Gabriels, 2004). This instrument is composed of five sections: introductory questions, communication, social development and play, repetitive and stereotyped behaviors, and general behavior problems (Walker et al., 2004). The ADI-R has been shown to be effective for children with a mental age of at least 18 months (Lord et al., 1994). Even the shortened version, which contains about 40 items, takes an experienced interviewer as much as 90 minutes to complete. This limits use of the instrument for screening purposes (Lord, 1997).

The Autism Diagnostic Observation Schedule—Generic (ADOS-G), which can be administered in about 40 minutes, is a structured, play-based observation of the child and assesses social and communication skills of children with a possible diagnosis of autism (Noland & Gabriels, 2004; Walker et al., 2004). The ADOS-G includes modules intended to assess children with various levels of language skills, as well as high-functioning adolescents and adults (Lord, 1997). De Bildt et al. (2004) stated that the ADOS-G is a well-developed, standardized instrument with good psychometric qualities, which utilizes direct observation to assess social and communicative behavior. Specialized training in administration and scoring is required.

It has been suggested that the ADOS-G and the ADI-R can be effectively used together. The ADOS-G can provide data on current behavior through observation, and the ADI-R parent interview can provide information on the child's history and development (de Bildt et al., 2004).

One of the most widely used assessments of adaptive behavior is the Vineland Adaptive Behavior Scales (Sparrow, Balla, & Cicchetti, 1984). This scale has been utilized extensively in the assessment of autism and developmental disabilities. It consists of five sections, assessing communication, daily living skills, socialization, motor skills, and maladaptive behavior (Walker et al., 2004). These domains are assessed via a semistructured interview administered to a parent or caregiver. A classroom edition to be used with teachers is also available (Klin, Carter, & Sparrow, 1997).

Evidence-Based Approaches to Intervention

Individual Therapies

Many treatments are available for children with autism; however, very few have any empirical evidence to support their use, and in fact some can be harmful (Smith, 1996). Several reviews of the literature have found that antiyeast treatments, facilitated communication, chelation treatments, sensory integration, psychotherapy, music therapy, and immunologic therapies have no scientific evidence to support their use (New York State Department of Health [NYSDOH], 1999; Smith, 1996). These treatments tend to get promoted when dramatic improvements have been seen in a single child, and the improvements are attributed to the given treatment. Many of these "miracle" cures have failed to produce significant effects when tested using standard scientific procedures or when tested with other children.

An example of a treatment that many children undergo despite a lack of evidence is the gluten-free casein-free (GFCF) diet. Proponents of the diet believe that children with autism are more likely to have gastrointestinal difficulties. It is proposed that children with autism are unable to process gluten and casein or that when these substances are processed in the stomach toxic byproducts similar to opioids are created that cause autistic behaviors. Black, Kaye, and Jick (2002) looked at children with autism and found they are no more likely to have intestinal problems than normally developing children. To date, there has been only one study evaluating the effects of the GFCF diet (Knivsberg, Reichelt, Hoien, & Nodland, 2002). The results indicated that children with autism showed no significant improvements on 3 of the 4 measures, and the only improvements observed were in "autistic traits," which were measured by a subjective rating scale and are therefore questionable. Furthermore, the diet can be difficult to adhere to and the GFCF foods are expensive and difficult to find. Children with autism already have selective eating habits; therefore, to ensure proper nutrition, restricted diets should be imposed only if warranted due to food allergies (Ahearn, Castine, Nault, & Green, 2001).

With the plethora of treatments advertised on the Internet using anecdotal evidence and personal endorsements as evidence of effectiveness, parents and social workers alike must be extremely careful to check the validity of these claims by searching the scientific literature *before* proceeding with any given treatment. Social workers can play a vital role in researching the evidence on a given treatment and sharing it with parents and other professionals.

There are only two treatments, applied behavior analysis (ABA) and psychopharmacology, that have strong evidence to support their effectiveness in the treatment of autism. Early intensive behavioral intervention (EIBI), based on the principles of ABA, views autism as a behavioral disorder marked by behavioral excesses (stereotyped behavior, tantrums) and deficits (in language, social skills, play skills) that, like all behaviors, can be modified if the proper contingencies are arranged. There are several different approaches based on ABA (discrete trials, the Lovaas method, verbal behavior, natural environment training, incidental teaching, pivotal response training), and they all share the same goals of reducing problem behaviors that interfere with learning and teaching appropriate alternative behaviors. As of yet there is no research to suggest any of the ABA variants is more effective than the others, and given their foundations in ABA they are all likely to be effective at different points in time. Typically, basic learning skills (sitting in a chair, following instructions, attending to others) that will enable the child to learn more advanced skills are taught first. Several excellent manuals exist that delineate the specific skills to teach, methods for teaching them, and the order in which to teach them (Leaf & McEachin, 1999; Lovaas, 2003; Maurice, Green, & Luce, 1996; Sundberg & Partington, 1998). Although these manuals are extremely user-friendly and many parents have reported being able to learn how to do basic therapy with their child after reading them, it is strongly recommended that parents seek out the assistance of a qualified behavior analyst to provide training and assistance.

More than 30 years of research exists showing that individuals with autism can make significant improvements, and in some cases fully recover, given an early diagnosis and implementation of EIBI (Birnbrauer & Leach, 1993; Lovaas, 1987; Matson, Benavidez, Stabinsky-Compton, Paclawskyj, & Baglio, 1996; McEachin, Smith, & Lovaas, 1993; Risley, 1968). In 1967, Lovaas and colleagues began the first evaluation of EIBI in which trained students provided 40 hours of therapy a week to children with autism who were under the age of 5, for 2 to 3 years in a clinic setting. Although many of the children made significant gains, it was found that when the children returned home their treatment gains were not maintained. In a subsequent and more well-known study, Lovaas (1987) conducted therapy at the child's home and parents were trained to conduct therapy. This study compared a group of children with autism who received EIBI for 40 hours a week to a similar group of children with autism that received 10 hours of therapy a week and another group who received no EIBI. The results showed that of the group receiving EIBI for 40 hours a week, 9 out of 19 (47%) fully recovered (i.e., were indistinguishable from normally developing peers and mainstreamed into regular education first-grade classrooms), 8 made significant gains (successfully completed first grade in a special education classroom), and 2 made minimal gains. Surprisingly, there was no significant difference in outcomes between the no-treatment control group and the group of children that received 10 hours of therapy a week. McEachin et al. found that of the 9 children in the best outcome group, 8 continued to have IQs in the normal range and remained in regular education classrooms 8 years later.

Several other studies have reported similar results from the use of EIBI in the treatment of autism. Anderson, Avery, DiPietro, Edwards, and Christian (1987) had parents and therapists provide 15 to 25 hours of EIBI a week to 13 children with autism (average age = 3.5 years) in their homes. Eight of the 13 made gains at a rate faster than their normally developing peers during the 2 years of treatment. Birnbauer and Leach (1993) evaluated the benefits of EIBI for 9 children with autism (average age = 3.25 years) who received an average of 19 hours of therapy a week. Their results, similar to those of Lovaas (1987), indicated that 44% made significant gains (IQs increased from untestable to 80), 44% made moderate gains, and 12% made minimal gains. Sheinkopf and Siegel (1998) compared matched pairs of children in which one child in each pair received an average of 20 hours of therapy a week while the other child served as a no-treatment control. Seven out of 10 receiving EIBI did better than the control group children, although the gains achieved by these children were much less than those of Lovaas and colleagues. Collectively these studies provide substantial evidence of the effectiveness of EIBI and ABA for the treatment of children with autism and highlight several factors that seem to be critical for achieving the best outcome possible.

First, early intervention is essential. Research has shown that the earlier EIBI is begun, the better, with treatment ideally starting by age 3. Second, the intensity of EIBI is important. Although 40 hours of therapy a week are optimum, cost and availability of resources may prohibit this level of treatment. Efforts should be made to provide as many hours of EIBI as possible. Third, parent involvement is critical. Studies have shown that EIBI is more effective when parents are trained to provide 5 to 10 hours of structured therapy a week. Fourth, the quality of therapy provided affects outcome. Parents need to carefully check a therapist's credentials and experience prior to beginning any treatment program. Ideally, the person in charge of the child's program should be a board-certified behavior analyst (BCBA; www.bacb.com), have at least 1 year of experience conducting behavior analysis with a variety of children with autism, have been supervised by a BCBA with 5 or more years experience working with children with autism, and have experience developing programs and training new therapists (see www.behavior.org and www.abainternational.org for more information). It should be noted that experience alone does not guarantee effectiveness. Unless the person in charge of training and supervision is proficient at specific training and supervisory skills, his or her trainees may not learn the new skills (McGimsey, Greene, & Lutzker, 1995), and as a result, the children will be unlikely to improve. A recent study looked at the effectiveness of qualified therapists training newer therapists and found that unless the trainer had received specific training in how to train, it took up to 6 months to get a new therapist's therapy skills up to proficiency (Peeler, Masincup, & Phillips, 2004). It is important to inform parents of these factors and their effect on outcome so that they can have a realistic picture of how much improvement their child will make. Although less intensive methods of delivering ABA services to children with autism (e.g., consultation, parent training, workshop presentations) are likely to produce benefits, there is little evidence to suggest that these methods would produce the same results as EIBI.

It has been estimated that 3 years of EIBI costs close to $100,000 (Jacobson et al., 1998); with inflation, the continued demand for services, and a shortage of qualified professionals, it is likely much higher now. However, a savings of approximately $300,000 to the educational system, and a savings of up to $2,816,535 across the lifetime in social services can be expected for children with autism who make full recovery or moderate gains (Jacobson et al., 1998). Only a few insurance companies currently fund ABA services, but Medicaid has a home- and community-based waiver program for persons with developmental disabilities that will pay for behavior analysis services on a limited basis. "Medwaiver" services also tend to be reserved for those cases in which there are significant and harmful behavior problems (e.g., self-injurious behavior, aggression).

Often used in conjunction with behavior analysis, some of the newer medications have been found to be effective at treating behavior problems in children with autism. A multisite study evaluating the effects of risperidone (i.e., Risperdal) found the medication helpful in decreasing aggression and self-injurious behavior; mild side effects included increased appetite, fatigue, drowsiness, dizziness, and drooling (McCracken et al., 2002). Traditionally, the medication of choice for children with autism was haloperidol, an antipsychotic medication shown to be helpful in decreasing stereotypies, irritability, and tantrums. Unfortunately, many of the children on haloperidol became more withdrawn and developed tardive dyskinesia (Anderson, Campbell, Adams, et al., 1989; Anderson, Campbell, Grega, et al., 1984). Clomipramine, a nonselective serotonin reuptake inhibitor, was found to decrease stereotyped behaviors, although several children had serious side effects, including tachycardia and grand mal seizures. Clomipramine is therefore not typically recommended in younger children, as it is less well tolerated (Gordon, State, Nelson, Hamburger, & Rapport, 1993).

Each child responds to medication differently, and as such it is often necessary for a psychiatrist to try several medications and dosages before the best one is found. It is important to work with a psychiatrist who has experience treating children with autism and is familiar with the most recent research and new medications. Unfortunately, children with autism often cannot report how well the medication is working or any side effects they are experiencing. This information must come from parents, who also may not be able to accurately describe the effects the medication is having on their child. Current evaluation techniques therefore include the use of standardized assessment tools and behavior checklists (Copeland, Wolraich, Lindgren, Milich, & Woolson, 1987). However, some caution that many of these have questionable reliability and validity (Schroeder, Rojahn, & Reese, 1997) and should therefore be combined with direct observations of the behaviors for which the medication was prescribed (Luiselli, Blew, Keane, Thibadeau, & Holzman, 2000).

Dietary supplements have been proposed as a better alternative to medications as they are often more natural and may be less likely to cause side effects (Rimland, 1987). More than 15 studies have found that 30% to 50% of children with autism receiving doses of B-6 ranging from 30 to 3,000 mg/day and magnesium doses ranging from 350 to 500 mg/day show improvements in behavior. Advocates believe that "children with autism have a genetic or acquired medical disorder (as yet unspecified) that increases their requirement for certain nutrients" (Smith, 1996, p. 54). However, there have been reports of nerve damage with doses of B-6 as low as 200 mg/day, and no research has been done on the long-term effects of such high doses of these vitamins.

Students with autism often receive speech and language therapy and occupational therapy as part of their individual education plan (IEP). There is virtually no research on the effectiveness of speech therapy in the treatment of children with autism; however, there are many effective communication interventions that are based on the principles of ABA (Goldstein, 2002). Without scientific evidence it is hard to say whether these treatments are beneficial or not. Other, equally popular treatments such as music therapy, sensory integration, and brushing therapy have no research to support their effectiveness (NYSDOH, 1999). It is possible that one or all of these therapies do in fact provide some type of benefit to children with autism, but perhaps for reasons other than those proposed. For example, in a study comparing the effects of contingent and noncontingent music (as might be done in music therapy), a child with autism showed increased responding during therapy under the contingent music condition as compared to the noncontingent condition (Sheppard, Armano, Elwood, & Peeler, 2004). However, the improvements were due to the effectiveness of music as a reinforcer as opposed to the amelioration of internal processing problems as suggested by music therapists. Such findings indicate the need for more research in this area.

Marital, Couple, and Family Therapies

When parents receive a diagnosis of autism for their child, they may go through a grieving process similar to the experience of parents who lose a child to death; they are grieving the typically developing child that this child will never be. The challenges presented by a child with autism extend beyond parenting the child to maintaining the marital relationship, the family, and the siblings' quality of life (Siegel, 1997). The use of a family systems perspective in assessment and intervention of marital and family problems places social workers in a unique position to assist families as they go through the grieving process. Social workers need to be alert to parent stress levels and provide resources to reduce stress whenever possible. Social workers should be aware of community resources, such as support groups for families of children with autism, early intervention programs, and educational options, and assist families in accessing these resources. Respite services have been found to reduce stress and improve parents' well-being (Lessenberry & Rehfeldt, 2004).

There is significant research indicating that parents of children with developmental disabilities experience high levels of stress (Hastings & Johnson, 2001; Kasari & Sigman, 1997; Keller & Honig, 2004; Smith, Oliver, & Innocenti, 2001). Parents of children with autism report higher levels of stress than parents of children with Down syndrome or children without disabilities (Lessenberry & Rehfeldt, 2004). Instruments designed to measure parental stress can be administered to parents as part of the family assessment and as an evaluation tool for an ongoing intervention plan.

The Parenting Stress Index (PSI) is a 120-item instrument that assesses the impact of the parenting role on stress level. The areas addressed are child characteristics, parent characteristics, and stressful life events. The child characteristics section and the parent section are subdivided into areas such as adaptability,

mood, distractibility/hyperactivity, attachment to child, social isolation, sense of competence in the parenting role, and parental
health. The child characteristics and parent characteristics scales
must be completed to obtain a valid score (Lessenberry & Rehfeldt, 2004).

The Parental Stress Scale also focuses on stress related to the
parenting role; it is made up of 18 items that rate the parent-child
relationship and the parents' feelings regarding that relationship
on a 5-point Likert scale (Lessenberry & Rehfeldt, 2004). Although this scale was not developed specifically for parents of children with disabilities, scores were able to discriminate between
parents of typically developing children and parents of children
with developmental delays, disabilities, and behavior problems
(Berry & Jones, 1995). Other instruments are available, such as
the Global Inventory of Stress, the Perceived Stress Scale, and the
Family Inventory of Life Events and Changes. Most of these scales
are easily administered and scored in a short time. Some have
computer scoring available (Lessenberry & Rehfeldt, 2004).

An important factor in helping families cope appears to be
approaching families from a strengths perspective and positive
adaptation rather than presuming or expecting family pathology
(Risdal & Singer, 2004). Smith et al. (2001) found that parental
stress was strongly correlated with family functioning variables, as
measured by the Family Support Scale, the Family Resource Scale,
and the Family Inventory of Life Events and Changes. This study
recommends parent training on effective use of existing financial
resources, development of outreach programs, respite services,
and financial assistance, and intervention strategies that address
multiple aspects of family functioning. In a study of maternal and
paternal stress in families with a child with a disability, Keller and
Honig (2004) found no significant difference in PSI scores of
mothers and fathers; however, scores were significantly different
on the Attachment subscale of the parent domain, with fathers reporting more difficulty establishing a close emotional relationship
with the child with a disability. These findings indicate a need to
involve fathers in support groups, educational planning, and activities that provide opportunities for fathers to interact with their
child. A family systems approach is vital in working with families
of children with autism. This approach considers the unique needs
of each family member as well as the system as a whole. "The influence of family harmony needs to be recognized as a strong mediator of parental stress for fathers and mothers" (p. 343).

Researchers have also looked at the adjustment of siblings of
children with autism and the quality of the relationships between
children with autism and their typically developing siblings. Studies that looked at adjustment in areas such as self-esteem, depression, behavior problems, and social competence have produced
inconsistent results. Social workers need to be cognizant of the

role of siblings in the family and consider their needs when interventions are planned. Use of the family systems approach involves recognizing sources of family stress that are harmful to the sibling relationship and identifying sources of support for siblings (Rivers & Stoneman, 2003).

Social workers must have knowledge of special education law and understand the process of evaluation and placement to work effectively with parents of children with autism. Assisting parents in advocating for appropriate educational services for their child is a role many social workers provide.

The education of children with special needs is governed by the Individuals with Disabilities Education Act (IDEA). Autism has been included in the list of eligible disabilities since 1990. A 1997 amendment delineated programs for children age 3 and older as Part B; services to children from birth to 3 were referred to as Part C (Noland & Gabriels, 2004). Educational programming for children with autism and other disabilities as defined by IDEA is driven by the individualized family services plan for children from birth to 3 and the IEP for children 3 and older (Turnbull, Wilcox, & Stowe, 2002).

Prior to a child turning 3 years of age, an assessment process will be completed by the school system to determine continued eligibility for services. Two criteria must be met: (1) having one or more of the disabilities listed in IDEA, and (2) as a result of the disability, needing special education and related services (Turnbull et al., 2002). There is a difference between the disability criteria under IDEA, which provides an educational diagnosis, and a clinical diagnosis provided by a physician or clinical psychologist. Parents have the right to obtain a clinical diagnosis from community providers if they so choose; however, the decision regarding provision of educational services rests with the school system (Noland & Gabriels, 2004). Placement decisions must be based on provision of services in the least restrictive environment that meets the child's needs. There is evidence to suggest that if children with autism have basic learning skills (e.g., ability to sit, follow instructions, work independently, observational learning skills) and basic social skills (e.g., asking for help, taking turns, conversation skills), then inclusion classrooms, which include disabled and typically developing children, can be beneficial (Smith, 1996). Children who do not possess these skills are unlikely to succeed in an inclusion classroom; therefore, a special education classroom would be more appropriate.

An important role of the social worker during this process is to assist the parents in developing a partnership with the school system that focuses on sharing of information and problem solving. Each member of the partnership has a unique role. Parents of children with autism are their child's best advocates. Often they have developed an extensive knowledge of the disorder and can provide valuable resources to the school personnel (Janzen, 1996).

Given the variety of services in the community and through school programs, there is a great need for better collaboration among service providers and scientific evaluations of such combined treatment approaches in autism. Schwartz, Sandall, McBride, and Boulware (2004) have proposed a model for an all-inclusive school-based approach to the treatment of autism. The model program, Project DATA, includes (a) a high-quality inclusive early childhood program, (b) extended instructional time, (c) technical and social support for families, (d) collaboration and coordination across services, and (e) transition support. Project DATA was not designed as a research project, and therefore little is known about the effectiveness of such a program. Given the rise in treatments available to children with autism and the number of services each child receives, the field of social work should strive to unify these services or at least facilitate the empirical evaluation of such multimodal treatment efforts.

Summary

The importance of early detection and early intervention in the treatment of children with autism needs to be reemphasized. Social workers can play several critical roles in helping children with autism and their families. First, they can help educate the medical community on early signs and detection of autism by sharing information on the best diagnostic tools. Second, once a diagnosis is made, social workers can play a pivotal role in providing parents and professionals with information on which treatments are effective and which are not. Thereafter, if the child is still having significant behavioral problems, discussions and efforts should turn to available medications and the supporting evidence (i.e., risperidone). Third, social workers can provide information about other therapies, such as vitamin therapies, which have less conclusive but significant evidence. Fourth, social workers can play the important role of service coordinator. All service providers approach treating autism from a different perspective; to the extent that a social worker can coordinate these services and promote collaboration among professionals, the services the child and parents receive are likely to be more effective.

Study Questions

1. Discuss the roles of social workers when intervening with families of children with autism.
2. Discuss the available assessment tools and their relative contributions in the identification of and diagnosis of Autistic Disorder.

3. Explain why the development of the M-CHAT is important in the diagnosis and subsequent treatment of Autistic Disorder.

4. Identify the proposed reasons for the increase in prevalence of Autistic Disorder in the past 10 years.

5. What does research show about the effectiveness of EIBI? What factors increase the effectiveness of EIBI techniques with children with Autistic Disorder?

6. Discuss the existing evidence regarding the effectiveness of psychopharmacological treatments in the treatment of autism.

7. Identify and discuss alternative treatments and where they fit within the scope of treatment for Autistic Disorder.

8. Discuss findings related to the effects of Autistic Disorder on families and relevant assessment tools.

References

Ahearn, W. H., Castine, T., Nault, K., & Green, G. (2001). An assessment of food acceptance in children with autism, or pervasive developmental disorder: not otherwise specified. *Journal of Autism and Developmental Disorders, 31,* 505–512.

American Psychiatric Association. (2000). *Diagnostic and statistical manual of mental disorders* (4th ed., text rev.). Washington, DC: Author.

Anderson, L. T., Campbell, M., Adams, P., Small, A. M., Perry, R., & Shell, J. (1989). The effects of haloperidol on discrimination and learning and behavioral symptoms in autistic children. *Journal of Autism and Developmental Disorders, 19,* 227–239.

Anderson, L. T., Campbell, M., Grega, D. M., Perry, R., Small, A. M., & Green, W. H. (1984). Haloperidol in the treatment of infantile autism: Effects on learning and behavioral symptoms. *American Journal of Psychiatry, 141,* 1195–1202.

Anderson, S. R., Avery, D. L., DiPietro, E. K., Edwards, G. L., & Christian, W. P. (1987). Intensive home based early-intervention with autistic children. *Education and Treatment of Children, 10,* 352–366.

Baird, G., Charman, T., Baron-Cohen, S., Cox, A., Swettenham, J., Wheelwright, S., et al. (2000). A screening instrument for autism at 18 months of age: A 6-year follow-up study. *Journal of the American Academy of Child and Adolescent Psychiatry, 39,* 694–702.

Berry, J. O., & Jones, W. H. (1995). The Parental Stress Scale: Initial psychometric evidence. *Journal of Social and Personal Relationships, 12,* 463–472.

Bertrand, J., Mars, A., Boyle, C., Bove, F., Yeargin-Allsop, M., & Decoufle, P. (2001). Prevalence of autism in a United States population. *Pediatrics, 108,* 1155–1161.

Birnbrauer, J. S., & Leach, D. J. (1993). The Murdoch Early Intervention Program after 2 years. *Behavior Change, 10,* 63–74.

Black, C., Kaye, J., & Jick, H. (2002). Relation of childhood GI disorders to autism: Nested case-control study using data from the UK General Practice Research Database. *British Medical Journal, 325,* 419–421.

Bryson, S. E., & Smith, I. M. (1998). Epidemiology of autism: Prevalence, associated characteristics, and service delivery. *Mental Retardation and Developmental Disabilities Research Reviews, 4,* 97–103.

Clark, C. (2004, April 25). Cases of child autism have increased 850 percent in Missouri. *Southeast Missourian.* Retrieved February 8, 2005, from http://www.semissourian.com/story.html$rec=136164.

Copeland, L., Wolraich, M., Lindgren, S., Milich, R., & Woolson, R. (1987). Pediatrician's reported practices in the assessment and treatment of attention deficit disorder. *Developmental and Behavioral Pediatrics, 8,* 191–197.

de Bildt, A., Sytema, S., Ketelaars, C., Kraijer, D., Mulder, E., Volkmar, F., et al. (2004). Interrelationship between Autism Diagnostic Observation Schedule—Generic (ADOS-G), Autism Diagnostic Interview-Revised (ADI-R), and the *Diagnostic and Statistical Manual of Mental Disorders* (*DSM-IV-TR*) classification in children and adolescents with mental retardation. *Journal of Autism and Developmental Disorders, 34,* 129–137.

Dobson, B., & Middleton, S. (1998). *Paying to care: The cost of childhood disability* (Report from the Joseph Rowntree Foundation). York, North Yorkshire, England: York Publishing Services.

Epstein, L. H., Doke, L. A., Sajwaj, T. E., Sorrell, S., & Rimmer, B. (1974). Generality and side effects of overcorrection. *Journal of Applied Behavior Analysis, 7,* 385–390.

Fombonne, E. (1998). Epidemiology of autism and related conditions. In F. R. Volkmar (Ed.), *Autism and pervasive developmental disorders* (pp. 32–63). Cambridge, England: Cambridge University Press.

Fombonne, E., & Chakrabarti, S. (2001). No evidence for a new variant of measles-mumps-rubella-induced autism. *Pediatrics, 108,* 58.

Fujiura, G. T., Roccoforte, J. A., & Braddock, D. (1994). Costs of family care for adults with mental retardation and related developmental disabilities. *American Journal of Mental Retardation, 99,* 250–261.

Goin, R. P., & Myers, B. J. (2004). Characteristics of infantile autism: Moving toward earlier detection. *Focus on Autism and Other Developmental Disabilities, 19,* 5–18.

Goldstein, H. (2002). Communication intervention for children with autism: A review of treatment efficacy. *Journal of Autism and Developmental Disorders, 32*(5), 373–396.

Gordon, C. T., State, R. C., Nelson, J. E., Hamburger, S. C., & Rapport, J. L. (1993). A double-blind comparison of clomipramine, desipramine, and placebo in the treatment of autistic disorder. *Archives of General Psychiatry, 50,* 441–447.

Guess, D., & Carr, E. (1991). Emergence and maintenance of stereotypy and self-injury. *American Journal of Mental Retardation, 96,* 299–329.

Hastings, R. P., & Johnson, E. (2001). Stress in UK families conducting intensive home-based behavioral intervention for their young child with autism. *Journal of Autism and Developmental Disorders, 31,* 327–336.

Hepworth, D. H., Rooney, R. H., & Larsen, J. A. (2002). *Direct social work practice: Theory and skills* (6th ed.). Pacific Grove, CA: Brooks/Cole.

Hviid, A., Stellfeld, M., Wohlfahrt, J., & Melbye, M. (2003). Association between thimerosal-containing vaccine and autism. *Journal of the American Medical Association, 290,* 1763–1766.

Jacobson, J. W., Mulick, J. A., & Green, G. (1998). Cost benefit estimates for early intensive behavioral intervention for young children with autism. *Behavioral Interventions, 13,* 201–226.

Janzen, J. E. (1996). *Understanding the nature of autism.* San Antonio, TX: Therapy Skill Builders.

Jarbrink, K., Fombonne, E., & Knapp, M. (2003). Measuring the parental, service, and cost impacts of children with autistic spectrum disorder: A pilot study. *Journal of Autism and Developmental Disorders, 33,* 395–402.

Jones, R. S. P., Wint, D., & Ellis, N. C. (1990). The social effects of stereotyped behavior. *Journal of Mental Deficiency Research, 34,* 261–268.

Kanner, L. (1943). Autistic disturbances of affective contact. *Nervous Child, 2,* 217–250.

Kasari, C., & Sigman, M. (1997). Linking parental perceptions to interactions in young children with autism. *Journal of Autism and Developmental Disorders, 27,* 39–57.

Keller, D., & Honig, A. S. (2004). Maternal and paternal stress in families with school-aged children with disabilities. *American Journal of Orthopsychiatry, 74,* 337–348.

Klin, A., Carter, A., & Sparrow, S. S. (1997). Psychological assessment. In D. J. Cohen & F. R. Volkmar (Eds.), *Handbook of autism and pervasive developmental disorders* (2nd ed., pp. 418–427). New York: Wiley.

Klin, A., Carter, A., Volkmar, F., Cohen, D., Marans, W. D., & Sparrow, S. (1997). Assessment issues in children with autism. In D. J. Cohen & F. R. Volkmar (Eds.), *Handbook of autism and pervasive developmental disorders* (2nd ed., pp. 411–418). New York: Wiley.

Knivsberg, A. M., Reichelt, K. L., Hoien, T., & Nodland, M. (2002). A randomised, controlled study of dietary intervention in autistic syndromes. *Nutritional Neuroscience, 5,* 251–261.

Koegel, R. L., & Covert, A. (1972). The relationship of self-stimulation to learning in autistic children. *Journal of Applied Behavior Analysis, 5,* 381–387.

Korvatska, E., Van de Water, J., Anders, T. F., & Gershwin, M. E. (2002). Genetic and immunologic considerations in autism. *Neurobiology of Disease, 9,* 107–125.

LaGrow, S. J., & Repp, A. C. (1984). Stereotypic responding: A review of intervention research. *American Journal of Mental Deficiency, 88,* 595–609.

Leaf, R., & McEachin, J. (1999). *A work in progress.* New York: DRL Books.

Lessenberry, B. M., & Rehfeldt, R. A. (2004). Evaluating stress levels of parents of children with disabilities. *Exceptional Children, 70,* 231–244.

Lord, C. (1997). Diagnostic instruments in autism spectrum disorders. In D. J. Cohen & F. R. Volkmar (Eds.), *Handbook of autism and pervasive developmental disorders* (2nd ed., pp. 460–483). New York: Wiley.

Lord, C., Rutter, M., & LeCouteur, A. (1994). Autism Diagnostic Interview-Revised: A revised version of a diagnostic interview for caregivers of individuals with possible pervasive developmental disorders. *Journal of Autism and Developmental Disorders, 24,* 659–685.

Lotter, V. (1966). Epidemiology of autistic conditions in young children. *Social Psychiatry, 1,* 124–137.

Lovaas, O. I. (1987). Behavioral treatment and normal educational and intellectual functioning in young autistic children. *Journal of Consulting and Clinical Psychology, 55,* 3–9.

Lovaas, O. I. (2003). *Teaching individuals with developmental delays: Basic intervention techniques.* Austin, TX: PRO-ED.

Luiselli, J. K., Blew, P., Keane, J., Thibadeau, S., & Holzman, T. (2000). Pharmacotherapy for severe aggression in a child with autism: "Open label" evaluation of multiple medications on response frequency and intensity of behavioral intervention. *Journal of Behavior Therapy and Experimental Psychiatry, 31,* 219–230.

Matson, J. L., Benavidez, D. A., Stabinsky-Compton, L., Paclawskyj, T., & Baglio, C. (1996). Behavioral treatment of autistic persons: A review of research from 1980 to the present. *Research in Developmental Disabilities, 17,* 433–465.

Maurice, C., Green, G., & Luce, S. (1996). *Behavioral interventions for young children with autism.* Austin, TX: PRO-ED.

McCracken, J. T., McGough, J., Shah, B., Cronin, P., Hong, D., Aman, M. G., et al. (2002). Risperidone in children with autism and serious behavioral problems. *New England Journal of Medicine, 347,* 314–321.

McEachin, J. J., Smith, T., & Lovaas, O. I. (1993). Long term outcome for children with autism who received early intensive behavioral treatment. *American Journal on Mental Retardation, 4,* 359–372.

McGimsey, J. F., Greene, B. F., & Lutzker, J. R. (1995). Competence in aspects of behavioral treatment and consultation: Implications for service delivery and graduate training. *Journal of Applied Behavior Analysis, 28,* 301–315.

Morrison, K., & Rosales-Ruiz, J. (1997). The effect of object preferences on task performance and stereotypy in a child with autism. *Research in Developmental Disabilities, 18,* 127–137.

Muhle, R., Trentacoste, S. V., & Rapin, I. (2004). The genetics of autism. *Pediatrics, 113,* 472–486.

New York State Department of Health. (1999). *Clinical practice guideline: Report of the recommendations—Autism/pervasive developmental disorders, assessment and intervention for young children (age 0–3 years)* (Publication No. 4215). Albany, NY: Author.

Noland, R. M., & Gabriels, R. L. (2004). Screening and identifying children with autism spectrum disorders in the public school system: The development of a model process. *Journal of Autism and Developmental Disorders, 34,* 265–277.

Peeler, C. M., Masincup, K., & Phillips, C. (2004). *Evaluation and training of basic therapy skills for therapists working with children with autism.* Manuscript submitted for publication.

Rellini, E., Tortolani, D., Trillo, S., Carbone, S., & Montecchi, F. (2004). Childhood Autism Rating Scale (CARS) and Autism Behavior Checklist (ABC) correspondence and conflicts with *DSM-IV* criteria in diagnosis of autism. *Journal of Autism and Developmental Disorders, 34,* 703–708.

Rimland, B. (1987). Megavitamin B6 and magnesium in the treatment of autistic children and adults. In E. Schopler & G. B. Mesibov (Eds.), *Neurobiological issues in autism* (pp. 390–405). New York: Plenum Press.

Risdal, D., & Singer, G. H. S. (2004). Marital adjustment in parents of children with disabilities: A historical review and meta-analysis. *Research and Practice for Persons with Severe Disabilities, 29,* 95–103.

Risley, T. R. (1968). The effects and side effects of punishing the autistic behaviors of a deviant child. *Journal of Applied Behavior Analysis, 1,* 21–34.

Rivers, J. W., & Stoneman, Z. (2003). Sibling relationships when a child has autism: Marital stress and support coping. *Journal of Autism and Developmental Disorders, 33,* 383–394.

Robins, D. L., Fein, D., Barton, M. L., & Green, J. A. (2001). The Modified Checklist for Autism in Toddlers: An initial study investigating the early detection of autism and pervasive developmental disorders. *Journal of Autism and Developmental Disorders, 31,* 131–144.

Schopler, E., Reichler, R. J., & Renner, B. R. (1988). *The Childhood Autism Rating Scale (CARS).* Los Angeles: Western Psychological Services.

Schroeder, S. R., Rojahn, J., & Reese, R. M. (1997). Brief report: Reliability and validity of instruments for assessing psychotropic medication effects on self-injurious behavior in mental retardation. *Journal of Autism and Developmental Disorders, 27,* 89–102.

Schwartz, I. S., Sandall, S. R., McBride, B. J., & Boulware, G. L. (2004). Project DATA (Developmentally Appropriate Treatment for Autism): An inclusive school-based approach to educating young children with autism. *Topics in Early Childhood Special Education, 24,* 156–168.

Sheinkopf, S. J., & Siegel, B. (1998). Home-based treatment of young children with autism. *Journal of Autism and Developmental Disorders, 28,* 15–23.

Sheppard, M., Armano, V. L., Elwood, C., & Peeler, C. M. (2004). *The effects of contingent versus noncontingent music on the stereotypic vocalizations of a child with autism.* Unpublished manuscript, Florida State University, Panama City.

Siegel, B. (1997). Coping with the diagnosis of autism. In D. J. Cohen & F. R. Volkmar (Eds.), *Handbook of autism and pervasive developmental disorders* (2nd ed., pp. 745–766). New York: Wiley.

Skuse, D., Warrington, R., Bishop, D., Chowdhury, U., Lau, J., Mandy, W., et al. (2004). The Developmental, Dimensional, and Diagnostic Interview (3DI): A novel computerized assessment for autism spectrum disorders. *Journal of the American Academy of Child and Adolescent Psychiatry, 43,* 548–558.

Smith, T. (1996). Are other treatments effective? In C. Maurice, G. Green, & S. C. Luce (Eds.), *Behavioral interventions for young children with autism* (pp. 45–59). Austin, TX: PRO-ED.

Smith, T. B., Oliver, M. N. I., & Innocenti, M. S. (2001). Parenting stress in families of children with disabilities. *American Journal of Orthopsychiatry, 71,* 257–261.

Sparrow, S. S., Balla, D. A., & Cicchetti, D. V. (1984). *Vineland Adaptive Behavior Scales.* Circle Pines, MN: American Guidance Service.

Stone, W. L., Coonrod, E. E., Turner, L. M., & Pozdol, S. L. (2004). Psychometric properties of the STAT for early autism screening. *Journal of Autism and Developmental Disorders, 34,* 691–701.

Strock, M. (2004). *Autism spectrum disorders (pervasive developmental disorders)* (NIH Publication No. NIH-04-551). Bethesda, MD: National Institutes of Health, U.S. Department of Health and Human Services.

Sundberg, M. L., & Partington, J. W. (1998). *Teaching language to children with autism or other developmental disabilities.* Pleasant Hill, CA: Behavior Analysts.

Turnbull, H. R., Wilcox, B. L., & Stowe, M. J. (2002). A brief overview of special education law with focus on autism. *Journal of Autism and Developmental Disorders, 32,* 479–493.

Volkmar, F. R., & Pauls, D. (2003). Autism. *Lancet, 362,* 1133–1141.

Wakefield, A. J., Murch, S. H., Anthony, A., Linnell, J., Casson, D. M., Malik, M., et al. (1998). Ileal-lymphoid-nodular hyperplasia, non-specific colitis, and pervasive developmental disorder in children. *Lancet, 351,* 637–641.

Walker, D. R., Thompson, A., Zwaigenbaum, L., Goldberg, J., Bryson, S. E., Mahoney, W. J., et al. (2004). Specifying PDD-NOS: A comparison of PDD-NOS, Asperger syndrome, and autism. *Journal of the American Academy of Child and Adolescent Psychiatry, 43,* 172–180.

Wing, L. (1993). The definition and prevalence of autism: A review. *European Child and Adolescent Psychiatry, 2,* 61–74.

Wing, L., & Gould, J. (1979). Severe impairments of social interaction and associated abnormalities in children. *Journal of Autism and Developmental Disorders, 9,* 11–29.

Yeargin-Allsop, M., Rice, C., Karapurkar, T., Doernberg, N., Boyle, C., & Murphy, C. (2003). Prevalence of autism in a U.S. metropolitan area. *Journal of the American Medical Association, 289,* 49–55.

—

Attention-Deficit/ Hyperactivity Disorder

David R. Dupper and Joy B. Musick

4

Chapter

Learning Objectives

After reading this chapter, the reader will be able to:

- Discuss the most current knowledge of best practices on the topic of Attention-Deficit/Hyperactivity Disorder in children.
- Discuss the most current evidence-based approaches to assessment and diagnosis of Attention-Deficit/Hyperactivity Disorder as well as examples of assessment tools that are used in practice settings.
- Present the state of the art of evidence-based interventions in Attention-Deficit/Hyperactivity Disorder in children.
- Discuss the practice implications of assessing and treating children suspected of having Attention-Deficit/Hyperactivity Disorder.

Overview of the Problem

Attention-Deficit/Hyperactivity Disorder (ADHD) is the most common childhood neurobehavioral disorder and among the most prevalent chronic health conditions affecting school-age children in the United States (American Academy of Pediatrics, 2000a). It is estimated that ADHD affects between 3% and 5% of children, or approximately 2 million children in the United States today (National Institute of Mental Health [NIMH], 2003). It has been estimated that at least one child in a classroom of 25 to 30 children will suffer from symptoms of ADHD (NIMH, 2003).

It appears that ADHD is more predominant among males than among females, especially among school-age children (Silverthorn, Firck, Kuper, & Ott, 1996). Barkley (1990) estimates a male-to-female ratio of a low of 6:1 to as high as 9:1 in school-age children. A recent American Academy of Pediatrics (2000a) study concluded that 9.2% of males and 2.9% of females are found to have behaviors consistent with ADHD. One explanation for this discrepancy is that boys are more likely to be referred to treatment. Current research has not found sex differences in the number and severity of ADHD symptoms (Berry, Shaywitz, & Shaywitz, 1985; Brown, Madan-Swain, & Baldwin, 1991; Horn, Wagner, & Ialongo, 1989; James & Taylor, 1990; Kashani, Chapel, Ellis, & Shekim, 1979). It has also been noted that prevalence rates vary significantly across the United States due to wide geographical differences in how ADHD is diagnosed (American Academy of Pediatrics, 2000a).

What causes ADHD? Four major theories have been promulgated. It has been theorized that ADHD is due to environmental agents, brain injury, food additives and sugar, and genetics (Center for Mental Health Services, 2000). However, several of these theories have been refuted. Specifically, very few children with ADHD have endured significant brain injury. Moreover, the National Institutes of Health found that only about 5% of children with ADHD were affected by diet restrictions, a finding that implies that ADHD in children is most likely not due to food additives and the amount of sugar a child consumes (Consensus Development Panel, 1982). Exposure to environmental toxins may contribute to behaviors that mimic ADHD (Blackman, 1999). These include pre-, peri-, and postnatal complications and malnutrition, diseases, trauma, and other neurologically compromising events that may occur during the development of the nervous system before and after birth (Barkley, 1998). Prenatal exposure to alcohol and tobacco smoke has been related to inattention and hyperactivity (Milberger, Biederman, Faraone, Chen, & Jones, 1996). Alcohol and tobacco smoke also affects parents of children with ADHD, even when not pregnant (Cunningham, Benness, & Siegel, 1988). Contrary to once popular belief, none of the following plays a role in the causes of ADHD: bad parenting, physical brain damage, nutrition, or allergies (Phelan, 1993). The genetics theory found that a child is three times more likely to have ADHD if the parent also has it. In addition, having a sibling with ADHD increases your chances 25% to 30% (Phelan, 1993). Such findings imply a possible genetically linked risk for executive function deficits in families that have ADHD children, even if symptoms of ADHD do not directly affect family members (Barkley, 1997).

For children, ADHD impacts peer and family relationships and academic performance. For example, children with ADHD tend to be viewed by peers as bossy, loud, forward, domineering, pushy, and disruptive. These behaviors affect the peer relationship because these children often are not liked by their peers. Barkley (1998) stated that children with ADHD make more argumentative statements and show more explosiveness and defiance than children without ADHD. Therefore, it is not surprising that Landau, Milich, and Diener (1998) found that as many as 50% of children with ADHD are often rejected by peers and may experience difficulties making and keeping friends. Peer rejection is very important, because peer rejection has very high correlations with aggression, delinquency, and school maladjustment in children (Parker & Asher, 1987). Also, when peer rejection is high and the number of friends is low, depression and low self-esteem should always be considered and assessed. Children with ADHD often see themselves as similar to nonreferred children in terms of self-perceived competence and global self-worth, and they deny responsibility for negative social events (Hoza, Pelham, Milich, Pillow, & McBride, 1993).

Families are also impacted by a child with ADHD. These families suffer higher levels of divorce, marital discord, and parent frustration compared to other families (Hoff, Doepke, & Landau, 2002). Family members often feel blame, anger, and frustration toward the child and, more important, toward themselves. In addition, parents and siblings express feelings of confusion, exhaustion, and being overwhelmed with coping with the effects of ADHD on their daily lives. Another issue impacting these families is parental guilt due to the realization that their child with ADHD will probably not attain the same goals as his or her peers on the same timetable (Research and Training Center on Family Support and Children's Mental Health, 2004). Treating a child with ADHD can also place a great financial burden on families. A child with ADHD is likely to be placed on medications, which can be very expensive. In the past 5 years, the average cost of an ADHD drug has nearly doubled, from $39.03 in 1999 to $76.49 in 2003 (Wellmark Bluecross Blueshield, 2005). Some of the price increase can be attributed to the newer drugs, which are more expensive. For example, the average cost of a 30-day prescription for Strattera in 2003 was nearly $108. The average cost of Ritalin LA was more than $73 (Wellmark Bluecross Blueshield, 2005). The Center for Mental Health Services (2000) found that "the mental health services and special education required by children and adolescents with ADHD cost millions of dollars each year." The Center also noted that "underachievement and lost productivity can cost these young people and their families even more."

In relation to academic performance, children with ADHD have been found to display deficits in executive processes or in organizing and monitoring output information rather than deficits in extracting and comprehending main ideas. For example, children with ADHD can comprehend and understand main ideas and points of a story but may experience difficulty reading a story from beginning to end or in writing a book review that is clearly organized into introduction, body, and conclusion sections (Tannock, Purvis, & Schachar, 1993).

Operational Definitions of the Problem

The *Diagnostic and Statistical Manual of Mental Disorders,* fourth edition, text revision (*DSM-IV-TR;* American Psychiatric Association, 2000) is a diagnostic tool used by many professionals in making mental health diagnoses. The *DSM-IV-TR* requires that five criteria be met to make a diagnosis of ADHD. A child with ADHD demonstrates a pattern of inattention, hyperactivity-impulsivity, or both, more than individuals without ADHD (American Psychiatric Association, 2000). According to the *DSM-IV-TR*, there are three types of ADHD: inattention, hyperactivity-impulsivity, and combined (American Psychiatric Association, 2000). For a detailed discussion of the symptoms and criteria for each type of ADHD, see the *DSM-IV-TR* (pp. 92–93).

A child with ADHD often struggles with details, listening to instructions, and organization; is easily distracted and forgetful; often makes careless mistakes; and has trouble waiting for his or her turn and engaging in mental effort tasks such as schoolwork (Fowler, 2002). Although ADHD is usually not diagnosed until the age of 9, symptoms typically begin before the child goes to school (Morrison, 1995, p. 515). Symptoms of ADHD may remit when the child reaches puberty, or they may continue into adulthood (Maxmen & Ward, 1995, p. 438). If any symptom disappears first, it is usually the disorder's major hallmark: hyperactivity (p. 438).

One of the difficulties in diagnosing ADHD in children is that ADHD shares many symptoms with other disorders. The five most common disorders that co-occur with ADHD are Oppositional Defiant Disorder (ODD), Conduct Disorder (CD), anxiety, depression, and learning disabilities (Fowler, 2002). Unlike children with ADHD, children with ODD tend to be disobedient, have recurrent fighting, and talk back to others (Markward, 1998). Also, ODD children tend to have a greater disregard for others' rights and a higher rate of problems with substances and the law (Markward, 1998). Early stages of Bipolar Disorder tend to produce symptoms (more talkative than usual, flight of ideas, distractibility, and attention too easily drawn to unimportant or irrelevant external stimuli) that look like ADHD (American Psychiatric Association, 2000). Pervasive Developmental Disorder and psychotic disorders such as Schizophrenia share symptoms similar to those of ADHD (Maxmen & Ward, 1995). It has been estimated that 10% to 50% of children with ADHD have some type of learning disability (Tannock et al., 1993). Also, Tourette's syndrome in the early stages reports symptoms of an inability to pay attention (Morrison, 1995). Major stressful life events, such as parental divorce, child abuse, and parental death, can also produce temporary symptoms that resemble ADHD. Because disorders such as Schizophrenia do not show their true form, severity, or symptoms until later in life, children, who are still developing, can be difficult to diagnose. The dilemma facing the practitioner is to be able to distinguish between transitory symptoms that will disappear over time and those symptoms that are indicative of a serious disorder that will only worsen if left untreated.

Evidence-Based Approaches to Assessment

The procedures used to diagnose ADHD in children are inconsistent. This inconsistency results in overdiagnosis and underdiagnosis of children with ADHD. For example, some practitioners do not use structured parent questionnaires, rating scales, or teacher or school input, and pediatricians, family practitioners, and psychiatrists tend to rely on parent rather than teacher input (National Institute of Health, 1998). Consequently, it is essential that practice parameters based on best practices be followed in assessing and diagnosing children with behavioral symptoms that suggest ADHD. The American Academy of Child and Adolescent Psychiatry (Dulcan, 1997) has issued practice parameters for the assessment and treatment of children and adolescents with ADHD, based on extensive review of the scientific literature and clinical consensus among experts.

In addition to these practice parameters, it is important to be aware of the fact that a given dose of psychostimulant medication may not exert the same therapeutic effect in all domains of functioning for a given child or across children (Hoff et al., 2002, p. 1140). It is also important to be aware of the fact that teachers seem to be increasingly more comfortable recommending to parents that their child could benefit from psychostimulant medication as a way to improve classroom behavior and academic performance (Ogan, 2001). This has led to the passage of legislation that prohibits all school personnel from suggesting psychiatric medications to parents. The intent of these state laws is to ensure that the first mention of medication comes from a physician (Ogan, 2001). Currently, nine states prohibit schools from coercing parents to have their child put on psychiatric drugs; eight states have established investigations and/or tracking systems for children being psychiatrically labeled and drugged; five states have increased parental consent rights; and four states have eliminated the threat of parents being criminally charged with " 'medical neglect' if they refuse to place their child on a psychiatric drug" (Ablechild Parents for Label and Drug Free Education, 2004). For more information about these legislative bills and states where they have been introduced or passed, please refer to the Ablechild Parents for Label and Drug Free Education web site (http://ablechild.org/slegislation.htm).

The following is a discussion of current evidence-based assessment approaches and techniques for assessing and diagnosing children who are suspected of having ADHD: structured teacher and student interviews, rating scales, and direct observations.

Structured Teacher and Student Interviews

Structured interviews "provide critical contextual information regarding rules, expectations, and supports available in the environments" in which children and youth must function. They allow for the gathering of information about strengths as well as problem behaviors. Interviews should also elicit information about "behavioral expectations of the classroom and broader school environment, past strategies (both successful and unsuccessful) used to address the problems, and current resources available to parents and teachers" (Hoff et al., 2002, p. 1142). The Semi-Structured Clinical Interview for Children and Adolescents (SCICA; McConaughy & Achenbach, 2001) is designed for use by trained interviewers and includes instructions, a protocol of questions and probes for ages 6 to 18, observation and self-report forms for rating what the child does and says during the interview, and a profile for scoring ratings (Achenbach System of Empirically Based Assessment [ASEBA], 2004b). The SCICA scoring profile includes eight syndrome scales (Aggressive/Rule-Breaking Behavior, Anxious, Anxious/Depressed, Attention Problems, Language/Motor Problems, Self-Control Problems, Somatic Complaints; ages 12 to 18 only); and Withdrawn/Depressed, as well as Internalizing, Externalizing, and separate Total Problems for Observation and Self-Report items (ASEBA, 2004b).

Rating Scales

Rating scales provide additional evidence that symptoms are sufficiently severe to warrant classification (Hoff et al., 2002). A careful review of rating scale data can be invaluable in planning interventions. Not only can the data from rating scales reveal specific concerns of each informant (e.g., mother reports more oppositional behavior than father does), but differences in symptom severity may indicate where interventions must be concentrated (e.g., the problem behavior may be situational or setting- or informant-specific; Hoff et al., 2002, pp. 1141–1142).

Five rating scales are most commonly used in assessing ADHD. The following is a brief description of each:

1. *Parent-Completed Child Behavior Checklist (CBCL):* The parent-completed CBCL is used to rate behaviors of children during the prior months (Goldman & Mitchell, 1990, p. 203). The CBCL/6–18 has 118 items that describe specific behavioral and emotional problems, plus two open-ended items for reporting additional problems (ASEBA, CBCL/6–18, 2004a). The reliability equals alphas that "ranged from .58 to .83 over subscales and total alpha equals .88" (Goldman & Mitchell, 1990, p. 203).

2. *The Teacher Report Form (TRF) of the Child Behavior Checklist:* The TRF is designed to obtain teachers' reports of children's academic performance, adaptive functioning, and behavioral and emotional problems (ASEBA, TRF, 2004c). Teachers rate the child's academic performance in each subject on a 5-point scale ranging from 1 (far below grade level) to 5 (far above grade level; ASEBA, TRF, 2004c). Teachers rate the child for how true each item is now or was within the past 2 months, using a 3-point response scale (ASEBA, TRF, 2004c).

3. *The Conners Parent and Teacher Rating Scales:* The Conners Parent and Teacher Rating Scales are used "to screen for hyperactivity in children" (Goldman & Mitchell, 1990, p. 195). The reliability rate equals alphas that "ranged from .61 to .94 across subscales (all but one alpha was below .76) [and the] validity of these scales ranged from .42 to .91 across studies" (p. 195).

4. *The ADD-H Comprehensive Teacher Rating Scale (ACTeRS):* The ACTeRS is designed to provide a reliable diagnostic measure of ADHD. The test items define three scales: Attention, Hyperactivity/Impulsivity, and Social Adjustment (Ullmann, Sleator, & Sprague, 1998). There are 35 self-report statements to which the examinee responds on a 5-point scale (Ullmann et al., 1998). Differences between male and female score patterns are insignificant, and reliability coefficients average .88 (Ullmann et al., 1998).

5. *The Barkley Home Situations Questionnaire and School Situations Questionnaire:* This questionnaire is an assessment tool to "give the clinician a quick appreciation for the pervasiveness and severity of the child's disruptive behavior across a variety of home and public situations" (Barkley, 1997, p. 46).

Direct Observations

Direct observation is a critical step in an assessment:

> *To determine why the problem is occurring and the onset and main-*
> *tenance of the behavior, it is important to identify antecedents (e.g.,*
> *task difficulty, teacher direction, student fight on the school bus),*
> *consequences (e.g., peer attention, escape from a difficult task), and*
> *other environmental variables (ecological and contextual factors)*
> *surrounding the problem behavior (e.g., parental divorce, excessive*
> *dose of medication, other life stressors, illness). (Hoff et al., 2002,*
> *p. 1137)*

In addition,

> *structured observations can verify information from indirect assess-*
> *ment methods such as rating scales and interviews and are useful in*
> *confirming or disconfirming initial hypotheses regarding causes of*
> *problematic behaviors. Structured observations not only clarify*
> *what the child is actually doing, but also provide important infor-*
> *mation about the settings and situations in which problem behav-*
> *iors occur. (p. 1144)*

Intervention planning should be linked directly to assessment data (e.g., functional behavioral assessment). Because all behavior serves a purpose, "even actions that adults view as inattentive, whenever possible, interventions should replace inattentive be-haviors with functionally equivalent" behaviors (DuPaul, Stoner, & O'Reilly, 2002, pp. 1124–1125).

Evidence-Based Approaches to Intervention

Most of the advances in the treatment of ADHD over the past 30 years have occurred in the area of psychopharmacology. We know that the stimulants methylphenidate (Ritalin), dextroampheta-mine, and pemoline result in short-term improvements in the core symptoms (e.g., inattention, hyperactivity/impulsivity, aggression) of ADHD and that these pharmacological treatments for ADHD are less expensive and "have much more short-term empirical support than psychosocial treatments" for children older than 5 years of age (Pelham, Wheeler, & Chronis, 1998, p. 191). The most commonly prescribed stimulants are methylphenidate (Ritalin, Concerta, Metadate CD, Focalin), d-amphetamine (Dexedrine or Dextrostat), d- and l-amphetamine combination (Adderall, Adderall XR), and pemoline (Cylert; Barkley, 2004). The effectiveness of these med-ications has led to their widespread use, estimated at 2.8% of the school-age population, with ADHD children (Kazdin, Esveldt-Dawson, French, & Unis, 1987). According to the American Association of Applied and Preventative Psychology, in 2001, nearly 20 million prescriptions were written for the psychopharmacological treatment of ADHD, and "various surveys reveal a six- to eight-fold increase in prescriptions during the 1990s" (Hoff et al., 2002, pp. 1133–1134).

However, medication is not always a viable option. For example, Barkley (2004) reported that between 8% and 25% of ADHD children do not respond positively to the stimulant medications. We also know that many parents are searching for alternatives to medication in treating ADHD due to the growing concern over the risks associated with long-term use of medication with children. For example, although there is no conclusive evidence that the careful therapeutic use of psychostimulants is harmful in the short term, very high doses of psychostimulants "may cause central nervous system damage, cardiovascular damage, and hypertension," and there is little information about the long-term effects of psychostimulants (National Institutes of Health, 1998, p. 13). Moreover, there is no empirical evidence to conclude that psychostimulant medication alone produces long-term changes in academic achievement or long-term changes in interpersonal relationships. More specifically, it has not been proven that simply medicating children with ADHD will improve other problems in daily living, including "poor academic performance and behavior at school, poor relationships with peers and siblings, failure to obey adult requests, and poor relationships with their parents" (Pelham & Gnagy, 1999, p. 226). In addition, there is little evidence that beneficial treatment effects from psychostimulants alone are maintained into adolescence (Pelham & Gnagy, 1999). As a result, it is essential that the comparative efficacy of psychosocial treatments be evaluated (Pelham et al., 1998; Whalen, 2001). Behavior modification is the *only* nonmedical, psychosocial treatment for ADHD with a large scientific evidence base (Barkley, 2004; Children and Adults with Attention-Deficit/Hyperactivity Disorder [CHADD], 2004). As a result, behavior modification, medication, and a combination of the two have strong empirical support as effective short-term treatments for ADHD (Pelham et al., 1998). Pelham and Gnagy (1999, p. 231) have discussed several advantages of combining pharmacological and behavioral treatments of ADHD: (a) "the behavioral component of treatment may be reduced in scope and complexity if combined with low dosages of medication"; (b) "the dose of medication for most children can be reduced by 50% to 75% when medication is combined with a behavioral intervention"; (c) "these treatments have complementary effects and are more comprehensive in coverage than either treatment alone"; and (d) "because the addition of a low dose of psychostimulant medication

enables relatively greater effects to be achieved with less restrictive and more natural behavior programs, a combined intervention may be more likely to be maintained by parents and
teachers." Treating ADHD in children often involves medical, educational, and behavioral interventions. This comprehensive approach to treatment is called "multimodal" and consists of parent
and child education about diagnosis and treatment, specific behavior management techniques, stimulant medication, and appropriate school programming and supports. According to findings
from the Multimodal Treatment Study of ADHD (MTA), children
who were treated with medication alone, which was carefully
managed and individually tailored, and children who received
both medication and behavioral treatment experienced the greatest improvements in their ADHD symptoms compared to behavior
modification therapy and the usual community comparison (MTA
Cooperative Group, 1999a, 1999b; NIMH, 2000).

The severity and type of ADHD may be factors in deciding
which "components are necessary. Treatment should be tailored to
the unique needs of each child and family" (CHADD, 2004). Two
psychosocial treatments that have been shown to be effective over
a period of 4 months or less when used in combination with a low
dose of psychostimulant medication are behavioral parent training
(BPT) and classroom applications of contingency management
techniques (Ollendick & King, 2004; Pelham et al., 1998). See Ollendick and King for a detailed description of the criteria established by the Society of Clinical Psychology Task Force on
Promotion and Dissemination of Psychological Procedures for
"well-established treatments," "probably efficacious treatments,"
and "experimental treatments."

Behavioral Parent Training

Behavioral parent training (BPT) has been documented to improve
both child ADHD behavior and maladaptive parenting behavior
(Chronis, Chacko, Fabiano, Wymbs, & Pelham, 2004). Behavioral
parent training is an organized, psychoeducational approach to
helping parents manage their child's behavior difficulties while simultaneously managing parents' reactions to their child's behavior
(Edwards, 2002). Edwards stated that the ultimate goal of BPT is to
"create a familial environment in which a child with ADHD can
become and remain successful." Consequently, a child's environment may need to be structured much differently from that of a
non-ADHD child for the child with ADHD to "negotiate typical developmental tasks for [his or her] age" (p. 130).

According to Pelham and Gnagy (1999), Pelham et al. (1998),
and Children and Adults with Attention-Deficit/Hyperactivity Disorder (2004), typical parent training programs use well-manualized
approaches over 8 to 16 weekly group sessions where parents are
given assigned readings and are taught standard behavioral tech-

niques (i.e., time-out, point systems, and contingent attention) as well as basic information about ADHD. Parenting sessions usually involve an instructional book or videotape on how to use behavioral management procedures with children. Homework assignments are given for parents to track behavior and practice techniques with their children and to bring results to the subsequent session for discussion. If the child is an adolescent, the behavioral techniques taught to parents are modified to be more age appropriate. For example, rather than using time-out as a consequence, parents are encouraged to use loss of privileges or assignment of work chores.

Children and Adults with Attention-Deficit/Hyperactivity Disorder (2004) outlined a series of topics that are typically covered in parent training sessions:

- Establishing house rules and structure
- Learning to praise appropriate behaviors (praising good behavior at least five times as often as bad behavior is criticized) and ignoring mild inappropriate behaviors (choosing your battles)
- Using appropriate commands
- Using "when . . . then" contingencies (withdrawing rewards or privileges in response to inappropriate behavior)
- Planning ahead and working with children in public places
- Time-out as positive reinforcement (using time-outs as a consequence for inappropriate behavior)
- Daily charts and point/token systems with rewards and consequences
- School-home note system for rewarding behavior at school and tracking homework

Although many of the ideas and techniques taught in behavioral parent training are commonsense parenting techniques and are very effective in improving ADHD symptoms, most parents need careful teaching and support to learn these skills and use them consistently. Pelham and Gnagy (1999, p. 230) have pointed out that "some parents and teachers are unable or are unwilling to implement a complicated behavioral intervention. Even when parents and teachers are willing to initiate elaborate interventions, they typically do not continue them without ongoing consultation."

Classroom Applications of Contingency Management Techniques

In addition to BPT, the application of contingency management techniques in the classroom has met the criteria for well-established treatments (Pelham et al., 1998). According to Barkley (2004), research focused on the application of behavior management methods in the classroom with ADHD children clearly indicates the effectiveness of behavioral techniques in the short-term treatment of academic performance problems (e.g., talking out of turn during class) in ADHD children. Through behavior management techniques, ADHD children will be more capable of "accruing a range of positive behaviors and verbal responses that will contribute to success in school, the community, and society at large" (Barkley, 2002, p. 167).

Many teachers have expertise in developing and implementing programs for students with ADHD, yet the majority of children with ADHD have regular education teachers who may know little about ADHD or behavior modification and will need assistance in learning and implementing the necessary programs (CHADD, 2004). Consequently, most of these programs are designed for regular or special education classroom teachers who also receive training and guidance from school support staff or outside consultants. Parents of children with ADHD should work closely with the teacher to support efforts in implementing classroom programs. DuPaul et al. (2002) have described the following preventive classroom interventions that are established *before* a student's inattentive behavior has a chance to occur: (a) adjusting curriculum to student instructional level, (b) classwide peer tutoring (CWPT), (c) computer-assisted instruction, (d) providing students with task choices, and (e) directed note-taking activities. A detailed description of each of these strategies can be found in DuPaul et al. It has been found that contingency management (CM) approaches produce very large effects in children with ADHD. Contingency management techniques range from "relatively potent components such as point/token economy reward systems, time-out, and response cost to less potent components such as manipulations of teacher attention, reprimands, and removal of privileges" (Pelham & Gnagy, 1999, p. 228). Specific techniques include the use of daily report cards, modifying classroom rules and instructional techniques, ignoring mild inappropriate behaviors, giving effective commands and reprimands, using "when-then" contingencies, implementing a response cost/reward point or token system, and using time-out procedures (Pelham & Gnagy, 1999). It is important to note that "prudent negative consequences (verbal reprimands, given consistently and immediately, backed up with time-out and loss of privileges) are an effective and necessary component of classroom behavioral interventions, whereas positive consequences are not" (p. 229). See Table 4.1 for a more detailed list of typical classroom behavioral management procedures arranged in order from mildest and least restrictive to more intensive and most restrictive. Some of these programs may be included in 504 plans or individualized educational programs for children with ADHD. Interventions are individualized and consist of several components based on the child's needs, classroom resources, and the teacher's skills and preferences.

Table 4.1 **Classroom Behavioral Management Procedures**

1. Classroom rules and structure
   - Use classroom rules such as:
     —Be respectful of others.
     —Obey adults.
     —Work quietly.
     —Stay in assigned seat/area.
     —Use materials appropriately.
     —Raise hand to speak or ask for help.
     —Stay on task and complete assignments.
   - Post the rules and review them before each class until learned.
   - Make rules objective and measurable.
   - Tailor the number of rules to developmental level.
   - Establish a predictable environment.
   - Enhance children's organization (folders/charts for work).
   - Evaluate rule-following and give feedback/consequences consistently.
   - Tailor the frequency of feedback to developmental level.

2. Praise of appropriate behaviors and choosing battles carefully
   - Ignore mild inappropriate behaviors that are not reinforced by peer attention.
   - Use at least five times as many praises as negative comments.
   - Use commands/reprimands to cue positive comments for children who are behaving appropriately—that is, find children who can be praised each time a reprimand or command is given to a child who is misbehaving.

3. Appropriate commands and reprimands
   - Use clear, specific commands.
   - Give private reprimands at the child's desk as much as possible.
   - Reprimands should be brief, clear, neutral in tone, and as immediate as possible.

4. Individual accommodations and structure for the child
   - Structure the classroom to maximize the child's success.
   - Place the student's desk near the teacher to facilitate monitoring.
   - Enlist a peer to help the student copy assignments from the board.
   - Break assignments into small chunks.
   - Give frequent and immediate feedback.
   - Require corrections before new work is given.

5. Proactive interventions to increase academic performance—Such interventions can prevent problematic behavior from occurring and can be implemented by individuals other than the classroom teacher, such as peers or a classroom aide. When disruptive behavior is not the primary problem, these academic interventions can improve behavior significantly.
   - Focus on increasing completion and accuracy of work.
   - Offer task choices.
   - Provide peer tutoring.
   - Consider computer-assisted instruction.

6. "When . . . then" contingencies (withdrawing rewards or privileges in response to inappropriate behavior)—Examples include recess time contingent upon completion of work, staying after school to complete work, assigning less desirable work prior to more

(continued)

Table 4.1 continued

desirable assignments, and requiring assignment completion in study hall before allowing free time.

7. Daily school-home report card (instruction packet available at http://wings.buffalo.edu/adhd)—This tool allows parents and teacher to communicate regularly, identifying, monitoring and changing classroom problems. It is inexpensive and minimal teacher time is required.
   - Teachers determine the individualized target behaviors.
   - Teachers evaluate targets at school and send the report card home with the child.
   - Parents provide home-based rewards; more rewards for better performance and fewer for lesser performance.
   - Teachers continually monitor and make adjustments to targets and criteria as behavior improves or new problems develop.

8. Behavior chart and/or reward and consequence program (point or token system)
   - Establish target behaviors and ensure that the child knows the behaviors and goals (e.g., list on index card taped to desk).
   - Establish rewards for exhibiting target behaviors.
   - Monitor the child and give feedback.
   - Reward young children immediately.
   - Use points, tokens or stars that can later be exchanged for rewards.

9. Classwide interventions and group contingencies—Such interventions encourage children to help one another because everyone can be rewarded. There is also potential for improvement in the behavior of the entire class.
   - Establish goals for the class as well as the individual.
   - Use points, tokens or stars that can later be exchanged for rewards.
   - Establish rewards for appropriate behavior that any student can earn (e.g., class lottery, jelly bean jar, wacky bucks).
   - Establish a class reward system in which the entire class (or subset of the class) earns rewards based on class functioning as a whole (e.g, Good Behavior Game) or the functioning of the student with AD/HD.
   - Tailor frequency of rewards and consequences to developmental level.

10. Time out—The child is removed, either in the classroom or to the office, from the ongoing activity for a few minutes (less for younger children and more for older) when he or she misbehaves.

11. Schoolwide programs—Such programs, which include schoolwide discipline plans, can be structured to minimize the problems experienced by children with AD/HD, while at the same time help manage the behavior of all students in a school.

Source: Reprinted with permission from Children and Adults with Attention-Deficit/ Hyperactivity Disorder (CHADD).

Summary

Social workers come into daily contact with children and adolescents with ADHD in health, mental health, judicial, educational, and community-based programs (Kottler, 2000). Social workers should bring state-of-the-art information related to the assessment, diagnosis, and treatment of ADHD to parents and other professionals. For example, social workers should work to ensure that the practice parameters developed by the American Academy of Child and Adolescent Psychiatry are followed in assessing and diagnosing ADHD in children. Following these best practices will help to rule out other psychiatric or environmental causes of symptoms and help prevent overdiagnosing or underdiagnosing children with ADHD. Social workers should be directly involved in several of these steps. For example, social workers can conduct an informal clinical observation of the referred child in the classroom setting and other, less structured settings to gather information about the child's behavior, the teacher's management style, and other characteristics of the academic environment that may be contributing to the child's misbehavior. Is the child's behavior situation specific, or does it occur across all settings and persons? Have all plausible factors that may explain the child's problematic behavior been ruled out? A comprehensive assessment involving multiple sources of information will help to ensure that other reasons for a child's restlessness, inattention, or impulsivity are not ignored and that children whose symptoms are of recent onset do not mistakenly receive the diagnosis of ADHD (Kottler, 2000).

As stated earlier, social workers must also be aware that teachers often recommend to parents that their child could benefit from psychostimulant medication as a way to improve classroom behavior and academic performance. It is important that the social worker explain to parents that the first mention of medication should come from a physician and that a number of states have passed laws to prohibit school personnel from suggesting psychiatric medications to parents.

Once a diagnosis has been made, social workers are often the first members of a treatment team to come into contact with the child or adolescent with ADHD and frequently must make a referral for a medication evaluation. Therefore, social workers should have up-to-date knowledge about the medications commonly used for ADHD, as questions may arise about their effects and side effects and the necessity of adhering to the medical regimen (Kottler, 2000). Social workers should inform parents about best practices and provide current information about the effectiveness of medication-only approaches to treatment. Children and adolescents with ADHD need the assistance of a social worker in understanding the cause of their troubles, in locating helpful resources, and in learning new skills (Kottler, 2000). For example, social workers should educate the child and parents about the basics of ADHD and its effect on behavior. As Kottler stated:

> *For many it is empowering to have an explanation for the difficulties they or their children have endured and to know that the manifestations of ADHD are no one's fault. Social workers can give examples of positive outcomes for people who have ADHD. (p. 2)*

Kottler also pointed out that social workers' knowledge of ADHD can provide valuable input to program planning. She stated that because a sizable percentage of those seeking social work intervention struggle with disorganization and poor attention regulation, social workers must consider the importance of planning programs in which expectations and protocols are clear and easy to follow.

Social workers should also be aware of online resources, organizations, model programs, publications, and other resources that have been designed for children and adolescents with ADHD and their parents. This information can be found in the appendix at the end of this chapter. It is hoped that the information presented in this chapter will assist social workers in providing the most up-to-date, state-of-the-art, empirically supported information related to the assessment, diagnosis, and treatment of children and adolescents with ADHD.

Study Questions

1. Is an etiology for ADHD clearly established?
2. What is generally meant by the term ADHD?
3. Describe two well-supported methods of assessment useful in ADHD.
4. How can the use of direct observations of persons diagnosed with presumptive ADHD be helpful in the assessment process?
5. Describe two evidence-based interventions for ADHD.
6. Describe the role of parents in the treatment of ADHD.
7. Describe the role of teachers in the treatment of ADHD.
8. Does the use of medications to treat presumptive ADHD imply an acceptance of a biological etiology for this problem? Why or why not?

Appendix

Internet Resources

- Children and Adults with Attention-Deficit/Hyperactivity Disorder (CHADD): www.chadd.org.

    CHADD is the leading nonprofit organization serving individuals with ADHD. Through collaborative leadership, advocacy, research, education, and support, CHADD provides science-based, evidence-based information about ADHD to parents, educators, professionals, the media, and the general public.

- Evidence-Based Medication Management for Children and Adolescents with AD/HD: http://www.chadd.org/fs/fs3.htm.

- Center for Children and Families, University at Buffalo: http://wings.buffalo.edu/adhd.

    The Center for Children and Families is an interdisciplinary center at the University at Buffalo that focuses on a tripartite mission of education, research, and service. Its goal is to increase the knowledge of mental health and learning problems in children and adolescents, to disseminate new information to the professional, educational, and family communities, and to provide state-of-the-art treatments for families whose children have mental health and learning problems.

- Comprehensive Treatment for Attention Deficit Disorder: http://ctadd.net.

    Comprehensive Treatment for Attention Deficit Disorder offers treatment manuals, program materials, and consulting to parents, teachers, and health care providers of children with ADHD.

Model Programs

- Contingencies for Learning Academic and Social Skills (CLASS).

    Hops, H., & Walker, H. M. (1988). *CLASS: Contingencies for Learning Academic and Social Skills manual.* Seattle, WA: Educational Achievement Systems.

- Community Parent Education Program (COPE): http://www.communityed.ca/training/cope.htm.

    Community parent education program is a large group parenting course with proven effectiveness. Community parent eduation program has been conducted for families of children with ADHD, Oppositional Disorders, and developmental disabilities.

    Cunningham, C. E., Cunningham, L. J., & Martorelli, V. (1997). *Coping with conflict at school: The collaborative student mediation project manual.* Hamilton, Ontario, Canada: COPE Works.

- The Early Risers Program: http://www.safeschools.stokes.k12.nc.us/SafeEarlyRisers.htm.

    The Early Risers Program is a science-based pilot program provided as one alternative to out-of-school suspension for elementary school students. This curriculum was written especially for grade school children to develop better thinking skills, more mature and responsible ways of behaving, and improved academic performance.

August, G. J., Realmuto, G. M., Hektner, J. M., & Bloomquist, M. L. (2001). An integrated components preventive intervention for aggressive elementary school children: The Early Risers Program. *Journal of Consulting and Clinical Psychology, 69,* 614–626.

- The Incredible Years: www.incredibleyears.com.

   The Incredible Years are research-based, proven effective programs for reducing children's aggression and behavior problems and increasing social competence at home and at school. These award-winning parent training, teacher training, and child social skills training approaches have been selected by the U.S. Office of Juvenile Justice and Delinquency Prevention as an "exemplary" best practice program and as a "Blueprints" program.

- Peabody Classwide Peer Tutoring Reading Methods.

   Mathes, P. G., Fuchs, D., Fuchs, L. S., Henley, A. M., & Sanders, A. (1994). Increasing strategic reading practice with Peabody Classwide Peer Tutoring. *Learning Disabilities Research and Practice, 9,* 44–48.

   Mathes, P. G., Fuchs, D., & Fuchs, L. S. (1995). Accommodating diversity through Peabody Classwide Peer Tutoring. *Intervention in School and Clinic, 31,* 46–50.

- Reprogramming Environmental Contingencies for Effective Social Skills (RECESS).

   Walker, H. M., Hops, H., & Greenwood, C. R. (1992). *RECESS manual.* Seattle, WA: Educational Achievement Systems.

- Triple P: Positive Parenting Program, www.triplep.net.

   The Triple P-Positive Parenting Program is a multi-level, parenting and family support strategy that aims to prevent severe behavioral, emotional and developmental problems in children by enhancing the knowledge, skills and confidence of parents.

Suggested Readings for Professionals

Barkley, R. A., & Murphy, K. R. (1998). *Attention-deficit hyperactivity disorder: A clinical workbook* (2nd ed.). New York: Guilford Press.

Chamberlain, P., & Patterson, G. R. (1995). Discipline and child compliance in parenting. In M. Bornstein (Ed.), *Handbook of parenting: Vol. 4. Applied and practical parenting* (pp. 205–225). Mahwah, NJ: Erlbaum.

Dendy, C. (2000). *Teaching teens with ADD and ADHD: A quick reference guide for teachers and parents.* Bethesda, MD: Woodbine House.

DuPaul, G. J., & Stoner, G. (2003). *AD/HD in the schools: Assessment and intervention strategies* (2nd ed.). New York: Guilford Press.

Forehand, R., & Long, N. (2002). *Parenting and the strong-willed child.* Chicago: Contemporary Books.

Haber, J. S. (2000). *ADHD: The great misdiagnosis.* Dallas, TX: Taylor Publishing Company.

Kazdin, A. E. (2001). *Behavior modification in applied settings* (6th ed.). Belmont, CA: Wadsworth/Thomson Learning.

Kendall, P. C. (2000). *Cognitive-behavioral therapy for anxious children: Therapist manual* (2nd ed.). Ardmore, PA: Workbook Publishing.

Martin, G., & Pear, J. (2002). *Behavior modification: What it is and how to do it* (7th ed.). Upper Saddle River, NJ: Prentice-Hall.

Mrug, S., Hoza, B., & Gerdes, A. C. (2001). Children with attention-deficit/hyperactivity disorder: Peer relationships and peer-oriented interventions. In D. W. Nangle & C. A. Erdley (Eds.), *The role of friendship in psychological adjustment: New directions for child and adolescent development* (pp. 51–77). San Francisco: Jossey-Bass.

Pelham, W. E., Greiner, A. R., & Gnagy, E. M. (1997). *Children's summer treatment program manual.* Buffalo, NY: Comprehensive Treatment for Attention Deficit Disorders.

Rief, S. F., & Heimburge, J. A. (2002). *How to reach and teach ADD/AD/HD children: Practical techniques, strategies, and interventions for helping children with attention problems and hyperactivity.* San Francisco: Jossey-Bass.

Wilen, T. (1999). *Straight talk about psychiatric medications for kids.* New York: Guilford Press.

Suggested Readings for Parents and Other Caregivers

Barkley, R. A. (1995). *Taking charge of AD/HD: The complete, authoritative guide for parents.* New York: Guilford Press.

Dendy, C. (1995). *Teenagers with ADD: A parents' guide.* Bethesda, MD: Woodbine House.

Forehand, R., & Long, N. (2002). *Parenting and the strong-willed child.* Chicago: Contemporary Books.

Forgatch, M., & Patterson, G. R. (1989). *Parents and adolescents living together: Pt. 2. Family problem solving.* Eugene, OR: Castalia.

Fowler, M. (2002, April). *Attention-deficit/hyperactivity disorder: Briefing paper.* Washington, DC: National Dissemination Center for Children with Disabilities.

Greene, R. (2001). *The explosive child: A new approach for understanding and parenting easily frustrated, chronically inflexible children.* New York: HarperCollins.

Kelley, M. L. (1990). *School-home notes: Promoting children's classroom success.* New York: Guilford Press.

Patterson, G. R., & Forgatch, M. (1987). *Parents and adolescents living together: Pt. 1. The basics.* Eugene, OR: Castalia.

Phelan, T. (1991). *Surviving your adolescents.* Glen Ellyn, IL: Child Management.

References

Ablechild Parents for Label and Drug Free Education. (2004). [Online]. Available from http://ablechild.org/slegislation.htm.

Achenbach System of Empirically Based Assessment. (2004a). *Child Behavior Checklist for Ages 6–18* (CBCL/6–18). Retrieved October 6, 2004, from http://www.aseba.org/products/cbcl6-18.html.

Achenbach System of Empirically Based Assessment. (2004b). *Semistructured Clinical Interview for Children and Adolescents* (SCICA). Retrieved October 6, 2004, from http://www.aseba.org/products/scica.html.

Achenbach System of Empirically Based Assessment. (2004c). *Teacher's Report Form for Ages 6–18* (TRF). Retrieved October 6, 2004, from http://www.aseba.org/products/trf.html.

American Academy of Pediatrics. (2000a). *Diagnosis and evaluation of the child with attention-deficit/hyperactivity disorder* (AC0002). Retrieved October 4, 2004, from http://aap.org/policy/ac0002.html.

American Academy of Pediatrics. (2000b). *Press release: AAP releases new guidelines for diagnosis of ADHD*. Retrieved October 4, 2004, from http://www.aap.org/advocacy/releases/mayadhd.htm.

American Psychiatric Association. (2000). *Diagnostic and statistical manual of mental disorders* (4th ed., text rev.). Washington, DC: Author.

Barkley, R. A. (1990). *Attention-deficit hyperactivity disorder: A handbook for diagnosis and treatment*. New York: Guilford Press.

Barkley, R. A. (1997). *Defiant children: A clinician's manual for assessment and parent training* (2nd ed.). New York: Guilford Press.

Barkley, R. A. (1998). *Attention-deficit hyperactivity disorder: A handbook for diagnosis and treatment* (2nd ed.). New York: Guilford Press.

Barkley, R. A. (2002). Psychosocial treatments for attention-deficit/hyperactivity disorder in children. *Journal of Clinical Psychiatry, 63,* 36–43.

Barkley, R. A. (2004). *Treating children and adolescents with ADHD: An overview of empirically*

based treatments. Retrieved October 6, 2004, from http://www.continuingedcourses.net/active/courses/courses006.php.

Berry, C. A., Shaywitz, S. E., & Shaywitz, B. A. (1985). Girls with attention deficit disorder: A silent minority? A report on behavioral and cognitive characteristics. *Pediatrics, 76,* 801–809.

Blackman, J. A. (1999). Attention-deficit hyperactivity disorder in preschoolers: Does it exist and should we treat it? *Pediatric Clinics of North America, 46,* 1011–1024.

Brown, R. T., Madan-Swain, A., & Baldwin, K. (1991). Gender differences in a clinic-referred sample of attention-deficit disordered children. *Child Psychiatry and Human Development, 22,* 111–128.

Center for Mental Health Services. (2000). *Attention-deficit/hyperactivity disorder in children and adolescents*. Retrieved October 4, 2004, from http://www.mentalhealth.org/publications/allpubs/Ca0008/ADHD.htm.

Children and Adults with Attention-Deficit/Hyperactivity Disorder. (2004). *CHADD fact sheet #9: Evidence-based psychosocial treatment for children and adolescents with AD/HD*. Retrieved October 6, 2004, from http://www.chadd.org/fs/fs9.htm.

Chronis, A. M., Chacko, A., Fabiano, G. A., Wymbs, B. T., & Pelham, W. E., Jr. (2004). Enhancements to the behavioral parent training paradigm for families of children with ADHD: Review and future directions. *Clinical Child and Family Psychology Review, 7,* 1–27.

Consensus Development Panel. (1982). Defined diets and childhood hyperactivity. *National Institutes of Health Consensus Development Conference Summary, 4*(3).

Cunningham, C. E., Benness, B. B., & Siegel, L. S. (1988). Family functioning, time allocation, and parental depression in the families of normal and attention-deficit hyperactivity children. *Journal of Clinical Child Psychology, 17,* 169–177.

Dulcan, M. (1997). Practice parameters for the assessment and treatment of children, adolescents, and adults with attention-deficit/hyperactivity disorder. *Journal of the American Academy of Child and Adolescent Psychiatry, 36,* S85–S121.

DuPaul, G. J., Stoner, G., & O'Reilly, M. J. (2002). Best practices in classroom interventions for attention problems. In A. Thomas & J. Grimes (Eds.), *Best practices in school psychology IV* (Vol. 2, pp. 1115–1127). Bethesda, MD: National Association of School Psychologists.

Edwards, J. H. (2002). Evidenced-based treatment for child ADHD: "Real-world" practice implications. *Journal of Mental Health Counseling, 24,* 126–139.

Fowler, M. (2002, April). *Attention-deficit/hyperactivity disorder: Briefing paper.* Washington, DC: National Dissemination Center for Children with Disabilities.

Goldman, B. A., & Mitchell, D. F. (1990). *Directory of unpublished experimental mental measures* (Vol. 5). Dubuque, IA: Brown.

Hoff, K. E., Doepke, K., & Landau, S. (2002). Best practices in the assessment of children with attention deficit/hyperactivity disorder: Linking assessment to intervention. In A. Thomas & J. Grimes (Eds.), *Best practices in school psychology IV* (Vol. 2, pp. 1129–1150). Bethesda, MD: National Association of School Psychologists.

Horn, W. F., Wagner, A. E., & Ialongo, N. (1989). Sex differences in school-aged children with pervasive attention deficit hyper-activity disorder. *Journal of Abnormal Child Psychology, 17,* 109–125.

Hoza, B., Pelham, W., Milich, R., Pillow, D., & McBride, K. (1993). The self-perceptions and attributions of attention deficit hyperactivity disordered and nonreferred boys. *Journal of Abnormal Child Psychology, 21,* 271–286.

James, A., & Taylor, E. (1990). Sex differences in the hyperkinetic syndrome of childhood. *Journal of Child Psychology and Psychiatry, 31,* 437–446.

Kashani, J., Chapel, J. L., Ellis, J., & Shekim, W. O. (1979). Hyperactive girls. *Journal of Operational Psychology, 10,* 145–148.

Kazdin, A. E., Esveldt-Dawson, K., French, N. H., & Unis, A. S. (1987). Effects of parent management training and problem-solving skills training combined in the treatment of antisocial child behavior.

Journal of the American Academy of Child and Adolescent Psychiatry, 26, 416–424.

Kottler, S. (2000, April–May). *Social work guide to attention-deficit hyperactivity disorder* (FOCUS Newsletter). Boston: National Association of Social Workers, MA Chapter.

Landau, S., Milich, R., & Diener, M. B. (1998). Peer relations of children with attention-deficit hyperactivity disorder. *Reading and Writing Quarterly: Overcoming Learning Difficulties, 14,* 83–105.

Markward, M. J. (1998). Attention deficit hyperactivity disorder. In B. A. Thyer & J. S. Wodarski (Eds.), *Handbook of empirical social work practice* (Vol. 1, pp. 55–73). New York: Wiley.

Maxmen, J., & Ward, N. (1995). *Essential psychopathology and its treatment* (2nd ed., revised for *DSM-IV*). New York: Norton.

McConaughy, S. H., & Achenbach, T. M. (2001). *Manual for the Semistructured Clinical Interview for Children and Adolescents* (2nd ed.). Burlington: University of Vermont, Center for Children, Youth, and Families.

Milberger, S., Biederman, J., Faraone, S. V., Chen, L., & Jones, J. (1996). Is maternal smoking during pregnancy a risk factor for attention deficit hyperactivity disorder in children? *American Journal of Psychiatry, 153,* 1138–1142.

Morrison, J. (1995). DSM-IV *made easy: The clinician's guide to diagnosis.* New York: Guilford Press.

MTA Cooperative Group. (1999a). A 14-month randomized clinical trial of treatment strategies for attention-deficit/hyperactivity disorder. *Archives of General Psychiatry, 56,* 1073–1086.

MTA Cooperative Group. (1999b). Moderators and mediators of treatment response for children with attention-deficit/hyperactivity disorder. *Archives of General Psychiatry, 56,* 1088–1096.

National Institute of Health. (1998, November 16–18). Diagnosis and treatment of attention deficit hyperactivity disorder (ADHD). *NIH Consensus Statement, 16*(2).

National Institute of Mental Health. (2000). *Research on treatment for attention deficit hyperactivity disorder (ADHD): The multimodal* treatment study—Questions and answers. Retrieved September 28, 2004, from www.nimh.nih.gov/childhp.

National Institute of Mental Health. (2003). *Attention-deficit hyperactivity disorder.* Retrieved October 4, 2004, from http://www .nimh.nih.gov/publicat/adhd.cfm.

Ogan, A. T. (2001, December). Psychosocial treatment of ADHD. *NASP Communique, 30*(4).

Ollendick, T. H., & King, N. J. (2004). Empirically supported treatments for children and adolescents: Advances toward evidenced-based practice. In P. M. Barrett & T. H. Ollendick (Eds.), *Handbook of interventions that work with children and adolescents: Prevention and treatment* (pp. 3–25). Hoboken, NJ: Wiley.

Parker, J. G., & Asher, S. R. (1987). Peer relations and later personal adjustment: Are low-accepted children at risk? *Psychological Bulletin, 102,* 357–389.

Pelham, W. E., & Gnagy, E. M. (1999). Psychosocial and combined treatments for ADHD. *Mental Retardation and Developmental Disabilities Research Reviews, 5,* 225–236.

Pelham, W. E., Wheeler, T., & Chronis, A. (1998). Empirically supported psychosocial treatments for attention deficit hyperactivity disorder. *Journal of Clinical Child Psychology, 27,* 190–205.

Phelan, T. W. (1993). *All about attention deficit disorder.* Glen Ellyn, IL: Child Management.

Research and Training Center on Family Support and Children's Mental Health. (2004, May). *Data trends #98: The effects of having a child with ADHD on family members and family management.* Retrieved October 4, 2004, from http://www.rtc.pdx.edu/pgDataTrends9 .shtml.

Silverthorn, P., Frick, P., Kuper, K., & Ott, J. (1996). Attention deficit hyperactivity disorder and sex: A test of two etiological models to explain the male predominance. *Journal of Clinical Child Psychology, 25,* 52–59.

Tannock, R., Purvis, K., & Schachar, R. (1993). Narrative abilities in children with attention deficit hyperactivity disorder and normal peers. *Journal of Abnormal Child Psychology, 21,* 103–117.

Ullmann, R. K., Sleator, E. K., & Sprague, R. L. (1998). *ADD-H Comprehensive Teacher/Parent Rating Scales (ACTeRS), teacher rating/profile forms.* Champaign, IL: MetriTech.

Whalen, C. K. (2001). ADHD treatment in the 21st century: Pushing the envelope. *Journal of Clinical Child Psychology, 30,* 136–140.

Wellmark Bluecross Blueshield. (2005). *Tenth in a series of special reports: Attention-deficit/ hyperactivity disorder drugs.* Retrieved January 15, 2004, from http://www.wellmark .com/health_improvement/reports/ADHD /about.htm.

Conduct Disorder

Carolyn Hilarski

5

Chapter

Learning Objectives

After reading this chapter, the reader will be able to:

- Implement the definition and diagnostic criteria for Conduct Disorder.
- Describe the prevalence, risk factors, and costs of Conduct Disorder.
- Locate and describe evidence-based assessment instruments used for acting-out or disruptive youth.
- Locate and describe evidence-based interventions for children and adolescents meeting the criteria for Conduct Disorder.

Overview of the Problem

Social workers often are asked to assess and/or treat children and adolescents who appear to meet the diagnostic criteria for Conduct Disorder (Bagley & Mallick, 2000; Barber, Bolitho, & Bertrand, 2001). This commonly encountered presenting problem represents significant diagnostic and interventive challenges (Wakefield, Pottick, & Kirk, 2002); challenges that are all the more meaningful given the long-term deleterious effects on youth who fail to receive effective care for this condition.

Operational Definitions of the Problem

Conduct Disorder is defined by the American Psychiatric Association (2000) as a repetitive and persistent pattern of distinctive behaviors occurring in individuals under the age of 18, where the basic rights of others or major societal norms or rules are violated. Fifteen behaviors are listed in the *Diagnostic and Statistical Manual of Mental Disorders,* fourth edition, text revision (*DSM-IV-TR;* American Psychiatric Association, 2000), as Conduct Disorder characteristics. These behaviors fall into any of the following four categories: aggressive conduct that causes or threatens physical harm to other people or animals, nonaggressive behaviors that cause property loss or damage, deceitfulness or theft, and serious violation of rules (e.g., truancy, staying out all night, or running away).

Conduct Disorder (CD) is classified as an Axis I disorder that is diagnosed in childhood or adolescence (Searight, Rottnek, & Abby, 2001). A CD diagnosis is indicated, according to the *DSM* (American Psychiatric Association, 2000), when three or more of the characteristic behaviors take place within a 12-month period, with at least one behavior present within the previous 6 months. An additional qualifier is the reporting of consequences from these behaviors that impede the youth's social, academic, or occupational functioning (American Psychiatric Association, 2000).

Additional Specifiers

Childhood Onset

Conduct Disorder with childhood onset is diagnosed when at least one CD criterion characteristic is observed before the age of 10 (American Psychiatric Association, 2000). Children in this trajectory can begin to show negative, argumentative, and oppositional behaviors as young as 24 months (Kingston & Prior, 1995). Generally, behaviors such as stubbornness, defiance, noncompliance, temper tantrums, irritability, blaming, annoying others, spitefulness, and anger (e.g., hitting and biting) dominate the picture in this early stage (Bassarath, 2001; Lahey et al., 1999).

As the disorder progresses, ages 6 to 10, the repertoire of disruptive behaviors expands to deceit, shoplifting, aggression, fire setting, swearing, cruelty to animals, rule breaking, and bullying (Bassarath, 2001; Lahey et al., 1999). Youth with CD rarely display the more severe antisocial behaviors (acts contrary to the norms and laws of society) without first showing the less severe oppositional behaviors at an earlier age (Frick, Kimonis, Dandreaux, & Farell, 2003).

Conduct Disorder with childhood onset is considered the more severe form of CD (Golden & Golden, 2001). Children with this diagnosis are more likely to have persistent CD and are at greater risk for developing adult Antisocial Personality Disorder (Broidy et al., 2003).

Adolescent Onset

Conduct Disorder with adolescent onset is specified when a youth or his or her collaterals report no CD behaviors before the age of 10. Instead, when these children reach adolescence, they suddenly begin to show a severe pattern of antisocial behavior, such as cruelty to others, stealing, running away from home, truancy, breaking and entering, and rape (Bassarath, 2001). Interestingly, the arrests and convictions for adolescent-onset CD are comparable to the arrests and convictions of adolescents who show the childhood-onset trajectory. In fact, adolescents with this late-onset pattern of CD outnumber youth showing the childhood onset at a rate of about 3 to 1 (Moffitt, Caspi, Dickson, Silva, & Stanton, 1996). Nonetheless, youth showing antisocial behaviors at a later onset when compared to childhood onset tend, generally, to be less aggressive and violent (Moffitt et al., 1996), have fewer cognitive and neuropsychological deficits, present equally between genders, and have more positive peer relationships (Moffitt & Lynam, 1994). It is possible that late-onset adolescents are attempting to obtain independence, respect, and adult advantage (Moffitt et al., 1996). With increasing age and earlier appropriate cognitive and social development, a subgroup of these youth will discontinue their acting-out behavior, although a significant portion will persist (Broidy et al., 2003).

Criteria for Severity of Conduct Disorder

- *Mild:* The youth's behavior and consequences minimally meet the CD diagnosis, and collaterals report few disturbing issues.
- *Moderate:* The youth's behavior may meet or moderately exceed the CD diagnostic criteria, and the resulting consequences may be reported as somewhat uncomfortable to disturbing for collaterals.
- *Severe:* The youth's behaviors and their consequences greatly exceed those needed for a CD diagnosis, with collaterals expressing alarm or grave concern over the youth's behavior (Atkins & McKay, 1996).

Comorbidity

Studies focusing on the tendency for disorders to co-occur (comorbidity) in adolescent samples have shown that Conduct Disorder rarely manifests in isolation (Costello, Mustillo, Erkanli, Keeler, & Angold, 2004; Frick, Bodin, & Barry, 2000; Lahey, Loeber, Burke, Rathouz, & McBurnett, 2002; Salekin, Leistico, Neumann, DiCicco, & Duros, 2004). Indeed, it has been well established that comorbid

CD, Attention-Deficit/Hyperactivity Disorder (ADHD), and Oppositional Defiant Disorder (ODD) are commonly found in population-based surveys and studies of clinically referred juveniles (Biederman, Newcorn, & Sprich, 1991; Kuhne, Schachar, & Tannock, 1997; McArdle, O'Brien, & Kolvin, 1995). In fact, there is some suspicion that these disorders are not independent of one another, with ODD and CD estimates ranging from 20% to 60%, and CD and ADHD from 60% to 90% (Abikoff & Klein, 1992). Other common patterns are CD and depression or anxiety, found in 25% to 50% of youth diagnosed with CD (Bird, 1993), and CD and substance use and abuse (Costello et al., 2004; Whitmore et al., 1997).

Prevalence

Among adolescents, the male prevalence rate for CD is 3.4% to 10.4% and the female is 0.8% to 8.0%. In preadolescent children, the prevalence rate drops to 1.9% to 8.0% for boys and 0 to 1.9% for girls (American Psychiatric Association, 1994). Thus, overall, Conduct Disorder is diagnosed in males far more than females, although this disparity diminishes toward midadolescence (Maughan, Rowe, Messer, Goodman, & Meltzer, 2004). Generally, adolescent females engage in covert (e.g., prostitution) behaviors, whereas males continue with aggressive acting out (Bardone et al., 1998), although there is a subgroup of females that engage in violent behavior that persists into adulthood (Kjelsberg, 1999).

Cost

Child and adolescent behavior problems are serious social challenges (Cottle, Lee, & Heilbrun, 2001). The magnitude of these problems, in terms of costs both to the individual and to society, have led prominent leaders to describe the phenomenon as a crisis of epic proportions (Stephens, Pitt, & Patrick, 1997). The numbers of serious violent crimes committed by adolescents have recently dropped. However, extreme violence by juveniles continues to be considerable and significantly exceeds the average of any previous decade (Snyder, 2001). Moreover, crimes are being committed by an increasingly younger segment of the population, as significant numbers of preadolescent children are involved in arson, vandalism, and sex offenses (Espiritu, Huizinga, Crawford, & Loeber, 2001). Five percent of those arrested for violent crimes in the year 2003 were children under the age of 15 (FBI, 2003).

Behavioral problems are associated with huge costs to the youth involved. First, these youth are at substantial risk for school failure. Research findings have indicated that children who engage in delinquent or criminal behavior are far more likely to fail or drop out of school (Dumas, Prinz, Smith, & Laughlin, 1999). This severs ties with one of society's most important agents for social-ization. Adolescent school dropouts miss opportunities to learn the basic skills for living as productive members of society, and they increase their risk for unemployment, poverty, and poor health (Wodarski & Wodarski, 1998).

The costs associated with child and adolescent behavior prob-lems are not only incurred by the youth involved, but also by society as a whole. Indeed, the cost of caring for one unsocialized or under-socialized child is estimated at $25,000 per year for life (Lykken, 1995). Communities also incur other tangible costs, including costs associated with property damage, with maintenance of a growing juvenile justice system, and with the provision of health care to those injured by a delinquent or substance-abusing youth. Estimates report that one delinquent youth costs society between $1.7 and $2.3 million during his or her lifetime (Cohen, Dugan, McLaughlin, & Soucar, 1995). Although tangible costs are great, the intangible costs may be the most devastating. These include the loss of poten-tially productive members of society, the propagation of fear and de-spair, and the disintegration of community.

Implications for Social Work

According to the American Psychiatric Association (1994, p. 88), "Conduct Disorder is one of the most frequently diagnosed condi-tions in outpatient and inpatient mental health facilities for chil-dren." Left untreated, children diagnosed with CD potentially face numerous problems, such as substance abuse, academic failure, criminal involvement, and suicidal behavior, in addition to having a high probability of premature death (Laub & Vaillant, 2000; Neeleman, Wessely, & Wadsworth, 1998).

Conduct Disorder is a persistent disorder that is difficult to treat. Youth with CD often live in families and communities with inadequate resources, challenging treatment plans to include mul-tiple system issues (Finkelhor & Asdigian, 1996). Moreover, *system issues*, such as legal mandates, can actually delay intervention, en-couraging chronicity and placing the youth at risk for develop-ment of adult psychopathology, such as antisocial personality (Kazdin, 2000).

Recent research has proposed that perspective taking and empathic response to others in distress can promote interper-sonal responsibility and inhibit negative acts (Greenberg, Kusche, Cook, & Quamma, 1995). In general, parental nurturance com-bined with nonphysical punishment and the teaching of desirable parenting skills, such as time-out and age-appropriate explana-tions of suitable behavioral patterns, have also been found to im-prove the likelihood of prosocial thinking and behaving in children (Webster-Stratton & Hammond, 1997; Webster-Stratton

& Herbert, 1993, 1994; Webster-Stratton & Lindsay, 1999). Clinical interventions that focus on enabling the parents of children diagnosed with Conduct Disorder to instill and encourage empathy may allow these children to avoid problems associated with CD. Such parents and their children are likely to develop and sustain much more satisfying and rewarding relationships.

Evidence-Based Approaches to Assessment

There are no known causes of CD behavior. However, researchers have discovered factors that appear associated with this disorder, such as difficult parent and child interactions, abuse, caregivers that engage in alcohol or drug abuse, academic problems, low self-esteem, head injury, and comorbidity (Hinshaw & Zupan, 1997). Such varying issues demand a comprehensive assessment that includes interviews with the youth, parents, teachers (together and separately), and other caregivers and family members, in addition to a social and medical history and a cognitive and psychiatric evaluation (King et al., 1996).

Person Interviews or Self-Reports

Historical information related to the youth's prenatal and birth history, including substance abuse by the mother and maternal infections and medications, in addition to the youth's developmental history regarding primary caregiver attachment, overall temperament, general level of aggression and oppositional behavior, attention, and impulse control is vital. The Child Behavior Checklist is helpful for obtaining some of this information (Achenbach, 1991).

In addition, assessment should include the following questions: Was the youth a victim or perpetrator of physical, verbal, emotional, or sexual abuse? Does the youth use mood-altering substances and/or engage in sexual activity? Is the youth exposed to community violence? What is the youth's ability to trust and empathize, experience guilt, accept responsibility? What are the youth's overall mood, sense of self, beliefs, suicide potential, peer relationships, and worldview? Instruments that may be helpful in gathering this information are discussed next.

The Weinberger Adjustment Inventory (Weinberger, 1997) is a 29-item Likert self-report measure for youth ages 10 to 17. The instrument may be administered to groups or an individual by an untrained examiner. The subscale scores include Anxiety, Depression, Low Self-Esteem, Low Well-being, Self-Restraint, Suppression of Aggression, Impulse Control, Responsibility, and Consideration of Others.

The Jesness Inventory (Jesness & Wedge, 1984) is a 160-item true/false self-report that provides important treatment-related information regarding personality subtypes for conduct disordered youths and adults age 8 and older.

The Carlson Psychological Survey (Carlson, 1981) is a 50-item questionnaire with a grade 4 reading level that takes 15 minutes for youths and adults to complete. The instrument includes five scales relating to Substance Abuse, Thought Disturbance, Antisocial Tendencies, Self-Depreciation, and Validity.

The Hare Psychopathy Checklist: Youth Version (Hare, 1991) is a 20 item semistructured interview meant to assess psychopathic traits in male and female delinquents ages 12 to 18. Output requires obtaining collateral information. The interviewer needs to be a trained professional in the area of forensics.

Collaterals

The Conners Parent-Teacher Rating Scales (Conners, Sitarenios, Parker, & Epstein, 1998) include a long (80 items, 10 scales) and short (27 items, 4 scales) parent form and a teacher long (59 items, 9 scales) and short (28 items, 4 scales) version. Indexes relate to anxiety, social problems, oppositional, hyperactive-impulsive, perfectionism, global index, and cognitive functioning. The scales are normed for ages 3 through 17.

Family Assessment

Understanding the family's coping style, strengths, stressors, structure, interactions, problem-solving abilities, worldview, and cognitions is vital (Frick, 2001). Is the parenting style harsh, abusive, permissive, inconsistent, coercive, neglectful, or reinforcing? Is there a history of primary caregiver antisocial behavior, learning disabilities, tic, mood, personality, somatization, or ADHD? How do the sibling systems function? Has there been a loss of employment, divorce, separation, or death in the family? Ignoring the influences of a youth's psychosocial context sabotages any meaningful work (Frick, 2001).

School Functioning

Interactions with the school principal, psychologist, teacher, and nurse will aid in obtaining intelligence and achievement test information in addition to overall academic performance, cognitive functioning, and behavioral reports. The Child Behavior Checklist (Achenbach, 1991) is a helpful teacher rating scale for behavioral information regarding the youth.

Physiological Evaluation

Obtaining a physical examination report that includes a pulse rate, especially if the youth is taking medications, a vision and hearing exam, medical history (Lahey, Hart, Pliszka, Applegate, & McBurnett, 1993), and somatization evaluation, in addition to a urine or blood screen (for substance use), is essential (Taylor & Carey, 1998).

Diagnostic Formulation

Once the CD criteria are met, further specification of whether the disorder began in childhood or adolescence is necessary. Additionally, subtyping (Loeber, Keenan, & Quanwu, 1997) of the CD may help to further define the assessment picture and point to specific objectives for prevention planning. For example, is the youth's presenting behavior overt (e.g., assaultive), covert (e.g., theft), or authority conflicted? Are the youth's behaviors under- or over-restrained? Overrestrained youth tend to be older, more socialized, deceptively mature, academically functional, more violent, and commit fewer CD behaviors than underrestrained youth (Loeber & Hay, 1997). Treatment needs revolve around anger management and emotional acceptance (Steiner, Petersen, Saxena, Ford, & Matthews, 2003).

If the CD behavioral criteria are only partially met, other issues should be considered, perhaps as primary and CD as secondary.

Evidence-Based Approaches to Intervention

Treatment outcome studies completed after 1980 revealed promising results for youth with CD behavior (Shamsie & Hluchy, 1991). Positive results were noted in one third of therapy programs that emphasized involvement of parents. Successful programs included those that provided family therapy (when addressing a family's unique needs), cognitive-behavioral interventions, anger management training, and specific individualized treatment approaches that addressed problems related to individual behavior, family dynamics, peer group, and the social system (Shamsie & Hluchy, 1991).

Individual Therapy

Although child-alone and parent-alone prevention models have shown limited effectiveness, a new generation of multicomponent models provides the promise of greater impact. Following the developmental models of risk and protection, interventions that target multiple environments and socialization agents (parents, teachers, peers) over extended developmental periods are necessary to alter the developmental trajectories of children who live in high-risk environments and are already showing signs of CD behavior (Reid, Eddy, Fetrow, & Stoolmiller, 1999).

The Preschool Child

Intervention objectives for this age group might examine the parent and child relationship concerning parental effectiveness (e.g., understanding the child's normative behaviors) and communication issues (Nixon, Sweeney, Erickson, & Touyz, 2004). Programs aimed at very young children deter the development of self-defeating behaviors and their consequences (Webster-Stratton & Taylor, 2001).

School-Age Children

Preadolescence is a critical period for prevention intervention efforts. Disruptive behaviors in middle childhood are shown to be antecedents to serious adolescent disorders, such as substance abuse and delinquency (Patterson, Forgatch, Yoerger, & Stoolmiller, 1998). At this age, improving peer relationships and problem-solving and academic skills, in addition to facilitating issues relating to authority figures, is helpful (Kazdin, 2000).

Child- and Parent-Focused and School-Based Interventions

The Adolescent Transitions Program (Dishion, Andrews, & Kavanagh, 1996) is based on an ecological model of antisocial behavior and targets both at-risk adolescents and their parents to prevent further escalation of self-defeating behaviors (Dishion & Kavanagh, 2000). The program is designed to improve teens' self-regulation by teaching problem-solving skills using videotapes, modeling, and tokens to reinforce newly acquired skills. The parent component of the program attempts to improve parent management skills. In addition, parents and teens work as a group to sort through their family structural issues (Dishion & Kavanagh, 2003).

Evaluation of this program has not shown significant improvement in school behavior, though parents in all groups reported improved family interaction (Dishion, Kavanagh, Schneiger, Nelson, & Kaufman, 2002).

Child-Focused and School-Based

The problem-solving skills training model (Spivack, Platt, & Shure, 1976) has been well researched. It is based on literature that demonstrates that youth with disruptive behaviors often show cognitive deficits and distortions that can lead to aggression. Altering the way the youth perceives environmental events and interprets the intent of the behavior of others reduces aggression. A youth works individually with the therapist to learn appropriate self-statements for interpersonal situations that lead to effective solutions to a problem. Prosocial solutions are fostered through the therapist's active role in treatment, which can include modeling, role-playing, coaching and practice, direct reinforcement, and mild punishment (e.g., loss of points). Over the course of treatment, the youth increasingly uses the new skills in real-life situations (Nash, Fraser, Galinsky, & Kupper, 2003).

Several outcome studies with preadolescents in clinic and inpatient settings have demonstrated significant reductions in aggressive and antisocial behavior at home, at school, and in the community. These gains were still evident at 1-year follow-up. However, this model has been relatively untested with the delinquent adolescent population (Nash et al., 2003).

Hudley et al. (1998) examined the Brain Power Program, designed to counteract attributional biases and reactive aggression in aggressive children. It was implemented in four elementary schools in southern California, with 384 African American and Latino 10- to 12-year-old males, who were paired with nonaggressive peers and exposed to a 12-lesson school-based intervention focusing on improving the accuracy of their perceptions and interpretations of others' actions. Teacher ratings indicated that the program improved the identified group's behavior. However, a 12-month follow-up showed diminished effects (Hudley et al., 1998).

The Intervention Campaign against Bully-Victim Problems (Olweus, 1991) is a universal prevention program that was originally implemented in Norway from 1983 to 1985 to reduce bullying and related victimization among elementary and middle school children. The program provided families with a 4-page pamphlet on bullying and teachers with a 32-page booklet that described in detail suggestions for reducing and preventing bullying, in addition to a 25-minute video containing vignettes of bullying situations. Finally, a brief questionnaire related to bullying was administered to students. The questionnaire was considered part of the intervention as it was intended to act as a mechanism for awareness and discussion of the problem of bullying. The study had a quasi-experimental (staggered cohort) design with 2,500 students in grades 4 to 7 from 42 elementary and middle schools. The students were divided into four age/grade-equivalent cohorts of 600 to 700 students, with roughly equal numbers of boys and girls in each. Results at 8 and 20 months postintervention showed reductions of 50% or more in bully and victim problems for boys and girls across all grades (4 to 9), with increased effects at the 2-year follow-up (Olweus, 1991).

Group Therapies

Children with Conduct Disorder behaviors show deficits in the way they process and respond to social information, which makes them susceptible to acting inappropriately in social contexts. Cognitive-behavioral skills training teaches youth, in a group format, to inhibit angry and impulsive responding, overcome deficits in social cognition, use more appropriate social problem-solving skills, and develop more appropriate social skills (Crick & Dodge, 1996).

Family Therapy

The risk of developing Conduct Disorder is increased or decreased by the social and family context within which the child develops (Frick, 1998). Parenting practices are viewed as one of the most important family correlates of Conduct Disorder (Frick et al., 2003). This is based on the view that the development of Conduct Disorder reflects a failure of the child or adolescent to be adequately socialized by parents, who are the primary socializing agents for youth (Loeber, Green, Lahey, Frick, & McBurnett, 2000).

Parent psychopathology and maladjustment, including criminal behavior and alcoholism as well as certain disciplinary practices and attitudes, have consistently been found to correlate with Conduct Disorder in youth (Kazdin, 2002). In addition, dysfunctional family relations have been noted. Parents of children with CD tend to be less accepting of their children and display less warmth, affection, and emotional support, as well as less attachment, than do the parents of nondiagnosed youth (Kazdin, 2002). Unhappy marital relations, interpersonal conflict, and aggression (Kazdin, 2002) further characterize the parental relations of youth diagnosed with CD.

Family-focused interventions have demonstrated their ability to affect the behavior of a youth with CD. These interventions require ongoing involvement of a parent or family member, and they require the parent to complete tasks or practice skills outside the treatment session. The immediate goal of the intervention is to develop specific skills in the parents that will alter the interactional patterns maintaining aggressive and antisocial behavior. The parent training approach teaches parents the benefits of refocusing their attention from the youth's negative to his or her positive behaviors. Parents also learn different behavioral techniques and practice these skills through structured role-play.

There is some evidence to support the use of parent training techniques based on social and behavioral learning theory for children with CD (Larson, 1998). However, parent training is more effective in reducing behavior problems in younger children than in older children, with optimal effects achieved before fourth grade, when such behaviors appear to become firmly entrenched through association with deviant peers. Family therapy models that incorporate parent management training have been shown to be more effective with adolescents with CD (Frick, 1998). The parents engage in developing contingency management programs for use in the home, which enhances parent and child interactions through improved communication, youth monitoring, and consistent discipline (Mabe, Turner, & Joseph-son, 2001).

Multisystemic Therapy

In multisystemic therapy (MST) problem behaviors are conceptual-ized as being linked with individual characteristics and with various aspects of the multiple systems in which the youth is entrenched, including family, peers, schools, and neighborhood. Multisystemic therapy is designed to intervene at all levels using treatment tech-niques most likely to (a) promote disengagement from deviant peers, (b) build stronger bonds to conventional groups such as the family and school, (c) enhance family management skills such as monitoring and discipline, and (d) develop greater social and aca-demic competence in the adolescent (Henggeler, Schoenwald, Bor-duin, Rowland, & Cunningham, 1998).

The specific treatment techniques used are individualized to the needs of the youth and his or her family. The treatment plan is based on an extensive assessment of all systems and their interre-lationships to identify the most salient contributors to the prob-lem. Therapists use a variety of demonstrated therapy techniques to change the systems supporting the problem behaviors, including family therapy, school consultation, and behavioral and cognitive-behavioral techniques (see Sutphen, Thyer, & Kurtz, 1995). Sev-eral studies have shown significant results in reducing negative behaviors and increasing family functioning with chronically vio-lent antisocial youth (Borduin et al., 1995). In addition, MST has been very successful in reducing substance abuse in juvenile ado-lescents, even at 6-month follow-up (Henggeler et al., 1998).

Community Interventions

Community-based residential programs for aggressive and delin-quent adolescents have been the treatment of choice for some time. However, the effectiveness of these programs are undecided, especially in the long term (Castellano & Soderstrom, 1992). They are quite expensive, as they require service for control and secu-rity. Moreover, limited research has shown that acting-out adoles-cents who are exposed to other deviant peers may increase their delinquent behavior (Larson, 1998). Finally, the behavior changes that may occur during the program frequently do not generalize to other milieus (Castellano et al., 1992).

The Head Start program, designed for preschool children, may help prevent antisocial behavior in a specific subgroup of children (Kaminski, Stormshak, Good, & Goodman, 2002). The program in-tervenes with children on multiple levels by providing the child with consistent structure, health care resources (Allen, Stuart, Everett, & Elangovan, 2004), education, and support for the care-giver (Baydar, Reid, & Webster-Stratton, 2003).

Additional prevention strategies in the school or neighborhood are community policing, supervised recreation, and mentoring.

Community Policing

Stringent enforcement of laws against illegal gun carrying has proven effective (Blumstein, 2002). Other effective policing strategies are increased patrol of high crime areas and arrests of repeat offenders and drunk drivers (Sherman, 1998). Policies found unsuccessful include neighborhood block watches, juvenile arrests for minor offenses, and drug sale arrests. Community policing programs must be dedicated to community problem solving and strengthening police and community alliances (Conway, 2002).

Supervised Recreational Programs

Juvenile crime occurs most often after school, when many children are unsupervised because parents are working (Farrell, Meyer, & Dahlberg, 1996). This void in child supervision is a community issue that needs attention if reducing juvenile crime is the community goal. Supervised *afterschool programs* help to intervene in this issue and need serious consideration in crime prevention planning (Nation et al., 2003). Programs that are supported by theory, include multiple levels of age-appropriate components, encourage prosocial relationships, are logistically convenient to the community, include trained staff and supervision, and are continually evaluated are more likely to succeed (Nation et al., 2003). Currently, however, there is a lack of empirical outcome research for the prudence of this intervention. Although several studies have demonstrated positive results regarding reducing juvenile crime and drug use (Schinke, Orlandi, & Cole, 1992; St. Pierre, Mark, & Kaltreider, 1997), further research is needed (Scott-Little, Hamann, & Jurs, 2002). An afterschool program would be helpful to incorporate into a multisystemic treatment plan, as one of the important protective factors for youth is a positive connection to the community with appropriate role models and circumstances that provide for practice of newly learned skills.

Mentoring

Mentoring is an inexpensive program in which adult (same-sex) volunteers spend time with children or adolescents (generally from single-parent homes), usually engaged in sports or educational activities (Rhodes, Grossman, & Resch, 2000; Rhodes, Grossman, & Roffman, 2002). The Big Brother/Big Sister mentoring program is an example. Empirical examination of this program by Tierney and colleagues (Tierney, Grossman, & Resch, 2000) showed that the mentored youths described less fighting in comparison to wait-list controls, in addition to a perception of positive family relations.

A noteworthy problem with mentoring interventions is retaining mentors long enough to sustain a meaningful relationship for considerable change to occur (DuBois, Holloway, Valentine, & Cooper, 2002). The best results come from a significant relationship that lasts at least 1 year (Grossman & Rhodes, 2002). Dreman and colleagues (Dreman, Aldor, & Katz, 1995) may have found one disconnection issue, namely, that the mentored child's mother expected mentors to fill a substitute parent role. A subgroup of Big Brother/Big Sister volunteers may feel overwhelmed by such responsibility.

Research has found that mentors who are flexible and relationship focused in their approach to mentoring retain their relationships longer than mentors who are more directive and tend to prescribe activities and topics of discussion (Morrow & Styles, 1995).

The issue of level and type of training for mentors is not answered. Some studies found that nondirective programs were not helpful to youth and their caregivers (DuBois et al., 2002; Roberts, Liabo, Lucas, Dubois, & Sheldon, 2004). Others found no significant differences in trained and minimally trained mentors (Cavell & Hughes, 2000).

Summary

Progress has been made in the clinical treatment of youth with a diagnosis of Conduct Disorder (Frick, 2001; Kazdin & Whitley, 2003). However, the absence of consistently effective interventions suggests that additional research could potentially contribute to a better understanding of the disorder and to intervention techniques that are more reliable and successful. Currently, no single treatment method has effectively ameliorated Conduct Disorder or its poor long-term prognosis (Kazdin & Whitley, 2003).

Study Questions

1. Discuss the most effective treatment for adolescents diagnosed with Conduct Disorder.
2. What evaluative instruments would you use for a *preadolescent* child referred with disruptive behavior? Explain your choice.
3. What evaluative instruments would you use for an *adolescent* youth referred with disruptive behavior? Explain your choice.
4. Discuss how family interventions are useful in treating a youth presenting with Conduct Disorder. Are there different family techniques used according to the age of the youth?

5. Discuss community interventions and rate their usefulness in treating a child with Conduct Disorder.

6. Discuss the long- and short-term consequences of Conduct Disorder with childhood onset and with adolescent onset.

7. When a youth presents with Conduct Disorder behavior, what family issues need to be assessed and why?

8. Describe the risk factors associated with Conduct Disorder behavior presenting in childhood and in adolescence.

References

Abikoff, H., & Klein, R. G. (1992). Attention-deficit hyperactivity and conduct disorder: Comorbidity and implications for treatment. *Journal of Consulting and Clinical Psychology, 60,* 881–892.

Achenbach, T. M. (1991). *Manual for the Child Behavior Checklist/4–18 and 1991.* Burlington: University of Vermont, Department of Psychiatry.

Allen, R. L., Stuart, A., Everett, D., & Elangovan, S. (2004). Preschool hearing screening: Pass/refer rates for children enrolled in a Head Start program in eastern North Carolina. *American Journal of Audiology, 13,* 29–38.

American Psychiatric Association. (1994). *Diagnostic and statistical manual of mental disorders* (4th ed.). Washington, DC: Author.

American Psychiatric Association. (2000). *Diagnostic and statistical manual of mental disorders* (4th ed., text rev.). Washington, DC: Author.

Atkins, M. S., & McKay, M. (1996). *DSM-IV* diagnosis of conduct disorder and oppositional defiant disorder: Implications and guidelines for school mental health teams. *Psychological Review, 25,* 274–284.

Bagley, C., & Mallick, K. (2000). Spiraling up and spiraling down: Implications of a long term study of temperament and conduct disorder for social work with children. *Child and Family Social Work, 5,* 291–301.

Barber, J. G., Bolitho, F. & Bertrand, L. (2001). Parent-child synchrony and adolescent adjustment. *Child and Adolescent Social Work Journal, 18,* 51–64.

Bardone, A. M., Moffitt, T. E., Caspi, A., Dickson, N., Stanton, W. R., & Silva, P. A. (1998). Adult physical health outcomes of adolescent girls with conduct disorder, depression, and anxiety. *Journal of the American Academy of Child and Adolescent Psychiatry, 37,* 594–601.

Bassarath, L. (2001). Conduct disorder: A biopsychosocial review. *Canadian Journal of Psychiatry, 46,* 609–616.

Baydar, N., Reid, M. J., & Webster-Stratton, C. (2003). The role of mental health factors and program engagement in the effectiveness of a preventive parenting program for Head Start mothers. *Child Development, 74,* 1433–1453.

Biederman, J., Newcorn, J., & Sprich, S. (1991). Comorbidity of attention deficit hyperactivity disorder with conduct, depressive, anxiety, and other disorders [see comments]. *American Journal of Psychiatry, 148,* 564–577.

Bird, H. R. (1993). Patterns of diagnostic comorbidity in a community sample of children aged 9 through 16 years. *Journal of the American Academy of Child and Adolescent Psychiatry, 32,* 361–368.

Blumstein, A. (2002). Youth, guns, and violent crime. *Future Child, 12*(2), 38–53.

Borduin, C. M., Mann, B. J., Cone, L. T., Henggeler, S. W., Fucci, B. R., Blaske, D. M., et al. (1995). Multisystemic treatment of serious juvenile offenders: Long-term prevention of criminality and violence. *Journal of Consulting and Clinical Psychology, 63,* 569–578.

Broidy, L. M., Nagin, D. S., Tremblay, R. E., Bates, J. E., Brame, B., Dodge, K. A., et al. (2003). Developmental trajectories of childhood disruptive behaviors and adolescent delinquency: A six-site, cross-national study. *Developmental Psychology, 39,* 222–245.

Carlson, K. A. (1981). *Manual: Carlson Psychological Survey.* London, Ontario, Canada: Research Psychologist Press.

Castellano, T. C., & Soderstrom, I. R. (1992). Therapeutic wilderness programs and juvenile recidivism: A program evaluation. *Journal of Offender Rehabilitation, 17*(3/4), 19–46.

Cavell, T. A., & Hughes, J. N. (2000). Secondary prevention as context for assessing change processes in aggressive children. *Journal of School Psychology, 38,* 199–235.

Cohen, S. W., Dugan, L. M., McLaughlin, R. H., & Soucar, E. (1995). "Prediction of antisocial behavior in attention-deficit hyperactivity disorder boys from aggression/defiant scores": Comment. *Journal of the American Academy of Child and Adolescent Psychiatry, 34,* 397–398.

Conners, C. K., Sitarenios, G., Parker, J. D., & Epstein, J. N. (1998). The revised Conners' Parent Rating Scale (CPRS-R): Factor structure, reliability, and criterion validity. *Journal of Abnormal Child Psychology, 26,* 257–268.

Conway, K. (2002). Booze and beach bans: Turning the tide through community action in New Zealand. *Health Promotion International, 17,* 171–177.

Costello, E. J., Mustillo, S., Erkanli, A., Keeler, G., & Angold, A. (2004). Prevalence and development of psychiatric disorders in childhood and adolescence. *Archives of General Psychiatry, 60,* 837–844.

Cottle, C. C., Lee, R. J., & Heilbrun, K. (2001). The prediction of criminal recidivism in juveniles: A meta-analysis. *Criminal Justice and Behavior, 28,* 367–394.

Crick, N. R., & Dodge, K. A. (1996). Social information-processing mechanisms in reactive and proactive aggression. *Child Development, 67,* 993–1002.

Dishion, T. J., Andrews, D. W., & Kavanagh, K. (1996). Preventive interventions for high-risk youth: The Adolescent Transitions Program. In D. V. Peters & R. J. McMahon (Eds.), *Preventing childhood disorders, substance abuse, and delinquency* (pp. 184–214). Thousand Oaks, CA: Sage.

Dishion, T. J., & Kavanagh, K. (2000). A multilevel approach to family-centered prevention in schools: Process and outcome. *Addictive Behaviors, 25,* 899–911.

Dishion, T. J., & Kavanagh, K. (2003). *Intervening in adolescent problem behavior: A family centered approach.* New York: Guilford Press.

Dishion, T. J., Kavanagh, K., Schneiger, A., Nelson, S., & Kaufman, N. K. (2002). Preventing early adolescent substance use: A family-centered strategy for the public middle school. *Preventive Science, 3,* 191–201.

Dreman, S., Aldor, R., & Katz, D. (1995). The big brother in the single parent family: Family, friend, or counselor. *Journal of Divorce and Remarriage, 24*(3/4), 59–70.

DuBois, D. L., Holloway, B. E., Valentine, J. C., & Cooper, H. (2002). Effectiveness of mentoring programs for youth: A meta-analytic review. *American Journal of Community Psychology, 30,* 157–197.

Dumas, J. E., Prinz, R. J., Smith, E. P., & Laughlin, J. (1999). The EARLY ALLIANCE prevention trial: An integrated set of interventions to promote competence and reduce risk for conduct disorder, substance abuse, and school failure. *Clinical Child and Family Psychology Review, 2,* 37–53.

Espiritu, R. C., Huizinga, D., Crawford, A., & Loeber, R. (2001). Epidemiology of self-reported delinquency. In R. Loeber & D. P. Farrington (Eds.), *Development, intervention, and service needs* (pp. 47–66). Thousand Oaks, CA: Sage.

Farrell, A. D., Meyer, A. L., & Dahlberg, L. L. (1996). Richmond youth against violence: A school-based program for urban adolescents. *American Journal of Preventive Medicine, 12*(5), 13–21.

Federal Bureau of Investigation. (2003). *Uniform crime reports for the United States.* Available from http://www.fbi.gov/ucr/ucr/htm.

Finkelhor, D., & Asdigian, N. L. (1996). Risk factors for youth victimization: Beyond a lifestyles/routine activities theory approach. *Violence and Victims, 11,* 3–19.

Frick, P. J. (1998). *Conduct disorders and severe antisocial behavior.* New York: Plenum Press.

Frick, P. J. (2001). Effective interventions for children and adolescents with conduct disorder. *Canadian Journal of Psychiatry, 46,* 597–608.

Frick, P. J., Bodin, D., & Barry, C. T. (2000). Psychopathic traits and conduct problems in community and clinic-referred samples of children: Further development of the Psychopathy Screening Device. *Psychological Assessment, 12,* 382–393.

Frick, P. J., Kimonis, E. R., Dandreaux, D. M., & Farell, J. M. (2003). The 4-year stability of psychopathic traits in non-referred youth. *Behavioral Science and the Law, 21,* 713–736.

Golden, Z. L., & Golden, C. J. (2001). Do early onset conduct disordered adolescents perform like brain injured or normal adolescents on cognitive tests? *International Journal of Neuroscience, 111,* 109–121.

Greenberg, M. T., Kusche, C. A., Cook, E. T., & Quamma, J. P. (1995). Promoting emotional competence in school-aged children: The effects of the PATHS curriculum. *Development and Psychopathology, 7,* 117–136.

Grossman, J. B., & Rhodes, J. E. (2002). The test of time: Predictors and effects of duration in youth mentoring relationships. *American Journal of Community Psychology, 30,* 199–219.

Hare, R. D. (1991). *Hare Psychopathy Checklist-Revised (PCL-R).* Toronto, Ontario, Canada: Multi-Health Systems.

Henggeler, S. W., Schoenwald, S. K., Borduin, C. M., Rowland, M. D., & Cunningham, P. B. (1998). *Multisystemic treatment of antisocial behavior in children and adolescents.* New York: Guilford Press.

Hinshaw, S. P., & Zupan, B. A. (1997). Assessment of antisocial behavior in children and adolescents. In E. J. Mash & R. A. Barkley (Eds.), *Child psychopathology* (pp. 36–50). New York: Guilford Press.

Hudley, C., Britsch, B., Wakefield, W. D., Smith, T., Demorat, M., & Cho, S.-J. (1998). An attribution retraining program to reduce aggression in elementary school students. *Psychology in the Schools, 35,* 271–282.

Jesness, C. F., & Wedge, R. F. (1984). Validity of a revised Jesness Inventory I-level classification with delinquents. *Journal of Consulting and Clinical Psychology, 52,* 997–1010.

Kaminski, R. A., Stormshak, E. A., Good, R. H., III, & Goodman, M. R. (2002). Pre-vention of substance abuse with rural Head Start children and families: Results of project STAR. *Psychology of Addictive Behaviors, 16*(Suppl. 4), 11–26.

Kazdin, A. E. (2000). Treatments for aggressive and antisocial children. *Child and Adolescent Psychiatric Clinics of North America, 9,* 841–858.

Kazdin, A. E. (2002). Family and parenting interventions for conduct disorder and delinquency: A meta-analysis of randomized controlled trials. *Journal of Pediatrics, 141,* 738.

Kazdin, A. E., & Whitley, M. K. (2003). Treatment of parental stress to enhance therapeutic change among children referred for aggressive and antisocial behavior. *Journal of Consulting and Clinical Psychology, 71,* 504–515.

King, C. A., Ghaziuddin, N., McGovern, L., Brand, E., Hill, E., & Naylor, M. (1996). Predictors of comorbid alcohol and substance abuse in depressed adolescents. *Journal of the American Academy of Child and Adolescent Psychiatry, 35,* 743–751.

Kingston, L., & Prior, M. (1995). The development of patterns of stable, transient, and school-age onset aggressive behavior in young children. *Journal of the American Academy of Child and Adolescent Psychiatry, 34,* 348–358.

Kjelsberg, E. (1999). Adolescence-limited versus life-course-persistent criminal behavior in adolescent psychiatric inpatients. *European Child and Adolescent Psychiatry, 8,* 276–282.

Kuhne, M., Schachar, R., & Tannock, R. (1997). Impact of comorbid oppositional or conduct problems on attention-deficit hyperactivity disorder. *Journal of the American Academy of Child and Adolescent Psychiatry, 36,* 1715–1725.

Lahey, B. B., Goodman, S. H., Waldman, I. D., Bird, H., Canino, G., Jensen, P., et al. (1999). Relation of age of onset to the type and severity of child and adolescent conduct problems. *Journal of Abnormal Child Psychology, 27,* 247–260.

Lahey, B. B., Hart, E. L., Pliszka, S. R., Applegate, B., & McBurnett, K. (1993). Neurophysiological correlates of conduct disorder: A rationale and a review.

Journal of Clinical and Child Psychology, 22, 141–153.

Lahey, B. B., Loeber, R., Burke, J., Rathouz, P. J., & McBurnett, K. (2002). Waxing and waning in concert: Dynamic comorbidity of conduct disorder with other disruptive and emotional problems over 7 years among clinic-referred boys. *Journal of Abnormal Psychology, 111,* 556–567.

Larson, J. (1998). Managing student aggression in high schools: Implications for practice. *Psychology in the Schools, 35,* 283–295.

Laub, J. H., & Vaillant, G. E. (2000). Delinquency and mortality: A 50 year follow up study of 1,000 delinquent and non-delinquent boys. *American Journal of Psychiatry, 157,* 96–102.

Loeber, R., Green, S. M., Lahey, B. B., Frick, P. J., & McBurnett, K. (2000). Findings on disruptive behavior disorders from the first decade of the Developmental Trends Study. *Clinical Child and Family Psychology Review, 3,* 37–60.

Loeber, R., & Hay, D. (1997). Key issues in the development of aggression and violence from childhood to early adulthood. *Annual Review of Psychology, 48,* 371–410.

Loeber, R., Keenan, K., & Quanwu, Z. (1997). Boy's experimentation and persistence in developmental pathways toward serious delinquency. *Journal of Child and Family Studies, 6,* 321–357.

Lykken, D. T. (1995). *The antisocial personalities.* Hillsdale, NJ: Erlbaum.

Mabe, P. A., Turner, M. K., & Josephson, A. M. (2001). Parent management training. *Child and Adolescent Psychiatric Clinics of North America, 10,* 451–464.

Maughan, B., Rowe, R., Messer, J., Goodman, R., & Meltzer, H. (2004). Conduct disorder and oppositional defiant disorder in a national sample: Developmental epidemiology. *Journal of Child Psychology and Psychiatry, 45,* 609–621.

McArdle, P., O'Brien, G., & Kolvin, I. (1995). Hyperactivity: Prevalence and relationship with conduct disorder. *Journal of Child Psychology and Psychiatry, 36,* 279–303.

Moffitt, T. E., Caspi, A., Dickson, N., Silva, P., & Stanton, W. (1996). Childhood-onset versus adolescent-onset antisocial conduct problems in males: Natural history from ages 3–18 years. *Development and Psychopathology, 8,* 399–424.

Moffitt, T. E., & Lynam, D. R. (1994). The neuropsychology of conduct disorder and delinquency: Implications for understanding antisocial behavior. In D. Fowles, P. Sutker, & S. Goodman (Eds.), *Psychopathy and antisocial personality: A developmental perspective* (Vol. 18, pp. 233–262). New York: Springer.

Morrow, K. V., & Styles, M. B. (1995). *Building relationships with youth in program settings: A study of Big Brothers/Big Sisters.* Philadelphia: Public/Private Ventures.

Nash, J. K., Fraser, M. W., Galinsky, M. J., & Kupper, L. L. (2003). Early development and pilot testing of a problem-solving skills-training program for children. *Research on Social Work Practice, 13,* 432–451.

Nation, M., Crusto, C., Wandersman, A., Kumpfer, K. L., Seybolt, D., Morrissey-Kane, E., et al. (2003). What works in prevention: Principles of effective prevention programs. *American Psychology, 58,* 449–456.

Neeleman, J., Wessely, S., & Wadsworth, M. (1998). Predictors of suicide, accidental death, and premature natural death in a general-population birth cohort. *Lancet, 351*(9096), 93–97.

Nixon, R. D., Sweeney, L., Erickson, D. B., & Touyz, S. W. (2004). Parent-child interaction therapy: One- and two-year follow-up of standard and abbreviated treatments for oppositional preschoolers. *Journal of Abnormal Child Psychology, 32,* 263–271.

Olweus, D. (1991). Bully/victim problems among school children: Basic facts and effects of a school-based intervention program. In D. J. Pepler & K. H. Rubin (Eds.), *The development and treatment of childhood aggression* (pp. 411–448). Hillsdale, NJ: Erlbaum.

Patterson, G. R., Forgatch, M. S., Yoerger, K. L., & Stoolmiller, M. (1998). Variables that initiate and maintain an early-onset trajectory for juvenile offending. *Development and Psychopathology, 10,* 531–547.

Reid, J. B., Eddy, J. M., Fetrow, R. A., & Stoolmiller, M. (1999). Description and immediate impacts of a preventive intervention for conduct problems. *American Journal of Community Psychology, 27,* 483–517.

Rhodes, J. E., Grossman, J. B., & Resch, N. L. (2000). Agents of change: Pathways through which mentoring relationships influence adolescents' academic adjustment. *Child Development, 71,* 1662–1671.

Rhodes, J. E., Grossman, J. B., & Roffman, J. (2002). The rhetoric and reality of youth mentoring. *New Directions for Youth Development, 93,* 9–20.

Roberts, H., Liabo, K., Lucas, P., DuBois, D., & Sheldon, T. A. (2004). Mentoring to reduce antisocial behavior in childhood. *British Medical Journal, 328*(7438), 512–515.

Salekin, R. T., Leistico, A. M., Neumann, C. S., DiCicco, T. M., & Duros, R. L. (2004). Psychopathy and comorbidity in a young offender sample: Taking a closer look at psychopathy's potential importance over disruptive behavior disorders. *Journal of Abnormal Psychology, 113,* 416–427.

Schinke, S. P., Orlandi, M. A., & Cole, K. C. (1992). Boys and Girls Clubs in public housing developments: Prevention services for youth at risk [Special issue]. *Journal of Community Psychology,* 118–128.

Scott-Little, C., Hamann, M. S., & Jurs, S. G. (2002). Evaluations of after school programs: A meta evaluation of methodologies and narrative synthesis of findings. *American Journal of Evaluation, 23,* 387–420.

Searight, H. R., Rottnek, F., & Abby, S. L. (2001). Conduct disorder: Diagnosis and treatment in primary care. *American Family Physician, 63,* 1579–1588.

Shamsie, J., & Hluchy, C. (1991). Youth with conduct disorder: A challenge to be met. *Canadian Journal of Psychiatry, 36,* 405–414.

Sherman, L. W. (1998). American policing. In M. H. Tonry (Ed.), *Handbook of crime and punishment* (pp. 429–456). London: Oxford University Press.

Snyder, H. N. (2001). Epidemiology of official offending. In R. Loeber & D. P. Farrington (Eds.), *Child delinquents: Development, intervention, and service needs* (pp. 25–46). Thousand Oaks, CA: Sage.

Spivack, G., Platt, J., & Shure, M. B. (1976). *The problem-solving approach to adjustment.* San Francisco: Jossey-Bass.

St. Pierre, T. L., Mark, M. M., & Kaltreider, D. L. (1997). Involving parents of high-risk youth in drug prevention: A 3-year longitudinal study in Boys and Girls Clubs. *Journal of Early Adolescence, 17,* 21–50.

Steiner, H., Petersen, M. L., Saxena, K., Ford, S., & Matthews, Z. (2003). Divalproex sodium for the treatment of conduct disorder: A randomized controlled clinical trial. *Journal of Clinical Psychiatry, 64,* 1183–1191.

Stephens, R. O., Pitt, P., & Patrick, J. (1997). Curing and killing [Letter]. *Canadian Medical Association Journal, 156,* 166–167.

Sutphen, R. D., Thyer, B. A., & Kurtz, P. D. (1995). Multisystemic treatment of high risk juvenile offenders. *International Journal of Offender Therapy and Comparative Criminology, 39,* 327–334.

Taylor, J., & Carey, G. (1998). Antisocial behavior, substance use, and somatization in families of adolescent drug abusers and adolescent controls. *American Journal of Drug and Alcohol Abuse, 24,* 635–646.

Tierney, J. P., Grossman, J. B., & Resch, N. I. (2000). *Making a difference: An impact study of Big Brothers Big Sisters.* Philadelphia: Public/Private Ventures.

Wakefield, J. C., Pottick, K. J., & Stuart, S. A. (2002). Should the DSM-IV diagnostic criteria for conduct disorder consider social context? *American Journal of Psychiatry, 159,* 380–386.

Webster-Stratton, C., & Hammond, M. (1997). Treating children with early-onset conduct problems: A comparison of child and parent training interventions. *Journal of Consulting and Clinical Psychology, 65,* 93–109.

Webster-Stratton, C., & Herbert, M. (1993). What really happens in parent training? *Behavior Modification, 17,* 407–456.

Webster-Stratton, C., & Herbert, M. (1994). Strategies for helping parents of children with conduct disorders. *Progress in Behavior Modification, 29,* 121–142.

Webster-Stratton, C., & Lindsay, D. W. (1999). Social competence and conduct problems in young children: Issues in assessment. *Journal of Clinical Child Psychology, 28,* 25–43.

Webster-Stratton, C., & Taylor, T. (2001). Nipping early risk factors in the bud: Preventing substance abuse, delinquency, and violence in adolescence through interventions targeted at young children (0 to 8 years). *Prevention Science, 2,* 165–192.

Weinberger, D. A. (1997). Distress and self-restraint as measures of adjustment across the life span: Confirmatory factor analyses in clinical and nonclinical samples. *Psychological Assessment, 9,* 132–135.

Whitmore, E. A., Mikulich, S. K., Thompson, L. L., Riggs, P. D., Aarons, G. A., & Crowley, T. J. (1997). Influences on adolescent substance dependence: Conduct disorder, depression, attention deficit hyperactivity disorder, and gender. *Drug and Alcohol Dependence, 47,* 87–97.

Wodarski, J. S., & Wodarski, L. A. (1998). *Preventing teenage violence.* New York: Springer.

Oppositional Defiant Disorder

Lisa A. Rapp-Paglicci

6

Chapter

Learning Objectives

After reading this chapter, the reader will be able to:

- Discuss empirical findings regarding the incidence and prevalence of Oppositional Defiant Disorder.
- Discuss empirical findings regarding comorbidity with Oppositional Defiant Disorder.
- Discuss empirical findings regarding assessment of Oppositional Defiant Disorder.
- Discuss empirical findings regarding intervention for Oppositional Defiant Disorder.

Overview of the Problem

Oppositional Defiant Disorder (ODD) is a relatively common diagnosis in young children, with studies indicating prevalence between 8% and 20% (Gadow, Sprafkin, & Nolan, 2001; Keenan, Shaw, Walsh, Delliquadri, & Giovannelli, 1997; Keenan & Wakschlag, 2004; Lavigne et al., 1996). Almost 90% of children with ODD are considered severely emotionally disturbed in multiple areas of living, including family relationships, peer relationships, and school performance, which is a rate higher than for other childhood disorders (Ford et al., 2000). Greene et al. (2002) found that the diagnosis of ODD was associated with

117

significantly higher rates of comorbid disorders, greater social impairment, and greater family dysfunction when compared with a group of clinically referred youth without ODD or Conduct Disorder (CD). The ODD youth had significantly higher family conflict and impaired social interactions. Males are diagnosed with this disorder three times more frequently than females (Markward & Bride, 2001; Maughan, Rowe, Messer, Goodman, & Meltzer, 2004). In addition, Ford et al. (1999) found children with ODD to be at a higher risk for traumatic victimization at some point in their lives.

The course and possible progression of ODD has been of significant concern and study. Recent studies have suggested that ODD is often a precursor to CD, but not all children with ODD continue to progress down this path; some outgrow their ODD behaviors and either develop other disorders or discontinue all symptoms of mental illness (August, Realmuto, Joyce, & Hektner, 1999; Lahey et al., 1994; Lavigne et al., 2001; Rowe, Maughan, Pickles, Costello, & Angold, 2002). Lavigne et al. found that 6- to 11-year-old children with ODD had an onset of the disorder during their preschool years. The relative risk of continued ODD is much higher if ODD is present in the preschool years.

Studies have also indicated a robust relationship between externalizing disorders, in that ODD, CD, and Attention-Deficit /Hyperactivity Disorder (ADHD) co-occur at levels greater than chance (Burt, Krueger, McGue, & Iacono, 2001). Youth with one of these diagnoses had at least one other diagnosis 29% to 71% of the time (Simonoff et al., 1997). However, evidence strongly suggests that those youth who have both ODD and ADHD have a significantly poorer prognosis, as evidenced by more serious clinical courses, poorer response to treatment, and poorer outcomes. Oppositional Defiant Disorder in addition to ADHD commonly progresses to CD (August et al., 1999; Burt et al., 2001; Clark, Prior, & Kinsella, 2000; Gadow & Nolan, 2002; Speltz, McClellan, DeKlyen, & Jones, 1999). Gadow and Nolan also found that children with ODD alone had more individual and family impairment than those with ADHD alone, further reinforcing the notion that ODD can no longer be considered a mild or placid diagnosis.

According to Reid, Webster-Stratton, and Hammond (2003), early-onset behavioral problems such as ODD are among the most costly mental disorders because such a large number of youth with ODD continue to be involved with mental health, social services, and criminal justice systems throughout their lives. For instance, early-onset ODD has been found to be a strong predictor of adolescent delinquency, violence, drug abuse, and school dropout (Snyder, 2001) and in some cases adult criminal behavior. Moreover, ODD has been identified as a highly heterogeneous disorder with varied presentations, emanating from disparate pathways, and developing into diverse disorders (Greene et al., 2002). In fact, ODD has been termed a "gateway disorder" because it often progresses into a wide variety of disorders, including CD, Antisocial Personality Disorder, Mood disorders, and Anxiety disorders (Lavigne et al., 2001; Maughan et al., 2004; Speltz et al., 1999).

Operational Definitions of the Problem

The *Diagnostic and Statistical Manual of Mental Disorders* (*DSM;* American Psychiatric Association, 2000, p. 119) describes Oppositional Defiant Disorder as:

> *a pattern of negativistic, hostile, and defiant behavior lasting at least 6 months during which four or more of the following are present:*
>
> *(1) often loses temper*
>
> *(2) often argues with adults*
>
> *(3) often actively defies or refuses to comply with adults' requests or rules*
>
> *(4) often deliberately annoys people*
>
> *(5) often blames others for his or her mistakes or misbehavior*
>
> *(6) is often touchy or easily annoyed by others*
>
> *(7) is often angry or resentful*
>
> *(8) is often spiteful or vindictive*

The recurrent pattern of defiant behavior must cause significant impairment in social, academic, or occupational functioning in the youth and is clearly distinguished from CD and ADHD (Angold & Costello, 1996; Loeber, Burke, Lahey, Winters, & Zera, 2000).

Evidence-Based Approaches to Assessment

Early disruptive behavior disorders can be difficult to differentiate due to symptom overlap, developmental changes as children mature, and the frequent comorbidity of these early disorders. These complex issues demand that evidence-based approaches to assessment be utilized. Because ODD consists of oppositional emotions and behaviors, and these exist on a continuum, it is imperative that multiple instruments be utilized for a comprehensive assessment.

The Eyberg Child Behavior Inventory (ECBI) and the Sutter-Eyberg Student Behavior Inventory-Revised (SESBI-R) are adult-report scales for assessing disruptive behaviors in children and younger adolescents. The ECBI is used for parent report and the SESBI-R is used for teacher report (Eyberg & Pincus, 1999). The ECBI contains 36 items closely related to *DSM* criteria, and the SESBI-R contains 38 items tailored to the classroom setting. Many studies have demonstrated strong psychometric properties for both scales (Eisenstadt, McElreath, Eyberg, & McNeil, 1994; Eyberg & Robinson, 1983; Webster-Stratton, 1988; Webster-Stratton & Eyberg, 1982). Both internal consistency and test-retest reliability are very good, as is validity. The two measures are well supported, and ECBI in particular demonstrates utility in varied settings (Collett, Ohan, & Myers, 2003). The only known disadvantages are that the normative data are specific to certain regions of the country and are not ethnically heterogeneous (Collett et al., 2003).

The Child Behavior Checklist (CBCL) is designed for use with children ages 2 to 18 (Achenbach & Edelbrock, 1983). The measure is a comprehensive inventory of behavior problems; other forms have been developed for parents, teachers, and youth. The checklist takes approximately 20 minutes to complete and contains questions regarding specific emotional and behavioral problems as well as competence items covering the child's activities, social relations, and school performance (Abolt & Thyer, 2002). Extensive studies have supported the CBCL as a reliable and valid checklist, but it should be stressed that it is not a direct measure of ODD, but simply a primary assessment tool for youth. However, it is easy and time- and cost-effective.

The New York Teacher Rating Scale for Disruptive and Antisocial Behavior (NYTRS) is a teacher report related to symptoms of ODD and CD (Miller, Klein, & Piacentini, 1995). The scale provides a thorough evaluation of ODD and CD symptoms as well as factors important to the development and maintenance of deviant behaviors. It is most useful for estimating the severity of behavioral problems in the school setting and tracking those behaviors over time or in response to treatment (Collett et al., 2003). Although it has had limited use as an outcome measure, it has been shown to be sensitive and able to detect mild to moderate treatment effects (R. Klein et al., 1997). The NYTRS demonstrates strong psychometric properties and is correlated with other, similar scales such as the Revised Behavior Problem Checklist and the Conners Teacher Rating Scale (Loney & Milich, 1982). It appears to be a useful and effective scale. Perhaps its only weakness is in relation to the minimal normative data collected thus far.

Home and School Situations Questionnaires (HSQ and SSQ) are unique adult-report scales that focus on the environmental context in which a youth's deviant behaviors occur rather than on the frequency of specific behaviors (Barkley, 1997). The scales can be used for 4- to 11-year-old youth, and modified versions have now been developed for adolescents. The HSQ contains 16 items and the SSQ includes 12 items; each takes only a few minutes to complete, making them useful as outcome measures. The psychometric properties of both scales are strong, and they have shown promise in understanding disruptive behaviors in the context of larger systems. These scales demonstrate how disruptive behaviors affect daily living in various settings and should be used in addition to other diagnosis-driven scales. Normative data are also limited with these two scales, warranting caution by the practitioner and researcher.

The Early Childhood Inventory 4 (ECI-4) includes parent and teacher rating scales developed to screen preschool children for emotional and behavioral disorders (Gadow & Sprafkin, 2000). There is a one-to-one correspondence between ECI-4 and *DSM* symptoms, with the parent version containing 108 items and the teacher version containing 77. The scales require only 15 minutes to complete and are most useful as a preinterview screen (Sprafkin, Volpe, Gadow, Nolan, & Kelly, 2002). The scales measure symptom count (categorical) and symptom severity (dimensional) for a wide range of emotional and behavioral disorders. The ECI-4 has strong reliability and validity and shows high correlations to other standardized scales. These scales may not be appropriate for use as outcome measures because they were developed as screening checklists and will produce some false positives. They should be used in conjunction with other measures.

The Diagnostic Interview Schedule for Children (DISC) is one of the most widely used structured interviews for youth. Developed by the National Institute of Mental Health, DISC questions focus on symptomatic and contextual variables derived from the *DSM* criteria (Friman et al., 2000). Trained interviewers administer the instrument. There are several versions for youth and parents, and the instrument has been revised several times based on large field trials and *DSM* criteria changes. It is a diagnostic instrument and thus covers more than 30 child and adolescent mental disorders. The instrument has shown good reliability and validity, and although it was designed to evaluate large community samples, new research has indicated that it also may have utility for the study of clinical populations (Friman et al., 2000).

The Amsterdam Scale of Oppositionality (ASO) is a new self-report instrument that measures the full range of oppositionality in early adolescents. The scale contains 30 items assessing oppositional emotions, oppositional behaviors, and oppositionality in varying contexts and situations. Scores can be obtained on all of those factors. The ASO has shown good internal reliability and good validity (Hoffenaar & Hoeksma, 2002) and has potential with further supporting research to be a helpful instrument in assessing ODD.

The Conners Rating Scale is useful for children ages 3 to 17 in identifying behavioral problems of impulsivity, oppositional behaviors, and inability to focus attention (Ronen, 2005). There are short and long forms as well as forms for children, parents, and teachers. The Conners scales have been found to be reliable and valid and to be a fairly quick and useful method for assessing ODD as well as other behavior problems (Lehmann & Dangel, 1998).

Evidence-Based Approaches to Intervention

Youth with ODD often have deficits in social skills, problem solving, anger control, and emotional regulation. Interventions that focus on these issues have shown promise with elementary and middle school ODD children. Typically, they involve teaching interpersonal problem-solving skills, training to modify unhealthy cognitions, practice in developing emotional regulation skills, and role-plays to apply these skills to real-life scenarios (Fraser & Williams, 2004). But like any successful intervention, the most efficacious approach to intervening with ODD children is a comprehensive or multifaceted intervention that addresses multiple systems, such as child, parents and family, school, and community. The most effective interventions are discussed in the following section.

Individual Interventions

Most interventions for youth with ODD are considered child training, that is, skill-based training as opposed to therapy. Many have been found to be effective with this population, several of which are highlighted here. It should be noted that pharmacological treatment of pure ODD is not usually considered except in cases where aggression is a significant and persistent problem (Aman & Brooks, 2004). Thus pharmacological treatment is not discussed here.

Feindler (1987) developed an anger control program for oppositional adolescents. The model teaches arousal management techniques and cognitive strategies to promote self-control (Lehmann & Dangel, 1998). The intervention was delivered in a group format in 10 sessions and included self-monitoring of anger provocations, relaxation training, coping self statements, self-reinforcement strategies, self-control contingencies, assertiveness, and problem-solving skills training (Feindler, 1987). The youth were taught common self-control strategies in addition to specific strategies for anger-promoting incidents. Evaluation indicated that the experimental group displayed fewer school suspensions and in-class fines in addition to better problem-solving skills and self-control than did the control group (Feindler, 1987).

Stress inoculation training (SIT), developed by Schlicter and Horan (1981), is another skills-based program geared to address anger control. Youth are educated about causes and consequences of anger and aggression as well as alternative control choices (Sprague & Thyer, 2002). The youth are also taught how to construct a 6-item anger hierarchy, specific coping skills, relaxation training, pleasant imagery, assertiveness skills, and self-reinforcement. Finally, they use modeling, practice, and feedback to master the anger control skills. Findings suggest that SIT reduced anger and verbal and physical aggression (Schlicter & Horan, 1981).

The I Can Problem-Solve program was designed for young children evincing disruptive behaviors. Teachers work with small groups of kindergarten children for about 20 minutes per day to teach problem-solving techniques. The children learn to think through problems, identify solutions, and learn about their own and other people's feelings (Shure, 1992). After 4 months of daily sessions, the experimental group reported significant increases in problem-solving techniques (Shure, 1993).

Group Interventions

Group therapy with children and youth with behavioral problems has been considered by practitioners as contraindicated due to concerns with increases in disruptive behaviors and the escalation of aggression when groups of oppositional children converge. However, many of the most effective interventions for ODD are delivered to children and youth in group settings. It is important to note that these interventions are not considered therapy and do not usually contain modules for processing or feeling expression; rather, they tend to be psychoeducational and skill based. Youth are often taught skills and then asked to practice these skills via role-plays and exercises. Consequently, there are no group therapy modalities found in the research literature for ODD children, but many of the individual-level interventions can be delivered to a small group of youths.

Family Interventions

Oppositional Defiant Disorder, like any other childhood disorder, must be addressed at the family level. Many parents feel that the child should be the sole focus of intervention; however, clinical wisdom as well as empirical evidence suggest otherwise. When parents are able to see that a change in their approach, interactions, and communications produces positive behavioral changes, most become willing participants of family intervention.

One of the most effective and well-researched interventions with families is parent training (PT). Parent training has been compared and shown to be superior to control groups, placebo groups, and family treatment and is considered by most experts to be the treatment of choice for ODD (Northey, Wells, Silverman, & Bailey, 2003). Since the 1970s researchers have found strong evidence for utilizing parenting skills training with parents of young children evincing oppositional behaviors (Eyberg & Boggs, 1998; Patterson, Chamberlain, & Reid, 1982; Peed, Roberts, & Forehand, 1977). There are numerous forms of PT, but the most effective ones address problematic family interaction patterns that contribute to and ultimately increase ODD behaviors. Parents are taught about child development and behavioral techniques. With this foundation they are then taught how to look for positive behavior and reinforce it. In addition, they are taught how to use techniques to handle noncompliance and disruptive behaviors. Parents also learn how to deliver clear directives to children and how to stay unemotional during conflict. After parents have learned these techniques and skills, there is a heavy emphasis on in vivo role-playing and practice sessions. Homework between sessions to practice skills with their own children and in real-life instances is utilized. These are a must for a full understanding and learning of skills.

Variations of the original conception of PT have emerged. All continue to focus on the skills just discussed; however, some programs have added components, such as coping skills and stress management for parents (Webster-Stratton, 1994), marital communication, and parent social isolation (Griest et al., 1982). These adjuncts have increased the efficacy and outcome for PT interventions (Northey et al., 2003). The empirical evidence for PT is clearly established, and there is currently an abundance of manualized PT programs available. Further research on PT should evaluate the long-term outcomes and perhaps the development of booster sessions for parents as children progress into older developmental ages.

Multisystemic therapy (MST), developed in the late 1980s, is a unique, interactional approach to problematic behavior by youth. It intervenes with multiple systems, such as the youth, family, peers, and school, and employs a comprehensive approach and team of experts (Henggeler et al, 1986). This team works with the youth and all of his or her systems by providing individual and family therapy, parenting skills training, case management for concrete resources, crisis intervention, school management plans and consultation, peer intervention, and marital therapy.

Multiple studies have shown appreciably positive results from the approach, especially for youth with disruptive behavior disorders, including ODD, CD, and serious offending behaviors. Specifically, MST has been found to reduce delinquent and offending behaviors, reduce affiliation with delinquent peers, improve school attendance and grades, and improve family relations (Borduin et al., 1995; Henggeler et al., 1986; Sutphen, Thyer, &

Kurtz, 1995). However, it must be noted that a recent systematic review of the effects of MST by Littell (2005) has produced a less favorable appraisal of its efficacy.

Functional family therapy (FFT) has also shown positive results for intervening with at-risk, ODD, and CD youth. Functional family therapy focuses on changing interactions, communication, and problem solving among family members. Initially, therapists work with the family to engage and motivate them to change their perceptions, beliefs, and interactions. Therapists help encourage hope, reduce negativism, and improve respect and alliances. Next, clinicians help develop and implement short- and long-term behavior change plans for all members of the family. Specific behaviors are modeled, and family members are assisted in achieving positive behavioral changes. Finally, family members are assisted in changing other problem areas and changes are maintained and supported. If necessary, FFT therapists intervene directly with larger systems (community, school, etc.); however, most of the time, family members are now capable of doing this on their own.

Functional family therapy has been shown to be highly successful with families with ODD and CD children (Sexton & Alexander, 2000). It was found to significantly reduce repeated behavioral problems in randomized and nonrandomized comparison group studies (Alexander, Pugh, Parsons, & Sexton, 2000). N. Klein, Alexander, and Parsons (1977) found that FFT also reduced behavioral problems in the siblings of youth with disruptive behavioral problems. Other studies have shown that when compared with no treatment, other family therapy, and traditional juvenile justice interventions, FFT was found to be the most efficacious by reducing rearrests by 20% to 60% (Barton, Alexander, Waldron, Turner, & Warburton, 1985; Gordon, Arbuthnot, Gustafson, & McGreen, 1988; Mendel, 2000).

Tuesday's Child is a comprehensive family program developed for children between 1 and 6 years of age. The program features a parent-training program which is delivered by previous parent graduates and supervised by professionals. Parents learn positive techniques to handle children as opposed to spanking and yelling and so on. In addition, children are all individually evaluated to identify any problems beyond ODD such as developmental or speech and language delays. Intervention is individualized to address each family's strengths and issues, and parents also attend a family support group (Markward & Bride, 2001).

Lavigne (1996) found considerable behavioral changes occurred for both children and parents in the Tuesday's Child program. Mothers who had been in the intervention group selectively attended to their children's positive behavior more often than those mothers who had not received the intervention. Consequently, their children showed improved compliance and cooperation at home and in school (Lavigne, 1996). This systems-focused program requires more study, but presently shows promise for families with ODD children.

Community and Multifaceted Programs

Most evidence-based interventions have now evolved to become what social workers have been doing for years: intervening with multiple systems. The field of social work has known that comprehensive interventions that address multiple client systems are the most thorough, most effective, and ultimately the most efficient, and now empirically based multifaceted programs are available. This section describes some highly effective programs that address multiple systemic levels, including the community level. The review of the literature indicates that there are no known empirically based, community-only interventions for children with ODD.

The Incredible Years intervention is targeted for children between 4 and 8 who are diagnosed with ODD and CD and for those who are beginning to evince some symptoms of ODD and CD. The program targets the children, their teachers, and parents (Webster-Stratton & Hammond, 1997) and is delivered in a group setting. Academic needs and social skills are the focus for the children, and parents are taught parenting skills and coping skills and are encouraged to collaborate with and become involved with the school. Teachers are trained to use behavioral management techniques and are also encouraged to develop home-school collaborations.

Studies indicate that parents receiving the intervention used consistent discipline and limit setting and fewer physical discipline techniques (Reid et al., 2003). In addition, they were significantly more involved with the school. Intervention children showed significant decreases in deviant and noncompliant behavior and increases in social competence, and teachers showed an increase in the use of positive behavioral management (Fraser & Williams, 2004). The Incredible Years program is a standardized and packaged program that has been shown to be effective and can be used as both an intervention and a prevention program.

Fast Track is another multicomponent program for young children who show some or all of the symptoms required for a diagnosis of ODD or CD. The program targets children, parents, and classrooms beginning in first grade and continuing through sixth grade (Conduct Problems Prevention Research Group [CPPRG], 1999). The goals of the child intervention include improving emotional regulation, academic achievement, and cognitive-behavioral skills. The family component focuses on behavioral parenting skills and parental involvement in school, and the classroom component delivers a curriculum to the children regarding understanding and communicating emotions and self-control (Fraser & Williams, 2004).

Empirical evaluations found significant differences between the experimental and control groups, with the experimental children exhibiting fewer disruptive behavior problems and fewer placements in special education programs. In addition, parents in the experimental groups used significantly more behavioral parenting techniques as compared to the control group (CPPRG, 2002).

Barrera et al. (2002) developed an early elementary school intervention to reduce conduct problems. The program provided supplemental reading instruction, social skills training, parent training, and an individualized classroom behavior management program for kindergarten through third-grade children. At 1-year follow-up the experimental group showed less coercive behavior and aggression at home than did the control group (Fraser & Williams, 2004).

The Seattle Social Development Project (SSDP) is another multicomponent intervention that has shown some of the highest rates of success of all comprehensive programs evaluated. It was originally conceived as a prevention program; however, its high rate of success has suggested that it may be useful as an early intervention for ODD youth. The SSDP contains child, parent, and classroom components for children from first through sixth grades (Hawkins et al., 1992). The classroom intervention focused on positive behavioral management by teachers, and the child component addressed social problem-solving skills and drug refusal skills. The parental component taught family management skills and encouraged collaboration with the school (O'Donnell, Hawkins, Catalano, Abbott, & Day, 1995).

Longitudinal studies indicate a significant difference between experimental and control groups, with the full intervention group showing a higher commitment and attachment to school, higher grade achievement and completion, less misbehavior and drinking, and fewer sexual partners, pregnancies, and violent offenses (Hawkins et al., 1992). The results suggest a very positive intervention when implementation is standardized, long lasting, and comprehensive.

Summary

Oppositional Defiant Disorder is a serious, early disruptive behavior disorder that has been termed a "gateway disorder" for mental illness in children. Although some children outgrow their behavioral problems, most continue to evince other types of disorders or more severe behavior disorders. Fortunately, there is a substantial body of research on ODD that provides social workers with clear guidance on accurate diagnosis, assessment, and intervention with ODD youth and their families. As always, there is more evidence to be obtained. Future research should further refine interventions, increase the number and types of multicomponent interventions, address ODD with different client groups such as ethnically diverse groups and females, and advance prevention efforts. Ironically, as research evidence regarding interventions continues to build, our communities and juvenile justice system have reduced their patience and tolerance for disruptive behaviors. This negative perception toward ODD youth will most likely only grow worse in the near future as our country continues to focus on "get tough" policies and adult penalties. It is essential that social workers intervene quickly and effectively with these children and families while strongly advocating for treatment, empowerment, and patience from the macrosystems that intersect with them. At this moment, it couldn't be more critical for social workers to utilize evidence-based practice.

Study Questions

1. The author reports that children with comorbid ODD and ADHD have a poorer prognosis than children with either ODD or ADHD alone. Describe why you think that is the case.

2. Review the diagnostic criteria for ODD, CD, and ADHD. How can the three diagnoses be differentiated?

3. Assessment is difficult with any client. Identify and describe some specific difficulties in assessment of ODD children and families.

4. The author found evidence suggesting that ODD children often have a history of traumatization. Why do you think that is? Explain.

5. As a practitioner, you are working with an ODD child with a history of trauma. How might that change your assessment, diagnosis, and intervention? Explain.

6. As an elementary school social worker, you are asked to intervene with several children who have ODD. You do not have time to work with each child and/or family individually. Describe the evidence-based intervention you would choose, and support your decision to use it as compared to others.

7. You have a Latina client, age 6, who meets the diagnostic criteria for ODD. Her parents are willing to participate but

speak very little English. Choose an evidence-based intervention, describe it, and then explain how you would modify the intervention for this particular client and family.

8. Describe how social workers can intervene to advocate for and improve the macrosystems that affect ODD children (specifically school systems and the juvenile justice system).

References

Abolt, T., & Thyer, B. (2002). Social work assessment of children with oppositional defiant disorder. *Social Work in Mental Health, 1,* 73–84.

Achenbach, T., & Edelbrock, C. (1983). *Manual for the Child Behavior Checklist and Revised Child Behavior Profile.* Burlington: University of Vermont, Department of Psychiatry.

Alexander, J., Pugh, C., Parsons, B., & Sexton, T. (2000). Functional family therapy. In D. S. Elliott (Ed.), *Blueprints for violence prevention* (2nd ed., pp. 167–184). Boulder, CO: Center for the Study and Prevention of Violence, Institute of Behavioral Science.

Aman, K., & Brooks, S. (2004). International consensus statement on attention-deficit/hyperactivity disorder (ADHD) and disruptive behavior disorders (DBD): Clinical implications and treatment practice suggestions. *European Neuropsychopharmacology, 14,* 11–28.

American Psychiatric Association. (2000). *Diagnostic and statistical manual of mental disorders* (4th ed., text rev.). Washington, DC: Author.

Angold, A., & Costello, J. (1996). Toward establishing an empirical basis for the diagnosis of oppositional defiant disorder. *Journal of the American Academy of Child and Adolescent Psychiatry, 35,* 1205–1212.

August, G., Realmuto, G., Joyce, T., & Hektner, J. (1999). Persistence and desistance of oppositional defiant disorder in a community sample of children with ADHD. *Journal of the American Academy of Child and Adolescent Psychiatry, 38*(10), 1262–1270.

Barkley, R. (1997). *Defiant children: A clinician's manual for assessment and parent training* (2nd ed.). New York: Guilford Press.

Barrera, M., Biglan, A., Taylor, T., Gunn, B., Smolkowski, K., Black, C., et al. (2002). Early elementary school intervention to reduce conduct problems: A randomized trial with Hispanic and non-Hispanic children. *Prevention Science, 3*(2), 83–94.

Barton, C., Alexander, J., Waldron, H., Turner, C., & Warburton, J. (1985). Generalizing treatment effects of functional family therapy: Three replications. *American Journal of Family Therapy, 13,* 16–26.

Borduin, C., Mann, B., Cone, L., Henggeler, S., Fucci, B., Blaske, D., et al. (1995). Multisystemic treatment of serious juvenile offenders: Long-term prevention of criminality and violence. *Journal of Consulting and Clinical Psychology, 63,* 569–578.

Burt, S., Krueger, R., McGue, M., & Iacono, W. (2001). Sources of covariation among attention-deficit/hyperactivity disorder, oppositional defiant disorder, and conduct disorder: The importance of shared environment. *Journal of Abnormal Psychology, 110*(4), 516–525.

Clark, C., Prior, M., & Kinsella, G. (2000). Do executive function deficits differentiate between adolescents with ADHD and oppositional defiant/conduct disorder? A neurological study using the Six Elements Test and Hayling Sentence Completion Test. *Journal of Abnormal Child Psychology, 28*(5), 403–414.

Collett, B., Ohan, J., & Myers, K. (2003). Ten-year review of rating scales, V: Scales assessing attention-deficit/hyperactivity disorder. *Journal of the American Academy of Child and Adolescent Psychiatry, 42,* 1015–1037.

Conduct Problems Prevention Research Group. (1999). Initial impact of the Fast Track prevention trial for conduct problems: I. The high-risk sample. *Journal of Consulting and Clinical Psychology, 67,* 631–647.

Conduct Problems Prevention Research Group. (2002). Evaluation of the first 3 years of the Fast Track prevention trial with children at high risk for adolescent conduct problems. *Journal of Abnormal Child Psychology, 30,* 19–35.

Eisenstadt, T., McElreath, L., Eyberg, S., & McNeil, C. (1994). Interparent agreement on the Eyberg Child Behavior Inventory. *Child and Family Behavioral Therapy, 16,* 21–27.

Eyberg, S., & Boggs, S. (1998). Parent-child interaction therapy: A psychosocial intervention for the treatment of young conduct-disordered children. In J. Briesmeister & C. Schaefer (Eds.), *Handbook of parent training: Parents as co-therapists for children's behavior problems* (2nd ed., pp. 61–97). New York: Wiley.

Eyberg, S., & Pincus, D. (1999). *Eyberg Child Behavior Inventory and Sutter-Eyberg Student Behavior Inventory-Revised, professional manual.* Odessa, FL: Psychological Assessment Resources.

Eyberg, S., & Robinson, E. (1983). Conduct problem behavior: Standardization of a behavior rating scale with adolescents. *Journal of Clinical Child Psychology, 12,* 347–354.

Feindler, E. (1987). Clinical issues and recommendations in adolescent anger control training. *Journal of Child and Adolescent Psychotherapy, 4,* 267–274.

Ford, J., Racusin, R., Daviss, W., Ellis, C., Thomas, J., Rogers, K., et al. (1999). Trauma exposure among children with oppositional defiant disorder (ODD) and attention deficit hyperactivity disorder (ADHD). *Journal of Consulting and Clinical Psychology, 67,* 786–789.

Ford, J., Racusin, R., Ellis, C., Daviss, W., Reiser, J., Fleischer, A., et al. (2000). Child maltreatment, other trauma exposure, and posttraumatic symptomatology among children with oppositional defiant and attention deficit hyperactivity disorders. *Child Maltreatment, 5*(3), 205–217.

Fraser, M., & Williams, M. (2004). Aggressive behavior. In L. Rapp-Paglicci, C. Dulmus,

& J. Wodarski (Eds.), *Handbook of preventive interventions for children and adolescents* (pp. 100–132). Hoboken, NJ: Wiley.

Friman, P., Handwerk, M., Smith, G., Larzelere, R., Lucas, C., & Shaffer, D. (2000). External validity of conduct and oppositional defiant disorders determined by the NIMH Diagnostic Interview Schedule for Children. *Journal of Abnormal Child Psychology, 28*(3), 277–286.

Gadow, K., & Nolan, E. (2002). Differences between preschool children with ODD, ADHD, and ODD+ADHD symptoms. *Journal of Child Psychology and Psychiatry, 43,* 191–201.

Gadow, K., & Sprafkin, J. (2000). *Early Childhood Inventory 4 screening manual.* Stony Brook, NY: Checkmate Plus.

Gadow, K., Sprafkin, J., & Nolan, E. (2001). *DSM-IV* symptoms in community and clinic preschool children. *Journal of the American Academy of Child and Adolescent Psychiatry, 40,* 1383–1392.

Gordon, D., Arbuthnot, J., Gustafson, K., & McGreen, P. (1988). Home-based behavioral-systems family therapy with disadvantaged juvenile delinquents. *American Journal of Family Therapy, 16,* 243–255.

Greene, R., Biederman, J., Zerwas, S., Monuteaux, M., Goring, J., & Faraone, S. (2002). Psychiatric comorbidity, family dysfunction, and social impairment in referred youth with oppositional defiant disorder. *American Journal of Psychiatry, 159,* 1214–1224.

Griest, D., Forehand, R., Rogers, T., Breiner, J., Furey, W., & Williams, C. (1982). Effects of parent enhancement therapy on the treatment outcome and generalization of a parent training program. *Behavior Research and Therapy, 20,* 429–436.

Hawkins, J., Catalano, R., Morrison, D., O'Donnell, J., Abbott, R., & Day, L. (1992). The Seattle Social Development Project: Effects of the first 4 years on protective factors and problem behaviors. In J. McCord & R. Tremblay (Eds.), *Preventing antisocial behavior in children: Intervention from birth through adolescence* (pp. 139–161). New York: Guilford Press.

Henggeler, S., Roddick, J., Borduin, C. Hanson, C., Watson, S., & Urey, J. (1986).

Multisystemic treatment of juvenile offenders: Effects on adolescent behavior and family interaction. *Developmental Psychology, 22,* 132–141.

Hoffenaar, P., & Hoeksma, J. (2002). The structure of oppositionality: Response dispositions and situational aspects. *Journal of Child Psychology and Psychiatry, 43,* 375–385.

Keenan, K., Shaw, D., Walsh, B., Delliquadri, E., & Giovannelli, J. (1997). *DSM-III-R* disorders in preschool children from low-income families. *Journal of the American Academy of Child and Adolescent Psychiatry, 36,* 620–627.

Keenan, K., & Wakschlag, L. (2004). Are oppositional defiant and conduct disorder symptoms normative behaviors in preschoolers? A comparison of referred and nonreferred children. *American Journal of Psychiatry, 161,* 356–358.

Klein, N., Alexander, J., & Parsons, B. (1977). Impact of family systems intervention on recidivism and sibling delinquency: A model of primary prevention and program evaluation. *Journal of Consulting and Clinical Psychology, 45,* 469–474.

Klein, R., Abikoff, H., Klass, E., Ganeles, D., Seese, L., & Pollack, S. (1997). Clinical efficacy of methylphenidate in conduct disorder with and without attention deficit hyperactivity disorder. *Archives of General Psychiatry, 54,* 1073–1080.

Lahey, B., Applegate, B., Barkley, R., Garfinkel, B., McBurnett, K., Kerdyk, L., et al. (1994). *DSM-IV* field trials for oppositional defiant disorder and conduct disorder in children and adolescents. *American Journal of Psychiatry, 151,* 1163–1171.

Lavigne, J. (1996). Tuesday's Child: An early intervention project to improve the parent-child relationship. In M. Roberts (Ed.), *Model programs in child and family mental health* (pp. 135–147). Mahwah, NJ: Erlbaum.

Lavigne, J., Cicchetti, C., Gibbons, R., Binns, H., Larsen, L., & DeVito, C. (2001). Oppositional defiant disorder with onset in preschool years: Longitudinal stability and pathways to other disorders. *Journal of the American Academy of Child and Adolescent Psychiatry, 40,* 1393–1400.

Lavigne, J., Gibbons, R., Christoffel, K., Arend, R., Rosenbaum, D., Binns, H., et al. (1996). Prevalence rates and correlates of psychiatric disorders among preschool children. *Journal of the American Academy of Child and Adolescent Psychiatry, 35,* 204–214.

Lehmann, P., & Dangel, R. (1998). Oppositional defiant disorder. In B. Thyer & J. Wodarski (Eds.), *Handbook of empirical social work practice* (Vol. 1, pp. 91–116). New York: Wiley.

Littell, J. (2005). Lessons from a systematic review of effects of multisystemic therapy. *Children and Youth Services Review, 27*(4), 445–463.

Loeber, R., Burke, J., Lahey, B., Winters, A., & Zera, M. (2000). Oppositional defiant and conduct disorder: Pt. I. A review of the past 10 years. *Journal of the American Academy of Child and Adolescent Psychiatry, 39*(12), 1468–1484.

Loney, J., & Milich, R. (1982). Hyperactivity, inattention, and aggression in clinical practice. In M. Wolraich & D. Routh (Eds.), *Advances in behavioral pediatrics* (pp. 72–97). New York: Plenum Press.

Markward, M., & Bride, B. (2001). Oppositional defiant disorder and the need for family-centered practice in schools. *Children and Schools, 23,* 73–84.

Maughan, B., Rowe, R., Messer, J., Goodman, R., & Meltzer, H. (2004). Conduct disorder and oppositional defiant disorder in a national sample: Developmental epidemiology. *Journal of Child Psychology and Psychiatry, 45,* 609–621.

Mendel, R. (2000). *Less hype, more help: Reducing juvenile crime, what works and what doesn't.* Washington, DC: American Youth Policy Forum.

Miller, L., Klein, R. G., & Piacentini, J. (1995). New York Teacher Rating Scale for disruptive and antisocial behavior. *Journal of the American Academy of Child and Adolescent Psychiatry, 41,* 114–122.

Northey, W., Wells, K., Silverman, W., & Bailey, C. (2003). Childhood behavioral and emotional disorders. *Journal of Marital and Family Therapy, 29,* 523–545.

O'Donnell, J., Hawkins, J., Catalano, R., Abbott, R., & Day, L. (1995). Preventing school failure, drug use, and delinquency among low-income children: Long-term intervention in elementary schools. *American Journal of Orthopsychiatry, 65,* 87–100.

Patterson, G., Chamberlain, P., & Reid, J. (1982). A comparative evaluation of a parent-training program. *Behavior Therapy, 13,* 638–650.

Peed, S., Roberts, M., & Forehand, R. (1977). Evaluation of the effectiveness of a standardized parent training program in altering the interaction of mothers and their noncompliant children. *Behavior Modification, 1,* 323–350.

Reid, M., Webster-Stratton, C., & Hammond, M. (2003). Follow-up on children who received the Incredible Years intervention for oppositional-defiant disorder: Maintenance and prediction of 2-year outcome. *Behavior Therapy, 34,* 471–491.

Ronen, T. (2005). Students' evidence-based practice intervention for children with oppositional defiant disorder. *Research on Social Work Practice, 15*(3), 165–179.

Rowe, R., Maughan, B., Pickles, A., Costello, E., & Angold, A. (2002). The relationship between *DSM-IV* oppositional defiant disorder and conduct disorder: Findings from the Great Smoky Mountains Study. *Journal of Child Psychology and Psychiatry, 43*(3), 365–373.

Schlicter, J., & Horan, J. (1981). Effects of stress inoculation on the anger and aggression management skills of institutionalized juvenile delinquents. *Cognitive Therapy and Research, 5,* 359–365.

Sexton, T., & Alexander, J. (2000). Functional family therapy. *OJJDP Juvenile Justice Bulletin.* Washington, DC: U.S. Department of Justice.

Shure, M. (1992). *I Can Problem Solve: An interpersonal cognitive problem-solving approach for kindergarten and primary grades.* Champaign, IL: Research Press.

Shure, M. (1993). I Can Problem Solve: Interpersonal problem solving for young children. *Early Child Development and Care, 96,* 49–64.

Simonoff, E., Pickles, A., Meyer, J., Silberg, J., Maes, H., Loeber, R., et al. (1997). The Virginia twin study of adolescent behavioral development. *Archives of General Psychiatry, 54,* 800–808.

Snyder, H. (2001). Epidemiology of official offending. In R. Loeber & D. Farrington (Eds.), *Child delinquents: Development, intervention, and service needs* (pp. 25–46). Thousand Oaks, CA: Sage.

Speltz, M., McClellan, J., DeKlyen, M., & Jones, K. (1999). Preschool boys with oppositional defiant disorder: Clinical presentation and diagnostic change. *Journal of the American Academy of Child and Adolescent Psychiatry, 38,* 838–845.

Sprafkin, J., Volpe, R., Gadow, K., Nolan, E., & Kelly, K. (2002). A *DSM-IV* referenced screening instrument for preschool children: The Early Childhood Inventory 4. *Journal of the American Academy of Child and Adolescent Psychiatry, 41*(5), 604–612.

Sprague, A., & Thyer, B. (2002). Psychosocial treatment of oppositional defiant disorder. *Social Work in Mental Health, 1,* 63–72.

Sutphen, R., Thyer, B., & Kurtz, P. D. (1995). Multisystemic treatment of high-risk juvenile offenders. *International Journal of Offender Therapy and Comparative Criminology, 39,* 327–334.

Webster-Stratton, C. (1988). Mothers' and fathers' perceptions of child deviance: Roles of parent and child behaviors and parent adjustment. *Journal of Consulting and Clinical Psychology, 56,* 909–915.

Webster-Stratton, C. (1994). Advancing videotape parent training: A comparison study. *Journal of Consulting and Clinical Psychology, 62,* 583–593.

Webster-Stratton, C., & Eyberg, S. (1982). Child temperament: Relationship with child behavior problems and parent-child interactions. *Journal of Clinical Child Psychology, 11,* 123–129.

Webster-Stratton, C., & Hammond, M. (1997). Treating children with early onset conduct problems: A comparison of child and parent training interventions. *Journal of Consulting and Clinical Psychology, 65,* 93–109.

Pica

Irma A. Molina, Matthew T. Theriot,
and Catherine N. Dulmus

7

Chapter

Learning Objectives

After reading this chapter, the reader will be able to:

- Demonstrate knowledge of diagnostic criteria for pica.
- Identify risk factors for pica.
- Identify evidence-based intervention approaches for pica.
- Identify and discuss research gaps related to assessment and treatment of pica.

Operational Definitions of the Problem

The *Diagnostic and Statistical Manual of Mental Disorders* (*DSM-IV*; American Psychiatric Association, 2000, p. 103) defines pica as the persistent eating of one or more nonnutritive substances for at least 1 month. To qualify as an eating disorder, this behavior must also meet other *DSM-IV* criteria, such as being developmentally inappropriate, not part of a culturally sanctioned practice, and not the symptom of another mental disorder. *Pica* is a Latin word for "magpie," a bird known for its voracious appetite. Some specific forms of pica are *pagophagia* (eating ice), *geomelophagia* (eating raw potato), *plumbophagia* (eating lead paint chips), *geophagia* (eating clay), *amylophagia* (eating laundry starch), *cautopyreiophagia* (eating burnt matches), *tricophagia* (eating hair), *lithopagia* (eating stone), and *coprophagia* (eating feces; Lacey, 1990). The etiology of this fascinating behavior remains unclear (Lanzkowsky, 1959; Roberts-Harewood & Davies, 2001), though pica is commonly associated with children, pregnant women, and people with developmental and intellectual disabilities. It is classified in the *DSM-IV* as a disorder usually first diagnosed in infancy, childhood, or adolescence (American Psychiatric Association, 1994). Certain risk factors for pica include female gender, childhood, mental retardation, and African American and aboriginal races (Philipps, Zaheer, & Drugas, 1998).

Overview of the Problem

Prevalence and Characteristics among Children

Ingesting nonedible substances is commonly observed among young children but is not considered abnormal unless it persists after 18 months of age. In Boston, the prevalence of pica among children 1 to 6 years of age was found to be between 18.5% and 32.1%, though the prevalence and range of objects ingested decreased with increasing age. Common pica objects included paper, clothing, dirt, and matches (Barltrop, 1966). In a similar longitudinal study on the maladaptive eating patterns of more than 800 children and their mothers in two New York counties, it was reported that younger children in the age range of 1 to 10 were more likely to ingest nonfood items, and pica did not differ between boys and girls. Pica in early childhood was also related to Bulimia Nervosa in later adolescence (Marchi & Cohen, 1990). A study of reports to a poison control center between 1988 and 1991 indicated that ingestion of tobacco-containing products among 700 children under 6 years of age who were entered in the study was relatively benign. Most of the children experienced vomiting and their symptoms resolved completely. No hazardous complications such as death, coma, or respiratory difficulties were reported (McGee, Brabson, McCarthy, & Piccioti, 1995).

Among a handful of international studies, in a study conducted in the United Kingdom with a small population of children who have sickle cell disease and pica for sponge, four children were found to have a positive family history of pica. The authors were not able to determine the reason for the children's pica behavior and argued that the behavior can be a learned behavior or a response to a nutritional deficit or that developmental and emotional issues may be involved (Roberts-Harewood & Davies, 2001). In China, one study looked into the hair and plasma zinc levels of 703 children ages 1 to 6 years, and these were correlated with their physical development. Of the 307 children with a variety of complaints, 75 had growth retardation, 47 had pica, and 91 complained of anorexia. These children had significantly lower values of zinc in their hair relative to the well-nourished children. Zinc supplementation was provided, resulting in improvement in their hair zinc levels and a reduction in pica and anorexia, as well as growth improvements. The authors concluded that zinc deficiency could lead to pica among young children (Xue-Cun et al., 1985).

Specific to geophagy, the prevalence among 156 primary school children in western Kenya was found to be 73.1%. Based on interviews, these children ate soil daily. Anemia and iron depletion were also associated with geophagy, although the study was not conclusive whether soil eating was the cause or consequence of anemia or iron depletion. No significant differences were found between geophageous and nongeophageous children in terms of age, sex, and socioeconomic measures (Geissler, Mwaniki, Thiong'o, Michaelsen, & Friis, 1998). In a study done in the Republic of Guinea, geophagia was found to be a risk factor for orally acquired nematode infections. Of the 286 children sampled in the study, one or more nematode parasite infections were identified in 53.5%. Parents reported that geophagia occurred in 57%, 53%, and 43% of children ages 1 to 5, 6 to 10, and 11 to 18 years, respectively (Glickman, Camara, Glickman, & McCabe, 1999).

Prevalence and Characteristics among Women

Among adults, pica is most common among pregnant women. In one literature review on two major forms of pica practiced during pregnancy, geophagia (clay) and amylophagia (starch), it was found that women who live in rural areas, are of African descent, and have a positive family history of pica were at a higher risk for pica. The prevalence of pica among pregnant White women was only one fourth the prevalence among pregnant African American women. This particular study concludes that, unless more evidence is available on the consequences of pica, pica during pregnancy should not be considered benign and that health care professionals who counsel pregnant women should recognize the increased prevalence of pica in certain groups (Grigsby, Thyer, Waller, & Johnston, 1999; Horner, Lackey, Kolasa, & Warren, 1991).

Among the African American population in rural Holmes County, Mississippi, it was reported that 57% of the women and 16% of the children practiced geophagy, but none of the adult males or adolescents did. Geophagia occurred in 28% of pregnant and postpartum women, and 19% of this group also engaged in other forms of pica such as eating laundry starch, dry powdered milk, and baking soda. Contrary to *DSM-IV* diagnostic criteria, cultural norms permitted young children of both sexes to consume clay, and mothers were found to be instrumental in transferring geophagia from one generation to the next. Although this practice was acceptable for younger children, it was discouraged as the child aged (Vermeer & Frate, 1979). For these reasons, the behavior of many of these children does not meet the technical definition of pica, though their behavior is problematic and unhealthy.

In a similar study done with 225 pregnant low-income Mexican-born women in Mexico and California, 44% in Mexico and 31% in California reported pica behavior. Many women reported that they replaced their strong cravings for traditional pica items (such as dirt) with "safer" substitutes (such as magnesium carbonate) because they worried that traditional items were dirty or unsanitary and thus dangerous to their fetus. "Cleaner" items that these women would eat include blocks of clay or magnesium carbonate, "bean stones" (little clods of dirt found among unwashed beans), and ice. Only the women in California reported ice eating, probably because none of the women in Mexico owned a refrigerator. Those who reported pica behavior also frequently had relatives who practiced pica. The reasons cited for engaging in pica were attraction to the taste, smell, and texture of the pica item in their mouth, for medicinal purposes, and because of advice received from another person. Although a quarter of the women believed that practicing pica could harm the fetus, most thought that not satisfying their craving for pica could result in miscarriage, illness, or a baby with unsatisfied needs. This study concludes that pica is common in low-income Mexican-born women (Simpson, Mull, Longley, & East, 2000).

In New York City, lead poisoning in 33 pregnant women was documented in blood tests reported to the New York City Department of Health between September 1996 and June 1999. Ninety percent of these women were foreign-born, with the majority being from Mexico. The three women with the highest blood lead levels (BLLs) received chelation therapy. Thirteen women (39%) reported pica, including the three women with the highest BLLs. Pica items included dirt (8 women), pulverized pottery (2 women), and both dirt and pulverized pottery (2 women). The imported pottery used for cooking by seven women tested positive for lead. Younger women, those who are more advanced in their pregnancies, and those with a shorter length of time in the United States had higher BLLs. Pica behavior was also directly associated with higher BLLs. The most important risk factors associated with lead poisoning were pica, use of imported pottery, and immigration. The incidence rates for lead poisoning among pregnant women living in New York City was calculated to be 8.8 per 100,000, which is lower than the rates reported by facilities conducting universal screening procedures (Klitzman, Sharma, Nicaj, Vitkevich, & Leighton, 2002).

In Kenya, soil eating was a widespread practice among pregnant women in the Kilifi district. Specifically, 73% of 52 pregnant women reported eating soil regularly, with an estimated daily intake of 41.5 grams. Geophagia was a common cultural practice, especially among pregnant women, and it was customary for women to carry soil with them when going to a place where their preferred soil was unavailable. Most of the women (72%) ate soil from the walls of houses (sedimental red loamy sand). This was preferred because of its smoky taste from the cooking fires inside the hut. Other types of favored soils include a gray clay soil (described as sweet), the "soft stones" from riverbeds, and soil attached by termites to the trunks of trees or poles of houses (liked for its salty taste). All soil, except for the gray clay, was characteristic of the Kenyan coast. Twenty-six women (68%) reported eating soil because they liked it and it was tasty. Although soil did not satisfy their hunger, they reported that they did not like their food unless they ate soil first. Twelve women (32%) reported having the urge to eat clay because of their pregnancy. Although they admitted to eating clay when not pregnant, strong cravings were felt more during pregnancy. Clay eating was a female habit linked to fertility and reproduction (Geissler et al., 1999).

In a study conducted among 553 pregnant African American women in Washington, DC, pica prevalence was reported to be 8.1% (45 women). The most frequently reported pica items were freezer frost (3.1%), ice (3.8%), and starch (1.4%). Geophagia was not observed in these women. Women with pica were found to have significantly lower serum ferritin concentrations and mean corpuscular hemoglobin compared to nonpica women. These women were also reported to have a significantly smaller support system than women who did not display pica (Edwards et al., 1994).

In a Texas study of 281 pregnant women with infants younger than 1 year of age who participated in the Special Supplemental Nutrition Program for Women, Infants, and Children (WIC), the prevalence of pica by substance was ice (53.7%); ice and freezer frost (14.6%); substances such as baking soda, baking powder, cornstarch, laundry starch, baby powder, clay, or dirt (8.2%); and no pica (23.5%). One consequence of pica was lower hemoglobin levels at delivery among women with pica than those without it; however, this was not associated with pregnancy outcomes. Specifically, no differences were found in mean birth weight or mean gestational age among the pica and nonpica women (Rainville, 1998).

In a correlational study conducted among 128 socioeconomically disadvantaged pregnant women attending prenatal care at one of two rural health agencies, the pica prevalence was 38% (48 women). Substances ingested included ice, laundry starch, cornstarch, clay, dirt, and baked clay dirt. Eleven women practiced *polypica* (ingestion of more than one substance). The majority of the women who practiced pica said that they had a "craving" for the substance. African American ethnicity was significantly associated with pica. Women who practiced pica daily had significantly lower hematocrit than women who did not practice pica or who practiced intermittent pica. Again, as with previous studies, pregnancy complications were not associated with pica practice (Corbett, Ryan, & Weinrich, 2003).

Prevalence and Characteristics among the Developmentally and Intellectually Disabled

Among children and adolescents with developmental disorders, individuals with exceptionally low intellectual functioning often practice pica (Hardan & Sahl, 1997). In a study of 991 mentally retarded individuals living in an institution who range in age from 11 to 88 years, the prevalence of pica was estimated to be 25.8%. Food pica accounted for 5.4% and nonfood pica for 16.7%. Food and nonfood pica combined for 3.7% of the population. The frequency of pica increased with the severity of retardation and decreased with age; however, the frequency of pica tended to increase again among individuals 70 years of age or older. The most frequently consumed nonfood items were strings and rags (31%); feces, vomit, and urine (18%); and paper, cigarettes, and soil (9%). Among food picas, excessive consumption of water topped the list (16%), followed by coffee and coffee grounds (13%) and food from trashcans (7%). The investigators also found that pica was an underreported problem, with only 37 of the 256 individuals with pica correctly identified in their records. Most medical complications also occurred with the pica population (Danford & Huber, 1982).

In a similar study, the prevalence of pica was 9.2% in a sample of 607 persons with metal retardation at a state institution. The prevalence of pica increased with the degree of mental retardation yet decreased with age. The highest occurrence of pica was in residents between 10 and 19 years old. No resident older than 44 exhibited pica. Most who engaged in pica were profoundly mentally retarded. Pica objects included clothes (30.5%); dirt, dust, or fluff off the floor (16.6%); toys (10.1%); paper (8.3%); grass (5.5%); metal, plastic, or concrete (4.6%); cigarettes and cigarette butts (4.6%); string (4%); buttons (4%); wood (2.7%); hair (2.7%); soil (2.7%); and straw, wire, and feces (2%; McAlpine & Singh, 1986).

In yet another study of individuals living at a state institution for developmentally disabled individuals, 10.8% of 749 participants exhibited pica behavior. Like the studies described earlier, pica behavior was strongly associated with the profoundly or severely mentally retarded, and individuals in the age range of 22 to 45 years had the highest pica prevalence. This age range also constituted the largest portion of the institution's population (Wakham, Burtner, McNeal, Garvey, & Bedinger, 1992).

Finally, other research on eating disorders has reported that 4% to 26% of adults with intellectual disability have pica. For this group, pica is associated with institutionalization, severe or profound intellectual disability, male sex, old age, autism and socialization problems, hyperactivity, food-related behavior problems (e.g., stealing, cravings, and smearing), self-injury, and other behavior problems (Gravestock, 2000).

Social and Financial Costs

It is difficult to estimate the social and financial costs of pica because it is a problematic and dangerous disorder that can lead to severe medical complications. Each of these complications can have substantial financial and social costs that can be temporary or permanent. These complications include intestinal obstruction (Anderson, Akmal, & Kittur, 1991; Danford & Huber, 1982; Phillips et al., 1998), abdominal pain and bloating (Yogev, Katz, & Phillip, 1997), perforation with peritonitis (Anderson et al., 1991), constipation and diarrhea (Robinson, Tolan, & Golding-Beecher, 1990), dental abrasion and serious dental complications such as injury to the periodontium or adjacent soft tissues in the mouth (Wakham et al., 1992), lead intoxication (Danford & Huber; 1982; Shannon & Graef, 1992; Siklar, Tanyer, Dallar, & Gunay, 2000), vomiting (McGee et al., 1995), severe toxicity (Calabrese, Stanek, James, & Roberts, 1997), parasitism (Glickman et al., 1999; Robinson et al., 1990), acute cerebral edema (Maslinski & Loeb, 2004), and even death (McLoughlin, 1988). Although anemia due to iron deficiency was seen more frequently in pica cases (Arbiter & Black, 1991; Estlin, 1993; Lanzkowsky, 1959; Mihailidou, Galanakis, Paspalaki, Borgia, & Mantzouranis, 2002; Robinson et al., 1990; Singhi & Singhi, 1983), the literature is inconclusive about whether anemia is the result or cause of pica. Gestational lead poisoning due to maternal pica has been reported in pregnant women (Lowry, 2004; Shannon, 2003), and pica in early childhood is a precursor to Bulimia Nervosa in later adolescence (Marchi & Cohen, 1990). Among institutionalized mentally retarded persons, pica represents a serious health hazard and is a life-threatening behavior problem (Foxx & Martin, 1975).

Evidence-Based Approaches to Assessment

Apart from the traditional clinical interview, behavioral observation is the most common method for assessing pica. Frequently, in studies done about people with pica, two independent observers will simultaneously score the frequency of pica or other target responses (Duker & Nielen, 1993; Fisher et al., 1994; Goh, Iwata, &

Kahng, 1999; Johnson, Hunt, & Siebert, 1994; Mace & Knight, 1986; Matson, Stephens, & Smith, 1978; Pace & Toyer, 2000; Rapp, Dozier, & Carr, 2001; Ricciardi, Luiselli, Terrill, & Reardon, 2003; Rojahn, McGonigle, Curcio, & Dixon, 1987; Singh & Winton, 1984, 1985; Smith, 1987; Winton & Singh, 1983; Woods, Miltenberger, & Lumley, 1996). Many other studies use an interval recording technique wherein an observer watches the subject for a specified interval and records any occurrence of pica or like behaviors (Duker & Nielen, 1993; Johnson et al., 1994; Mace & Knight, 1986; Paniagua, Braverman, & Capriotti, 1986; Rojahn et al., 1987; Singh & Winton, 1984, 1985; Winton & Singh, 1983; Woods et al., 1996). Other methods for assessing pica are the use of video cameras to record behavior (Duker & Nielen, 1993; Rapp et al., 2001; Woods et al., 1996), the inspection of subjects' hands and mouth for any scavenging or pica behavior (Foxx & Martin, 1975), and the use of an event recording system (Hirsch & Smith-Myles, 1996). Interviews with primary caregivers (Singhi & Singhi, 1983), hospital and institutional staff (Danford & Huber, 1982), and the subjects themselves (Edwards et al., 1994; Geissler et al., 1999; Rainville, 1998; Simpson et al., 2000) have also been used.

Additionally, physiological measures can be useful for assessing pica. Examples include analysis of stool specimens (Foxx & Martin, 1975; Glickman et al., 1999; Robinson et al., 1990; Stanek & Calabrese, 1995), obtaining hemoglobin values (Lanzkowsky, 1959; Robinson et al., 1990; Singhi & Singhi, 1983; Yogev et al., 1997), X-ray (Anderson et al., 1991; Estlin, 1993; Phillips et al., 1998), dental examinations (Wakham et al., 1992), rectal exams (Anderson et al., 1991), measures of serum ferritin and serum folate concentrations (Edwards et al., 1994), blood tests (Klitzman et al., 2002), and measuring zinc concentrations in hair and blood (Xue-Cun et al., 1985).

Evidence-Based Approaches to Intervention

Overcorrection Procedure

Foxx and Martin (1975) report on an overcorrection procedure to treat the scavenging behavior, pica, and coprophagy (ingesting fecal matter) of four profoundly retarded adults. The procedure emphasizes correction of the scavenging act, accepting responsibility for the action, and teaching alternative, appropriate behavior. The overcorrection procedure consists of the following: an oral hygiene training (10 minutes), a personal hygiene training (10 minutes), and cleaning up the area (10 minutes). The oral hygiene training requires subjects to brush their mouth, gums, and teeth gently with a soft toothbrush that has been soaked in an oral antiseptic (mouthwash). Following this, subjects are given a personal hygiene training that consists of washing and scrubbing their fingernails in warm soapy water with a soft fingernail brush. Next, subjects are guided to the area where they were discovered eating and handling the feces and are then required to clean the area with disinfectant. The entire procedure lasts 30 minutes. In this study, the overcorrection procedure eliminated the scavenging and pica behavior of the four subjects almost completely and improved their grooming behaviors and personal appearance. The appearance and condition of their teeth and gums also significantly improved, and three of the coprophagic scavengers were rid of intestinal parasites.

Singh and Winton (1985) used three components of an overcorrection procedure (tidying, oral hygiene, and personal hygiene) to treat the pica behavior of two mentally retarded patients. An alternating-treatments design was used to compare the individual effects of the three components across a variety of settings: the dayroom, the sunroom, and the dining room. Tidying requires the patients to spit out the inedible object, put it in the trashcan, pick up the trash on the floor, and throw away the contents of the trashcan. These procedures are similar to those described by Foxx and Martin (1975). Oral hygiene was found to be the most effective treatment procedure; both patients had lowest rates of pica when the oral hygiene procedure was used during the alternating-treatments phase. No pica was observed in each subject for 5 consecutive days during all three daily sessions.

Similar results occurred when an overcorrection procedure was used with a profoundly retarded woman who ingested cigarette butts (Matson et al., 1978). In addition to sweeping the floor, emptying trashcans, and picking up cigarette butts and debris, the woman was required to brush her mouth, teeth, and gums with a mild solution of water and hot sauce for 44 days. The solution was then increasingly diluted with water. This overcorrection procedure reduced pica behavior for this woman by 90% from the baseline level. She was also observed to pick up trash and place it in the garbage can on her own—a behavior not observed before treatment.

Negative Practice (Mild Punishment)

Duker and Nielen (1993) used a negative practice method to treat the pica behaviors of a severely mentally retarded female (*K*) suffering from Prader-Willi syndrome. She would bite off and chew inedible objects such as pieces of jigsaw puzzles, pencils, and paper clips. The target behavior was defined as each time *K* brought the inedible object to her mouth. Contingent upon each occurrence of the target behavior, the therapist would approach *K* and say,

"Good, *K*, chew on it!" At the same time, the therapist would take her hand holding the inedible object and press the object in her hand without letting her bite on it. This position was held for 2 minutes. Any attempt to escape this procedure by pushing away the therapist's hand was met with negative reinforcement. For *K*, pica was reduced to a near zero level for several months while the procedure continued.

Rojahn et al. (1987) compared the effects of contingent water mist spray and aromatic ammonia inhalation on the pica behavior of a 16-year-old autistic and severely retarded female at a child-adolescent psychiatric facility. During the aromatic ammonia condition, when the female attempted to engage in pica, the therapist would crush a capsule containing a minimum of 0.33 cc alcohol directly under the client's nose and hold it there for 3 seconds. The water mist condition consisted of spraying a room-temperature water mist to the client's face from a distance of approximately 15 cm. After 13 sessions, the ammonia procedure was eliminated, leaving only the water mist procedure. This latter procedure was highly effective in reducing the pica to a near-zero level. This treatment effect was maintained for a period of 3 months and was consistent across different settings and with different therapists. Although possibly effective, interventions using punitive consequences are usually recommended only if less aversive methods had been given a legitimate trial and shown not to be effective, and if the adverse effects of the pica are judged sufficiently harmful.

In one more example of negative practice, Singh and Winton (1984) evaluated the effects of a response-contingent blindfold on the pica of a 24-year-old profoundly retarded institutionalized woman. Each occurrence of pica would result in the woman being physically guided to remove the object form her mouth (but not from her hand, if she so desired). A blindfold then would be placed on her eyes for 1 minute, and her release from the blindfold was contingent on a 1-minute period of nondisruptive behavior. During the initial treatment phase, the blindfold contingency was in effect for 8 hours each day. Then the treatment was discontinued and the woman's behavior was observed for a 6-month follow-up period. It was found that the blindfold contingency rapidly decreased pica behaviors as well as the picking and handling of inedible objects (antecedents to pica) during the treatment and follow-up periods.

Brief Physical Restraint

Though the use of physical restraint is often discouraged in social work practice, Winton and Singh (1983) found that the use of brief physical restraint (without any verbal reprimand) was effective at reducing pica in two profoundly retarded boys. Specifically, any occurrence of pica would lead to an instruction for the boys to remove the inedible object from their mouth, physically guiding them to do so if necessary, and restraining their arms at their side. One boy was restrained for either 30 seconds or 10 seconds, and the other boy was restrained for either 10 seconds or 3 seconds. The 10-second restraint was found to be most effective with both subjects and was associated with substantial reduction in pica behavior.

Noncontingent Reinforcement

The previous sections described contingent intervention methods, or those actions taken in response to an occurrence of pica behavior. Noncontingent reinforcement interventions are less reactive. Hirsch and Smith-Myles (1996), for example, evaluated the effectiveness of a pica box in controlling the behavior of a 10-year-old female with autism. The pica box contained both edible and inedible items that were safe for her to chew, mouth, and ingest. She was given the pica box every morning when she appeared calm and was instructed that it was her pica box, containing items safe for her to put in her mouth. She was then allowed to choose two items from the pica box. Whenever she attempted pica, she was removed from the area and taken by the hand to her pica box. She was then assisted with opening the box and selecting appropriate edible items. Through the course of the study, the introduction of the pica box did decrease the mean number of daily pica behaviors. Yet, because pica behaviors were not eradicated, the authors conclude that the pica box is helpful but not a cure for pica.

In a somewhat more complicated study, Piazza, Hanley, and Fisher (1996) applied functional analysis methods to treat the pica for cigarette butts of a 17-year-old male with severe mental retardation and autism. After it was determined that tobacco was this male's preferred part of the cigarette and that his pica was maintained independent of social consequences (pica occurred primarily when alone or with minimal supervision), the effects of preferred foods and a response-interruption procedure were measured. Two conditions were evaluated: a noncontingent food (NCF) condition and an NCF plus interrupt condition. During the NCF condition, appropriate edible items were placed on a table and the youth was instructed to eat the food and not touch the cigarette butts. No consequence was delivered for consuming cigarette butts. During the second condition (the NCF plus interrupt condition), in addition to the preferred food items, a piece of purple paper was taped on the wall so that these specific contingencies would be associated with the purple paper. The therapist then delivered a verbal reprimand of "No butts" whenever the subject touched a cigarette butt. Though presenting preferred foods alone was not successful in decreasing the consumption of cigarette butts, providing verbal reprimands that interrupted the pica behavior did effectively eliminate the dangerous cigarette butt consumption. Finally, during a stimulus control assessment session, either a yellow or a purple card was given to the subject before treatment sessions. The response interruption procedure was not implemented. This was to determine if the purple card would be associated with lower rates of pica in its absence. As expected, the purple card was indeed related to reduced pica compared to when the yellow card was given. The use of a purple card was subsequently shown to be effective across multiple settings.

Differential Reinforcement of Incompatible Behavior

Smith (1987) examined the effectiveness of differential reinforcement of incompatible behavior (DRI) to treat pica in a young, profoundly retarded and autistic man at a nonsheltered place of employment. In this study, behaviors incompatible with pica are reinforced with food, drink, and praise. Such praiseworthy behaviors included keeping his hands on his work area or his work activity, keeping his mouth clean, and staying in his assigned work area. After 9 days of baseline observation, the man was exposed to 32 days of DRI. There was then another baseline observation period (12 days) and then 29 more days of DRI. Smith found that pica behaviors decreased during the DRI treatment compared to the first baseline, increased during the second baseline period, but decreased again during the second wave of DRI intervention. The author concludes that, although the number of pica behaviors per day did not decrease to zero, they were controlled to the extent that the client could function in the community without risk of serious injury to self or others.

Donnelly and Olczak (1990) reached parallel conclusions when DRI was used with two mentally retarded males residing in a residential program facility who had a pica for cigarettes. The incompatible behaviors to be reinforced (determined by an assessment of the males' preferred food items) were chewing sugarless mint gum and drinking small amounts of decaffeinated instant coffee. Using an A-B-A-B study design similar to Smith's (1987) study, both subjects had a rapid reduction of pica to near-zero levels during the intervention periods, but the pica behaviors returned to near-baseline levels between intervention phases. As the training progressed, the latency of pica as well as the number of sessions in which pica did not occur increased. The authors therefore conclude that DRI can be an effective treatment.

Finally, Ricciardi et al. (2003) found that repeatedly interrupting one autistic child's pica actions and teaching the child to discard the item in a trash receptacle led to lasting reductions in the mean number of daily pica behaviors.

Discrimination Training with Punishment Component

Johnson et al. (1994) evaluated a treatment package that included a discrimination training procedure to treat the pica and scavenging behavior of two profoundly retarded adolescents. The treatment package had both reinforcement and punishment components intended to help the youths discriminate safe from unsafe food items by ingesting only those items placed on a specified placemat. The mild punishments for pica behavior consisted of a 15-second face wipe with a cool damp cloth for the first adolescent and brief physical restraint (forced to stand with his arms at his side for 15 seconds) or a face wipe for the second adolescent. Subjects were conversely praised for selecting and ingesting the safe food items. The treatment package led to an almost complete elimination of pica behavior for both subjects, and the occurrence of pica behaviors remained low at 7- and 10-week follow-ups. Compared to brief physical restraint, the face wipe appeared to be a more effective punishment for both adolescents.

Fisher et al. (1994) utilized a similar intervention strategy and found like results with three mentally retarded children. The children showed marked reductions in pica combined with more appropriate eating habits throughout a 9-month follow-up period.

A Combination of Noncontingent Reinforcement and Differential Reinforcement of Alternative Behavior

Goh et al. (1999) tested a combined noncontingent reinforcement and differential reinforcement of alternative behavior strategy to change the cigarette pica behavior of four developmentally disabled individuals. The first phase of the study was a thorough assessment of the subjects' preferred cigarette components and preferred edible food items. As with other studies beginning with a detailed assessment, this allowed for the subsequent intervention to be customized for each individual. When offered cigarettes and food items, three people selected the edible items and one selected cigarette components. The second phase then evaluated the different treatment procedures. During the noncontingent reinforcement stage, preferred food items were delivered on a fixed time interval and cigarettes were also available. Success was achieved if pica was absent for several minutes across multiple sessions. During the differential reinforcement of alternative behaviors stage, participants were taught to exchange found cigarettes for preferred food items. To determine whether an independent (unprompted) exchange would occur when a cigarette was available, the food item was delivered only if cigarettes were discarded without physical prompting. It was found that noncontingent reinforcement was effective for two individuals, but these effects were not maintained when treatment conditions were altered. Conversely, the differential reinforcement approach was effective for three participants, and these benefits extended across multiple therapists and settings. Neither intervention approach was effective at reducing the pica of one participant, who showed preference for cigarettes rather than food items. This suggests that preference for edible food items is predictive of treatment effectiveness.

Simplified Habit Reversal

Woods et al. (1996) reported on a simplified habit reversal treatment for pica-related chewing in a 6-year-old boy with normal intelligence and a pica diagnosis. This treatment resembles both noncontingent and differential reinforcement interventions and consists of awareness training, competing response training, and social support. In awareness training, the boy learned to recognize his pica during live treatment sessions and by watching a videotaped recording of his chewing behavior. The competing response training for his chewing behavior involved removing the object from his mouth and pursing his lips for 1 minute. Social support then consisted of praise from his family when he correctly implemented the competing response and reminders to use the competing response when he engaged in problematic chewing behaviors. During the first intervention period, the chewing behavior became almost nonexistent. However, 30 weeks after the treatment, when the subject was no longer using the competing response, the problematic chewing returned to pretreatment levels. Following a second implementation of the treatment, the chewing behavior again decreased.

Use of Social Interactions without Aversive Stimuli

Mace and Knight (1986) emphasized staff-client interaction and physical contact when designing an effective intervention without aversive components to treat the pica of a 19-year-old profoundly retarded man. The young man was also fitted with a physician-prescribed helmet to further inhibit the ingestion of inedible objects. Pretreatment assessment and observation showed that the male exhibited less pica behavior during periods of interaction with staff. Therefore, whenever the subject engaged in pica, staff members would remove the object without reprimands and avoided eye contact. This procedure was then paired with the following interaction conditions: frequent interaction, limited interaction, and no interaction. The second phase of the intervention was an analysis of helmet conditions. This was done to empirically determine the minimum level of protection needed to discourage pica. The procedures were identical to the limited interaction phase, with the following variations: the helmet with face shield condition, helmet without face shield condition, and the no helmet condition. After evaluating each of these treatment conditions (interaction and helmet), the researchers found that frequent interaction with the man and wearing no protective equipment were associated with less pica behavior. The authors conclude that social interaction without the use of aversive stimuli leads to lower levels of pica. Stated differently, higher levels of social interaction are associated with lower levels of pica, and lower levels of social interaction are associated with higher levels of pica.

Use of a Comprehensive Treatment Package

Combining several different intervention approaches, Paniagua et al. (1986) investigated the effect of a comprehensive treatment package to manage the pica and self-stimulation of a 4-year-old profoundly mentally retarded girl. This package consists of a verbal reprimand, removal of objects (or fingers) from the subject's mouth, physical restraint, differential reinforcement of other behavior, response interruption, and positive practice overcorrection. During a baseline period, the girl freely engaged in self-stimulation and pica but was prompted (physically and with modeling) by the therapist to play with her toys. Praise was then given when she used a toy. During a subsequent intervention period, the treatment package was introduced. A verbal reprimand (a loud "No!") was given for each occurrence of pica. The pica object was then removed from her mouth, followed by an immediate physical restraint (holding her arms down for 30 seconds). The differential reinforcement consisted of praise when she would not engage in pica behavior for a 1-minute interval. This treatment package resulted in rapid and dramatic reduction in the levels of pica across multiple settings, including at inpatient and outpatient treatment facilities and at the girl's home.

Rapp et al. (2001) similarly combined several treatment approaches when they evaluated the effectiveness of progressing from less to more intrusive interventions with a 6-year-old girl diagnosed with autism and persistent pica. Like several other studies reviewed in this chapter, this intervention began with a thorough assessment that included an examination of the girl's pica behavior and an evaluation of foods that competed with her pica cravings. Beginning with mild intervention, slightly lower levels of pica were observed when a therapist delivered a verbal reprimand each time the girl engaged in pica. This effect decreased over time, though, and the pica increased. Next, the young girl was provided noncontingent access to rice cakes (her preferred food item identified in assessment). Access was initially intense, then subsequently thinned. This approach too was ineffective, so the researchers initiated a multielement intervention. This consisted of access to noncontingent food, brief physical restraint of the girl's hands when she attempted to eat pica items, verbal reprimands and statements of disapproval, and contingent auditory stimulation wherein she wore a yellow wristwatch intended to provide inhibitory stimulus control over pica by pairing it with auditory stimulus. Because the noncontingent food, physical blocking, and verbal reprimands failed to generate substantial reduction in pica behaviors alone, the use of the contingent auditory stimulation became the treatment of choice. It yielded zero or near-zero rates of pica and an increase in the duration of toy manipulation.

Iron Therapy and Vitamin Supplement

In one study of 12 children with average intelligence and pica living in Cape Town, South Africa, all were found to have iron deficiency anemia. These children ingested a wide variety of substances: white sand, black soil, pieces of brick stones, wood, black coal, and clay. Furthermore, 83% of the children had a positive history of ascaris infestation, and five children who had radiological examinations showed opaque material interpreted as sand or stones in the large bowel. Given these characteristics and needs, Lanzkowsky (1959) investigated the effects of iron therapy to reduce the children's pica behaviors. Following the start of intramuscular iron therapy, all 12 children showed no further pica within 1 to 2 weeks. Moreover, several of the children who had previously eaten sand or stones continued to play with these items but had no inclination to eat them. Many children also had increased appetite and an improved sense of well-being.

Pace and Toyer (2000) expanded this iron therapy to include a multivitamin in treating the pica of a 9-year-old girl with severe mental retardation, iron deficiency, and anemia. Although her pica decreased during times when she was taking the vitamins and iron supplement, the results were inconclusive because it was not clear if the vitamins provided a deficient mineral to the girl or if they simply aided in the absorption of iron.

Summary

There is considerable evidence from the literature that a number of interventions effectively reduce pica: the use of behavioral interventions such as differential reinforcement or brief physical restraint, the use of social interactions, and use of comprehensive treatment packages, among others. Two studies effectively used iron and vitamin supplements. Specific to people with developmental disabilities, physical restraint, mild punishment, and aversive stimulation have proven to be effective forms of treatment. Although the use of such methods is sometimes controversial in social work practice, its effectiveness has been consistently demonstrated in several studies. It is imperative that these intrusive interventions be used appropriately and safely. Therefore, professionals uncomfortable or unsure about their use should utilize other, more reinforcement-based approaches as first-choice treatments and resort to applying more aversive techniques if the first, less restrictive methods fail.

Several studies demonstrate the importance of developing interventions that are customized to the specific client. For example, Piazza et al. (1996) made efforts to determine the client's preferred part of the cigarette and thus were able to develop an effective intervention that specifically addressed this desired stimulus. In other studies, researchers determined what types of punishment were least enjoyable for the client (such as face wiping) and which alternative behaviors were most enjoyable (e.g., chewing gum or rice cakes). The data obtained from such pretreatment assessments were instrumental in developing more systematic and effective interventions. Essentially, knowing the variables that maintain or discourage pica is crucial for developing less intrusive and more acceptable forms of intervention.

According to Stokes and Baer (1977, cited in McAdam, Sherman, Sheldon, & Napolitano, 2004), the clinical significance of pica reductions depend not only on the magnitude of the reduction but also on the intervention's impact across time and its generalization to different behaviors and behavior-change agents. Of the studies reviewed in this chapter, many demonstrated consistent changes across settings and some reported consistency across settings and therapists. Unfortunately, most of the studies did not evaluate intervention effectiveness across substantial periods of time. Plus, most of the studies were done in controlled environments (e.g., institutions); therefore, the demonstrated effectiveness and successful outcomes reported by the researchers have yet to be proven in more naturalistic settings. The small sample size of all of the studies must also be noted. Generalization is further limited as most studies use samples of only one or two participants. For all of these reasons, conclusions about treatment effectiveness should be made with caution.

Despite these potential limitations, several treatment approaches and options have been detailed throughout this chapter. This is especially true regarding the treatment of people with development and intellectual disabilities. Because these clients can be among the most challenging and difficult to serve, the available literature has special significance for social work practice with this population. Nonetheless, more research is needed evaluating the effectiveness of behavioral interventions with pregnant women and people with normal intelligence. Future research should therefore be conducted that assesses the frequency of pica and the prevalence of specific types of pica in these groups and tests different intervention strategies. By expanding the scope of pica research, it will be possible to better serve all persons afflicted with this unusual and dangerous disorder.

Study Questions

1. According to the *DSM*, what are the diagnostic criteria for pica?
2. What are some specific forms of pica (and the substances associated with each)?
3. What are common risk factors for pica?
4. Describe the most common methods for assessing pica behavior.
5. List and describe the steps in an overcorrection procedure as done by Foxx and Martin (1975), Singh and Winton (1985), and Matson et al. (1978).
6. What are the similarities and differences between contingent and noncontingent interventions for pica?
7. What are some of the limitations of the available pica research?
8. To better understand and treat pica, what are some topics and areas needing further study? Why might more research on these topics be important?

References

American Psychiatric Association. (1994). *Diagnostic and statistical manual of mental disorders* (4th ed.). Washington, DC: Author.

American Psychiatric Association. (2000). *Diagnostic and statistical manual of mental disorders* (4th ed., text rev.). Washington, DC: Author.

Anderson, J. E., Akmal, M., & Kittur, D. S. (1991). Surgical complications of pica: Report of a case of intestinal obstruction and a review of the literature. *American Surgeon, 57,* 663–667.

Arbiter, E. A., & Black, D. (1991). Pica and iron-deficiency anaemia. *Child Care, Health, and Development, 17,* 231–234.

Barltrop, D. (1966). The prevalence of pica. *American Journal of the Diseases of the Child, 112,* 116–123.

Calabrese, E. J., Stanek, E. J., James, R. C., & Roberts, S. M. (1997). Soil ingestion: A concern for acute toxicity in children. *Environmental Health Perspectives, 105,* 1354–1358.

Corbett, R. W., Ryan, C., & Weinrich, S. (2003). Pica in pregnancy: Does it affect pregnancy outcomes? *American Journal of Maternal/Child Nursing, 28,* 183–189.

Danford, D. E., & Huber, A. M. (1982). Pica among mentally retarded adults. *American Journal of Mental Deficiency, 87,* 141–146.

Donnelly, D. R., & Olczak, P. V. (1990). The effect of differential reinforcement of incompatible behaviors (DRI) on pica for cigarettes in persons with intellectual disability. *Behavior Modification, 14,* 81–96.

Duker, P. C., & Nielen, M. (1993). The use of negative practice for the control of pica behavior. *Journal of Behavior Therapy and Experimental Psychiatry, 24,* 249–253.

Edwards, C. H., Johnson, A. A., Knight, E. M., Oyemade, U. J., Cole, O. J., Westney, O. E., et al. (1994). Pica in an urban environment. *Journal of Nutrition, 124,* S954–S962.

Estlin, E. J. (1993). Childhood pica [Letter to the editor]. *Journal of Paediatrics and Child Health, 30,* 80–81.

Fisher, W. W., Piazza, C. C., Bowman, L. G., Kurtz, P. F., Sherer, M. R., & Lachman, S. R. (1994). A preliminary evaluation of empirically derived consequences for the treatment of pica. *Journal of Applied Behavior Analysis, 27,* 447–457.

Foxx, R. M., & Martin, E. D. (1975). Treatment of scavenging behavior (coprophagy and pica) by overcorrection. *Behavior Research and Therapy, 13,* 153–162.

Geissler, P. W., Mwaniki, D. L., Thiong'o, F., Michaelsen, K. F., & Friis, H. (1998). Geophagy, iron status, and anaemia among primary school children in western Kenya. *Tropical Medicine and International Health, 3,* 529–534.

Geissler, P. W., Prince, R. J., Levene, M., Poda, C., Beckerleg, S. E., Mutemi, W., et al. (1999). Perceptions of soil-eating and anaemia among pregnant women on the Kenyan coast. *Social Science and Medicine, 48,* 1069–1079.

Glickman, L. T., Camara, A. O., Glickman, N. W., & McCabe, G. P. (1999). Nematode intestinal parasites of children in rural Guinea, Africa: Prevalence and relationship to geophagia. *International Journal of Epidemiology, 28,* 169–174.

Goh, H. L., Iwata, B. A., & Kahng, S. W. (1999). Multicomponent assessment and treatment of cigarette pica. *Journal of Applied Behavior Analysis, 32,* 297–316.

Gravestock, S. (2000). Eating disorders in adults with intellectual disability. *Journal of Intellectual Disability Research, 44,* 625–637.

Grigsby, R. K., Thyer, B. A., Waller, R. J., & Johnston, G. A. (1999). Chalk eating in middle Georgia: A culture-bound syndrome of pica? *Southern Medical Journal, 92,* 190–192.

Hardan, A., & Sahl, R. (1997). Psychopathology in children and adolescents with developmental disorders. *Research in Developmental Disabilities, 18,* 369–382.

Hirsch, N., & Smith-Myles, B. S. (1996). The use of a pica box in reducing pica behavior in a student with autism. *Focus on Autism and Other Developmental Disabilities, 11,* 222–226.

Horner, R. D., Lackey, C. J., Kolasa, K., & Warren, K. (1991). Pica practices of pregnant women. *Journal of the American Dietetic Association, 91,* 34–38.

Johnson, C. R., Hunt, F. M., & Siebert, M. J. (1994). Discrimination training in the treatment of pica and food scavenging. *Behavior Modification, 18,* 214–229.

Klitzman, S., Sharma, A., Nicaj, L., Vitkevich, R., & Leighton, J. (2002). Lead poisoning among pregnant women in New York City: Risk factors and screening practices. *Journal of Urban Health: Bulletin of the New York Academy of Medicine, 79,* 225–237.

Lacey, E. P. (1990). Broadening the perspective of pica: Literature review. *Public Health Reports, 105,* 29–35.

Lanzkowsky, P. (1959). Investigation into the aetiology and treatment of pica. *Archives of Disease in Childhood, 34*(174), 140–148.

Lowry, L. K. (2004, April 15). Maternal pica is suspected in a case of infant lead poisoning. *Blood Weekly,* 54–55.

Mace, F. C., & Knight, D. (1986). Functional analysis and treatment of severe pica. *Journal of Applied Behavior Analysis, 19,* 411–416.

Marchi, M., & Cohen, P. (1990). Early childhood eating behaviors and adolescent eating disorders. *Journal of the American Academy of Child and Adolescent Psychiatry, 29,* 112–117.

Maslinski, P. G., & Loeb, J. A. (2004). Pica-associated cerebral edema in an adult. *Journal of the Neurological Sciences, 225,* 149–151.

Matson, J. L., Stephens, R. M., & Smith, C. (1978). Treatment of self-injurious behavior with overcorrection. *Journal of Mental Deficiency Research, 22,* 175–178.

McAdam, D. B., Sherman, J. A., Sheldon, J. B., & Napolitano, D. A. (2004). Behavioral interventions to reduce the pica of persons with developmental disabilities. *Behavior Modification, 28,* 45–72.

McAlpine, C., & Singh, N. N. (1986). Pica in institutionalized mentally retarded persons. *Journal of Mental Deficiency Research, 30,* 171–178.

McGee, D., Brabson, T., McCarthy, J., & Picciotti, M. (1995). Four-year review of cigarette ingestions in children. *Pediatric Emergency Care, 11,* 13–16.

McLoughlin, I. J. (1988). Pica as a cause of death in three mentally handicapped men. *British Journal of Psychiatry, 152,* 842–845.

Mihailidou, H., Galanakis, E., Paspalaki, P., Borgia, P., & Mantzouranis, E. (2002). Pica and the elephant's ear. *Journal of Child Neurology, 17,* 855–856.

Pace, G. M., & Toyer, E. A. (2000). The effects of a vitamin supplement on the pica of a child with severe mental retardation. *Journal of Applied Behavior Analysis, 33,* 619–622.

Paniagua, F. A., Braverman, C., & Capriotti, R. M. (1986). Use of a treatment package in the management of a profoundly mentally retarded girl's pica and self-stimulation. *American Journal of Mental Deficiency, 90,* 550–557.

Phillips, M. R., Zaheer, S., & Drugas, G. T. (1998). Gastric trichobezoar: Case report and literature review. *Mayo Clinic Proceedings, 73,* 653–656.

Piazza, C. C., Hanley, G. P., & Fisher, W. W. (1996). Functional analysis and treatment of cigarette pica. *Journal of Applied Behavior Analysis, 29,* 437–450.

Rainville, A. J. (1998). Pica practices of pregnant women are associated with lower maternal hemoglobin level at delivery. *Journal of the American Dietetic Association, 98,* 293–296.

Rapp, J. T., Dozier, C. L., & Carr, J. E. (2001). Functional assessment and treatment of pica: A single case experiment. *Behavioral Interventions, 16,* 111–125.

Ricciardi, J. N., Luiselli, J. K., Terrill, S., & Reardon, K. (2003). Alternative response training with contingent practice as intervention for pica in a school setting. *Behavioral Interventions, 18,* 219–226.

Roberts-Harewood, M., & Davies, S. C. (2001, December). Pica in sickle cell disease: "She ate the headboard" [Letter to the editor]. *Archives of Disease in Childhood, 85,* 510–511.

Robinson, B. A., Tolan, W., & Golding-Beecher, O. (1990). Childhood pica: Some aspects of the clinical profile in Manchester, Jamaica. *West Indian Medical Journal, 39,* 20–26.

Rojahn, J., McGonigle, J. J., Curcio, C., & Dixon, M. J. (1987). Suppression of pica by water mist and aromatic ammonia. *Behavior Modification, 11,* 65–74.

Shannon, M. (2003). Severe lead poisoning in pregnancy. *Ambulatory Pediatrics, 3*(1), 37–39.

Shannon, M., & Graef, J. (1992). Lead intoxication in infancy. *Pediatrics, 89,* 87–90.

Siklar, Z., Tanyer, G., Dallar, S., & Gunay, S. (2000, October). Pica and intoxication in childhood [Letter to the editor]. *Clinical Pediatrics, 39,* 624–625.

Simpson, E., Mull, J. D., Longley, E., & East, J. (2000). Pica during pregnancy in low-income women born in Mexico. *Western Journal of Medicine, 173,* 20–24.

Singh, N. N., & Winton, A. S. W. (1984). Effects of a screening procedure on pica and collateral behaviors. *Journal of Behavior Therapy and Experimental Psychiatry, 15,* 59–65.

Singh, N. N., & Winton, A. S. W. (1985). Controlling pica by components of an overcorrection procedure. *American Journal of Mental Deficiency, 90,* 40–45.

Singhi, P., & Singhi, S. (1983). Nutritional status and psycho-social stress in children with pica. *Indian Pediatrics, 20,* 345–349.

Smith, M. D. (1987). Treatment of pica in an adult disabled by autism by differential reinforcement of incompatible behavior. *Journal of Behavior Therapy and Experimental Psychiatry, 18,* 285–288.

Stanek, E. J., III., & Calabrese, E. J. (1995). Daily estimates of soil ingestion in children. *Environmental Health Perspectives.* Retrieved October 29, 2004, from http://ehp.niehs.nih.gov/cgi-bin/simpleprint.pl.

Vermeer, D. E., & Frate, D. A. (1979). Geophagia in rural Mississippi: Environmental and cultural contexts and nutritional implications. *American Journal of Clinical Nutrition, 32,* 2129–2135.

Wakham, M. D., Burtner, P., McNeal, D. R., Garvey, T. P., & Bedinger, S. (1992). Pica: A peculiar behavior with oral involvement. *Special Care in Dentistry, 12,* 207–210.

Winton, A. S. W., & Singh, N. N. (1983). Suppression of pica using brief-duration physical restraint. *Journal of Mental Deficiency Research, 27,* 93–103.

Woods, D. W., Miltenberger, R. G., & Lumley, V. A. (1996). A simplified habit reversal treatment for pica-related chewing. *Journal of Behavior Therapy and Experimental Psychiatry, 27,* 257–262.

Xue-Cun, C., Tai-An, Y., Jin-Sheng, H., Qiu-Yan, M., Zhi-Min, H., & Li-Xiang, L. (1985). Low levels of zinc in hair and blood, pica, anorexia, and poor growth in Chinese preschool children. *American Journal of Clinical Nutrition, 42,* 694–700.

Yogev, Y., Katz, M., & Phillip, M. (1997). An 8-year-old girl with an abdominal mass. *European Journal of Pediatrics, 156,* 243–244.

SUBSTANCE-RELATED DISORDERS

Alcohol Abuse

Nancy J. Smyth and Charles D. Syms

8

Chapter

Learning Objectives

After reading this chapter, the reader will be able to:

- Define alcohol abuse, alcohol dependence, and heavy drinking.
- Discuss strategies for assessing an alcohol problem and how they can inform intervention.
- Identify the role pharmacological interventions should play in alcohol treatment.
- Describe which interventions for alcohol problems have the strongest research support.

Operational Definitions of the Problem

Alcohol problems can take many forms and can be defined in many ways. Most often they are defined by diagnosis; however, recently there has been more focus on the health risks of heavy drinking, irrespective of whether an individual qualifies for an alcohol-related diagnosis (Heather, 1993).

Moderate and Risky or Heavy Drinking

Moderate drinking has been defined by the U.S. Department of Agriculture and the U.S. Department of Health and Human Services as no more than two drinks a day (or 14 per week, with not more than four per day) for most men, and one drink a day (or seven per week, with not more than three per day) for most women (National Institute on Alcohol Abuse and Alcoholism [NIAAA], 1992). NIAAA (2005) defines heavy drinking as five or more drinks per day or 15 or more drinks per week for men, and four or more drinks per day or eight or more drinks per week for women. Heavy drinking is also called risky drinking (Moyer & Finney, 2004–2005).

Alcohol-Related Disorders

Alcohol-related disorders are divided into two major categories by the *Diagnostic and Statistical Manual of Mental Disorders* (*DSM*; American Psychiatric Association, 2000): alcohol use disorders and alcohol-induced disorders. The latter includes such diagnoses as alcohol-withdrawal delirium and alcohol-induced anxiety disorder; the former includes two diagnoses, alcohol abuse and alcohol dependence, the second of which is considered more severe. This chapter focuses primarily on alcohol use disorders because they are more commonly of concern in social work practice.

To qualify for a diagnosis of *alcohol abuse,* individuals must, within a 1-year period, demonstrate a "maladaptive pattern of . . . use leading to clinically significant impairment or distress" (American Psychiatric Association, 2000, p. 198) in one of four ways: (1) failure, as a recurrent consequence of drinking, to adequately complete one's major responsibilities in some significant life role or setting (e.g., work, school, family); (2) repeated alcohol use in physically dangerous situations (e.g., drinking heavily and then driving); (3) continuing to drink despite having social or interpersonal problems that result from, or are worsened by, drinking; and (4) experiencing repeated difficulties with the law as a result of drinking. Qualifying for a diagnosis of alcohol dependence is an exclusion criterion for the diagnosis of alcohol abuse.

A *DSM* diagnosis of *alcohol dependence* is assigned if an individual experiences three or more of the following seven symptoms within a 1-year period: (1) withdrawal symptoms; (2) tolerance, that is, needing more alcohol to achieve the same effect or finding that the same amount of alcohol has a markedly reduced effect; (3) drinking more than planned or for a longer period of time than planned; (4) failed attempts to reduce or control drinking or a persistent wish to do so; (5) spending a lot of time acquiring alcohol, drinking, or recovering from drinking; (6) decreasing or giving up "important social, occupational or recreational activities" (American Psychiatric Association, 2000, p. 197) due to drinking; and (7) continuing to drink in spite of knowing that drinking causes or exacerbates a physical or psychological problem.

The term *alcohol problem* is often used to refer to any negative consequence resulting from alcohol use or abuse. This clearly includes the diagnoses of alcohol abuse and alcohol dependence; it also includes those situations that do not qualify for either diagnosis, such as someone with one or two alcohol dependence symptoms.

People with Alcohol Problems

A wide range of terms are used to refer to people who have problems with alcohol, specifically alcohol abusers, alcoholics, and problem drinkers. The distinctions between these terms can be confusing, and different people may use them differently. *Alcohol abuser* is usually applied to people who meet the diagnostic criteria for alcohol abuse, although sometimes it refers to anyone with an alcohol problem. *Alcoholic* is a label applied to people with more chronic alcohol problems. Some people use the term for anyone who meets *DSM* alcohol dependence criteria, others apply it only to those who meet those criteria and who also meet criteria for physical dependence on alcohol (withdrawal or tolerance). *Problem drinker* is often used to refer to people with alcohol abuse or dependence, particularly without significant withdrawal symptoms or significant physical deterioration due to alcohol use. In light of the variable use of these terms, the phrases *people with alcohol problems, alcoholics, alcohol abusers,* and *problem drinkers* are used interchangeably in this chapter.

Prevalence, Incidence, and Social and Financial Costs

Just over 22% of the U.S. adult (>18 years old) population report never drinking alcohol, 15% identify themselves as former drinkers, and 13.2% as infrequent drinkers, leaving slightly less than half (49.5%) of adults identifying themselves as current drinkers (Centers for Disease Control and Prevention [CDC], 2004). In the U.S. general population, 4.7% qualify for a current diagnosis of alcohol abuse, 3.8% for alcohol dependence, and 8.5% for either alcohol dependence or alcohol abuse (Grant et al., 2004). In examining rates for current alcohol abuse or dependence among subpopulations, Native American males have the highest combined rates (15.9%), followed by White males (12.8%), with Hispanic (12.1), Black (10.8%), and Asian (6.8%) following. Among females, Native Americans (8.8%) show the highest combined rate, followed by White females (Grant et al., 2004). The age group with the highest rates of combined alcohol abuse and dependence is 18- to 29-year-olds (16.2%; Grant et al., 2004).

Although not all heavy drinkers experience current alcohol-related problems, they are at risk of developing future problems (NIAAA, 1992, 2005), and 1 in 4 qualifies for a current diagnosis of alcohol abuse or dependence (NIAAA, 2005). Among all people who reported some alcohol use, 17.7% reported experiencing at least one alcohol-related problem in the past year (Substance Abuse and Mental Health Services Administration [SAMHSA], 1995). Among heavy drinkers, this rate was reported at 70.3% (SAMHSA, 1995).

Alcohol use and abuse play a significant role in many problems, including a wide range of medical diseases, accidental deaths and injuries, suicides and attempted suicides, homicides, family violence, criminal behavior, birth defects, and job productivity losses (NIAAA, 2000). For example, 40% of all fatal crashes in 2003 were alcohol related (CDC, 2005). Alcohol involvement among emergency room patients ranges from 15% to 25% (NIAAA, 1994). The incidence of Fetal Alcohol Syndrome, a cluster of birth defects attributable to maternal alcohol use during pregnancy, is estimated at 0.5 to 3.0 cases per 1,000 births in the United States, although the rate for some special populations can be much higher (NIAAA, 1999). To illustrate, some Native American populations in the United States have rates at 10 per 1,000 births, and rates as high as 120 per 1,000 have been reported among Canadian Indians (NIAAA, 1994). Taken together, the direct and indirect economic costs of alcohol problems in the United States were projected to be $184,636 million for the year 1998 (NIAAA, 2000).

Relevance of Social Work's Involvement

Social workers can be involved in assessment and intervention with alcohol problems in one of two ways: in alcohol and other drug practice settings or through contact with alcohol-involved clients in other practice settings (Smyth, 1995). Because alcohol abuse may affect people in any number of ways, people with alcohol problems (and their family members) often seek services for a wide range of presenting problems, including family conflict, depression, anxiety, financial difficulties, legal problems, declining school or work performance, and illness (Smyth, 1995). Therefore, social workers employed in child welfare, family services, health, mental health, criminal justice, employee assistance, school, and private practice settings frequently encounter clients who are experiencing alcohol-related problems, either as a result of their own use of alcohol or because of alcohol abuse by someone they know.

In many cases, clients do not connect their use of alcohol to the cause of their difficulties, so they may not volunteer information about their alcohol and other drug use. For these reasons, it is essential for social workers in all practice settings to be familiar with how alcohol abuse can affect individuals and families. Alcohol and other drug use information should also, therefore, be routinely gathered. However, in one recent survey of the National Association of Social Workers (2001) members, only 43% reported screening for substance abuse problems among their clients, suggesting that the majority of social workers are not yet meeting this goal.

Evidence-Based Approaches to Assessment

As with all good social work practice, the assessment of alcohol problems provides the foundation for case conceptualization and treatment planning; as such, it should take place in the context of a comprehensive biopsychosocial-spiritual assessment of clients and their environments. Factors such as social support, family environment, psychopathology, use of drugs other than alcohol, and employment all affect the client's probability of success in addressing an alcohol problem (Moos, Finney, & Cronkite, 1990). As a general rule, the more aspects of clients' lives that are impaired, whether due to alcohol use or other problems, the more involved and comprehensive treatment will need to be.

In addition to conducting clinical interviews, there are many different types of assessment strategies that can be employed to facilitate the assessment process, including structured interviews, computerized assessment tools, self-report methods, observation, and biological methods. An excellent source book on assessment, assessment methods, and scales and interviews is available from the NIAAA (Allen & Columbus, 2003). Unless indicated otherwise, all of the assessment instruments discussed here have demonstrated good psychometric characteristics; that is, they have demonstrated reliability and validity.

Structured Clinical Interviews

There are several structured clinical interviews that can be used in alcohol assessment and treatment. The alcohol section of the Diagnostic Interview Survey IV (Robins, Helzer, Croughan, & Ratcliff, 1981) is often used to establish a reliable and valid diagnosis of alcohol abuse or dependence. A structured interview often used for treatment planning or measurement of treatment outcome is the Addiction Severity Index (ASI; McLellan, Kushner, et al., 1992). The ASI yields composite and severity scores in seven areas of client functioning: alcohol use, drug use, medical, employment, legal, family/social, and psychiatric (McLellan, Kushner, et al.,

1992). The Comprehensive Problem Drinker Profile (Miller & Marlatt, 1984) is another structured interview that provides useful information for treatment planning.

Computerized Assessment Methods

There are computerized versions available of many of the assessment scales discussed in this chapter. Among the structured interviews, a computerized version of the Diagnostic Interview Survey (Robins et al., 1981) exists. The computerized version of the Time Line Followback (Sobell & Sobell, 1995c), an alcohol consumption assessment tool, greatly facilitates the collection and scoring of this information. Many of the self-report assessment instruments, such as the Inventory of Drinking Situations (Annis, Graham, & Davis, 1987), also have computerized versions.

Self-Report Methods

There are many self-report methods that are used in the assessment and treatment of alcohol abuse and dependence, although they can be conceptualized in three major categories: measures of alcohol consumption, screening and diagnostic measures, and measures of characteristics of drinking that are helpful in the treatment planning process. Accurate self-reports are more likely when interviews are conducted under the following conditions: Clients are alcohol-free, confidentiality is ensured, questions are objective and clear, memory aides are utilized, and interviews are conducted in clinical or research settings (versus legal settings; Sobell & Sobell, 2003).

Alcohol Consumption Measures

Common measures of alcohol consumption include the Alcohol Timeline Followback method (TLFB; Sobell & Sobell, 1995a), a range of quantity-frequency measures (Room, 1990), and use of diaries or self-monitoring logs (Miller, Westerberg, & Waldron, 1995). All measures evaluate drinking in terms of the number of standard drinks. One standard drink is equivalent to 6 oz of ethyl alcohol. Alcoholic beverages vary in the amount of alcohol contained in each; the following beverages are approximately one standard drink: one 12 oz beer or wine cooler; 8 to 9 oz of a malt liquor (a full 12 oz glass would be 1.5 standard drinks); 5 oz of table wine or 3.5 oz of a fortified wine; and 2.5 oz of a cordial liqueur, or 1.5 oz of brandy or 80 proof liquor (NIAAA, 2005, p. 13).

Diaries and drinking self-monitoring logs are useful for collecting current and prospective levels of drinking, as clients can fill this out on a day-by-day basis. Log entries usually include information about the situation in which alcohol is consumed, the client's mood or thoughts at the time, and the amount and type of alcoholic beverage consumed (Sobell & Sobell, 1995b). In addition to providing information about levels of consumption, this assessment method can provide useful clinical information about drinking antecedents, which, in turn, can facilitate treatment planning.

Quantity-frequency measures usually retrospectively assess an average pattern of alcohol use based on the average number of drinks per drinking occasion and the average frequency of drinking occasions, although the frequency of the maximum quantity of drinking also may be measured. These measures provide information about total alcohol consumption and number of drinking days, but because they assume that drinking is constant, they do not provide information about the variation in drinking over time (Sobell & Sobell, 1995b). This distinction is important because different drinking patterns, with similar rates of consumption, may yield different risks to health (Sobell & Sobell, 2003).

The TLFB method utilizes a calendar to collect detailed information about an individual's past daily drinking over a designated time period, anywhere from 30 days to 12 months prior to the interview (Sobell & Sobell, 1995a). Several memory aids are used to enhance accurate recall, and the test can be administered by a trained interviewer or self-administered by clients in either paper-and-pencil or computerized formats (Sobell & Sobell, 1995a, 1995c).

Screening and Diagnostic Measures

Screening and diagnostic measures aid in the determination of the existence and severity of an alcohol problem. Screening measures are designed to detect people with alcohol problems who have not yet been identified as having an alcohol problem, for example, people seeking primary health care. For this reason, they are usually brief (Connors, 1995). Diagnostic measures are used to assess the severity of an alcohol problem among clinical populations. Some instruments, such as the Michigan Alcoholism Screening Test (MAST; Selzer, 1971), are sometimes used for both screening and diagnosis.

Two common brief screening tools are the MAST (Selzer, 1971), and the CAGE (Mayfield, McLeod, & Hall, 1974). There are several brief versions of the MAST, including a 10-item, a 13-item, and a 24-item version (Allen & Columbus, 2003). CAGE is the simplest of the screening tools; it involves asking the following four questions about alcohol use (two positive responses are clinically significant):

C Have you ever felt you should **C**ut-down on your drinking?

A Have people **A**nnoyed you by criticizing your drinking?

G Have you ever felt bad or **G**uilty about your drinking?

E Have you ever had a drink first thing in the morning to steady your nerves or to get rid of a hangover? (**E**ye-opener; Mayfield et al., 1974, p. 1121)

Both the CAGE and the MAST inquire about lifetime alcohol problems, so they are best used to identify individuals who need further assessment and not to determine a current drinking problem. However, the CAGE does not appear to be as sensitive with women and minorities (NIAAA, 2002). For this reason, it is recommended that questions about quantity and frequency be added to improve detection of alcohol problems (NIAAA, 2002). One test that does this is the Alcohol Use Disorders Identification Test (Saunders, Aasland, Babor, de la Fuente, & Grant, 1993), a 10-item screening tool developed by the World Health Organization that assesses recent drinking with questions on quantity and frequency, alcohol problems, and alcohol dependence. Research suggests that it is free of cultural and gender bias and may also be valid with adolescents (NIAAA, 2002).

Finally, some screening instruments have been designed for detection of alcohol problems in special populations. Among these are the Tolerance, Worried, Eye Opener, Amnesia, K/Cut Down (TWEAK; Russell, Czarnecki, Cowan, McPherson, & Mudar, 1991) for women; the Rutgers Alcohol Problem Index (White & Labouvie, 1989) for adolescents; and the Short Michigan Alcoholism Screening Test—Geriatric Version (Blow & Barry, 2003) for older adults.

Diagnostic measures are used to assess the severity of an alcohol problem; they are more often employed in situations where an alcohol problem is already suspected, as in the case of evaluation interviews conducted in an alcohol treatment clinic. Common diagnostic measures are the Alcohol Dependence Scale (ADS; Horn, Skinner, Wanberg, & Foster, 1984), an instrument that assesses severity of alcohol dependence; the Impaired Control Scale (Heather, Tebbut, Mattick, & Zamir, 1993), a measure of actual and perceived control over drinking; and the DrInc (Miller, Tonigan, & Longabaugh, 1995), a scale that measures the consequences of alcohol use. Information from these measures can be useful in making some clinical decisions. For example, the ADS can be used to determine if a moderate drinking (versus abstinence) treatment goal is likely to be successful for a particular client (Skinner & Horn, 1984).

Treatment Planning Tools
There are many instruments that can inform treatment planning. Among these are instruments that assess a client's motivation to change, alcohol-related beliefs, drinking relapse risk, and self-efficacy (Donovan, 1995). Others, like the Addiction Sever-

ity Index (McLellan, Carise, et al., 1992), were developed for substance abuse problems but can be used for alcohol problems as well.

One key factor that should be assessed is client motivation and readiness to change. The Readiness to Change Questionnaire (Heather, Gold, & Rollnick, 1991) and the Stages of Change Readiness and Treatment Eagerness Scale (Miller & Tonigan, 1994) are two instruments that assess clients according to the stages-of-change model developed by Prochaska and associates (Prochaska & DiClemente, 1984; Prochaska, DiClemente, & Norcross, 1992). Their research identified five stages of change that people go through in changing addictive behaviors: precontemplation, contemplation, preparation/determination, action, and maintenance (Prochaska & DiClemente, 1984). Clients in the earlier stages of precontemplation and contemplation should receive interventions designed to move them from one stage to the next (Prochaska et al., 1992).

Clients' beliefs or expectancies about alcohol use also are important to consider in assessment; research indicates that people with alcohol problems hold different alcohol expectancies than people without these problems (Donovan, 1995). When expectancies maintain problematic drinking, they should be specifically targeted for change through cognitive and/or behavioral interventions. Among the many scales used to assess alcohol expectancies are the Alcohol Effects Questionnaire (Rohsenow, 1983) and the Alcohol Beliefs Scale (Connors & Maisto, 1988).

Relapse risk is often assessed through examination of two aspects of clients' behavior: situational patterns of heavy drinking and self-efficacy, that is, beliefs about their ability to successfully maintain changes in their drinking (Dimeff & Marlatt, 1995). Two assessment instruments that are frequently used for these respective purposes are the Inventory of Drinking Situations (Annis et al., 1987) for patterns of drinking and the Situational Confidence Questionnaire (Annis & Graham, 1988). Both scales are based on relapse research conducted by Marlatt and colleagues (1985) that identifies the following common situations for relapse risk: unpleasant emotions, physical discomfort, pleasant emotions, testing personal control, urges or temptations to use, conflict with others, social pressure to use, and pleasant times with others.

Observational Methods

Observational methods are not used as frequently in the assessment and treatment of alcohol abuse as they are in clinical research, where observation in simulations, such as a simulated bar, may be used. The most common observational method relevant to practice is that of observing clients in role-play scenarios. Although practitioners can develop client-specific scenarios, there are several role-play tests that have been developed for this purpose. One such instrument is the Alcohol-Specific Role Play Test (Monti et al., 1993), a 10-situation role-play that is used to assess relapse risk in intrapersonal and interpersonal situations.

Physiological Measures
Many physiological measures of acute and chronic alcohol use exist; most involve testing blood or urine for specific biological markers (Anton, Litten, & Allen, 1995). One exception to this rule is the alcohol breath test, or breathalyzer, a test that measures the amount of alcohol on the breath. This test often is used in clinical as well as legal settings to determine if an individual is under the influence of alcohol, and is normally reported as a blood alcohol count or blood alcohol level. In addition, there are physiological markers that can detect damage due to chronic alcohol intake. There are laboratory tests for five biomarkers; gamma glutamyltransferase (GGT), macrocytic volume, carbonhydrate-deficient transferring, aspartate aminotransferase, and alanine aminotransferase. Gamma glutamyltransferase is most often used but can produce many false positives. A combination of biochemical measures is recommended (Allen, Sillanaukee, Strid, & Litten, 2003). Unlike the breathalyzer, which is often utilized by social workers and other nonmedical personnel, laboratory tests tend to be utilized by medical personnel or researchers.

Evidence-Based Approaches to Intervention

There are many evidenced-based approaches available for intervening with alcohol problems. However, it has often been the case that alcohol treatment agencies do not use treatment approaches that have research support; instead, many agencies have relied on approaches that either have not been effectively tested or have been shown to be less effective than other methods (Hester & Miller, 2003; Miller, Brown, et al., 1995; Miller & Hester, 1986).

Although most alcohol treatment agencies identify abstinence as the goal of treatment, research indicates that moderate drinking is a realistic goal for some problem drinkers (Connors, 1993). Generally, research indicates that stable, positive, and moderate drinking outcomes are more likely for low to moderate severity problem drinkers than for severely dependent alcoholics (Connors, 1993). There are several other variables that should also be considered in evaluating the goal of moderate drinking: (a) The person should be in good health, physically and mentally; (b) there should be no signs of cognitive impairment; (c) the person should have a stable social history with good social supports; and (d) the person should have a relatively short drinking history, at least less than 5 years (Westermeyer, n.d.). There is now online software available to evaluate and assist people in meeting moderation goals (Moderation Management, 2005).

Natural recovery, sometimes called spontaneous remission, is essentially the resolution of problematic drinking without formal treatment, either through abstinence or moderate drinking. There are some things that practitioners can learn from research on these populations. People who successfully quit on their own had spousal, family, and social support; used Alcoholics Anonymous; and had stable employment (Yalisove, 2004). Those who successfully moderated their use were less severely dependent, more highly educated, high in self-esteem, and in supportive relationships (Yalisove, 2004).

Among the most important trends in alcohol treatment research in the 1990s was an emphasis on matching clients to alcohol treatments, that is, recognizing that no one treatment approach works for everyone (Allen & Kadden, 1995; Institute of Medicine, 1990). Project MATCH was a large, multisite NIAAA-funded study to determine if matching clients with specific characteristics to specific interventions would produce better outcomes. Three treatment protocols were evaluated: cognitive-behavioral coping skills, motivational enhancement, and a 12-step-based intervention. Participants were randomly assigned one of these three conditions. Sixteen patient-treatment matches were evaluated, with researchers finding only one of these matches to be significant (NIAAA, 1997). The researchers concluded that participants receiving any of the interventions saw improvement, and treatment matching added little to the outcomes. However, because the study excluded all participants with a concurrent (past year) drug dependence diagnosis other than marijuana, the lack of matching findings could be due to having screened out those clients who would have responded differentially to the treatments (Smyth, 2004). McLellan et al. (NIAAA, 2000) looked at matching client problems, in addition to their alcohol use, that contributed to that use versus those who received standard alcohol treatment. Rates of abstinence were similar, yet those receiving enhanced treatment were working more, stayed in treatment longer, had fewer family difficulties, and were less likely to be arrested or be readmitted for treatment.

One of the most promising approaches to treatment may be combining psychosocial and pharmacological treatments. Project COMBINE, a NIAAA-sponsored clinical trial, will evaluate the effectiveness of combining behavioral (low and/or moderate intensity) treatments with medications (naltrexone or acamprosate) or a placebo (Bradley, 2001); findings may be reported in the near future. A recent meta-analysis of international studies indicated that the strongest treatment results occurred when naltrexone was combined with cognitive-behavioral treatments (compared to either treatment by itself), and that preliminary studies of acamprosate suggest the same finding (Bergland, 2005).

Individual Therapies

Most alcohol treatment settings provide some type of individual counseling. However, many place a greater emphasis on group and self-help approaches (Straussner, 1993). Brief intervention of alcohol problems is receiving increasing attention in the treatment literature, particularly for clients with low or moderate alcohol dependence; for this population it seems to be more effective than no treatment and as effective as more extensive treatment (Heather, 1995; Miller & Wilbourne, 2002). Brief treatment most often involves some assessment of clients' drinking, followed by the provision of personalized feedback about their drinking; this can include a physician simply giving someone advice to cut down on drinking as well as a clear message about the nature of sensible and problematic drinking (Babor, Ritson, & Hodgson, 1986). There is more evidence supporting brief intervention than any other type of alcohol treatment (Miller & Wilbourne, 2002).

Motivational interventions are a specialized type of brief intervention designed to enhance people's commitment to changing their drinking. The most well known of these approaches, motivational interviewing (Miller & Rollnick, 2002), synthesizes elements of several effective motivational strategies. The goal of motivational interviewing is to assist clients in recognizing they have problems with alcohol and to help them decide to change and move toward making desired changes in their lives. Miller and Rollnick identify five basic principles of motivational interviewing: (1) Express empathy, (2) develop discrepancy between individuals' perceptions of where they are and where they want to be, (3) avoid argumentation, (4) roll with resistance, and (5) support the client's sense of self-efficacy. Motivational interviewing utilizes many of the principles of empathic and nondirective communication in a systematic effort to facilitate change. Client resistance is managed through empathy, reflection, and paraphrasing instead of by challenging it directly. The practitioner attempts to engage the client in a collaborative, mutual exploration of his or her drinking using active listening skills to reinforce any information related to a drinking problem. Labels (e.g., alcoholic, problem drinker, having an alcohol problem) are de-emphasized and are not envisioned as necessary for change to occur.

Outcome research on motivational interventions indicates that they are quite effective; Hester and Miller (2003) ranked these strategies second in terms of cumulative evidence on their effectiveness. Results from Project MATCH, a nine-site national study funded by the NIAAA, indicated that four sessions of motivational enhancement therapy (Miller, Zweben, DiClemente, &

Rychtarik, 1992) were as effective as 12 sessions of the comparative treatments, coping skills training, and 12-step facilitation (Project MATCH Research Group, 1996).

Behavioral self-control training (BSCT) is a treatment method that can be used for either abstinence or moderation drinking goals and can be delivered in individual or group treatment formats (Hester, 2003). Behavioral self-control training involves setting limits on drinking, self-monitoring of drinking, utilizing moderation strategies such as drink refusal and drinking rate control skills, designing reward systems for goal achievement, analysis of the antecedents for overdrinking, and development of alternative coping skills to manage overdrinking trigger situations (Hester, 1995). Overall, BSCT has strong empirical support (Hester, 1995; Miller, Brown, et al., 1995); those times when it hasn't performed well have been because it was compared to brief interventions (Miller, Brown, et al., 1995). These findings suggest that BSCT should be provided after efforts with brief intervention have failed (Hester, 1995; Miller, Brown, et al., 1995); in addition, research indicates that moderation goals may be appropriate for some problem drinkers but are not recommended for severely dependent alcoholics (Hester, 1995).

Relapse prevention is a treatment approach that has been offered in individual, family, and group treatment formats, although it has been most consistently evaluated as part of group treatment (Dimeff & Marlatt, 1995). Therefore, it is discussed in the section on group therapies.

Pharmacological interventions primarily used for alcohol problems are interventions for alcohol withdrawal (detoxification) and treatment. Benzodiazepines such as diazepam and chlorodiazepoxide (Anton, 1994) are generally used for detoxification. Medications are not recommended for treatment of alcohol problems by themselves; however, they can provide important supplements to other treatment (Anton, 1994; Swift, 2003). The most well known drug used in alcoholism treatment is disulfiram (Antabuse), a medication that causes one to become ill if alcohol is ingested (Fuller, 1995). In addition to disulfiram, research on naltrexone and acamprosate suggests that when used as an adjunct to treatment they reduce cravings, which may prevent alcoholism relapse (Swift, 2003) and contribute to overall better treatment outcomes than psychosocial treatment alone (Berglund, 2005). Both medications have been approved for the treatment of alcoholism in the United States.

Group Therapies

Although many practitioners consider group therapy to be the treatment of choice for people with alcohol problems (Galanter, Castaneda, & Franco, 1991), the comparative effectiveness of group versus other treatment modalities has not been systematically examined (Cartwright, 1987). One study of problem drinkers found no difference between the two treatment modalities, although group therapy clients achieved their gains earlier in treatment than those in individual therapy (Duckert, Amundsen, & Johnsen, 1992). Another study compared individual and group guided self-change treatment, a motivationally based four-session BSCT, and found no differences in treatment outcome, treatment retention, or client satisfaction (Sobell, Sobell, Brown, Cleland, & Buchan, November 1995).

As was noted earlier, relapse prevention (RP) is often provided in a group. Its components include self-monitoring of drinking or drinking urges, identifying high-risk situations, assessment of current coping skills and resources and self-efficacy, developing coping strategies and a plan to manage high-risk situations, and developing and strengthening lifestyle balance with regard to shoulds and wants (Dimeff & Marlatt, 1995). Evaluation of the research on relapse prevention more recently suggests that RP may not be as effective as once believed (Miller & Wilbourne, 2002). Some research suggests that RP is most likely to benefit people with moderate to severe alcohol dependence (Dimeff & Marlatt, 1995) and alcoholics with differentiated (versus undifferentiated) drinking profiles, that is, drinking that varies over different types of situations (Annis & Davis, 1989).

Coping and social skills training (Monti, Abrams, Kadden, & Cooney, 2002) for treating alcohol problems has been most often delivered and investigated as a group intervention, although it has been adapted for individual treatment as well (Monti et al., 2002). This method usually includes interpersonal and mood management skills, particularly as they relate to alcohol use (Monti et al., 2002). Topics include coping with alcohol cravings and drinking-related thoughts, problem solving, managing anger, assertiveness, giving and receiving criticism, planning for emergencies, coping with a lapse, and managing negative thinking. Social skills training has empirical support; however, some coping skills training, such as relaxation and stress management training, has less support (Miller, Brown, et al., 1995; Miller & Wilbourne, 2002; Miller, Wilbourne, & Hettema, 2003).

No discussion of group treatment would be complete without self-help groups. The largest and most widely known group is Alcoholics Anonymous (AA), but there are others, including Rational Recovery (RR), Secular Organizations for Sobriety/Save Our Selves, Women for Sobriety, and Self-Management and Recovery Training (SMART; Horvath, 1996; McCrady & Delaney, 1995). There is some research on the type of individuals likely to affiliate with AA and RR. Specifically, AA affiliates are likely to have severe drinking histories and experience loss of control and anxiety over their drinking (Emrick, Tonigan, Montgomery, & Little, 1993). Rational Recovery affiliates often place a high value on rationality and a low value on spirituality (Galanter, Egelko, & Edwards, 1993).

Most alcohol treatment settings and treatment professionals refer clients to AA, yet there is little strong evidence supporting the effectiveness of AA as an intervention by itself (McCrady & Delaney, 1995). A review of studies examining AA's effectiveness as an adjunct to treatment indicated that AA attendance was associated with modest improvements in outcome (Emrick et al., 1993). There have been a very small number of studies looking at SMART recovery versus 12-step-oriented self-help. The results have shown differences in participants' locus of control (Li, Feifer, & Strohm, 2000). Similar clinical outcomes were found in another study (Brooks & Penn, 2003).

Marital and Family Therapies

Marital and family treatment (MFT) of alcohol problems, particularly behavioral MFT, has relatively strong empirical support for its effectiveness (Miller et al., 2003; O'Farrell, 1995). Clients who accept and complete MFT are most likely to (a) be employed full-time, if able and wishing to work; (b) have a minimum of a high school education; (c) have serious alcohol problems with relatively long duration; (d) be older; (e) come into treatment after a crisis, usually one that threatens the marriage; and (f) live with a spouse, or be willing to reconcile during treatment (O'Farrell & Fals-Stewart, 2003a). There are four factors that might contraindicate MFT: (1) The client or the significant other presents with current psychosis; (2) there is immediate risk of severe family violence; (3) a court order requires no contact, until such order has been rescinded or modified by the court; (4) the client and other family members are concurrently misusing substances (O'Farrell & Fals-Stewart, 2003a).

Marital and family treatment can be divided into two major categories. The first set of interventions, for the couple, is designed to work with spouses of treatment-resistant alcoholics. The second set is interventions used when the alcoholic is in treatment.

Marital and Family Treatment Interventions
for Treatment-Resistant Alcoholics

One intervention targeting spouses of treatment-resistant alcoholics is unilateral family therapy (UFT), an intensive, 4- to 6-month approach that works with spouses of alcoholics to enhance their coping skills and family functioning, as well as how to encourage problem drinkers' sobriety or acceptance of treatment

(Barber & Gilbertson, 1996; Fals-Stewart, O'Farrell, & Birchler, 2003; Thomas, 1994). Preliminary trials evaluating UFT have supported its effectiveness in decreasing spouses' distress, increasing marital satisfaction, and facilitating alcoholics' entry into treatment (O'Farrell, 1995; Thomas, Santa, Bronson, & Oyserman, 1987). However, further study is needed to demonstrate its effectiveness (O'Farrell & Fals-Stewart, 2003a).

Unilateral family therapy can involve several months of treatment. In an effort to develop a brief unilateral intervention, Barber and Crisp (1995) developed the pressures to change approach, a five- or six-session treatment method that teaches the spouse or partner behavioral strategies to encourage the alcohol abuser to either reduce drinking or seek treatment. When compared to both a control group and to Alanon, partners receiving the pressures to change approach were more likely to have a spouse who reduced drinking and entered treatment (Barber & Gilbertson, 1996).

Another form of unilateral intervention is the community reinforcement approach and family training (CRAFT), a strategy for the significant other or family members to motivate an uncooperative alcoholic to alter his or her drinking or engage in treatment. The principal components of CRAFT are (a) motivational strategies, (b) functional analysis of the alcohol abuser's drinking behavior, (c) communications training, (d) using small rewards to reinforce recovery-oriented behavior, (e) discouraging using behavior, (f) self-reinforcement training for the nonusing individual, (g) domestic safety, and (h) treatment suggestions. Although more independent research is needed, preliminary research suggests that CRAFT may be effective (Smith & Meyers, 2004).

A relational intervention sequence for engagement (ARISE; Fals-Stewart et al., 2003; Landau et al., 2004) is a three-step intervention to help motivate the resistant problem drinker to begin treatment. Step 1, usually a telephone call from a concerned other asking for help, focuses on gathering background information, supporting the concerned other, and inviting the problem drinker's social network and the problem drinker to a meeting where it is hoped that the problem drinker will accept help. If the problem drinker refuses to attend the meeting or refuses treatment, the ARISE clinician moves to other steps that involve implementing specific consequences to influence the problem drinker to seek help. Preliminary treatment outcomes on ARISE are promising and warrant further study (Landau et al., 2004).

The Johnson Institute intervention model (JII; Johnson, 1973) involves educating and preparing family members to confront the alcohol abuser and to implement specific consequences to push the person into treatment. This model is generally not supported by research; it results in high dropout rates (Liepman, Nirenberg, & Begin, 1989; O'Farrell & Fals-Stewart, 2003a) and low treatment engagement rates (O'Farrell & Fals-Stewart, 2003a). Only one retrospective study found that JII referrals were more likely to complete treatment than voluntary clients (Loneck, Garrett, & Banks, 1996b).

Self-help groups for family members of alcoholics also exist, specifically Alanon (for adult family members), Alateen and Alatot (for children), and ACOA—Adult Children of Alcoholics, for adults who grew up in an alcoholic family (McCrady & Delaney, 1995). Of these groups, only Alanon has received any study, and that has been minimal (O'Farrell, 1995). In two controlled studies of Alanon (O'Farrell & Fals-Stewart, 2003b), participants had fewer personal problems than control participants. However, as was noted earlier, Alanon was not as effective in helping spouses facilitate their partner's entry into treatment when compared to the pressures to change approach. Al-Anon facilitation therapy is a therapist-driven, manualized intervention that encourages involvement with the 12-step program (O'Farrell & Fals-Stewart, 2003b). Two controlled studies (O'Farrell & Fals-Stewart, 2003b) reported reductions in spousal emotional stress and increases in coping behavior and reductions in spousal emotional stress and family conflict as well as enhancements in family cohesion and relationship happiness for spouses and parents. Finally, there also have been several uncontrolled, correlational studies reporting positive outcomes for wives who participated in Alanon (O'Farrell, 1995).

Marital and Family Treatment Interventions
When the Alcoholic Is in Treatment

Alcohol treatment agencies often treat couples by enrolling the spouse and alcoholic in separate, concurrent treatment; however, there are no controlled studies evaluating the effectiveness of this treatment approach (O'Farrell, 1995). In contrast, there is quite a bit of research on the effectiveness of conjoint MFT when the alcoholic is enrolled in treatment (O'Farrell, 1995). As noted earlier, most of the effective MFT interventions are behavioral approaches. However, there also is some empirical support for nonbehavioral couples' group treatment compared to treating the alcoholic only (O'Farrell & Fals-Stewart, 2003b).

Behavioral couples therapy (BCT), a form of behavioral martial and family therapy (BMFT), can be conducted with one couple or with a group of couples; it generally includes communication skills training, problem-solving training, and teaching constructive strategies for changing a spouse's behavior, as well as a focus on drinking and alcohol-related interaction (O'Farrell, 1995). Behavioral couples therapy can also include disulfiram or sobriety contracts. Here the alcoholic is positively reinforced in a statement by his or her partner for taking the medication, in the case of disulfiram, or for not drinking that day, in the case of the sobriety contract (O'Farrell & Fals-Stewart, 2003b). A review of treatment studies on BMFT/BCT indicated that they are more effective in treating alcoholics than individual-based interventions (O'Farrell & Fals-Stewart, 2003a).

Community Interventions

Community interventions can range from interventions that utilize environmental components in the treatment of individuals to interventions that target population subgroups or whole communities for intervention. Many of the communitywide interventions for alcohol problems focus on preventing the development of alcohol problems (primary prevention) as opposed to intervention with people with early-stage or more serious alcohol problems (NIAAA, 1994).

The community reinforcement approach (CRA; Meyers & Smith, 1995; Smith & Meyers, 1995) is a broad-spectrum behavioral treatment method that utilizes environmental reinforcers (social, recreational, vocational, familial) to intervene in alcohol and other drug problems. Treatment strategies are chosen from a wide array of options, including coping skills training, job training, social clubs, marital therapy, relapse prevention, disulfiram, and social and recreational counseling, depending on the assessment of the antecedents and consequences of an individual's drinking. In a comprehensive review of alcohol treatment research, CRA was rated as sixth (among 46 different modalities) in the amount of cumulative evidence that supports its effectiveness (Miller & Wilbourne, 2002).

A different type of community intervention applies brief interventions in community settings such as hospitals and primary health care settings. These interventions may be conducted as part of health screening programs or regular physical exams or in the context of a medical hospitalization (Heather, 1995; Zweban, Rose, Stout, & Zywiak, 2003). As with brief intervention in general, these community-based brief treatment approaches have strong research support (Heather, 1995). Brief interventions have also been utilized successfully by mailing information about alcohol effects and strategies for low-risk drinking to individuals who responded to a newspaper advertisement (Sobell et al., 2002).

Intervention with offenders arrested for driving under the influence (DUI) is another area for community intervention. A meta-analysis of DUI remediation programs concluded that such programs are generally successful in preventing recidivism (Wells-Parker, Bangert-Drowns, McMillen, & Williams, 1995). The best combination of interventions was identified as education, psychotherapy, and probation contact (Wells-Parker et al.,

1995). An approach to intervening with multiple DUI offenders, the probation alcohol treatment approach, integrates alcoholism treatment and probation into a single intervention. A 10-year follow-up study found that DUI offenders who successfully completed this program were significantly less likely to be rearrested for a drinking and driving offense; those in the program also committed fewer other crimes than a no-treatment control group (Nochajski, Bell, & Augustino, 1995).

Summary

Social workers have at their disposal a range of evidence-based interventions for providing interventions to persons with alcohol problems. In the United States there continues to be a sizable gap between evidence-based alcohol treatment interventions and treatment offered in clinical practice. Social workers are well positioned to provide leadership to ensure that clients have access to interventions with demonstrated effectiveness, both in alcohol treatment settings and in other service settings.

Study Questions

1. What are the different ways that problems with alcohol can manifest themselves?

2. What is the difference between a screening tool and a diagnostic tool? Identify an example of each and the types of client situations where you might use each.

3. Identify the different methods used to assess an alcohol problem.

4. You've been asked to help the staff of a mental health clinic integrate some alcohol screening and/or treatment strategies into their clinic. What do you think should be used, and why?

5. What are the questions that make up the CAGE?

6. The CAGE is even more sensitive if questions about quantity and frequency are added to it. What questions might you ask that would elicit information from clients about quantity and frequency of alcohol use? When would be the most effective point in the assessment process to ask these questions? Why?

7. What types of alcohol treatments discussed in this chapter are available in your community? What types are missing?

What strategies could be used at a regional level to encourage the development of those missing services?

References

Allen, J. P., & Columbus, M. (Eds.). (2003). *Assessing alcohol problems: A guide for clinicians and researchers* (2nd ed., NIAAA, NIH Publication No. 03-3745). Bethesda, MD: U.S. Department of Health and Human Services.

Allen, J. P., & Kadden, R. M. (1995). Matching clients to alcohol treatments. In R. K. Hester & W. R. Miller (Eds.), *Handbook of alcoholism treatment approaches* (2nd ed., pp. 170–182). Boston: Allyn & Bacon.

Allen, J. P., Sillanaukee, P., Strid, N., & Litten, R. Z. (2003). Biomarkers of heavy drinking. In J. P. Allen & M. Columbus (Eds.), *Assessing alcohol problems: A guide for clinicians and researchers* (2nd ed., pp. 37–54, NIAAA Treatment Handbook, NIH Publication No. 03-7003). Bethesda, MD: U.S. Department of Health and Human Services.

American Psychiatric Association. (2000). *Diagnostic and statistical manual of mental disorders* (4th ed., text rev.). Washington, DC: Author.

Annis, H. M., & Davis, C. S. (1989). Relapse prevention. In R. K. Hester & W. R. Miller (Eds.), *Handbook of alcoholism treatment approaches* (pp. 278–291). New York: Pergamon Press.

Annis, H. M., & Graham, J. M. (1988). *Situational Confidence Questionnaire (SCQ-39): User's guide*. Toronto, Ontario, Canada: Addiction Research Foundation.

Annis, H. M., Graham, J. M., & Davis, C. S. (1987). *Inventory of Drinking Situations (IDS): User's guide*. Toronto, Ontario, Canada: Addiction Research Foundation.

Anton, R. F. (1994). Medications for treating alcoholism. *Alcohol Health and Research World, 18,* 265–271.

Anton, R. F., Litten, R. Z., & Allen, J. P. (1995). Biological assessment of alcohol consumption. In J. P. Allen & M. Columbus (Eds.), *Assessing alcohol problems: A guide for clinicians and researchers* (NIAAA Treatment Handbook, Series 4, NIH Publication No. 95-3745, pp. 31–39). Bethesda, MD: U.S. Department of Health and Human Services.

Barber, J. G., & Crisp, B. R. (1995). The pressures to change approach to working with the partners of heavy drinkers. *Addiction, 90,* 269–276.

Barber, J. G., & Gilbertson, R. (1996). An experimental study of brief unilateral intervention for the partners of heavy drinkers. *Research on Social Work Practice, 6,* 325–336.

Babor, T. F., Ritson, E. B., & Hodgson, R. J. (1986). Alcohol-related problems in the primary health care setting: A review of early intervention strategies. *British Journal of Addiction, 81,* 23–46.

Berglund, M. (2005). A better widget? Three lessons for improving addiction treatment from a meta-analytical study. *Addiction, 100,* 742–750.

Blow, F. C., & Barry, K. L. (2003, June). *Use and misuse of alcohol among older women.* Retrieved July 11, 2005, from http://pubs.niaaa.nih.gov/publications/arh26-4/308-315.htm.

Bradley, A. (2001, March 8). NIAAA launches COMBINE clinical trial (National Institute on Alcohol Abuse and Alcoholism). Retrieved July 14, 2005, from http://www.niaaa.nih.gov/press/2001/combine3-01.htm.

Brooks, A. J., & Penn, P. E. (2003). Comparing treatments for dual diagnosis: Twelve step and self-management and recovery training. *American Journal of Drug and Alcohol Abuse, 29,* 359–383.

Cartwright, A. (1987). Group work with substance abusers: Basic issues and future research. *British Journal of Addiction, 82,* 951–953.

Centers for Disease Control and Prevention. (2004). *Health, United States, 2004, with chartbook on trends in the health of Americans* (DHHS Publication No. 2004-1232). Hyattsville, MD: U.S. Department of Health and Human Services, Centers for Disease Control and Prevention. Retrieved July 25, 2005, from http://www .cdc.gov/nchs/data/hus/hus04trend.pdf# pref.

Centers for Disease Control and Prevention. (2005). *Impaired driving.* Retrieved July 25, 2005, from http://www.cdc.gov /ncipc/factsheets/drving.htm.

Connors, G. J. (1993). Drinking moderation training as a contemporary therapeutic approach. In G. J. Connors (Ed.), *Innovations in alcoholism treatment* (pp. 117–134). Binghamton, NY: Haworth Press.

Connors, G. J. (1995). Screening for alcohol problems. In J. P. Allen & M. Columbus (Eds.), *Assessing alcohol problems: A guide for clinicians and researchers* (NIAAA Treatment Handbook, Series 4, NIH Publication No. 95-3745, pp. 17–29). Bethesda, MD: U.S. Department of Health and Human Services.

Connors, G. J., & Maisto, S. A. (1988). The Alcohol Beliefs Scale. In M. Hersen & A. S. Bellack (Eds.), *Dictionary of behavioral assessment techniques* (pp. 24–26). New York: Pergamon Press.

Dimeff, L. A., & Marlatt, G. A. (1995). Relapse prevention. In R. K. Hester & W. R. Miller (Eds.), *Handbook of alcoholism treatment approaches* (2nd ed., pp. 176–194). Boston: Allyn & Bacon.

Donovan, D. (1995). Assessments to aid in the treatment Planning process. In J. P. Allen, & M. Columbus (Eds.), *Assessing alcohol problems: A guide for clinicians and researchers* (NIAAA Treatment Handbook, Series 4, NIH Publication No. 95-3745). Bethesda, MD: U.S. Department of Health and Human Services.

Duckert, E., Amundsen, A., & Johnsen, J. (1992). What happens to drinking after therapeutic intervention? *British Journal of Addiction, 87,* 1457–1467.

Emrick, C. D., Tonigan, S., Montgomery, H., & Little, L. (1993). Alcoholics Anonymous: What is currently known. In B. S. McCrady & W. R. Miller (Eds.), *Research on Alcoholics Anonymous: Opportunities and alternatives* (pp. 41–79). New Brunswick, NJ: Alcohol Research Documentation, Inc., Rutgers University.

Fals-Stewart, W., O'Farrell, J., & Birchler, G. R. (2003). Family therapy techniques. In F. Rotgers, J. Morgenstern, & S. T. Walters (Eds.), *Treating substance abuse problems: Theory and technique* (2nd ed., pp. 140–165). New York: Guilford Press.

Fuller, R. K. (1995). Antidipsotropic medications. In R. K. Hester & W. R. Miller (Eds.), *Handbook of alcoholism treatment approaches* (2nd ed., pp. 123–133). Boston: Allyn & Bacon.

Galanter, M., Castaneda, R., & Franco, H. (1991). Group therapy and self-help groups. In R. J. Frances & S. I. Miller (Eds.), *Clinical textbook of addictive disorders* (pp. 431–451). New York: Guilford Press.

Galanter, M., Egelko, S., & Edwards, H. (1993). Rational Recovery: Alternative to AA for addiction. *American Journal of Drug and Alcohol Abuse, 19,* 499–510.

Grant, B. F., Dawson, D. A., Stinson, F. S., Chou, S. P., Dufour, M. C., & Pickering, R. P. (2004). The 12-month prevalence and trends in *DSM-IV* alcohol abuse and dependence: United States, 1991–1992 and 2001–2002. *Drug and Alcohol Dependence, 74,* 223–234.

Heather, N. (1993). Application of harm-reduction principles to the treatment of alcohol problems. In N. Heather, A. Wodak, E. Nadelmann, & P. O'Hare (Eds.), *Psychoactive drugs and harm reduction: From faith to science* (pp. 168–183). London: Whurr.

Heather, N. (1995). Brief intervention strategies. In R. K. Hester & W. R. Miller (Eds.), *Handbook of alcoholism treatment approaches* (2nd ed., pp. 105–122). Boston: Allyn & Bacon.

Heather, N., Gold, R., & Rollnick, S. (1991). *Readiness to Change Questionnaire: User's manual* (Technical Report 15). Kensington, Australia: National Drug and Alcohol Research Center, University of New South Wales.

Heather, N., Tebbutt, J. S., Mattick, R. P., & Zamir, R. (1993). Development of a scale for measuring impaired control over alcohol consumption: A preliminary report. *Journal of Studies on Alcohol, 54,* 700–709.

Hester, R. K. (1995). Behavioral self-control training. In R. K. Hester & W. R. Miller (Eds.), *Handbook of alcoholism treatment approaches* (2nd. ed., pp. 148–159). Boston: Allyn & Bacon.

Hester, R. K. (2003). Behavioral self-control training. In R. K. Hester & W. R. Miller (Eds.), *Handbook of alcoholism treatment approaches: Effective alternatives* (3rd ed., pp. 152–164). Boston: Allyn & Bacon.

Hester, R. K., & Miller, W. R. (Eds.). (2003). *Handbook of alcoholism treatment approaches: Effective alternatives* (3rd ed.). Boston: Allyn & Bacon.

Horn, J. L., Skinner, H. A., Wanberg, K., & Foster, F. M. (1984). *Alcohol Dependence Scale (ADS)*. Toronto, Ontario, Canada: Addiction Research Foundation.

Horvath, A. T. (1996, July). Is SMART as effective as AA? *SMART Recovery: News and Views,* 1–2.

Institute of Medicine. (1990). *Broadening the base of treatment for alcohol problems*. Washington, DC: National Academy Press.

Johnson, V. A. (1973). *I'll quit tomorrow*. New York: Harper & Row.

Landau, J., Stanton, M. D., Brinkman-Sull, D., Ikle, D., McCormick, D., Garrett, J., et al. (2004). Outcomes with the ARISE approach to engaging reluctant drug- and alcohol-dependent individuals in treatment. *American Journal of Drug and Alcohol Abuse, 30,* 711–748.

Li, E. C., Feifer, C., & Strohm, M. (2000). A pilot study: Locus of control and spiritual beliefs in Alcoholics Anonymous and SMART Recovery members. *Addictive Behaviors, 25*(4), 633–640.

Liepman, M. R., Nirenberg, T. D., & Begin, A. M. (1989). Evaluation of a program designed to help family and significant others to motivate resistant alcoholics into recovery. *American Journal of Drug and Alcohol Abuse, 15,* 209–221.

Loneck, B., Garrett, J. A., & Banks, S. M. (1996b). The Johnson intervention and relapse during outpatient treatment. *American Journal of Drug and Alcohol Abuse, 22,* 363–375.

Marlatt, G. A. (1985). Situational determinants of relapse and skill-training interventions. In G. A. Marlatt & J. R. Gordon (Eds.), *Relapse prevention: Maintenance strategies in the treatment of addictive behaviors* (pp. 71–127). New York: Guilford Press.

Mayfield, D., McLeod, G., & Hall, P. (1974). The CAGE questionnaire: Validation of a new alcoholism screening instrument. *American Journal of Psychiatry, 131,* 1121–1123.

McCrady, B. S., & Delaney, S. I. (1995). Self-help groups. In R. K. Hester & W. R. Miller (Eds.), *Handbook of alcoholism treatment approaches* (2nd ed., pp. 160–175). Boston: Allyn & Bacon.

McCrady, B. S., Horvath, A. T., & Delaney, S. I. (2003). Self-help groups. In R. K. Hester & W. R. Miller (Eds.), *Handbook of alcoholism treatment approaches* (3rd ed., pp. 165–187). Boston: Allyn & Bacon.

McLellan, A. T., Carise, D., Coyne, T. H., & Jackson, T. R. (1992). *Addiction Severity Index* (5th ed.). Retrieved August 1, 2005, from http://www.sounddatasource.org/downloads.html.

McLellan, A. T., Kushner, H., Metzger, D., Peters, R., Smith, I., Grissom, G., et al. (1992). The 5th ed. of the Addiction Severity Index: Historical critique and normative data. *Journal of Substance Abuse, 9,* 199–213.

Meyers, R. J., & Smith, J. E. (1995). *Clinical guide to alcohol treatment: The community reinforcement approach*. New York: Guilford Press.

Miller, W. R., Brown, J. M., Simpson, T. L., Handmaker, N. S., Bien, T. H., Luckie, L. F., et al. (1995). What works? A methodological analysis of the alcohol treatment outcome literature. In R. K. Hester & W. R. Miller (Eds.), *Handbook of alcoholism treatment approaches* (2nd. ed., pp. 12–44). Boston: Allyn & Bacon.

Miller, W. R., & Hester, R. K. (1986). The effectiveness of alcoholism treatment: What research reveals. In W. R. Miller & N. Heather (Eds.), *Treating addictive behaviors: Processes of change* (pp. 121–174). New York: Plenum Press.

Miller, W. R., & Marlatt, G. A. (1984). *Manual for the Comprehensive Drinker Profile*. Odessa, FL: Psychological Assessment Resources.

Miller, W. R., & Rollnick, S. (2002). *Motivational interviewing: Preparing people to change addictive behavior* (2nd ed.). New York: Guilford Press.

Miller, W. R., & Tonigan, J. S. (1994). *Assessing drinker's motivation for change: The Stages of Change Readiness and Treatment Eagerness Scale (SOCRATES).* Unpublished manuscript, Center on Alcoholism, Substance Abuse, and Addictions, University of New Mexico, Albuquerque.

Miller, W. R., Tonigan, J. S., & Longabaugh, R. (1995). *The Drinker Inventory of Consequences (DrInC): An instrument for assessing adverse consequences of alcohol abuse—Test manual* (NIAAA Project MATCH Monograph Series, Vol. 4., NIH Publication No. 95-3911). Washington, DC: U.S. Government Printing Office.

Miller, W. R., Westerberg, V. S., & Waldron, H. B. (1995). Evaluating alcohol problems in adults and adolescents. In R. K. Hester & W. R. Miller (Eds.), *Handbook of alcoholism treatment approaches* (2nd ed., pp. 61–88). Boston: Allyn & Bacon.

Miller, W. R., & Wilbourne, P. L. (2002). Mesa Grande: A methodological analysis of clinical trials of treatments for alcohol use disorders. *Addiction, 97,* 265–277.

Miller, W. R., Wilbourne, P. L., & Hettema, J. E. (2003). What works? A summary of alcohol treatment outcome research. In R. K. Hester & W. R. Miller (Eds.), *Handbook of alcoholism treatment approaches: Effective alternatives* (3rd ed., pp. 13–63). Boston: Allyn & Bacon.

Miller, W. R., Zweben, A., DiClemente, C. C., & Rychtarik, R. G. (Eds.). (1992). *Motivational enhancement therapy manual: A clinical research guide for therapists treating individuals with alcohol abuse and dependence* (NIAAA Project MATCH Monograph Series, Vol. 2, DHHS Publication No., ADM, 92-1894). Washington, DC: U.S. Government Printing Office.

Moderation Management. (2005, August). *Suggested software and interactive websites.* Retrieved August 14, 2005, from http://www.moderation.org/software/MMSoftware.shtml.

Monti, P. M., Abrams, D. A., Kadden, R. M., & Cooney, N. L. (2002). *Treating alcohol dependence: A coping skills guide* (2nd ed.). New York: Guilford Press.

Monti, P. M., Rohsenow, D. J., Abrams, D. B., Zwick, W. R., Binkoff, J. A., Munroe, S. M., et al. (1993). Development of a behavior analytically derived alcohol-specific role-play assessment instrument. *Journal of Studies on Alcohol, 54,* 710–721.

Moos, R. H., Finney, J. W., & Cronkite, R. C. (1990). *Alcoholism treatment context, process and outcome.* New York: Oxford University Press.

Moyer, A., & Finney, J. W. (2004–2005). Brief interventions for alcohol problems: Factors that facilitate intervention. *Alcohol Research and Health: Screening and Brief Intervention Part I—An Overview, 28*(1), 44–55.

National Association of Social Workers. (2001). PRN datagram: Substance abuse treatment activities. *PRN 1*(4). Retrieved August 27, 2005, from http://www.naswdc.org/naswprn/surveyOne/substance.pdf.

National Institute on Alcohol Abuse and Alcoholism. (1992, April). *Moderate drinking: Alcohol alert* (DHHS Publication No. 16). Rockville, MD: Alcohol, Drug Abuse, and Mental Health Administration.

National Institute on Alcohol Abuse and Alcoholism. (1994). *Eighth special report to the U.S. Congress on alcohol and health* (NIH Publication No. 94-3699). Alexandria, VA: U.S. Department of Health and Human Services.

National Institute on Alcohol Abuse and Alcoholism. (1997, April). *Patient-treatment matching.* Retrieved July 11, 2005, from http://www.niaaa.nih.gov/publications/aa36.htm.

National Institute on Alcohol Abuse and Alcoholism. (1999). *Identification and care of fetal alcohol-exposed children: A guide for primary-care providers* (NIH Publication No. 99-4369). Rockville, MD: National Institute on Alcohol Abuse and Alcoholism (Office of Research on Minority Health) and National Institutes of Health.

National Institute on Alcohol Abuse and Alcoholism. (2000). *Tenth special report to the U.S. Congress on alcohol and health.* Alexandria, VA: U.S. Department of Health and Human Services.

National Institute on Alcohol Abuse and Alcoholism. (2002). Screening for alcohol problems: An update. *Alcohol Alert*

(DHHS Publication No. 56). Rockville, MD: Alcohol, Drug Abuse, and Mental Health Administration.

National Institute on Alcohol Abuse and Alcoholism. (2005). *Helping patients who drink too much: A clinician's guide.* Retrieved July 5, 2005, from http://www.niaaa.nih .gov/publications/Practitioner/guide.pdf.

Nochajski, T. H., Bell, A. B., & Augustino, D. K. (1995, August). *Impact of treatment on DWI offenders: A 10-year follow-up.* Retrieved July 7, 2005, from http://druglibrary.org /schaffer/Misc/driving/s28p5.htm.

O'Farrell, T. J. (1995). Marital and family therapy. In R. K. Hester & W. R. Miller (Eds.), *Handbook of alcoholism treatment approaches* (2nd ed., pp. 195–220). Boston: Allyn & Bacon.

O'Farrell, T. J., & Fals-Stewart, W. (2003a). Marital and family therapy. In R. K. Hester & W. R. Miller (Eds.), *Handbook of alcoholism treatment approaches* (3rd ed., pp. 188–212). Boston: Allyn & Bacon.

O'Farrell, T. J., & Fals-Stewart, W. (2003b). Alcohol abuse. *Journal of Marital and Family Therapy, 29*(1), 121–146.

Prochaska, J. O., & DiClemente, C. C. (1984). *The transtheoretical approach.* Homewood, IL: Dorsey Press.

Prochaska, J. O., DiClemente, C. C., & Norcross, J. C. (1992). In search of how people change: Applications to addictive behaviors. *American Psychologist, 47*(9), 1102–1114.

Project MATCH Research Group. (1996). Matching alcoholism treatments to client heterogeneity: Project MATCH posttreatment drinking outcomes. *Journal of Studies on Alcohol, 58,* 7–29.

Robins, L. N., Helzer, J. E., Croughan, J., & Ratcliff, K. S. (1981). National Institute of Mental Health Diagnostic Interview Schedule. *Archives of General Psychiatry, 38,* 381–389.

Rohsenow, D. J. (1983). Drinking habits and expectancies about alcohol's effects for self versus others. *Journal of Consulting and Clinical Psychiatry, 55,* 411–417.

Room, R. (1990). Measuring alcohol consumption in the United States: Methods and rationales. In L. T. Kozlowski, H. M. Annis, H. D. Cappell, F. B. Glaser, M. S.

Goodstadt, Y. Israel, et al. (Eds.), *Research advances in alcohol and drug problems* (Vol. 10, pp. 39–80). New York: Plenum Press.

Russell, M., Czarnecki, D. M., Cowan, R., McPherson, E., & Mudar, P. (1991). Measures of maternal alcohol use as predictors of development in early childhood. *Alcoholism: Clinical and Experimental Research, 15,* 991–1000.

Saunders, J. B., Aasland, O. G., Babor, T. F., de la Fuente, J. R., & Grant, M. (1993). Development of the Alcohol Use Disorders Screening Test (AUDIT): Pt. II. WHO collaborative project on early detection of persons with harmful alcohol consumption. *Addiction, 88,* 791–804.

Selzer, M. L. (1971). The Michigan Alcoholism Screening Test: The quest for a new diagnostic instrument. *American Journal of Psychiatry, 127,* 1653–1658.

Skinner, H. A., & Horn, J. L. (1984). *Alcohol Dependence Scale: User's guide.* Toronto, Ontario, Canada: Addiction Research Foundation.

Smith, J. E., & Meyers, R. J. (1995). The community reinforcement approach. In R. K. Hester & W. R. Miller (Eds.), *Handbook of alcoholism treatment approaches* (2nd ed., pp. 251–266). Boston: Allyn & Bacon.

Smith, J. E., & Meyers, R. J. (2004). *Motivating substance abusers to enter treatment: Working with the family.* New York: Guilford Press.

Smyth, N. J. (1995). Substance abuse: Direct practice. In R. L. Edwards, J. G. Hopps, L. D. Bernard, D. D. DiNitto, P. L. Ewalt, M. Frumkin, et al. (Eds.), *Encyclopedia of social work* (19th ed., pp. 2328–2337). Washington, DC: National Association of Social Workers.

Smyth, N. J. (2004, April). *Research 101: Making sense out of research.* Presentation at the 27th annual Training Conference for ATOD Treatment and Prevention Specialists, Atlantic City, NJ.

Sobell, L. C., & Sobell, M. B. (1995a). *Alcohol Timeline Followback (TLFB): User's manual.* Toronto, Ontario, Canada: Addiction Research Foundation.

Sobell, L. C., & Sobell, M. B. (1995b). Alcohol consumption measures. In J. P. Allen & M. Columbus (Eds.), *Assessing alcohol problems: A guide for clinicians and researchers* (NIAAA

NIH Publication No. 03-3745, 2nd ed., pp. 75–101). Bethesda, MD: U.S. Department of Health and Human Services.

Sobell, L. C., & Sobell, M. B. (1995c). *Timeline followback computer software*. Toronto, Ontario, Canada: Addiction Research Foundation.

Sobell, L .C., & Sobell, M. B. (2003). Alcohol consumption measures. In J. P. Allen & M. Columbus (Eds.), *Assessing alcohol problems: A guide for clinicians and researchers* (2nd ed., NIH Publication No. 03-3745). Bethesda, MD: U.S. Department of Health and Human Services, National Institute on Alcohol Abuse and Alcoholism.

Sobell, L. C., Sobell, M. B., Brown, J. C., Cleland, P. A., & Buchan, G. (1995, November). *A randomized trial comparing group versus individual guided self-change treatment for alcohol and drug abusers*. Poster presented at the 29th annual meeting of the Association for Advancement of Behavior Therapy, Washington, DC.

Sobell, L. C., Sobell, M. B., Leo, G. I., Agrawal, S., Johnson-Young, L., & Cunningham, J. (2002). Promoting self-change with alcohol abusers: A community-level mail intervention based on natural recovery studies. *Alcoholism Clinical and Experimental Research, 26*(6), 936–948.

Straussner, S. L. (1993). Assessment and treatment of clients with alcohol and other drug problems: An overview. In S. L. Straussner (Ed.), *Clinical work with substance-abusing clients* (pp. 3–30). New York: Guilford Press.

Substance Abuse and Mental Health Services Administration. (1995). *National household survey on drug abuse: Main findings 1993*. Rockville, MD: U.S. Department of Health and Human Services.

Swift, R. M. (2003). Medications. In R. K. Hester & W. R. Miller (Eds.), *Handbook of alcoholism treatment approaches* (3rd ed., pp. 259–281). Boston: Allyn & Bacon.

Thomas, E. J. (1994). Appendix B: The unilateral treatment program for alcohol abuse—Background, selected procedures, and case applications. In J. Rothman & E. J. Thomas (Eds.), *Intervention research, design and development for human service* (pp. 427–447). New York: Haworth Press.

Thomas, E. J., Santa, C. A., Bronson, D., & Oyserman, D. (1987). Unilateral family therapy with spouses of alcoholics. *Journal of Social Service Research, 10,* 145–162.

Wells-Parker, E., Bangert-Drowns, R., McMillen, R., & Williams, M. (1995). Final results from a meta-analysis of remedial interventions with drink/drive offenders. *Addiction, 90,* 907–926.

Westermeyer, R. W. (n.d.). *Harm reduction and moderation as an alternative to heavy drinking*. Retrieved July 11, 2005, from http://www .habitsmart.com/cntrldnk.html.

White, H. R., & Labouvie, E. W. (1989). Toward a multisource approach. In C. E. Stout, J. L. Levitt, & D. H. Ruben (Eds.), *Handbook for assessing and treating addictive disorders* (pp. 83–96). New York: Greenwood.

Yalisove, D. (2004). *Introduction to alcohol research: Implications for treatment, prevention, and policy*. Boston: Allyn & Bacon.

Zweben, A., Rose, S. J., Stout, R. L., & Zywiak, W. H. (2003). Case monitoring and motivational style brief interventions. In R. K. Hester & W. R. Miller (Eds.), *Handbook of alcoholism treatment approaches: Effective approaches* (3rd ed., pp. 113–130). Boston: Allyn & Bacon.

Cannabis-Related Disorders

Melissa Radey and Laura Hopson

9

Chapter

Learning Objectives

After reading this chapter, the reader will be able to:

- Recognize the different forms of cannabis and signs of misuse.
- Identify the populations most affected by cannabis disorders.
- Identify evidence-based approaches to treating cannabis disorders.
- Understand the evidence-based approaches to assessment of cannabis disorders.

Overview of the Problem

Prevalence and Incidence

Cannabis has been used for centuries and its prevalence has increased and decreased in popularity over time. Use was at its height in the late 1970s and then steadily declined until 1995 (McDowell & Spitz, 1999). According to the 2002 National Household Survey on Drug Abuse, marijuana, a form of cannabis, is the most commonly used illicit drug, with about 14.6 million individuals who reportedly used marijuana in the past month prior to being surveyed. Of current illicit drug users, 75% reported using marijuana. Fifty-four percent of illicit drug users reported using only marijuana, 21% used marijuana in combination with other drugs, and 25% reported using an illicit drug other than marijuana. Thus, the majority of illicit drug users report using marijuana by itself or in conjunction with other drugs. Of the 6.8 million Americans diagnosed with dependence or abuse of illicit drugs in 2003, 4.2 million (61%) were classified as being dependent on or abusing marijuana (Substance Abuse and Mental Health Services Administration [SAMHSA], 2003).

In terms of lifetime prevalence, approximately 41% of the population age 12 years and older reported using marijuana during their lifetime (SAMHSA, 2004). In 2001, 2.6 million individuals started marijuana use, well above the 1.6 million new users in 1990. In 2002, approximately 54% of adults reported that they had used marijuana in their lifetime. Marijuana is also prevalent among adolescents. Twenty-two percent of individuals ages 12 to 17 reported that they had used marijuana in their lifetime (SAMHSA, 2003).

In terms of current use, more than 25 million Americans age 12 years and older reported using marijuana at least once in the past year, and 14 million Americans reported usage in the past month. Of individuals who used marijuana in the past year, 12% used marijuana on 300 or more days. With these statistics, there are approximately 3.1 million people who use marijuana almost every day (SAMHSA, 2004). The rates of current use are highest among young adults (18 to 25 years), accounting for 20% of all users, followed by youth (under 12 to 18 years) at 11% and adults (26 and older) at 6.5% (SAMHSA, 2004). Although youth constitute a remarkable proportion of the marijuana-using population, the rates among youth dropped 20% between 2002 and 2003 among both casual and heavy users. The number of daily users dropped from 358,000 to 282,000, and the number of youth who had smoked marijuana 20 or more days in a month dropped from 603,000 to 482,000. This decline may be due in part to a greater perception of the risk of marijuana that surveyed youth reported (SAMHSA, 2004).

Social and Financial Costs

Marijuana use can negatively influence school and work performance among adolescents and adults. Students who smoke marijuana are less likely to graduate from high school than their nonsmoking counterparts, and daily marijuana users are more likely to be unemployed than users who use marijuana less than daily and nonusers (Brook, Balka, & Whiteman, 1999; SAMHSA, 2004). In addition, marijuana use decreases the ability to learn and retain information, thus causing individuals to fall behind their peers in both intellectual and job skills. In terms of job performance, smoking increases absences, tardiness, accidents, worker's compensation claims, and job turnover, thus lowering productivity and morale (Lehman & Simpson, 1992). In a study of adolescents measuring problem-solving and emotional skills, marijuana users in eighth grade did not make the same gains in psychological skills by the 12th grade, such as goal pursuit and confidence maintenance, when compared with their nonsmoking peers (Scheier & Botvin, 1996). Research also indicates that the drug's impact on learning and memory remains compromised after use is discontinued among almost-daily marijuana users. Although recall returned after 4 weeks of abstinence, heavy users remained impaired even though they had not smoked within the past 24 hours (Pope & Yurgelun-Todd, 1996). Marijuana use is also associated with depression, anxiety, and personality disturbances (Ellickson, Martino, & Collins, 2004).

The negative impact of marijuana can also be seen on the societal level. Marijuana use, and drug use more broadly, is associated with death due to overdose or other complications of drug use; effects on the unborn children of pregnant users; the spread of infectious diseases, such as HIV/AIDS and Hepatitis C, through sexual intercourse; and increased crime and homelessness (National Institute on Drug Abuse [NIDA], 2005). During 2002, according to the Drug Abuse Warning Network, marijuana was recorded during emergency department visits 119,474 times, up 24% from 2000. Of illicit drugs mentioned, marijuana was mentioned most often after cocaine (SAMHSA, 2003). Marijuana also adds to the prison population, with approximately half of all U.S. drug arrests for marijuana-related offenses (Federal Bureau of Investigation [FBI], 2002). In 2003, 5.5% of drug abuse arrests were for marijuana sale or manufacturing and 39.5% were for marijuana possession (FBI, 2004). Over 20% of arrests by the Drug Enforcement Administration in fiscal year 2003 were related to marijuana (Bureau of Justice Statistics, 2004).

The economic costs of marijuana to society are also notable. Recent studies indicate that law enforcement aimed solely at marijuana use and possession consumes 25% to 40% of the $31 billion annual costs for the "war on drugs" (NORML, 2002; Schlosser, 2003). The use of illegal drugs more generally cost the United States nearly $161 billion in 2000. The decrease in productivity from premature death, drug-abuse-related illness, institutionalization or hospitalization, being a victim of a crime, incarceration, and having a criminal career costs approximately $110 billion; health care alone costs $12.9 billion. The remaining costs ($35 billion) include prevention efforts and other efforts to minimize drug use (Office of National Drug Control Policy, 2001).

Social Work Involvement

Because marijuana use can affect multiple dimensions of users' lives, social work practitioners provide a natural gateway to treatment and services. With this gateway, users may enter treatment for other problems, such as family conflict, depression, anxiety, financial problems, legal problems, school or work issues, or physical disabilities (Smyth, 1995). Although clients may not specify marijuana as a primary or even secondary concern, proper assessment can help practitioners provide the most applicable services to their clients. Through direct practice with individuals, families, and groups, community-oriented practice, and social policy development, social workers can prevent marijuana abuse and treat current users.

Over the past decade, social workers have become increasingly interested in treating individuals with marijuana problems as well as with substance problems more generally. The creation of a special section of the National Association of Social Workers (NASW, 2005) illustrates this increased interest, which may reflect the increased demand. Even with the problems of screening and assessing the use of marijuana, in 2002, 14% of admissions to specialty drug and alcohol treatment facilities were marijuana admissions, and the percentage continues to rise (SAMHSA, 2002). These increases indicate that clinicians see more marijuana-using clients and can benefit from more competence in recognizing and assessing marijuana problems. Assessment can improve if social workers ask directly about marijuana use, even when clients are referred for other problems.

Operational Definitions of the Problem

Cannabis refers to a range of substances obtained from the cannabis plant. Marijuana or bhang refers to the product of cannabis leaves, tops, and steps dried and rolled into cigarettes. The leaves and tops excrete a resinlike substance called hashish, which may then be concentrated and distilled to create hashish oil. Sensimilla is a more potent form of cannabis. Although cannabis is usually smoked, it is also consumed orally by mixing it with tea or food. Delta-9-tetrahydrocannabinol (THC) is the substance in cannabis that is responsible for most of its psychoactive properties. The THC content of marijuana varies widely and has generally increased over time in samples of illicit marijuana users (American Psychiatric Association, 2000).

The diagnostic criteria for cannabis intoxication according to the *Diagnostic and Statistical Manual of Mental Disorders* (*DSM;* American Psychiatric Association, 2000) include the following:

- The individual has recently used cannabis.

- During or shortly after use, there are significant behavioral or psychological changes such as poor coordination, euphoria, anxiety, poor judgment, and social withdrawal.

- Two or more of the following within 2 hours of use:
  —Changes to the eye's mucous membrane.
  —Increased appetite.
  —Dry mouth.
  —Rapid heart beat.
- The symptoms are not a result of a medical condition or other mental disorder.

Signs of withdrawal may include anxiety, irritability, tremors, perspiration, nausea, appetite changes, and poor sleep quality.

As with other substances, cannabis-related disorders can be classified as dependence or abuse. Drug tolerance and withdrawal symptoms distinguish cannabis dependence from abuse. Abuse is associated with recurrent use that results in failure to fulfill obligations, legal problems, and interpersonal difficulties, but is not typically associated with withdrawal symptoms. Individuals who are dependent on cannabis have developed tolerance to the drug and need increased amounts to achieve the same effects. They may experience withdrawal symptoms if they discontinue use. Dependence is also characterized by a tendency to structure daily activities around obtaining and using cannabis (American Psychiatric Association, 2000).

Evidence-Based Approaches to Assessment

Assessment of substance abuse problems is inherently difficult because client problems are often multifaceted, with no one clear trigger creating a client's presenting problem. The debate surrounding the medical and social consequences, positive or negative, about marijuana complicate assessment and treatment (Joy, Watson, & Benson, 1999). Yet with these difficulties, marijuana assessment is critical and can be extremely helpful in identifying substance users. Fleming (2002) found that clinicians will be able to detect over 80% of drug users if they limit their initial screening questions to marijuana.

The Culture Surrounding Marijuana Use

Often the media, television, Hollywood stars, and politicians give the message that marijuana use is not harmful, but acceptable (Office of National Drug Control Policy Media Campaign, 2002). Although recreational marijuana use remains illegal in all states, national polls indicate that the majority of the American public oppose current marijuana policies, favor decriminalization, and favor the legalization of medical marijuana (Stein, 2002). Nine states have legalized medical marijuana, and several medical organizations, including the American Medical Association,

managed care companies, and numerous medical journals, endorse its use (NORML, 2002). Yet the White House Drug Policy
director voiced the perception that the safety of marijuana use is
the wrong message (Chatterjee, 2002). The National Institute of
Drug Abuse (2005) emphasizes the negative consequences, including the adverse mental, physical, emotional, and behavioral
changes of the potentially addictive drug. The mixed messages in
American culture complicate marijuana assessment because the
differences among "experimental," "normal," "regular," and
"problematic" users become blurred (Fleming, 2002). In seeking
social justice, social workers must consider the context of marijuana use in assessing whether the use is problematic (Alexander, 2003c).

Marijuana Use and Adolescence

Although adults enter treatment for cannabis, it is often the drug
of choice among adolescents. Much research has examined the
negative consequences of marijuana use with this population
(e.g., Brook et al., 1999; Ellickson et al., 2004; Fergusson, Horwood, & Swain-Campbell, 2002). Although the consequences of
marijuana on the health of adults is highly debated (Alexander,
2003c), consensus exists regarding the drug's detrimental outcomes among teens who are still developing (NORML, 2002). Frequent use of marijuana is associated with lower levels of
achievement and lower expectations for success, family problems,
and a greater likelihood of using other drugs (Brook, Gordon,
Brook, & Brook, 1989; Kandel, 2003). Marijuana users are also
susceptible to cognitive impairments and higher levels of anxiety,
depression, and suicide ideation (Fergusson et al., 2002; Sherman,
Roth, Gong, & Tashkin, 1991). In an examination of how adolescent marijuana use predicts outcomes at age 29, Ellickson and
colleagues (2004) found that young adolescent heavy marijuana
users had the least favorable socioeconomic, behavioral, and
health outcomes, whereas abstainers experienced the most favorable outcomes.

Overview of Assessment Instruments

Because the short substance abuse screening tools do not differentiate among the variety of illegal substances, many practitioners use the same screening tools to assess for marijuana as for
other illegal substance use. For adult assessment of marijuana,
the Diagnostic Interview Schedule (DIS), the Structured Clinical
Interview for the *DSM* (SCID), the Substance Abuse Subtle
Screening Inventory (SASSI-3), the Drug Abuse Screening Test
(DAST), the Substance Abuse Problem Checklist (SAPC), the
Drug Use Screening Inventory (DUSI), and the Drug Lifestyle

Screening Interview (DLSI) are common tools available (for descriptions, see Chapter 11, "Opioid-Related Disorders"). Although adolescents and adults alike use cannabis, the following
section outlines diagnostic interviews and screening instruments specific to adolescents because of marijuana's overwhelming presence and negative consequences with this
population. The assessment of substance abuse generally includes short pencil-and-paper self-assessment tests and longer
tests administered by a clinician. After a review of the adoles-
cent-specific instruments, a discussion of instruments specific
to marijuana concludes this section.

Diagnostic Interviews

Similar to the many interview schedules for diagnosis of substance abuse problems for adults, several diagnostic interviews aid
in the assessment of children and adolescents.

The Adolescent Diagnostic Interview (ADI) schedule includes sections on sociodemographic information, mental health,
substance abuse history, and signs of abuse or dependence covering all major drug categories. In addition to specific drug information, the ADI covers possible problems affecting other areas of
functioning, such as school performance, peer and family relationships, leisure activities, and legal difficulties (Winters &
Stinchfield, 1995). Research studies support the reliability and the
validity of the ADI (Winters & Henly, 1993; Winters, Stinchfield,
Fulkerson, & Henly, 1993).

The Adolescent Drug Abuse Diagnosis (ADAD) tool is
drawn from the well-researched and well-documented Addiction Severity Index (ASI) for adults (for description, see Chapter
11, "Opioid-Related Disorders"). It is conducted by a clinician
and contains 150 items covering the following dimensions: medical status, drug and alcohol use, legal status, family background
and problems, school or employment, social activities and peer
relations, and psychological status. The clinician rates the client
on a 10-point scale to assess the need for additional treatment.
The drug use section contains a drug use frequency checklist and
questions that examine drug involvement, such as drug use at
school, attempts at abstinence, and withdrawal symptoms (Winters & Stinchfield, 1995). Research indicates that the ADAD is a
reliable and valid assessment instrument for adolescent substance abuse (Friedman & Utada, 1989).

Based on the ASI for adults, Kaminer, Bukstein, and Tarter
(1991) developed the Teen Addiction Severity Index, which
examines the seven dimensions of chemical use, school status,
employment-support status, family relationships, legal status,
peer-social relationships, and psychiatric status. Both clients
and interviewers rate each of the dimensions on a 5-point scale.

Available research demonstrates adequate interrater agreement for the seven scales, but validity remains uncertain (Kaminer et al., 1991; Winters & Stinchfield, 1995).

Assessment Specific to Cannabis

Although practitioners often use a four question screener regarding use including Cut down, Annoyed, Guilty, and Eye opener (CAGE), the SAPC, the DAST, and the DUSI to identify problems with marijuana, none of these short instruments discuss marijuana specifically. Longer screening instruments, such as the SASSI and ASI, only mention marijuana among other drugs or have a couple of items specific to marijuana use. In a review of the literature, Alexander (2003c) identifies why these tools are inappropriate for the assessment of marijuana: its widespread use, the culturally confusing messages about marijuana's acceptability or harmfulness, the current debate over legalization and decriminalization, scientific debates about its risks and medical benefits, and the difficulty in assessing diagnosis using *DSM-IV.* In addition, clients rarely mention marijuana use as a primary or secondary problem, the marijuana quantity and frequency clinical risk guidelines are not clear, and lab tests and general drug use questionnaires do not appropriately assess marijuana use patterns (Alexander, 2003b).

The profession of social work generally recognizes that substance-using clients must be assessed in their environment to meet the client's needs and develop an appropriate treatment plan. As previously mentioned, the attitude and culture surrounding marijuana use is anything but straightforward. Although there are three marijuana questionnaires, none was designed for the initial assessment of marijuana use: the Marijuana Effect Expectancy Questionnaire assesses the expectancy of effects associated with marijuana, the Marijuana Craving Questionnaire was developed to assess the "craving" concept associated with relapse, and the Marijuana Quit Questionnaire examines the difficulties associated with quitting the use of marijuana (Alexander, 2003c). Thus, Alexander (2003a) recently proposed a new instrument specifically to address marijuana use, rather than other drugs.

The development of the Marijuana Screening Inventory—Experimental Version (MSI-X) is currently under way (Alexander, 2003b). The purpose of the MSI-X is to detect whether marijuana use is a problem. The assessment tool contains 34 yes/no questions and five numerical frequency items relevant to assessing marijuana use based on the evidence-based literature. Preliminary clinical scoring cutoffs based on a convenience sample suggest that a score above 6 indicates that marijuana use is a problematic risk. A score of 3 or less indicates experimental or normal use. Although the MSI-X remains in the developmental stages, the initial evaluations of the instrument indicate future hope and success in the assessment of marijuana use (Alexander, 2003a; Alexander & Leung, 2004).

Biological Assessment Measures

Physiological measures, such as urinalysis and hair analysis, provide alternative or supplemental measures to self-reported measures. Because denial is popular among marijuana users, especially adolescents, biological measures in the clinical setting allow for the identification of drug users and the adequate provision of their treatment (Verebey & Buchan, 1997). Confirmation of evidence in certain subpopulations may be particularly helpful. Kim, Fendrich, and Wislar (2000) found that urinalysis results uncovered significantly higher rates of marijuana use in boys than in girls, yet self-reported measures indicated similar rates of use. Thus, boys may be less likely to accurately report their marijuana usage. Faced with a biological check for substance use, clients may more readily admit their use. Despite these advantages, biological assessment methods are often inferior with regard to sensitivity and specificity when compared to self-report and can create major barriers to practitioner-client rapport (Johnson, 2004; Richter & Johnson, 2001). In addition, false-positive results can occur without confirmation from expensive analytic methods (Meyers et al., 1999).

Urinalysis, the most common drug screen, uses client urine to detect the recent or current use of substances. Despite its popularity, the routine thin-layer chromatography (TLC) drug screen is often not sensitive enough to detect marijuana use. A negative drug screen means there is not evidence of high dose in the past 30 days or recent casual use of marijuana in the past 1 to 3 days. However, the TLC test is not likely to detect low levels of marijuana, and false negatives (someone who has used marijuana recently tests negative for drug use) are common. Therefore, if marijuana use is suspected, practitioners must specifically request that a marijuana screen be completed (Verebey & Buchan, 1997).

Urinalysis is unaffected by social desirability or demand characteristics, but it detects only recent or current marijuana use in the past 2 weeks. Although urinalysis often uncovers daily or near daily users, the method often misses intermittent binge users (Jaffe, 1998). In addition, it does not provide information about the existence of a problem, use patterns, history, or any other contextual information that is necessary for an appropriate assessment.

Hair analysis examines a client's 3.9 centimeter-long strand of hair for substance use. The advantages of hair analysis include a time frame from 1 to 6 months for detection, ease of collection without embarrassment, and little time for tampering. Although hair analysis can be useful, the test may not detect use within the past week (Verebey & Buchan, 1997). In addition, Dembo et al. (1999) found that urinalysis is a more sensitive test for clients with short hair. The newness of hair analysis creates a strong need for improved appropriate cutoff concentrations and improved interpretation of results in terms of dosage and frequency of substance use (Mangura, Laudet, & Goldberger, 1999). In addition, environmental contamination of hair strands may yield a false-positive result (Verebey & Buchan, 1997).

Saliva tests can also detect marijuana. Saliva provides a non-invasive test, but has a detection window between 12 and 24 hours. In addition, the collection can become easily contaminated and the collection process can influence the pH and s/p ratios in the saliva, possibly altering the results. Overall, saliva is used minimally at the current time, but as technology improves, its usage could increase in the future for short-term detection, such as testing automobile drivers in accidents (Verebey & Buchan, 1997).

Computerized Assessment Methods

Computer-assisted self-interviews (CASIs) are advantageous for assessing substance abuse problems with some clients. These instruments allow clients to enter their responses automatically and answer only applicable questions through the use of skip patterns. They lower confusion by presenting one item at a time, alert clients to inconsistencies in their answers, and often give clients a greater sense of confidentiality (Richter & Johnson, 2001). Although comparisons of CASIs with paper-and-pencil tests revealed similar rates of student substance abuse, Hallfors, Khatapoush, Kadushin, Watson, and Saxe (2000) found that CASI increased the speed of data processing and resulted in fewer missing data. The quicker processing with additional data of computers may override the lack of opportunity to gain rapport with clients (Weber, Miracle, & Skehan, 1994). Thus, although computerized assessment can assist practitioners, the in-depth clinical interviewing is still needed in the collection of sensitive and socially undesirable behavior, including substance use (Morrison, McCusker, Stoddard, & Bigelow, 1995).

Evidence-Based Approaches to Intervention

Until recently, few studies have focused on treatment of cannabis disorders. This may be due to perceptions that individuals do not become dependent on marijuana and that adverse drug use rarely occurs with marijuana alone. The culture surrounding marijuana may normalize its use and further contribute to the lack of marijuana treatments. An increasing awareness that marijuana dependence is more common and problematic than once thought has led to a greater number of clinical studies evaluating interventions for reducing marijuana use (McRae, Budney, & Brady, 2003). Because marijuana is often the drug of choice for adolescents who use illicit drugs, many interventions focus on treating this population. This is especially true for family interventions. Recent research indicates, however, that many adults would like treatment for cannabis misuse. Just as this trend has increased focus on creating cannabis-specific assessment instruments, it may lead to development of more interventions that specifically address cannabis use.

Individual Therapies

Motivational enhancement therapy (MET) is a well-researched treatment approach that focuses on reducing ambivalence to engaging in drug therapy and abstaining from drug use. The approach consists of an initial assessment and two to four individual treatment sessions that aim to increase internal motivation for change while motivational interviewing strategies are used to develop coping skills and a plan for change. Throughout the intervention, the therapist monitors changes in the client's behavior, reviews strategies, and provides encouragement. Research indicates that participation in MET is associated with decreased marijuana use (Stephens, Roffman, & Simpson, 1994). This therapy may also be used with other approaches. A multicomponent intervention consisting of MET, cognitive-behavioral therapy, and case management resulted in greater decreases in marijuana use than MET alone. Both conditions resulted in significant decrease in marijuana use compared with the control condition (Marijuana Treatment Project Research Group, 2004).

Relapse prevention (RP) is a cognitive-behavioral approach that can be administered as an individual or group intervention. The approach assumes that there are cognitive, behavioral, and emotional processes that underlie drug use and relapse. In RP treatment, clients learn strategies that improve self-control, such as exploring the consequences of drug use and self-monitoring to identify triggers that lead to drug use. Irvin, Bowers, Dunn, and Wang (1999) conducted a meta-analysis of studies evaluating RP and found that it is generally effective for alcohol and substance abuse. It is most effective when used to treat alcohol and polysubstance abuse and when combined with medication. The effect sizes were similar for both individual and group modalities of RP.

Pharmacological Interventions

Pharmacological interventions are beginning to receive more attention for treatment of marijuana dependence. Although few studies have evaluated such interventions, there are some promising findings. In a study evaluating a treatment for alcoholics who use marijuana, participants who received fluoxetine reduced their marijuana use more than those who did not receive the medication (Cornelius et al., 1998). Nefazodone has also been shown to decrease anxiety and muscle pain associated with marijuana withdrawal (Haney, Hart, Ward, & Foltin, 2003). Divalproex sodium is another medication that has been used to decrease marijuana use, but its efficacy has not been confirmed in clinical trials (Levin et al., 2004).

Group Therapies

Behavioral therapy for adolescents employs techniques of modeling and rewarding desired behavior to reduce use of drugs, including marijuana. During group sessions, adolescents complete behavioral tasks, rehearse desired behaviors, and record their progress. Group leaders give praise and other rewards when participants meet their goals. Azrin and associates (1996, 1994) found that behavioral therapy was effective in reducing drug use and helping adolescents maintain abstinence from drugs, including marijuana.

Relapse prevention groups help participants learn cognitive-behavioral strategies to identify and change problematic behaviors (NIDA, 1999). The group begins by increasing motivation to abstain from marijuana use. Participants also practice exercises, such as relaxation and assertiveness training, and complete homework assignments that focus on using coping skills and eliciting the support of others. Stephens et al. (1994) found that adults participating in relapse prevention groups reduced marijuana use. Groups consisted of 12 to 15 participants and met weekly for 8 weeks and every other week for the following 4 weeks. Men receiving RP were more likely than men in a social support comparison group to report reduced marijuana use with no problems 3 months following the intervention. In a more recent study, adults participating in RP groups had significantly higher abstinence rates than those in a delayed treatment group. These rates were not significantly higher than a group receiving individual motivational therapy, however (Stephens, Roffman, & Curtin, 2000).

Family Therapies

Research demonstrates that family therapy interventions effectively reduce drug use among adolescents. Brief strategic family therapy has effectively reduced adolescent substance use and risk behavior and has improved family relationships in clinical trials (Santisteban et al., 2003). The approach aims to identify and change family interactions that are linked with the adolescent's drug use. Santisteban et al. found that Hispanic adolescents whose families participated in this therapy reported significant decreases in marijuana use compared with those participating in group counseling.

Multisystemic therapy (MST) is a home-based family intervention that has successfully reduced delinquency, sexual offenses, and drug use. It has also improved family relations among high-risk youth, such as juvenile offenders (Borduin, Henggeler, Blaske, & Stein, 1990; Henggeler, Pickrel, Brondino, & Crouch, 1996). The approach was designed for children and adolescents who exhibit antisocial behaviors and use drugs. Multisystemic therapy aims to reduce risk and build protective factors by providing intense treatment in adolescents' natural environments, such as homes and schools. The approach has effectively reduced drug use among adolescents in clinical trials (Hengeeler et al., 1991, 1996). In their meta-analysis, Curtis, Ronan, and Borduin (2004) found that those treated with MST were functioning better than 70% of those receiving an alternative treatment. Multisystemic therapy produced larger effect sizes on measures of family relations than on measures of individual adjustment.

Multidimensional family therapy assumes that adolescent drug use is a result of a large network of influences at the individual, peer, family, and community levels. The approach includes individual and family sessions in which adolescents learn to communicate thoughts and feelings and cope with stressors, and parents learn developmentally appropriate strategies for helping their child. Schmidt, Liddle, and Dakof (1996) found that adolescents completing 16 sessions of multidimensional family therapy experienced decreased drug use, and parents demonstrated improvements in parenting skills.

Another promising family approach is family network therapy (FNT), a multicomponent approach that incorporates family therapy, parent education, and case management. It was developed for use with motivational enhancement therapy. Although FNT itself has limited research support, the approach was created based on research studies that demonstrate the benefits of family involvement on treatment outcomes for adolescent drug users. The goals of FNT are to include family members in treatment, enhance the quality of family relationships, help parents learn behavioral skills, and increase both adolescents' and parents' commitment to recovery from drug abuse. In a study comparing multiple approaches to reducing drug use, participants in an FNT condition demonstrated improved abstinence from drug use, but the treatment was not more effective than other evidence-based treatments (Dennis et al., 2004).

Community Interventions

The therapeutic community approach (described in Chapter 11, "Opioid-Related Disorders") has been successfully adapted for use with adolescents. As in the traditional approach, adolescents reside in the therapeutic community and participate in a structured routine of responsibilities and activities. Research indicates that completing the residential phase of treatment significantly decreased the frequency of drug use among adolescents whose primary drug of abuse was marijuana (Jainchill, Hawke, De Leon, & Yagelka, 2000).

Summary

Although the media and popular culture often romanticize marijuana, the use of cannabis in any form can interfere in multiple dimensions of a client's life. The popularity and ambiguous culture surrounding marijuana often complicates assessment. Because marijuana often is not presented as the primary problem, social work practitioners can gain critical information about their clients by asking specifically about the use of marijuana. As the most commonly used illicit drug, cannabis is particularly popular among adolescents. Assessment and treatment among these younger users is important because of marijuana's negative consequences for the growing brain. Although the evidence-based tools for assessing and treating marijuana are in the early stages of development, newly available tools illustrate that the scientific community recognizes the therapeutic gains available when clinicians correctly assess and treat clients for cannabis-related disorders.

Study Questions

1. Your client expresses concern about his recent marijuana use. What would be your first step in assessing this client, and why?

2. How would your approach to cannabis assessment differ for adolescents and adults?

3. You are interested in engaging an adolescent's family in her treatment for cannabis abuse. What approach would you use and why?

4. Explain some of the differences in family treatment approaches for reducing cannabis abuse.

5. What behavioral characteristics would make you concerned that someone is dependent on cannabis?

6. Identify the social and financial costs to society of marijuana.

7. As a social work practitioner, in which practice settings might you need to be most vigilant for cannabis disorders?

8. Do you think assessment tools specific to marijuana are necessary? Please explain.

References

Alexander, D. (2003a). Clinical pilot experiences using the Marijuana Screening Inventory (MSI-X): Screening guidelines and case illustrations. *Journal of Social Work Practice in the Addictions, 3,* 29–51.

Alexander, D. (2003b). A marijuana screening inventory (experimental version): Description and preliminary psychometric properties. *American Journal of Drug and Alcohol Abuse, 29,* 619–646.

Alexander, D. (2003c). A review of marijuana assessment dilemmas: Time for marijuana specific screening methods? *Journal of Social Work Practice in the Addictions, 3,* 5–28.

Alexander, D., & Leung, P. (2004). The Marijuana Screening Inventory (MSI-X): Reliability, factor structure, and scoring criteria with a clinical sample. *American Journal of Drug and Alcohol Abuse, 30*(2), 321–351.

American Psychiatric Association. (2000). *Diagnostic and statistical manual of mental disorders* (4th ed., text rev.). Washington, DC: Author.

Azrin, N. H., Acierno, R., Kogan, E. S., Donohue, B., Besalel, V. A., & McMahon, P. T. (1996). Follow-up results for supporting versus behavioral therapy for illicit drug use. *Behavior Research and Therapy, 34,* 41–46.

Azrin, N. H., McMahon, P. T., Donohue, B., Besalel, V. A., Lapinski, K. J., Kogan, E. S., et al. (1994). Behavior therapy for drug abuse: A controlled treatment outcome study. *Behavior Research and Therapy, 32,* 857–866.

Borduin, C. M., Henggeler, S. W., Blaske, D. M., & Stein, R. (1990). Multisystemic treatment of adolescent sexual offenders. *International Journal of Offender Therapy and Comparative Criminology, 35,* 105–114.

Brook, J., Balka, E., & Whiteman, M. (1999). The risks for late adolescence of early adolescent marijuana use. *American Journal of Public Health, 89,* 1549–1554.

Brook, J., Gordon, A., Brook, A., & Brook, D. (1989). The consequences of marijuana use on intrapersonal and interpersonal functioning in Black and White adolescents. *Genetic, Social, and General Psychology Monographs, 115,* 349–369.

Bureau of Justice Statistics. (2004). *Sourcebook of criminal justice statistics.* Washington, DC: U.S. Department of Justice.

Chatterjee, S. (2002, September 6). Young Americans' drug use spikes. *Houston Chronicle,* 17A.

Cornelius, J. R., Salloum, I. M., Haskett, R. F., Ehler, J. G., Jarrett, P. J., Thase, M. E., et al. (1998). Fluoxetine versus placebo for the marijuana use of depressed alcoholics. *Addictive Behaviors, 24,* 111–114.

Curtis, N. M., Ronan, K. R., & Borduin, C. M. (2004). Multisystemic treatment: A meta-analysis of outcome studies. *Journal of Family Psychology, 18,* 411–419.

Dembo, R., Shemwell, M., Guida, J., Schmeidler, J., Baumgartner, W., Ramirez-Garnica, G., et al. (1999). A comparison of self-report, urine sample, and hair sample testing for drug use: A longitudinal study. In T. Mieczkowski (Ed.), *Drug testing technology* (pp. 91–108). New York: CRC Press.

Dennis, M., Godley, S. H., Diamond, G., Tims, F. M., Babor, T., Donaldson, J., et al. (2004). The Cannabis Youth Treatment (CYT) study: Main findings from two randomized trials. *Journal of Substance Abuse Treatment, 27,* 197–213.

Ellickson, P., Martino, S., & Collins, R. (2004). Marijuana use from adolescence to young adulthood. *Health Psychology, 23,* 299–307.

Federal Bureau of Investigation. (2002). *Uniform crime report for 2001.* Retrieved January 11, 2005, from http://www.fbi.gov/01ucr/cius.

Federal Bureau of Investigation. (2003). *Crime in the United States, 2003.* Retrieved August 22, 2006, from http://www.fbi.gov/ucr/cius_03/pdf/toc03.pdf.

Federal Bureau of Investigation. (2004). *Uniform crime report for 2003.* Retrieved January 11, 2005, from http://www.fbi.gov/03ucr/cius.

Fergusson, D., Horwood, J., & Swain-Campbell, N. (2002). Cannabis use and psychosocial adjustment in adolescence and young adulthood. *Addiction, 97,* 1123–1135.

Fleming, M. (2002). Screening, assessment, and intervention for substance use disorders in general health care settings. In M. Haack & A. Hoover (Eds.), Executive summary strategic plan for interdisciplinary faculty development: Arming the nation's health professional workforce for a new approach to substance use disorders. *Substance Abuse, 23*(Suppl. 3), 319–340.

Friedman, A., & Utada, A. (1989). A method for diagnosing and planning the treatment of adolescent drug abusers (Adolescent Drug Abuse Diagnostic Instrument). *Journal of Drug Education, 19,* 285–312.

Hallfors, D., Khatapoush, S., Kadushin, C., Watson, K., & Saxe, L. (2000). A comparison of paper versus computer-assisted self-interview for alcohol, tobacco, and other drug surveys. *Evaluation and Program Planning, 23,* 149–155.

Haney, M., Hart, C. L., Ward, A. S., & Foltin, R. W. (2003). Nefazodone decreases anxiety during marijuana withdrawal in humans. *Psychopharmacology, 2,* 157–165.

Henggeler, S. W., Borduin, C. M., Melton, G. B., Mann, B. J., Smith, L., Hall, J. A., et al. (1991). Effects of multisystemic therapy on drug use and abuse in serious juvenile offenders: A progress report from two outcome studies. *Family Dynamics of Addiction Quarterly, 1,* 40–51.

Henggeler, S. W., Pickrel, S. G., Brondino, M. J., & Crouch, J. L. (1996). Eliminating (almost) treatment dropout of substance abusing or dependent delinquents through home-based multisystemic therapy. *American Journal of Psychiatry, 153,* 427–428.

Irvin, J., Bowers, C. A., Dunn, M. E., & Wang, M. C. (1999). Efficacy of relapse prevention: A meta-analytic review. *Journal of Consulting and Clinical Psychology, 67,* 563–570.

Jaffe, S. (1998). Adolescent substance abuse: Assessment and treatment. *Adolescent Psychiatry: Developmental and Clinical Studies, 23,* 61–71.

Jainchill, N., Hawke, J., De Leon, G., & Yagelka, J. (2000). Adolescents in TCs: One year post-treatment outcomes. *Journal of Psychoactive Drugs, 32,* 81–94.

Johnson, J. (2004). *Fundamentals of substance abuse practice.* Belmont, CA: Thomson Brooks/Cole.

Joy, J., Watson, S., & Benson, J. (Eds.). (1999). *Marijuana and medicine: Assessing the science base.* Washington, DC: Institute of Medicine, National Academy Press.

Kaminer, Y., Bukstein, O., & Tarter, R. (1991). The Teen Addiction Severity Index: Rationale and reliability. *International Journal of Addictions, 26,* 219–226.

Kandel, D. (2003). Does marijuana use cause the use of other drugs? *Journal of the American Medical Association, 289,* 482–483.

Kim, J., Fendrich, S., & Wislar, J. (2000). The validity of juvenile arrestees' drug use reporting: A gender comparison. *Journal of Research in Crime and Delinquency, 37,* 419–432.

Lehman, W., & Simpson, D. (1992). Employee substance abuse and on-the-job behaviors. *Journal of Applied Psychology, 77,* 309–321.

Levin, F. R., McDowell, D., Evans, S. M., Nunes, E., Akerele, E., Donovan, S., et al. (2004). Pharmacotherapy for marijuana dependence: A double-blind, placebo-controlled pilot study of divalproex sodium. *American Journal of Addiction, 13,* 21–32.

Mangura, S., Laudet, A., & Goldberger, B. (1999). Improving the validity of behavior drug abuse research through drug testing. In T. Mieczkowski (Ed.), *Drug testing technology* (pp. 91–108). New York: CRC Press.

Marijuana Treatment Project Research Group. (2004). Brief treatments for cannabis dependence: Findings from a randomized multisite trial. *Journal of Consulting and Clinical Psychology, 72,* 455–466.

McDowell, D., & Spitz, H. (1999). *Substance abuse: From principles to practice.* Philadelphia: Taylor & Francis.

McRae, A. L., Budney, A. J., & Brady, K. T. (2003). Treatment of marijuana dependence: A review of the literature. *Journal of Substance Abuse Treatment, 24,* 369–376.

Meyers, K., Hagan, T., Zanis, D., Webb, A., Frantz, J., Ring-Kurtz, S., et al. (1999). Critical issues in adolescent substance abuse assessment. *Drug and Alcohol Dependence, 55,* 235–246.

Morrison, C., McCusker, J., Stoddard, A., & Bigelow, C. (1995). The validity of behavioral data reported by injection drug users on a clinical risk assessment. *International Journal of Addictions, 30,* 889–899.

National Association of Social Workers. (2005). *Specialty sections.* Retrieved January 11, 2005, from http://www.naswdc.org/sections/default.asp.

National Institute on Drug Abuse. (1999). *Scientifically based approaches to drug addiction treatment.* Retrieved January 25, 2005, from http://www.nida.nih.gov /PODAT/PODAT10.html.

National Institute on Drug Abuse. (2005). *Ask Dr. Nida: Marijuana.* Retrieved January 11, 2005, from http://teens.drugabuse .gov/drnida/drnida_mj1.asp.

NORML. (2002). Marijuana crop reports. *NORML home page library, medical marijuana.* Retrieved January 8, 2005, from www.norml.org.

Office of National Drug Control Policy. (2001). *Economic costs of drug abuse in the United States, 1992–1998* (Publication No. NCJ-190636). Washington, DC: Executive Office of the President.

Office of National Drug Control Policy Media Campaign. (2002). *Communication Strategy Statement.* Retrieved August 23, 2005, from http://www.mediacampaign .org/publications/strat_statement/contents .html.

Pope, H., & Yurgelun-Todd, D. (1996). The residual cognitive effects of heavy marijuana use in college students. *Journal of the American Medical Association, 272,* 521–527.

Richter, L., & Johnson, P. (2001). Current methods of assessing substance use: A review of strengths, problems, and developments. *Journal of Drug Issues, 31,* 809–832.

Santisteban, D. A., Coatsworth, J. D., Perez-Vidal, A., Kurtines, W. M., Schwartz, S. J., LaPerriere, A., et al. (2003). Efficacy of brief strategic family therapy in modifying Hispanic adolescent behavior problems and substance use. *Journal of Family Psychology, 17,* 121–133.

Scheier, L., & Botvin, G. (1996). Effects of early adolescent drug use on cognitive efficacy in early-late adolescence: A developmental structural model. *Journal of Substance Abuse, 7,* 397–404.

Schlosser, E. (2003). *Reefer madness: Sex, drugs, and cheap labor in the American black market.* New York: Houghton Mifflin.

Schmidt, S. E., Liddle, H. A., & Dakof, G. A. (1996). Effects of multidimensional family therapy: Relationship of changes in parenting practices to symptom reduction in adolescent substance abuse. *Journal of Family Psychology, 10,* 1–16.

Sherman, M., Roth, M., Gong, H., & Tashkin, D. (1991). Marijuana smoking, pulmonary function, and lung macrophage oxidant release. *Pharmacology, Biochemistry, and Behavior, 40,* 663–669.

Smyth, N. (1995). Substance abuse: Direct practice. In R. L. Edwards (Ed.), *Encyclopedia of social work* (19th ed., pp. 2328–2337). Washington, DC: National Association of Social Workers.

Stein, J. (2002). The new politics of pot. *Time, 160,* 56–61.

Stephens, R. S., Roffman, R. A., & Curtin, L. (2000). Comparison of extended versus brief treatments for marijuana use. *Journal of Consulting and Clinical Psychology, 68,* 898–908.

Stephens, R. S., Roffman, R. A., & Simpson, E. E. (1994). Treating adult marijuana dependence: A test of the relapse prevention model. *Journal of Consulting and Clinical Psychology, 62,* 92–99.

Substance Abuse and Mental Health Services Administration. (2002). *The DASIS report: Marijuana admissions increase: 1993–1999.* SAMHSA Drug and Alcohol Services Information System: Office of Applied Studies, January 18, 2002, updated April 10, 2002. Retrieved January 11, 2005, from http:// www.drugabusestatistics.samhsa.gov.

Substance Abuse and Mental Health Services Administration. (2003). *Results from the 2002 National Survey on Drug Use and Health: National findings* (Office of Applied Studies, NHSDA Series H-22, DHHS Publication No. SMA 03-3836). Rockville, MD: Author.

Substance Abuse and Mental Health Services Administration. (2004). *Results from the 2003 National Survey on Drug Use and Health: National findings* (Office of Applied Studies, NSDUH Series H-25, DHHS Publication No. SMA 04-3964). Rockville, MD: Author.

Verebey, K., & Buchan, B. (1997). Diagnostic laboratory: Screening for drug abuse. In J. Lowinson, P. Ruiz, R. Millman, & J. Langrod (Eds.), *Substance abuse: A comprehensive textbook* (pp. 564–578). Baltimore, MD: Williams & Wilkins.

Weber, L., Miracle, A., & Skehan, T. (1994). Interviewing early adolescents: Some methodological considerations. *Journal of Sociology and Applied Anthropology, 53,* 42–47.

Winters, K., & Henly, G. (1993). *Personal Experience Inventory Test and user's manual.* Los Angles: Western Psychological Services.

Winters, K., & Stinchfield, R. (1995). Current issues and future needs in the assessment of adolescent drug abuse. *NIDA Research Monograph, 156,* 146–171.

Winters, K., Stinchfield, R., Fulkerson, J., & Henly, G. (1993). Measuring alcohol and cannabis use disorders in an adolescent clinical sample. *Psychology of Addictive Behaviors, 7,* 185–196.

Cocaine-Related Disorders

Patrick S. Bordnick, Hilary L. Copp,
and Bruce A. Thyer

10
Chapter

Learning Objectives

After reading this chapter, the reader will be able to:

- Gain an overview of cocaine abuse and dependence in the United States.
- Understand the *DSM-IV-TR* diagnostic criteria for cocaine abuse and dependence.
- Increase knowledge of assessment and diagnostic instruments used in treating cocaine-using clients.
- Understand current empirical status of cocaine treatment approaches.

Overview of the Problem

Over the past 100 years, the popularity of stimulants in general and cocaine in particular has waxed and waned. Globally it is estimated that 13.4 million people are impacted by cocaine use (Gorelick, Gardner, & Xi, 2004). The prevalence of cocaine abuse in the United States gradually increased from the 1970s (Manschreck, 1993) to a peak marked by the introduction of crack cocaine in the mid-1980s (National Institute on Drug Abuse [NIDA], 1993). In the following years, several NIDA surveys indicated a decrease in use from the mid-1980s (5.7 million

201

current cocaine users) to the early 1990s, with a relative stabilization from the early 1990s to the present (1.7 million current cocaine users; Sofuoglu & Kosten, 2005; U.S. Department of Health
and Human Services, 2004). Currently, 33.9 million Americans
age 12 and over are estimated to have tried cocaine (U.S. Department of Health and Human Services, 2004). In 2002, it was estimated that 1.6 million persons age 12 or older had used crack
cocaine, and 5.9 million reportedly used cocaine during the previous year (U.S. Department of Health and Human Services, 2004).
It is estimated that, among adults, approximately 25% of those
ages 25 to 34 have used cocaine (Manschreck, 1993), and by age
28, 33% have tried cocaine (Johnston, O'Malley, & Bachman,
1994). It has been estimated that between 5% and 6% of first-
time users of cocaine become dependent on the drug within 24
months after initial use (M. S. O'Brien & Anthony, 2005), with
smoking crack cocaine appearing to be even more addictive than
nasal insufflation of the powdered cocaine hydrochloride (Chen &
Anthony, 2003). Even with the downward trends in overall usage,
millions of Americans are abusing cocaine and may require varying degrees of intervention.

The cocaine-related costs to society are high, with drug-
related crime and health issues representing the greatest burden.
According to the Drug Abuse Warning Network survey of admissions at emergency rooms in 21 metropolitan areas, the number
of cocaine-related emergency room admissions increased by 37%
from 1988 (80,335) to 1991 (110,335; U.S. Department of Health
and Human Services, 1992). During this time period, the total
number of cocaine-related fatalities quadrupled. By 1991, cocaine
was the primary drug mentioned in reports of drug-related deaths
(U.S. Department of Health and Human Services, 1992). As of
2001, cocaine-related emergency room admissions had reached
193,034 (Gorelick et al., 2004); the number increased again in
2002 to 199,198 (Office of National Drug Control Policy, 2003).

More recent statistics from the 2004 National Survey on
Drug Use and Health found that some 34.2 million Americans ages
12 and older had tried cocaine at least once in their lifetime (about
14.2% of this population). About 2.4% had used cocaine during
the past year and 0.8% within the past month. It is particularly
worrying that among 12th graders during 2005, 2.3% reported
using cocaine within the previous month and 8% during their lifetime. The corresponding figures for college students were 2.4%
during 2004 and 9.5% during their lifetime, and for young adults,
2.2% (past month) and 15.2% (lifetime) also for 2004 (data obtained from Office of National Drug Control Policy, 2006).

Cocaine-related criminal activity is a major concern to society. In 2000, the National Institute of Justice found that 30.9% of
a national sample representing 188,815 male arrestees tested positive for cocaine at the time of arrest (National Institute of Justice,

2003). Of female arrestees (drawn from a significantly smaller sample size), 33.1% tested positive for cocaine at the time of arrest. Thus the link between cocaine abuse and criminal behavior seems significant.

Social workers have been involved in various roles with regard to cocaine abuse. A large number of clinicians providing assessment and treatment services to cocaine-abusing patients are licensed social workers and social work students. For this reason, social workers need to keep abreast of the current state-of-the-science assessment and treatments for cocaine-abusing patients to provide the most efficacious interventions available. Treatment research in cocaine abuse has not historically been a strong role for social workers, as is evident in the sparse number of research outcome studies published in the literature by social workers. However, social workers are beginning to realize the vital role that research plays in providing effective practice, and this could lead to more participation in empirically based treatment outcome research on cocaine and other drugs of abuse. Among the contributions to the professional literature on cocaine abuse authored by social workers are a number of conceptual works (e.g., Mattaini, 1991); some exhortative articles, urging social workers to become more involved in this field (e.g., Berger, Gendler, Sorensen, & Fitzsimmons, 1990; Worthington, 1987); methodological contributions (e.g., Wambach, 1999); some descriptive research (e.g., Barth, 1991; Pelham & DeJong, 1992); a study on the accuracy of urine assays in detecting cocaine use (Schilling, Bidassie, & El-Bassel, 1999); and some very rare empirical outcome studies (e.g., Bordnick, Elkins, Orr, Walters, & Thyer, 2004; Bordnick, Graap, et al., 2004; Bordnick & Schmidtz, 1998; Jansson, Svikis, Breon, & Cieslak, 2005; Schinke, 1991). Social worker Carl Leukefeld has coedited a highly regarded monograph on cocaine treatment as well (Tims & Leukefeld, 1993). The clinical research of social workers Robert Schilling and Nabila El-Bassel (Edlin et al., 1994; El-Bassel, Gilbert, Schilling, & Wada, 2000; El-Bassel, Ivanoff, Schilling, & Gilbert, 1995; El-Bassel, Simoni, Cooper, Gilbert, & Schilling, 2001; Fernando, Schilling, Fontdevila, & El-Bassel, 2003; Schilling, Ivanoff, El-Bassel, & Soffa, 1997; Schilling, Mares, & El-Bassel, 2004) related to a series of investigations on the correlates and predictors of substance abuse, including cocaine, is a particularly noteworthy contribution from the discipline of social work.

Operational Definitions of the Problem

Several categories in the *Diagnostic and Statistical Manual of Mental Disorders,* fourth edition, text revision (*DSM-IV-TR;* American Psychiatric Association, 2000) pertain to cocaine use. Substance Use and Substance-Induced Disorders are the two major groups listed for cocaine-related disorders. *Substance Use Disorders* are divided into two classes: Cocaine Dependence (304.20) and Cocaine Abuse (305.60). The major difference between these diagnostic categories is that Cocaine Dependence involves repeated administration that leads to tolerance, withdrawal, or compulsive drug use behavior. Also, cocaine use is less frequent and less intense in individuals who meet the criteria for Cocaine Abuse. *Cocaine-Induced Disorders* encompass problems that are associated with cocaine use, such as withdrawal, intoxication, and physiological and psychological problems that manifest during use episodes (American Psychiatric Association, 2000).

Evidence-Based Approaches to Assessment

Currently, a variety of physiological and psychological assessment methods are being used to assess and evaluate treatment outcome in cocaine abusers, including self-report methods, behavioral assessment, and physiological measures.

Self-Report Methods

The Addiction Severity Index (ASI; A. T. McLellan, Luborsky, Woody, & O'Brien, 1980) is an instrument that assesses substance use and the severity of difficulties in the following areas: medical, employment, drug and alcohol, legal, family and social, and psychiatric problems; both the past 30 days and lifetime history are assessed. The ASI has high reliability and validity but does require training to administer. The ASI can provide the clinician with a vast amount of information regarding substance use history and the impact of that use on several areas of the patient's life (A. T. McLellan et al., 1980).

A new multimedia version of the ASI has been developed and represents a valid and reliable alternative to the standard ASI. Reliability and validity data are satisfactory for the ASI-MV (Butler et al., 2001), a cost- and time-effective computer-administered and -scored assessment that does not require extensive training to use (Inflexxion, Inc., 2001). New versions are available in Spanish and for criminal justice and follow-up; there is also a "lite" version. The ASI-MV can be found at www.asimv.com.

The Cocaine Relapse Inventory (CRI) is a structured clinical interview that purports to measure several factors (onset, course, and termination) of cocaine relapse episodes (Wiegmann, Stanny, McKay, Neri, & McCardie, 1996). The CRI must be administered by trained personnel; it takes approximately 30 minutes to complete all six sections. The CRI provides detailed accounts of the relapse episode, how the patient handled the relapse, and what happened after the relapse. Clinicians can use this information to assess the patient's potential reasons for returning to use and what skills, if any, the patient utilized to terminate use. The initial psychometric properties of the CRI appear to be acceptable (Wiegmann et al., 1996).

The University of Minnesota Cocaine Craving Scale (CCS) is a rapid assessment instrument designed to measure the intensity, frequency, and duration of a craving episode (Halikas, Kuhn, Crosby, Carlson, & Crea, 1991). The CCS can be administered daily, weekly, or at other set intervals. Intense levels of craving have been shown to be related to future levels of cocaine use (Bordnick & Schmitz, 1998). Clinicians who encounter patients with high levels of craving can adjust their treatment to potentially decrease future relapse episodes. However, caution should be used when utilizing this or other craving instruments due to the lack of reliability and validity of the data regarding craving measures.

Another measure of cocaine drug withdrawal symptoms is the Cocaine Selective Severity Assessment (CSSA; Kampman et al., 1998). CSSA scores appears to have good interrater reliability and scale internal consistency, and its scores are highly correlated with recent cocaine use and ASI scores. CSSA scores decline over time for clients who continue in treatment and remain abstinent, suggestive of its usefulness as a repeated measure of dependence severity.

A less resource-intensive measure of craving is the use of a single-item visual analogue scale completed by clients that attempts to measure cocaine craving right now and for the past week (Lee, Brown, Perantie, & Bobadilla, 2002), but this approach may not correlate well with actual drug use and it is not yet recommended as a primary outcome measure. Freedman, Lester, McNamara, Milby, and Schumacher (2006) have demonstrated that the naturalistic evaluation of cocaine craving via self-report can be undertaken by giving cell phones to homeless cocaine-addicted patients in treatment. Periodically, the phone would ring and the clients would be asked to rate their craving using a computerized survey delivered by the phone. This assessment also led the participants to report being more aware of the environmental precipitants evoking craving and suggested the usefulness of this assessment method as a potential treatment.

Weiss et al. (2003) have developed a very simple Cocaine Craving Scale that consists of only three items:

1. Please rate how strong your desire was to use cocaine during the past 24 hours.

2. Please imagine yourself in the environment in which you previously used drugs and/or alcohol. If you were in this

environment today, what is the likelihood that you would use cocaine?

3. Please rate how strong your urges are for cocaine when something in the environment reminds you of it.

Responses can vary from zero (no desire/likelihood of use) to nine (strong desire/likelihood; Weiss et al., 2003, p. 1321). This simple measure has been shown to be a modest predictor of cocaine use during the subsequent week among individuals in treatment, and that selected drug abuse treatments can weaken the link between craving and relapse.

The Substance Dependence Severity Scale (SDSS) is a semi-structured clinical interview designed to assess the severity of dependence across multiple drug categories, including cocaine, and to suggest a *DSM-IV* diagnosis (Miele et al., 2000b). The SDSS assesses only dependence on substances used during the previous 30 days and does not address any lifetime history of other substance dependence. Psychometric properties of the SDSS appear to be acceptable (Miele et al., 2000a, 2000b). Clinicians can use the SDSS to assess both treatment outcome and severity of dependence on a particular substance or across a range of substances.

Clients with particularly severe dependence on cocaine may experience cocaine-induced delusions or hallucinations. The Scale for the Assessment of Positive Symptoms for Cocaine-Induced Psychosis may be a clinically useful measure of these phenomena, most likely present during the early stages of treatment but not necessarily expected over the long-term care of such clients (see Cubells et al., 2005).

Behavioral Assessment

Virtual Reality-Based Assessment

In the past 3 years, advancements in computer technology have led to the design and development of virtual reality-based programs to assess drug craving and reactions. The first of these programs was developed for smoking by Dr. Patrick Bordnick in collaboration with Virtually Better, Inc., a research and therapy firm specializing in virtual reality technology. The general idea was to create realistic situations in virtual reality that allow smokers to experience high-risk smoking situations that would be generalizable to real-world experiences, allowing real-time assessment of craving and physiological reactivity. Dr. Bordnick's team created two interactive virtual environments: a room with smoking paraphernalia (i.e., cigarette packs, burning cigarettes in ashtrays, coffee pot, and alcohol beverages) and a party setting where people were smoking and drinking and offer a cigarette to the participant (Figure 10.1). In a controlled clinical trial comparing reactions of smokers, it was found that VR smoking environments led to significant increases

Figure 10.1

Screen Shots of Virtual Reality Cue Reactivity Smoking Environment

Virtual smoking party   Virtual cigarettes in ashtray

in craving compared to VR neutral environments (situations or places without cigarettes or associated stimuli; see Bordnick, Graap, et al., 2004).

After success in nicotine dependence, Virtually Better, Inc., paired with Drs. Rothbaum and Saladin to create a VR crack cocaine assessment program. The VR crack cocaine program consisted of a crack house in which participants see people smoking crack, experience a drug raid, and are offered crack for purchase. Pictures of the crack house are depicted in Figure 10.2. The crack program was tested in a controlled trial comparing crack environments to neutral environments and found a 400% increase in craving for cocaine situations compared to noncocaine interactions (Graap et al., 2004). Rothbaum (2005) emphasizes that the use of virtual reality-based technology is a useful *adjunct* to therapy but should not be seen (at least not at present) as a replacement for conventional treatment of cocaine abusers.

Physiological Measures

The standard in evaluating outcome, for example, of recent drug use, is urine analysis. Urine samples are collected from patients and analyzed to detect the level of cocaine metabolites present. The metabolite levels are compared with a cutoff value and are deemed

Figure 10.2

Screen Shots of Virtual Reality Crack Cocaine Cue Reactivity Environment

Virtual crack house   Virtual crack pipe made from soda can

Figures 10.3

Saliva Drug Screen and Urine Drug Screen

Photos courtesy of Branan Medical Corporation (www.brananmedical.com).

Oratectii™ saliva drug screen

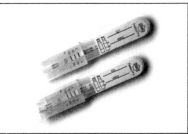

Fastect Ii™ urine dipstick screen

either positive or negative. Urine drug screens are the most effective means of evaluating treatment outcome. Due to advances in drug screen methodology, several products are easily utilized in a clinical setting and provide a rapid and valid measure of drug use. In addition to urine screens, new saliva-based drug screens have come to market. Saliva drug screens require users to insert a test strip in their mouth for collection of a sample. Photos of typical saliva and urine drug screen tests are depicted in Figure 10.3. The saliva is automatically collected and tested for several drugs of abuse. Several self-report instruments are also valuable in evaluating cocaine-dependent patients, if they are used in conjunction with the urine or saliva screens.

A more recent development in the physiological assessment of the use of cocaine or other illicit substances is through the radioimmunoassay analysis of hair samples, an approach that appears even more accurate in detecting actual cocaine use than urine testing (Swartz, Swanson, & Hannon, 2003) or client self-report of drug use (Appel et al., 2001). Hair analysis is best used in the assessment of longer term use of cocaine (past month or longer) as opposed to more recent use (e.g., past few days). Moreover, the technology for this means of assessment is not yet widely available, so its incorporation into clinical practice may be some years off.

Evidence-Based Approaches to Intervention

An extensive review of the treatment literature was undertaken to determine current state-of-the-science interventions for Cocaine Dependence and Cocaine Abuse. This review focused on empirically supported interventions that have been shown to offer effective strategies for treating cocaine-dependent individuals. Currently, interventions to treat Cocaine Abuse cover a wide range of inpatient and outpatient therapies, including, but not limited to, psychotherapy, behavior therapy, pharmacotherapy, and various combinations of these therapeutic approaches.

Although some progress has been made in finding effective pharmacological and psychosocial interventions, more work needs to be done (Gorelick et al., 2004; Leukefeld & Tims, 1993; Silva de Lima, Garcia de Oliveira Soares, Alves Pereira Reisser, & Farrell, 2002; Sofuoglu & Kosten, 2005). Currently, there appears to be little consensus with regard to the treatment of Cocaine Dependence (Gorelick et al., 2004; Silva de Lima et al., 2002; Sofuoglu & Kosten, 2005). A large-scale study was reported by Simpson, Joe, and Broome (2002) on the 5-year treatment outcomes for individuals meeting the criteria for cocaine dependence. Although moderate reductions in cocaine use were obtained following treatment, at 5 years following treatment about 25% of patients (of a sample of 708 from 45 programs in 8 cities across the United States) continued to use cocaine weekly. Obviously the field needs further advances in developing more consistently effective interventions.

The following subsections review psychosocial and psychopharmacological approaches to the treatment of Cocaine Dependence, with the empirical status of each. Studies selected for review represent current state-of-the-science outcome evaluations in Cocaine Abuse and Cocaine Dependence treatment.

Individual Therapies

Psychotherapy

Currently, an arsenal of psychotherapies can be applied to treat clients with cocaine dependence, ranging from 12-Step model approaches (i.e., Cocaine Anonymous) to peer-led counseling programs, used on both an inpatient and an outpatient basis. However, the efficacy of most psychotherapeutic approaches to treatment of cocaine addiction is largely unknown, as most psychotherapeutic treatments for Cocaine Abuse have not been subjected to controlled trials (Carroll, Rounsaville, & Gawin, 1991; Van Horn & Frank, 1998). Prior to 1997, the treatment literature contained only one randomized clinical trial evaluating purely verbal psychotherapeutic approaches for Cocaine Abuse (Carroll et al., 1991).

Outpatient Therapy

In an uncontrolled study, Washton (1987) reported data on 63 outpatients who were treated with a combination of intervention strategies. They reported that 51 patients were presently abstinent at 7- to 19-month follow-up, but that half of those patients had used cocaine without returning to compulsive use.

In an evaluation of supportive expressive individual therapy, structural family therapy, and peer-led group therapy on a sample of 148 cocaine abusers, Kleinman et al. (1991) determined from data analysis that the three therapies offered were insufficient to produce remission in a large majority of those patients.

Carroll et al. (1991) compared interpersonal psychotherapy to cognitive-behavioral relapse prevention treatments on 42 patients in outpatient therapy. Overall, 23 of the 42 subjects failed to achieve abstinence, defined in this study as not using cocaine for 3 weeks while in treatment. Difference in abstinence rates between the two treatments was not statistically significant. The investigators found that patients who were rated *high severity* at pretreatment were more likely to become abstinent if they were given the relapse prevention intervention. These results indicate that drug severity may be an important treatment-matching variable. Unfortunately, no conclusions regarding the overall relative efficacy of interpersonal psychotherapy versus relapse prevention can be offered on the basis of these findings. However, aside from having a small sample size, this study has fewer methodological shortcomings than previously reviewed studies. In particular, the researchers used random assignment to treatment condition, manual-driven therapy, and biological verification of drug use.

In a study to determine the efficacy of psychotherapy, family therapy, and group therapy, 168 patients were treated, and follow-up data were collected at 6 to 12 months posttreatment (Kang et al., 1991). Findings revealed that only 23 patients became abstinent. The abstinence criteria were defined as having a negative urine test and reporting abstinence for the prior 3 months. The investigators concluded that the interventions tested do not appear to be effective on a weekly visit basis for cocaine use disorders.

A manual-driven treatment referred to as a neurobehavioral model, utilizing a combination of psychotherapeutic and behavioral methods according to presumed stages in cocaine recovery, has been practiced by the Matrix Center since 1985 (Rawson, Obert, McCann, & Ling, 1993). In an open trial of this treatment model involving 486 patients at two locations in California (Rancho Cucamonga and Beverly Hills), self-report and urinalysis revealed abstinence rates of 40% and 44%, respectively, for the two sites (Rawson et al., 1993). A controlled trial with 100 cocaine abusers compared the Matrix treatment to community-based inpatient and outpatient treatments (Rawson et al., 1995). Results revealed that subjects in both treatment conditions significantly reduced their cocaine use. No differences were found between the two treatment conditions. Subjects in the Matrix treatment had higher rates of treatment retention and participation, which were positively related to improvements on several psychosocial measures and urine results (Rawson et al., 1995). Although promising, this multicomponent treatment approach has not been shown to be superior to other treatment approaches. Research continues on the utility of this model as an outpatient treatment.

Motivational enhancement treatment (MET) is a fairly new therapy being applied to clients with an array of problems, including cocaine abuse. Rohsenow et al. (2004) conducted a comparison of MET and group-coping skills training for 165 clients receiving care in a day-treatment program that was based on a learning theory and 12-Step orientation. Motivational enhancement treatment seemed to be more beneficial for the less motivated clients than the well-motivated ones, but overall the results were less than striking for this new technique. A more recent randomized controlled trial of a brief motivational intervention for cocaine users found similarly meager outcomes (Marsden et al., 2006). While it would be premature to conclude that this method holds little promise, it would be similarly premature to recommend it as a first choice or empirically supported therapy.

Wells, Peterson, Gainey, Hawkins, and Catalano (1994) compared cognitive-behavioral relapse prevention and the 12-Step approach in a sample of 110 cocaine-abusing outpatients. The results failed to demonstrate differences in outcome between the two treatments. One interesting finding was a significant decrease in alcohol use in the relapse prevention group. The investigators also found that the length of time spent in treatment had an effect on use. Again, the results are clouded with various methodological problems. The authors noted that the treatments were not manual-based and may have been inadvertently similar in the two groups. Also, the confound of concurrent history as a probable cause for improvements and the provision of a control group comparison would indeed improve, if not clarify, these results.

A more recent evaluation of 12-Step based intervention for cocaine dependent clients was reported by Weiss et al. (2005), who examined the association between attending 12-Step groups and drug use, finding that such attendance was not a predictor of an individual's future likelihood of using cocaine. However, those who actively participated in 12-Step group meetings were found to use less cocaine. Thus simply referring a client to a 12-Step program, absent their active participation during the meetings, was of little value. Given the wide-spread use of 12-Step-oriented programs in the treatment of substance abusers, considerable additional evaluation research is needed to further determine the presumptive benefits of these approaches.

Inpatient Therapy
The drug abuse treatment community appears to be turning away from inpatient services for substance abusers, perhaps because studies have found virtually no differences in outcome that favor inpatient treatment. However, it has been suggested that patients with significant physical or psychiatric problems, or those prone to drop out, might particularly benefit from inpatient stays (Volpicelli, Alterman, Hayasgida, & O'Brien, 1992). Miller (1993) indicates that the literature of the past 20 years reveals that inpatient and residential settings have consumed the bulk of treatment dollars, even though studies have concluded that inpatient settings

offer no overall benefit above outpatient settings (Annis, 1985; U.S. Congress, Office of Technology Assessment, 1983).

Empirical research with regard to the efficacy of inpatient cocaine treatment is virtually nonexistent and mostly consists of uncontrolled studies. Miller, Millman, and Keskinen (1990) studied 1,627 inpatients admitted for polysubstance abuse (alcohol, alcohol and other drugs, and cocaine and other drugs) and found that a sample of patients who responded to a survey of treatment reported abstinence rates of 76% at 6 months and 62% at 12 months.

Another treatment setting is the day hospital program. Galanter, Egelko, De Leon, and Rohrs (1993) evaluated a day hospital program having both peer-led and professional treatment components; they found that 59 patients, out of 150 who had completed treatment or were still involved in the program, had acceptable outcomes. An acceptable outcome was defined as three consecutive negative urine samples immediately before termination.

A comparison of the costs of inpatient and day hospital treatment for 111 patients found that 50% of the patients in the sample were abstinent from cocaine 7 months after admission (confirmed with urine samples) and that the two treatments were equally effective (Volpicelli et al., 1992). The results of this study provide important information with regard to the cost-effectiveness of inpatient versus outpatient treatment. The cost of inpatient treatment in this study was 1.5 to 3.0 times greater than outpatient care, leading to the suggestion that only patients with significant physical or psychological problems should be admitted for inpatient treatment (Volpicelli et al., 1992).

Research on inpatient treatment for cocaine abuse provides little support for the hospitalization of patients for drug abuse treatment in the absence of acute hospitalization for related medical problems. Results from the preceding review indicate that inpatient treatment programs do not offer an advantage over outpatient programs. The costs of inpatient treatment programs are approximately double the costs of outpatient programs, and the additional costs are not justified. Inpatient programs should be utilized for only the most severe cases or when patients suffer from significant physical or psychological problems.

Behavior Analysis and Therapy

Treatment strategies in the behavioral arena have deep conceptual roots in the processes of classical conditioning (Pavlov, 1927) and operant learning (Skinner, 1953) in both humans and animals. The role of conditioned responses to drug-related stimuli was originally proposed by Wikler (1948) and continues to form the basis for various behavior therapy approaches, such as cue exposure (Childress, Ehrman, McLellan, & O'Brien, 1988), coping skills training (Marlatt, 1988), and aversion procedures (Rimmele, Howard, & Hilfrink, 1995; Smith, 1982). This subsection reviews the empirical findings from studies testing these behaviorally based treatments.

OPERANT APPROACHES Operant-based treatment approaches focus on eliminating cocaine use by decreasing its reinforcing effects (e.g., using contrived negative consequences) or increasing the positive consequences of alternative abstinence-oriented behaviors (e.g., the community reinforcement approach). The operant conditioning paradigm or model views drug use as behavior that operates on the environment and is at least partially maintained by the pharmacological and psychosocial consequences associated with drug use (Grabowski, Higgins, & Kirby, 1993). Drugs themselves can serve as powerful unlearned reinforcers for abusers (Grabowski et al., 1993), and interventions usually involve implementing changes in the patient's environment, changes in the consequences associated with drug use, or both. Researchers have continued to use operant principles in developing new interventions. These strategies, as described in the literature, are reviewed and evaluated next.

Contingency Management. In the contingency management approach, the drug-abusing patient agrees to the implementation of certain positive or negative consequences, contingent on abstinence or drug use. Contingency management procedures are used to ultimately reinforce abstinence (Higgins et al., 1993). Bigelow, Stitzer, Griffiths, and Liebson (1981) have discussed the role of reinforced operant behaviors and believe that drug self-administration behaviors can be positively changed with the contingency management approach. Several studies utilizing the contingency management approach have offered findings of possible efficacy for cocaine abusers.

Anker and Crowley (1982) and Crowley (1984) used a contingency management approach coupled with psychotherapy or pharmacotherapy if needed. The contingency program consisted of a contract with the patient that if a urine test was positive for cocaine, letters would be mailed to specific individuals or agencies, which could result in various negative legal and other consequences. Results on a sample of 67 patients indicated that of the 32 patients who used contingency contracts, 31 remained abstinent in treatment, whereas the 35 patients who did not participate continued to use cocaine (Anker & Crowley, 1982).

Budney, Higgins, Delaney, Kent, and Bickel (1991) utilized a contingency management approach in a trial with two patients who were abusing marijuana and cocaine. Patients could earn vouchers contingent on cocaine and marijuana abstinence. Abstinence was measured by urine samples, which were collected on a fixed schedule 2 to 4 times per week and analyzed immediately. The patient and therapist jointly selected items or activities that were bought with the earned vouchers. During the first phase of treatment, vouchers were contingent on negative urine sample tests for cocaine. Both patients were abstinent from cocaine use but continued to use marijuana during this phase. In the next phase of treatment, vouchers were contingent on the urine samples testing negative for both cocaine and marijuana. During this phase, the two patients' samples were 96% and 100% negative, respectively, for cocaine and marijuana. Urine testing at 1- and 5-month post-treatment follow-up revealed continued cocaine abstinence in both patients but resumption of marijuana use (Budney et al., 1991).

Roll, Chermack, and Chudzynski (2004) examined the effectiveness of a contingency management approach to decrease cocaine abuse among three persons with Schizophrenia. A voucher-based reinforcement therapy was provided wherein vouchers redeemable for desired goods or services could be earned. The more consecutive drug-free samples that were provided, the greater the monetary value of the vouchers. This proved effective in reducing cocaine use among all three participants. Similar results using a contingency management approach among persons with Schizophrenia and cocaine abuse were obtained by Shaner et al. (1997), who provided cash instead of vouchers redeemable for goods or services. Given the propensity for individuals with chronic mental illness to abuse drugs such as cocaine, and for illicit substance abuse to lead to problems with reliably taking antipsychotic medications, finding psychosocial interventions to deter cocaine use among persons with chronic mental illness is an important area of practice research. The results of these early uncontrolled trials appear promising, but extensive follow-up research is required.

Such work on the long-term effects of contingency contracting is being undertaken, and a surprising number of outcome studies with positive results have recently appeared in print (e.g., Lewis & Petry, 2005; Martin, Petty, & Simcic, 2005; Petry, Alessi, Marz, & Tardiff, 2005; Petry, Peirce, et al., 2005; Poling et al., 2006; Rawson et al., 2002; Roll, Chermack, & Chudzynski, 2004; Rowan-Szal, Bartholomew, Chatham, & Simpson, 2005). This promising body of literature is now sufficiently large and impressive to warrant clinicians involved in the treatment of cocaine-abusing clients to give this research very serious consideration as an emerging evidence-based practice.

Respondent Conditioning

CUE EXPOSURE   The principles of respondent (Pavlovian) conditioning have been used in studies directed toward eliminating conditioned responses that are elicited by conditioned stimuli (see Rohsenow, Childress, Monti, Niaura, & Abrams, 1991). Ehrman, Robbins, Childress, McLellan, and O'Brien (1991) demonstrated that cues relevant to a specific drug user play a role in maintaining abuse and appear to be conditioned. In studies comparing nonusers to cocaine abusers, several investigators have found marked physiological responses (changes in skin temperature, galvanic skin response, and heart rate) to cocaine-related cues (videotapes of cocaine use and handling of paraphernalia) in abusers, whereas nonusers did not display these responses (Childress, Ehrman, et al., 1988; Negrete & Emil, 1992; Svanum & Ehrmann, 1992).

Passive cue exposure (extinction) treatment involves repeatedly exposing the patient to cocaine-related stimuli without allowing the exposure to be followed by drug use (Childress et al., 1993). During this treatment, patients receive individual sessions involving the presentation of cocaine-related stimuli (e.g., pipes, razor blades, white powder, mirrors, and syringes), while discussing their feelings and thoughts during this exposure. Craving ratings are taken periodically. These sessions are repeated until conditioned cravings diminish. Cue exposure may be combined with other behavioral treatments or traditional psychotherapeutic treatments.

Extinction of cocaine-related cues was studied in 60 detoxified cocaine patients to determine if adding passive cue exposure to drug counseling or psychotherapy would be beneficial (Childress, Ehrman, et al., 1988; Childress, McLellan, & O'Brien, 1988). Results indicated that patients who received passive exposure had better retention in treatment and more negative urine tests for cocaine use. Results also indicated that repeated cue exposure produced a nearly complete reduction in self-reported craving.

Similar preliminary results were reported comparing extinction programs combined with either psychotherapy or standard drug counseling to psychotherapy or standard drug counseling without extinction. The results indicated that subjects in therapies combined with extinction had more negative urine screens for cocaine compared to the nonextinction programs and had better retention in treatment (C. P. O'Brien, Childress, McLellan, & Ehrman, 1990).

In a study of 16 cocaine-abusing outpatients, Childress (1991) found that craving for cocaine may be reduced with a treatment program combining passive cue exposure, relaxation, and imagery techniques. The results of the extinction studies should be interpreted with caution because most of the patients resumed or never stopped using, despite reporting reduced craving on exposure to specific stimuli after treatment (Childress, McLellan, et al., 1988). It can be argued from previous research that cues may be an important element for some patients but not for others. Based on past trials, results of the extinction programs are varied, so definite conclusions regarding their efficacy cannot yet be made.

Aversion Therapy

The respondent model has led to the testing of aversion treatments to eliminate craving, induce an aversion to drugs, and potentially increase abstinence rates in cocaine abusers. Aversion treatments have been utilized in the study of alcohol abuse and are currently being investigated for their efficacy on cocaine abuse. Aversion therapy involves the repeated pairing of the abused drug and associated paraphernalia with an aversive stimulus (such as shock or nausea) to eliminate pleasant associations (T. A. McLellan & Childress, 1985; Smith, 1982). By pairing the aversive experience with cocaine use and associated stimuli, the addict should develop an aversion to the sight, smell, taste, thoughts, and other cues associated with the use of the drug. The three forms of aversion therapy presently utilized in substance abuse treatment are chemical aversion (emetic), electrical aversion (faradic), and verbal aversion (covert sensitization).

Bordnick, Elkins, et al. (2004) used a randomized experimental design to evaluate the relative effectiveness of three different aversion therapies (faradic, emetic, and covert sensitization) versus a relaxation control condition in the treatment of drug craving among 70 male cocaine abusers being treated at an inpatient Veterans Administration hospital. All three aversion therapies proved superior in reducing craving for cocaine compared to relaxation treatment, with emetic-based aversion yielding the greatest reductions. This study was the first controlled trial of aversion therapy for cocaine abuse, and these initially promising results indicate the need for further investigations of this type. Although craving for cocaine has been strongly implicated in relapse, it has yet to be demonstrated that an anticraving-based treatment such as aversion therapy actually reduces subsequent drug use.

Pharmacological Treatments

The development of medications for cocaine abusers has been on the rise and trials are continuing. The research on medications to combat cocaine abuse focuses on the neurobiological aspects of cocaine use. In 1988, $2.8 billion was allocated by legislators for the war on drugs, of which $10 million was used for medication research; that budget item has increased over time (Johnson & Vocci, 1993). Several drugs are being studied that are presumed to affect different brain systems (e.g., dopaminergic and serotonergic) or aspects of behavior and are being used to treat addiction, withdrawal, and craving and to maintain abstinence.

Although there have been a number of studies, no pharmacological agent has been approved for management of Cocaine Dependence (Gorelick et al., 2004; Johnson & Vocci, 1993; C. P. O'Brien, 2005; Silva de Lima et al., 2002; Sofuoglu & Kosten, 2005). Currently, a variety of medication trials are demonstrating potentially promising results, but the data supporting these results are limited and not uniform (Schmitz, Stotts, Sayre, DeLaune, & Grabowski, 2004; Sofuoglu & Kosten, 2005). A number of review articles provide a more detailed analysis of medication treatments for cocaine abuse (Mendelson & Mello, 1996; Silva de Lima et al., 2002; Sofuoglu & Kosten, 2005; Tutton & Crayton, 1993).

CURRENT RESEARCH   The NIDA Clinical Research Efficacy Screening Trial has recommended several dopaminergic medications (agents that act on the dopamine system) for Phase II trials (Gorelick et al., 2004). Currently, only disulfiram has been found to be effective (Gorelick et al., 2004; Sofuoglu & Kosten, 2005). Further research must be conducted, however, before disulfiram can be considered an effective treatment. GABA, a neurotransmitter, is thought to have an effect on the dopamine system and cocaine effects (Sofuoglu & Kosten, 2005), and several GABAergic medications are currently under investigation. Tiagabine, gabapentin, and baclofen have been found to have potential merit in clinical trials (Sofuoglu & Kosten, 2005), though additional clinical trials are needed to determine their ultimate effectiveness. Preliminary studies of adrenoceptor antagonists, vasodilators, immunotherapies (vaccine), and sustained-release stimulant medications have also been conducted, with mixed results (Gorelick et al., 2004; Sofuoglu & Kosten, 2005).

L-type calcium channel blockers have been shown in ongoing research to attenuate cocaine's toxic effects in the brain and reduce some of its subjective effects (Johnson & Vocci, 1993; Muntaner, Kumor, Nagoshi, & Jaffe, 1991). These results suggest that L-type calcium channel blockers may be useful in treatment of the behavioral and toxic effects of cocaine (Johnson et al., 1997).

The opiate antagonist naltrexone has been shown to reduce alcohol use and craving (Volpicelli et al., 1992). Dr. Joy Schmitz and her research team at the University of Texas Medical School, Houston, are currently investigating naltrexone for its effect on Cocaine Dependence in a double-blind placebo-controlled study comparing relapse prevention versus direct counseling therapies.

Another medical approach, one not focused on the administration of drugs intended to reduce the craving for cocaine, has been the development of a cocaine vaccine, a preventive injection that would protect at-risk individuals from developing an addiction to the drug (see Hall & Carter, 2004, for a discussion of the ethics of such an approach). Several clinical trails of potential cocaine vaccines are under way in the United Kingdom.

In some, perhaps many circumstances, clinicians combine pharmacological and psychosocial treatments, but the relative effectiveness of these combined approaches versus a unimodal therapy regimen has not been clearly isolated. One promising approach appears to be combining contingency management approaches (monetary vouchers earned for providing drug-free urine tests) with medication regimens (e.g., Schottenfeld et al., 2005).

As stated at the beginning of this subsection, no medication has been proven to be efficacious in the treatment of Cocaine Abuse. The results of present and ongoing research appear promising, but more replications with larger samples and strict experimental controls are needed before definitive conclusions can be reached.

Group Therapies

Another mechanism discussed in cocaine treatment is the use of self-help groups, such as Drugs Anonymous, Narcotics Anonymous, and Cocaine Anonymous. These groups closely parallel the Alcoholics Anonymous format. Spitz and Rosecan (1987) state that these groups provide emotional support to members and serve a vital therapeutic function. Washton and Stone-Washton (1987) claim that thousands of addicts around the world have benefited from these groups, and they encourage all patients to get involved. However, this approach suffers from a lack of empirical study, so information regarding the efficacy of the strategy is sparse. However, the view that self-help groups are opposed to research on their efficacy is changing (Schaiberger, Kennedy, Miller, Gal, & Petty, 1993). Information claiming the beneficial nature of these groups is rampant in the research and self-help literatures, but it is based primarily on anecdotal case reports and patient testimonials.

The multisite NIDA Collaborative Cocaine Treatment Study has found that group drug counseling combined with individual drug counseling, supportive-expressive psychotherapy, cognitive therapy, or alone is effective in decreasing cocaine use, with group drug counseling plus individual drug counseling producing the most significant outcomes (Barber, Foltz, Crits-Cristoph, & Chittams, 2004). Stotts, Schmitz, Rhoades, and Grabowski (2001) conducted a pilot study of motivational interviewing (MI) with 105 cocaine-dependent outpatients enrolled in a detoxification program. No difference was found in completion rates between the MI and control (a detox program) group; however, patients in the MI group submitted fewer cocaine-positive urine samples (Stotts et al., 2001).

Weiss et al. (2005) evaluated the role of 12-Step group attendance and participation on drug use outcomes among 487 cocaine-dependent outpatients, one of the very few empirical studies of this type of intervention. 12-Step group attendance *did not* predict subsequent drug use, but active participation in these groups during a given month was associated with decreased cocaine use the subsequent month. 12-Step individual counseling also had a moderately beneficial effect. It remains to be seen if these initially promising results will be replicated, but it is encouraging to see empirical evaluations of this widely used model being published.

Community Interventions

Community Reinforcement Approach

Roozen et al. (2004) conducted a review of published outcome studies utilizing the community reinforcement approach (CRA) in treatment of alcohol, cocaine, and opioid addiction. The CRA behavioral program consists of the following components, which may be selectively employed according to the patient. First, patients receive points for negative urine tests, which can be exchanged for various reinforcers: favorable consequences, tangible items, or activities. Second, drug use (a positive urine test) results in the loss of positive reinforcement (i.e., points). Third, by agreement with the patient, significant others in the patient's life who have agreed to participate are notified of the urine test results. Fourth, patients are instructed on how to identify antecedents and consequences of their drug use. Fifth, adjunctive pharmacotherapies may be used. For example, disulfiram therapy may be used if alcohol is causing problems in achieving cocaine abstinence. The main goal of CRA is to increase the number of natural sources of reinforcement for non-drug-using prosocial behavior and abstinence (Higgins, Budney, Bickel, & Badger, 1994). Roozen et al. found that CRA with reinforcers (incentives) was more effective than non-CRA cocaine treatment, and that making the incentives contingent on abstinence further increased effectiveness.

A controlled trial comparing the effectiveness of behavioral treatment based on CRA with a 12-Step program demonstrated that 3 of 13 patients in the behavioral group achieved 12 consecutive weeks of abstinence, compared to none of 12 patients in the 12-Step program group (Higgins et al., 1991). These positive, yet preliminary, results were later replicated in a larger study involving 38 patients. Higgins et al. (1993) compared the CRA with 12-Step counseling and found that significantly more patients in the CRA group remained in treatment. At 16 weeks in treatment, significantly more patients were abstinent in the CRA group (42%) than in the 12-Step group (5%), and the use of other drugs did not differ significantly between groups.

In a further assessment, Higgins, Budney, Bickel, Foerg, et al. (1994) compared a CRA with incentives to a CRA without incentives, using a sample of 40 patients. The incentives included, but were not limited to, sporting equipment, gift certificates for restaurants, fishing licenses, and educational materials.

The incentive group showed greater abstinence rates according to urine test data at 5-, 10-, and 20-week intervals compared to the nonincentive group, thus demonstrating that the CRA with incentives is helpful in achieving significant periods of abstinence during treatment (Higgins, Budney, Bickel, Foerg, et al., 1994). The authors discuss two limitations of the study: The incentive group was in treatment longer, and the cost of utilizing this approach may not be practical (Higgins, Budney, Bickel, Foerg, et al., 1994). Thus, long-term outcome data from two clinical trials for the CRA (Higgins, Budney, Bickel, Foerg, et al., 1994; Higgins et al., 1993) have been reported. One-year follow-up data in both trials revealed that the CRA combined with incentives was more efficacious than controls (Higgins et al., 1995).

Higgins et al. (2005) report a more recent appraisal of the CRA for cocaine-dependent outpatients in a comprehensive study of 100 drug abusers randomly assigned to CRA + vouchers or to a vouchers-alone treatment condition. The vouchers were given to clients contingent on their submitting cocaine-free urine samples and could be redeemed for various retail items. The longer a client submitted cocaine-free drug samples, the greater the monetary value of the vouchers. CRA + vouchers was shown to considerably augment the effectiveness of vouchers alone in producing cocaine abstinence, improving employment behavior, decreasing depression, and leading to fewer hospitalizations and legal problems during follow-up. On balance, the CRA combined with vouchers to cocaine-abusing or -dependent clients seems one of the better supported psychosocial interventions available to social workers active in this area of practice.

Summary

Clearly, a universally effective intervention has not been developed from the previously described psychotherapeutic, biological, and behavioral approaches. That is not to say that some patients have not been successfully treated, but those who have been represent a small minority of cocaine abusers. Interpreting the results is difficult when faced with the methodological problems that plague most of the investigations. Generalizing results from patient studies to various populations is problematic, due to the fact that the vast majority of studies use sample groups that are all White males.

Investigators are still unsure of exactly what to address when providing interventions. Some have concentrated on withdrawal symptoms, others have targeted abstinence behaviors, and still others have treated both. Combining therapies to create a more extensive approach (i.e., combining both biological and behavioral treatments) may increase the efficacy rates in future treatment research trials. There is a consensus among researchers that treatment development needs to take into account different types of patient characteristics. The matching of patient to treatment may be crucial to achieving positive outcomes (Pearsall & Rosen, 1992). Clinicians working with patients who abuse crack need to change strategies or develop new ones for assessing and assigning patients to treatment (Marlatt, 1988).

Currently, the recommendation is to use those interventions that have been shown to be the most efficacious in empirically based outcome evaluations. Indeed, it can be argued that to apply treatments for which there are no efficacy or effectiveness data is unethical, or borders on it. In this period of search and research, each clinic is obligated to keep current on knowledge and the application rationale for particular techniques and should closely monitor programs under clearly defined regimens. Behavioral treatment approaches that include contingent reinforcement, skills training, and situational analysis of behavior appear to provide the most effective interventions. Relapse prevention and community reinforcement approaches that utilize these behavioral strategies have been shown to be the most effective in achieving abstinence in cocaine-dependent subjects. Withers, Pulvirenti, Koob, and Gillin (1995) propose that treatments that combine medications and behavior or cognitive therapies based on current research may offer the most efficacious intervention approaches. However, further trials are needed to determine the efficacy of these combined approaches before definitive conclusions can be reached.

Much more information with regard to the treatment of Cocaine Abuse needs to be learned if an effective treatment for Cocaine Dependence is to be discovered. Controlled treatment outcome evaluation research is needed so that more definitive conclusions can be reached regarding the efficacy of interventions, due to the fact that no specific intervention strategy has been shown to be effective. Combining multiple strategies appears to be warranted based on the current research. Future research on cocaine dependence also needs to focus on treatment development to provide more effective interventions for this complex problem. We conclude with a quotation from a recent review:

> *The level of progress in the behavioral treatment of drug abuse in recent years has exceeded what many researchers and practitioners had believed possible. Efficacious behavioral treatments exist, and conditions for which efficacious medications exist can be treated with combinations of behavioral and pharmacological treatments that have even greater potency than either type of treatment alone. (Carroll & Onken, 2005, p. 1457)*

Study Questions

1. How has cocaine negatively impacted society (economic, social, public health)?
2. What is the major difference between cocaine abuse and dependence?
3. List the two criteria for cocaine dependence.
4. How can craving be explained by respondent conditioning?
5. Describe how cocaine dependence can be treated using a combination of medications and cognitive therapy.
6. Discuss two problems with self-report assessment outcome measures in treatment settings.
7. Look up some recent citations evaluating the community reinforcement approach to drug abuse treatment. Critically evaluate the merits of this approach.

References

American Psychiatric Association. (2000). *Diagnostic and statistical manual of mental disorders* (4th ed., text rev.). Washington, DC: Author.

Anker, A., & Crowley, T. J. (1982). Use of contingency contracts in specialty clinics for cocaine abusers. In L. S. Harris (Ed.), *Proceedings of the 43rd annual scientific meeting, the Committee on Problems of Drug Dependence, Inc., National Institute on Drug Abuse Research Monograph No. 41: Problems of drug dependence 1981* (pp. 452–459). Washington, DC: National Institute of Health.

Annis, H. M. (1985). Is inpatient rehabilitation of the alcoholic cost effective? Con position. *Advances in Alcohol and Substance Abuse, 5,* 175–190.

Appel, P. W., Hoffman, J. H., Blane, H. T., Frank, B., Oldak, R., & Burke, M. (2001). Comparison of self-report and hair analysis in detecting cocaine use in a homeless /transient sample. *Journal of Psychoactive Drugs, 33,* 47–55.

Barber, J. P., Foltz, C., Crits-Christoph, P., & Chittams, J. (2004). Therapists' adherence and competence and treatment discrimination in the NIDA Collaborative Cocaine Treatment Study. *Journal of Clinical Psychology, 60,* 29–41.

Barth, R. P. (1991). Educational implications of prenatally drug-exposed children. *Social Work in Education, 13,* 130–136.

Berger, C. S., Gendler, B., Sorensen, L., & Fitzsimmons, J. (1990). Cocaine and pregnancy: A challenge for health care providers. *Health and Social Work, 15,* 310–316.

Bigelow, G. E., Stitzer, M. L., Griffiths, R. R., & Liebson, I. A. (1981). Contingency management approaches to drug self-administration and drug abuse: Efficacy and limitations. *Addictive Behaviors, 6,* 241–252.

Bordnick, P. S., Elkins, R. L., Orr, T. E., Walters, P., & Thyer, B. A. (2004). Evaluating the relative effectiveness of three aversion therapies designed to reduce craving among cocaine abusers. *Behavioral Interventions, 19,* 1–24.

Bordnick, P. S., Graap, K. M., Copp, H., Brooks, J., Ferrer, M., & Logue, B. (2004). Utilization of virtual reality to standardize nicotine craving research: A pilot study. *Addictive Behaviors, 29,* 1889–1894.

Bordnick, P. S., & Schmitz, J. M. (1998). Cocaine craving: An evaluation across treatment phases. *Journal of Substance Abuse, 10,* 9–17.

Budney, A. J., Higgins, S. T., Delaney, D. D., Kent, L., & Bickel, W. K. (1991). Contingent reinforcement of abstinence with individuals abusing cocaine and marijuana. *Journal of Applied Behavior Analysis, 24,* 657–665.

Butler, S. F., Budman, S. H., Goldman, R. J., Newman, F. J., Beckley, K. E., Trottier, D., et al. (2001). Initial validation of a computer-administered addiction severity index: The ASI-MV. *Psychology of Addictive Behaviors, 15,* 4–12.

Carroll, K. M., & Onken, L. S. (2005). Behavioral therapies for drug abuse. *American Journal of Psychiatry, 162,* 1452–1460.

Carroll, K. M., Rounsaville, B. J., & Gawin, F. H. (1991). A comparative trial of psychotherapies for ambulatory cocaine abusers: Relapse prevention and interpersonal psychotherapy. *American Journal of Drug and Alcohol Abuse, 17,* 229–247.

Chen, C.-Y., & Anthony, J. C. (2003). Epidemiological estimates of risk in the process of becoming dependent upon cocaine: Cocaine hydrochloride powder versus crack cocaine. *Psychopharmacology, 172,* 78–86.

Childress, A. R. (1991, January). *Integrating cue exposure techniques with standard psychosocial treatments for cocaine dependence.* Paper presented at the National Institute on Drug Abuse Symposium Research and Treatment: "Alliance for the 21st Century," Washington, DC.

Childress, A. R., Ehrman, R., McLellan, A. T., & O'Brien, C. P. (1988). Conditioned craving and arousal in cocaine addiction: A preliminary report. In L. S. Harris (Ed.), *Proceedings of the 49th annual scientific meeting, the Commission on Problems of Drug Dependence, Inc., National Institute on Drug Abuse Research Monograph No. 81: Problems of drug dependence 1987* (pp. 74–80). Washington, DC: National Institute of Health.

Childress, A. R., Hole, A. V., Ehrman, R. N., Robbins, S. J., McLellan, A. T., & O'Brien, C. P. (1993). Cue reactivity and cue reactivity interventions in drug dependence. In L. S. Onken, J. D. Blaine, & J. J. Boren (Eds.), *National Institute on Drug Abuse Research Monograph No. 137: Behavioral treatment for drug abuse and de-*

pendence (pp. 73–95). Washington, DC: National Institute of Health.

Childress, A. R., McLellan, A. T., & O'Brien, C. P. (1988). Classically conditioned responses in cocaine and opioid dependence: A role in relapse. In B. A. Ray (Ed.), *National Institute on Drug Abuse Research Monograph No. 84: Learning factors in substance abuse* (pp. 25–43). Washington, DC: National Institute of Health.

Crowley, T. J. (1984). Contingency contracting treatment of drug-abusing physicians, nurses, and dentists. In J. Grabowski, M. Stitzer, & J. Henningfield (Eds.), *National Institute on Drug Abuse Research Monograph No. 46: Behavioral intervention techniques in drug abuse treatment* (pp. 68–83). Washington, DC: National Institute of Health.

Cubells, J. F., Feinn, R., Pearson, D., Burda, J., Tang, Y., Farrer, L. A., et al. (2005). Rating the severity and character of transient cocaine-induced delusions and hallucinations with a new instrument, the Scale for Assessment of Positive Symptoms for Cocaine-Induced Psychosis (SAPS-CIP). *Drug and Alcohol Dependence, 80,* 23–33.

Edlin, B. R., Irwin, K., Faruque, S., McCoy, C., Word, C., Serrano, Y., et al. (1994). Intersecting epidemics: Crack cocaine use and HIV infection among inner city young adults. *New England Journal of Medicine, 331,* 1422–1427.

Ehrman, R. N., Robbins, S. J., Childress, A. R., McLellan, A. T., & O'Brien, C. P. (1991). Responding to drug-related stimuli in humans as a function of drug use history. In R. A. Glennon, T. Jarbe, & J. Frankenhein (Eds.), *National Institute on Drug Abuse Research Monograph No. 116: Drug discrimination: Applications to drug abuse research* (pp. 231–244). Washington, DC: National Institute of Health.

El-Bassel, N., Gilbert, L., Schilling, R., & Wada, T. (2000). Drug abuse and partner violence among women in methadone treatment. *Journal of Family Violence, 15,* 209–228.

El-Bassel, N., Ivanoff, A., Schilling, R., & Gilbert, L. (1995). Correlates of problem drinking among drug-using incarcerated women. *Addictive Behaviors, 20,* 359–369.

El-Bassel, N., Simoni, J., Cooper, D., Gilbert, L., & Schilling, R. F. (2001). Sex trading and psychological distress among women on methadone. *Psychology of Addictive Behaviors, 15,* 177–184.

Fernando, D., Schilling, R. F., Fontdevila, J., & El-Bassel, N. (2003). Predictors of sharing drugs among injection drug users in the South Bronx: Implications for HIV transmission. *Journal of Psychoactive Drugs, 35,* 227–236.

Freedman, M. J., Lester, K. M., McNamara, C., Milby, J. B., & Schumacher, J. E. (2006). Cell phones for ecological momentary assessment with cocaine-addicted homeless patients in treatment. *Journal of Substance Abuse Treatment, 30,* 105–111.

Galanter, M., Egelko, S., De Leon, G., & Rohrs, C. (1993). A general hospital day program combining peer-led and professional treatment of cocaine abusers. *Hospital and Community Psychiatry, 44,* 644–649.

Gorelick, D. A., Gardner, E. L., & Xi, Z. X. (2004). Agents in development for the management of cocaine abuse. *Drugs, 64,* 1547–1573.

Graap, K. M., Rothbaum, B. O., Saladin, M., Brady, K., Ferrer, M., & Brooks, J. (2004, November). *Virtual reality cue exposure for crack cocaine dependence.* Paper presented at the Association for the Advancement of Behavior Therapy, New Orleans, LA.

Grabowski, J., Higgins, S. T., & Kirby, K. C. (1993). Behavioral treatments of cocaine dependence. In F. M. Tims & C. G. Leukefeld (Eds.), *National Institute of Health Research Monograph No. 135: Cocaine treatment: Research and clinical perspectives* (pp. 133–149). Washington, DC: National Institute of Health.

Halikas, J. A., Kuhn, K. L., Crosby, R., Carlson, G., & Crea, F. (1991). The measurement of craving in cocaine patients using the Minnesota Cocaine Craving Scale. *Comprehensive Psychiatry, 32,* 22–27.

Hall, W., & Carter, L. (2004). Ethical issues in using a cocaine vaccine to treat and prevent cocaine abuse and dependence. *Journal of Medical Ethics, 30,* 337–340.

Higgins, S. T., Budney, A. J., Bickel, W. K., & Badger, G. J. (1994). Participation of significant others in outpatient behavioral treatment predicts greater cocaine abstinence. *American Journal of Drug and Alcohol Abuse, 20,* 47–56.

Higgins, S. T., Budney, A. J., Bickel, W. K., Badger, G. J., Foerg, F. E., & Ogden, D. (1995). Outpatient behavioral treatment for cocaine dependence: One-year outcome. *Experimental and Clinical Psychopharmacology, 3,* 205–212.

Higgins, S. T., Budney, A. J., Bickel, W. K., Foerg, F. E., Donham, R., & Badger, G. J. (1994). Incentives improve outcome in outpatient behavioral treatment of cocaine dependence. *Archives of General Psychiatry, 51,* 568–576.

Higgins, S. T., Delaney, D. D., Budney, A. J., Bickel, W. K., Hughes, J. R., Foerg, F., et al. (1991). A behavioral approach to achieving initial cocaine abstinence. *American Journal of Psychiatry, 148,* 1218–1224.

Higgins, S. T., Rush, C. R., Bickel, W. K., Hughes, J. R., Lynn, M., & Capeless, M. A. (1993). Acute behavioral and cardiac effects of cocaine and alcohol combinations in humans. *Psychopharmacology, 111,* 285–294.

Higgins, S. T., Sigmon, S. C., Wong, C. J., Heil, S. H., Badger, G. J., Donham, R., et al. (2005). Community reinforcement therapy for cocaine-dependent outpatients. *Archives of General Psychiatry, 60,* 1043–1052.

Inflexxion, Inc. (2001). Addiction Severity Index—Multimedia Version (ASI-MV) [Computer software]. Newton, MA: Author.

Jansson, L. M., Svikis, D. S., Breon, D., & Cieslak, R. (2005). Intensity of case management services: Does more equal better for drug dependent women and their children? *Social Work in Mental Health, 3*(4), 63–78.

Johnson, D. N., & Vocci, F. J. (1993). Medications development at the National Institute on Drug Abuse: Focus on cocaine. In F. R. Tims & C. G. Leukefeld (Eds.), *National Institute on Drug Abuse Research Monograph No. 135: Cocaine treatment: Research and clinical perspectives* (pp. 57–70). Washington, DC: National Institute of Health.

Johnston, L. D., O'Malley, P. M., & Bachman, J. G. (1994). *National survey results on drug use from the Monitoring the Future study, 1975–1993: Vol. 2. College students and young adults.* Washington, DC: National Institute on Drug Abuse.

Kampman, K. M., Volpicelli, J. R., McGinnis, D. E., Alterman, A. I., Weinreib, R. M.,

D'Angelo, L. D., et al. (1998). Reliability and validity of the Cocaine Selective Severity Assessment. *Addictive Behaviors, 23,* 449–461.

Kang, S., Kleinman, P. H., Woody, G. E., Millman, R. B., Todd, T. C., Kemp, J., et al. (1991). Outcomes for cocaine abusers after once-a-week psychosocial therapy. *American Journal of Psychiatry, 148,* 630–636.

Kleinman, P. H., Woody, G. E., Todd, T. C., Millman, R. B., Kang, S., Kemp, J., et al. (1991). Crack and cocaine abusers in outpatient psychotherapy. In L. S. Onken & J. D. Blaine (Eds.), *National Institute on Drug Abuse Research Monograph No. 104* (pp. 24–35). Washington, DC: National Institute of Health.

Kosten, T., Poling, J., & Oliveta, A. (2003). Effects of reducing contingency management values on heroin and cocaine use for buprenorphine and desipramine-treated patients. *Addiction, 98,* 665–671.

Lee, J. W., Brown, E. S., Perantie, D. C., & Bobadilla, L. (2002). A comparison of single-item visual analog scales with a multi-item Likert-type scale for assessment of cocaine craving in persons with bipolar disorder. *Addictive Disorders and Their Treatment, 1,* 140–142.

Leukefeld, C. G., & Tims, F. M. (1993). Treatment of cocaine abuse and dependence: Directions and recommendations. In C. G. Leukefeld & F. M. Tims (Eds.), *National Institute on Drug Abuse Research Monograph No. 135: Cocaine treatment: Research and clinical perspectives* (pp. 260–266). Washington, DC: National Institute of Health.

Lewis, M. W., & Petry, N. M. (2005). Contingency-management treatments that reinforce completion of goal-related activities: Participation in family activities and its association with outcomes. *Drug and Alcohol Dependence, 79,* 267–271.

Manschreck, T. C. (1993). The treatment of cocaine abuse. *Psychiatric Quarterly, 64,* 183–197.

Marlatt, G. A. (1988). Matching client to treatment: Treatment models and stages of change. In D. M. Donovan & G. A. Marlatt (Eds.), *Assessment of addictive behaviors* (pp. 474–483). New York: Guilford Press.

Marsden, J., Stillwell, G., Barlow, H., Boys, A., Taylor, C., Hunt, N., et al. (2006). An evaluation of a brief motivational intervention among young ecstasy and cocaine users: No effect on substance and alcohol use outcomes. *Addictions, 101,* 1014–1027.

Martin, B., Petty, N. M., & Simcic, F. (2005). Prize reinforcement contingency management for cocaine dependence: Integration with group therapy in a methadone clinic. *Journal of Consulting and Clinical Psychology, 73,* 354–359.

Mattaini, M. A. (1991). Choosing weapons in the war on "crack": An operant analysis. *Research on Social Work Practice, 1,* 188–213.

McLellan, A. T., Luborsky, L., Woody, G. E., & O'Brien, C. P. (1980). An improved diagnostic evaluation instrument for substance abuse patients: The Addiction Severity Index. *Journal of Nervous and Mental Diseases, 168,* 26–33.

McLellan, T. A., & Childress, A. R. (1985). Aversive therapies for substance abuse: Do they work? *Journal of Substance Abuse Treatment, 2,* 187–191.

Mendelson, J. H., & Mello, N. K. (1996). Drug therapy: Management of cocaine abuse and dependence. *New England Journal of Medicine, 334,* 965–972.

Miele, G. M., Carpenter, K. M., Cockerham, M. S., Trautman, K. D., Blaine, J., & Hasin, D. S. (2000a). Concurrent and predictive validity of the Substance Dependence Severity Scale (SDSS). *Drug and Alcohol Dependence, 59,* 77–88.

Miele, G. M., Carpenter, K. M., Cockerham, M. S., Trautman, K. D., Blaine, J., & Hasin, D. S. (2000b). Substance Dependence Severity Scale (SDSS): Reliability and validity of a clinician-administered interview for *DSM-IV* substance use disorders. *Drug and Alcohol Dependence, 59,* 63–75.

Miller, N. S., Millman, R. B., & Keskinen, S. (1990). Outcome at 6 and 12 months post inpatient treatment for cocaine and alcohol dependence. *Advances in Alcohol and Substance Abuse, 9,* 101–120.

Miller, W. R. (1993). Behavioral treatments for drug problems: Where do we go from here? *National Institute on Drug Abuse Research Monograph, 137,* 303–321.

Muntaner, C., Kumor, K. M., Nagoshi, C., & Jaffe, J. H. (1991). Effects of nifedipine pretreatment on subjective and cardiovascular responses to intravenous cocaine in humans. *Psychopharmacology, 105,* 37–41.

National Institute of Justice. (2003). *2000 arrestee drug abuse monitoring: Annual report* (No. NCJ 193013). Washington, DC: Author.

National Institute on Drug Abuse. (1993). *Capsules: Cocaine abuse.* Washington, DC: National Institute of Health.

Negrete, J. C., & Emil, S. (1992). Cue-evoked arousal in cocaine users: A study of variance and predictive values. *Drug and Alcohol Dependence, 30,* 187–192.

O'Brien, C. P. (2005). Anticraving medications for relapse prevention: A possible new class of psychoactive medications. *American Journal of Psychiatry, 162,* 1423–1431.

O'Brien, C. P., Childress, A. R., McLellan, T., & Ehrman, R. (1990). Integrating systematic cue exposure with standard treatment in recovering drug dependent patients. *Addictive Behaviors, 15,* 355–365.

O'Brien, M. S., & Anthony, J. C. (2005). Risk of becoming cocaine dependent: Epidemiological estimates for the United States, 2000–2001. *Neuropsychopharmacology, 30,* 1006–1018.

Office of National Drug Control Policy. (2003). *ONDCP drug policy information clearinghouse fact sheet: Cocaine.* Rockville, MD.

Office of National Drug Control Policy. (2006). *Drug facts: Cocaine.* Washington, DC: Author. Retrieved March 7, 2006, from http://www.whitehousedrugpolicy.gov/drugfact/cocaine.

Pavlov, I. P. (1927). *Conditioned reflexes.* London: Oxford University Press.

Pearsall, H. R., & Rosen, M. I. (1992). Inpatient treatment of cocaine addiction. In T. R. Kosten & H. D. Kleber (Eds.), *Clinician's guide to cocaine addiction* (pp. 314–334). New York: Guilford Press.

Pelham, T. L., & DeJong, A. R. (1992). Nationwide practices for screening and reporting prenatal cocaine abuse: A survey of teaching programs. *Child Abuse and Neglect, 16,* 763–770.

Petry, N. M., Alessi, J., Marz, M. A., & Tardiff, M. (2005). Vouchers versus prizes: Contingency management treatment of substance abusers in community settings. *Journal of Consulting and Clinical Psychology, 73,* 1005–1014.

Petry, N. M., Peirce, J. M., Stitzer, M. L., Blaine, J., Roll, J. M., Cohen, A., et al. (2005). Effect of prize-based incentives on outcomes in stimulant abusers in outpatient psychosocial treatment programs: A National Drug Abuse Treatment Clinical Trials Network study. *Archives of General Psychiatry, 62,* 1148–1156.

Petry, N. M., Tedford, J., Austin, M., Nich, C., Carroll, K. M., & Rounsaville, B. J. (2004). Prize reinforcement contingency management for treating cocaine abusers: How low can we go and with whom? *Addiction, 99,* 349–360.

Poling, J., Oliveto, A., Petry, N., Sofuoglu, M., Gonsai, K., Gonzalez, G., et al. (2006). Six-month trial of buprorion with contingency management for cocaine dependence in a methadone-maintained population. *Archives of General Psychiatry, 63,* 219–228.

Rawson, R. A., Huber, A., McCann, M., Shoptaw, S., Farabee, D., Reiber, C., et al. (2002). A comparison of contingency management and cognitive-behavioral approaches during methadone maintenance treatment for cocaine dependence. *Archives of General Psychiatry, 59,* 817–824.

Rawson, R. A., Obert, J. L., McCann, M. J., & Ling, W. (1993). Neurobehavioral treatment for cocaine dependence: A preliminary evaluation. In F. R. Tims & C. G. Leukefeld (Eds.), *National Institute on Drug Abuse Research Monograph No. 135: Cocaine treatment: Research and clinical perspectives* (pp. 92–115). Washington, DC: National Institute of Health.

Rawson, R. A., Shoptaw, S. J., Obert, J. L., McCann, M. J., Hasson, A. L., Marinelli-Casey, P. J., et al. (1995). An intensive outpatient approach for cocaine abuse treatment: The MATRIX model. *Journal of Substance Abuse Treatment, 12,* 117–127.

Rimmele, C. T., Howard, M. O., & Hilfrink, M. L. (1995). Aversion therapies. In R. K. Hester & W. R. Miller (Eds.), *Handbook of alcoholism treatment approaches: Effective alter-*

natives (pp. 134–147). Needham Heights, MA: Allyn & Bacon.

Rohsenow, D. J., Childress, A. R., Monti, P. M., Niaura, R. S., & Abrams, D. B. (1991). Cue reactivity in addictive behaviors: Theoretical and treatment implications. *International Journal of the Addictions, 25,* 957–993.

Rohsenow, D. J., Monti, P. M., Martin, R. A., Colby, S. M., Myers, M. G., Gulliver, S. B., et al. (2004). Motivational enhancement and coping skills training for cocaine abusers: Effects on substance use outcomes. *Addiction, 99,* 862–874.

Roll, J. M., Chermack, S. T., & Chudzynski, J. E. (2004). Investigating the use of contingency management in the treatment of cocaine use among individuals with schizophrenia: A feasibility study. *Psychiatry Research, 125,* 61–64.

Roozen, H. G., Boulogne, J. J., van Tulder, M. W., van den Brink, W., De Jong, C. A. J., & Kerkhof, J. F. M. (2004). A systematic review of the effectiveness of the community reinforcement approach in alcohol, cocaine, and opioid addiction. *Drug and Alcohol Dependence, 74,* 1–13.

Rothbaum, B. O. (2005). Commentary. *CyberPsychology and Behavior, 8,* 239–240.

Rowan-Szal, G. A., Bartholomew, N. G., Chatham, L. R., & Simpson, D. D. (2005). A combined cognitive and behavior intervention for cocaine-using methadone clients. *Journal of Psychoactive Drugs, 37,* 75–84.

Schaiberger, P. H., Kennedy, T. C., Miller, F. C., Gal, J., & Petty, T. L. (1993). Pulmonary hypertension associated with long-term inhalation. *Chest, 104*(2), 614–616.

Schilling, R. F., Bidassie, B., & El-Bassel, N. (1999). Detecting cocaine and opiates in urine: Comparing three commercial assays. *Journal of Psychoactive Drugs, 31,* 305–313.

Schilling, R. F., Ivanoff, A., El-Bassel, N., & Soffa, F. (1997). HIV-related behaviors in transitional correctional settings. *Criminal Justice and Behavior, 24,* 256–277.

Schilling, R. F., Mares, A., & El-Bassel, N. (2004). Women in detoxification: Loss of guardianship of their children. *Children and Youth Services Review, 26,* 463–480.

Schinke, S. P. (1991). *The effectiveness of Boys and Girls Clubs on alcohol and other drug use*

and related problems in public housing: Final research report. New York: Boys Clubs of America.

Schmitz, J. M., Stotts, A. L., Sayre, S. L., DeLaune, K. A., & Grabowski, J. (2004). Treatment of cocaine-alcohol dependence with naltrexone and relapse prevention therapy. *American Journal of Addictions, 13,* 333–341.

Schottenfeld, R. S., Chawarski, M. C., Pakes, J. R., Pantalon, M. V., Carroll, K. M., & Kosten, T. R. (2005). Methadone versus buprenorphine with contingency management or performance feedback for cocaine and opioid dependence. *American Journal of Psychiatry, 162,* 340–349.

Shaner, A., Roberts, L. J., Eckman, T. A., Tucker, D. E., Tsuang, J. W., Wilkins, J. N., et al. (1997). Monetary reinforcement of abstinence from cocaine among mentally ill patients with cocaine dependence. *Psychiatric Services, 48,* 807–810.

Silva de Lima, M., Garcia de Oliveira Soares, B., Alves Pereira Reisser, A., & Farrell, M. (2002). Pharmacological treatment of cocaine dependence: A systematic review. *Addiction, 97,* 931–949.

Simpson, D. D., Joe, G. W., & Broome, K. M. (2002). A national 5-year follow-up of treatment outcomes for cocaine dependence. *Archives of General Psychiatry, 59,* 538–544.

Skinner, B. F. (1953). *Science and human behavior.* New York: Macmillan.

Smith, J. W. (1982). Treatment of alcoholism in aversion conditioning hospitals. In E. M. Pattison & E. Kaufman (Eds.), *Encyclopedic handbook of alcoholism* (pp. 874–884). New York: Gardener Press.

Sofuoglu, M., & Kosten, T. R. (2005). Novel approaches to the treatment of cocaine addiction. *CNS Drugs, 19*(1), 13–25.

Spitz, H. I., & Rosecan, J. S. (1987). *Cocaine abuse: New directions in treatment and research.* New York: Brunner/Mazel.

Stotts, A. L., Schmitz, J. M., Rhoades, H. M., & Grabowski, J. (2001). Motivational interviewing with cocaine-dependent patients: A pilot study. *Journal of Consulting and Clinical Psychology, 69*(5), 858–862.

Svanum, S., & Ehrmann, L. C. (1992). Alcoholic subtypes and the MacAndrew Alcoholism

Scale. *Journal of Personality Assessment, 58,* 411–422.

Swartz, M. S., Swanson, J. W., & Hannon, M. L. (2003). Detection of illicit substance use among persons with schizophrenia by radioimmunoassay of hair. *Psychiatric Services, 54,* 891–895.

Tims, F. M., & Leukefeld, C. G. (Eds.). (1993). *National Institute of Health Research Monograph No. 135: Cocaine treatment: Research and clinical perspectives.* Rockville, MD: National Institute of Health.

Tutton, C. S., & Crayton, J. W. (1993). Current pharmacotherapies for cocaine abuse: A review. *Journal of Addictive Diseases, 12,* 109–127.

U.S. Congress, Office of Technology Assessment. (1983). *The effectiveness and costs of alcoholism treatment.* Washington, DC: U.S. Government Printing Office.

U.S. Department of Health and Human Services. (1992). *Annual emergency room data: Data from the drug abuse network* (DHHS Publication No. 94–3017). Rockville, MD: Author.

U.S. Department of Health and Human Services. (2004). *NIDA infofacts: Crack and cocaine.* Rockville, MD: National Institutes of Health.

Van Horn, D. H. A., & Frank, A. F. (1998). Psychotherapy for cocaine addiction. *Psychology of Addictive Behaviors, 12*(1), 47–61.

Volpicelli, J. R., Alterman, A. I., Hayasgida, M., & O'Brien, C. P. (1992). Naltrexone in the treatment of alcohol dependence. *Archives of General Psychiatry, 49,* 876–880.

Wambach, K. G. (1999). The utility of "tree-generating" statistics in applied social work research. *Evaluation and Program Planning, 22,* 375–385.

Washton, A. M. (1987). Outpatient treatment techniques. In A. M. Washton & M. S. Gold (Eds.), *Cocaine: A clinicians' handbook* (pp. 106–117). New York: Guilford Press.

Washton, A. M., & Stone-Washton, N. (1991). Outpatient treatment of cocaine addiction: Suggestions to increase its effectiveness. *International Journal of the Addictions, 25,* 1421–1429.

Weiss, R. D., Griffin, M. L., Gallop, R. J., Najavits, L. M., Frank, A., Crits-Christoph, P., et al. (2005). The effect of 12-step self-help group attendance and participation on drug use outcomes among cocaine-dependent patients. *Drug and Alcohol Dependence, 77,* 177–184.

Weiss, R. D., Griffin, M. L., Mazurick, M. L., Berkman, B., Gastfriend, D. R., Frank, A., et al. (2003). The relationship between cocaine craving, psychosocial treatment, and subsequent cocaine use. *American Journal of Psychiatry, 160,* 1320–1325.

Wells, E. A., Peterson, P. L., Gainey, R. R., Hawkins, J. D., & Catalano, R. F. (1994). Outpatient treatment for cocaine abuse: A controlled comparison of relapse prevention and 12-step approaches. *American Journal of Drug and Alcohol Abuse, 20,* 1–17.

Wiegmann, D. A., Stanny, R. R., McKay, D. L., Neri, D. F., & McCardie, A. H. (1996). Methamphetamine effects on cognitive processing during extended wakefulness. *International Journal of Aviation Psychology, 6*(4), 379–397.

Wikler, A. (1948). Recent progress in research on the neurophysiological basis of morphine addiction. *American Journal of Psychiatry, 105,* 328–338.

Withers, N. W., Pulvirenti, L., Koob, G. F., & Gillin, J. C. (1995). Cocaine abuse and dependence. *Journal of Clinical Psychopharmacology, 15,* 63–78.

Worthington, T. (1987, September 7). The crack challenge from across the Atlantic. *Social Work Today, 21,* 20–21.

Opioid-Related Disorders

Laura Hopson and Melissa Radey

11

Chapter

Learning Objectives

After reading this chapter, the reader will be able to:

- Recognize the different forms and signs of the misuse of opiates.
- Identify the populations most affected by opioid disorders.
- Identify evidence-based approaches to treating opioid disorders.
- Understand the evidence-based approaches to assessment of opioid disorders.

Overview of the Problem

Prevalence and Incidence

Misuse of opioids exacts an enormous toll on users and on our society as a whole. The use of heroin, the most commonly abused opioid, has decreased in recent years but continues to threaten many lives. According to a 2002 survey by the Community Epidemiology Work Group, which collects information about illicit drug use in 21 U.S. cities, admissions for heroin treatment accounted for 62% to 82% of all admissions for illicit drug use in participating northeastern cities (National Institute on Drug Abuse [NIDA], 2004).

In the 2004 National Survey of Drug Use and Health (NSDUH) conducted by the Substance Abuse and Mental Health Services Administration (SAMHSA), 398,000 respondents over the age of 12 reported heroin use, compared with 314,000 in 2003. In 2004, 21,000 children between the ages of 12 and 17 reported heroin use, compared with 12,000 in 2003 (SAMHSA, 2005). In 2003 heroin abuse was involved in 8% of emergency department cases (NIDA, 2006). Heroin users are predominantly White men over the age of 30 living in cities (Office of National Drug Control Policy [ONDCP], 2002).

Although reported heroin use has declined, the number of NSDUH respondents reporting nonmedical use of pain relievers has increased. Opioids among these pain relievers include Oxy-Contin and methadone (SAMHSA, 2004). The number of new users of pain relievers for nonmedical purposes increased from 600,000 in 1991 to 2 million in 2001. In 2002, almost 30 million people reported using pain relievers for nonmedical reasons at least once. Young adults ages 18 to 25 were about twice as likely as children or older adults to have used pain relievers nonmedically. Nonmedical use was higher among males than females and higher among Whites than other racial/ethnic groups (SAMHSA, 2004).

Social and Financial Costs

Although the amount that Americans spent on heroin has decreased since 1990, Americans spent $10 billion on the drug in 2000. Opioids also impose heavy costs in the form of resources dedicated to drug-related arrests and convictions. The Drug Enforcement Agency reported 3,557 arrests for opioids out of 38,411 total drug arrests between October 1999 and September 2000. During 2001, 1,757 federal drug offenders were convicted of a crime involving heroin (ONDCP, 2003).

Illicit use of opioids such as heroin causes serious medical complications that result from abuse. Chronic heroin users may suffer from collapsed veins, bacterial infections of blood vessels, soft tissue infections, and liver or kidney disease. Poor respiration makes chronic heroin users susceptible to pneumonia and tuberculosis. Injection drug use also greatly increases risk for HIV/AIDS and hepatitis B and C (ONDCP, 2003). Death rates for those dependent on opioids may be as high as 2% per year. Death from opioid dependence most often results from overdose, injuries, AIDS, or other medical problems (*Diagnostic and Statistical Manual of Mental Disorders* [*DSM-IV-TR*]; American Psychiatric Association, 2000).

Social Work Involvement

Substance abuse affects many of the clients that social workers traditionally serve (DiNitto, 2002). Social workers in mental health, health, and child welfare settings are likely to find that many of their clients are affected by drug use. Because chronic drug use is influenced by individual, family, community, and societal factors, the ecological perspective shared by social workers is particularly useful for assessment and treatment. Social workers have the versatility to take on multiple roles that include clinician, mediator, and advocate. All of these roles are helpful in treating substance abuse because it affects functioning in many different areas of a client's life (Sun, 2004). The strengths-based perspective that social workers bring to treatment is also important for treating substance abuse problems because it may help increase clients' motivation to address their substance abuse. This is critical because lack of motivation is one reason cited by drug users for discontinuing treatment (Ashery, Carlson, Falck, & Siegal, 1995).

Operational Definitions of the Problem

Opioids are classified as natural, semisynthetic, and synthetic. Morphine and opium are natural opioids; heroin is semisynthetic; methadone and codeine are synthetics. Opioids may be prescribed in the form of cough suppressants, analgesics, antidiarrheal medication, and anesthetics. Heroin is the most commonly abused drug in the opioid family and is typically injected, although it may also be smoked or snorted in powder form. Opioid intoxication is characterized by euphoria followed by apathy, impaired judgment and social functioning, and psychomotor agitation or retardation. Drowsiness and slurred speech are also common. The *DSM-IV* (American Psychiatric Association, 2000) specifies the following diagnostic criteria for opioid intoxication:

- Recent use of an opioid.
- Clinically significant behavioral or psychological changes, which may include euphoria followed by apathy, agitation or psychomotor retardation, and impaired judgment, and social functioning.
- Constricted pupils, or dilated pupils in the case of a severe overdose, and at least one of the following:
  —Drowsiness or coma.
  —Slurred speech.
  —Poor attention or memory.
- The above symptoms are not due to a medical condition or another mental disorder.

Symptoms of withdrawal from opioids can be life threatening and include dysphoria, nausea, muscle aches, dilated pupils, fever, sweating, diarrhea, and insomnia (American Psychiatric Association, 2000).

Opioid dependence is characterized by tolerance, a need for increased amounts of the drug to achieve the same effects. Withdrawal symptoms occur when use is discontinued abruptly. Individuals who are dependent on opioids may structure their daily activities around obtaining and using them. In contrast to opioid dependence, abuse is characterized by less frequent use of the drug and the absence of withdrawal symptoms with discontinued use. Abuse is associated with recurrent use that results in failure to fulfill obligations, legal problems, and interpersonal difficulties (American Psychiatric Association, 2000).

Evidence-Based Approaches to Assessment

Timely, comprehensive, and ongoing assessment that examines the many dimensions of a client's life provides the foundation for social work treatment of a substance abuse problem (Johnson, 2004). Fundamental to treatment, practitioners must gain rapport with their clients and engage their clients to become active partners in the treatment process. No one theory explains chemical dependency, thus practitioners should develop a multisystemic approach to address client issues. Through interviewing the client, taking a history of the problem, and administering psychological tests, practitioners can determine the nature and causes of a client's problem which can help to determine a treatment plan that fits both the client and the social worker. The assessment of the problem can dramatically affect treatment. Long- and short-term goals are affected by the extent and seriousness of the problem, the client's motivation, the setting, the projected treatment time, client and therapist preferences, and the cooperation of others (Lewis, Dana, & Blevins, 2002).

As with the assessment of any client's problem, an assessment for opioid abuse must include a clear and accurate description of the client's life, including problems, strengths, and recommendations for the client to create and maximize successful changes (Gambrill, 1997). To gain the most complete picture of a client, Johnson (2004) outlines nine important dimensions of assessment: (1) client description, including presenting problem and the context of the referral; (2) treatment history; (3) substance abuse history; (4) medical history; (5) basic needs; (6) psychological and emotional functioning; (7) family history and structure; (8) the community and macro context; and (9) the client's motivation. In addition to these specific dimensions, practitioners must also consider what role cultural context plays in the client's strengths and areas for improvement. The influence of culture on the assessment instrument results, including translation, measured constructs, cultural characteristics, and acculturation and biculturation, must be considered (Kurtines & Szapocznik, 1995).

The opportunity for clients to self-report their substance use is a helpful mechanism in assessment. The validity of self-report relies on a variety of contextual and interpersonal factors (Meyers et al., 1999). Studies on self-report have found good validity in situations where clients are sober, feel safe, and are in a clinical rather than legal setting (Sobell & Sobell, 1990, 1995). Self-report methods are easy to administer, easy to quantify and analyze, inexpensive, and can be used in a variety of ways, including by a clinician, by the client, over the telephone, by mail, or by computer (Patrick et al., 1994; Richter & Johnson, 2001).

Along with the advantages of self-report methods for substance use assessment, clinicians must consider the disadvantages. Client characteristics can affect the validity of self-report. When considering the use of self-reported drug use, McAllister and Makkai (1991) found that adults underreport the use of drugs less frequently than adolescents, and younger adolescents underreport use less frequently than older adolescents. By design, clients can present themselves as they want on self-report questionnaires to meet demand characteristics and appear more socially desirable. Thus, clients can mask their substance abuse, complicating treatment. Although the formula of the diagnostic instrument increases quantifiability, it does not consider the client's motivation and context, fundamental elements in competent social work practice.

In addition to completing general clinical interviews, a variety of both self-report and biological strategies can be used to gain a fuller picture of the opioid-using client. Among these are structured interviews, screening questionnaires, computerized assessment tools, self-report methods, and biological methods. This section outlines the usefulness and precautions for use of these various methods.

Structured Clinical Interviews

An assortment of structured clinical interviews can be used with clients to provide a valid and reliable assessment of substance abuse or dependence. Although not specific to opioid use, several interview schedules include a substance abuse section, for example, the Diagnostic Interview Survey (DIS; Robins, Helzer, Croughan, & Ratcliff, 1981) and the Structured Clinical Interview for *DSM-IV* Axis I Disorders (SCID; First, Spitzer, Gibbon, & Williams, 1996). The DIS and the SCID contain questions regarding presence of substances and problems with substances in clients' lives to yield a specific psychiatric diagnosis. However, the

Addiction Severity Index (ASI) and the Substance Dependence Severity Scale (SDSS) were designed with special attention to substance use problems.

Although originally designed as a research instrument, the ASI (McLellan et al., 1992) is increasingly accepted as a valid and reliable screening tool to assess for substance abuse problems (Treatment Research Institute, 1990). The instrument is designed to determine a client's need for treatment from severity ratings that the practitioner assigns based on a semistructured interview. The interview examines eight problem areas: medical status, employment, social support, drug use, alcohol use, legal status, family/social status, and psychiatric status. The ASI examines use in the past 30 days and does not detect the history or severity of longer term use. The scores range from 0 (no treatment necessary) to 9 (treatment needed to intervene in life-threatening situation). Although the ASI has been used on many populations, including the homeless, pregnant women, gamblers, and prisoners, its reliability and validity have been tested only on adults seeking treatment for substance abuse problems (McLellan, Randall, Joseph, & Alterman, 1991) and people with alcoholism and serious mental illness (Teitelbaum & Carey, 1996).

Miele et al. (2000b) designed the SDDSS to assess the severity of substance disorders according to standard diagnostic criteria and to assess the severity of multiple substances when applicable. The SDSS is a semistructured interview administered by a clinician that examines *DSM-IV* dependence and abuse for alcohol and illicit drugs. The interview examines the dimensions of the frequency of symptoms and the severity of symptoms in the 30 days before the interview. Results indicate that the SDSS is a reliable and valid instrument for assessing opioid abuse and dependence (Miele et al., 2000a, 2000b).

Structured interviews provide a clinician with an outline of questions to determine assessment and diagnosis. Clinicians are also able to consider the client's motivation and context when assessing the client and situation. Along with these strengths, clinicians must consider the biases of the interview approach. When clinicians interpret results, they may record client responses differently based on their preconceived notions or stereotypes (Richter & Johnson, 2001). As with all social work practice, clinicians must remember not to make assumptions about their clients. Instead, asking additional questions and probing clients can help to illuminate a client's situation.

Screening Questionnaires

Many screening instruments exist for the assessment of alcohol abuse, but the tools for accessing drug use are less prevalent and sophisticated. Although new tools are constantly being designed and tested, the limited use of screening instruments for opioids at the present time may be attributable to the stronger reliance on biological measures (A. Abbott & Wood, 2000). This section outlines the most commonly used assessment instruments for substance abuse more generally and opioids more specifically when applicable.

The CAGE was developed by Ewing and Rouse (1974) originally to detect alcoholism and continues to be widely used to detect both alcohol and substance abuse because of its simplicity and ease of use (Ewing, 1984). It contains four questions:

C   Have you tried to **C**ut down on your drinking/drug use?

A   Have people **A**nnoyed you by criticizing your drinking/drug use?

G   Have you ever felt **G**uilty about your drinking/drug use?

E   Have you ever used alcohol/drugs in the morning as an **E**ye-opener?

Clients answering yes to two or more of the questions are likely to be alcohol or drug dependent; clients answering yes to one question require more assessment.

This Substance Abuse Subtle Screening Inventory 3, developed by G. Miller (1983), is a relatively short screening tool based on client self-report of lifetime substance abuse. Clients can complete the drug scales and the 52 true/false assessment questions alone or through an interview. The instrument combines measures of obvious substance abuse with signs and symptoms of subtle items seemingly unrelated to substance abuse. It covers the dimensions of symptoms, values, attitudes, defensiveness, family dynamics, and involvement with the criminal justice system. It also screens for random answer patterns to detect randomness, faking, or comprehension problems during assessment (Johnson, 2004). There are versions for both adults and adolescents. A review of studies finds the instrument valid to detect chemical dependency (Kerr, 1994).

Similar to the Michigan Alcoholism Screening Test for alcoholism assessment, the Drug Abuse Screening Test is a self-administered questionnaire designed to reveal problems with drug use. Research studies support the use of the test, with sensitivity levels of 85% and alpha coefficients between .88 and .92 (Gavin, Ross, & Skinner, 1989; Saltstone, Hallivell, & Hayslip, 1994; Skinner, 1982).

Designed by J. Carroll (1984), the self-administered Substance Abuse Problem Checklist contains 377 items grouped into eight areas: motivation, health problems, personality, social relationships, job, leisure time, religion/spirituality, and legal issues.

This Drug Use Screening Inventory-Revised, developed by Tarter (1990), contains 149 yes/no questions covering 10 domains: substance abuse, psychiatric disorders, health status, behavior problems, peer relations, social competence, school, work, family, and leisure. The instrument indicates the intensity of the problems specific to each of these areas. Preliminary testing reports adequate validity (Tarter, Mezzich, Kirisci, & Kaczynksi, 1992).

The Drug Lifestyle Screening Inventory seeks to uncover serious drug misuse by examining four behavioral dimensions associated with drug use: irresponsibility or pseudo-responsibility, stress or coping imbalance, interpersonal triviality, and social rule breaking or bending (Walters, 1994). Walters (1995) found the instrument to have adequate interrater reliability, internal consistency, and concurrent validity.

The Severity of Dependence Scale contains five instruments designed to tap into the subjective aspects of drug dependence. The questions examine a client's concerns about stopping, anxiety regarding missing a dose, and perceived difficulty in quitting the drug. Out of a possible 15 points, a score of 4 has been recommended as a cutoff point for heroin users (Swift, Copeland, & Hall, 1998). The instrument is useful as a quick assessment in a clinical setting (Swift et al., 1998; Teesson, Degenhardt, & Hall, 2002).

Assessment Specific to Opioids

In addition to the variety of assessment tools for substance use in general, the Severity of Opiate Dependence Questionnaire (SODQ) and the Opiate Treatment Index (OTI) were designed specifically for the assessment of opioids. Sutherland et al. (1986) developed the SODQ as an opiate version of the Severity of Alcohol Dependence Questionnaire. The SODQ is a self-administered questionnaire in five sections: the quantity and pattern of opiate use, physical symptoms of withdrawal, affective symptoms of withdrawal including craving, withdrawal-relief drug taking, and rapidity of reinstatement of withdrawal symptoms after a period of abstinence. Research indicates that the instrument is both reliable and valid.

The OTI is an easily administered instrument with good psychometric properties (Darke, Ward, Zador, & Swift, 1991). The instrument assesses opiate use by examining basic demographics, treatment history and drug use consumption measures, assessments of HIV risk-taking behavior, social functioning, criminality, health, and psychological adjustment (Teesson et al., 2002). The resulting index is a simple checklist to provide a global assessment of the health status of drug users. Darke and colleagues designed the instrument and have shown its reliability and validity (Darke, Baker, Dixon, Wodak, & Heather, 1992; Darke et al., 1991).

Physiological Measures

Physiological measures, such as urinalysis and hair analysis, provide alternative or supplemental measures to self-report measures. Although denial among opioid users is less common than for users of other drugs (Mangura & Lipton, 1988), the biological test may assist clients in admitting to their substance use, knowing their usage will be uncovered in any case. Despite these advantages, biological assessment methods are often inferior with regard to sensitivity and specificity when compared to self-report and can create major barriers to practitioner-client rapport (Johnson, 2004; Richter & Johnson, 2001). In addition, false-positive results can occur without confirmation from expensive analytic methods (Meyers et al., 1999).

Urinalysis, the most common drug screen, uses client urine to detect the recent or current use of opioids. Specifically, the screen detects morphine and 6-acetylmorphine in the urine. A negative drug screen for opioids means that there is no evidence of use in the past 1 to 3 days. This can create problems in monitoring opioid use among clients seen on a less frequent basis (Verebey & Buchan, 1997). In addition, the cutoff concentration for positive use is 300 ngs/µl (nanograms per micro liter). Clients who approach this cutoff could test as false negatives (although they did use opioids, they tested negative for use), complicating their treatment and the client-practitioner relationship. In addition, urinalysis does not provide information about use patterns, history, or any other contextual information that is necessary for an appropriate assessment.

Hair analysis examines a client's strand of hair for substance use. Although urinalysis has a brief detection window of a couple of days for opioids, the examination of a 4-centimeter-long strand of hair extends the time to over a month, depending on the severity of use. With this longer detection time, hair analysis may miss opioid use in the past week. Also, hair strands may yield a false-positive result if environmentally contaminated (Verebey & Buchan, 1997). Hair analysis also becomes problematic for clients with short hair (Dembo et al., 1999). In addition, hair analysis is a relatively new technique, and therefore appropriate cutoff concentrations and appropriate result interpretations in terms of dosage and frequency of substance use remain under consideration (Magura, Laudet, & Goldberger, 1999).

Saliva tests can also detect opioids. Saliva provides a noninvasive test, but has a detection window between 12 and 24 hours. In addition, the collection can become easily contaminated and the collection process can influence the pH and s/p ratios in the saliva, possibly altering the results. Overall, saliva is used minimally at the current time, but as technology improves its usage could increase in the future for short-term detection, such as testing automobile drivers in accidents (Verebey & Buchan, 1997).

Research indicates that morphine can be detected in sweat (Cone, 1993). Routine sweat collection is difficult because its production is highly contingent on environmental conditions and there is a lack of sweat detection devices. In response to these problems, a patch, similar to a Band-Aid, was developed to collect sweat for up to 2 weeks to detect the use of drugs. Although there is high intersubject variability, the use of the patch looks promising (Verebey & Buchan, 1997).

Computerized Assessment Methods

For some opioid-using clients, computer-assisted self-interviews (CASIs) can assist in the detection of misuse. These instruments give clients a greater sense of confidentiality by allowing them to enter their responses automatically. The presentation of one item at a time often lowers confusion among clients, and computerized skip patterns ensure that clients answer only applicable questions. In addition, CASIs will alert clients if they enter answers that contradict each other (Richter & Johnson, 2001). When compared with pencil-and-paper tests, research found that CASIs increased the speed of data processing and resulted in fewer missing data (Hallfors, Khatapoush, Kadushin, Watson, & Saxe, 2000). The speed and unbiased accuracy may make up for the loss of rapport and trust with clients (Weber, Miracle, & Skehan, 1994). Thus, although practitioners can use computerized assessment to gain information about a client's opioid-using behavior in a confidential setting, clinicians will still need to complete the in-depth clinical interview to help some clients to recognize and admit to their drug misuse (Morrison, McCusker, Stoddard, & Bigelow, 1995).

Evidence-Based Approaches to Intervention

A range of interventions are available to treat addiction to opioids, especially heroin. The National Institutes of Health recommends the following improvements to opioid addiction treatment:

- *Better access to methadone maintenance programs.*
- *Removal of federal and state regulations that impede access to methadone maintenance.*
- *Including substance abuse counseling, psychosocial therapies, and supportive services in treatment. (NIDA, 2006)*

Because successful treatment of opioids is affected by a range of factors, including the client's family, peer group, employment, and financial situation, multicomponent interventions may be necessary.

Research has demonstrated the effectiveness of several individual, group, and family interventions. However, few settings that serve clients with drug abuse problems use evidence-based practices. Some of the barriers to implementing these practices in community settings include the costs of implementation, the organization's philosophy, and beliefs among practitioners that the intervention will not help their clients (Robbins, Bachrach, & Szapocznik, 2002). The current focus on bridging the gap between practice and research may encourage stronger partnerships between practice and research settings and ultimately result in greater use of evidence-based practices.

Individual Therapies

Supportive-expressive psychotherapy (SEP) is an individual counseling approach to reducing opioid abuse. The approach consists of two main components: supportive techniques to encourage an open discussion about clients' personal experiences and expressive techniques that assist clients in identifying and addressing interpersonal relationship issues. In both of these areas, the sessions focus on the impact of drug use on clients' behavior and finding approaches to solving problems without drug use.

Supportive-expressive psychotherapy has been evaluated with clients who have psychiatric problems and are receiving methadone treatment. Clients who received SEP required less methadone treatment than those who received standard drug counseling, but opioid use was similar in both groups. In an earlier study, clients addicted to opioids who received both drug counseling and SEP experienced better outcomes in methadone treatment than those who received drug counseling alone (Woody, McLellan, Luborsky, & Brien, 1987, 1995).

Individualized drug counseling is another approach that has successfully reduced opioid use. This intervention focuses on stopping the client's drug use while addressing other areas of functioning, such as employment problems and social relations. The intervention employs short-term behavioral goals and individualized counseling to assist the client in developing coping strategies and tools for abstaining from drug use. The client is also encouraged to participate in a 12-step program. Research findings indicate that opioid users receiving methadone treatment in addition to individualized drug counseling had significantly greater reductions in opioid use compared with those who received methadone treatment alone (McLellan, Arndt, Metzger, Woody, & O'Brien, 1993).

Motivational interviewing has been used to address a range of alcohol and substance abuse disorders. The therapist works collaboratively with the client using empathy, questioning, and reflective listening. The goal of therapy is to increase motivation by identifying discrepancies between present behavior and goals (W. R. Miller, 1996). Saunders, Wilkenson, and Phillips (1995) found that heroin addicts participating in motivational interviewing complied with treatment and abstained from drug use longer than those in the control group.

Voucher-based reinforcement therapy uses vouchers as an incentive to abstain from drug use while receiving methadone maintenance treatment. Clients receive vouchers when their routine urine samples are drug free. The vouchers can be used to obtain goods and services that are consistent with treatment goals. To reward continued abstinence, the value of the vouchers is low at the beginning of treatment and increases with the number of consecutive drug-free urine samples. A drug-positive sample results in reducing the value of vouchers to the low starting value. Research indicates that participation in the voucher program is associated with significant decreases in heroin-positive urine samples (Silverman et al., 1996).

Detoxification is a process of systematically withdrawing a client from opioid use under the care of a physician. It is used as a precursor to drug treatment to reduce the physiological effects of withdrawal. Because the side effects of withdrawal from opioids are dangerous and can be fatal, detoxification is often necessary for chronic users. However, the approach does not address psychological, behavioral, and social issues associated with addiction and is unlikely to result in long-term recovery (Kleber, 1996).

Pharmacological Interventions

Methadone maintenance treatment is the most commonly prescribed pharmacological intervention for opioid addiction. Methadone is a synthetic opioid that blocks the effects of heroin for approximately 24 hours. It effectively reduces opioid use when prescribed in the correct dose. Like methadone, Levo-alphacetylmethadol (LAAM) is a synthetic opioid that inhibits the effects of other opioids. Because its effects last up to 72 hours, clients can take the drug three times a week instead of daily (NIDA, 2005).

Naltrexone is often used to block the effects of morphine, heroin, and other opioids. Following detoxification clients are administered doses of naltrexone three times per week, usually in conjunction with group therapy sessions. In addition to helping clients cope with the effects of withdrawal, the medication blocks the euphoric effects of heroin and other opioids, and therefore helps to prevent relapse (Matthias, 2003). The approach is most successful when combined with voucher-based reinforcement therapy, outlined earlier (K. M. Carroll et al., 2001).

Buprenorphine is a drug that allows greater flexibility in treatment scheduling. It is prescribed in a doctor's office, and therefore helps integrate treatment for opioid addiction with mainstream health services. The drug may also be prescribed in combination with naloxone, a drug that is often used to treat opioid overdose. Because it appears to have a lower potential for abuse, buprenorphine may be preferable to methadone for many clients (NIDA, 2006). Research indicates that clients receiving a combination of buprenorphine and naloxone experienced greater reductions in opioid abuse than those who received a placebo (NIDA, 2004).

Group Therapies

Network therapy (NT) engages family members and friends in treatment to support participation in therapy and reduced drug use. Behavioral skills training and medication monitoring are included in treatment, and the client is often referred to a 12-step program as well. The approach has been used successfully to improve compliance with addiction treatment. In a study evaluating the efficacy of NT compared with medication management using buprenorphine, heroin addicts receiving NT had fewer drug-positive urine samples than those receiving medication management (Galanter et al., 2004).

Programs such as Alcoholics Anonymous (AA) and Narcotics Anonymous (NA) are 12-step self-help programs that promote abstinence from drug use. The principles that are central to the 12 steps of treatment in NA include admitting that the drug use is a problem, seeking help, engaging in self-examination, disclosing drug use, making amends for any harm done to others, and helping others with their addiction (Narcotics Anonymous, 2005).

Although there are few studies examining the effectiveness of 12-step programs, they are often used in conjunction with evidence-based drug treatment. The limited research evaluating 12-step programs focuses predominantly on AA programs. In the early 1990s, a Methadone Anonymous (MA) group was founded in Maryland. A survey found that members felt that MA affiliation was more helpful than services provided by their methadone maintenance service providers (Gilman, Galanter, & Dermatis, 2001). Another study found that serving as a sponsor for another member in a 12-step program was associated with decreased injection drug use, although having a sponsor was not associated with decreased use (Crape, Latkin, Laris, & Knowlton, 2002).

Couples and Family Therapies

Behavioral couples therapy (BCT) typically engages the substance abuser and spouse in 15 to 20 couples sessions over the course of about 6 months. The model assumes that ending the substance abuse is the couple's primary goal and uses problem-solving and communication skills training in highly structured sessions to enhance relationship functioning and decrease substance abuse. At the beginning of treatment, the couple agrees to a behavioral contract which states that they will abstain from drug use and engage in a brief daily discussion about trust and drug use. The couple is also asked to complete behavioral homework assignments before the next session (Fals-Stewart, Birchler, & O'Farrell, 1996).

Fals-Stewart et al. (1996) found that men who participated in BCT reported less drug use and longer periods of abstinence than those in a comparison group. Husbands receiving BCT also reported fewer negative consequences resulting from drug use.

Community Interventions

The therapeutic community (TC) is an intensive, comprehensive treatment approach to treating addiction. Clients reside in the TC, which aims to immerse them in a lifestyle that promotes abstinence and identifies negative behaviors that can lead to drug use. The earliest communities relied on punishments, contracts, and peer pressure to change behavior, although these approaches have been modified over time. Clients now are taught values that encourage living in the present and changing the way they relate to peers, significant others, and society. They are expected to perform jobs within the TC to help maintain its daily operations. Residing in a TC usually means being physically excluded from external influences in order to reinforce the sense of community within the TC. Residents receive individual counseling and participate in group activities, seminars, and opportunities to interact with other residents formally and informally (SAMHSA, 1999). Research conducted by NIDA found that participation in a TC was associated with lower levels of heroin and other drug use as well as a reduction in criminal behavior, unemployment, and symptoms of depression (NIDA, 2002).

The community reinforcement approach (CRA) aims to help clients make lifestyle adjustments that reduce drug abuse. The approach focuses on changing environmental factors that may be related to substance abuse, such as employment, recreation, and family involvement. Although the approach has been studied more often with cocaine-addicted rather than opioid-addicted individuals, a few studies indicate its effectiveness in reducing opioid use and completing treatment (Roozen et al., 2004). One study found that those receiving CRA were more likely to finish treatment than those receiving usual care in a detoxification program, and were able to abstain from drug use for more consecutive weeks (Bickel, Amass, Higgins, Badger, & Esch, 1997). In another study, those receiving CRA provided more consecutive drug-negative urine samples than those receiving usual care in a methadone maintenance program (P. J. Abbott, Moore, Weller, & Delaney, 1998).

Treatment Accountability and Safer Communities (TASC) is a community intervention that provides an alternative to incarceration for drug-addicted individuals in the criminal justice system. The program provides counseling, medical care, parenting skills training, job training, and employment services. It coordinates drug treatment with criminal justice, assesses criminal offenders for drug use, and makes appropriate treatment referrals, monitors drug use, and uses legal sanctions to induce offenders to continue treatment. Research indicates that participation in TASC is associated with significant reductions in drug relapse and criminal recidivism (Inciardi, Martin, Butzin, Hooper, & Harrison, 1997).

Summary

This chapter has provided a description of opioids and the populations that report opioid misuse. The chapter also describes evidence-based approaches to assessment and treatment of opioid disorders. Social workers are likely to encounter individuals who are struggling with their own substance use or that of someone in their social network. For this reason, it is critical that social workers understand the most effective ways of proceeding with these clients. By promoting the use of evidence-based practices in community settings, social workers will play an important role in bridging the gap that exists between research and practice in treating opioid disorders.

Study Questions

1. After an initial assessment, you determine that your client meets the diagnostic criteria for opioid dependence. How would you proceed with this client, and why?
2. Discuss the advantages and disadvantages of self-reported assessment in comparison to computerized assessment.
3. What behavioral characteristics would make you concerned that someone is dependent on opioids?
4. Describe a community intervention that is effective for treating opioid abuse.
5. Why might you choose a couples intervention over an individual intervention to address opioid abuse?
6. Explain the strengths and limitations of using physiological measures for opioid detection as opposed to self-report measures.

7. How would you know if a person was experiencing opioid withdrawal, and how would you proceed?

8. Are self-report measures for opioids reliable methods for detecting opioid misuse? Why or why not?

References

Abbott, A., & Wood, K. (2000). Assessment: Techniques and instruments for data collection. In A. Abbott (Ed.), *Alcohol, tobacco, and other drugs: Challenging myths, assessing theories, individualizing interventions* (pp. 159–186). Washington, DC: NASW Press.

Abbott, P. J., Moore, B. A., Weller, S. B., & Delaney, H. D. (1998). AIDS risk behaviors in opioid dependent patients treated with community reinforcement approach, and relationships with psychiatric disorders. *Journal of Addictive Diseases, 17,* 33–48.

American Psychiatric Association. (2000). *Diagnostic and statistical manual of mental disorders* (4th ed., text rev.). Washington, DC: Author.

Ashery, R. S., Carlson, R., Falck, R. S., & Siegal, H. (1995). Injection drug users, crack-cocaine users, and human services utilization: An exploratory study. *Social Work, 40,* 75–82.

Bickel, W. K., Amass, L., Higgins, S. T., Badger, G. J., & Esch, R. A. (1997). Effects of adding behavioral treatment to opioid detoxification with buprenorphine. *Journal of Consulting and Clinical Psychology, 65,* 803–810.

Carroll, J. (1984). Substance abuse problem checklist: A new clinical aid for drug and/or alcohol treatment dependency. *Journal of Substance Abuse Treatment, 1,* 31–36.

Carroll, K. M., Ball, S. A., Nich, C., O'Connor, P. G., Eagan, D. A., Frankforter, T. L., et al. (2001). Targeting behavioral therapies to enhance naltrexone treatment of opioid dependence: Efficacy of contingency management and significant other involvement. *Archives of General Psychiatry, 58,* 755–761.

Cone, E. (1993). Saliva testing for drugs of abuse. *Annals of the New York Academy of Science, 694,* 91–127.

Crape, B. L., Latkin, C. A., Laris, A. S., & Knowlton, A. R. (2002). The effects of sponsorship in 12-step treatment of injection drug users. *Drug and Alcohol Dependence, 65,* 291–301.

Darke, S., Baker, A., Dixon, J., Wodak, A., & Heather, N. (1992). Drug use and HIV risk-taking behavior among clients in methadone maintenance treatment. *Drug and Alcohol Dependence, 29,* 263–268.

Darke, S., Ward, J., Zador, D., & Swift, G. (1991). A scale for estimating the health status of opioid users. *British Journal of Addiction, 86,* 1317–1322.

Dembo, R., Shemwell, M., Guida, J., Schmeidler, J., Baumgartner, W., Ramirez-Garnica, G., et al. (1999). A comparison of self-report, urine sample, and hair sample testing for drug use: A longitudinal study. In T. Mieczkowski (Ed.), *Drug testing technology* (pp. 91–108). New York: CRC Press.

DiNitto, D. M. (2002). War and peace: Social work and the state of chemical dependency treatment in the United States. *Journal of Social Work Practice in the Addictions, 2*(3–4), 7–29.

Ewing, J. (1984). Detecting alcoholism: The CAGE questionnaire. *Journal of the American Medical Association, 252,* 1905–1907.

Ewing, J., & Rouse, B. (1974). Alcohol sensitivity and ethnic background. *American Journal of Psychiatry, 131,* 206–210.

Fals-Stewart, W., Birchler, G. R., & O'Farrell, T. J. (1996). Behavioral couples therapy for male substance-abusing patients: Effects of relationship adjustment and drug-using behavior. *Journal of Consulting and Clinical Psychology, 64,* 959–972.

First, M., Spitzer, R., Gibbon, M., & Williams, J. (1996). *Structured Clinical Interview for DSM-IV Axis I Disorders: Patient edition* (SCID-I/P, Version 2.0). New York: Biometrics Research Development.

Galanter, M., Dermatis, H., Glickman, L., Maslansky, R., Sellers, M. B., Neumann, E., et al. (2004). Network therapy: Decreased secondary opioid use during buprenorphine maintenance. *Journal of Substance Abuse Treatment, 26,* 313–318.

Gambrill, E. (1997). *Social work practice: A critical thinker's guide.* New York: Oxford University Press.

Gavin, D., Ross, H., & Skinner, H. (1989). Diagnostic validity of the Drug Abuse Screening Test in the assessment of *DSM-III* drug disorders. *British Journal of Addictions, 84,* 301–307.

Gilman, S. M., Galanter, M., & Dermatis, H. (2001). Methadone Anonymous: A 12-step program for methadone maintained heroin addicts. *Substance Abuse, 22,* 247–256.

Hallfors, D., Khatapoush, S., Kadushin, C., Watson, K., & Saxe, L. (2000). A comparison of paper versus computer-assisted self-interview for alcohol, tobacco, and other drug surveys. *Evaluation and Program Planning, 23,* 149–155.

Inciardi, J. A., Martin, S. S., Butzin, C. A., Hooper, R. M., & Harrison, L. D. (1997). An effective model of prison-based treatment for drug-involved offenders. *Journal of Drug Issues, 27,* 261–278.

Johnson, J. (2004). *Fundamentals of substance abuse practice.* Belmont, CA: Thomson Brooks/Cole.

Kerr, B. (1994). Review of Substance Abuse Subtle Screening Inventory (SASSI). In J. Conoley & J. Impara (Eds.), *The supplement to the eleventh mental measurements yearbook* (pp. 249–251). Lincoln: University of Nebraska Press.

Kleber, H. D. (1996). Outpatient detoxification from opiates. *Primary Psychiatry, 1,* 42–52.

Kurtines, W. M., & Szapocznik, J. (1995). Cultural competence in assessing Hispanic youths and families: Challenges in the assessment of treatment needs and treatment evolution for Hispanic drug-abusing adolescents. In E. Rahdert & D. Czechowicz (Eds.), *Adolescent drug abuse: Clinical assessment and therapeutic interventions* (NIDA Research Monograph 156, pp. 172–189). Washington, DC: U.S. Government Printing Office.

Lewis, J., Dana, R., & Blevins, G. (2002). *Substance abuse counseling.* Pacific Grove, CA: Thomson Brooks/Cole.

Mangura, S., Laudet, A., & Goldberger, B. (1999). Improving the validity of behavior drug abuse research through drug testing. In T. Mieczkowski (Ed.), *Drug testing technology* (pp. 91–108). New York: CRC Press.

Mangura, S., & Lipton, D. (1988). The accuracy of drug use monitoring in methadone treatment. *Journal of Drug Issues, 18,* 317–326.

Matthias, R. (2003). New approaches seek to expand naltrexone use in heroin treatment. *NIDA Notes, 17*(6). Retrieved January 20, 2005, from http://www.drugabuse.gov/NIDA_notes/NNVol17N6/Approaches.html.

McAllister, I., & Makkai, T. (1991). Correcting for the underreporting of drug use in opinion surveys. *International Journal of Addictions, 26,* 945–961.

McLellan, A., Kushner, H., Metzger, D., Peters, R., Smith, I., Grissom, G., et al. (1992). The 5th edition of the Addiction Severity Index: Historical critique and normative data. *Journal of Substance Abuse, 9,* 199–213.

McLellan, A., Randall, M., Joseph, N., & Alterman, A. (1991). Using the ASI to compare cocaine, alcohol, opiate, and mixed substance abusers. In L. Harris (Ed.), *Problems with drug dependence 1990* (NIDA Research Monograph, pp. 227–135). Washington, DC: U.S. Government Printing Office.

McLellan, A. T., Arndt, I. O., Metzger, D. S., Woody, G. E., & O'Brien, C. P. (1993). The effects of psychosocial services in substance abuse treatment. *Journal of the American Medical Association, 269,* 1953–1959.

Meyers, K., Hagan, T., Zanis, D., Webb, A., Frantz, J., Ring-Kurtz, S., et al. (1999). Critical issues in adolescent substance abuse assessment. *Drug and Alcohol Dependence, 55,* 235–246.

Miele, G., Carpenter, K., Sockerham, M., Trautman, K., Blaine, J., & Hasin, D. (2000a). Concurrent and predictive validity of the Substance Dependence Severity Scale (SDSS). *Drug and Alcohol Dependence, 59,* 77–88.

Miele, G., Carpenter, K., Sockerham, M., Trautma, K., Blaine, J., & Hasin, D.

(2000b). Substance Dependence Severity Scale (SDSS): Reliability and validity of a clinician-administered interview for *DSM-IV* substance use disorders. *Drug and Alcohol Dependence, 59,* 63–75.

Miller, G. (1983). *Substance Abuse Subtle Screening Inventory (SASSI).* Bloomington, IN: SASSI Institute.

Miller, W. R. (1996). Motivational interviewing: Research, practice, and puzzles. *Addictive Behaviors, 21,* 835–842.

Morrison, C., McCusker, J., Stoddard, A., & Bigelow, C. (1995). The validity of behavioral data reported by injection drug users on a clinical risk assessment. *International Journal of Addictions, 30,* 889–899.

Narcotics Anonymous. (2005). *Information about NA.* Retrieved January 25, 2005, from http://www.na.org/bulletins/berbull .htm.

National Institute on Drug Abuse. (2002). *Research report series: Therapeutic community.* Retrieved January 25, 2005, from http://www.drugabuse.gov/Research Reports/Therapeutic/default.html.

National Institute on Drug Abuse. (2004). *NIDA InfoFacts: Nationwide Trends,* Retrieved August 25, 2006, from http://www .drugabuse.gov/Infofacts/nationtrends.html.

National Institute on Drug Abuse. (2005). *Research Report Series: heroin abuse and addiction.* Retrieved August 25, 2006, from http://www.drugabuse.gov/ResearchReports /Heroin/Heroin.html.

National Institute on Drug Abuse. (2006). *InfoFacts: Heroin.* Retrieved August 25, 2006, from http://www.drugabuse.gov /infofacts/heroin.html.

Office of National Drug Control Policy. (2002). *Pulse check: Trends in drug abuse April 2002.* Retrieved January 20, 2005, from http://www.whitehousedrugpolicy.gov /publications/drugfact/pulsechk/apr02 /heroin.html.

Office of National Drug Control Policy. (2003). *Drug Policy Information Clearinghouse fact sheet, June, 2003.* Rockville, MD: Drug Policy Information Clearinghouse. Retrieved January 25, 2005, from www .whitehousedrugpolicy.gov.

Patrick, D., Cheadle, A., Thompson, D., Diehr, P., Koepsell, T., & Kinne, S. (1994). The validity of self-reported smoking: A re-

view and meta-analysis. *American Journal of Public Health, 84,* 1086–1093.

Richter, L., & Johnson, P. (2001). Current methods of assessing substance use: A review of strengths, problems, and developments. *Journal of Drug Issues, 31,* 809–832.

Robbins, M. S., Bachrach, K., & Szapocznik, J. (2002). Bridging the research-practice gap in adolescent substance abuse treatment: The case of brief strategic family therapy. *Journal of Substance Abuse Treatment, 23,* 123–132.

Robins, L., Helzer, J., Croughan, J., & Ratcliff, K. (1981). National Institute of Mental Health Diagnostic Interview Schedule. *Archives of General Psychiatry, 38,* 381–389.

Roozen, H. G., Boulogne, J. J., van Tulder, M. W., van den Brink, W., De Jong, C. A. J., & Kerkhof, A. J. F. M. (2004). A systematic review of the effectiveness of the community reinforcement approach in alcohol, cocaine, and opioid addiction. *Drug and Alcohol Dependence, 74,* 1–13.

Saltstone, R., Halliwell, S., & Hayslip, M. A. (1994). A multivariate evaluation of the Michigan Alcoholism Screening Test and the Drug Abuse Screening Test in a female offender population. *Addictive Behavior, 19,* 445–462.

Saunders, B., Wilkinson, C., & Phillips, M. (1995). The impact of a brief motivational intervention with opiate users attending a methadone programme. *Addiction, 90,* 415–424.

Silverman, K., Wong, C., Higgins, S., Brooner, R., Montoya, I., Contoreggi, C., et al. (1996). Increasing opiate abstinence through voucher-based reinforcement therapy. *Drug and Alcohol Dependence, 41,* 157–165.

Skinner, H. (1982). The drug abuse screening test. *Addictive Behaviors, 7,* 363–371.

Sobell, L., & Sobell, M. (1990). Self-report issues in alcohol abuse: State of the art and future directions. *Behavioral Assessment, 12,* 77–90.

Sobell, L., & Sobell, M. (1995). Alcohol consumption measures. In J. P. Allen & M. Columbus (Eds.), *Assessing alcohol problems: A guide for clinicians and researchers* (NIAAA Treatment Handbook, Series 4 NIH 95–3745, pp. 55–73). Bethesda, MD:

U.S. Department of Health and Human Services.

Substance Abuse and Mental Health Services Administration. (1999). *Tip 32: Treatment of adolescents with substance use disorders.* Retrieved January 25, 2005, from http://www.ncbi.nlm.nih.gov/books/bv.fcgi?rid=hstat5.chapter.56031.

Substance Abuse and Mental Health Services Administration. (2004). *Results from the 2003 National Survey on Drug Use and Health: National findings* (Office of Applied Studies, NSDUH Series H–25, DHHS Publication No. SMA 04-3964). Rockville, MD: Author.

Substance Abuse and Mental Health Services Administration. (2005). Overview of findings from the 2004 National Survey on Drug Use and Health (Office of Applied Studies, NSDUH Series H-27, DHHS Publication No. SMA 05-4061). Rockville, MD: Author.

Sun, A. (2004). Principles for practice with substance-abusing pregnant women: A framework based on the five social work intervention roles. *Social Work, 49,* 383–394.

Sutherland, G., Edwards, G., Taylor, C., Phillips, G., Gossop, M., & Brady, R. (1986). The measurement of opiate dependence. *British Journal of Addiction, 81,* 485–494.

Swift, W., Copeland, J., & Hall, W. (1998). Choosing a diagnostic cut-off for cannabis dependence. *Addiction, 93,* 1681–1692.

Tarter, R. (1990). Evaluation and treatment of adolescent substance abuse: A decision tree method. *American Journal of Drug and Alcohol Abuse, 16*(1–2), 1–46.

Tarter, R., Mezzich, A., Kirisci, L., & Kaczynksi, N. (1992). Reliability of the drug use screening inventory among ado-lescent alcoholics. *Journal of Child and Adolescent Substance Abuse, 3,* 25–36.

Teesson, M., Degenhardt, L., & Hall, W. (2002). *Addictions.* New York: Psychology Press.

Teitelbaum, L., & Carey, K. (1996). Alcohol assessment in psychiatric patients. *Clinical Psychology: Science and Practice, 3,* 323–338.

Treatment Research Institute. (1990). *The Addiction Severity Index manual and question by question guide.* Retrieved January 15, 2005, from http://www.research.org.

Verebey, K., & Buchan, B. (1997). Diagnostic laboratory: Screening for drug abuse. In J. Lowinson, P. Ruiz, R. Millman, & J. Langrod (Eds.), *Substance abuse: A comprehensive textbook* (pp. 367–376). Baltimore, MD: Williams & Wilkins.

Walters, G. (1994). Discriminating between high and low substance abusers by means of the Drug Lifestyle Screening Interview. *American Journal of Drug and Alcohol Abuse, 20,* 19–33.

Walters, G. (1995). Predictive validity of the Drug Lifestyle Screening Interview: A 2-year follow-up. *American Journal of Drug and Alcohol Abuse, 21,* 187–194.

Weber, L., Miracle, A., & Skehan, T. (1994). Interviewing early adolescents: Some methodological considerations. *Journal of Sociology and Applied Anthropology, 53,* 42–47.

Woody, G. E., McLellan, A. T., Luborsky, L., & O'Brien, C. P. (1987). Twelve month follow-up of psychotherapy for opiate dependence. *American Journal of Psychiatry, 144,* 590–596.

Woody, G. E., McLellan, A. T., Luborsky, L., & O'Brien, C. P. (1995). Psychotherapy in community methadone programs: A validation study. *American Journal of Psychiatry, 152,* 1302–1308.

SCHIZOPHRENIA AND OTHER PSYCHOTIC DISORDERS

Schizophrenia

Kia J. Bentley, Joseph Walsh,
A. Suzanne Boyd, and Melissa Floyd Taylor

12

Chapter

Learning Objectives

After reading this chapter, the reader will be able to:

- Identify historical developments in the diagnosis of Schizophrenia and the characteristic symptoms currently used to describe it, including identified subtypes.

- Describe the emotional, social, and economic costs of the disorder and articulate the role and relevance of social work practice in assisting individuals and families suffering with this disorder.

- Distinguish the available options used by clinicians and researchers for formally assessing the nature, quality, and severity of common characteristics or symptom patterns.

- Critically discuss the range of psychosocial approaches used in communities or agencies with individuals with Schizophrenia and their families that have garnered consensus in the field for their effectiveness and usefulness.

Overview of the Problem

Schizophrenia has been described in contemporary terms as "a genetically mediated neurodevelopmental disorder" (Lieberman et al., 2001, p. 884) but also more simply and colloquially as "one of today's best known and most common forms of madness" (Gottesman, 1991, p. 1). It is specifically a disorder of thought and considered, along with other disorders such as Bipolar Disorder and unipolar depression, to be one of the major mental disorders. The term "major" implies a high degree of severity and a pervasive negative impact on the everyday lives of those who struggle with symptoms, particularly those whose illness runs a chronic course necessitating long-term treatment.

Operational Definitions of the Problem

The diagnosis of Schizophrenia is made on the basis of the existence of an array of symptoms in an individual over time. Often, formal diagnosis is preceded by months or years of prodromal or early warning symptoms, such as distractibility, irritability, superstitiousness, bizarre or obsessive behavior, or social withdrawal (Lieberman et al., 2001). Schizophrenia is also considered a "diagnosis of exclusion," meaning that all other potential diagnoses, such as organic disorders, substance abuse, and affective disorders, should be ruled out before this one is applied. The current *Diagnostic and Statistical Manual of Mental Disorders* (*DSM;* American Psychiatric Association, 2000) warns about the difficulty in diagnosing Schizophrenia in the context of other cultures and the need to be sensitive to differences in an individual's presentation and communication style.

In general, there are thought to be two defining groups of symptoms in Schizophrenia. The first is psychosis, characterized by lack of reality testing and manifested by hallucinations ("false" perceptions such as hearing voices, seeing things that are not objectively there), delusions ("false" beliefs centered around, e.g., grandiosity, persecution, or personal reference), unusual behavior (bizarre or inappropriate actions), disturbed thinking (such as thought insertion or thought broadcasting), and disorganized speech (e.g., tangential, illogical, loose associations). In recent years this set of symptoms has come to be known as *positive* symptoms because they reflect *excesses or distortions* of typical human functioning. Second, Schizophrenia is characterized by so-called deficit or *negative symptoms* that reflect a *loss* of typical functioning, such as social withdrawal, avolition, and a flattening or restricting of affect often resulting in marked problems in interpersonal functioning. Some might say metaphorically that positive symptoms seem to reflect those symptoms the disorder "gives" and negative symptoms are those things the disorder "takes" from the person with Schizophrenia. For the diagnosis to be applied, the criteria require symptoms to be present for 6 months, with 1 month in an active phase (American Psychiatric Association, 2000). If a person's disorder is characterized more by positive symptoms, he or she is said to be Type 1, whereas those with primarily negative symptoms are considered to be suffering from Type 2. The distinctions of positive and negative have proved especially meaningful in distinguishing medication effects.

The *DSM* also provides a separate and slightly older list of subtypes of Schizophrenia, also based on the predominant features in a presenting individual. These are *paranoid,* characterized by persecutory delusions; *disorganized,* characterized by inappropriate affect; *catatonic,* characterized by bizarre body movements, posturing, or lack of responsiveness to the environment; *undifferentiated,* which means the individual does not meet the criteria of other subtypes; and finally, *residual,* meaning the individual has had a previous episode but currently has no prominent positive symptoms. Some in the field suggest that studies using neuroimaging, brain mapping, and other techniques in molecular biology and genetics will eventually yield better information with respect to subtypes (Amador & Ratakonda, 1996), with important implications for understanding the causes and course of Schizophrenia. It should also be noted that others, including social work scholars, are becoming more vocal in their critique of the potential of the heavy, often exclusive, emphasis on disease models and biological interventions for what they conceptualize as more complex *biopsychosocial* phenomena (Cohen, 2002; Kiesler, 2000).

The *DSM* is but one of the models of operational criteria used to define and describe Schizophrenia. The history of epidemiology is largely a history of debates about language, the emphasis given certain symptoms, and the appropriate breadth of definition (Amador & Ratakonda, 1996). For example, Bleuler, whose broad description of Schizophrenia replaced Kraepelin's more narrow dementia praecox around 1911, described the fundamental symptoms as the "4 As": *autism* (inappropriate) *affect, ambivalence* and (loose) *associations.* This characterization seems to emphasize what we now call negative symptoms. The Present State Examination (see later discussion) might be said to emphasize positive symptoms. No matter what the emphasis, the term Schizophrenia, chosen to reflect the split (schism or incongruence) between affect, behavior, and thought, may have led to widespread confusion of this disorder with "split personality," known today as Dissociative Identity Disorder (Sadock & Sadock, 2003). Of particular importance, in the context of a biological revolution and in spite of the hope of a discovered chemical or anatomical "definitive neuropathology," Schizophrenia is "still diagnosed today as it was at the turn of the century": through clinical judgment about observations of "abnormal patterns of thought and perception as inferred from language and behavior" (Gottesman, 1991, p. 17).

Although a considerable amount of evidence suggests strong roles for genetic and other biological factors (e.g., prenatal insult) in the etiology of Schizophrenia, no single element or combination of such elements have been conclusively demonstrated to be the cause of Schizophrenia. Indeed, the role of environmental stressors has also been strongly implicated in the onset of this disorder.

Prevalence, Incidence, Social and Economic Costs

Data from the Epidemiologic Catchment Area research, sponsored by the National Institute of Mental Health, shows the lifetime prevalence of Schizophrenia (total numbers who have or will have the disorder) to be 1.3% of the population in the United States. The incidence (in 1 year) is estimated at 0.025% to 0.05% of the population. There are now thought to be over 2 million people in America who have or will have Schizophrenia.

Males tend to have their first episode of Schizophrenia in their late teens and early 20s; this happens a bit later, in their late 20s, for females. In general, however, there are equal prevalence rates for males and females and an even geographical distribution in the United States and throughout the world. In addition, people with Schizophrenia tend to be born in winter or early spring. These statistics apparently seem to hold across time (past 200 years) and space (pastoral villages to industrial societies), with only modest variations by culture. Sadly, given the many effective medications and psychosocial interventions available (see later discussion), it is estimated that only about half of people with Schizophrenia receive treatment.

Complete and total remission in Schizophrenia is thought to be relatively uncommon, and most would describe the outlook in general terms as "guarded" (Zide & Gray, 2001, p. 43). Although not considered a progressive illness, in that it does not automatically get worse over a lifetime (indeed, the opposite is true), its course is typically described as variable. This is usually reflected in either a chronic course, with symptoms being less or more florid but never really disappearing, or one in which periods of substantial symptomatology are interspersed with periods of remission. As with many physical and mental disorders, though a typical course can be described, reliable and accurate prediction of any individual's course is still impossible. Some of the risk factors for a poorer prognosis are poor premorbid functioning, gradual onset, earlier age at onset, being male, a long active phase, existence of structural brain abnormalities, abnormal neurological functioning, having a history of Schizophrenia in the family, single marital status, and social isolation. This information can tell us only so much, however, because studies show that risk factors can account for only 38% of the variance in outcome (Black, Yates, & Andreason, 1988). In other words, we still don't know so much more than we do know with respect to the outcome and course of Schizophrenia.

Black and colleagues (1988) summarize 80 years of research on the devastating personal and social costs of the illness. Many people with Schizophrenia live under extreme social and economic limits. For example, 66% of people with Schizophrenia never marry, and only 34% live in their own home or in a relative's home. The social drift hypothesis explains the higher concentrations of people with Schizophrenia in poverty by noting the impairments in vocational functioning and the impact of stigma. Perhaps most startling (and underreported) is that 50% of people with Schizophrenia attempt suicide; 10% succeed, contributing to the lower life expectancy of people with this disorder. These statistics approach those of persons with affective disorders. In fact, suicide is the number one cause of premature death in Schizophrenia (Fenton, McGlashan, Victor, & Blyer, 1997).

It is estimated that 25% of all hospital beds are filled with someone diagnosed with Schizophrenia. Total societal costs are put at 2% of our gross national product. In today's dollars, that is close to $100 *billion*. This includes direct costs such as treatment and public assistance as well as indirect costs such as the loss of employment productivity by persons with Schizophrenia (Black et al., 1988). Emotional costs and family burden have been widely discussed in personal account literature and elsewhere. Stigma contributes to the difficulties faced by individuals and families in even openly discussing the disorder with those in their personal circles (Miller & Mason, 2002).

Relevance of Social Work Involvement

In spite of the grim picture painted thus far of the symptoms and costs of this disorder, many would say we are in a time of great optimism with respect to Schizophrenia. The expanding knowledge base relates to new brain imaging techniques, related discoveries in neurotransmission, brain anatomy, brain function, and genetics, and the seemingly constant introduction of new types of antipsychotic medications. Along with this influx of mainly biological knowledge and interventions, there is also a growing appreciation of psychosocial influences on onset, course, and treatment. These include stress, life events, early trauma, and the quality of the living environment. As we will see later in this chapter, the newer diagnostic and assessment techniques and effectiveness research in Schizophrenia are also causes for tremendous hope for all people with Schizophrenia, their families, and all providers in mental health.

Social workers, the largest professional group of providers in public and nonprofit mental health agencies, have been participating in these developments since Edith Horton, a graduate of what is now Columbia University School of Social Work, was sent out as an aftercare agent for two mental hospitals in 1904. Developments in the first 50 years of the past century—such as the rise of social psychiatry, the aftercare and mental hygiene movements and two World Wars—set the stage for expanded social work roles in mental health and mental illness. Today, social workers provide services to people with Schizophrenia in state and private hospitals, psychiatric units, community mental health centers, private clinics, residential treatment centers, group homes, rehabilitation centers, psychosocial clubhouses, and drop-in centers. They function as therapists, discharge planners, case managers, counselors, brokers, advocates, educators, group leaders, community organizers, researchers, program planners and evaluators, and, most important, as *partners* with people diagnosed with Schizophrenia, their families, and other providers who are trying to help improve the quality of human life.

Evidence-Based Approaches to Assessment

Described in this section are a range of instruments that may be used by social workers to assess symptoms, symptom changes, quality of life, levels of social functioning, and medication side effects for persons with Schizophrenia. We focus on instruments that are relatively short and have utility in clinical as well as research settings. First, however, we briefly describe several well-known instruments that are generally used in large-scale research studies.

Instruments Used in Research Studies

Schizophrenia can be diagnosed with the Schedule for Affective Disorders and Schizophrenia (Endicott & Spitzer, 1978), the Diagnostic Interview Schedule (Robins, Helzer, Croughan, & Ratcliff, 1981), the Present State Examination (Manchanda & Hirsch, 1986; Wing, Cooper, & Sartorius, 1974), and the Structured Clinical Interview (Spitzer, Williams, Gibbon, & First, 1992). The Quality of Life Questionnaire measures a client's general happiness, satisfaction of needs, and actualization of abilities (D. A. Bigelow, Gareau, & Young, 1990). The Katz Adjustment Scale is a self-report inventory about clients' social functioning that exists in two forms, one for use by clients and the other by close relatives (Katz & Lyerly, 1963; Platt, 1986). Both forms rate symptoms and social behavior, performance of socially expected activities, extent of free-time activities, and relatives' satisfaction with client functioning. The Social Behavior and Adjustment Scale assesses a client's performance of major life roles and the effects of that performance on members of the client's household (Platt, 1986; Platt,

Weyman, Hirsch, & Hewett, 1980). Large service system intervention outcomes can be measured with a new scale, the Schizophrenia Care and Assessment Program Health Questionnaire, which attends to clients' symptom levels, functional status, health status, quality of life, and safety (Lehman, Fischer, et al., 2003).

Symptom Measures for Use in Clinical Settings

The Brief Psychiatric Rating Scale (BPRS) measures symptom changes in persons with Schizophrenia (Overall & Gorman, 1962). It is not a diagnostic tool but provides a clinical profile at a single point in time. There are several versions of this instrument, but the most well-known includes 18 items, each rated on a 7-point scale. The BPRS includes 12 items specific to Schizophrenia and 6 for depression. The scale is constructed to measure symptoms of Schizophrenia, but along with the depression items it may also be considered a schizoaffective scale. Scores for the four domains of thinking disturbance, withdrawal/retardation, hostility/suspicion, and anxiety/depression can be calculated. It includes cutoff scores for evaluating symptom severity. The social worker is instructed to assess most client symptoms at the time of the interview, but six items may be rated on the basis of conditions during the prior 3 days. No standard interview protocol is included with this instrument, although it is recommended that the task be completed within 30 minutes. Reliability for the BPRS was established through Spearman intraclass coefficients of seven raters, with resulting scores ranging from .74 to .83 (Andersen et al., 1989). Concurrent validity was established by an overall correlation of .93 with one other rating scale in a study that included 475 clients.

The Psychiatric Symptoms Assessment Scale (PSAS; L. B. Bigelow & Berthot, 1989) is a revised version of the BPRS. The 23-item scale uses behavioral anchor points as guides for the social worker's decision making about ratings. The instrument includes the 18 BPRS items (although five are renamed), with 4 items added to expand the range of ratings for depression, mania, and Schizophrenia. A global "loss of functioning" item has also been added. The items, all of which include guidelines and examples, are rated on a 7-point scale. The order of items is arranged to reflect the sequence in which information is usually gathered in a clinical interview, and the social worker is instructed to rate the quality of a given behavior rather than its duration. In reliability tests, intraclass correlation coefficients for individual PSAS items fell between .33 (this was the only item below .63) and .87. Interrater reliability for overall PSAS scores was .93. Predictive validity was tested by assessing 60 clients with Schizophrenia while on medication and then after their medications were discontinued.

Scores of all but four items changed significantly in the predicted direction.

The Manchester Scale (Krawiecka, Goldberg, & Vaughan, 1977) is a short, easy-to-administer instrument, sensitive to symptom change, for monitoring persons with Schizophrenia. It consists of eight items with a 5-point rating scale that cover the three domains of positive symptoms, negative symptoms, and affect (anxiety and depression). The first four ratings are based on client responses to questions (no interview guidelines are provided), and the other four on observations made during the interview. A manual offers probe questions and rating guidelines. The scale is not intended to be used blindly; familiarity with the client's history is desirable. Interrater reliability for the Manchester Scale has been assessed at greater than .80, and concurrent validity was demonstrated through positive correlations of total scores with various external symptom severity criteria.

Classifying clients on the basis of symptoms that are predominantly positive or negative can have implications for intervention. The Scale for the Assessment of Negative Symptoms (SANS) and the Scale for the Assessment of Positive Symptoms (SAPS) are used to quantify these client characteristics (Andreasen, 1982; Andreasen & Olsen, 1982). The SANS is a 25-item instrument, rated along a 6-point scale, with five subscales (Affect, Poverty of Speech, Apathy, Anhedonia, and Impairment of Attention). The SAPS is a 35-item instrument with four subscales (Hallucinations, Delusions, Bizarreness, and Positive Thought Disorder) and one global assessment of affect. Subscales for both instruments contain a global rating index. Symptom ratings are to be considered within a time frame of 1 month. The SANS and SAPS are designed to be used in conjunction with client interviews, clinical observations, family member observations, and reports from professionals. Regarding reliability, the internal consistency for total scores was .90 for the SANS and .86 for the SAPS. Intraclass correlations averaged .83 to .92 for the global summaries and total scores for both instruments. Regarding validity, factor analysis indicated that the instruments measure independent symptom dimensions. Criterion validity was supported by the fact that higher functioning clients had less severe positive and negative symptoms than did lower functioning clients.

The Positive and Negative Syndrome Scale for Schizophrenia (PANSS) measures both types of symptoms, the relative predominance of one type to the other, and a measure of global pathology (Kay, Fiszbein, & Opler, 1987). The PANSS includes 18 items adapted from the BPRS and 12 items derived from another source. Seven items represent each of the positive and negative symptom scales, and 16 items represent general pathology. Each item includes a definition and anchoring criteria for the 7-point ratings. Positive and Negative Syndrome Scale for Schizophrenia ratings are based on information specific to a time period, usually the previous week. The social worker derives information primarily from the clinical interview but may also utilize input from other professionals and family members. The 30- to 40-minute semiformal interview consists of four prescribed phases: rapport development; probes of themes of pathology; questions about mood, anxiety, orientation, and reasoning; and a probing of areas where the client seems ambivalent. Instrument reliability has been demonstrated with Cronbach's alphas of .73 for the Positive Symptom subscale, .83 for the Negative Symptom subscale, and .79 for the General Pathology subscale. Construct validity was supported by the inverse correlation of positive and negative subscale scores. Criterion validity was supported by the relationship of the scale to a variety of external client variables.

Scales Measuring Quality of Life

Measures of the life quality and social functioning of persons with Schizophrenia acknowledge the importance of comprehensive community services for these clients. The Quality of Life Interview (QOLI), perhaps the best-known scale, is a structured, 45-minute instrument for use with persons who have serious mental illness, including Schizophrenia (Lehman, 1988). The QOLI can provide quality of life measures at a single point in time or measures of change in any of nine domains: living situation, family relations, social relations, leisure, work, finances, legal and safety concerns, and physical and mental health. The social worker first asks the client for a rating of general life satisfaction and then proceeds through the life domains, asking about objective life conditions and satisfaction with those conditions. The interview concludes with another question about life satisfaction and some open-ended probes. Clients receive scaled or dichotomous scores in all domains. The QOLI is highly structured to minimize interviewer effects, but the social worker must set limits as needed on a respondent's tendency to digress and judge whether a respondent can tolerate the interview and provide valid responses. In reliability testing, levels of internal consistency ranged from .44 to .90 for the subscales, and test-retest correlations ranged from .29 to .98. Content validity was established by selecting scale items from a variety of existing measures. Satisfactory construct validity was argued by (a) comparing intercorrelations of QOLI measures within each domain, (b) correlating general life satisfaction scores with QOLI domain scores, and (c) correlating general life satisfaction scores with another measure of psychopathology. Predictive validity was established by comparing overall predictive capacity of the model with other indicators of clients' life situations.

The Quality of Life Scale (QLS) is a 21-item instrument utilizing a semistructured interview to assess and monitor changes in deficit symptoms specific to Schizophrenia (Heinrichs, Hanlon, & Carpenter, 1984). The conceptual framework of the QLS asserts that symptom fluctuations occur in the areas of intrapsychic, interpersonal, and instrumental functioning. These domains are supported by factor analysis along with a fourth domain reflecting the client's participation in routine activity patterns. The QLS elicits information on symptoms and functioning during the preceding 4 weeks. It is scored on a 7-point scale and requires approximately 45 minutes to administer. The process is organized similarly to that of a clinical interview, and the social worker is instructed to use his or her own probes or prompts to elicit needed information. In a study involving five trained professionals, interrater reliability correlations were .88 for total scores and between .84 and .94 for each of the four domains. Construct validity was demonstrated by a factor analysis of 111 clients that supported the four scale dimensions for both males and females.

Social Functioning Scales

The Social Adjustment Scale II (SAS-II) consists of 52 items that measure interpersonal and instrumental performance in the five areas of work, relationships with household members, relationships with other relatives, performance of leisure and recreational activities, and personal well-being (Weismann, Sholomskas, & John, 1981). Global ratings of the domain areas are also included. Each item is rated on a 5-point scale based on information obtained during a 1-hour semistructured interview with the client or a significant other. Scores can be combined to yield an average performance per area or role. Ten factors have been statistically derived for the SAS-II from a large sample of persons with Schizophrenia: personal anguish, intimate relations, parental role, primary relationship, social relationships, work affect, sexual practices, major role performance, self-care, and economic independence. Interrater reliability for the scale was assessed at .98 in a study of 56 persons with Schizophrenia and their partners.

The University of California at San Diego Performance-Based Skills Assessment is a measure of social functioning for middle-aged and elderly persons with Schizophrenia living in the community (Patterson, Goldman, McKibbin, Hughs, & Jeste, 2001). The instrument measures the five domains of household chores (cooking and shopping), communication (use of the telephone), finances (counting change and paying bills), transportation (use of public transportation), and planning recreational activities (several outings). Each domain is assessed through standardized role-play tasks that are assigned to the participant for completion in the presence of the interviewer. The social worker rates the client's successful completion of each task on a Likert scale that ranges between 0 to 4 and 0 to 9, depending on the measure. Summary scores are calculated for each domain and a total score is also calculated. The assessment procedure requires 30 minutes for administration. Reliability and validity of the instrument was tested with the participation of 50 persons with Schizophrenia and 20 controls. Interrater reliability was assessed at .91, and concurrent validity was established through a high correlation ($r = .86$) of total scores with scores from two other established measures of functioning.

The Multidimensional Scale of Independent Functioning can be used to rate functional disability in psychiatric clients through discreet ratings of role responsibility, presence and level of support, and performance quality in the context of a client's work, educational, and residential domains (Jaeger, Berns, & Czobor, 2003). Ratings are made by applying a set of detailed anchors on a 7-point Likert scale to information obtained in a semistructured interview with the client. External sources of information may be used when available, including family members, employers, and other professional staff. Global ratings within each environment are also made to reflect the client's overall level of functioning. The scale is intended to capture the client's functioning during the past month. The information is then coded for each applicable environment in each of the three dimensions. In a study involving 18 clients, the scale demonstrated an interrater reliability range of .74 to 1.0 for discrete items, .91 to .98 for global ratings within each environment, and .90 for overall global rating. Criterion validity was established in a study of 113 clients as scale items correlated from .78 to .86 with SAS-II global ratings. Further, the subscales performed as expected with regard to external validators such as hours of employment, earned income, supported versus nonsupported employment, and housing and educational status.

Assessing the Adverse Effects of Medication

People with Schizophrenia are almost always prescribed antipsychotic medications. Although these drugs may help to relieve many symptoms of the disorder, they also tend to produce a variety of adverse physical effects. Some of these are classified as movement disorders and are related to drug effects on the consumer's extrapyramidal nerve pathways. Symptoms may include a reduction in the range of facial and arm movements, muscle rigidity, shuffling gait, drooling, and difficulty starting or stopping movements (Parkinsonian effects); restlessness and muscle discomfort (akathesia); uncoordinated and involuntary movements produced by muscle spasms (dystonias); and a distortion of voluntary movements (dyskinesia). Because it is important for social workers to participate in the monitoring of the client's experience of adverse effects, several useful scales are described here.

The Simpson-Angus Neurological Rating Scale was developed to provide an objective method for rating many extrapyramidal symptoms of the antipsychotic drugs (Simpson & Angus, 1970). The scale includes 10 items pertaining to the presence or absence of tremor and salivation and concerns about movements in the client's gait, arms, shoulders, elbows, wrists, legs, and head. Each item is rated on a 5-point Likert scale that can be completed in 10 minutes. A consumer's score is determined by adding the numbers endorsed on each item and dividing by 10. The scale's validity was assessed in part by examining the scores for consumers receiving various doses of medication. Interrater reliability was assessed with two physicians examining a variety of consumers in a double-blind study, with resulting correlation coefficients for all items ranging between .71 and .96.

The Abnormal Involuntary Movement Scale (AIMS), developed by the National Institute of Mental Health, is a 10-item instrument that assesses abnormal movements related to the adverse effects of antipsychotic medication, including dyskinesia, dystonias, and akathesia (Alcohol, Drug Abuse, and Mental Health Administration, 1985). The scale includes two additional items that are intended to correct for movements that may be related to a consumer's mental status. The practitioner rates the presence and severity of symptoms involving the face, mouth, extremities, and trunk on a 5-point scale. Three items provide for global judgments of the severity of abnormal movements, the consumer's level of incapacitation due to these movements, and his or her awareness of the abnormal movements. The AIMS can be completed in 5 to 10 minutes, and because of its simplicity it is said to be the most widely used such scale (Cassady, Thaker, Summerfelt, & Tamminga, 1997). Interrater reliability has been established for the instrument, and though its face and content validity is asserted, other tests of validity have not been done.

The Barnes Akathesia Scale was designed to facilitate a more reliable differential diagnosis of akathesia (motor restlessness) from other drug-induced movement disorders (Barnes, 1989). Scale items evaluate the client's restless movements, awareness of this restlessness, and any distress associated with the symptoms. The Barnes scale can be completed in 15 minutes. Reliability coefficients for scale items range between .74 and .96. Predictive validity is based on comparing results with symptoms identified in previous studies involving outpatients with Schizophrenia who receive antipsychotic medication.

The Maryland Psychiatric Research Center Scale (MPRC) is designed to measure the dyskinesia and Parkinsonism induced by antipsychotic medications (Cassady et al., 1997). Comprised of 29 items, it offers a global rating of dyskinesia in each of 11 body areas and two ratings related to the consumer's gait. Fifteen

Parkinsonian ratings are made on areas of concern in the client's arms, fingers, feet, and legs. A single global rating for dyskinesia, Parkinsonism, and akathesia completes the scale. The MPRC utilizes an 8-point Likert scale. It can be administered by any mental health professional and can be completed in less than 30 minutes. The MPRC has undergone extensive testing for validity and reliability. It has demonstrated construct validity by establishing distinct dyskinetic and Parkinsonian statistical factors; convergent validity through its degree of correlation with the AIMS; discriminant validity by comparing clients with and without movement disorders on total dyskinesia and total Parkinsonism scores; criterion validity through score associations with clinicians' global judgments of overall severity; and predictive validity by using scores to predict physicians' diagnoses of tardive dyskinesia. Reliability for the MPRC has been established with Cronbach's alpha scores (.80 for dyskinetic and .78 for Parkinsonian items), inter-rater reliability (.81 for total dyskinesia and .90 for total Parkinsonian scores), and 1-week test-retest reliability (.92 for dyskinesia and .96 for the global score; .83 for appropriate Parkinsonian items and .65 for the global score).

Evidence-Based Approaches to Intervention

Effective interventions for Schizophrenia are those that have been shown through repeated, reputable research studies to improve selected outcomes for individuals and their families. Some of these outcomes include decreased positive or negative symptoms, increased participation in activities of daily living, decreased hospital days, and improved interpersonal relationships and cognitive skills. Psychiatric medications are most often the primary intervention in the treatment of Schizophrenia, and certainly social workers should be familiar with these medications to effectively function in multidisciplinary treatment teams (see Bentley & Walsh, 2006). This section, however, deals with those effective interventions that can be categorized as primarily psychosocial modalities. These interventions are important because "a multitude of controlled studies" demonstrate that certain psychosocial interventions have been found to prevent relapse and improve the course of the disorder when provided in conjunction with a psychopharmacological treatment plan (Brenner & Pfammatter, 2000, p. 74; Lehman, Leiberman, et al., 2004). In particular, a 1998 meta-analysis of 106 studies found that individuals who are treated with a combination of somatic—such as psychotropic medications or electroconvulsive therapy—and psychosocial interventions were more improved than 65% of individuals treated with somatic methods only (Mojtabai, Nicholson, & Carpenter, 1998). Interestingly, this same meta-analysis found higher effect sizes for individuals with Schizophrenia in the chronic stage versus those in an acute phase, implying that psychosocial treatments may be particularly useful with those individuals who have persistent problems with the symptoms of Schizophrenia.

In the face of these efficacy studies and the reality of the devastating effects of the negative symptoms of Schizophrenia on an individual's level of functioning, studying which psychosocial interventions hold the most promise is essential. The following three subsections on individual interventions, group and family approaches, and community interventions explore common psychosocial interventions and their levels of effectiveness. The American Psychiatric Association's *Practice Guidelines for the Treatment of Patients with Schizophrenia,* second edition, completed in 2004, is an excellent compilation of the latest empirical inquiry in psychosocial treatments (Lehman, Lieberman, et al., 2004, p. 70). The authors ranked interventions based on having an "adequate evidence base" or a "limited evidence base." This information is incorporated in what follows.

Individual Interventions

Four major approaches to individualized treatment with persons who have Schizophrenia have been studied over the years: psychodynamic psychotherapy, supportive treatment, case management, and behavioral skills training/cognitive problem-solving strategies (Hogarty et al., 1997a, 1997b). Of these, psychodynamic psychotherapy has been largely dismissed due to lack of demonstrated effectiveness with persons with Schizophrenia, and case management and supportive therapy have shown some positive but variable effects. Skills training has shown consistently positive outcomes (Hogarty et al., 1997a; Lehman, Lieberman, et al., 2004).

It should be pointed out that choice of treatment intervention will vary based on the phase of the illness and the time in a person's life. For example, in an acute phase of Schizophrenia, individual intervention may consist only of supportive approaches that emphasize reassurance and reality testing; during a stable phase of the illness, an individual may benefit from more skills-based or cognitive-behavioral approaches. Likewise, a newly diagnosed individual and his or her family may need a more supportive approach aimed at education about and acceptance of the diagnosis and treatment adherence, whereas people who have dealt with their Schizophrenia for years may benefit from more in-depth approaches emphasizing relationship building, stress management, problem solving, or vocational exploration. Interestingly, it can be concluded from meta-analyses that there is a "considerable additive effect for psychosocial treatment approaches," suggesting that many individuals with Schizophrenia may benefit from more than one of the interventions described here (Brenner & Pfammatter, 2000, p. 74).

Supportive Therapy
Personal therapy is a supportive approach with skills-training elements that was designed to be a disorder-relevant, individual, psychological approach to Schizophrenia (Hogarty et al., 1997a, 1997b). It is an individualized, long-term, psychosocial intervention that is contained within a larger treatment program with psychopharmacological and family intervention alongside material and psychological support (Hogarty, et al., 1997a, 1997b; Lehman, Lieberman, et al., 2004). Psychiatric stability is the main objective of personal therapy. This includes stress management and the development of adaptive coping skills to improve social reintegration (Mueser et al., 2002). Specifically, personal therapy encourages internal coping by helping the individual to recognize the experience of stress and develop a response. Although hopes were high for demonstrable positive outcomes of personal therapy, these have not yet materialized beyond initial study results, especially in the area of protection against late relapse (Hogarty et al., 1997a, 1997b). Risk of relapse was reduced only for persons who lived with their family; however, the good news is that recipients of personal therapy experienced improved social functioning regardless of where they lived (Hogarty et al., 1997a, 1997b; Mueser et al., 2002). Because the results have been somewhat mixed and remain unreplicated, personal therapy is considered to have a very limited evidence base by the American Psychiatric Association for the treatment of Schizophrenia (Lehman, Lieberman, et al., 2004).

Social Skills Training
Social skills training is aimed at teaching skills that increase a client's social competence, thereby decreasing social distress and anxiety and aiding in everyday functioning (Brenner & Pfammatter, 2000). Training is behavioral in nature, is targeted to specific situations, and is normally provided through small groups (Lehman, Lieberman, et al., 2004). The efficacy of social skills training as an intervention in Schizophrenia to improve social role functioning has been consistently supported by clinical trials and therefore is considered to have a "substantial evidence base" (Lehman, Lieberman, et al., 2004, p. 69). Effects over time (e.g., after 1 year) are not as clear. Similarly, a clear effect on reduction of Schizophrenia symptoms and general relapse rates is not as clear, particularly with those clients who have persistent negative symptoms (Kopelowicz, Liberman, Mintz, & Zarate, 1997). Additionally, better mechanisms for transferring skills acquired during

social skills training to everyday environments are thought to be needed (Brenner & Pfammatter, 2000).

Cognitive-Behavioral Interventions

A range of cognitive behavioral techniques are often used with persons who have Schizophrenia, with the goal of decreasing symptoms and increasing and strengthening coping strategies. These interventions normally occur on a one-to-one basis and contain supportive elements along with other strategies, such as belief modification (where delusional beliefs are challenged in a supportive manner), focusing or reattribution (where symptoms are related to normal life, aiding the individual to attribute the symptom to an internal rather than an external source), and normalizing the psychotic experience (Lehman, Lieberman, et al., 2004). In one meta-analysis, cognitive behavioral interventions were found to be particularly effective in treating Schizophrenia, particularly in the alleviation of persistent positive symptoms (Mojtabai et al., 1998). In a review of 19 trials, cognitive-behavioral interventions were found to be of value, particularly in the short term, but the authors concluded that there is need for further evaluation as the studies to date are not entirely conclusive (Jones, Cormac, da Mota Neto, Silveira, & Campbell, 2004).

In a cognitive-behavioral approach called behavioral tailoring, which is designed to increase medication adherence, people are encouraged to pair their medication with another daily routine such as toothbrushing, or the medication routine is simplified in some other way (Mueser et al., 2002). Behavioral tailoring is similar to cognitive adaptation training, which is described next, in that it provides a way to compensate for cognitive deficits, such as memory problems, which can be common for some individuals with Schizophrenia.

Cognitive Adaptation Training

In cognitive adaptation training, individuals are taught compensatory strategies for cognitive deficits associated with Schizophrenia by learning how to alter their physical environment (Velligan et al., 2000; Velligan, Mahurin, True, Lefton, & Flores, 1996). Cognitive adaptation training has been used successfully for years in other fields, for example, with individuals who have head injury or mental retardation (Velligan et al., 2000). The training frequently entails using signs, labels, and electronic devices, as well as organization and simplification strategies to enhance adaptive skills. The efficacy of cognitive adaptation training is so far a bit unclear (Brenner & Pfammatter, 2000), as many studies have had small sample sizes and were noncontrolled. The American Psychiatric Association practice guidelines for Schizophrenia refers to studies on cognitive remediation strategies as "promising" (Lehman, Lieberman, et al., 2004, p. 75) but recommends that they still be regarded as experimental until better durability and generalizability of gains in cognitive functioning are demonstrated in studies with improved control.

Family Approaches and Group Therapies

Group Interventions

The evidence for the efficacy of generic group therapies in assist-   –ᵥℓℓe
ing people who have Schizophrenia is not considered strong. Lehman, Lieberman, et al.'s (2004) review points to only "modest evidence" for efficacy in improved social adjustment and coping skills. No evidence supports insight-oriented groups for hospitalized consumers in acute phases of Schizophrenia. Similarly, a meta-analysis of 106 studies was pessimistic about the promise of generic group therapies as it found the smallest effect sizes for this modality, but also stipulated that these results could possibly be a confound (as they disappear with multiple regression analyses) and suggest further study on this popular form of treatment (Mojtabai et al., 1998). Given these findings, it is tempting to suggest that when possible, interventions with persons who have Schizophrenia and their families be delivered on an individual basis. However, because in the current mental health climate limited resources often necessitate group service delivery, care should be taken to utilize content in the group, such as skills training or cognitive-behavioral methods, which has a strong effectiveness track record.

An important aside in the findings about group modalities is the recent increase in peer support groups. Lehman, Lieberman, et al. (2004, p. 75) define peer support as "social, emotional, and sometimes instrumental support that is mutually offered or provided by persons having a mental health condition to others sharing a similar mental health condition to bring about a desired social or personal change" (also see Gartner & Riessman, 1982). Several evaluations have found some evidence that self-help groups may improve symptoms, increase quality of life, and have positive effects on social networks (Lehman, Lieberman, et al., 2004; see also Davidson et al., 1999), but overall, these types of groups have not been well studied to date. However, they should not be discounted in their potential to positively impact consumers with Schizophrenia through a modality that increases personal and peer empowerment. A more thorough discussion of peer approaches is found later in the chapter.

Family Education

The American Psychiatric Association Practice Guidelines for the Treatment of Patients with Schizophrenia states, "All evidenced-based approaches emphasize the value of family participation in treatment and stress the importance of working together in a collaborative endeavor" (Lehman, Lieberman, et al., 2004, p. 70). Relatedly, it is important to define the family as broadly as possible to honor close support systems that may not be blood relatives but are key people in the lives of clients (Mueser et al., 2002). Notably, an emphasis on family intervention is consistent with social work's historic focus on the person-in-environment.

The original goal of interventions with families was the decrease in relapse rates of individuals with Schizophrenia. Of particular importance, recent research also emphasizes goals such as improved client functioning, decreased family burden, and improved family functioning (Lehman, Lieberman, et al., 2004). In their research review of 40 controlled studies, Mueser et al. (2002) echo others in finding that family psychoeducation is well supported by the evidence. In a meta-analyses of family intervention studies, a consistent reduction of relapse rates has been found, with the most effective programs being highly structured, lasting longer than 9 months, and including participation by a psychiatrist (Brenner & Pfammatter, 2000; Lehman, Lieberman, et al., 2004; Mojtabai, et al., 1998). A 2002 review of 10 studies where psychoeducation was provided with clients and at least one family member, the reviewers similarly concluded that psychoeducation reduced relapse (Pekkala & Merinder, 2002). An added benefit of coping-oriented family interventions is that they are cost-effective, in addition to having a substantial evidence base (Brenner & Pfammatter, 2000).

A number of models of family education and psychoeducation are discussed in the literature. A common theme is that increased coping and competence is achieved through education and shared experiences rather than through sudden insight or manipulated changes in the family structure. One established education course for family members of people with Bipolar Disorder and Schizophrenia developed in Virginia, Mutual Education Support and Advocacy, relies on coleadership among families and professionals (Cubine, Bentley, Poe, & McCafferty, 2001). Recently the National Alliance for the Mentally Ill has especially touted its Family to Family Education model, which was originated by Joyce Burland a decade ago in Vermont. Like most of the programs, the 12-week course provides information on the nature of mental illness, medications, problem solving, and communication skills training with family members (www.nami.org). Researchers at George Warren Brown School of Social Work at Washington University are in the midst of validating a new model of family education that stresses family participation in the design and choice of curriculum topics. Their 24-session model, called Psychoeducation Responsive to Families, is showing impressive short- and long-term impact on knowledge and understanding of illness, family burden, and family morale (Pollio, McClendon, & North, 2005).

An important consideration in applying family interventions is whether the intervention should be in the form of individual or multiple family groups. According to Lehman, Lieberman, et al. (2004), the jury is still out concerning this, although one study (McFarlane, 1994) found slightly higher protection against relapse among a multiple-family group. Another consideration is whether peer-taught groups for families are more effective in that they can help validate and normalize the experiences of family members dealing with the journey that constitutes recovery from severe mental illness (Baxter & Diehl, 1998).

Community Interventions

The empirical knowledge base on the effectiveness of community interventions for people with Schizophrenia has flourished during the past 20 years. Many believe these interventions hold promise for strengthening the individual's ability to manage the symptoms of Schizophrenia and to live successfully within the community with limited inpatient hospitalizations. This section reviews four community interventions that have demonstrated effectiveness for people with Schizophrenia, including consumer-operated services (i.e., drop-in centers, businesses, and housing programs), case management (including consumer case management and assertive community treatment), vocational rehabilitation (including supported employment), and supported education.

Consumer-Operated Services

Consumer-operated mental health programs are "services that are planned, delivered, and evaluated by consumers themselves," that is, individuals with Schizophrenia and a range of other psychiatric disorders who "consume"—receive or have received—mental health services (Van Tosh, Ralph, & Campbell, 2000, p. 12). Professionals are included in some activities at the discretion of the respective consumer-operated organization. Receiving increasing attention in the literature, they represent one of the newest and most innovative community interventions for people with Schizophrenia. It is thought that "working with peers can facilitate a sense of individual empowerment and can offer role-modeling opportunities through exposure to others who have faced similar obstacles" (Cook & Razzano, 2000, p. 98). The Community Support Program of the National Institute of Mental Health funded local consumer-operated services demonstration projects from 1988 to 1991. A result of these early efforts included more involvement of mental health consumers in traditional service roles, developing

Positive outcomes but need more evidence and providing peer support, evaluating services, and crafting policy (Van Tosh et al., 2000). Now, consumer-operated services are rapidly expanding, diversifying, and maturing as part of the mental health service continuum (Holter, Mowbray, Bellamy, MacFarlane, & Dukarski, 2004). Although very early study findings suggest that such programs may improve the quality of life, symptoms, and social support (Campbell & Salzer, 2004), published reports of these programs are still primarily descriptive in nature and often involve process evaluations or consumer satisfaction surveys (Lefley, 1997). Thus, they clearly warrant further investigation, especially into their impact (Boyd, in press).

Two literature reviews assessed what is known specifically about the effectiveness of consumer-provided services (Solomon & Draine, 2001) and peer support among mental health consumers (Davidson et al., 1999). Both suggest promising outcomes of consumer-delivered services in general, yet "no [firm] conclusions can be reached about the effectiveness of consumer provided services" (Solomon & Draine, 2001, p. 26). As consumer-operated services continue to expand and develop, funders may increasingly demand demonstrated proof of effectiveness and greater accountability (Salzer & Shear, 2002).

Consumer-operated drop-in centers (CODICs) represent one of the more popular consumer-operated models among a diverse array of consumer-operated services, which include housing programs, businesses, and case management programs. A CODIC is defined by the self-help group, Justice In Mental Health Organization, as "a place which provides a critical social support function for high-risk hospital users with . . . recreational and social activities where individuals and center staff assist each other in solving their social, recreational, housing, transportation, and vocational problems" (Mowbray & Tan, 1992, p. 19). Consumer-operated drop-in centers are based on an ideology of empowerment and improving the participant's quality of life (Boyd & Bentley, 2005) through mutual support from peers. Holter and colleagues (2004) note their essential purpose as providing a safe, supportive, and normalizing environment and an atmosphere of acceptance. One of the main benefits of consumer-operated services such as CODICs is that they reach people with Schizophrenia and other psychiatric diagnoses who may be reluctant to participate in more traditional mental health services.

The positive processes (and, to a lesser degree, outcomes) for participants utilizing CODICs in particular have been described in the literature. The first known process evaluation of a CODIC reported in the literature documenting the operations of a program was published 15 years ago (Mowbray & Tan, 1992). A total of 120 consumers were interviewed from six centers and asked about service utilization and their likes and dislikes about the center. Over half (53.3%) reported that they went to the center for "people-related" reasons such as having friends there, a chance to socialize, and a sense of family. When asked how the CODIC had changed their lives, 79% of the respondents indicated that they gained more friends. In Virginia, the results of a survey of 140 CODIC participants found that their needs for friendship and support were also reportedly being met (Silverman, Blank, & Taylor, 1997). In Pennsylvania, a survey involving nine centers found that CODIC participants enjoyed the center's "relaxed atmosphere" as well as social activities (Kaufmann, Ward-Colasante, & Farmer, 1993). In general, CODIC participants have reported high levels of empowerment (Boyd & Bentley, 2005), employment assistance (Chamberlin, Rogers, & Ellison, 1996), and an increase in overall quality of life and social support (Mowbray & Tan, 1992).

A consumer-operated business (COB) is a strategy of recovery whereby individuals with psychiatric disorders manage and operate their own businesses with little or no involvement from mental health providers (Trainor & Trembley, 1992). The outcome literature on COB is very limited, but it will most likely expand with an increasing focus on the vocational rehabilitation for people with Schizophrenia. An early report by Mowbray, Chamberlain, Jennings, and Reed (1988) described Winners Janitorial Services, a for-profit consumer-operated janitorial service located in a suburban area that regrettably had to close due to high overhead costs, unsuccessful marketing, and lack of business experience of the director. Trainor and Trembley (1992) however, reported more promising results for COBs in Canada. Among consumer participants involved in five different consumer-run businesses in Ontario, reductions were reported in hospital admissions, contacts with crisis services, in-patient days, and visits to private physicians.

Consumer-operated housing programs (COHPs) are housing arrangements wherein a group of mental health consumers live together and supervise themselves, with the involvement of mental health providers determined by each housing program. Consumer-operated housing programs emphasize self-determination and group self-management, reflecting the belief "that a therapeutic relationship is the strengthening movement of two [consumers] reaching across, as equals" (Zinman, 1982, p. 4). Not surprisingly, studies on the housing preferences of people with mental illness have found that the majority prefer to live in independent living situations (Minsky, Riesser, & Duffy, 1995; Yeich, Mowbray, Bybee, & Cohen, 1994). However, there are few evaluative or descriptive studies on COHPs in the literature. One from 25 years ago describes the experience of a group of mental health consumers defining and implementing a small client-run residence that operated for 1.5 years (Zinman, 1982).

The national Consumer-Operated Service Program Multisite Research Initiative (COSP MRI) that began in 1998 may address some of the methodological shortcomings previously identified in the research literature in earlier studies on the effectiveness of consumer-operated services. Funded by the Substance Abuse and Mental Health Services Administration, COSP MRI is a "national effort to assess to what extent consumer-operated programs as an adjunct to traditional mental health services are effective in improving the outcomes of adults with serious mental illness" (Campbell & Salzer, 2004). The COSP MRI utilizes randomized experimental design and includes seven study sites funded for 4 years and eight program sites funded for 6 years. The main hypothesis is that participants who are offered both traditional mental health services and consumer-operated services will demonstrate greater improvement in well-being over time compared to participants offered only traditional mental health services. The preliminary results indicate that the addition of consumer-operated services to traditional mental health services "adds incrementally to well-being" (Johnsen, Teague, & McDonel-Herr, 2004). The initial study results provide further support for including consumer-operated services in the mental health service delivery continuum. The pending results of the national COSP project will have a significant impact on the future direction of the proliferation and financial support of consumer-operated services, specifically their place in the larger continuum of mental health services.

Case Management

Case management (CM), a widely recognized community-based service delivery model for people with Schizophrenia, is considered to be an integral component in public mental health services for this population (U.S. Department of Health and Human Services, 1999) and represents "a range of strategies for enhancing continuity of care and functioning in the community" (Lehman, 1999, p. 265). In essence, CM can be considered a process by persons with Schizophrenia are assisted in their negotiation and procurement of desired services (Anthony, Cohen, Farkas, & Cohen, 2000).

Ziguras and Stuart (2000) conducted a meta-analysis to study the effectiveness of CM based on 44 published studies between 1980 and 1998, specifically to compare clinical case management and Assertive Community Treatment (ACT) outcomes (discussed later). Positive outcomes were reported with regard to family satisfaction with services, family burden, and cost of care, and both ACT and clinical case management were more effective when compared to usual treatment. Similarly, Rapp and

Goesha (2004, p. 319) examined 21 CM studies employing quasi-experimental or experimental designs to "identify the common denominators of case management interventions that produced statistically significant positive outcomes for people with psychiatric disabilities," including persons with Schizophrenia. They conclude that the "strengths model" of CM demonstrated desired impacts on nonhospitalization outcomes, such as symptoms, housing, social functioning, vocational pursuits, quality of life, leisure time, and social contact. They found the simpler "broker model" of CM, which relies on only indirect service coordination, to be ineffective and suggested that this model be abandoned. On the up side, they offer a number of principles for effective CM in mental health and argue that these should act as the core in the design of CM services. These principles include the notions that case managers should foster choice and deliver as much of the help or service as possible, rather than making referrals to multiple formal services, and that caseload sizes should be small enough to allow for a relatively high frequency of contact, be time-unlimited (if necessary), and be available 24 hours a day. An important caveat, according to Draine (1997), is that technical challenges associated with conducting randomized trials of CM, including inadequately defined conceptual frameworks, participant attrition, and inadequate statistical analyses, impact the validity of CM research.

Consumer case management (CCM), a rapidly developing area of consumer-centered services, occurs when consumers are employed as a full-fledged case manager or aide for other people with a serious mental illness to assist them in obtaining needed social, vocational, financial, and other supports and thereby successfully living in the community. Solomon and Draine (1995) report on the 1-year outcomes of a randomized trial of CCM with 91 clients with serious mental illness using a pretest-posttest experimental design. They hypothesized, and indeed found, that consumers who received CM services from a CCM team would have the *same outcomes* as consumers who received CM services from a nonconsumer CM team on quality of life, various clinical and social outcomes such as housing, homelessness, size of social network, and level of functioning, and behavioral symptoms.

The CM literature also reports examples of consumers working as advocates or peer specialists on CM teams. Dixon, Krauss, and Lehman (1994), for example, reported on the experience of employing two full-time consumer advocates as part of an experimental ACT team that provided services to persons who were homeless and had a severe mental illness. Consumer advocates served as role models for recovery and played an important role in the engagement of clients and sensitizing team staff to consumer experiences. Felton et al. (1995) examined 104 clients served by teams that included these peer specialists and found a reduction in the number of major life problems experienced and greater improvement in multiple areas of quality of life.

Assertive community treatment was initially developed in the late 1970s by Leonard Stein and Mary Ann Test in Madison, Wisconsin (Lehman, Buchanan, et al., 2003). This initial experiment essentially moved the inpatient, multidisciplinary treatment team of the state hospital into the community setting (Stein & Test, 1980). It is a model of direct, intensive, and aggressive outreach to clients in the community. The model emphasizes a person's strengths in adapting to community life, providing consultation and support to a person's natural support networks, including families, employers, peers and friends, and community agencies, and encourages clients to remain in the program and maintain adherence to medications (Lehman, Kreyenbuhl, et al., 2004; McReynolds, Ward, & Singer, 2002; Phillips et al., 2001). Caseloads are low for providers and there is high-frequency contact with much flexibility in terms of services and activities. The program is strongly endorsed by the National Alliance for the Mentally Ill and other family advocacy groups (Lehman, 1999).

Studies have consistently demonstrated the efficacy of the ACT model in both improving the living conditions for a person with Schizophrenia and reducing symptoms and the length of hospitalizations (Bond, Drake, Mueser, & Latimer, 2001; Lehman, Dixon, Kernan, DeForge, & Postrado, 1997; Salkever et al, 1999). Gains in both quality of life and functional status are also frequently reported as outcomes (Dixon, 2000). In addition, the effectiveness research on ACT has shown that this model improves the quality of life and increases housing stability for people experiencing the most severe and persistent forms of mental illness (Phillips et al., 2001). For example, Mueser, Bond, Drake, and Resnick (1998) reviewed the literature on ACT programs serving people with serious mental illness. Housing stability was indicated in 9 out of 11 studies. A decrease in the amount of time spent in the hospital occurred in 14 out of 22 studies. Indeed, due to a solid history of effectiveness, Lehman, Kreyenbuhl, et al. (2004) state that people with Schizophrenia should have an ACT program in their system of care. The available evidence for ACT also suggests that it is a less costly intervention for high mental health service users, and participants report high levels of satisfaction with services (Lauriello, Bustillo, & Keith, 1999; Mueser & McGurk, 2004). Less evidence exists for demonstrating ACT's impact on social functioning and competitive employment (Lauriello, Lenroot, & Bustillo, 2003).

One caveat: Despite a general consensus within the professional and self-help community that ACT is an effective psychosocial intervention, this appraisal may be biased by authors who support the program philosophy, and evaluators may be confusing workers' efforts for clients' efforts. That is, some positive outcomes may be due to administrators refusing some services such as hospitalization to clients as an option. In summary, then, ACT programs and other forms of intensive community intervention for persons with Schizophrenia do produce positive outcomes, but some questions remain as to the influence of resource availability (fewer hospital beds, more short-term crisis residences) and the more pervasive presence of case managers in clients' lives.

Vocational Rehabilitation

Difficulty with employment continues to be one of the debilitating effects of Schizophrenia (Lauriello et al., 2003). Persons with Schizophrenia experience competitive employment rates as low as 10% to 20% (Mueser & McGurk, 2004). As such, competitive employment is a major rehabilitation goal for persons with this disorder (Gioia & Brekke, 2003), although many persons with psychiatric disabilities remain unemployed, though they have the potential to be employed (Bedell & Rivera, 1999). The residual effects of unemployment for people with Schizophrenia are vast (e.g., increasing dependence on family supports, low self-esteem, economic instability, use of public assistance, social marginalization). However, research suggests that people with Schizophrenia who possess the following characteristics may reap benefits from vocational interventions: (a) a competitive employment history, (b) minimal psychiatric hospitalization history, (c) identification of competitive employment as a goal, and (d) good work skills, as judged on the basis of a formal vocational assessment (Lehman, 1999).

Vocational rehabilitation (VR) for individuals with Schizophrenia provides them with an opportunity to participate in normalizing daily living activities, like meaningful, productive work or activity, and to be financially compensated for their services. These models include a variety of approaches, such as sheltered workshops, psychosocial rehabilitation, transitional employment, and supported employment. Several research-based ideals of VR for persons with psychiatric disabilities are endorsed currently, including situational assessment, competitive or supported employment (rather than sheltered or unpaid work), rapid placement, ongoing individualized support, and job tailoring (Cook & Razzano, 2000).

In terms of outcomes of VR programs, there is good news and bad news. The bad news is that, in general, the evidence suggests that VR interventions are not as effective for people with Schizophrenia compared to people with other psychiatric disorders (Cook & Razzano, 2000). Although VR programs, such as sheltered workshops, do enhance job-related activities for people with Schizophrenia and other mental illnesses, most programs have thus far failed to demonstrate long-term impacts on independent, competitive employment rates (Lauriello et al., 1999; Lehman, 1995).

However, the good news is that the positive symptoms associated with a diagnosis of Schizophrenia do not preclude persons from success in work (Yankowitz, 1990). In addition, some VR programs are associated with positive outcomes for persons with Schizophrenia. For example, a study investigating the clinical benefits of paid work activity among 150 participants with Schizophrenia or Schizoaffective Disorder randomly assigned participants to a pay or no-pay condition in 6-month work placements in the Department of Veterans Affairs. The results reveal that the pay participants had a lower rehospitalization rate and demonstrated a much greater decline in their total symptom severity from intake to 5-month follow-up, as compared to participants in the no-pay condition (Bell, Lysaker, & Milstein, 1996).

Supported Employment
Several community-based programs have been developed to assist people with Schizophrenia in finding and maintaining ongoing employment (Lauriello et al., 2003), such as supported employment (SE) and individual placement and support (IPS) models. Originally, SE developed as an alternative to the effective "train and place" VR model for people with developmental disabilities and mental retardation (Yankowitz, 1990). Supported employment programs place individuals quickly and train them while on the job, in addition to placing them in integrated employment settings with at least minimum wage compensation. Job placement is tailored to an individual's interest and preferences, while providing ongoing unlimited vocational support and treatment team collaboration with a supervisor and coworkers (Twamley, Jeste, & Lehman, 2003).

The research evidence on the effectiveness of SE programs has accumulated at a rapid pace, especially during the past 10 years. This evidence suggests a promising outlook (Lauriello et al., 1999) for this community intervention. When compared to traditional VR interventions for people with Schizophrenia, supported employment programs and IPS interventions have consistently reported better outcomes in terms of competitive employment and employment of any type (Twamley et al., 2003). The existing evidence supporting the effectiveness of SE programs includes improved rates of competitive employment, wages earned, and hours worked (Mueser & McGurk, 2004). Competitive employment rates are higher for SE program participants; however, the effects are short term (Lauriello et al., 1999). For example, Bond and colleagues (Bond, Drake, Mueser, & Becker, 1997) reviewed six randomized controlled SE studies for persons with serious mental illness. Out of the study samples, between 35% and 66% of the persons were diagnosed with Schizophrenia. The authors found that the mean rate for obtaining competitive employment was almost three times higher (58%) when compared to the rate for traditional VR programs (21%). However, persons tended to cease competitive employment by the end of 6 months, ranging from 41% to 71%. Similarly, McGurk, Mueser, Harvey, LaPuglia, and Marder (2003) found that during a 2-year follow-up period after an SE program, only 50% ($n = 15$) of the people worked competitively, with an average time in competitive employment of 140 days ($SD = 131$) and the average wage of \$6,007 ($SD = 5,770$). There was not a significant change in either the symptoms or cognitive functioning over the 2-year follow-up period.

Overall, the recent reviews of nine randomized controlled trials of the SE model for people with serious mental illness (Bond, 2004) suggest that SE should be considered as an evidence-based practice due to improved symptom control and improved self-esteem, both of which are examples of benefits to people with mental illness who hold competitive jobs for an ongoing period of time. In fact, Lehman, Kreyenbuhl, et al. (2004) state that SE should be offered to people with Schizophrenia who have the goal of employment. However, more research is needed to further identify the benefits of employment on nonvocational outcomes, such as improved quality of life, empowerment, and symptom reduction (Lauriello et al., 2003; Mueser et al., 2004).

Supported Education
In addition to the interruption of vocational opportunities, the onset of Schizophrenia during early adulthood frequently interrupts the postsecondary educational and training trajectory for people with Schizophrenia. As one of the newest psychosocial rehabilitation interventions for people with psychiatric disabilities, supported education (SEd) programs provide preparation, assistance, and supports to those who wish to pursue postsecondary training or education (McReynolds et al., 2002; Mowbray, Collins, & Bybee, 1999). This model has emerged as a valuable intervention. Programs incorporate the values and principles of hope, normalization, self-determination, support and relationships, and systems change (Mowbray et al., 2005). In 1997, SEd was identified as an exemplary practice by the Center for Mental Health Services, Substance Abuse and Mental Health Services Administration (Mowbray et al., 1999).

Data suggest that both men and women actively participate in SEd programs and participants reflect the ethnic and racial diversity of their communities. They tend to have low incomes, be in their early 30s, and meet the criteria for a serious mental illness diagnosis (Mowbray et al., 2005). Earlier studies demonstrated that SEd assists mental health consumers in making therapeutic gains (Bateman, 1997), such as increased self-worth (Egnew, 1993) and increased self-esteem (Cook & Solomon, 1993; Unger, Anthony, Sciarappa, & Rogers, 1991). Participants indicate satisfaction with such programs (Mowbray et al., 2005). Mowbray and colleagues' (1999) review of the existing evidence of the effectiveness of SEd programs in helping adults succeed in postsecondary education concluded that although the programs contribute to positive outcomes (e.g., increases in the competitive employment and college enrollment rates), there is a range of reported outcomes. A model SEd program, the Michigan Supported Education Research Project, funded from 1992 to 1996, addressed the methodological shortcomings of earlier SEd studies by employing a true experimental design. The Michigan project enrolled a total of 397 persons with long-term, serious mental illness who were randomly assigned to one of three conditions: classroom, group support, or individual (control) conditions. The 12-month follow-up results reveal that for the classroom and group conditions, 21% to 28% were enrolled in vocational training or college and 39% to 46% were engaged in some type of job or school activity. The Michigan program continues to serve about 200 participants per year (Mowbray et al., 1999).

In sum, study outcomes in the research literature continue to demonstrate the effectiveness of SEd programs in "help[ing] people with psychiatric disabilities gain access to and complete postsecondary education" (Mowbray et al., 2005, p. 13). A suggested area for future study of the effectiveness of SEd programs is to examine the long-term outcomes on the extent to which participants have completed certificate programs or academic degrees (Mowbray et al., 2005).

Summary

Very recently a group of international psychiatrists noted that "over the past decade, Schizophrenia has become more treatable than ever," and the continuing development of medications and psychosocial interventions has helped "to create an evidence-based climate of optimism" in the treatment of Schizophrenia (Royal Australian and New Zealand College of Psychiatrists, 2005, p. 1). They specify some seemingly simple essentials of treatment:

- Optimistic attitudes by all providers throughout the provision of care, with services delivered by a multidisciplinary team.

- Early detection and assertive, comprehensive treatment of first episodes, as well as during the 3 to 5 years following.

- Cautious and targeted use of antipsychotic medications.
- Comprehensive and routine use of psychosocial interventions with individuals with Schizophrenia and their families, tailored to phase and stage of illness, gender, and cultural background.
- Genuine involvement of individuals with Schizophrenia and their families in service development and delivery.
- Maintenance of good physical health by individuals with Schizophrenia.

Of course, there is recognition of serious barriers to individuals receiving this type and quality of care, including the interactions among such factors as the lack of a full and explicit understanding of the causes of Schizophrenia, the underfunding of mental health systems, stigma, and provider resistance or inexperience with new recovery-oriented strategies. To keep such evidence-based practices, which center on illness management, from "languishing on the academic shelf and yielding little effect in routine" settings, Mueser et al. (2002, p. 1279) urge the development of user-friendly treatment manuals, supportive policies and program standards, ongoing education, and, of course, the allocation of greater resources. Clearly, the work needs to continue in order to ensure uncomplicated, affordable, and reliable access to effective, comprehensive, and high-quality services and treatment for people with Schizophrenia today.

Study Questions

1. What are the obvious and the hidden costs of Schizophrenia to individuals, families, communities, and society?
2. What is the potential for subtyping in the diagnosis of Schizophrenia to help or hurt the practice (or research) enterprise?
3. What are some of the most important real-world barriers to using the assessment devices discussed in this chapter? Important facilitating forces?
4. Few social workers are credited with developing interventions for Schizophrenia, and our visibility in the practice community with the population seems less than ideal. Do you agree? What do you make of that? How might social workers change the status quo in regard to developing or disseminating interventions and practice approaches?
5. What approaches reviewed here are the easiest for you to visualize yourself using, and why? The most difficult, and why? What will you do next to better prepare yourself to

utilize or implement the approaches described here in your everyday practice?

6. What information in the chapter served to combat myths about Schizophrenia and its treatment? Did anything serve to perpetuate myths?

7. What effect will dimensions of the current service delivery climate (managed care and other financial restrictions, increased litigation, publicized incidents of violent consumers, rise of technology and evidence-based practice, differing views and controversies around medication) have on agency selection of interventions?

References

Alcohol, Drug Abuse, and Mental Health Administration. (1985). *NIMH Treatment Strategies in Schizophrenia Study* (Publication No. ADM-117). Washington, DC: Department of Health and Human Services, Public Health Service.

Amador, X. F., & Ratakonda, S. (1996). The diagnosis of schizophrenia: Past, present, and future. In C. A. Kaufman & J. M. Gorman (Eds.), *Schizophrenia: New directions for clinical research and treatment (pp. 5–15)*. Larchmont, NY: Mary Ann Liebert.

American Psychiatric Association. (2000). *Diagnostic and statistical manual of mental disorders* (4th ed., text rev.). Washington, DC: Author.

Andersen, J., Larsen, J. K., Schultz, V., Nielsen, B. M., Korner, A., Behnke, K., et al. (1989). The Brief Psychiatric Rating Scale: Dimension of schizophrenia—Reliability and construct validity. *Psychopathology, 22,* 168–176.

Andreasen, N. C. (1982). Negative symptoms of schizophrenia: Definition and reliability. *Archives of General Psychiatry, 39,* 784–788.

Andreasen, N. C., & Olsen, S. (1982). Negative versus positive schizophrenia: Definition and validation. *Archives of General Psychiatry, 39,* 789–794.

Anthony, W. A., Cohen, M., Farkas, M., & Cohen, B. F. (2000). Clinical care update: The chronically mentally ill—Case management: More than a response to a dysfunctional system. *Community Mental Health Journal, 36,* 97–106.

Barnes, T. R. E. (1989). A rating scale for drug-induced akathesia. *British Journal of Psychiatry, 154,* 672–676.

Bateman, M. (1997). The development of a statewide supported education program: Assessing consumer and family needs. *Psychiatric Rehabilitation Journal, 21,* 16–23.

Baxter, E. A., & Diehl, S. (1998). Emotional stages: Consumers and family members recovering from the trauma of mental illness. *Psychiatric Rehabilitation Journal, 21,* 349–356.

Bedell, J., & Rivera, J. (1999). An evaluation of seven job stressors for persons with serious mental illness. *Psychiatric Rehabilitation Skills, 3,* 11–20.

Bell, M. D., Lysaker, P. H., & Milstein, R. M. (1996). Clinical benefits of paid work activity in schizophrenia. *Schizophrenia Bulletin, 22,* 51–67.

Bentley, K. J., & Walsh, J. (2006). *The social worker and psychotropic medication: Toward effective collaboration with mental health clients, families and providers* (3rd ed.). Monterey, CA: Brooks/Cole.

Bigelow, D. A., Gareau, M. J., & Young, D. J. (1990). A quality of life interview. *Psychosocial Rehabilitation Journal, 14,* 94–98.

Bigelow, L. B., & Berthot, B. D. (1989). The Psychiatric Symptom Assessment Scale

(PSAS). *Psychopharmacology Bulletin, 25,* 168–179.

Black, D. W., Yates, W. R., & Andreasen, N. C. (1988). Schizophrenia, schizophreniform disorder, and delusional (paranoid) disorders. In J. A. Talbott, R. E. Hales, & S. C. Yudofsky (Eds.), *American Psychiatric Press textbook of psychiatry* (pp. 357–402). Washington, DC: American Psychiatric Press.

Bond, G. R. (2004). Supported employment: Evidence for an evidence-based practice. *Psychiatric Rehabilitation Journal, 27,* 345–359.

Bond, G. R., Drake, R. E., Mueser, K. T., & Becker, D. R. (1997). An update on supported employment for people with severe mental illness. *Psychiatric Services, 48,* 335–346.

Bond, G. R., Drake, R. E., Mueser, K. T., & Latimer, E. (2001). Assertive community treatment for people with severe mental illness: Critical ingredients and impact on clients. *Disease Management and Health Outcomes, 9,* 141–159.

Boyd, A. S. (in press). Consumer- and peer-operated services: An overview and assessment of the current state of knowledge. In S. J. Rosenberg & J. Rosenberg (Eds.), *Community mental health: Current perspectives.* Philadelphia: Brunner/Routledge.

Boyd, A. S., & Bentley, K. J. (2005). The relationship between the level of personal empowerment and quality of life among psychosocial clubhouse members and consumer-operated drop-in center participants. *Social Work in Mental Health, 4*(2), 67–93.

Brenner, H. D., & Pfammatter, M. (2000). Psychological therapy in schizophrenia: What is the evidence? *Acta Psychiatrica Scandinavica, 102*(Suppl. 407), 74–77.

Campbell, J., & Salzer, M. (2004, November). *COSP MRI organization, design, and study methods from the SAMHSA/CMHS Consumer-Operated Service Program (COSP) Multisite Research Initiative.* Paper presented at the annual meeting of the American Public Health Association, Washington, DC.

Cassady, S. L., Thaker, G. K., Summerfelt, A., & Tamminga, C. A. (1997). The Maryland Psychiatric Research Center Scale and the characterization of involuntary movements. *Psychiatry Research, 70,* 21–37.

Chamberlin, J., Rogers, J. A., & Ellison, M. L. (1996). Self-help programs: A description of their characteristics and their members. *Psychiatric Rehabilitation Journal, 19*(3), 33–42.

Cohen, D. (2002). Research on drug treatment of schizophrenia: A critical appraisal and implications for social work education. *Journal of Social Work Education, 38*(2), 217–239.

Cook, J. A., & Razzano, L. (2000). Vocational rehabilitation for persons with schizophrenia: Recent research and implications for practice. *Schizophrenia Bulletin, 26,* 87–103.

Cook, J. A., & Solomon, M. L. (1993). The Community Scholar Program: An outcome study of supported education for students with severe mental illness. *Psychosocial Rehabilitation Journal, 17*(1), 83–97.

Cubine, T., Bentley, K. J., Poe, J., & McCafferty, P. T. (2001). The MESA model of family education: Virginia's experience in enhancing collaboration between families and CMHC providers. *Arete, 25*(2), 46–57.

Davidson, L., Chinman, M., Kloos, B., Weingarten, R., Stayner, D., & Tebes, J. (1999). Peer support among individuals with severe mental illness: A review of the evidence. *Clinical Psychology: Science and Practice, 6,* 165–187.

Dixon, L. (2000). Assertive community treatment: Twenty-five years of gold. *Psychiatric Services, 51,* 759–765.

Dixon, L., Krauss, N., & Lehman, A. (1994). Consumers as service providers: The promise and challenge. *Community Mental Health Journal, 30,* 615–625.

Draine, J. (1997). A critical review of randomized field trials of case management for individuals with serious and persistent mental illness. *Research on Social Work Practice, 7,* 32–52.

Egnew, R. C. (1993). Supported education and employment: An integrated approach. *Psychosocial Rehabilitation Journal, 17*(1), 121–128.

Endicott, J., & Spitzer, R. L. (1978). A diagnostic interview: The Schedule for Affective Disorders and Schizophrenia. *Archives of General Psychiatry, 35,* 837–844.

Felton, C. J., Stastny, P., Shern, D., Blanch, A., Donahue, S. A., Knight, E., et al. (1995). Consumers as peer specialists on intensive case management teams: Impact on client outcomes. *Psychiatric Services, 46,* 1037–1044.

Fenton, W. S., McGlashan, T. H., Victor, B. J., & Blyler, C. R. (1997). Symptoms, subtypes, and suicidality of patients with schizophrenia spectrum disorders. *American Journal of Psychiatry, 154,* 199–204.

Gartner, A. J., & Riessman, F. (1982). Self-help and mental health. *Hospital and Community Psychiatry, 33,* 631–635.

Gioia, D., & Brekke, J. S. (2003). Knowledge and use of workplace accommodations and protections by young adults with schizophrenia: A mixed method study. *Psychiatric Rehabilitation Journal, 27*(1), 59–68.

Gottesman, I. I. (1991). *Schizophrenia genesis: The origins of madness.* New York: Freeman.

Heinrichs, D. W., Hanlon, T. E., & Carpenter, W. T. (1984). The Quality of Life Scale: An instrument for rating the schizophrenic deficit syndrome. *Schizophrenia Bulletin, 10,* 388–398.

Hogarty, G. E., Kornblith, S. J., Greenwald, D., DiBarry, A. L., Cooley, S., Ulrich, R. F., et al. (1997a). Three-year trials of personal therapy among schizophrenic patients living with or independent of family: Pt. I. Description of study and effects on relapse rates. *American Journal of Psychiatry, 154,* 1504–1513.

Hogarty, G. E., Kornblith, S. J., Greenwald, D., DiBarry, A. L., Cooley, S., Ulrich, R. F., et al. (1997b). Three-year trials of personal therapy among schizophrenic patients living with or independent of family: Pt. II. Effects on adjustment of patients. *American Journal of Psychiatry, 154,* 1514–1524.

Holter, M. C., Mowbray, C. T., Bellamy, C. D., MacFarlane, P., & Dukarski, J. (2004). Critical ingredients of consumer run services: Results of a national survey. *Community Mental Health Journal, 40,* 47–63.

Jaeger, J., Berns, S. M., & Czobor, P. (2003). The Multidimensional Scale of Independent Functioning: A new instrument for measuring functional disability in psychiatric populations. *Schizophrenia Bulletin, 29,* 153–167.

Johnsen, M., Teague, G., & McDonel-Herr, E. (2004, November). *Measuring peer-run mental health programs from the SAMHSA/CMHS Consumer-Operated Service Program (COSP) Multisite Research Initiative.* Paper presented at the annual meeting of the American Public Health Association, Washington, DC.

Jones, C., Cormac, I., da Mota Neto, J. I., Silveira, J. I., & Campbell, C. (2004). Cognitive behavior therapy for schizophrenia. *Cochrane Database of Systematic Reviews* (Issue 4, Art. No. CD000524. DOI: 10.1002/14651858.CD000524.pub2).

Katz, M. M., & Lyerly, S. B. (1963). Methods for measuring adjustment and social behavior in the community: Pt. I. Rationale, description, discriminative validity and scale development. *Psychological Reports, 13,* 502–535.

Kaufman, C. L., Ward-Colasante, C., & Farmer, J. (1993). Development and evaluation of drop-in centers operated by mental health consumers. *Hospital and Community Psychiatry, 44,* 675–678.

Kay, S. R., Fiszbein, A., & Opler, L. A. (1987). The Positive and Negative Syndrome Scale for schizophrenia. *Schizophrenia Bulletin, 13,* 261–275.

Kiesler, D. J. (2000). *Beyond the disease model of mental disorders.* Westport, CT: Praeger.

Kopelowicz, A., Liberman, R. P., Mintz, J., & Zarate, R. (1997). Comparison of efficacy of social skills training for deficit and non-deficit negative symptoms in schizophrenia. *American Journal of Psychiatry, 154,* 424–425.

Krawiecka, M., Goldberg, D., & Vaughan, M. (1977). A standardized psychiatric assessment scale for rating chronic psychotic patients. *Acta Psychiatrica Scandinavica, 55,* 299–308.

Lauriello, J., Bustillo, J., & Keith, S. J. (1999). A critical review of research on psychosocial treatment of schizophrenia. *Biological Psychiatry, 46,* 1409–1417.

Lauriello, J., Lenroot, R., & Bustillo, J. R. (2003). Maximizing the synergy between pharmacotherapy and psychosocial therapies for schizophrenia. *Psychiatric Clinics of North America, 26,* 191–211.

Lefley, H. P. (1997). The consumer recovery vision: Will it alleviate family burden? *American Journal of Orthopsychiatry, 67,* 210–219.

Lehman, A. F. (1988). A quality of life interview for the chronically mentally ill. *Evaluation and Program Planning, 11,* 51–62.

Lehman, A. F. (1995). Vocational rehabilitation in schizophrenia. *Schizophrenia Bulletin, 21,* 645–656.

Lehman, A. F. (1999). Improving treatment for persons with schizophrenia. *Psychiatric Quarterly, 70,* 259–272.

Lehman, A. F., Buchanan, R. W., Dickerson, F. B., Dixon, L. B., Goldberg, R., Green-Paden, L., et al. (2003). Evidence-based treatment for schizophrenia. *Psychiatric Clinics of North America, 26,* 939–954.

Lehman, A. F., Dixon, L. B., Kernan, E., De-Forge, B. R., & Postrado, L. T. (1997). A randomized trial of assertive community treatment for homeless persons with severe mental illness. *Archives of General Psychiatry, 54,* 1038–1043.

Lehman, A. F., Fischer, E. P., Postrado, L., Delahanty, J., Johnstone, B. M., Russo, P. A., et al. (2003). The Schizophrenia Care and Assessment Program Health Questionnaire (SCAP-HQ): An instrument to assess outcomes of schizophrenia care. *Schizophrenia Bulletin, 29,* 247–256.

Lehman, A. F., Kreyenbuhl, J., Buchanan, B. W., Dickerson, F. B., Dixon, L. B., Goldberg, R., et al. (2004). The Schizophrenia Patient Outcomes Research Team (PORT): Updated treatment recommendations 2003. *Schizophrenia Bulletin, 30,* 193–217.

Lehman, A. F., Lieberman, J. A., Dixon, L. B., McGlashan, T. H., Miller, A. L., Perkins, D. O., et al. (2004). *Practice guidelines for the treatment of patients with schizophrenia* (2nd ed.). Washington, DC: American Psychiatric Association.

Lieberman, J. A., Perkins, D., Bleger, A., Chakos, M., Jarskog, F., Boteva, K., et al. (2001). The early stages of schizophrenia: Speculations on pathogenesis, pathophysiology, and therapeutic approaches. *Society for Biological Psychiatry, 50,* 884–897.

Manchanda, R., & Hirsch, S. R. (1986). Rating scales for clinical studies on schizophrenia. In P. B. Bradley & S. R. Hirsch (Eds.), *The psychopharmacology and treatment of schizophrenia* (pp. 234–260). New York: Oxford University Press.

McFarlane, W. R. (1994). Multiple-family groups and psycho-education in the treatment of schizophrenia. *New Directions for Mental Health Services, 62,* 13–22.

McGurk, S. R., Mueser, K. T., Harvey, P. D., LaPuglia, R., & Marder, J. (2003). Cognitive and symptom predictors of work outcomes for clients with schizophrenia in supported employment. *Psychiatric Services, 54,* 1129–1135.

McReynolds, C. J., Ward, D. M., & Singer, O. (2002). Stigma, discrimination, and invisibility: Factors affecting successful integration of individuals diagnosed with schizophrenia. *Journal of Applied Rehabilitation Counseling, 33*(4), 32–39.

Miller, R., & Mason, S. E. (Eds.). (2002). *Diagnosis schizophrenia: A comprehensive resource for patients, families, and helping professionals.* New York: Columbia University Press.

Minsky, S., Riesser, G. G., & Duffy, M. (1995). The eye of the beholder: Housing preferences of inpatients and their treatment teams. *Hospital and Community Psychiatry, 46,* 173–176.

Mojtabai, R., Nicholson, R. A., & Carpenter, B. N. (1998). Role of psychosocial treatments in management of schizophrenia: A meta-analytic review of controlled outcome studies. *Schizophrenia Bulletin, 24,* 569–587.

Mowbray, C. T., Chamberlain, P., Jennings, M., & Reed, C. (1988). Consumer-run mental health services: Results from five demonstration projects. *Community Mental Health Journal, 24,* 151–156.

Mowbray, C. T., Collins, M. E., Bellamy, C. D., Megivern, D. A., Bybee, D., & Szilvagyi, S. (2005). Supported education for adults with psychiatric disabilities: An innovation for social work and psychosocial rehabilitation practice. *Social Work, 50,* 7–20.

Mowbray, C. T., Collins, M., & Bybee, D. (1999). Supported education for individuals with psychiatric disabilities: Long-term outcomes from an experimental study. *Social Work Research, 23,* 89–101.

Mowbray, C. T., & Tan, C. (1992). Evaluation of an innovative consumer-run service model: The drop-in center. *Innovations and Research, 1*(2), 19–24.

Mueser, K. T., Bond, G. R., Drake, R. E., & Resnick, S. G. (1998). Models of community care for severe mental illness: A review of research on case management. *Schizophrenia Bulletin, 24,* 37–74.

Mueser, K. T., Clark, R. E., Haines, M., Drake, R. E., McHugo, G. J., Bond, G. R., et al. (2004). The Hartford study of supported employment for persons with severe mental illness. *Journal of Consulting and Clinical Psychology, 72,* 479–490.

Mueser, K. T., Corrigan, P. W., Hilton, D. W., Tanzman, B., Schaub, A., Gingerich, S., et al. (2002). Illness management and recovery: A review of the research. *Psychiatric Services, 53,* 1272–1284.

Mueser, K. T., & McGurk, S. R. (2004). Schizophrenia. *Lancet, 363,* 2063–2072.

Overall, J. E., & Gorman, D. R. (1962). The Brief Psychiatric Rating Scale. *Psychological Reports, 10,* 799–812.

Patterson, T. L., Goldman, S., McKibbin, C. L., Hughs, T., & Jeste, D. V. (2001). UCSD Performance-Based Skills Assessment: Development of a new measure of everyday functioning for severely mentally ill adults. *Schizophrenia Bulletin, 27*(2), 235–245.

Pekkala, E., & Merinder, L. (2002). Psychoeducation for schizophrenia. *Cochrane Database of Systematic Reviews* (Issue 2, Art. No. CD002831. DOI: 10.1002/14651858 .CD002831).

Phillips, S. D., Burns, B. J., Edgar, E. R., Mueser, K. T., Linkings, K. W., Rosenheck, R. A., et al. (2001). Moving assertive community treatment into standard practice. *Psychiatric Services, 52,* 771–779.

Platt, S. (1986). Evaluating social functioning: A critical review of scales and their underlying concepts. In P. B. Bradley & S. R. Hirsch (Eds.), *The psychopharmacology and treatment of schizophrenia* (pp. 263–284). New York: Oxford University Press.

Platt, S., Weyman, A., Hirsch, S., & Hewett, S. (1980). The Social Behavior Assessment Schedule (SBAS): Rationale, contents, scoring, and reliability of a new interview schedule. *Social Psychiatry, 15,* 43–55.

Pollio, D., McClendon, J., & North, C. S. (2005, January 14). "Psychoeducation Re-sponsive to Families": 12 month and 24 month family-level outcomes of a randomized clinical trial. Paper presented at the Society for Social Work Research annual conference, Miami, FL.

Rapp, C. A., & Goesha, R. J. (2004). The principles of effective case management of mental health services. *Psychiatric Rehabilitation Journal, 27*(4), 319–333.

Robins, L. N., Helzer, J. E., Croughan, J., & Ratcliff, K. S. (1981). National Institute of Mental Health Diagnostic Interview Schedule: Its history, characteristics, and validity. *Archives of General Psychiatry, 38,* 381–390.

Royal Australian and New Zealand College of Psychiatrists. (2005). Royal Australian and New Zealand College of Psychiatrists clinical practice guidelines for the treatment of schizophrenia and related disorders. *Australian and New Zealand Journal of Psychiatry, 39*(1/2), 1–30.

Sadock, B. J., & Sadock, V. A. (2003). *Kaplan and Sadock's synopsis of psychiatry: Behavioral sciences, clinical psychiatry* (9th ed.). Baltimore: Williams & Wilkins.

Salkever, D., Domino, M. E., Burns, B., Santos, A. B., Deci, P. A., Dias, J., et al. (1999). Assertive community treatment for people with severe mental illness: The effect on hospital use and costs. *Health Services Research, 34,* 577–601.

Salzer, M. S., & Shear, S. L. (2002). Identifying consumer-provider benefits in evaluations of consumer-delivered services. *Psychiatric Rehabilitation Journal, 25,* 281–288.

Silverman, S., Blank, M., & Taylor, L. C. (1997). On our own: Preliminary findings from a consumer-run service model. *Psychiatric Rehabilitation Journal, 21*(2), 151–159.

Simpson, G. M., & Angus, J. W. S. (1970). A rating scale for extrapyramidal side effects. *Acta Psychiatrica Scandinavia, 212*(Suppl.), 11–19.

Solomon, P., & Draine, J. (1995). Consumer case management and attitudes concerning family relations among persons with mental illness. *Psychiatric Quarterly, 66,* 249–261.

Solomon, P., & Draine, J. (2001). The state of knowledge of the effectiveness of consumer provided services. *Psychiatric Rehabilitation Journal, 25*(1), 20–27.

Spitzer, R. L., Williams, J. B., Gibbon, M., & First, M. B. (1992). The structured clinical interview for *DSM-III-R* (SCID) I: History, rationale, and description. *Archives of General Psychiatry, 49,* 624–629.

Stein, L. I., & Test, M. A. (1980). Alternative to mental hospital treatment: Pt. I. Conceptual model, treatment program, and clinical evaluation. *Archives of General Psychiatry, 37,* 392–397.

Trainor, J., & Tremblay, J. (1992). Consumer/survivor businesses in Ontario: Challenging the rehabilitation model. *Canadian Journal of Community Mental Health, 11,* 65–71.

Twamley, E. W., Jeste, D. V., & Lehman, A. F. (2003). Vocational rehabilitation in schizophrenia and other psychotic disorders: A literature review and meta-analysis of randomized controlled trials. *Journal of Nervous and Mental Diseases, 191,* 515–523.

Unger, K. V., Anthony, W. A., Sciarappa, K., & Rogers, E. S. (1991). A supported education program for young adults with long-term mental illnesses. *Hospital and Community Psychiatry, 42,* 838–842.

U.S. Department of Health and Human Services. (1999). *Mental health: A report of the surgeon general—Executive summary.* Rockville, MD: U.S. Department of Health and Human Services, Substance Abuse and Mental Health Administration, Center for Mental Health Services, National Institutes of Health, National Institute of Mental Health.

Van Tosh, L., Ralph, R. O., & Campbell, J. (2000). The rise of consumerism. *Psychiatric Rehabilitation Skills, 4,* 383–409.

Velligan, D. I., Bow-Thomas, C. C., Huntzinger, C., Ritch, J., Ledbetter, N., Prihoda, T. J., et al. (2000). Randomized controlled trial of the use of compensatory strategies to enhance adaptive functioning in outpatients with schizophrenia. *American Journal of Psychiatry, 157,* 1317–1328.

Velligan, D. I., Mahurin, R. K., True, J. E., Lefton, R. S., & Flores, C. V. (1996). Preliminary evaluation of cognitive adaptation training to compensate for cognitive deficits in schizophrenia. *Psychiatric Services, 47*(4), 415–417.

Weismann, M., Sholomskas, D., & John, K. (1981). The assessment of social adjustment: An update. *Archives of General Psychiatry, 38,* 1250–1258.

Wing, J. K., Cooper, J. E., & Sartorius, N. (1974). *The measurement and classification of psychiatric symptoms.* Cambridge, England: Cambridge University Press.

Yankowitz, R. B. (1990). Employment programming and psychiatric disabilities. *New Directions for Mental Health Services, 45,* 37–48.

Yeich, S., Mowbray, C. T., Bybee, D., & Cohen, E. (1994). The case for a "supported housing" approach: A study of consumer housing and support preferences. *Psychosocial Rehabilitation Journal, 18,* 75–86.

Zide, M. R., & Gray, S. W. (2001). *Psychopathology: A competency based assessment model for social workers.* Pacific Grove, CA: Brooks/Cole.

Ziguras, S. J., & Stuart, G. W. (2000). A meta-analysis of the effectiveness of mental health case management over 20 years. *Psychiatric Services, 51,* 1410–1421.

Zinman, S. (1982). A patient-run residence. *Psychosocial Rehabilitation Journal, 6*(1), 3–11.

PART IV

MOOD DISORDERS

Major Depressive Disorder

Michael J. Holosko, Nansy Jean-Baptiste,
Trang Le, Allison Eaton, and Lisa Power

13

Chapter

Learning Objectives

After reading this chapter, the reader will be able to:

- Describe the prevalence of Major Depressive Disorder in different populations and understand its economic costs and social work's involvement in its treatment and prevention.

- Name and describe the major symptoms associated with Major Depressive Disorder, as presented in the *DSM*.

- Describe the main methods of assessment of Major Depressive Disorder, including the evidence supporting the use of each method type.

- Describe and choose among different treatment options for persons with Major Depressive Disorder, based on empirically tested results.

Overview of the Problem

Epidemiological studies of the prevalence, incidence, and costs of major depression in the United States abound. Some have compared major depression to the "common cold" of mental illness because of its prevalence. The problems most commonly associated with major depression are increased risks of hospitalization and suicide. In its 1999 report, the Office of the U.S. Surgeon General found that major depression was the number one cause of worldwide disability, and that a majority of persons with depression go undiagnosed and even visit physicians to find other explanations for their somatic symptoms.

Greenberg et al. (2003) found that for the estimated 30 million Americans who will get depression in their lifetime, the average number of days missed in a year was 35. Further, they found that 59% were impaired in their social functioning. Stewart, Ricci, Chee, Hahn, and Morganstein (2003) estimated that depression cost $12 billion a year in medical costs and an additional $32 billion in loss of work productivity. This number is estimated to be three times higher than the normal range for nondepressed U.S. workers.

Further, Murray and Lopez (1995) from the World Health Organization found that, in industrialized countries, the burden of major depression as a disease was second only to ischemic heart disease. In their review, Üstün and Kessler (2002) found that most depressions have a mean duration of 23 to 30 weeks.

Dunlop, Song, Lyons, Manheim, and Chang (2003) report an estimated 12-month prevalence of 10.8% for persons ages 15 to 54. Lewinsohn, Rohde, Seeley, Klein, and Gotlib (2003) reported higher rates for adolescents: 35% of female adolescents and 19% of male adolescents will have experienced major depression before they reach age 20. These rates are much higher than those reported for children.

Depression may be especially problematic for seniors, as some studies report that it is more persistent in this age group and can lead to more functional impairments (including an increased risk of heart attack), even if actual prevalence rates are lower with increasing age (Mojtabai & Olfson, 2004). These lower rates may be the result of instruments not sensitive enough to detect the different symptoms of depression among seniors.

Gender Differences

In a review of published refereed articles, Waraich, Goldner, Somers, and Hsu (2004) found the same disproportionate distribution of depression across genders: rates for lifetime and 12 months were 1.5 to 2.5 times higher for women than for men. Kuehner (2003) reported that women tend to have higher relapse and nonremission rates than men, despite women being more likely to seek treatment for their depressive symptoms (Kornstein, 2003).

Across studies, it was found that more than half of the persons diagnosed with and recovered from major depression will be felled by at least one other episode of the disorder. Number of previous depressive episodes is the best predictor of future relapse (Segal, Pearson, & Thase, 2003). Based on previous findings, treatment should be tailored differently for those persons most likely to have recurrences of depression: persons with previous episodes of depression, persons with histories of sexual abuse, and persons high in neuroticism (Segal et al., 2003).

Most authors agree that the differential reporting of symptoms does not seem to be a valid explanation for gender differences and thus recommend a focus on biological and social factors that may lead to depression instead. Galambos, Leadbeater, and Barker (2004) found that gender differences in the prevalence of depression begin during early adolescence (ages 13 to 15), which would support the hypothesis that sex hormones do have an effect on the rates of depression among women. It may also explain the higher rates of depression among postpartum women. However, both of these conditions are also associated with great changes in roles and a narrowing of accepted behavior for females (Kuehner, 2003).

Galambos et al.'s (2004) results are based on longitudinal, population-based data. They found that social support was associated with lower levels of depression, although causality was hard to establish. More established findings reported that these differences might be due to the higher use of rumination as a coping technique for females (e.g., Grant, Lyons, Finkelstein, Conway, & Reynolds, 2004) and the higher prevalence of stressful life events on females (especially when it comes to sexual abuse; e.g., Molnar, Buka, & Kessler, 2001). Other factors are higher prevalence of poverty in women, lower education, and, at the societal level, a lack of control and inequities in workload, especially for working women (Kuenher, 2003).

Ethnic Minority Issues

In 1999, the Office of the U.S. Surgeon General reported that ethnic minorities in the United States were less likely to be treated for depression. Ialongo et al. (2004) report that fewer than 10% of their participants (all African Americans) had received appropriate mental health specialty services while depressed. This is further compounded by the fact that Blazer, Kessler, McGonagle, and Swartz (1994) reported higher prevalence rates for different ethnic groups. These authors reported an 8.1% 30-day prevalence rate for Hispanics ages 15 to 54, a 4.7% prevalence rate for Caucasians, and a 3.8% rate for African Americans.

Dunlop et al. (2003) found higher prevalence of risk factors for depression among ethnic minority participants, for example, chronic health conditions, physical limitations, living alone, lack of education, lower income, and caring for a relative. After controlling for such variables, these authors found that African Americans had lower rates of depression than Caucasians, and Hispanics became more similar to the latter group.

Ialongo et al. (2004) postulated that the discrepancy in prevalence rates for African Americans might be due to their experiences of discrimination. As such, African Americans have had their achievement thwarted by racism, and thus historically experience greater distress overall.

Clearly, depression is undertreated not only for ethnic minorities, where it is more pronounced, but for all persons affected with major depression. Simon, Fleck, Lucas, Bushnell, and the LIDO Group (2004) studied barriers to treatment of depression across different regions of the world. They reported that males, ethnic minorities, and persons with less severe symptoms were less likely to receive treatment. They also found that the most common barrier was financial, and treatment by pharmacotherapy was most prominent. Ironically, even after the participants' physicians were informed of the diagnosis, most went untreated.

Operational Definitions of the Problem

The central features of Major Depressive Disorder (MDD) as described in the *Diagnostic and Statistical Manual of Mental Disorders* (*DSM*; American Psychiatric Association, 2000) are negative mood (which in children and adolescents can take the form of irritability), loss of interest in day-to-day activities that are normally found to be enjoyable, cognitive impairment in the areas of memory and concentration, and great indecisiveness. These symptoms must have occurred on most days for at least 2 weeks (American Psychiatric Association, 2000). Also included are symptoms of irrational guilt and a sense of worthlessness. Somatic symptoms often associated with MDD include either weight gain or loss without dieting (accompanied by an increase or decrease in appetite); sleep disturbances (too little or too much), fatigue, or psychomotor agitation (American Psychiatric Association, 2000).

It is important to note that a person cannot be diagnosed with MDD if he or she has been diagnosed previously with Bipolar Disorder, Schizoaffective Disorder, or Schizophrenia (American Psychiatric Association, 2000). Further, all possible biological explanations (such as hypothyroidism and substance abuse) must first be eliminated. Finally, if the depressed mood can be accounted for by life events (e.g., bereavement), then an MDD diagnosis should be postponed (American Psychiatric Association, 2000).

Other important but less common symptoms include psychoses, suicidal ideation or attempts or preoccupation with thoughts of death, and psychomotor retardation. These latter symptoms are associated with greater severity of depression

(American Psychiatric Association, 2000). New to the fourth edition of the *DSM* is that, to diagnose depression, symptoms must significantly impair day-to-day functioning of the client.

Evidence-Based Approaches to Assessment

Self-Report Methods and Other Administered Interview Guides

The most commonly used method to assess depression, and the gold standard against which other measures are compared, is the clinical interview. Some clinicians use a traditional diagnostic assessment method that is unstructured. This consists of interviewing the client and asking questions to assess the problem. P. R. Miller, Dasher, Collins, Griffiths, and Brown (2001) found that the diagnostic accuracy of structured interviews such as the Structured Clinical Interview for the *DSM* (SCID) and the Computer Assisted Diagnostic Interview for *DSM*—Clinical Version both had excellent agreement among expert ratings and were statistically significantly better than the traditional assessment in diagnosing depression. These authors found that interviewers who did not use the structured interviews tested for only 53% of the "key criteria" and were thus more likely to miss information that could lead to a more complete diagnosis (p. 262).

The most popular structured interview is the SCID, along with earlier versions based on *DSM-III* criteria (First, Spitzer, Gibbon, & Williams, 1995). There are currently reliability studies that support the continued use of the SCID *DSM-IV* version (Ventura, Liberman, Green, Shaner, & Mintz, 1998). Ventura et al. described in detail the standardized administration and training procedures, which allow for higher reliability and interrater agreement across interviewers, including better than 90% agreement on final diagnosis. The SCID usually takes between 1 and 2 hours to administer. It should not be used on clients with mental retardation, and results may be invalid for those who are too ill to properly answer all questions. For those who do not speak English fluently, parts of the SCID have been translated into other languages. This questionnaire is best used by experienced clinicians or health professionals. An average of 20 hours of training is required for fluency in its administration.

Another often used, well-known, semistructured interview is the Hamilton Rating Scale for Depression (HRSD; Hamilton, 1960) and the Modified Hamilton Rating Scale for Depression. Both have been validated and found to be reliable (I. W. Miller, Bishop, Norman, & Maddever, 1985). These questionnaires were designed for use by experienced health professionals and they combine interview questions and observations of symptoms.

For cross-cultural use, the University of Michigan Composite International Diagnostic Interview has been shown to be valid and reliable across different nationalities (Tacchini, Coppola, Musazzi, Altamura, & Invernizzi, 1994; Wittchen, 1994). It can easily be administered by most interviewers in 1 to 2 hours and requires minimal training (Farmer, McGuffin, & Williams, 2002).

A recent article by Joiner, Walker, Pettit, Perez, and Cukrowicz (2005) provides a particularly fine overview of evidence-based assessment methods for depression occurring among adults.

For Youth and Adolescents

The Children's Depression Inventory has been widely validated and tested for use with younger age groups. Lewinsohn et al. (2003) concluded that, contrary to what is found when diagnosing children, parental assessment was not necessary for the diagnosis of depression in adolescents. The scales recommended for the assessment of depression in this age group are the Kiddie-Sads-Present and Lifetime Version (K-SADS), the Structured Clinical Interview, the Diagnostic Interview for Children and Adolescents (Welner, Reich, Herjanic, & Jung, 1987), and the Revised Diagnostic Interview Schedule for Children (Schwab-Stone, Fisher, Piacentini, & Shaffer, 1993). Some adult tests can be used with adolescents; please refer to administration manuals for more information. All of the preceding diagnostic tools are semistructured interviews and yield similar diagnostic rates when administered in person or by phone (Lewinsohn et al., 2003).

Self-Report Interviews and Self-Administered Methods

In terms of self-report measures, the most popular is the Beck Depression Inventory (BDI; Beck, Ward, Mendelson, Mock, & Erbaugh, 1961). The BDI detects only depression and can be administered aurally or by paper and pencil. It has been extensively validated and has been shown to yield similar factor structures across different ethnic groups (Contreras, Fernandez, Malcarne, Ingram, & Vaccarino, 2004). Another measure that has been validated is the Inventory to Diagnose Depression (IDD; Zimmerman, Coryell, Corenthal, & Wilson, 1986), created for the purpose of diagnosing as well as evaluating the severity of depressive symptoms. The Center for Epidemiological Studies Depression Scale (CES-D) is also in the public domain. This scale has been widely found to be reliable and valid in population-based studies (Radloff, 1977). However, it was not found to be stable across ethnic groups (Crockett, Randall, Shen, Russell, & Driscoll, 2005). It is important to note that the previous measures should be used mainly as a first step, with the final diagnosis being reserved until after a complete interview is conducted.

For Adolescents

The CES-D, the BDI, and the HRSD have all been found to be reliable and valid with adolescents (e.g., Motl, Dishman, Birnbaum, & Lytle, 2005; Osman, Kopper, Barrios, Gutierrez, & Bagge, 2004; Roberts, Andrews, Lewinsohn, & Hops, 1990). However, adolescents are more likely to endorse items in the CES-D and the BDI. Thus, Lewinsohn et al. (2003) recommend the use of a cutoff score of 24 for female and 22 for male adolescents on the CES-D, and using 11 for female and 15 for male adolescents with the BDI.

Evidence-Based Approaches to Intervention

It used to be assumed that the longer a client was in therapy, the greater the improvements in his or her mental health. But short-term therapy has been found to be just as effective as longer therapy. However, Shapiro, Rees, Barkham, and Hardy (1995) found that both cognitive-behavioral therapy (CBT) and interpersonal psychotherapy (IPT) required a minimum number of sessions to be effective, and they recommend a length of at least 16 sessions for both. These authors found that IPT gains were maintained at that number of sessions, and the CBT was superior at that number of sessions.

Biological and Biochemical Interventions

Antidepressant pharmacotherapy is the most rigorously studied treatment for all forms of depression. This is partly because it is easy to conceive of a placebo or control group in clinical trials, and also because pharmaceutical companies invest significant resources in such trials. Currently, there are three classes of antidepressant medications: tricyclic antidepressants (TCAs), monoamine oxidase inhibitors (MAOIs), and selective serotonin reuptake inhibitors (SSRIs). All have proven more effective than placebos in controlled clinical trials (Hollon, Thase, & Markowitz, 2002). The type of antidepressant currently most prescribed is the SSRI class, a newer class of drugs, because of their "low nuisance side effects and safety in overdose" (Hollon, Muñoz, et al., 2002, p. 615). For example, clients who take MAOIs have dietary restrictions, and both MAOIs and TCAs have risks of overdose (which is especially problematic for depressed patients). Overall, each type of medication has shown advantages over the others in different types of depression, but SSRIs are a good first-line intervention (Hollon, Thase, et al., 2002).

Although it is already available, a new type of antidepressant medication is currently undergoing more rigorous clinical testing. Bupropion has fewer side effects than SSRIs and is now easier to take because it is available in sustained-release form (Hollon, Thase, et al., 2002).

For depressed individuals who have not responded to antidepressants and psychotherapy, as well as for those with psychotic episodes during depression, electroconvulsive therapy (ECT) is efficacious (Hollon, Thase, et al., 2002). In ECT, patients have grand mal seizures induced by electrical shocks. The new forms of treatment are nothing like the early methods and are now very safe (Hollon, Muñoz, et al., 2002). Side effects may include memory loss and decline in cognitive abilities (Hollon, Muñoz, et al., 2002).

Combination Therapies

It is often believed by clinicians and physicians that combining pharmacotherapy with psychotherapy yields the best overall outcomes for clients. Newer studies have examined the ideal combination, focusing on the optimal timing of each type of therapy; some have even questioned the use of both therapies. Fava and Ruini (2005) reported on a recent study that found that an optimal treatment for the prevention of relapse in depression was the use of pharmacotherapy during the acute stage of depression and later the use of psychotherapy to address residual symptoms. Segal, Vincent, and Levitt (2002) also found greater efficacy of crossover and sequential treatments for depression. According to Fava and Ruini (2005, p. 93), the effectiveness of this sequential approach lies in the "fact that the psychotherapeutic approach is applied when the most severe symptoms of depression have abated on pharmacological treatment and when the potential for learning has thus increased." Questions remain concerning which types of depression are most amenable to which types of treatment (Areán & Cook, 2002).

Areán and Cook (2002) noted that a focus on combination therapy can have deleterious effects on certain types of clients: (a) those who cannot afford both therapies, (b) those who do not have access to one of these therapies and may thus be offered therapy not based on evidence of efficacy, and (c) clients who are already taking a certain number of other medications, which can increase the risk of unintended interactions or side effects.

Individual Therapies

Cognitive-behavioral therapy and interpersonal psychotherapy are the two approaches with the strongest evidence in support of their efficacy (King & Heyne, 2000). The most popular treatment for depression is currently a CBT approach. This approach is also the one that is most strongly supported by evidence of its efficacy. Although the issue is complicated by type of symptom and severity of depression, clients treated with CBT have half the likelihood of recurrence of depression compared to clients treated solely with pharmacotherapy (Hensley, Nadiga, & Uhlenhuth, 2004). Hollon (2003) reported that studies have shown its efficacy with most age groups. One of the most popular and evidence-based treatment manuals was written by Beck, Rush, Shaw, and Emery (1979), entitled *Cognitive Therapy for Depression: A Treatment Manual.* It is important to note that all their research supports the use of CBT, but that the lack of strong evidence for other therapies is not equivalent to their ineffectiveness.

Recent reviews have also supported the effectiveness of IPT and short-term psychodynamic therapy for depression (e.g., Leichsenring, 2001). These studies did not find a significant difference in percentage of clients considered remitted between cognitive, cognitive-behavioral, and short-term psychodynamic therapies in rates of remission. Although the same author reported that the effect size for all these therapies was small.

Interpersonal psychotherapy combines elements of psychodynamic therapy and CBT and usually lasts between 12 and 16 weeks (Markowitz, 1999). One of the main focus points of IPT is the resolution of role conflicts currently causing distress in clients, with a focus on depression as an illness, and thus a removal of self-blame for the symptoms and the inability to simply get over it (Markowitz, 1999). Interpersonal psychotherapy can be learned through reading the manual, and certification in its use is available but not considered necessary, as peer supervision is an alternative (Markowitz, 1999). Overall, it is a fairly simple technique to master (Markowitz, 1999). Sotsky, Glass, Shea, and Pilkonis (1991) found that IPT seems more appropriate than CBT for clients with lower levels of social dysfunction and higher baseline levels of depression, as well as those with cognitive and memory impairments. Maintenance psychotherapeutic treatment is also recommended for the prevention of relapse.

Interpersonal psychotherapy has been shown to be effective for adolescents (e.g., Mufson et al., 2004) and seniors (e.g., Reynolds et al., 1999; Sholomskas, Chevron, Prusoff, & Berry, 1983). One problem, however, is that IPT has been evaluated on mostly healthy Caucasian clients, and thus these results may not be generalizable to other populations (Areán & Cook, 2002). Two texts are recommended for more information: the *Comprehensive Guide to Interpersonal Psychotherapy* by Weissman, Markowitz, and Klerman (2000) and *Mastering Depression: A Patient Guide to Interpersonal Psychotherapy* by Weissman (1995) for clients in IPT.

Social problem-solving therapy may help resolve depressive symptomatology by showing clients techniques to help them solve problems at psychological and social levels (Hegel, Barrett, & Oxman, 2000). This treatment has been shown to be effective for young and older adults, as well as with persons who are mentally retarded (Hegel et al., 2000). This therapy typically requires 10 to 12 sessions and should be administered by a person with training in CBT. With some modifications, this technique has been shown to be effective when administered by other health professionals in primary care settings (Hegel et al., 2000). Social problem-solving therapy has also demonstrated superiority to simple supportive therapy in treating seniors with cognitive impairments (Alexopoulos, Raue, & Areán, 2003). This brings hope to social workers and other health professionals who are constantly faced with the challenge of helping persons with cognitive impairments.

Primary care settings are now increasingly prescribing physical exercise as treatment for depression. In their review, Craft and Landers (1998) found a significant effect of exercise on depression levels. Craft (2005) found that the main mechanism for the decrease of mood disturbance seems to be through increases in self-efficacy derived from exercising successfully (for long-term, moderately [47.3 months] depressed participants). The changes occurred as early as 3 weeks after the beginning of the moderate exercise regimen (Craft, 2005). She also found that women who exercised were less likely to ruminate and more likely to use distraction to cope with their negative thoughts.

Group Therapies

Morrison (2001) reviewed the literature on the effectiveness of cognitive-behavioral group therapy for the treatment of depression and concluded that group therapy was almost always as effective as individual therapy, and that the decreases in costs associated with group therapy make up for any differences in outcome. Most of these groups run from 12 to 20 sessions, usually lasting from 90 minutes to 2 hours (Morrison, 2001). The most effective therapies were preceded by individual evaluations to gauge the severity and type of symptoms in each group member before assignment into appropriate groups. Morrison also pointed out that a few clients fared very poorly in these treatment conditions. More research is clearly needed to identify the clients who are least likely to benefit from group therapy.

Morrison (2001) further reported that most authors concur that group therapy should be run with a cotherapist because of the amount of work that has to be done in each session. She also states that, if therapists offer sessions on their own, six participants is the maximum number a therapist can practically manage. Advantages of group therapy include the ability to treat more clients in the same amount of time, cohesiveness among group members, "imitative behavior," learning interpersonal skills within the group, and recognition of disordered thoughts in others, which makes application to the self easier (p. 314).

In terms of disadvantages, the therapist must ensure that every group member has an equal opportunity to speak, that group members do not become confrontational, that (unfavorable) comparisons are not made of group members who do not progress as fast as the others, that clients do not self-censor in front of others, that the group discussion doesn't devolve into social talk, and that the group doesn't break up into different subgroups. Purely logistical issues, such as arranging a convenient meeting time for all, can also present problems.

Hoberman, Lewinsohn, and Tilson (1988) found that the Coping with Depression course was effective in treating depression. This course is a psychoeducational, 12-session treatment that uses social learning theory to design the intervention. Group cohesion, existing social support, and higher level of reading ability were predictive of positive outcomes. Just like the adult version, the Adolescent Coping with Depression Course has found empirical support for its effectiveness (Lewinsohn et al., 2003).

There are a few training and user manuals available for cognitive-behavioral educational group programs. Lewinsohn, Antonuccio, Steinmetz, and Teri (1984) describe such an evidence-based program in *The Coping with Depression Course: A Psycho-Educational Intervention for Unipolar Depression.*

A recent review of mindfulness-based stress reduction (MBSR) therapy found that across a variety of conditions, including physical pain and depression, participants in these studies improved significantly: an average effect size of .5, which clinically is considered moderate improvement (Grossman, Niemann, Schmidt, & Walach, 2004). Mindfulness-based stress reduction teaches clients to observe their thoughts and emotions from a more detached perspective, making it less likely that they will get caught up in negative thought cycles (Day & Horton-Deutsch, 2004). (For more information on the treatment of depression with mindfulness meditation, refer to *Full Catastrophe Living: Using the Wisdom of Your Body and Mind to Face Stress, Pain, and Illness* by Kabat-Zinn, 1990.)

Teasdale changed some components of MBSR specifically to treat depression and added cognitive components to this new treatment. This treatment mode is called mindfulness-based cognitive therapy (MBCT) and consists of an 8-week group program (Ma & Teasdale, 2004). A training manual entitled *Mindfulness-Based Cognitive Therapy for Depression: A New Approach to Preventing Relapse* by Segal, Williams, and Teasdale (2002) is available. Compared with clients who received their usual treatment, those who engaged in MBCT had half of the relapse rate. Ramel, Goldin, Carmona, and McQuaid (2004) found that this method worked mainly by reducing rumination in previously depressed participants, and thus reduced the risk of recurrence of depression. Their participants had all been previously treated with CBT; they thus concluded that MSBR has effects that are additive to CBT treatment alone. Because of these findings, the authors hypothesized that mindfulness-based treatment modes will be more effective for depression caused by cognitive style as opposed to that due to significant negative life events. However, overall compliance in this method was found to be poor for participants.

For Seniors

Cognitive-behavioral therapy, behavioral therapy, brief dynamic therapy, and problem-solving therapy have all been found to be effective with different groups of seniors, at the individual as well as at the group levels (Areán & Cook, 2002). But there is at least one form of therapy that was developed specifically for seniors (Areán & Cook, 2002). Reminiscence therapy is most often offered in the form of group therapy but can also be used in individual therapy. A recent review of the literature found this type of therapy useful for depressed seniors (Hsieh & Wang, 2003). Reminiscence therapy is based on Erikson's theory and is cognitive in structure (Hsieh & Wang, 2003). It aims to increase self-esteem and self-efficacy by focusing the client on past events that were successfully navigated, and thus integrate all previous experiences (Areán, Perri, Nezu, & Schein, 1993). It is considered relatively cost-effective and has been found to also have positive effects on family members of the depressed client (Comana, Brown, & Thomas, 1998). Hsieh and Wang found no differences in effectiveness based on modality or location of the treatment, and there was no difference based on number of sessions (from 3 to 16). However, Areán et al. reported that problem-solving therapy had better outcomes than reminiscence therapy in general. For more information on reminiscence therapy, *Critical Advances in Reminiscence Work: From Theory to Application,* edited by Webster and Haight (2002), offers a good review.

Marital, Couple, and Family Therapies

Research has shown an association between depression and divorce. A recent longitudinal study explored the directionality of this effect. Whisman and Bruce (1999) found that marital problems were more likely to cause depression, not the other way around. Twelve months after the baseline interview, individuals who had not been depressed but had reported marital problems were almost 3 times as likely to meet criteria for MDD.

According to a recent review, the strongest evidence supports the use of behavioral marital therapy (BMT), although its efficacy over every type of individual therapy has not been demonstrated empirically (Gupta, Coyne, & Beach, 2003). Behavioral marital therapy focuses on increasing the intimacy and reducing the amount of conflict between the couples in treatment, as well as increasing problem-solving and communication skills

(p. 323). One advantage to BMT, or BMT combined with CBT, is the fact that all couples in such treatments showed improvement in marital satisfaction. Thus, although the effect on depression from CBT and BMT was similar, there was an additional gain to using BMT.

Community Interventions

As reported earlier, poverty is a risk factor for depression, as is ethnic minority status and previous history of victimization (e.g., Katon & Ludman, 2003). However, studies have shown that, in the United States, persons without medical insurance have difficulty accessing appropriate mental health services. This is even more difficult considering the fact that depressed individuals often do not have the energy to advocate for themselves. Clearly, social work has its challenges in this area.

Another important problem is the stigma associated with mental illness, especially MDD (Katon & Ludman, 2003). Katon and Ludman recommend using a new model, wherein one health professional (e.g., a social worker) works with an interdisciplinary team to act as the advocate for the depressed client, but also to make sure that the client follows through with the different treatments. This approach fits nicely with social work's current case management orientation. Using this model, the authors found that clients needed fewer psychotherapeutic interventions and that the model increased adherence to medication and led to a "75% recovery in intervention patients" (p. 116). This treatment model was found to be even more efficacious among minority clients. Erickson and Muramatsu (2004) also reported that social workers can act as team leaders and add to the multidisciplinary team through their ability to closely follow clients and by informing other health professionals of the possible barriers faced by the client (such as lack of transportation, the prohibitive cost of the medications, the intolerability of side effects).

Another proactive step must be the education of the population regarding the effectiveness and especially the availability of treatments for MDD (Collins, Westra, Dozois, & Burns, 2004). As noted previously, the majority of depressed individuals do not receive appropriate care. Interventions also need to focus on educating health care professionals regarding the symptoms and prevalence of depression. Further, evidence supports the assertion that early diagnosis and treatment of depression will decrease the severity of the symptoms and the subsequent risk of recurrence.

Some authors argue that mental health professionals must develop new methods of delivering services to reach wider audiences (Hollon, Muñoz, et al., 2002). Trials have been conducted providing such services online, using bibliotherapy, using television programs, through phone and mail communication, as well as providing programs in other languages (Hollon, Muñoz, et al., 2002).

Summary

Major Depressive Disorder is one of the most common mental illnesses in North America. It is both debilitating and treatable. Because of its prevalence and costs to society, social workers will have to rise to the challenge of most effectively treating this disorder. There is currently a research-practice gap in this area. After reviewing more than 300 articles on the evidence-based treatment for depression, the authors of this chapter found that the overwhelming majority of empirical studies originated from the discipline of psychology, not social work. The profession of social work needs to address this shortfall in empirical research on effective psychosocial services for depressed individuals.

Study Questions

1. Explain the differences and/or similarities between men and women who are suffering or have suffered from Major Depressive Disorder. Why do you think these differences and/or similarities occur?

2. What risk factors associated with higher rates of depression are described throughout the chapter? How do these affect social work interventions?

3. From what you have read about depression assessment methods, which method do you think is the most valid for the population you intend to work with? Why?

4. Explain which interventions are most commonly used with adolescents, seniors, and adults. Which intervention would you feel comfortable working with, and why?

5. Which client or group characteristics are most likely to influence the outcome of treatment in depression?

6. What interventions would you choose if you were aiming to lower the prevalence of Major Depressive Disorder in the general population? In women? In ethnic minorities?

7. Can you think of innovative ways of informing specific populations about the symptoms and the treatment of depression? Would they work better than the current methods? Why?

8. List five challenges confronting social workers working with clients who have Major Depressive Disorder.

References

Alexopoulos, G. S., Raue, P., & Areán, P. (2003). Problem-solving therapy versus supportive therapy in geriatric major depression with executive dysfunction. *American Journal of Geriatric Psychiatry, 11,* 46–52.

American Psychiatric Association. (2000). *Diagnostic and statistical manual of mental disorders* (4th ed., text rev.). Washington, DC: Author.

Areán, P. A., & Cook, B. L. (2002). Psychotherapy and combined psychotherapy/pharmacotherapy for late life depression. *Biological Psychiatry, 52,* 293–303.

Areán, P. A., Perri, M. G., Nezu, A. M., & Schein, R. L. (1993). Comparative effectiveness of social problem-solving therapy and reminiscence therapy as treatments for depression in older adults. *Journal of Consulting and Clinical Psychology, 61,* 1003–1010.

Beck, A. T., Rush, A. J., Shaw, B. E., & Emery, G. (1979). *Cognitive therapy of depression: A treatment manual.* New York: Guilford Press.

Beck, A. T., Ward, C. H., Mendelson, M., Mock, J., & Erbaugh, J. (1961). An inventory for measuring depression. *Archives of General Psychiatry, 4,* 561–571.

Blazer, D. G., Kessler, R. C., McGonagle, K. A., & Swartz, M. S. (1994). The prevalence and distribution of major depression in a national community sample: The national co-morbidity survey. *American Journal of Psychiatry, 151,* 979–986.

Collins, K. A., Westra, H. A., Dozois, D. J. A., & Burns, D. D. (2004). Gaps in accessing treatment for anxiety and depression: Challenges for the delivery of care. *Clinical Psychology Review, 24,* 583–616.

Comana, M. T., Brown, V. M., & Thomas, J. D. (1998). The effect of reminiscence therapy on family coping. *Journal of Family Nursing, 4,* 182–197.

Contreras, S., Fernandez, S., Malcarne, V. L., Ingram, R. E., & Vaccarino, V. R. (2004). Reliability and validity of the Beck depression and anxiety inventories in Caucasian Americans and Latinos. *Hispanic Journal of Behavioral Sciences, 26,* 446–462.

Craft, L. L. (2005). Exercise and clinical depression: Examining two psychological mechanisms. *Psychology of Sport and Exercise, 6,* 151–171.

Craft, L. L., & Landers, D. M. (1998). The effect of exercise on clinical depression and depression resulting from mental illness: A meta-analysis. *Journal of Sport and Exercise Psychology, 20,* 339–357.

Crockett, L. J., Randall, B. A., Shen, Y., Russell, S. T., & Driscoll, A. K. (2005). Measurement equivalence of the Center for Epidemiological Studies Depression Scale for Latino and Anglo adolescents: A national study. *Journal of Consulting and Clinical Psychology, 73,* 47–58.

Day, P. O., & Horton-Deutsch, S. (2004). Using mindfulness-based therapeutic interventions in psychiatric nursing practice: Pt. I. Description and empirical support for mindfulness-based interventions. *Archives of Psychiatric Nursing, 18,* 164–169.

Dunlop, D. D., Song, J., Lyons, J. S., Manheim, L. M., & Chang, R. W. (2003). Racial/ethnic differences in rates of depression among pre-retirement adults. *American Journal of Public Health, 93,* 1945–1952.

Erickson, C. L., & Muramatsu, N. (2004). Parkinson's disease, depression, and medication adherence: Current knowledge and social work practice. *Journal of Gerontological Social Work, 42*(3–4), 3–18.

Farmer, A., McGuffin, P., & Williams, J. (2002). *Measuring psychopathology.* New York: Oxford University Press.

Fava, G. A., & Ruini, C. (2005). What is the optimal treatment of mood and anxiety disorders? *Clinical Psychology: Science and Practice, 12,* 92–96.

First, M. B., Spitzer, R. L., Gibbon, M., & Williams, J. B. W. (1995). *Structured Clinical Interview for* DSM-IV. New York: Biometrics Research Department.

Galambos, N. L., Leadbeater, B. J., & Barker, E. T. (2004). Gender differences in and risk factors for depression in adolescence: A 4-year longitudinal study. *International Journal of Behavioral Development, 28,* 16–25.

Grant, K. E., Lyons, A. L., Finkelstein, J. S., Conway, K. M., & Reynolds, L. K. (2004). Gender differences in rates of depressive symptoms among low-income, urban,

African American youth: A test of two mediational hypotheses. *Journal of Youth and Adolescence, 33,* 523–533.

Greenberg, P. E., Kessler, R. C., Birnbaum, H. G., Leong, S. A., Lowe, S. W., Berglund, P. A., et al. (2003). The economic burden of depression in the United States: How did it change between 1990 and 2000? *Journal of Clinical Psychiatry, 64,* 1465–1475.

Grossman, P., Niemann, L., Schmidt, S., & Walach, H. (2004). Mindfulness-based stress reduction and health benefits: A meta-analysis. *Journal of Psychosomatic Research, 57,* 35–43.

Gupta, M., Coyne, J. C., & Beach, S. R. H. (2003). Couples treatment for major depression: Critique of the literature and suggestions for some different directions. *Journal of Family Therapy, 25,* 317–346.

Hamilton, M. (1960). A rating scale for depression. *Journal of Neurology, Neurosurgery, and Psychiatry, 23,* 56–61.

Hegel, M. T., Barrett, J. E., & Oxman, T. E. (2000). Training therapists in problem-solving treatment of depressive disorders in primary care: Lessons learned from the "treatment effectiveness project." *Families, Systems, and Health, 18,* 423–435.

Hensley, P. L., Nadiga, D., & Uhlenhuth, E. H. (2004). Long-term effectiveness of cognitive therapy in major depressive disorder. *Depression and Anxiety, 20,* 1–7.

Hoberman, H. M., Lewinsohn, P. M., & Tilson, M. (1988). Group treatment of depression: Individual predictors of outcome. *Journal of Consulting and Clinical Psychology, 56,* 393–398.

Hollon, S. D. (2003). Does cognitive therapy have an enduring effect? *Cognitive Therapy and Research, 27,* 71–75.

Hollon, S. D., Muñoz, R. F., Barlow, D. H., Beardslee, W. R., Bell, C. C., Bernal, G., et al. (2002). Psychosocial intervention development for the prevention and treatment of depression: Promoting innovation and increasing access. *Biological Psychiatry, 52,* 610–630.

Hollon, S. D., Thase, M. E., & Markowitz, J. C. (2002). Treatment and prevention of depression. *Psychological Science in the Public Interest, 3*(2), 39–77.

Hsieh, H., & Wang, J. (2003). Effect of reminiscence therapy on depression in older adults: A systematic review. *International Journal of Nursing Studies, 40,* 335–345.

Ialongo, N., McCreary, B. K., Pearson, J. L., Koenig, A. L., Schmidt, N. B., Poduska, J., et al. (2004). Major depressive disorder in a population of urban, African American young adults: Prevalence, correlates, comorbidity and unmet mental health service need. *Journal of Affective Disorders, 79,* 127–136.

Joiner, T. E., Jr., Walker, P. L., Pettit, J. W., Perez, M., & Cukrowicz, K. C. (2005). Evidence-based assessment of depression in adults. *Psychological Assessment, 17*(3), 267–277.

Kabat-Zinn, J. (1990). *Pain and illness.* New York: Delacorte.

Katon, W. J., & Ludman, E. J. (2003). Improving services for women with depression in primary care settings. *Psychology of Women Quarterly, 27,* 114–120.

King, N. J., & Heyne, D. (2000). Promotion of empirically validated psychotherapies in counseling psychology. *Counseling Psychology Quarterly, 13,* 1–12.

Kornstein, S. G. (2003). Gender, depression, and antidepressant treatment. *Primary Psychiatry, 10,* 58–61.

Kuehner, C. (2003). Gender differences in unipolar depression: An update of epidemiological findings and possible explanations. *Acta Psychiatrica Scandinavica, 108,* 163–174.

Leichsenring, F. (2001). Comparative effects of short-term psychodynamic psychotherapy and cognitive-behavioral therapy in depression: A meta-analytic approach. *Clinical Psychology Review, 21,* 401–419.

Lewinsohn, P. M., Antonuccio, D., Steinmetz, J. L., & Teri, L. (1984). *The coping with depression course: A psychoeducational intervention for unipolar depression.* Eugene, OR: Castalia Press.

Lewinsohn, P. M., Rohde, P., Seeley, J. R., Klein, D. N., & Gotlib, I. H. (2003). Psychosocial functioning of young adults who have experienced and recovered from major depressive disorder during adolescence. *Journal of Abnormal Psychology, 112,* 353–363.

Ma, S. H., & Teasdale, J. D. (2004). Mindfulness-based cognitive therapy for depression: Replication and exploration of differential relapse prevention effects. *Journal of Consulting and Clinical Psychology, 72,* 31–40.

Markowitz, J. C. (1999). Developments in interpersonal psychotherapy. *Canadian Journal of Psychiatry, 44,* 556–561.

Miller, I. W., Bishop, S. B., Norman, W. H., & Maddever, H. (1985). The Modified Hamilton Rating Scale for Depression: Reliability and validity. *Psychiatry Research, 14,* 131–142.

Miller, P. R., Dasher, R., Collins, R., Griffiths, P., & Brown, F. (2001). Inpatient diagnostic assessments: Pt. 1. Accuracy of structured versus unstructured interviews. *Psychiatry Research, 105,* 255–264.

Mojtabai, R., & Olfson, M. (2004). Major depression in community-dwelling middle-aged and older adults: Prevalence and 2- and 4-year follow-up symptoms. *Psychological Medicine, 34,* 623–634.

Molnar, B. E., Buka, S. L., & Kessler, R. C. (2001). Child sexual abuse and subsequent psychopathology: Results from the national co-morbidity survey. *American Journal of Public Health, 91,* 753–760.

Morrison, N. (2001). Group cognitive therapy: Treatment of choice or sub-optimal option? *Behavioral and Cognitive Psychotherapy, 29,* 311–332.

Motl, R. W., Dishman, R. K., Birnbaum, A. S., & Lytle, L. A. (2005). Longitudinal invariance of the Center for Epidemiologic Studies Depression Scale among girls and boys in middle school. *Educational and Psychological Measurement, 65,* 90–108.

Mufson, L., Dorta, K. P., Wickramaratne, P., Nomura, Y., Olfson, M., & Weissman, M. (2004). A randomized effectiveness trial of interpersonal psychotherapy for depressed adolescents. *Archives of General Psychiatry, 61,* 577–584.

Murray, C. J. L., & Lopez, A. D. (1995). Progress and directions in refining the global burden of disease approach: A response to Williams. *Health Economics, 9,* 69–82.

Osman, A., Kopper, B. A., Barrios, F., Gutierrez, P. M., & Bagge, C. L. (2004). Reliability and validity of the Beck Depression Inventory-II with adolescent psychiatric

inpatients. *Psychological Assessment, 16,* 120–132.

Radloff, L. S. (1977). The CES-D scale: A self-report depression scale for research in the general population. *Applied Psychological Measurement, 1,* 385–401.

Ramel, W., Goldin, P. R., Carmona, P. E., & McQuaid, J. R. (2004). The effects of mindfulness meditation on cognitive processes and affect in patients with past depression. *Cognitive Therapy and Research, 28,* 433–455.

Reynolds, C. F., III, Frank, E., Perel, J. M., Imber, S. D., Cornes, C., Miller, M. D., et al. (1999). Nortriptyline and interpersonal psychotherapy as maintenance therapies for recurrent major depression: A randomized controlled trial in patients older than 59 years. *Journal of the American Medical Association, 281,* 39–45.

Roberts, R. E., Andrews, J. A., Lewinsohn, P. M., & Hops, H. (1990). Assessment of depression in adolescents using the Center for Epidemiologic Studies Depression Scale. *Psychological Assessment, 2,* 122–128.

Schwab-Stone, M., Fisher, P. W., Piacentini, J., & Shaffer, D. (1993). The Diagnostic Interview Schedule for Children: Revised version (DISC-R): Pt. II. Test retest reliability. *Journal of the American Academy of Child and Adolescent Psychiatry, 32,* 651–657.

Segal, Z. V., Pearson, J. L., & Thase, M. E. (2003). Challenges in preventing relapse in major depression: Report of a National Institute of Mental Health workshop on state of the science of relapse prevention in major depression. *Journal of Affective Disorders, 77,* 97–108.

Segal, Z. V., Vincent, P., & Levitt, A. (2002). Efficacy of combined, sequential, and crossover psychotherapy and pharmacotherapy in improving outcomes in depression. *Journal of Psychiatry and Neuroscience, 27,* 281–290.

Segal, Z. V., Williams, J. M. G., & Teasdale, J. D. (2002). *Mindfulness-based cognitive therapy for depression: A new approach to preventing relapse.* New York: Guilford Press.

Shapiro, D. A., Rees, A., Barkham, M., & Hardy, G. (1995). Effects of treatment duration and severity of depression on the maintenance of gains after cognitive-behavioral and psychodynamic-interpersonal psychotherapy. *Journal of Consulting and Clinical Psychology, 63,* 378–387.

Sholomskas, A. J., Chevron, E. S., Prusoff, B. A., & Berry, C. (1983). Short-term interpersonal therapy (IPT) with the depressed elderly: Case reports and discussion. *American Journal of Psychotherapy, 37,* 552–566.

Simon, G. E., Fleck, M., Lucas, R., Bushnell, D. M., & LIDO Group. (2004). Prevalence and predictors of depression treatment in an international primary care study. *American Journal of Psychiatry, 161,* 1626–1634.

Sotsky, S. M., Glass, D. R., Shea, M. T., & Pilkonis, P. A. (1991). Patient predictors of response to psychotherapy and pharmacotherapy: Findings in the NIMH treatment of depression collaborative research program. *American Journal of Psychiatry, 148,* 997–1008.

Stewart, W. F., Ricci, J. A., Chee, E., Hahn, S. R., & Morganstein, D. (2003). Cost of lost productive work time among U.S. workers with depression. *Journal of the American Medical Association, 289,* 3135–3144.

Tacchini, G., Coppola, M. T., Musazzi, A., Altamura, A. C., & Invernizzi, G. (1994). [Multinational validation of the composite international diagnostic interview (CIDI)]. *Minerva Psichiatrica, 35,* 63–80. (Original work Italian)

Üstün, T. B., & Kessler, R. C. (2002). Global burden of depressive disorders: The issue of duration. *British Journal of Psychiatry: Journal of Mental Science, 181,* 181–183.

Ventura, J., Liberman, R. P., Green, M. F., Shaner, A., & Mintz, J. (1998). Training

and quality assurance with structured clinical interview for *DSM-IV* (SCID-I/P). *Psychiatry Research, 79,* 163–173.

Waraich, P., Goldner, E. M., Somers, J. M., & Hsu, L. (2004). Prevalence and incidence studies of mood disorders: A systematic review of the literature. *Canadian Journal of Psychiatry, 49,* 124–138.

Webster, J. D., & Haight, B. K. (2002). *Critical advances in reminiscence work: From theory to application.* New York: Springer.

Weissman, M. M. (1995). *Mastering depression: A patient guide to interpersonal psychotherapy.* Albany, NY: Graywind.

Weissman, M. M., Markowitz, J. C., & Klerman, G. L. (2000). *Comprehensive guide to interpersonal psychotherapy.* New York: Basic Books.

Welner, Z., Reich, W., Herjanic, B., & Jung, K. G. (1987). Reliability, validity, and parent-child agreement studies of the Diagnostic Interview for Children and Adolescents (DICA). *Journal of the American Academy of Child and Adolescent Psychiatry, 26,* 649–653.

Whisman, M. A., & Bruce, M. L. (1999). Marital dissatisfaction and incidence of major depressive episode in a community sample. *Journal of Abnormal Psychology, 108,* 674–678.

Wittchen, H. U. (1994). Reliability and validity studies of the WHO-Composite International Diagnostic Interview (CIDI): A critical review. *Journal of Psychiatric Research, 28,* 57–84.

Zimmerman, M., Coryell, W., Corenthal, C., & Wilson, S. (1986). A self-report scale to diagnose major depressive disorder. *Archives of General Psychiatry, 43,* 1076–1081.

Dysthymic Disorder

Michael J. Holosko, Trang Le,
Nansy Jean-Baptiste, Lisa Power,
and Allison Eaton

Learning Objectives

After reading this chapter, the reader will be able to:

- Describe the prevalence rates of Dysthymic Disorder in different populations.
- Describe the social and financial costs of Dysthymic Disorder.
- Distinguish the *DSM* criteria for Dysthymic Disorder from those more solidly based in empirical research.
- Distinguish between Dysthymic Disorder and Major Depressive Disorder.
- Identify evidence-based assessment methods for Dysthymic Disorder.
- Identify evidence-based interventions for Dysthymic Disorder.

Overview of the Problem

With the increase in diagnoses of dysthymia, and the negative consequences typically associated with this disorder, it is imperative that social work and health care professionals understand how to properly identify, assess, and treat such individuals. Although dysthymia is often mistaken or referred to as neurotic depression, minor depression, or depressive personality, it is classified in the *Diagnostic and Statistical Manual of Mental Disorders* (*DSM*; American Psychiatric Association, 2000) as a mood/affective disorder that is

307

less severe than major depression but more enduring. It is characterized by a depressive mood that persists throughout the day, with more depressive moments than not, and is normally displayed by an individual for approximately 2 years. Identifying characteristics of individuals diagnosed with dysthymia include seeing themselves as being uninteresting or incompetent and at the same time experiencing social withdrawal, guilt, irritability, and excessive anger. Early intervention is important, for the social impairment appears to be persistent and detrimental. Due to the characteristics and the higher levels of depression, individuals with this disorder are more likely to have poor social skills, which deteriorate healthy relationships; employment difficulties that decrease job satisfaction and job loss; and pessimism, or hopelessness, which decreases self-esteem and motivation.

Prevalence

It is estimated that 8 million Americans will suffer from dysthymia at some point in their lifetime (Gwirtsman, 1994). That translates into a lifetime prevalence rate of 3.2% for the general population (Gwirtsman, 1994). According to the *DSM*, the lifetime prevalence rate of Dysthymic Disorder (with or without superimposed Major Depressive Disorder) is higher, at 6% (American Psychiatric Association, 2000). In addition, the point prevalence rate, or the prevalence at any given point in time, is approximately 3% (American Psychiatric Association, 2000). The prevalence rate differs between settings. In primary care settings, it has been reported at 2.1% for Dysthymic Disorder (with or without superimposed Major Depressive Disorder) and 1.3% for dysthymia alone (Lecrubier & Weiller, 1998).

The prevalence of dysthymia appears to decrease with age. For example, Beekman et al. (2004) investigated dysthymia in later life and found an overall prevalence of 4.61%, which is comparable to the general population. However, when these rates were examined by age group a trend was observed. For males, the rate decreased from 3.51% (55 to 64 years old) to 2.64% (75 to 85 years old), and for females it decreased from 10.80% (55 to 64 years old) to 3.05% (75 to 85 years old).

Prevalence rates appear to be different between women and men. Women are 2 to 3 times more likely than men to develop the disorder in their lifetime (American Psychiatric Association, 2000). Waraich, Goldner, Somers, and Hsu (2004) reported in a review of the dysthymia literature a disproportionate distribution of dysthymia between genders. Specifically, they found that prevalence rates ranged from 1.5 to 5 times higher for women than for men. Likewise, according to the Epidemiologic Catchment Area study, a multisite endeavor with more than 18,000 participants, the lifetime prevalence rates for dysthymia was 4.1%

for women and 2.2% for men. In older adults, the rate is also higher in females (5.82% lifetime prevalence) than males (3.00% lifetime prevalence; Beekman et al., 2004). Among adolescent and young adult populations, the lifetime rate is 2.3%, again with a higher rate for females (3%) than for males (1.7%; Pezawas et al., 2003).

Also, there are racial and ethnic differences in rates for dysthymia. Hispanics appear to be most at risk for developing dysthymia, with a 4.4% lifetime prevalence, followed by Caucasians with a 3.3% rate, and African Americans at 2.5% (Gwirtsman, 1994). Asian countries report the lowest rates of dysthymia (Waraich et al., 2004).

Social Impairment

There is some evidence in the literature to suggest that dysthymia is associated with greater social impairment than major depression and nondysthymic conditions (De Lisio, Maremmani, Perugi, & Cassano, 1986; Friedman, 1993; Klein et al., 1988). Compared to healthy adults, acutely depressed out-patient clients (including dysthymics) are more impaired in five social domains: work, social leisure, extended family involvement, marital, and parental (Weissman, 1978). Further, acutely depressed out-patient clients had the greatest overall social impairment compared to healthy adults, alcoholics, and schizophrenics (Weissman, Prusoff, Thompson, Harding, & Myers, 1978). In a sample of 176 depressed clients (38% of which were dysthymic), De Lisio et al. (1986) noted that social impairment was greatest in the work and in family spheres.

Conversely, Leader and Klein (1996) found that, after controlling for comorbid disorders (such as anxiety, substance abuse, and personality disorders), dysthymics were less likely than persons with double depression or episodic major depression to report that the depression had impaired their work functioning. Leader and Klein also reported that dysthymics were less likely than other groups to be impaired in relationships with extended family. All groups, however, were more impaired in work functioning, relationships with significant others, children, extended family, and social and leisure activities than control participants without depression (Leader & Klein, 1996).

Subjective social impairment appears to be a persistent feature of dysthymia, as evidenced by social functioning after treatment. For example, J. W. Stewart, Quitkin, McGrath, and Rabkin (1988) found that clients who improved with 6 weeks of antidepressant medication continued to rate themselves as functioning poorly. In a sample of 99 depressed clients (13% dysthymic), Perugi et al. (1988) found that at 3-month follow-up, impairments in leisure activities continued despite improvement in depressive symptoms. It appears that there are other factors involved in predicting outcomes of treatment for depression. Seivewright, Tyrer, and Johnson (2004) followed dysthymics over a period of 12 years and found that at posttreatment, residual social functioning problems were most closely associated with higher levels of self-reported depression, comorbid personality disorders, low socioeconomic status, and never having been married.

Lost Productivity and Economic Costs

Dysthymia is associated with lost productivity in the workforce and higher economic costs. W. F. Stewart, Ricci, Chee, Hahn, and Morganstein (2003) estimated that 3.6% of American employees met the criteria for dysthymia and that this type of depression led to an average loss of 3.3 hours of work per week, as opposed to 1.5 hours for nonclinically depressed employees (Lerner et al., 2004). Kessler (2002), found that 29% of persons with dysthymia report chronic limitations to their activity levels, and 16% report missing work to stay in bed during the previous week. A study comparing persons with dysthymia to psychologically healthy control participants in a primary care setting found that persons with dysthymia changed jobs more frequently, decreased the number of hours they worked, took positions that paid less, and were more likely to stop working for periods of 30 days or more (Adler et al., 2004). Further, when dysthymics attended work, their loss of productivity was calculated to be 6.3%, which amounted to $1,598 per year more than for the control group (2.8% lost productivity; Adler et al., 2004). Other reported on-the-job difficulties were problems with managing time efficiently, mental and interpersonal demands of the job, and "output demands" (p. 274).

Treatment Costs

The chronic and persistent course of dysthymia indicates greater and longer term use of medical and mental health services. In terms of medical services, Ohayon, Shapiro, and Kennedy (2000) found that persons with a mood disorder (including dysthymia) consulted physicians more (5 times in the past year) than clients without a mood disorder (3.7 times in the past year). Those with both mood and anxiety disorders averaged 8.7 consultations in the past year (Ohayon et al., 2000). In addition, more than two-thirds of the sample were not being treated by their physicians for dysthymia.

When dysthymia is comorbid with another disturbance, treatment costs can be great. For example, Westermeyer, Eames, and Nugent (1998) investigated the financial costs of substance-related and nonsubstance-related treatment in a group of 347 substance abuse clients with and without comorbid dysthymia. They found that dysthymics with substance abuse problems spent

4.5 years in treatment for substance-related disorders, compared to 0.9 years for substance abuse clients without dysthymia. They estimated substance-related treatment costs for dysthymics with comorbid substance abuse to be 4.7 times higher than for substance abuse clients ($292,037 versus $62,169). These findings suggest that screening for comorbid dysthymia in substance abuse clients may prove to be a cost-effective measure.

Operational Definitions of the Problem

According to the *DSM*, Dysthymic Disorder is an affective disorder characterized by a depressed mood occurring for most of the day and for more days than not. This can be relayed by the subjective account of the suffering individual or by observations made by others. This mood must occur for at least 2 years, and symptom-free periods must not last longer than 2 months. In children and adolescents, the mood can be irritable rather than depressed, and it must last for at least 1 year. Within the first 2 years of having the disorder (1 year for children and adolescents) a Major Depressive Episode must not have occurred and should not be better accounted for by Major Depressive Disorder, or Major Depressive Disorder in partial remission. After the initial 2 years of having Dysthymic Disorder, a Major Depressive Episode may be present; in which case, both Dysthymic Disorder and Major Depressive Disorder are diagnosed. In addition to having a depressed mood (or irritability in children and adolescents), at least two of the following symptoms must be present: poor appetite or overeating, insomnia (lack of sleeping) or hypersomnia (sleeping excessively), low energy or fatigue, low self-esteem, poor concentration or difficulty making decisions, or feelings of hopelessness. As well, the *DSM* includes differential diagnoses. For a diagnosis of Dsythymic Disorder there must never have been a Manic Episode, a Mixed Episode, or a Hypomanic Episode, and the criteria must never have been met for Cyclothymic Disorder. Dysthymic Disorder must not occur only during the course of a chronic psychotic disorder such as Schizophrenia or Delusional Disorder. The symptoms of Dysthymic Disorder must not be better accounted for by the direct physiological effects of a drug or by a general medical condition. Onset may be early (before age 21 years) or late (after age 21 years), and atypical features (outlined in the *DSM*) may be present.

Individual suffering from dysthymia typically describe their mood as sad or "down in the dumps." They tend to have pronounced low interest and be very self-critical. They often see themselves as boring, uninteresting, or incompetent. Clients are likely to have these feelings on a daily basis, and thus consider them a fundamental part of their identity. Therefore, interviewers should be diligent in obtaining this type of information by directly asking clients about them. Some associated features of the disorder are similar to that of Major Depressive Disorder, the most common of which are feelings of inadequacy, social withdrawal, guilt or ruminating about past events, irritability or excessive anger, and decreased productivity (American Psychiatric Association, 2000).

Associated features in older adults may include lower educational attainment, an external locus of control (believing that one's life is controlled by factors outside oneself), a greater number of chronic illnesses such as chronic lung disease and rheumatoid arthritis, functional limitations, limited social support, a greater number of recent adverse events, family history of mood disorders, having had a mood disorder in the past, continued conflict with significant others, having a partner with a serious illness, having suffered extreme events during World War II, and having a history of childhood abuse (Beekman et al., 2004). Among children, Dysthymic Disorder is associated with Attention-Deficit /Hyperactivity Disorder, Conduct Disorder, anxiety disorders, learning disorders, and mental retardation (American Psychiatric Association, 2000).

In addition, there appear to be associated features specific to early- and late-onset dysthymia. Barzega, Maina, Venturello, and Bogetto (2001) found in a sample of 84 outpatients with dysthymia that early-onset dysthymia was associated with being single, being female, having a longer duration of illness, and having a history of major depression. As well, early-onset dysthymics were more likely to have comorbid social phobia, Panic Disorder, and Conversion Disorder. Riso et al. (1996) found that early-onset dysthymics are more likely than nondysthymics to have a co-occurring Cluster B personality disorder (antisocial, narcissistic, borderline, or histrionic), or have relatives with Cluster B personality disorders. Pepper et al. (1995) found that, compared to those with Major Depressive Disorder, early-onset dysthymics were more likely to have comorbid personality disorders. Klein, Taylor, Dickstein, and Harding (1998) and Akiskal and Cassano (1997) found that early-onset dysthymics were more likely to have greater chronicity (dysthymia lasting longer), a relatively poor prognosis, and a greater likelihood of a family history of mood disorders compared to individuals with Major Depressive Disorder. On the other hand, Barzega et al. (2001) found that late-onset dysthymics were likely to have had at least one stressful life event in the year before the onset of disturbance. Late-onset dysthymics were more likely to have comorbid substance abuse, Generalized Anxiety Disorder, and Somatization Disorder.

Although vegetative symptoms such as sleep, appetite, or weight changes are included in the *DSM* criteria, there has been much research to suggest that these symptoms are less common in Dysthymic Disorder. The National Institute of Mental Health

(NIMH) held a conference in 1997 to develop recommendations and standards by which to assess dysthymia. An outcome of this conference was a list of symptom criteria that excluded the vegetative symptoms, part of the *DSM* criteria list. The NIMH criteria came about as a result of comparing six symptom lists, including the *DSM-IV* checklist (American Psychiatric Association, 2000) and the *DSM-IV* Field Trial Committee Report (Klein et al., 1996). The resulting set of major symptoms included low self-esteem, pessimism or hopelessness, social withdrawal, irritability or excessive anger, concentration or thinking problems, and low energy or initiative.

There is a high rate of comorbidity between mood and anxiety disorders (Ohayon et al., 2000). In Ohayon et al.'s sample, 43.7% of the participants had both (around 3% of the population). Gwirtsman (1994) reported that only 8% of the persons with dysthymia interviewed in the National Comorbidity Survey did not have a comorbid Axis I disorder. Other comorbid disorders include Borderline, Histrionic, Narcissistic, Avoidant, and Dependent Personality Disorders and substance dependence and chronic psychosocial stressors (American Psychiatric Association, 2000).

Traditionally, Dysthymic Disorder was considered a form of character pathology and was called neurotic depression. That is, the affective disturbance was thought to be a type of personality disturbance. Although dsythymia currently is included in the Axis I disorders of the *DSM-IV* as a mood disorder, there is still controversy in the literature about the overlap between dsythymia and Depressive Personality Disorder. Ryder, Bagby, and Dion (2001) suggested that Depressive Personality Disorder might be a milder subtype of dysthymia. They argued that the symptom criteria for Depressive Personality Disorder (chronic, early onset, mild depression with an emphasis on cognitive and interpersonal features) are very narrow and can potentially fall under the early-onset specifier for dysthymia. Awareness of this controversy is especially important for treatment planning.

Evidence-Based Approaches to Assessment

Sufferers of dysthymia experience serious social impairments and make up a large portion of treatment costs in both mental and medical health systems. The first step to providing effective treatment is the efficient and accurate identification of dysthymia. Gwirtsman (1994) reported on the findings of the NIMH Conference, and subsequently Guelfi and Corruble (1997) discussed methodological issues about the assessment of dysthymia. From this work, four well-established instruments were identified as the most commonly used to assess dysthymia: the Beck Depression

Inventory (BDI; Beck, Ward, Mendelson, Mock, & Erbaugh, 1961), the Hamilton Rating Scale for Depression (HRSD; Hamilton, 1960), the Cornell Dysthymia Rating Scale (CDRS; Cohen, 1997; Mason, 1989), and the Structured Clinical Interview for *DSM-IV-TR* (SCID; Kroenke, Spitzer, & Williams, 2003).

Self-Report Instruments

The BDI was developed to evaluate the efficacy of cognitive-behavioral therapies (Beck et al., 1961). Today, it is widely used in both clinical (Lee & Lee, 1996) and nonclinical (e.g., Lesperance, Frasure-Smith, & Talajic, 1996; Lustman, Clouse, Griffith, Carney, & Freedland, 1997) populations and has shown good psychometric properties. As well, it has been used to assess the efficacy of other types of psychotherapies for depression, such as interpersonal therapy (Stravynski, Shahar, & Verreault, 1991). The BDI has been successfully employed in different cultures and different languages (e.g., Byrne, Baron, & Campbell, 1994; Canals, Bladé, Carbajo, & Doménech-LLabería, 2001; Lee & Lee, 1996) and in adult and adolescent age groups. For example, Canals et al. investigated the utility of a Spanish version of the BDI in a population of 304 nonclinical Spanish-speaking adolescents. They found that the BDI was a reliable and valid instrument for screening nonclinical adolescents for depression.

The BDI is a 21-item, 4-degree self-report measure of the intensity of depressive symptoms. It assess four components of depression: cognitive, behavioral, affective, and somatic. Each of the 21 items consists of four statements that are rated on a Likert-type scale from 0 to 3. Respondents are asked to choose the statement that best describes their current experience. The highest score possible on the BDI is 36.

There have been several proposed cutoff scores for the identification of dysthymia using the BDI. The Center for Cognitive Therapy proposed the following guidelines for clinical populations with affective disorders: < 10 = No or minimal depression, 11 to 18 = Mild to moderate depression, 19 to 29 = Moderate to severe depression, and 30 to 36 = Severe depression. Canals et al. (2001) suggested that a cutoff score of 10 was best for the identification of dysthymia. Markowitz (1994) reported on treatment outcome studies that used BDI scores (de Jong et al., 1986; McCullough, 1991; Stravynski et al., 1991). De Jong et al. used a BDI cutoff score of 14 or less to indicate a positive response to cognitive-behavioral treatment for dysthymia.

Observer-Rating Scales

The HAMD was developed in the late 1950s to evaluate the effectiveness of pharmacological treatment of depression (Hamilton, 1960). Currently, it is the standard instrument for psychopharmacological treatment efficacy studies and is the most commonly used measure of depression (Demyttenaere & De Fruyt, 2003; Williams, 2001). The HAMD has demonstrated good psychometric properties. Bagby, Ryder, Schuller, and Marshall (2004) reviewed the psychometric properties of the HAMD and reported an estimated internal reliability (Cronbach's alpha) range of $\alpha = .46$ to .97, an interrater reliability (Pearson's r) ranging from .82 to .98, and test-retest reliability (Pearson's r) ranging from .81 to .98. Similar to the BDI, the HAMD has been successfully used in different cultures, languages (Aben, Verhey, Lousberg, Lodder, & Honig, 2002; Entsuah, Shaffer, & Zhang, 2002), clinical and nonclinical populations (Demitrack, Faries, Herrera, DeBrota, & Potter, 1998; Kobak & Reynolds, 1999), and age populations (Berard & Ahmed, 1995; Hammond, 1998; Shain, Naylor, & Alessi, 1990).

The HAMD is a 17-item interviewer-rated measure with items on either a 3-point (0 to 2) or 5-point (0 to 4) Likert-type scale yielding scores ranging from 0 to 50. Interviewers are asked to rate interviewees on these items, with a rating of 0 indicating "absent" to a rating of 2 (on 3-point) or 4 (5-point) indicating "severe." The HAMD assesses severity on 17 symptoms: depressed mood, feelings of guilt, suicide, insomnia early, insomnia middle, insomnia late, work and activities, retardation, agitation, anxiety/psychic, anxiety/somatic, somatic symptoms/GI, somatic symptoms/general, genital symptoms, hypochondriasis, loss of weight, and insight.

Proposed cutoff scores for the HAMD have been reported in a review by Guelfi and Corruble (1997), and Guelfi (1993) suggested a score falling between 7 and 15 to indicate dysthymia. Bakish et al. (1993) reported using an inclusion score of >13, whereas Vallejo, Casto, Catalan, and Salamero (1987) use a score of >16 for inclusion.

To date, only one rating scale has been developed specifically for assessing treatment efficacy for dysthymia. The CDRS was developed in 1993 by Mason et al. to be "more sensitive to the chronic and less severe symptomatology of dysthymia" (p. 628) compared to major depression. The CDRS is a 20-item interviewer-rated scale that assesses severity of symptoms on 5 interval-level degrees, ranging from none to severe. It excludes items shown to be uncommon in dysthymia as compared to major depression, such as psychomotor agitation or retardation and appetite changes (Keller, Klein, Hirschfeld, & Kocsis, 1995). According to Hellerstein, Batchelder, Lee, and Borisovskaya (2002), the CDRS may be a more sensitive rating instrument than the HAMD to assess dysthymia. More research on the CDRS's reliability and validity is required before widespread use is warranted.

Semistructured Interviews

The SCID-I is a semistructured interview for the diagnosis of Axis I disorders based on *DSM-IV* criteria (First, Spitzer, Gibbon, &

Williams, 1995). The SCID-I is divided into six self-contained modules that can be administered in sequence: mood episodes; psychotic symptoms; psychotic disorders; mood disorders; substance use disorders; and anxiety, adjustment, and other disorders. The SCID-I was designed to be administered by clinicians or trained mental health professionals. An Axis I SCID with a psychiatric client usually takes between 1 and 2 hours to complete, depending on the complexity of the psychiatric history and the subject's ability to clearly describe episodes of current and past psychopathology. A SCID with a nonclient takes .5 to 1.5 hours (http://www.scid4.org/scidfaq.htm). The interrater reliability of the SCID-I for Dysthymic Disorder ranges between $r = .76$ and .88 (Skre, Onstad, Torgersen, & Kringlen, 1991; Zanarini et al., 2000).

Evidence-Based Approaches to Intervention

Several interventions have been developed for the treatment of dysthymia. Individual interventions include cognitive-behavioral therapy (CBT), interpersonal therapy (IPT), and the cognitive-behavioral analysis system of psychotherapy (CBASP). Couples interventions include behavioral marital therapy (BMT) and cognitive marital therapy. Group interventions include cognitive-behavioral group therapy. Community interventions include the Program to Encourage Active, Rewarding Lives for Seniors (PEARLS) and a school-based group intervention program for children.

Individual Interventions

Cognitive-behavioral therapy is the most studied psychotherapy for the treatment of depression. It is a structured, manualized, time-limited psychotherapy that was developed by Beck, Rush, Shaw, and Emery in the late 1970s (Beck, Rush, Shaw, & Emery, 1979). It is based on cognitive theory, which posits that depression is maintained and generated by a number of dysfunctional processes, such as automatic negative thoughts (Teasdale, 1988). The role of the therapist is to build a collaborative relationship with the client and to help him or her learn new ways of thinking and acting. The therapist helps the client become aware of and make conscious efforts to change or control negative thoughts, thereby alleviating the depression.

There are many different configurations of CBT implemented for the treatment of dysthymia (Furlong & Oei, 2002). Variations typically consist of differences in the number of sessions. Treatment typically involves 8 to 12 individual weekly sessions of approximately 50 minutes each. Each session is highly structured and consists of reviewing homework, introducing themes for the session, explaining and practicing tasks, and assigning homework. The tasks are tailored to the client's individual needs, and an array of techniques are available in the appendixes of the manual (Beck et al., 1979). Park and Goodyer (2000) outline the components of a typical 8-session course of CBT treatment taken from Harrington, Wood, and Verduyn (1998). Table 14.1 outlines the 8 components of CBT. Sessions typically consist of introducing the treatment, providing education on emotions, and learning a number of skills, such as self-monitoring, self-reinforcement, social skills, problem-solving skills, and cognitive reframing.

There is much evidence to support the use of CBT in the treatment of dysthymia. Markowitz (1994) reported on seven studies of CBT for dysthymia from 1985 to 1992. Although the number of clients treated may be small ($N = 116$), the results appear to support the use of CBT for dysthymia. For example, de Jong, Treiber, and Henrich (1986) studied the efficacy of CBT (activity scheduling, social competence training, and cognitive restructuring) in a group of 30 unmedicated in-clients with double depression (dysthymia with superimposed Major Depressive Episode) over the course of 2 to 3 months. They found that 60% of the sample responded to CBT treatment compared to cognitive restructuring alone (30%) and wait-list status (10%). Stravynski et al. (1991) treated six clients with Dysthymic Disorder using 15 1-hour sessions of CBT. They observed significant improvement, with decreased scores on the HAMD and the BDI after treatment

Table 14.1 Components of Cognitive Behavior Therapy

1. *Introducing CBT:* The rationale, goals, and structure of CBT are explained to the client.

2. *Emotional education:* The client is educated on different emotions and is helped to distinguish between emotions and link emotions to actual events.

3. *Self-monitoring:* The client is asked to monitor his or her thoughts and feelings and link them to events using a diary or daily journal.

4. *Self-reinforcement:* The client is taught to reward himself or herself for desired behavior, and an activity schedule is introduced.

5. *Social skills:* The client's social skills deficits are determined and worked on and social interactions are encouraged through behavioral homework tasks to improve self-esteem.

6. *Problem solving:* The client role-plays to solve social and interpersonal problems.

7. *Cognitive reframing:* The client is encouraged to become aware of and challenge automatic thoughts using the Socratic method. For example, the client is encouraged to ask what the evidence is for an automatic thought. The client is also helped to identify the causes and consequences of events and the influence of mood on thinking.

8. *Ending therapy:* The themes and patterns that have emerged and the overall aims of treatment are reviewed with the client. Also, areas that require more attention from the client are discussed.

and at 6-month follow-up. In addition, four clients no longer met criteria for Dysthymic Disorder after treatment.

Another therapy that has shown promise for the treatment of dysthymia is IPT. Interpersonal therapy is a time-limited, manualized, life-event-based psychotherapy that originally was used only in research interventions. Its success in clinical trials moved it from the research domain to an integral part of the mood disorders treatment repertoire. Markowitz (2003) outlined the theoretical assumptions of IPT: (a) Depression is a treatable medical illness in which the client is not held responsible and is able to take on the sick role, and (b) mood and life events are linked temporally. In other words, a recent life event, presumably a negative one, triggers a depressive episode in a vulnerable person, or a depressive episode creates interpersonal problems and distressing life events. Treatment focuses on one of four interpersonal problem areas—grief, role dispute, role transition, or interpersonal deficits—and connects it to the current mood episode. Treatment typically consists of 12 to 16 weekly sessions that focus on some interpersonal crises related to the current mood problem. The goal of IPT is to solve the interpersonal problem that will result in relief from depressive symptoms. It is especially indicated for Dysthymic Disorder because interpersonal dysfunction is a salient feature of the disorder and dysthymics tend to have diminished support networks (American Psychiatric Association, 2000).

A typical course of IPT occurs in three sequential phases (Park & Goodyer, 2000):

1. *Initial phase* (sessions 1 to 4): After assessment and diagnosis, a detailed review of the client's relationships and recent life events is done to identify problem areas to focus on for treatment. The therapist explains the limited sick role the client will take and sets the parameters of the treatment contract.

2. *Middle phase* (sessions 5 to 8): The treatment focus is narrowed to one of the four interpersonal problem areas (role dispute, role transition, interpersonal deficit, or grief). Problem-solving strategies are generated to solve this area. The therapist is active in encouraging independent implementation of strategies and providing support and direction.

3. *Termination phase* (sessions 9 to 12): The client is reminded of the termination date at session 9. Treatment focuses on concluding problems and reviewing treatment thus far, such as changes in the client's life, skills learned, and future applications of new skills. Connections are made between termination problems and the problem area, and further treatment needs are discussed.

Some difficulties with treating dysthymics with traditional IPT have been noted. Dysthymics tend to have difficulty remembering significant negative events in their lives due to the chronicity of their symptoms. They tend to feel as though they have always been this way and view their symptoms as part of their overall personality makeup. Thus, therapists may have difficulty identifying one recent life event to focus on in treatment. An adaptation of IPT for dysthymia has been developed and involves framing clients' transition from viewing their difficulty as a fundamental part of themselves to viewing their difficulty as a treatable medical condition. In this way, therapists can help clients assume a limited sick role and focus on role transition as the interpersonal problem (Markowitz, 2003). By reframing the problem, treatment focuses on teaching the client interpersonal skills needed for the new role (e.g., happy person role), such as assertiveness skills, appropriate use of anger, and taking social risks.

Research on the efficacy of IPT in the treatment of dysthymia is nominal but encouraging. Markowitz (2003) reported on studies that involved IPT. A pilot study conducted by investigators at Cornell University Medical College examined the use of IPT in the treatment of 17 early-onset dysthymic clients, half of whom met criteria for double depression. They received 16 sessions of IPT-D (for depression). They found that 65% of the clients achieved remission after treatment and none of the clients became worse.

Browne et al. (2002) conducted a large study on the efficacy of sertraline alone, IPT alone, and a combination of sertraline and IPT. Their sample consisted of more than 700 participants with early- and late-onset Dysthymic Disorder or double depression (approximately one-third). They found that 60% responded to sertraline alone, 58% responded to combined treatment, and 47% responded to IPT alone. The interesting finding was that at 6-month and 2-year follow-ups, clients treated with combined therapy had much lower health and social services costs than those in the other treatment conditions. The finding is important because most individuals with depressive disorders referred for psychotherapy are also likely to be concurrently treated with antidepressants. These findings are encouraging, but more research is needed on the efficacy of IPT for dysthymic populations.

Another promising recent development in treatment for dysthymia is an integrative psychotherapy combining elements of behavioral, cognitive, interpersonal, and psychodynamic psychotherapy (McCullough et al., 2000). Cognitive-behavioral analysis system of psychotherapy is a time-limited (16 to 20 sessions), manualized psychotherapy for depression. The main goals are to help clients change patterns of coping, improve interpersonal skills, and understand consequences of behavior. Components of cognitive and behavioral therapies include a highly structured format, a focus on social problem-solving skills, and the use of homework assignments. It is similar to IPT in its focus on interpersonal problems and borrows from psychodynamic therapies the idea that the therapist helps clients become aware of their influence on others and to discriminate between adaptive and maladaptive relationships (McCullough et al., 2000).

In CBASP, there are three main components: (1) situational analysis (SA), (2) interpersonal discrimination exercise (IDE), and (3) behavioral skill training and rehearsal (McCullough et al., 2000). The main exercise in CBASP, situational analysis, involves identifying a recent, upsetting, interpersonal situation and examining it with the therapist. There are three phases in the SA technique: elicitation, remediation, and generalization. In the elicitation phase, clients describe the interpersonal event, give their interpretation of what occurred, and explain how they behaved, what the outcome was, what the desired outcome would be, and whether the desired outcome was achieved. In the remediation phase, the client works with the therapist to change interpretations, behaviors, and desired outcome to increase the likelihood of achieving the desired outcome. The generalization phase involves reviewing what has been learned and how new skills can be applied to past or future situations (McCullough et al., 2000).

In the IDE, clients are asked to describe persons who have significantly influenced the course of their lives either positively or negatively. The therapist then uses these descriptions to make transference hypotheses about the client (i.e., ways the client may view or treat the therapist because of past experiences with a significant other). Using this information, the therapist helps clients make connections between their past experiences, how they are viewing the therapist currently, and how the therapist is different from past significant others in terms of treatment of the client. From this exercise, clients learn to differentiate between the significant other who treated them poorly and other people in their lives. The last component, behavioral skill training and rehearsal, involves teaching clients skills related to their skill deficits determined in the SA exercise. These can be assertiveness skills, management of affect, or relaxation training.

Research on CBASP is sparse because of its relatively recent development. However, existing studies provide preliminary support for its use with individuals with dysthymia and other forms of chronic depression. Keller et al. (2000) conducted a study on a sample of 681 chronically depressed clients, including some with double depression. They compared the effectiveness of 12 weeks of nefazodone (an antidepressant), 16 to 19 weeks of CBASP, or a combination of both. Of the 519 clients who completed therapy, 55% responded to nefazodone, 52% responded to CBASP, and 85% responded to the combined treatment. These findings suggest that CBASP alone is as effective as nefazodone alone, and is most effective when combined with nefazodone. A problem with this study is that there was no control group. Despite this, the findings are promising for CBASP as an effective treatment for chronic depressions. Further research is required to solidify the preliminary evidence.

Couples Therapy

Dysthymic Disorder negatively affects many domains of interpersonal functioning, including the marital domain. As noted earlier, individuals with the disorder have diminished social support networks and poorer social skills, resulting in frequent isolation and exacerbation of the disorder. In addition, many studies have shown that martial discord is associated with the presence of depression (e.g., O'Leary & Beach, 1990; Whisman, 2001). Thus, it is important for mental health professionals to consider the marital or romantic relationships when treating clients with Dysthymic Disorder to minimize further loss of social support and maximize current social supports for the client. Evidence-based couples therapy approaches include cognitive marital therapy and behavioral marital therapy.

In cognitive marital therapy, the focus is on how couples perceive their marriage. They are taught to think about and understand their relationship in a less destructive way, a process called cognitive restructuring. This may include helping individuals consider alternative reasons for why their partner behaves in a certain way, or to reconceptualize realistic standards for marriage (Baucom, Shoham, Mueser, Daiuto, & Stickle, 1998). In terms of treating dysthymia, Waring, Chamberlaine, McCrank, and Stalker (1988) investigated the efficacy of combined cognitive marital therapy and antidepressant medication compared to placebo in a sample of 12 dysthymic women. Cognitive marital therapy consisted of encouraging self-disclosure between partners in a supportive and educational manner. They found that after 10 weeks of treatment, there was a significant reduction in depression for the combined treatment group. They posited that the presence of a supportive partner, in this case the male partner, was a major contributor to symptom reduction.

Behavioral marital therapy is the most widely researched couples therapy. It is a skills-based approach focusing on the couple's need for basic skills and an understanding of relationship interactions to improve their marriage. Therapy focuses on teaching couples communication skills and problem-solving skills and helping them negotiate plans and make contracts to change behavior to increase pleasurable interactions and minimize destructive interactions (e.g., increasing caring or loving acts toward the partner, increasing activities such as taking walks together or having special dinners together). Some treatment manuals are available (e.g., Baucom & Epstein, 1990; Jacobson, 1980; Jacobson &

Margolin, 1979) for this therapy. Behavioral martial therapy has shown efficacy in treating depression in the context of marital discord. In a sample of 36 maritally distressed couples, O'Leary and Beach (1990) compared the efficacy of standard behavioral marital treatment ($n = 12$), individual cognitive therapy ($n = 12$) for the treatment of depression (major depression $n = 32$, dysthymia $n = 4$) in the female spouse, and wait-list control group ($n = 12$). They found that both BMT and individual cognitive therapy were equally more effective than the wait-list condition in alleviating depression.

Group Interventions

As discussed, the financial costs of treating Dysthymic Disorder are considerable. Group therapies provide relatively effective treatment while minimizing the costs of administration. Effective group treatments include group cognitive-behavioral therapy and group interpersonal therapy.

Group cognitive-behavioral therapy uses the same principles as individual CBT and has been successful in treating dysthymia. For example, Norman and Lowry (1995) investigated the use of group CBT implemented by social workers combined with antidepressant medication in a sample of 40 women meeting *DSM-III-R* criteria for major depression ($n = 21$) or dysthymia with superimposed major depression ($n = 19$). The CBT treatment consisted of 2 weeks of daily 90-minute sessions focused on psychoeducation; sharing common experiences of depression; teaching self-monitoring of self-talk; examining underlying beliefs; increasing participation in pleasurable activities; teaching relapse-prevention skills, social skills, problem-solving skills, and relaxation skills; managing medication; and providing adherence counseling. Norman and Lowry found a significant decrease in depression scores on the BDI and the HAMD from pre- to posttreatment, and clients maintained these improvement at follow-up (on average, 11.77 months after discharge). The results of such a brief form of CBT are encouraging for social work practice, as clients are rarely seen in such settings for lengthy periods of time.

Community Interventions

Community interventions for dysthymia are particularly relevant for the elderly population. Independent mobility is more difficult for older adults, and depression occurs in 15% to 20% of elderly Americans (Karel, Ogland-Hand, Gatz, & Unützer, 2002; Koenig & Blazer, 1996; Lebowitz, 1996). One such intervention, called the Program to Encourage Active, Rewarding Lives for Seniors (Ciechanowski et al., 2004), has shown reductions in depressive symptoms in elderly populations. In a sample of 138 clients over the age of 60 with depression (minor depression = 54%, dysthymia = 48.6%), Ciechanowski et al. compared the PEARLS (*n* = 72) to usual care (*n* = 66). The PEARLS condition consisted of phone calls or in-home visits, where therapists (three MSWs) provided problem-solving treatment, social and physical education, and potential collaboration with physicians about antidepressant medications. Participants received eight 50-minute in-home sessions over 19 weeks, after which therapists maintained monthly phone contact. Results indicated that at 12 months PEARLS participants were approximately 5 times more likely to have at least a 50% reduction in depressive symptoms (43% versus 15%), were almost 5 times as likely to be in remission (45% versus 12%), and had greater improvements in functional and emotional well-being.

Community interventions are equally important for children. As discussed earlier, early-onset depression, particularly dysthymia, is associated with a more chronic course, greater social impairments, and poorer overall prognosis (Akiskal & Cassano, 1997; Klein et al., 1998). Stark, Swearer, Kurowski, Sommer, and Bowen (1996) developed a school-based cognitive-behavioral program to treat depression in children. It focused on social skills training that included assertiveness training, appropriate expressions of emotions, problem-solving skills, and turn taking. Social skills were taught in a group format through a number of techniques, including role-playing, rehearsal, and guided practice.

Summary

Dysthymic Disorder is a psychosocial problem commonly experienced by the clients of social workers. There are a variety of evidence-based approaches to assessment and to intervention that afford considerable guidance for practitioners to consider in undertaking the treatment of chronically depressed persons.

Study Questions

1. What are the primary characteristics of Dysthymic Disorder, and how do you see them affecting an individual's everyday life? Provide examples.

2. What are the main social impairments for individuals with dysthymia, and what roles do you think a social worker can play in assisting with decreasing these impairments?

3. Why do you believe it is necessary for social workers to identify, assess, and treat individuals with dysthymia differently from individuals with major depression?

4. What challenges or barriers may occur when working with individuals with dysthymia, and how would you as a social worker address these issues?

5. What roles do you believe a social worker can play in the process of assessing and treating individuals with dysthymia?

6. In your own words, briefly describe one of the four instruments used to assess individuals with dysthymia and why you think this instrument could be used in a social work setting.

7. Choose one intervention method and examine the theory behind this intervention. Why would a social worker want to use this method in practice?

8. Which form of intervention do you feel best fits your values and theories as a social worker?

9. Compare and contrast individual therapy to group therapy. Do you see one having more success than the other?

10. Based on the information presented in this chapter, what additional information do you believe social workers need to know to serve their clients?

11. What are some examples of best practices your agency could develop to help treat persons with Dysthymic Disorder?

References

Aben, I., Verhey, F., Lousberg, R., Lodder, J., & Honig, A. (2002). Validity of the Beck Depression Inventory, Hospital Anxiety and Depression Scale, SCL-90 and Hamilton Depression Rating Scale as screening instruments for depression in stroke clients. *Psychosomatics: Journal of Consultation Liaison Psychiatry, 43,* 386–393.

Adler, D. A., Irish, J., McLaughlin, T. J., Perssinotto, C., Chang, H., Hood, M., et al. (2004). The work impact of dysthymia in a primary care population. *General Hospital Psychiatry, 26,* 269–276.

Akiskal, H. S., & Cassano, G. B. (Eds.). (1997). *Dysthymia and the spectrum of chronic depressions.* New York: Guilford Press.

American Psychiatric Association. (2000). *Diagnostic and statistical manual of mental disorders* (4th ed., text rev.). Washington, DC: Author.

Bagby, R. M., Ryder, A. G., Schuller, D. R., & Marshall, M. B. (2004). The Hamilton Depression Rating Scale: Has the gold standard become a lead weight? *American Journal of Psychiatry, 161,* 2163–2177.

Bakish, D., Lapierre, Y. D., Weinstein, R., & Klein, J. (1993). Ritanserin, imipramine, and placebo in the treatment of dysthymic disorder. *Journal of Clinical Psychopharmacology, 13,* 409–414.

Barzega, G., Maina, G., Venturello, S., & Bogetto, F. (2001). Dysthymic disorder: Clinical characteristics in relation to age at onset. *Journal of Affective Disorders, 66,* 39–46.

Baucom, D. H., & Epstein, N. (1990). *Cognitive-behavioral marital therapy.* Philadelphia: Brunner/Mazel.

Baucom, D. H., Shoham, V., Mueser, K. T., Daiuto, A. D., & Stickle, T. R. (1998). Empirically supported couple and family interventions for marital distress and adult mental health problems. *Journal of Consulting and Clinical Psychology, 66,* 53–88.

Beck, A. T., Rush, A. J., Shaw, B. E., & Emery, G. (1979). *Cognitive therapy of depression: A treatment manual.* New York: Guilford Press.

Beck, A. T., Ward, C. H., Mendelson, M., Mock, J., & Erbaugh, J. (1961). An inventory for measuring depression. *Archives of General Psychiatry, 4,* 561–571.

Beekman, A. T. F., Deeg, D. J. H., Smit, J. H., Comijs, H. C., Braam, A. W., de Beurs, E., et al. (2004). Dysthymia in later life: A study in the community. *Journal of Affective Disorders, 81,* 191–199.

Berard, R. M. F., & Ahmed, N. (1995). Hospital Anxiety and Depression Scale (HADS) as a screening instrument in a depressed adolescent and young adult population. *International Journal of Adolescent Medicine and Health, 8,* 157–166.

Browne, G., Steiner, M., Roberts, J., Gafni, A., Byrne, C., Whittaker, S., et al. (2002). Sertraline and/or interpersonal psychotherapy for patients with dysthymic disorder in primary care: Six-month comparison with longitudinal 2-year follow-up of effectiveness and costs. *Journal of Affective Disorders, 68*(2/3), 317–330.

Byrne, B. M., Baron, P., & Campbell, T. L. (1994). The Beck Depression Inventory (French version): Testing for gender-invariant factorial structure for nonclinical adolescents. *Journal of Adolescent Research, 9,* 166–179.

Canals, J., Bladé, J., Carbajo, G., & Doménech-LLabería, E. (2001). The Beck Depression Inventory: Psychometric characteristics and usefulness in nonclinical adolescents. *European Journal of Psychological Assessment, 17,* 63–68.

Ciechanowski, P., Wagner, E., Schmaling, K., Schwartz, S., Williams, B., Diehr, P., et al. (2004). Community-integrated home-based depression treatment in older adults: A randomized controlled trial. *Journal of the American Medical Association, 291,* 1569–1577.

Cohen, J. (1997). Assessment and treatment of dysthymia: The development of the Cornell Dysthymia Rating Scale. *European Psychiatry, 12,* 190–193.

de Jong, R., Treiber, R., & Henrich, G. (1986). Effectiveness of two psychological treatments for inclients with severe and chronic depressions. *Cognitive Therapy and Research, 10,* 645–663.

De Lisio, G., Maremmani, I., Perugi, G., & Cassano, G. B. (1986). Impairment of work and leisure in depressed outclients: A preliminary communication. *Journal of Affective Disorders, 10,* 79–84.

Demitrack, M. A., Faries, D., Herrera, J. M., DeBrota, D. J., & Potter, W. Z. (1998). The problem of measurement error in multisite clinical trials. *Psychopharmacology Bulletin, 34,* 19–24.

Demyttenaere, K., & De Fruyt, J. (2003). Getting what you ask for: On the selectivity of depression rating scales. *Psychotherapy and Psychosomatics, 72,* 61–70.

Entsuah, R., Shaffer, M., & Zhang, J. (2002). A critical examination of the sensitivity of unidimensional subscales derived from the Hamilton Depression Rating Scale to antidepressant drug effects. *Journal of Psychiatric Research, 36,* 437–448.

First, M. B., Spitzer, R. L., Gibbon, M., & Williams, J. B. W. (1995). *Structured Clinical Interview for* DSM-IV. New York: Biometrics Research Department.

Friedman, R. A. (1993). Social impairment in dysthymia. *Psychiatric Annals, 23,* 632–637.

Furlong, M., & Oei, T. P. S. (2002). Changes to automatic thoughts and dysfunctional attitudes in group CBT for depression. *Behavioral and Cognitive Psychotherapy, 30,* 351–360.

Guelfi, J. D. (1993). The comorbidity of anxiety/depression and its treatment. *Encephale, 19,* 397–404.

Guelfi, J. D., & Corruble, E. (1997). Methodological issues raised by clinical trials on dysthymia: Assessment instruments and response criteria. *European Psychiatry, 12,* 183–189.

Gwirtsman, H. E. (1994). Overview of the diagnosis, prevalence, and comorbidity of dysthymia. *Psychopharmacology Bulletin, 30,* 45–51.

Hamilton, M. (1960). A rating scale for depression. *Journal of Neurology, Neurosurgery, and Psychiatry, 23,* 56–61.

Hammond, M. F. (1998). Rating depression severity in the elderly physically ill client: Reliability and factor structure of the

Hamilton and the Montgomery-Asberg Depression Rating Scales. *International Journal of Geriatric Psychiatry, 13,* 257–261.

Harrington, R., Wood, A., & Verduyn, C. (1998). Clinically depressed adolescents. In P. J. Graham (Ed.), *Cognitive-behavior therapy for children and families* (pp. 156–193). New York: Cambridge University Press.

Hellerstein, D. J., Batchelder, S. T., Lee, A., & Borisovskaya, M. (2002). Rating dysthymia: An assessment of the construct and content validity of the Cornell Dysthymia Rating Scale. *Journal of Affective Disorders, 71,* 85–96.

Hellerstein, D. J., Little, S., Samstag, L. W., Muran, J. C., Fedak, M., Kreditor, D., et al. (2001). Adding group psychotherapy to medication treatment in dysthymia: A randomized prospective study. *Journal of Psychotherapy Practice and Research, 10,* 93–103.

Jacobson, N. S. (1980). Behavioral marital therapy: Current trends in research, assessment and practice. *American Journal of Family Therapy, 8*(2), 3–5.

Jacobson, N. S., & Margolin, G. (1979). *Marital therapy: Strategies based on social learning and behavior exchange principles.* New York: Brunner/Mazel.

Karel, M. J., Ogland-Hand, S., Gatz, M., & Unützer, J. (2002). *Assessing and treating late-life depression: A casebook and resource guide.* New York: Basic Books.

Keller, M. B., Klein, D. N., Hirschfeld, R. M. A., & Kocsis, J. H. (1995). Results of the *DSM-IV* mood disorders field trial. *American Journal of Psychiatry, 152*(6), 843–849.

Keller, M. B., McCullough, J. P., Klein, D. N., Arnow, B., Dunner, D. L., Gelenberg, A. J., et al. (2000). A comparison of nefazodone, the cognitive behavioral-analysis system of psychotherapy, and their combination for the treatment of chronic depression. *New England Journal of Medicine, 342,* 1462–1470.

Kessler, R. C. (2002). Epidemiology of depression. In C. L. Hammen & I. H. Gotlib (Eds.), *Handbook of depression* (pp. 23–42). New York: Guilford Press.

Klein, D. N., Kocsis, J. H., McCullough, J. P., Holzer, C. E., Hirschfeld, R. M. A., & Keller, M. B. (1996). Symptomatology in dysthymic and major depressive disorder. *Psychiatric Clinics of North America, 19,* 41–53.

Klein, D. N., Taylor, E. B., Dickstein, S., & Harding, K. (1988). Primary early-onset dysthymia: Comparison with primary nonbipolar nonchronic major depression on demographic, clinical, familial, personality, and socioenvironmental characteristics and short-term outcome. *Journal of Abnormal Psychology, 97,* 387–398.

Kobak, K. A., & Reynolds, W. M. (1999). Hamilton Depression Inventory. In M. E. Maruish (Ed.), *The use of psychological testing for treatment planning and outcomes assessment* (2nd ed., pp. 935–969). Mahwah, NJ: Erlbaum.

Koenig, H. G., & Blazer, D. G. (1996). Minor depression in late life. *American Journal of Geriatric Psychiatry, 4*(4, Suppl. 1), S14–S21.

Kroenke, K., Spitzer, R. L., & Williams, J. B. W. (2003). The Patient Health Questionnaire-2: Validity of a two-item depression screener. *Medical Care, 41,* 1284–1292.

Leader, J. B., & Klein, D. N. (1996). Social adjustment in dysthymia, double depression, and episodic major depression. *Journal of Affective Disorders, 37,* 91–101.

Lebowitz, B. D. (1996). Diagnosis and treatment of depression in late life: An overview of the NIH consensus statement. *American Journal of Geriatric Psychiatry, 4*(4, Suppl. 1), S3–S6.

Lecrubier, Y., & Weiller, E. (1998). Characteristics, recognition and treatment of dysthymics in primary care. *European Psychiatry, 13,* 198–202.

Lee, A. M., & Lee, S. (1996). Disordered eating and its psychosocial correlates among Chinese adolescent females in Hong Kong. *International Journal of Eating Disorders, 20,* 177–183.

Lerner, D., Adler, D. A., Chang, H., Lapitsky, L., Hood, M. Y., Perissinotto, C., et al. (2004). Unemployment, job retention, and productivity loss among employees with depression. *Psychiatric Services, 55,* 1371–1378.

Lesperance, F., Frasure-Smith, N., & Talajic, M. (1996). Major depression before and after myocardial infarction: Its nature and consequences. *Psychosomatic Medicine, 58,* 99–110.

Lustman, P. J., Clouse, R. E., Griffith, L. S., Carney, R. M., & Freedland, K. E. (1997). Screening for depression in diabetes using the Beck Depression Inventory. *Psychosomatic Medicine, 59,* 24–31.

Markowitz, J. C. (1994). Psychotherapy of dysthymia. *American Journal of Psychiatry, 151,* 1114–1121.

Markowitz, J. C. (2003). Interpersonal psychotherapy for chronic depression. *Journal of Clinical Psychology, 59,* 847–858.

Mason, B. J., Kocsis, J. H., Leon, A. C., Thompson, S., Frances, A. J., Morgan, R. O., et al. (1993). Measurement of severity and treatment response in dysthymia. *Psychiatric Annals, 23,* 625–631.

McCullough, J. P. (1991). Psychotherapy for dysthymia: A naturalistic study of ten clients. *Journal of Nervous and Mental Diseases, 179,* 734–740.

McCullough, J. P., Klein, D. N., Keller, M. B., Holzer, C. E., Davis, S. M., Kornstein, S. G., et al. (2000). Comparison of DSM-III-R chronic major depression and major depression superimposed on dysthymia (double depression): Validity of the distinction. *Journal of Abnormal Psychology, 109,* 419–427.

Norman, J., & Lowry, C. E. (1995). Evaluating inclient treatment for women with clinical depression. *Research on Social Work Practice, 5,* 10–19.

Ohayon, M. M., Shapiro, C. M., & Kennedy, S. H. (2000). Differentiating *DSM-IV* anxiety and depressive disorders in the general population: Comorbidity and treatment consequences. *Canadian Journal of Psychiatry, 45,* 166–172.

O'Leary, K. D., & Beach, S. R. (1990). Marital therapy: A viable treatment for depression and marital discord. *American Journal of Psychiatry, 147,* 183–186.

Park, R. J., & Goodyer, I. M. (2000). Clinical guidelines for depressive disorders in childhood and adolescence. *European Child and Adolescent Psychiatry, 9,* 147–161.

Pepper, C. M., Klein, D. N., Anderson, R. L., Riso, L. P., Ouimette, P. C., & Lizardi, H. (1995). *DSM-III-R* Axis II comorbidity in dysthymia and major depression. *American Journal of Psychiatry, 152,* 239–247.

Pezawas, L., Wittchen, H.-U., Pfister, H., Angst, J., Lieb, R., & Kasper, S. (2003). Recurrent brief depressive disorder reinvestigated: A community sample of adolescents and young adults. *Psychological Medicine, 33,* 407–418.

Riso, L. P., Klein, D. N., Ferro, T., Kasch, K. L., Pepper, C. M., Schwartz, J. E., et al. (1996). Understanding the comorbidity between early-onset dysthymia and Cluster B personality disorders: A family study. *American Journal of Psychiatry, 153,* 900–906.

Ryder, A. G., Bagby, R. M., & Dion, K. L. (2001). Chronic, low-grade depression in a nonclinical sample: Depressive personality or dysthymia? *Journal of Personality Disorders, 15,* 84–93.

Seivewright, P. T., & Johnson, T. (2004). Persistent social dysfunction in anxious and depressed patients with personality disorder. *Acta Psychiatrica Scandinavica, 109,* 104–109.

Shain, B. N., Naylor, M., & Alessi, N. (1990). Comparison of self-rated and clinician-rated measures of depression in adolescents. *American Journal of Psychiatry, 147,* 793–795.

Skre, I., Onstad, S., Torgersen, S., & Kringlen, E. (1991). High interrater reliability for the Structured Clinical Interview for *DSM-III-R* Axis I (SCID-I). *Acta Psychiatrica Scandinavica, 84,* 167–173.

Stark, K. D., Swearer, S., Kurowski, C., Sommer, D., & Bowen, B. (1996). Targeting the child and the family: A holistic approach to treatment of child and adolescent depressive disorders. In E. D. Hibbs & P. S. Jensen (Eds.), *Psychosocial treatments for child and adolescent disorders: Empirically based strategies for clinical practice* (pp. 207–238). Washington, DC: American Psychological Association.

Stewart, J. W., Quitkin, F. M., McGrath, P. J., & Rabkin, J. G. (1988). Social functioning in chronic depression: Effect of 6 weeks of antidepressant treatment. *Psychiatry Research, 25,* 213–222.

Stewart, W. F., Ricci, J. A., Chee, E., Hahn, S. R., & Morganstein, D. (2003). Cost of lost productive work time among U.S. workers with depression. *Journal of the American Medical Association, 289,* 3135–3144.

Stravynski, A., Shahar, A., & Verreault, R. (1991). A pilot study of the cognitive treatment of dysthymic disorder. *Behavioral Psychotherapy, 19*, 369–372.

Teasdale, J. D. (1988). Cognitive vulnerability to persistent depression. *Cognition and Emotion: Special Information Processing and the Emotional Disorders, 2*, 247–274.

Vallejo, J., Casto, C., Catalan, R., & Salamero, M. (1987). Double-blind study: Imipramine-phenelzine in neurotic depression. *British Journal of Psychiatry, 151*, 639–642.

Waraich, P., Goldner, E. M., Somers, J. M., & Hsu, L. (2004). Prevalence and incidence studies of mood disorders: A systematic review of the literature. *Canadian Journal of Psychiatry, 49*, 124–138.

Waring, E. M., Chamberlaine, C. H., McCrank, E. W., & Stalker, C. A. (1988). Dysthymia: A randomized study of cognitive marital therapy and antidepressants. *Canadian Journal of Psychiatry, 33*, 96–99.

Weissman, M. M., Prusoff, B. A., Thompson, W. D., Harding, P. S., & Myers, J. K. (1978). Social adjustment by self-report in a community sample in psychiatric outclients. *Journal of Nervous Mental Disorders, 166*, 317–326.

Westermeyer, J., Eames, S. L., & Nugent, S. (1998). Comorbid dysthymia and substance disorder: Treatment history and cost. *American Journal of Psychiatry, 155*, 1556–1560.

Whisman, M. A. (2001). Marital adjustment and outcome following treatments for depression. *Journal of Consulting and Clinical Psychology, 69*, 125–129.

Williams, J. B. W. (2001). Standardizing the Hamilton Depression Rating Scale: Past, present, and future. *European Archives of Psychiatry and Clinical Neuroscience, 251*, 116–112.

Zanarini, M. C., Skodol, A. E., Bender, D., Dolan, R., Sanislow, C., Schaefer, E., et al. (2000). The collaborative longitudinal personality disorders study: Reliability of Axis I and II diagnoses. *Journal of Personality Disorders, 14*, 291–299.

ANXIETY DISORDERS

Panic Disorder and Agoraphobia

Joseph A. Himle, Daniel J. Fischer,
and Laura M. Lokers

15
Chapter

Learning Objectives

After reading this chapter, the reader will be able to:

- Distinguish between Panic Disorder and Agoraphobia, and describe the relationship that often exists between these two conditions.
- Locate and describe evidence-based approaches to assessing clients with presumptive Panic Disorder and Agoraphobia.
- Locate and describe current evidence-based approaches to treating clients with these conditions.

Overview of the Problem

The *Diagnostic and Statistical Manual of Mental Disorders* (*DSM*; American Psychiatric Association, 2000) defines a panic attack as a discrete period of intense fear or discomfort, in which 4 of 13 symptoms develop abruptly and reach a peak within 10 minutes of the onset of the episode. Panic attack symptoms include palpitations, pounding, or accelerated heart rate; sweating; trembling or shaking; shortness of breath or smothering; feeling of choking; chest pain or discomfort; feeling dizzy, unsteady, lightheaded, or faint; derealization or depersonalization; fear of losing control or going crazy; fear of dying; numbness or tingling sensations; and chills or hot flushes. The *DSM* describes Panic Disorder as recurrent, unexpected, panic attacks where at least one attack is followed by 1 month (or more) of at least one of the following: persistent concern about having additional attacks, worry about the implications of the attack or its consequences, or a significant change in behavior related to the attacks. There are two types of Panic Disorder: Panic Disorder without Agoraphobia and Panic Disorder with Agoraphobia.

Agoraphobia is a condition often related to Panic Disorder and is defined in the *DSM-IV* as anxiety about being in places or situations from which escape might be difficult (or embarrassing) or in which help may not be available, in the event of having a panic attack or experiencing paniclike symptoms. Agoraphobic fears include anxiety about being outside the home alone; being in a crowd or standing in a line; being on a bridge; traveling in a bus, train, or automobile; visiting a mall or grocery store; going to the theater; eating in a restaurant; and visiting places where panic attacks have occurred previously. Formally, the diagnosis of agoraphobia is present in two varieties, Panic Disorder with Agoraphobia and Agoraphobia without history of Panic Disorder.

Panic Disorder and Agoraphobia are both relatively common conditions. According to the National Comorbidity Survey, Panic Disorder without Agoraphobia is present in about 2% of the population, whereas Panic Disorder with Agoraphobia is somewhat less common, with 1.5% of the general population meeting diagnostic criteria (all rates are lifetime prevalence; Eaton, Kessler, Wittchen, & Magee, 1994). Agoraphobia without Panic Disorder is the most common of this group of anxiety disorders, at 5.2% (Eaton et al., 1994; Magee, Eaton, Wittchen, McGonagle, & Kessler, 1996). As with most psychiatric disorders, a range of impairment is noted among persons meeting criteria for Agoraphobia and Panic Disorder. However, it is clear that when both are present, impairment is often substantial (Magee et al., 1996; Welkowitz, Welkowitz, Struening, Hellman, & Guardino, 2004).

The average age of onset for Panic Disorder and Agoraphobia has consistently ranged from the mid- to late 20s across studies from several treatment centers and in epidemiological surveys (Magee et al., 1996; Ost, 1987a; Thyer, Himle, Curtis, Cameron, & Nesse, 1985). Females, compared to males, are roughly twice as likely to meet criteria for Panic Disorder (0.4% of males, 1% of females), Panic Disorder with Agoraphobia (0.4% of males, 1.0% of females), and Agoraphobia without history of Panic Disorder (1.0% of males, 2.1% of females; prevalence rates based on month prior to interview; Eaton et al., 1994; Magee et al., 1996). Fifty percent of people with Panic Disorder also develop symptoms of Agoraphobia, often as a result of attempting to protect themselves from future panic attacks (Gassner, 2004). Several disorders commonly co-occur with Panic Disorder and Agoraphobia. Depression is often present among clients with panic attacks and/or Agoraphobia

(Magee et al., 1996; Robins, Locke, & Regier, 1991). Panic Disorder and/or Agoraphobia also often coexist with other anxiety disorders, such as specific and social phobia (Magee et al., 1996; Welkowitz et al., 2004). Finally, alcohol abuse/dependence is common among subjects meeting criteria for Panic Disorder with Agoraphobia and Panic Disorder but not among those clients meeting criteria for Agoraphobia without Panic Disorder (Himle & Hill, 1991; Thyer, McNeece, & Miller, 1987; Thyer et al., 1986).

Two general treatment strategies, medication and cognitive-behavioral therapy (CBT), have been shown to be effective in the treatment of Panic Disorder and Agoraphobia. Tricyclic anti-depressants (Mavissakalian, 1990), monoamine oxidase inhibitors (Sheehan, Ballenger, & Jacobsen, 1980; van Vliet, den Boer, West-enberg, & Slaap, 1996), selective serotonin reuptake inhibitors (Bourin, Chue, & Guillon, 2001; den Boer & Westenberg, 1988; Stahl, Gergel, & Li, 2003), and the high-potency benzodiazapine alprazolam (Ballenger et al., 1988) have been shown to be effective in reducing the frequency and intensity of panic attacks. An extensive amount of research has been conducted which clearly demonstrates the effectiveness of behavioral therapies in reducing agoraphobic avoidance (see Barlow, 2001; Thyer, 1987b). These behavioral treatments involve prolonged and repetitive exposures to agoraphobic situations. More recently, various cognitive and be-havioral strategies have been developed which have been shown to significantly reduce the frequency and severity of panic attacks (Barlow, Gorman, Shear, & Woods, 2000). Other psychosocial in-terventions have not been empirically tested in the treatment of Panic Disorder and Agoraphobia and therefore are not reviewed in this chapter. It is the purpose of this chapter to describe the em-pirically based psychosocial treatments for Panic Disorder and Agoraphobia. Each of the empirical treatments described would generally be identified as a behavioral or cognitive treatment.

Evidence-Based Approaches to Assessment

At the most basic level, the task of the social worker evaluating a person suffering from Panic Disorder/Agoraphobia involves devel-oping an understanding of three main areas: the nature of the panic symptoms, the extent of phobic avoidance, and the triggering events and circumstances that elicit panic attacks and avoidance.

Clinical Interview

Structured clinical interviews such as the Structured Clinical Interview for *DSM* Axis I Disorders (SCID; First, Spitzer, Gibbon, & Williams, 1995) and the Anxiety Disorders Interview

Schedule—Revised (ADIS-R; Di Nardo et al., 1985) provide the interviewer with a checklist of panic attack symptoms and questions regarding phobic avoidance which can aid in establishing the diagnosis of Panic Disorder and Agoraphobia. The ADIS-R also provides information to the social worker regarding onset, course, and degree of interference in client functioning, as well as an inventory of thoughts related to panic attacks. Beyond the structured interview, a detailed assessment of phobic avoidance is conducted. In this assessment, the social worker and the client review situations that the client avoids, and an attempt is made to place these situations in a hierarchy progressing from easier to more difficult. It is also important to gather information on other variables that trigger panic and avoidance, such as distorted thinking, physiological sensations, interpersonal interactions, and affective states. In addition, it is important that the social worker discuss the impact of the client's panic attacks and avoidant behavior on his or her work life, family functioning, and romantic relationships.

As in assessment of any condition, the clinical interview should include a detailed review of the onset and course of the presenting complaint, a comprehensive review of other comorbid psychiatric conditions, and a thorough investigation of the client's medical, family, and social history.

Clinician-Rated and Self-Report Measures

One commonly used clinician-rated outcome measure is the Multicenter Collaborative Panic Disorder Severity Scale (Shear et al., 1997). This 7-item scale measures panic frequency, distress associated with panic, anticipatory anxiety, agoraphobic fear/avoidance, interoceptive fear/avoidance, work impairment/distress, and social impairment and distress. This scale has been shown to have excellent interrater reliability and moderate internal consistency and is sensitive to change (Shear et al., 1997). A second commonly used clinician-rated scale that measures the severity of panic and Agoraphobia is the Panic and Agoraphobia Scale (Bandelow, 1999). This scale also has acceptable reliability and validity.

Self-rating inventories have been developed to assess the symptoms present during a panic attack, including those designed to assess fear of panic symptoms, such as the Anxiety Sensitivity Index (Peterson & Reiss, 1987; Taylor & Cox, 1998) and the Body Sensations Questionnaire (Chambless, Caputo, Bright, & Gallagher, 1984). In addition, panic attack diaries have been developed to record panic frequency and symptoms present during attacks (Rapee, Craske, & Barlow, 1990). Self-report scales used to measure the extent of phobic avoidance include the Fear Questionnaire (Marks & Mathews, 1979), the Agoraphobia Scale (Ost, 1990), and the Mobility Inventory for Agoraphobia (Chambless, Caputo, Jasin, Gracely, & Williams, 1985).

Behavioral Avoidance Test

An additional method of assessing phobic behavior is the behavioral avoidance test (Barlow, O'Brien, & Last, 1984; Williams & Rappoport, 1983). During the behavioral avoidance test, clients are accompanied by the social worker and are instructed to approach a predetermined series of naturalistic situations of increasing difficulty, such as visiting a mall, going to church, or eating at a restaurant. Prior to the behavioral avoidance test, the situations to be encountered are determined using one of two methods. The first method involves the social worker and client constructing together an individualized hierarchy of feared situations. A second method involves the use of a predetermined series of challenging situations created by the social worker for use with several agoraphobic clients. During the behavioral avoidance test, the social worker records whether the client refuses the task (avoidance), partially completes the task (escape), or successfully completes the task. In addition, the client also rates the degree of anxiety he or she experiences on encountering each situation.

A recent review article by Antony and Rowa (2005) provides a very nice discussion of contemporary evidence-based approaches to assessing anxiety disorders among adults and is particularly recommended.

Evidence-Based Approaches to Intervention

Real-Life Exposure to External Cues

Agoraphobic behavior includes avoidance of a variety of situations and circumstances that serve as triggers to panic and extreme anxiety. Real-life exposure therapy is designed to reduce anxiety and avoidance by systematically asking clients to confront feared situations or circumstances until the fear subsides. Marks (1987) suggests that to ensure optimal effectiveness, exposure should be repeated and prolonged and the client should be encouraged to focus his or her attention on the phobic stimulus. The initial task in conducting successful exposure treatment is for the client to identify situational triggers that are avoided as well as those triggers that elicit anxiety but are not avoided. Once this is completed, the situations are arranged in a hierarchical fashion from least to most feared. Clients are taught to rate and monitor the degree of anxiety they experience using a subjective units of distress scale (SUDS; Wolpe, 1973). A SUDS scale is typically a 100-point scale with 0 representing calm and 100 representing extreme anxiety. This simple self-report method of quantifying subjective anxiety has been shown to correlate reasonably well with physiological indices of fear, such as heart rate and skin temperature (Thyer, Papsdorf, Davis, & Vallecorsa, 1984). Clients rate each item on the graded hierarchy with this scale. In practice, clients may find it easier to generate their hierarchy of feared situations by listing one item at a time and rating its anxiety, without initially attempting to list items hierarchically. Later, the feared situations can be arranged in ascending order.

Once a fear hierarchy has been established, clients are given exposure assignments in which they confront the situations they fear and avoid. Exposure assignments are determined in a collaborative effort between client and social worker, with the client ultimately dictating the pace of the exposure tasks. As previously mentioned, the keys to effective exposure are that trials must be frequent and prolonged, with the ideal being daily practice totaling at least 90 minutes per day (Marks, 1987). The more often clients practice, the more rapidly they will improve. Exposure trials are designed to purposefully increase and sustain the client's level of anxiety, until anxiety decreases naturally. This process, whereby an individual becomes less anxious after prolonged contact with fearful stimuli, is known as *habituation*. Movement from one major item in the hierarchy to the next (e.g., bus rides to shopping malls) is typically done after the client has mastered the previous step. During exposure trials, clients are asked to focus their attention on the task at hand, as research has shown that distraction reduces the therapeutic effect of exposure (Sartory, Rachman, & Grey, 1982). It is not uncommon for clients to report that they have attempted their own version of real-life exposure without success. Common reasons for their failure include not fully focusing their attention on the exposure task or terminating exposure prematurely.

One method of real-life exposure involves exposure trials conducted with the social worker present, supplemented by daily homework assignments that are carried out by the client between sessions. However, research suggests that clients can also progress well by conducting all their exposure sessions without the social worker. This can be achieved by using therapy sessions to develop assignments that the client carries out alone or by the client utilizing self-help books or computer-generated instruction without direct social worker assistance (Ghosh & Marks, 1987). Whichever treatment method is selected, exposure to external cues is of critical importance in reducing agoraphobic fear and avoidance. Additional clinical descriptions of implementation of exposure therapy can be found in the social work literature (e.g., Thyer, 1983, 1985).

Exposure to Internal Cues (Interoceptive Exposure)

Beyond repetitive exposure to external stimuli that prompt panic attacks, researchers (Barlow, Craske, Cerny, & Klosko, 1989) have demonstrated that exposure to internal body sensations associated with panic episodes is also of therapeutic benefit in the treatment of Panic Disorder. Barlow and Cerny (1988) suggest that after certain internal states (e.g., dizziness, increased heart rate, shortness of breath) have been associated with panic attacks, these sensations themselves can serve as conditioned triggers of panic episodes. Many clients with Panic Disorder closely scrutinize internal bodily sensations and often avoid activities that would elicit feelings associated with panic.

Using methods similar to those of treatment programs aimed at external panic triggers, Barlow and Cerny (1988) were first to develop a treatment program aimed at exposing clients in a gradual and repetitive manner to internal sensations (e.g., running in place, whirling about, hyperventilating, confronting hot places, staring at one's hand or a spot on a wall). Clients are thought to habituate to these exercises in a manner similar to that seen during therapeutic exposure to external cues. The individual internal cue exposure exercises can be combined (e.g., spinning about while hyperventilating and running in place) after clients become comfortable confronting one cue at a time.

Internal cue exposures are often initiated in the social worker's office and then given to the client as homework. Initially, it is not uncommon for clients to experience panic attacks when practicing their internal cue exercises. These attacks can be alarming to both the client and the social worker. However, with continued practice, attacks become less frequent and decrease in severity, both in the office and in the natural environment. In the authors' experience, internal cue exposure sessions need to be conducted somewhat differently from exposure sessions aimed at external triggers. Rarely can clients hyperventilate, run in place, and whirl about for hours at a time, as is often expected for sessions at the mall or theater. Instead, clients can be asked to practice repeated shorter trials of exposure with accompanying rest periods. In the authors' clinic, clients are typically asked to practice their internal cue exposures three times daily in 15-minute sessions. These exercises are often added to longer external cue exposure sessions to meet the general guideline of 1.5 to 2 hours of daily exposure.

In determining which internal cue exercises to select, the general rule of focusing on the "first" and the "worst" applies well here. The authors suggest that clients target those symptoms that they notice first during a panic attack and those that are most frightening. Although each client presents a symptom profile that is somewhat different, certain exercises appear to be especially valuable. In the authors' experience, voluntary hyperventilation is an especially challenging exercise for many clients, and mastery over it often results in substantial improvement. Asking the client to breathe rapidly and deeply through the mouth at a rate

of about one breath per second is all that is required. Also of particular interest and importance is the production of feelings of
unreality common during panic attacks. Several exercises, such
as staring at one's hand or a point on a wall or staring at a light
and attempting to read, can trigger feelings of unreality similar to
those experienced during naturally occurring panic attacks. Once
this unreality trigger has been identified, repetitive exposure
can begin.

It is important to note that although internal cue exposure
may elicit anxiety and often proves helpful, not all panic disordered clients respond to these exercises with feelings of anxiety.
In fact, some clients find that physical exertion actually reduces
their panic feelings. It is advisable that social workers present the
technique of exposure to internal cues to their panic clients as a
method that may or may not be used depending on whether the
exercises prompt anxiety.

Cognitive Therapy

A cognitive model of Panic Disorder has been described in which
inappropriate and catastrophic thinking exacerbates physiological
symptoms present during panic attacks (Clark, 1986). Ottaviani
and Beck (1987) found that clients often report thoughts that
they are about to die, collapse, go crazy, lose control, or have a
heart attack during panic attacks. These self statements are
thought to maintain a positive feedback loop where disordered
thinking exacerbates physical symptoms, which leads to further
catastrophic misinterpretations of bodily sensations, followed by
further worsening physical symptoms. As a result, clients often
pay close attention to internal sensations and external situations
previously associated with panic attacks and follow these triggers
with inaccurate thinking. Cognitive therapy for Panic Disorder involves the social worker and the client working together in a collaborative relationship to address the accuracy of these thoughts
and to replace them with more appropriate interpretations of
bodily sensations.

Clearly, one source of information that a social worker can
use to assess the accuracy of a client's thinking during a panic attack is the client's own history. By the time most clients seek therapy for Panic Disorder, they have already experienced several
attacks of varying severity. Most clients report catastrophic thinking (e.g., heart attack, stroke, death, going crazy) of one sort or
another during these attacks. Almost by definition, the feared
consequences have not come to pass. The social worker can gently
question clients and help them to recount how often they have
had panic attacks, erroneously predicted disaster, yet somehow
escaped it. Clients can use this information to counter thoughts

about panic attacks causing catastrophe. A second source of information that the social worker can utilize is knowledge about other clients with Panic Disorder. The social worker can educate the client about other panic clients he or she has seen, as well as about clients at other centers, informing the client about the high prevalence of predicted catastrophe and the near absence of truly deleterious consequences. Another form of assistance that can aid the client in countering irrational thinking is to provide information about the physiology of panic attacks. Clients who worry about fainting can be informed that heart rate and blood pressure are higher during panic attacks, whereas fainting requires low heart rate and blood pressure. Clients who worry about smothering and those who experience dizziness or tingling in the extremities can be instructed in the physiology of hyperventilation and the symptoms it typically produces. Clients can be instructed in the causes of heart attacks and how their efforts to prevent them during panic attacks (e.g., fleeing, having a drink of water, distraction) would have no effect if a real heart attack were on the way.

A fourth source of information is often referred to as a behavioral test. It is sometimes puzzling to clinicians why clients maintain the belief that terrible consequences will come from panic attacks when most clients seem to have had several opportunities to discover that panic attacks are not harmful. In fact, most clients do not allow themselves to learn that panic attacks do *not* lead to catastrophe because they engage in several behaviors (e.g., distraction, fleeing, taking a pill, taking a drink of water, supporting themselves) to protect themselves from disaster. Behavioral tests involve asking clients to experience entire attacks from start to finish without engaging in any such rescuing behaviors. The technique allows the client to discover that the panic attack only *seems* to signal true danger. Repetitive behavioral tests can sometimes involve the addition of deliberate attempts to aggravate panic (e.g., running in place during a panic attack) to build an even more convincing argument that panic attacks will not lead to catastrophic consequences. The four sources of information previously described can be used by the client and the social worker to argue against the negative thoughts often present during attacks and thus reduce the frequency and severity of the episodes.

Given the high prevalence of Panic Disorder and Agoraphobia, the potential exists to have a number of clients in treatment at the same time. This suggests the possible role of therapy and support groups in the provision of treatment. Both the psychoeducational aspects of cognitive therapy and the exposure treatment elements lend themselves well to delivery in small groups. The segue into supportive therapy is obvious; often, clients spontaneously develop phone networks to support each others' homework efforts, and they may pair themselves up to practice difficult exposure tasks together, independent of time spent with the social worker. Penava and colleagues (Penava, Otto, Maki, & Pollack, 1998) and others (Thyer, 1987a) describe the conduct of such groups for clients with these conditions.

Anxiety Management Techniques

When a person experiences a panic attack, the anxiety experienced involves three response classes: (1) a behavioral response (escape or avoidance), (2) a cognitive response (patterns of catastrophic thinking), and (3) a physiological response (e.g., heart palpitations, dizziness, shortness of breath, muscle tension). As has been discussed, behavioral strategies are helpful in ameliorating escape/avoidance patterns through the use of frequent and prolonged exposure to feared situations or body sensations. Cognitive restructuring is helpful in reducing anxiety by assisting clients in developing more accurate thinking about the physiological symptoms of panic. A third approach is to help clients learn strategies to manage and control the physiological component of their anxiety. Applied relaxation and breathing control training are two methods clients can use to manage the physiological symptoms of panic.

Applied relaxation training is a method devised by Ost (1987b) that involves teaching clients a graded method of relaxation using several steps. The initial step (session 1) is designed to increase the client's awareness of the specific early signs of arousal and panic, which then serve as cues for relaxation. Increasing awareness is accomplished by clients keeping a daily record of their panic attacks. The panic diary records situations where panic attacks occurred, physiological symptoms experienced, and ratings of panic intensity.

The second step (sessions 2 and 3) involves instructing clients in a progressive relaxation technique in which the client produces initial muscle tension followed by muscle relaxation. Muscle groups are tensed and relaxed, beginning with the hands and progressing through the arms, shoulders, face, neck, trunk, back, and down through the legs and feet. By alternating tension with relaxation, clients are taught to distinguish between a state of relaxation and muscle tension. They are instructed to rate their level of tension before and after the procedure using a 0 to 100 scale. Tension is typically applied for 5 to 10 seconds, followed by 10 to 15 seconds of relaxation.

The short version of progressive relaxation, release-only, is introduced during session 4. The goal of this stage is to further decrease the amount of time it takes to relax by omitting the tension portion of the exercise. The social worker instructs the client to relax each muscle group using a progression similar to that established during the tension/release phase. Muscle tension is used only if the client has difficulty relaxing a particular muscle group.

Cue-controlled or conditioned relaxation, which further reduces the time it takes for the client to achieve a state of relaxation, is introduced in session 5. This stage focuses on establishing a conditioned relationship between the self-instruction "Relax" and a state of increased relaxation. The session begins by having the client use release-only relaxation until a satisfactory level of relaxation is achieved. Following the client's breathing pattern, the social worker gives verbal cues to inhale, and then, just before the client exhales, the social worker gives the verbal cue "Relax." Eventually, the client is instructed to continue this breathing pattern on his or her own, replacing the social worker's verbal cues with self-generated statements.

Differential relaxation is introduced in session 6 and continued in session 7. The primary goal of this technique is to teach the client to relax while engaged in everyday activities. Session 6 starts with the client using cue-controlled relaxation while sitting comfortably on a chair or couch. The client is then instructed to move parts of the body while continuing to relax. Once the client has practiced these body movements while sitting in a comfortable chair, these same movements are practiced while sitting at a desk, standing, and eventually while walking. By the end of this phase of treatment, it is hoped that clients are able to relax in 60 to 90 seconds.

Sessions 8 and 9 are used to develop and practice rapid relaxation. Rapid relaxation, which further reduces the amount of time (20 to 30 seconds) it takes for the client to relax, teaches clients how to relax in stressful but nonpanic situations. In rapid relaxation, the client and social worker identify a series of cues (e.g., making a telephone call or looking at a watch) that remind the client to relax. When relaxing, the client is taught to take 1 to 3 deep breaths, then to think "Relax" before exhaling, all the while scanning the body for tension and trying to relax as much as possible.

Finally, sessions 10, 11, and 12 are used for application training in natural situations and for maintenance instruction. Application training involves teaching the client to apply the learned relaxation skills in stressful, panic-inducing situations. Practice usually involves frequent but brief (10 to 15 minutes) exposure to a variety of anxiety-producing stimuli and applying relaxation at the first signs of arousal. Clients are encouraged to scan their bodies for tension at least once daily and to practice differential or rapid relaxation regularly to maintain these skills. During each phase of applied relaxation training, clients are asked to practice the relaxation techniques at home between sessions.

A second commonly used anxiety management procedure for Panic Disorder is breathing retraining. Barlow and Cerny (1988) describe a breathing control technique that is useful as a method of managing initial symptoms associated with panic attacks, as well as controlling symptoms during the attacks themselves. The breathing control program involves instructing clients in slow-paced respirations coupled with a meditation counting technique to time the breathing frequency. Clients are instructed to count during each inhalation and to say the word "Relax" to themselves while exhaling. The goal of this technique is to gradually slow the client's respiratory rate to about 3 seconds devoted to inhalation and 3 seconds to exhalation. This practice limits breathing to around 10 breaths per minute, making it difficult to hyperventilate. Often, clients will mistakenly accelerate their breathing and gasp in large amounts of air as they begin to practice the breathing control technique. However, with practice, clients can learn to slow their counting, take in normal volume breaths, and thus appropriately regulate their ventilation.

To date, dozens of controlled studies exist documenting the efficacy of repetitive and prolonged exposure to agoraphobic situations (see Barlow, 2001; Marks, 1987). Many studies involve treatment in which the social worker is present during real-life exposure sessions or guides exposure homework exercises from the office without accompanying the client in the field. Clearly, it is beyond the scope of this chapter to review in detail the numerous studies documenting the benefits of exposure therapy, but it is important to note that this technique has limitations. Jansson and Ost (1982), reviewed several studies and found the average dropout rate for exposure treatment to be 12%. A second limitation is that approximately 30% to 40% of agoraphobics who complete exposure treatment fail to benefit (Barlow, 1988). Finally, exposure to agoraphobic situations does not apply for those panic disordered clients without Agoraphobia.

Beyond studies examining the effectiveness of external cue exposure in the treatment of Agoraphobia, a growing body of research has demonstrated the efficacy of other cognitive-behavioral strategies targeting panic attacks directly. Barlow and colleagues (1989) first studied a group of clients with Panic Disorder assigned to one of four groups: (1) progressive muscle relaxation, (2) panic control treatment (a combined CBT that includes internal cue exposure and cognitive restructuring), (3) panic control treatment plus relaxation, or (4) wait list (control group). Each active treatment was superior to the wait-list control group. Treatments that included panic control treatment were superior to relaxation therapy alone. The superiority of the panic control treatment was also demonstrated at up to 2 years posttreatment (Craske, Brown, & Barlow, 1991). The most definitive study of Barlow and Craske's (1994) CBT for Panic Disorder was recently completed (Barlow et al., 2000). In this study, a large group of clients with Panic Disorder (with or without mild Agoraphobia) were randomly assigned to receive CBT, imipramine, placebo, CBT plus imipramine, or CBT plus placebo. Cognitive-behavioral therapy was superior to placebo at the end of acute treatment and was especially durable at 6-month follow-up.

Several studies have sought to evaluate the relative effects of various cognitive-behavioral interventions. Clark and colleagues (1994) compared the effects of cognitive restructuring, applied relaxation (following Ost, 1987b), imipramine, and wait-list control among a group of clients with Panic Disorder. All three treatment conditions included weekly self-conducted external cue exposure. Cognitive-behavioral therapy was superior to all other treatment conditions in reducing panic attacks and avoidance at both the end of treatment and at 1-year follow-up. Imipramine and applied relaxation, although less effective than cognitive restructuring, were more helpful than the wait-list control group.

In contrast, Ost and associates (Ost, Westling, & Hellstrom, 1993) found similar rates of improvement when comparing applied relaxation, real-life external cue exposure, and cognitive therapy in a group of Panic Disorder clients. Like previous studies, all clients also performed self-conducted external cue exposure exercises, making it impossible to determine how effective these treatments would be without this component. However, there are three studies comparing CBT and relaxation that did not include external cue exposure. In the first of these studies, Ost and Westling (1994) found essentially equal efficacy for both CBT and applied relaxation. Beck, Stanley, Baldwin, Deagle, and Averill (1994) also investigated the differential effects of relaxation therapy (a version including progressive muscle relaxation and controlled breathing) and CBT and found both therapeutic conditions to be helpful. However, the CBT group exceeded the relaxation group in the percentage of subjects classified as treatment responders. The last of these studies without real-life exposure, conducted by Arntz and Van Den Hout (1996), found superior outcomes for clients randomly assigned to receive CBT compared to those given applied relaxation. One strength of this study is that it included only clinically referred clients compared to other studies with participants recruited from advertisements, suggesting that the results of this study may more closely replicate results likely to be found in the real world.

Other attempts to parse out the relative effects of various cognitive-behavioral strategies used in Panic Disorder have focused on the utility of internal cue exposure and breathing retraining. Margraf and colleagues (Margraf, Barlow, Clark, & Telch, 1993) found that internal cue exposure exercises enhance outcome when combined with other cognitive-behavioral methods. However, recent research has brought the value of incorporating breathing retraining into CBT for Panic Disorder somewhat into question. Schmidt and colleagues (2000) found lower levels of improvement for clients randomly assigned to receive CBT, internal cue exposure, real-life external cue exposure, plus breathing retraining compared to those assigned to receive these interventions without breathing retraining. Otto and Deveney (2005) suggest that these reduced outcomes may be due to breathing retraining and other interventions focused on controlling anxiety inadvertently encouraging escape behavior, distraction, and avoidance of anxiety.

Summary

To the benefit of the many who suffer from Panic Disorder and Agoraphobia, a substantial and growing body of empirical research exists to guide the social worker in selecting treatment approaches. The dilemma that presents itself to the social worker is how to select from the two major treatment approaches, medication and CBT. At times, the decision is simple: The client either refuses medication or cognitive-behavioral treatment, leaving the social worker to begin with what was not ruled out. More often, the client leaves it up to the social worker to decide what is best. The research literature does not give the social worker a clear choice between the two major treatments, as studies have not indicated that one treatment is clearly superior to the other (Black, Wesner, Bowers, & Gabel, 1993; Klosko, Barlow, Tassinari, & Cerny, 1990; Mavissakalian, 1989). Findings from Barlow et al.'s (2000) recent multicenter randomized trial of CBT, imipramine, placebo, CBT plus imipramine, and CBT plus placebo are consistent with these studies finding similar pre/postoutcomes for CBT and medication. However, combined CBT and imipramine had an advantage at follow-up, suggesting that combined treatment may be the most efficacious choice. Durability benefits from combined medication and CBT have also been reported elsewhere (Bruce, Spiegel, & Hegel, 1999; Massimo & Picardi, 2003). Recent research also supports the value of considering CBT or medication sequentially. Cognitive-behavioral therapy has been shown to be helpful for clients who did not respond well to a prior trial of medication (Otto, Pollack, Penva, & Zucker, 1999), and conversely, medications have been shown to enhance outcomes for patients who initially fail CBT (Kampman, Keijsers, Hoogduin, & Hendriks, 2002).

Combined CBT and medication may be especially beneficial when the client suffers from significant comorbid depression. Cognitive-behavioral treatments typically require the client to expend a substantial amount of effort, which is sometimes very difficult for clients with severe depression. Clinical experience suggests that antidepressant medications can be helpful in improving mood and consequently increasing the likelihood that clients will be able to complete their cognitive-behavioral assignments.

The standard practice in the authors' clinic is to encourage all clients to participate in either group or individual CBT, even if they wish to use medication. Part of the reasoning behind this practice is that most clients will likely wish to stop their medication at some point, out of either necessity (e.g., pregnancy) or preference. In addition, a limited amount of research suggests that clients will have greater success discontinuing medication if they have also participated in CBT (Otto, Pollack, Meltzer-Brody, & Rosenbaum, 1992; Spiegel, Bruce, Gregg, & Nuzzarello, 1994).

Recent research has also demonstrated that the benefits of CBT for Panic Disorder and Agoraphobia can be attained in service settings other than specialty centers focusing on the treatment of anxiety disorders. Stuart, Treat, and Wade (2000) found positive outcomes comparable to those observed in efficacy trials conducted in specialty care clinics for clients with Panic Disorder treated in a community mental health setting. Addis and colleagues (2004) and Roy-Byrne et al. (2005) both found that CBT delivered in primary care settings outperformed treatment as usual control groups for clients with Panic Disorder. Finally, Ghosh and Marks (1987) were first to demonstrate that many persons with Panic Disorder and Agoraphobia can also benefit from self-exposure therapy guided by computer instructions or a self-help book. Hecker and colleagues (Hecker, Losee, Fritzler, & Fink, 1996) confirmed this finding, showing that persons diagnosed with Panic Disorder or Panic Disorder with Agoraphobia showed similar levels of improvement with self-directed versus therapist-directed CBT. However, Marks (1987) notes that some clients require more guidance than others, at times making therapist-assisted exposure sessions necessary, provided that the social worker gradually withdraw, leaving clients to conduct exposure on their own.

Recent technological advances have also been utilized to deliver or enhance outcomes with CBT for Panic Disorder and Agoraphobia. Internet-based (Carlbring, Ekselius, & Andersson, 2003; Richards, Klein, & Carlbring, 2003), virtual reality (Pull, 2005), and palmtop-computer-assisted (Kenardy et al., 2003; Newman, Kenardy, Herman, & Taylor, 1997) CBT have all shown promise in the treatment of Panic Disorder and Agoraphobia.

In sum, the past 3 decades have produced an extensive body of research literature which has introduced exciting developments in the treatment of Panic Disorder and Agoraphobia. Given current efforts to further these developments, it is important for clinicians to remain up to date with future empirical studies and to adjust their practices accordingly.

Study Questions

1. What is the most common relationship between the conditions of Panic Disorder and those of Agoraphobia?
2. Describe two evidence-based approaches to assessing someone who may meet the criteria for Panic Disorder or Agoraphobia.
3. Describe how the gradual, structured exposure of persons to real-life external cues that evoke anxiety may be therapeutic.
4. How can one arrange for a client's exposure to internal cues that evoke anxiety?
5. Describe a cognitive approach to therapy for Panic Disorder.
6. Describe the process called breathing retraining.

References

Addis, M. E., Hatgis, C., Krasnow, A. D., Jacob, K., Bourne, L., & Mansfield, A. (2004). Effectiveness of cognitive-behavioral treatment for panic disorder versus treatment as usual in a managed care setting. *Journal of Consulting and Clinical Psychology, 72,* 625–635.

American Psychiatric Association. (2000). *Diagnostic and statistical manual of mental disorders* (4th ed., text rev.). Washington, DC: Author.

Antony, M. M., & Rowa, K. (2005). Evidence-based assessment of anxiety disorders in adults. *Psychological Assessment, 17,* 256–266.

Arntz, A., & Van Den Hout, M. (1996). Psychological treatments of panic disorder without agoraphobia: Cognitive therapy versus applied relaxation. *Behavior Research and Therapy, 34,* 113–121.

Ballenger, J. C., Burrows, G., DuPont, R. L., Lesser, I. M., Noyes, R., Pecknold, J. C., et al. (1988). Alprazolam in panic disorder and agoraphobia: Results from a multicenter trial: Pt. 1. Efficacy in short-term treatment. *Archives of General Psychiatry, 45,* 413–422.

Bandelow, B. (1999). *Panic and Agoraphobia Scale.* Seattle, WA: Hogrefe & Huber.

Barlow, D. H. (1988). *Anxiety and its disorders.* New York: Guilford Press.

Barlow, D. H. (2001). *Anxiety and its disorders: The nature and treatment of anxiety and panic* (2nd ed.). New York: Guilford Press.

Barlow, D. H., & Cerny, J. A. (1988). *Psychological treatment of panic.* New York: Guilford Press.

Barlow, D. H., & Craske, M. G. (1994). *Mastery of your anxiety and panic (Pt. II).* San Antonio, TX: Graywind Publications.

Barlow, D. H., Craske, M. G., Cerny, J. A., & Klosko, J. S. (1989). Behavioral treatment of panic disorder. *Behavior Therapy, 20,* 261–282.

Barlow, D. H., Gorman, J. M., Shear, M. K., & Woods, S. W. (2000). Cognitive-behavioral therapy, imipramine, or their combination for panic disorder: A randomized controlled trial. *Journal of the American Medical Association, 283,* 2529–2536.

Barlow, D. H., O'Brien, G. T., & Last, C. G. (1984). Couples treatment of agoraphobia. *Behavior Therapy, 15,* 41–58.

Beck, J. G., Stanley, M. A., Baldwin, L. E., Deagle, E. A., & Averill, P. M. (1994). A comparison of cognitive therapy and relaxation training for panic disorder. *Journal of Consulting and Clinical Psychology, 62,* 818–826.

Black, D. W., Wesner, R., Bowers, W., & Gabel, J. (1993). A comparison of fluvoxamine, cognitive therapy, and placebo in the treatment of panic disorder. *Archives of General Psychiatry, 50,* 44–50.

Bourin, M., Chue, P., & Guillon, Y. (2001). Paroxetine: A review. *CNS Drug Reviews, 7,* 25–47.

Bruce, T. J., Spiegel, D. A., & Hegel, M. T. (1999). Cognitive-behavioral therapy helps prevent relapse and recurrence of panic disorder following alprazolam discontinuation: A long-term follow-up of the Peoria and Dartmouth studies. *Journal of Consulting and Clinical Psychology, 67,* 151–156.

Carlbring, P., Ekselius, L., & Andersson, G. (2003). Treatment of panic disorder via the Internet: A randomized trial of CBT versus applied relaxation. *Journal of Behavior Therapy and Experimental Psychiatry, 34,* 129–140.

Chambless, D. L., Caputo, G. C., Bright, P., & Gallagher, R. (1984). Assessment of fear in agoraphobics: The Body Sensations Questionnaire and the Agoraphobic Cognitions Questionnaire. *Journal of Consulting and Clinical Psychology, 52,* 1090–1097.

Chambless, D. L., Caputo, G. C., Jasin, S. E., Gracely, E. J., & Williams, C. (1985). The mobility inventory for agoraphobia. *Behavior Research and Therapy, 23,* 33–44.

Clark, D. M. (1986). A cognitive approach to panic. *Behavior Research and Therapy, 24,* 461–470.

Clark, D. M., Salkovskis, P. M., Hackmann, A., Middleton, H., Anastasiades, P., & Gelder, M. (1994). A comparison of cognitive therapy, applied relaxation, and imipramine in the treatment of panic disorder. *British Journal of Psychiatry, 164,* 759–769.

Craske, M. G., Brown, T. A., & Barlow, D. H. (1991). Behavioral treatment of panic disorder: A 2-year follow-up. *Behavior Therapy, 22,* 289–304.

den Boer, J. A., & Westenberg, H. G. M. (1988). The effect of serotonin and noradrenaline uptake inhibitor in panic disorder: A double blind comparative study with fluvoxamine and maprotiline. *International Journal of Clinical Psychopharmacology, 3,* 59–74.

Di Nardo, P. A., Barlow, D. H., Cerny, J., Bermilyea, B. B., Himadi, W., & Waddell, M. (1985). *Anxiety Disorders Interview Schedule-Revised (ADIS-R).* Albany: State University of New York, Phobia and Anxiety Disorders Clinic.

Eaton, W. W., Kessler, R. C., Wittchen, H.-U., & Magee, W. J. (1994). Panic and panic disorder in the United States. *American Journal of Psychiatry, 151,* 413–420.

First, M. B., Spitzer, R. L., Gibbon, M., & Williams, J. B. (1995). *Structured Clinical Interview for* DSM-IV *Axis 1 Disorders (SCID).* New York: New York State Psychiatric Institute, Biometrics Research Department.

Gassner, S. M. (2004). The role of traumatic experience in panic disorder and agoraphobia. *Psychoanalytic Psychology, 2,* 222–243.

Ghosh, A., & Marks, I. M. (1987). Self-directed exposure for agoraphobia: A controlled trial. *Behavior Therapy, 18,* 3–16.

Hecker, J. E., Losee, M. C., Fritzler, B. K., & Fink, C. M. (1996). Self-directed versus therapist-directed cognitive-behavioral treatment for panic disorder. *Journal of Anxiety Disorders, 10,* 253–265.

Himle, J., & Hill, E. (1991). Alcohol abuse and the anxiety disorders. *Journal of Anxiety Disorders, 5,* 237–245.

Jansson, L., & Ost, L. G. (1982). Behavioral treatments for agoraphobia: An evaluative review. *Clinical Psychology Review, 2,* 311–336.

Kampman, M., Keijsers, G. P., Hoogduin, C. A., & Hendriks, G. J. (2002). A randomized, double blind, placebo controlled study of the effects of adjunctive paroxetine in panic disorder patients unsuccessfully treated with cognitive-behavioral therapy alone. *Journal of Clinical Psychiatry, 63,* 772–777.

Kenardy, J. A., Dow, M. G., Johnston, D. W., Newman, M. G., Thomson, A., & Taylor, C. (2003). A comparison of delivery methods of cognitive behavioral therapy for panic disorder: An international multicenter trial. *Journal of Consulting and Clinical Psychology, 71,* 1068–1075.

Klosko, J. S., Barlow, D. H., Tassinari, R., & Cerny, J. A. (1990). A comparison of alprazolam and behavior therapy in the treatment of panic disorder. *Journal of Consulting and Clinical Psychology, 58,* 77–84.

Magee, W. J., Eaton, W. W., Wittchen, H.-U., McGonagle, K. A., & Kessler, R. C. (1996). Agoraphobia, simple phobia, and social phobia in the National Comorbidity Survey. *Archives of General Psychiatry, 53,* 159–168.

Margraf, J., Barlow, D. H., Clark, D. M., & Telch, M. J. (1993). Psychological treatment of panic: Work in progress on outcome, active ingredients, and follow-up. *Behavior Research and Therapy, 31,* 1–8.

Marks, I., & Mathews, A. M. (1979). Brief standard self-rating for phobic clients. *Behavior Research and Therapy, 17,* 263–267.

Marks, I. M. (1987). *Fears, phobias, and rituals.* New York: Oxford University Press.

Massimo, B., & Picardi, A. (2003). Increased probability of remaining in remission from panic disorder with agoraphobia after drug treatment in patients who received concurrent cognitive-behavioral therapy: A follow up study. *Psychotherapy and Psychosomatics, 72,* 34–42.

Mavissakalian, M. (1989). Differential effects of imipramine and behavior therapy on panic disorder with agoraphobia. *Psychopharmacology Bulletin, 25,* 27–29.

Mavissakalian, M. (1990). Sequential combination of imipramine and self-directed exposure in the treatment of panic disorder with agoraphobia. *Journal of Clinical Psychiatry, 51,* 184–188.

Newman, M. G., Kenardy, J., Herman, S., & Taylor, C. (1997). Comparison of palm-top-computer-assisted brief cognitive-behavioral treatment to cognitive behavioral treatment for panic disorder. *Journal of Consulting and Clinical Psychology, 65,* 173–178.

Ost, L. G. (1987a). Age of onset of different phobias. *Journal of Abnormal Psychology, 96,* 223–229.

Ost, L. G. (1987b). Applied relaxation: Description of a coping technique and review of controlled studies. *Behavior Research and Therapy, 25,* 397–410.

Ost, L. G. (1990). The Agoraphobia Scale: An evaluation of its reliability and validity. *Behavior Research and Therapy, 28,* 323–329.

Ost, L. G., & Westling, B. E. (1994). Applied relaxation versus cognitive behavior therapy in the treatment of panic disorder. *Behavior Research and Therapy, 33,* 145–158.

Ost, L. G., Westling, B. E., & Hellstrom, K. (1993). Applied relaxation, exposure *in vivo,* and cognitive methods in the treatment of panic disorder with agoraphobia. *Behavior Research and Therapy, 31,* 383–394.

Ottaviani, R., & Beck, A. T. (1987). Cognitive aspects of panic disorders. *Journal of Anxiety Disorders, 1,* 15–28.

Otto, M. W., & Deveney, C. (2005). Cognitive-behavioral therapy and the treatment of panic disorder: Efficacy and strategies. *Journal of Clinical Psychiatry, 66,* 28–32.

Otto, M. W., Pollack, M. H., Meltzer-Brody, S., & Rosenbaum, J. F. (1992). Cognitive behavioral therapy for benzodiazepine discontinuation in panic disorder clients. *Psychopharmacology Bulletin, 28,* 123–130.

Otto, M. W., Pollack, M. H., Penva, S. J., & Zucker, B. G. (1999). Group cognitive-behavior therapy for patients failing to respond to pharmacotherapy for panic disorder: A clinical case series. *Behavior Research and Therapy, 37,* 763–770.

Penava, S. J., Otto, M. W., Maki, K. M., & Pollack, M. H. (1998). Rate of improvement during cognitive-behavioral group treatment for panic disorder. *Behavior Research and Therapy, 36,* 665–673.

Peterson, R. A., & Reiss, S. (1987). *Anxiety Sensitivity Index manual.* Worthington, OH: IDS Publishing.

Pull, C. B. (2005). Current status of virtual reality exposure therapy in anxiety disorders. *Current Opinion in Psychiatry, 18,* 7–14.

Rapee, R. M., Craske, M. G., & Barlow, D. H. (1990). Subject described features of panic attacks using a new self-monitoring form. *Journal of Anxiety Disorders, 4,* 171–181.

Richards, J., Klein, B., & Carlbring, P. (2003). Internet-based treatment for panic disorder. *Cognitive Behavior Therapy, 32,* 125–135.

Robins, L. N., Locke, B. Z., & Regier, D. A. (1991). An overview of psychiatric disorders in America. In L. N. Robins & D. A. Regier (Eds.), *Psychiatric disorders in America: The Epidemiologic Catchment Area study* (pp. 328–366). New York: Free Press.

Roy-Byrne, P. P., Craske, M. G., Stein, M. B., Sullivan, G., Bystritsky, A., Katon, W., et al. (2005). A randomized effectiveness trial of cognitive-behavioral therapy and medication for primary care panic disorder. *Archives of General Psychiatry, 62,* 290–298.

Sartory, G., Rachman, S., & Grey, S. (1982). Return of fear: The role of rehearsal. *Behavior Research and Therapy, 20*, 123–133.

Schmidt, N. B., Woolaway-Bickel, K., Trakowski, J., Santiago, H., Storey, J., Koselka, M., et al. (2000). Dismantling cognitive-behavioral treatment for panic disorder: Questioning the utility of breathing retraining. *Journal of Consulting and Clinical Psychology, 68*, 417–424.

Shear, M. K., Brown, T. A., Barlow, D. H., Money, R., Sholomskas, D. E., Woods, S. W., et al. (1997). Multicenter Collaborative Panic Disorder Severity Scale. *American Journal of Psychiatry, 154*, 1571–1575.

Sheehan, D. V., Ballenger, J. C., & Jacobsen, G. (1980). Treatment of endogenous anxiety with phobic, hysterical, and hypochondriacal symptoms. *Archives of General Psychiatry, 37*, 51–59.

Spiegel, D. A., Bruce, T. J., Gregg, S. F., & Nuzzarello, A. (1994). Does cognitive behavior therapy assist slow taper alprazolam discontinuation in panic disorder? *American Journal of Psychiatry, 151*, 876–881.

Stahl, S. M., Gergel, I., & Li, D. (2003). Escitalopram in the treatment of panic disorder: A randomized, double-blind, placebo-controlled trial. *Journal of Clinical Psychiatry, 64*, 1322–1327.

Stuart, G. L., Treat, T. A., & Wade, W. A. (2000). Effectiveness of an empirically based treatment for panic disorder delivered in a service clinic setting: One-year follow-up. *Journal of Consulting and Clinical Psychology, 68*, 506–512.

Taylor, S., & Cox, B. J. (1998). An expanded Anxiety Sensitivity Index: Evidence for a hierarchic structure in a clinical sample. *Journal of Anxiety Disorders, 12*, 463–483.

Thyer, B. A. (1983). Treating anxiety disorders with exposure therapy. *Social Casework, 64*, 77–82.

Thyer, B. A. (1985). The treatment of phobias in their natural contexts. *Journal of Applied Social Sciences, 9*, 73–78.

Thyer, B. A. (1987a). Community-based self-help groups in the treatment of agoraphobia. *Journal of Sociology and Social Welfare, 14*, 135–141.

Thyer, B. A. (1987b). *Treating anxiety disorders.* Newbury Park, CA: Sage.

Thyer, B. A., Himle, J., Curtis, G. C., Cameron, O. G., & Nesse, R. M. (1985). A comparison of panic disorder and agoraphobia with panic attacks. *Comprehensive Psychiatry, 26*, 208–214.

Thyer, B. A., McNeece, A. C., & Miller, M. A. (1987). Alcohol abuse among agoraphobics: A community-based replication. *Alcoholism Treatment Quarterly, 4*, 61–67.

Thyer, B. A., Papsdorf, J. D., Davis, R., & Vallecorsa, S. (1984). Automatic correlates of the Subjective Anxiety Scale. *Journal of Behavior Therapy and Experimental Psychiatry, 15*, 3–7.

Thyer, B. A., Parrish, R. T., Himle, J., Cameron, O. G., Curtis, G. C., & Nesse, R. M. (1986). Alcohol abuse among clinically anxious patients. *Behavior Research and Therapy, 24*, 357–359.

van Vliet, I. M., den Boer, J. A., Westenberg, H. G., & Slaap, B. R. (1996). A double-blind comparative study of brofaromine and fluvoxamine in outpatients with panic disorder. *Journal of Clinical Psychopharmacology, 16*, 299–306.

Welkowitz, J., Welkowitz, L. A., Struening, E., Hellman, F., & Guardino, M. (2004). Panic and anxiety symptoms in a national anxiety screening sample: Implications for clinical interventions. *Psychotherapy, Theory, Research, Practice Training, 41*, 69–75.

Williams, S. L., & Rappoport, J. A. (1983). Cognitive treatment in the natural environment for agoraphobics. *Behavior Therapy, 14*, 299–313.

Wolpe, J. (1973). *Practice of behavior therapy.* New York: Pergamon Press.

Agoraphobia without History of Panic Disorder

Bruce M. Hyman

16
Chapter

Learning Objectives

After reading this chapter, the reader will be able to:

- Describe the *DSM* diagnostic criteria for Agoraphobia without a history of Panic Disorder.
- Identify the diagnostic distinctions between Agoraphobia without a history of Panic Disorder and Panic Disorder with and without Agoraphobia.
- Identify some of the demographic characteristics of clients with Agoraphobia without history of Panic Disorder, including population prevalence, average age of onset, gender differences, and typical life course of the disorder.
- Identify the four functions of clinical assessment.
- Describe the major evidence-based approaches to the treatment of Agoraphobia without history of Panic Disorder.
- Identify the contribution or role of the extended social system, including the family or significant other, in the treatment of Agoraphobia without history of Panic Disorder.
- Identify four ways that assisted cognitive-behavioral therapy employing the motivated spouse or partner has distinct benefits over unassisted cognitive-behavioral therapy for the treatment of Agoraphobia.
- Identify the role of new technologies, including the Internet, in assisting agoraphobic clients.

Overview of the Problem

goraphobia is a Greek word that literally means "fear of the marketplace." The German neurologist Westphal first coined the term in 1871 to describe a group of patients who experienced unexpected and situational panic attacks in squares, on empty streets, on bridges, and in crowds. They suffered from anticipatory anxiety and a fear of sudden incapacitation.

Operational Definitions of the Problem

The modern definition of Agoraphobia as defined in the *Diagnostic and Statistical Manual of Mental Disorders* (*DSM*; American Psychiatric Association, 2000) is anxiety, fear, and avoidance about being in places or situations from which escape might be difficult, embarrassing, or not readily available. The term "agoraphobia" is actually a misnomer, in that the agoraphobic may experience feelings of panic not only in public places, but in countless situations where escape is perceived to be difficult. These may include traveling in a train, riding in elevators, buses, or automobiles, sitting in church, visiting a barber or hairdresser, being in crowded shopping malls or grocery stores, eating in restaurants, standing in line, being on a bridge, or visiting any place, indoors or out, where panic symptoms had previously occurred.

The degree of disability from Agoraphobia can range from mild situational discomfort to being severely housebound, unable to leave the home unless accompanied by a trusted friend or family member. Should these severely afflicted persons venture out of their home, it is often reluctantly and with anxious anticipation of discomfort, apprehensively looking forward to their return to the safety of home. For those who are not housebound, it is not uncommon for agoraphobic persons to establish a geographic perimeter encircling their home, be it a few blocks or a few miles, within which they feel safe to venture.

Agoraphobia is most commonly related to Panic Disorder. Persons with Panic Disorder experience sudden, intense episodes of fear or discomfort, accompanied by various somatic and cognitive symptoms (Barlow, 2002). These most often include palpitations, chest pain, sweating, trembling, shortness of breath, and numbness or tingling in the hands, as well as fears of dying, losing control, or going crazy. Although feelings of panic can occur as a feature of almost any anxiety disorder, Panic Disorder is distinguished by these feelings seemingly random, unpredictable, "out-of-the blue" occurrence (Barlow, 2002). According to *DSM* criteria (American Psychiatric Association, 2000), the attacks must include at least four panic symptoms, peak in severity within 10 minutes, and be followed by a minimum of 1 month of persistent worry about having a future attack. It is the seemingly random nature of the attacks that makes it impossible for the person to predict in what situations another attack will occur. This unpredictability results in the avoidance of any situation where a panic attack is perceived as likely to occur. Not only are specific places avoided, but agoraphobics may manifest avoidance of specific substances (e.g., caffeine, alcohol, medications) or physical activities (e.g., exercise, sex) that produces physical sensations resembling the symptoms associated with panic attacks.

Most clinical research of the past 20 years supports the theory that the anticipation of spontaneous, random panic attacks precedes the development of most cases of Agoraphobia (Katerndahl & Realini, 1997; Swinson, 1986; Thyer & Himle, 1985, 1987). Panic Disorder may occur either with or without the presence of Agoraphobia. In cases where situational avoidance is minimal, Panic Disorder without Agoraphobia is diagnosed. When the degree of situational avoidance results in marked social and occupational impairment, Panic Disorder with Agoraphobia is the chosen diagnosis.

Agoraphobia is present to varying degrees in many cases of Panic Disorder, yet the converse may not be true. When agoraphobic avoidance occurs in the absence of full-blown panic symptoms, or is accompanied by milder attacks with fewer than four paniclike symptoms (termed a "limited symptom attack"), the diagnosis Agoraphobia without history of Panic Disorder, or AWOPD, is used (American Psychiatric Association, 2000). In approximately 57% of cases of AWOPD (Goisman et al., 1995), the person typically presents with a limited number of paniclike symptoms. Others present with persistent situational avoidance surrounding the occurrence of some potential physical catastrophe such as a heart attack or embarrassment such as loss of bladder control, having diarrhea, or vomiting in public places (Barlow, 2002). In commenting on the features of patients presenting with a diagnosis of Agoraphobia without panic attacks, Thyer, Himle, Curtis, Cameron, and Nesse (1985, p. 209) observed that this group "often suffered from some somatic ailment of an unpredictable or spasmodic nature, such as epilepsy or colitis. This physical illness often served as the functional equivalent to panic attacks in terms of agoraphobic restrictions." See also the work of Pinto (1972) in this regard.

The diagnosis of AWOPD is a controversial one that is not well understood. Some clinical researchers argue that it does not represent a distinct diagnosis but rather a milder, uncomplicated subtype of Panic Disorder (Goisman et al., 1995). Based on community samples of persons reporting agoraphobic symptoms, epidemiological researchers (Wittchen, Reed, & Kessler, 1998) argued that panic attacks occurred in only a minority (32%) of

941 agoraphobic respondents, and therefore constituted a distinct diagnostic category. What accounts for this discrepancy of opinion? It appears, in part, to be due to the differences in the populations studied. Studies of clinical populations (those actively seeking treatment for psychiatric disorders) reveal an overwhelming prevalence of panic symptoms among agoraphobics. On the other hand, community samples of agoraphobics (those not necessarily seeking treatment) have found a much lower prevalence of panic symptoms (Weissman, 1985; Weissman, Leaf, Blazer, Boyd, & Florio, 1986). These differences can, in part, be accounted for by the idea that people with panic symptoms are more likely to seek treatment, and those who do are often impaired with multiple symptoms (Boyd, 1986). Also, there is evidence that community-based epidemiologic studies may have overestimated the prevalence of AWOPD due to misdiagnosis (Barlow, 2002). Methodological problems inherent in epidemiological surveys, including the use of lay interviewers rather than seasoned clinicians, may limit their usefulness in understanding AWOPD (Horwath, Lish, Johnson, Hornig, & Weissman, 1993). For example, the Epidemiologic Catchment Area survey of the prevalence of mental disorders in 18,000 Americans living in diverse communities (Weissman, 1985) mistakenly diagnosed people living in poor neighborhoods who reported being naturally fearful of venturing out into unsafe areas as having AWOPD. What may actually have been cases of normal fear-induced avoidance was mistaken for Agoraphobia. In addition, there is evidence that these interviewers consistently failed to distinguish between Agoraphobia and other anxiety disorders, such as specific phobias (Horwath, Lish, Johnson, Hornig, & Weissman, 1993; McNally, 1994; Wittchen et al., 1998).

Despite the ambiguity of the diagnosis of AWOPD, the best estimates of its prevalence are that it is quite common, with a lifetime rate of 5.3% of the population (Eaton, Kessler, Wittchen, & Magee, 1994; Kessler et al., 1994; Magee, Eaton, Wittchen, McGonagle, & Kessler, 1996). The average age of onset of AWOPD is not clear; however, due to its relationship to Panic Disorder, it may be assumed to be a disorder of early adulthood. Marked gender differences exist, with females outnumbering males by more than 2 to 1 (Bekker, 1996; Kessler et al., 1994). Other gender differences exist as well. A study of 96 women and 58 men with Panic Disorder with Agoraphobia (PDA) by Turgeon, Marchand, and Dupuis (1998) found that women with PDA reported more severe agoraphobic symptoms than men with PDA, including greater avoidance, more catastrophic thoughts, more feared bodily sensations, and more frequent comorbid diagnoses of either Social Phobia or Posttraumatic Stress Disorder.

Various hypotheses have been offered to explain this gender discrepancy, the most well-supported being the greater cultural acceptability of women to report being afraid and to manage this fear through avoidance. A study by Chambless and Mason (1986) found that agoraphobic avoidance by either males or females was significantly inversely correlated with higher masculinity scores on a measure of sex roles. That is, the less one endorsed traditionally masculine traits in oneself, the more a tendency toward agoraphobic avoidance. Studies by Pierce and Kirkpatrick (1992) and Ginsburg and Silverman (2000) confirmed that males in samples of young adults and children consistently underreport feeling fearful.

Significant gender differences can also be found in the manner in which men and women cope with anxiety. Many more men than women self-medicate with alcohol or nicotine as a means to endure rather than avoid feared situations (Barlow, 2002). Alcohol abuse, alcohol dependence, and nicotine dependence are much more prevalent among persons with Panic Disorder with Agoraphobia (Amering et al., 1999; Himle & Hill, 1991; Thyer, McNeece, & Miller, 1987). Levels of alcohol abuse in AWOPD are lower than in PDA (Himle & Hill, 1991), perhaps reflecting the less severe, debilitating nature of this diagnosis. There is evidence that panic and agoraphobic symptoms may worsen during the premenstrual and postpartum period due to hormonal alterations affecting the experience of somatic sensations (Barlow, 2002).

Cultural differences may influence the presentation of panic and agoraphobic symptoms. Studies have found consistent levels of Panic Disorder and Agoraphobia among African American, Hispanic American, and European American groups (Eaton et al., 1991; Horwath, Johnson, & Hornig, 1993), but African Americans are underrepresented in treatment settings for these disorders. It is theorized that African Americans use different coping strategies to gain relief from anxiety, including religiosity and help seeking for standard medical complaints (Paradis, Hatch, & Friedman, 1994). It is not clear to what extent socioeconomic status or availability of social support factors may account for these differences.

Due to the ambiguity of the AWOPD diagnosis, there is simply not sufficient research evidence to specify the course of the disorder, nor the degree of social and occupational impairment from AWOPD. Nor are we able to accurately describe the costs of this level of impairment to society. Based on its relationship to PDA, as a type of PDA "lite," we can assume that clients with AWOPD likely suffer from levels of social, occupational, and physical disability comparable, but perhaps not equal, to clients with Panic Disorder and Agoraphobia. Because clients with AWOPD do not tend to present for treatment (Antony & Swinson, 2000), the cost to society in terms of worker productivity and increased health care cannot be determined. The lifetime course of AWOPD has not been specified through research; however, it is assumed to be a chronic disorder. Obviously, much more research is needed to clarify the nature of the AWOPD diagnosis and its impact on its sufferers and society as a whole.

Evidence-Based Approaches to Assessment

The purpose of assessment is fourfold: (1) to confirm or establish the clinical diagnosis and to rule out competing, alternative diagnoses; (2) to measure the severity of the presenting problem and associated problems; (3) to aid in the selection of the appropriate treatment strategies; and (4) to measure the individual's response to treatment (Antony & Swinson, 2000).

The assessment of the agoraphobic client is complicated by the fact that the condition itself often prevents comfortable travel outside of a specific geographic range, and therefore many sufferers will either not seek help or, if they do, will require a Herculean effort to get to the clinician's office or treatment setting. Not infrequently, a request is made to conduct an evaluation by phone or in the client's home. Services provided by phone are controversial in that the lack of face-to-face contact leaves important clinical information about the client, such as attitude, mood, and affect, unattainable by the evaluating clinician. It should be considered only in the absence of all other options. Assessment performed in the agoraphobic client's home can provide a potentially rich source of clinical information about the problem and how it affects daily functioning and lifestyle. Despite its usefulness, therapist liability as well as the limitations on therapist's available time may discourage the routine use of in-home evaluation services for the agoraphobic client. Online evaluation over the Internet using webcam equipment that enables the client and therapist to see and hear each other in real time is a useful and increasingly available option. Such technology may be a potential godsend for some agoraphobics.

Semistructured Diagnostic Interviews

The Anxiety Disorders Interview Schedule IV (Di Nardo, Brown, & Barlow, 1994) and the Structured Clinical Interview for *DSM-IV* (SCID; First, Spitzer, Gibbon, & Williams, 1995) are commonly used and empirically supported clinician-administered semistructured interviews. They assess the full range of anxiety disorders, as well as mood, substance use, and other common comorbid disorders. Because the SCID was developed by psychiatrists, it also includes a medical history and screens for psychotic disorders. Among the data obtained by both are the frequency, intensity, and duration of anxiety symptoms, their antecedents, and patterns of avoidance behavior, including Agoraphobia. Unfortunately, due to the length of administration (2 to 4 hours), these instruments may not be practical for nonresearch settings.

Unstructured Clinical Interviews

The unstructured clinical interview is the most commonly used method of collecting information about the person presenting with Agoraphobia without history of Panic Disorder. First, a detailed review of the presenting complaint, including the onset and course of the most troubling symptoms, should be conducted to establish or confirm the diagnosis. Data are gathered about symptom frequency and intensity and impact on the person's daily functioning. Stressful life events and traumatic experiences that preceded the onset of symptoms are revealing, as is the client's level of functioning prior to the onset of symptoms (premorbid functioning). Physiological sensations such as dizziness and shortness of breath that cause discomfort are noted. Data about patterns of agoraphobic avoidance should be gathered, including distorted ideas, beliefs, and attitudes that engender agoraphobic avoidance. Measures taken to ward off discomfort when venturing beyond one's safety zone are noted, such as always carrying bottles of water, a cell phone, or antianxiety medications or sitting near exits when attending movies or at restaurants.

The developmental history of the symptoms is ascertained by questions about when and in what manner the symptoms first appeared and evolved into the present situation. Developmental factors such as early parenting and other family issues can help the clinician and client gain a more complete understanding of both the factors that contributed to the development of the presenting problem and the beliefs, attitudes, and behaviors that maintain the problem. For example, an early behavioral pattern of avoiding rather than confronting psychological discomfort, or being raised by parents who overfocused on potential dangers in the environment, may provide clues about the early life spawning of later life agoraphobic avoidance.

Questions about the impact of the symptoms on work, career, family functioning, and romantic relationships may provide clues as to the presence of secondary gains from avoidance of travel, such as dependency on other family members for transportation. A review of the client's medical, family, and social history, in addition to other psychiatric conditions that may be present, such as depression or substance abuse, should be conducted to better target the overall treatment strategy.

Throughout the entire assessment process, the social worker gathers information to be used in the formulation of an intervention strategy that will subsequently be used in psychosocial treatment, such as cognitive-behavior therapy.

Self-Report Measures

Self-rating inventories enable the clinician to measure the levels of key dimensions of the overall agoraphobic problem. Frequently used scales include the Agoraphobic Scale (Ost, 1990) and the Mobility Inventory for Agoraphobia (Chambless, Caputo, Jasin, Gracely, & Williams, 1985). The Agoraphobic Cognitions Questionnaire (Chambless, Caputo, Bright, & Gallagher, 1984) was designed to assess beliefs (e.g., "I am going to pass out" and "I am going to go crazy") associated with panic anxiety in Agoraphobia.

Due to the frequent presence of at least some level of panic symptoms in AWOPD, measures such as the Anxiety Sensitivity Index (Peterson & Reiss, 1993) and the Body Sensations Questionnaire (Chambless et al., 1984) can be used to measure the extent to which an individual is fearful of the sensations associated with anxiety and panic attacks or attributes neutral bodily sensations in a biased or catastrophic manner.

Behavioral Avoidance Tests

The behavioral avoidance test (BAT) is a commonly used form of behavioral assessment for anxiety disorders during which the client, accompanied by the therapist, is asked to enter or approach situations that are typically avoided, while his or her reactions are observed and measured (Barlow, O'Brien, & Last, 1984; Williams & Rappoport, 1983). Prior to the BAT, therapist and client determine a list of challenging situations rated according to increasing difficulty. The situations typically avoided by agoraphobic clients include visiting a shopping mall, sitting in a darkened theater, and eating in a restaurant. During the BAT, the therapist records the actual level of discomfort and avoidance engendered by the task using a client-rated scale called the subjective units of distress scale (SUDS). The client rates from 0 to 10 the degree of discomfort encountered in each situation, with 10 describing overwhelming anxiety and avoidance, and 0 no discomfort or avoidance at all. This information is ranked in order of levels of fear and avoidance generated, and is used by the therapist to construct a road map for subsequent practice during exposure-based treatment.

Evidence-Based Approaches to Intervention

Social workers have for decades been in the forefront of research, development, and utilization of evidence-based approaches to the treatment of anxiety disorders, including Agoraphobia, in academic, public, and private clinical settings. Evidence-based treatments for Panic Disorder without history of Agoraphobia include psychosocial treatment, mainly cognitive-behavior therapy, and biological agents including antianxiety and antidepressant medication. Although it is beyond the scope of this chapter to provide details, it is important that social workers be knowledgeable about biological approaches and their role in the evidence-based treatment of anxiety disorders. This section focuses primarily on psychosocial treatment, which is the realm of clinical social work. However, it is important that social workers, as members of the clinical treatment team, appreciate the importance of collaboration with other mental health professionals (e.g., psychiatrists, psychologists) to utilize their expertise to provide optimum client care.

Evidence-based psychosocial treatments for Agoraphobia without history of Panic Disorder include five main types of cognitive-behavioral strategies: (1) in vivo, or real-life, exposure to feared situations, such as walking alone in a shopping mall or riding public transportation; (2) interoceptive exposure to panic-related bodily sensations, for example, breathing hard through a straw to both evoke and habituate to the fear of dizziness and breathlessness; (3) cognitive strategies to challenge anxiety and fear/avoidance-generating beliefs and attitudes; (4) self-regulation strategies such as progressive relaxation training and breathing retraining exercises to effectively slow down or attenuate anxious physiological responses; and (5) involving the spouse or significant other in cognitive-behavioral treatment. It goes without saying that if the client experiences some sort of somatic ailment whose episodes serve as the functional equivalent to panic attacks (e.g., epilepsy, spastic colon), the underlying physical condition requires successful management, if not resolution, prior to undertaking the treatment of the secondary condition of Agoraphobia.

In Vivo Exposure: Overcoming Fear of External Situations

In vivo exposure as a treatment for Agoraphobia was first described in the clinical literature in the early 1960s (Marks & Gelder, 1965; Meyer & Gelder, 1963). Its technique has evolved and been refined over the decades to its current usage. Its effectiveness has been demonstrated repeatedly in controlled experiments comparing it to either no treatment or a placebo treatment, with 60% to 70% showing enduring clinical benefit (Burns, Thorpe, & Cavallaro, 1986; Cohen, Monteiro, & Marks, 1984; Emmelkamp & Kuipers, 1979; Jansson, Jerremalm, & Öst, 1986; Mathews, 1978; Mavissakalian & Barlow, 1981; O'Brian & Barlow, 1984).

In vivo exposure reduces anxiety and avoidance by systematically challenging clients to repeatedly confront situations that are feared and avoided, until the anxiety or discomfort subsides. Research has demonstrated that optimal effectiveness of in vivo exposure is achieved when exposure is prolonged and allows for maximal reduction in anxiety over the course of the exposure session (Marks, 1978; Marshall, 1985). Clients should be encouraged to limit distractions by focusing their full attention on the anxiety-provoking situation (Craske, Street, & Barlow, 1989). Safety signals, such as the presence of a safe person, or overprotective behaviors, such as carrying a cell phone, bottled water, or vial of medication when venturing out of the home, lead to short-term reductions in fear, but in the long term help to maintain agoraphobic avoidance. To achieve maximum benefit from exposure sessions, all safety behaviors should be limited or eliminated completely (Barlow, 2002).

It is important to plan the exposure strategy well in advance. Implementing successful in vivo exposure requires a fairly precise road map of structured exercises that are derived from the initial assessment. External situations that trigger discomfort or avoidance (such as going to a shopping mall or standing in line) are ranked in order of difficulty from least to most in what is termed an *anxiety hierarchy.* Clients are instructed in the use of the SUDS (Wolpe, 1973) to monitor the anxiety they experience in exposure situations. Typically the SUDS is a 100-point scale, where 0 represents minimal or no anxiety and 100 represents the worst state of anxiety imaginable. Then, starting with the situations that evoke a moderate degree of anxiety, around 50 to 60 SUDS, the client practices discomfort arousal directly in that situation. Exposure practice requires that the client remain in the situation for as long as it takes for the natural process of anxiety reduction, or *habituation,* to occur. Typically 90 minutes is required for complete habituation to occur, but not infrequently more or less time is needed, depending on the client's response. The exposure is repeated daily until SUDS levels aroused in the situation are consistently 20 or less. The client similarly challenges each successive situation on the anxiety hierarchy until habituation has been achieved for all items. The intensity of exposures should be considered carefully, as different approaches have their strengths and weaknesses and studies have been equivocal regarding their benefits. At levels of low intensity, the effects of exposure will not generalize to more difficult situations (Antony & Swinson, 2000). A study by Foa, Blau, Prout, and Latimer (1977) found that induction of very intense stress (versus moderate stress) during exposures does not lead to increased improvement. Feigenbaum (1988), on the other hand, found that very intensive, ungraded exposure was clearly more effective than graded, gradual exposure at 5-year follow-up and, contrary to previous studies, had lower attrition rates (though selection bias may have scared away more skittish subjects reluctant to participate in the intensive exposure). For practical purposes, it is recommended that for maximal effectiveness, the intensity should be in the moderate to high range, of around 70 SUDS or even more as the client can tolerate.

Due to the degree of discomfort generated in the exposure sessions, especially the initial ones, it is highly advisable practice for the social worker to accompany the client. This has several benefits. First, it provides comforting assistance to the client, who is attempting to do something highly uncomfortable and unpleasant for perhaps the first time in a long time, thus increasing compliance with the overall treatment effort. Second, the social worker can monitor whether the client is doing the exposure correctly as far as pacing, length, and intensity of the exposure. Avoidance, distraction, safety, and overprotective behaviors, known to decrease the effectiveness of the exposure, can be modified quickly and directly. Third, the social worker can model adaptive coping skills and appropriate risk-taking behaviors for the agoraphobic client, such as walking into a crowded mall or standing in a crowded elevator. It is important, however, to fade the social worker's direct assistance during exposures and encourage the client's independence and self-efficacy by requiring daily solo home exposure practice between sessions. Friends and family members can serve as helpful coaches for particularly fearful clients doing exposures when the social worker is not available. They can provide useful social support for the client's efforts to persist in exposure practices. A caveat is that they, too, must eventually limit and then curtail their involvement to avoid reinforcing dependency on them as safety signals.

Overall, it is recommended that clients practice exposure frequently. There is evidence that daily exposure sessions, conducted over a relatively short period of time, are more effective than one session per week conducted over many weeks (Foa, Jameson, Turner, & Payne, 1980).

Interoceptive Exposure: Overcoming Fear of Internal Sensations

As mentioned in a preceding section, Agoraphobia without history of Panic Disorder may involve fears of internal bodily sensations similar to those of clients with Panic Disorder with Agoraphobia. However, instead of the fear of an actual panic attack as seen in Panic Disorder clients, those with AWOPD may fear and avoid bodily sensations associated with medical conditions that may cause shame, humiliation, or embarrassment in public. Examples include fears of choking or fainting in public and losing bladder control. The client with AWOPD closely scrutinizes his or her body for sensations associated with fear, potential embarrassment, or humiliation. The sensations themselves serve as cues for agoraphobic avoidance.

Interoceptive exposure (exposure to sensations arising *from within the body*) was developed by Barlow and Craske (1994) as a method of helping agoraphobic clients overcome the fear of bodily sensations (e.g., dizziness, racing heart) that lead to agoraphobic avoidance. Conducted in a manner similar to in vivo exposure, the client is systematically exposed to avoided physical sensations. First a series of *symptom-induction tests* are conducted whereby the client elicits various avoided sensations in the presence of the social worker and measures the SUDS arising from those sensations. Client and therapist target for testing those sensations considered most relevant to the client's agoraphobic concerns. These may involve such activities as hyperventilating (to simulate light-headedness), shaking one's head from side to side (to simulate dizziness), spinning around in a circle (dizziness), running in place (palpitations), breathing rapidly through a straw (suffocation), staring into a light or a spot on the wall (depersonalization), applying a tongue depressor (choking), drinking a caffeinated beverage (racing heart), or drinking a large quantity of water (urinary urgency). The social worker then rank-orders the level of SUDS elicited by the most uncomfortable sensations to form an *anxiety hierarchy*. Then, beginning with the least threatening sensations (around 60 to 70 SUDS), the client practices repeatedly eliciting targeted sensations, both in the office and at home. Due to the fatigue that often accompanies interoceptive exposures, sessions may be shorter in length, say 15 minutes each, and repeated 3 to 4 times per day until SUDS reduces to 20 or less for all targeted interoceptives.

Interoceptive exposure is then combined with in vivo exposure in the actual avoided external settings, such as shopping malls, theaters, and restaurants. Exposure practice is most effective if done for approximately 1.5 to 2 hours per day over a period 1 to 3 weeks. Like in vivo exposure, it is important that, over time, the therapist fade his or her accompanying the client during exposures to foster greater self-reliance and self-efficacy. After progress is achieved, the client is encouraged to become a "discomfort junkie"—making exposure a daily part of life by voluntarily bringing on uncomfortable sensations in any and all naturalistic settings: standing in line, riding on an elevator, or driving. Examples of purposely eliciting sensations include walking briskly up a flight of stairs (pounding heart), wearing something tight around the neck (gagging), and standing up suddenly from a prone position (dizziness).

Typical Problems

Problems that typically arise doing exposure therapy with agoraphobic clients frequently involve several common issues. Clients occasionally refuse to do an exposure or complain that it's too difficult for them. It is important for the social worker to remain positive and encourage the client to try a simpler, less anxiety-provoking exposure—trying even smaller baby steps. Failure of clients to habituate to external and interoceptive cues is frequently due to the client engaging in subtle avoidance, overprotective, and/or safety behaviors such as distraction, "numbing out," or covert use of antianxiety medication. These are considered maladaptive impediments to progress and should be discouraged. Occasionally, a medical condition such as an inner ear disorder, mitral valve prolapse, asthma, or poor night vision may contribute to the failure of avoidance to lessen with exposure.

Sometimes the client lacks adequate information about the feared condition or situation that is the focus of the agoraphobic avoidance. Corrective information about, for example, the physiology of fainting or choking or the survival value and harmlessness of paniclike symptoms can be useful.

Environmental stress factors such as job termination, marital distress, and family illness can interfere with the best treatment efforts and are frequent causes of dropping out (Grilo et al., 1998). It is important for the social worker to remain attuned to these outside sources of interference and distraction and address them with the client to assess their potential impact. Due to the great emotional and time demands required by cognitive-behavioral therapy (CBT), there are times where CBT should be prudently suspended until the client's environment has stabilized. Taken up at a later time when the sole focus can be on the treatment, there is much greater chance of success.

Cognitive Strategies

Cognitive therapy is an important component in the treatment of Agoraphobia without history of Panic Disorder. It is based on a model of psychopathology that views the avoidance-based behaviors of Agoraphobia as founded in the distorted negative thoughts, assumptions, beliefs, and predictions about the imminence of catastrophic harm or danger (Antony & Swinson, 2002). The process of cognitive therapy encourages the client to replace automatic distorted thoughts with more balanced and realistic predictions and assumptions. Thus, by altering the thoughts, beliefs, and assumptions that precede anxiety responses, fear responses to both internal sensations and external situations can be modified.

Common distorted beliefs among persons with AWOPD involve inaccurate appraisals about the meaning of bodily sensations and situations as preludes to catastrophic events. These beliefs can be organized into a number of overlapping cognitive styles that represent the information-processing biases inherent in anxious thinking (Antony & Swinson, 2000): (a) Arbitrary inference involves deriving conclusions that are drawn with little or no supporting evidence or making overestimations of the likelihood of negative events occurring; (b) selective abstraction involves the client paying too much attention to information that confirms his or her anxious beliefs, while ignoring other important or relevant information; (c) catastrophic thinking involves assuming that should a particular event or consequence occur, it would be unmanageable; (d) all-or-nothing thinking is a perfectionist style of thinking whereby clients hold unreasonably high, rigid standards regarding their own behavior and is reflected in clients' excessive use of terms such as "should," "always," and "never."

Examples of distorted thoughts are listed in Table 16.1. In some cases, the categories overlap.

Cognitive therapy involves four steps in a process known as "cognitive restructuring" (Antony & Swinson, 2000). First, through a series of open-ended questions, the social worker assists the client to identify his or her anxious beliefs and derives the client's fearful predictions of catastrophic events, as exemplified in Table 16.1. Second, the social worker assists the client to generate alternative beliefs, for example, alternative reasons for dizziness (such as hunger, having a cold or flu) other than heart attack, or alternative consequences of being anxious in public other than social humiliation. At times, the social worker must provide corrective information by educating the client regarding, for example, the medical likelihood of fainting or the safety of flying or riding an elevator. Corrective information that is relevant to the client's fears can help the client overcome ingrained distorted beliefs and assumptions.

Table 16.1 Common Distorted Beliefs among People with Agoraphobia

My racing heart is a sure sign I'm having a heart attack (arbitrary inference, selective abstraction).

I always must have an escape plan for every place I go in case I get anxious (catastrophic thinking, all-or-nothing thinking).

If I get anxious, people will think that I'm crazy (arbitrary inference).

If I don't leave a situation when I feel anxious, my fear will spiral out of control (catastrophic thinking).

If I'm dizzy, I will definitely faint (catastrophic thinking; all-or-nothing thinking).

If I faint, I'll be so embarrassed I'll never show my face again (catastrophic thinking).

I must always remain completely calm while in public (all-or-nothing thinking).

I will suffocate if I'm stuck in an elevator (arbitrary inference).

If I'm not always within eyeshot of a bathroom, I'll lose control and urinate on myself (catastrophic thinking).

If I choke on food, I'll make a fool of myself (catastrophic thinking, arbitrary inference).

The next step in cognitive therapy ̶ to regard their beliefs as hypotheses or g̶ things are and to thoughtfully examine the ev̶ porting or contradicting their fearful beliefs. Thr̶ known as a "Socratic dialogue," clients are taught to g̶ ternative beliefs, explanations, and predictions that may̶ or contradict their original beliefs and assumptions. The follo̶ are examples (Antony & Swinson, 2000) of the type of question̶ that can generate alternative explanations and beliefs:

- Do I know for sure that my prediction will come true?
- What does my past experience tell me about the likelihood of my prediction coming true?
- Are there times when I have made the same prediction and it did not come true?
- Are there facts or statistics that can help me decide whether my prediction is likely to come true?
- What are some other possible interpretations for this situation?
- How might another person interpret this situation?

As described earlier, a common thinking bias in agoraphobic clients involves assuming that should a particular outcome occur it would be terrible and unmanageable (catastrophic thinking). Challenging catastrophic thinking involves guiding the agoraphobic client to imagine the most feared outcome and generate possible ways to actually cope with it, rather than emphasizing the awfulness of it. Examples are examining the feared versus the actual consequences of sweating in a crowded room, having to leave a crowded movie theater, and fainting in a shopping mall.

A cognitive therapy technique that is useful to assist clients during acute periods of fear and anxiety is the use of *rational self-statements*. These are statements made to remind oneself of alternative, nonanxious beliefs in situations where it may not be practical to go through the complete steps of cognitive restructuring. Examples of rational self-statements useful for agoraphobia are the following:

- Anxiety is uncomfortable, but not dangerous.
- If I wait it out, eventually my anxiety will reduce on it's own.
- If the worst thing happens, I'll just deal with it then.
- Just because something bad could happen does not make it likely to happen.

It is often a good idea to have clients write down these mantras on pieces of paper and place them in accessible places, for example, in a wallet or on the bathroom mirror, for easy reference.

Clients are encouraged to use diaries and monitoring forms and to challenge their anxiety-generating thoughts and beliefs on

⟩rm for Agoraphobia (Example)

History of Panic Disorder

365

involves teaching clients

esses about the way

dence either sup-

gh a process

nerate al-

modify

	Fearful Thought and Prediction	Rational Response	Outcome
g	I must leave immediately or I'll faint!	This is a very familiar feeling and I've never fainted. Even if I did faint, it would be brief and I'd be fine. Others may notice, but my self-consciousness would soon pass.	After a few minutes, I was fine. Much ado about nothing. SUDS = 20
10/4 6:00 P.M. 85	Stuck in traffic driving home from work, no available exits.	I'll get sick here in the car, have to stop, and be rescued by EMT.	I could get sick right here, but even if I do, I'll just continue driving until I get to an exit. I'll take care of my problem then.	I felt bad, but the feeling passed. I exited the highway as I normally do. SUDS = 30.

a daily basis. Such forms (see Table 16.2), while varying in specific organization and focus, typically instruct the client to identify anxiety-provoking situations, measure the level of anxiety (using the SUDS scale), identify the fearful, automatic beliefs and automatic assumptions that accompany the fearful reactions, and then challenge the dysfunctional appraisals with more rational responses, interpretations, and predictions.

Through daily, persistent practice clients can effectively incorporate these alternative beliefs and predictions into a newly emerging, alternative cognitive scheme that empowers them to cope with anxiety more effectively.

Self-Regulation Strategies Reconceptualized

Helping clients control the physiological responses to anxiety has long been a component of effective treatment for anxiety disorders, including Agoraphobia. Two of the more established methods include *progressive relaxation training* and *breathing retraining.* Progressive relaxation, developed by Jacobson (1938), employs a method of alternating voluntary muscle tension and release in seven muscle groups. The method is designed to be used to both lower overall state anxiety and to establish alternative responses to counteract panic and avoidance. Breathing retraining (BRT), developed by Barlow and Cerny (1988), is a breathing control technique that combines slow-paced breathing (counting inhales and exhales) with a particular focus on originating the breath from the diaphragm rather than from the upper chest. When practiced regularly, it has been found to be a useful means of controlling anxiety symptoms such as hyperventilation with its associated symptoms of dizziness, light-headedness, and fainting (Garssen, de Ruiter, & Van Dyke, 1992).

Although these techniques have a long history in the arsenal of strategies used to assist clients with anxiety disorders including Agoraphobia, recent reconceptualizations of such techniques have cast their usefulness in doubt. First, empirical studies have failed to show significant differences between BRT and placebo as to their effects on patients with Panic Disorder and Agoraphobia (Garssen et al., 1992; Hibbert & Chan, 1989). A study by Schmidt et al. (2000) concluded that BRT did not add any clear benefits to a treatment package consisting of psychoeducation, cognitive restructuring, and exposure-based techniques (in vivo and interoceptive exposure). The investigators concluded that by teaching clients to control their anxiety, the social worker is unwittingly sanctioning avoidance and/or distraction from the anxiety-related sensations, which, according to the theoretical model of cognitive-behavior therapy, is maladaptive (Barlow, 2002) and should not be *routinely* included in treatment for Agoraphobia.

According to Antony and Swinson (2000), breathing retraining may be useful for the client who frequently hyperventilates during exposure sessions. This can be observed by the social worker especially if the client complains of light-headedness and feelings of fainting during exposure work. Another situation is when the client specifically requests to be taught a relaxation method. Being armed with a coping tool to manage anxiety in exposure situations can have a psychologically powerful motivating effect, thereby encouraging compliance to CBT. Clients who refuse to practice exposures without a coping strategy should be taught BRT. A helpful description of the entire breathing retraining procedure can be found in Zuercher-White (1999).

Spouse or Significant Other Involvement in Cognitive-Behavioral Therapy

It has been observed by clinicians treating agoraphobic clients that progress in treatment not infrequently results in marital difficulties as the sufferer becomes more independent and less reliant on his or her partner (Hafner, 1984). Furthermore, relationship problems have been shown to predict relapse in clients who receive CBT for Agoraphobia (Bland & Hallam, 1981, cited in Antony &

Swinson, 2000). Therefore, it is vital that the social worker consider the social system that provides the context for the treatment of Agoraphobia, the natural province of social work. Many investigators have studied the inclusion of significant others or partners in the cognitive-behavioral treatment of Agoraphobia (Barlow et al., 1984; Daiuto, Baucom, Epstein, & Dutton, 1998). The investigators hypothesized that involving a motivated partner had distinct benefits above unassisted CBT for the following reasons: (a) The partner, trained as a potential coach, can provide a level of support for the agoraphobic, especially during the initially fearful stages of in vivo exposure; (b) by their involvement in the treatment process, partners gain a better understanding of Agoraphobia and the subtle ways they may be reinforcing agoraphobic behaviors (e.g., their role as safe persons); and (c) by their active involvement they may be less likely to feel threatened by their partner's success and independence.

Not all investigators found support for the inclusion of significant others in treatment (e.g., Emmelkamp et al., 1992 in Barlow), and sometimes the best partner may not be the client's spouse. An adult child or close friend or neighbor can be helpful in the supportive role (Barlow, 2002). However, most studies generally confirm the usefulness of enlisting partners and significant others for support during treatment for Agoraphobia (Barlow, 2002).

Summary

Fortunately, social workers who counsel and treat clients with anxiety disorders have a substantial body of empirical knowledge available to guide them in making decisions as to how best to intervene. Those studies provide solid support for the use of cognitive-behavioral procedures, including in vivo and interoceptive exposure and cognitive restructuring (Antony & Swinson, 2000). There is also considerable support for the role of pharmacologic treatment, with the use of antidepressants (tricyclic antidepressants and selective serotonin reuptake inhibitors) and anxiolytic agents (benzodiazepines) for reducing agoraphobic avoidance (Ballenger et al., 1988). Clearly, the social worker has an important role as a member of the treatment team helping anxiety disordered clients.

However, in the case of clients with Agoraphobia without history of Panic Disorder, the choices are not so clear. Given the statistical and theoretical ambiguity of the diagnosis, there is little if any research that addresses treatment procedures specific to the diagnosis of AWOPD. Almost all of the available studies on the efficacy of psychosocial and biological treatments target patients with Panic Disorder with Agoraphobia, and in most of those studies, the patients *suffered from no more than mild to moderate Agoraphobia* (Barlow, 2002). It is against this backdrop of ambiguity regarding both the diagnosis of AWOPD and the lack of available studies that the social worker must make choices as to how best to intervene with clients with AWOPD. If the clinician assumes (based on evidence presented in this chapter) that AWOPD is most likely related to Panic Disorder with Agoraphobia rather than a distinct disorder unto itself, studies of efficacy of various forms of CBT for PDA provide at least tentative support for the use of cognitive-behavioral procedures as the basis for intervening for AWOPD clients.

Considering the evidence supporting the use of pharmacological treatments for Agoraphobia, the social worker is often faced with the decision when to refer for medication evaluation and when to begin CBT. Many times, clients will make the decision themselves, either by refusing medication in favor of CBT or refusing CBT and insisting on medication. In either case, in studies of clients with Panic Disorder with Agoraphobia, both CBT and pharmacological treatments have been shown to be about equally effective, at least in the short term (Barlow & Craske, 1994; Barlow, Gorman, Shear, & Woods, 2000). For clients who present with severe, comorbid depression, a stronger case can be made for the overall effectiveness of the use of antidepressant medication in relieving painful depressive symptoms. Depressive symptoms interfere significantly with the ability to focus, concentrate, and therefore benefit from CBT. Therefore, a referral to a psychiatrist for medication evaluation seems most appropriate before beginning CBT.

Not infrequently, clients with anxiety disorders resist treatments, especially medication, that could potentially provide significant relief. This can be a source of frustration to the social worker's efforts to help the client. In the author's experience, agoraphobic clients, due to their personality penchant for needing to be in control, often manifest fears of external influence that is beyond their control. Taking a medication poses such a threat—that a pharmacological agent would be unleashed within the body and affect them in a manner that is uncontrollable and unpredictable and therefore dangerous. The social worker who is well-versed in psychopharmacology of anxiety disorders can dispel some of the misconceptions agoraphobic clients often have about medications: their side effects, dosages, and course of treatment. Bentley and Walsh (2000) is recommended in this regard. Calm reassurance, factual information, and encouragement can often spur motivation in the client reluctant to pursue potentially beneficial medication options.

Surprisingly, combining CBT with pharmacological treatment is about as effective as either approach alone (Barlow et al., 2000). However, clients given both treatments who attribute their progress to medication may be more vulnerable to relapse when medication, for whatever reason, must be discontinued (Basoglu, Marks, Kilic, Brewin, & Swinson, 1994). There is evidence that the benefits of CBT are much more enduring and relapse rates tend to be higher for patients receiving medication alone than for those receiving CBT alone (Barlow et al., 2000).

Considering all the evidence, the first-line treatment for most clients with Agoraphobia without history of Panic Disorder appears to be CBT, with in vivo exposure being an essential component of the treatment package. Cognitive therapy may be added to enhance the effectiveness of exposure. Teaching self-regulation methods such as breathing retraining appears to have little support except in limited circumstances. Medications should be considered an appropriate option for clients who do not respond to an adequate trial of CBT alone, who are likely to be noncompliant with treatment procedures, or who have a significant comorbid depression.

Another important resource for the sufferer of Agoraphobia that should not be overlooked by the social worker is the peer-conducted anxiety disorders support group, conducted both online (unmoderated and moderated peer-to-peer groups on the Internet) and offline (in hospitals, churches, and schools, conducted live, face-to-face). A number of research studies over the past 25 years have confirmed the value and benefits of self-help mutual aid groups (Kurtz, 1988; Kyrouz, Humphreys, & Loomis, 2002; Raiff, 1984). Through mutual sharing and camaraderie, the groups promote a sense of empowerment through fostering a sense of community, discouraging isolation, providing opportunities for emotional expression, promoting self-acceptance, dispelling misconceptions and myths surrounding the disease, providing relevant treatment information, and encouraging compliance with medical treatment. Likewise, there has been considerable research into online/Internet-based support groups, and though not nearly as extensive as for offline groups, the available evidence likewise points to significant benefits for patients with a variety of diseases and psychiatric disorders (Eysenbach, Powell, Englesakis, Rizo, & Stern, 2004; Finn, 1995, 1999; Perron, 2002; Weinberg, Uken, Schmale, & Adamek, 1995). Online support groups are conducted as chat rooms, newsgroups, message boards, and e-mail mailing lists. They offer the advantage over offline groups of flexibility (clients can participate on their own schedule), added confidentiality (no one sees you if you don't want to be seen), diversity (there are groups for every specific disorder imaginable), and convenience (clients can log on in the comfort of their own home). More research needs to be done to clarify both the advantages and disadvantages of online support groups. However, considering that anxiety disorders, including Agoraphobia, are very isolating conditions that provoke shame and embarrassment among its sufferers, online support groups may be of particular value to the housebound agoraphobic client. Via the virtual medium of the Internet, agoraphobic clients can gain valuable information, support, and human interaction with the world beyond the constraints of their disorder in ways previously unimaginable.

Study Questions

1. Twice as many women present with symptoms of Agoraphobia than men. What evidence from studies in the social and behavioral science literature can be cited to account for these differences?

2. Agoraphobia without history of Panic Disorder is a controversial diagnosis. What is the basis for this controversy? In your argument, cite evidence derived from the epidemiological and clinical survey literature on Panic Disorder and Agoraphobia.

3. African Americans are underrepresented in settings that treat anxiety disorders such as Agoraphobia without history of Panic Disorder. What theories of African American help-seeking behavior are used to explain this observation? What personal observations can you cite from your own experiences to either support or refute these explanations?

4. There is evidence that social reinforcement and secondary gain factors may contribute to the appearance and maintenance of agoraphobic symptoms. Cite the evidence supporting this view.

5. Evidence-based psychosocial treatments for Agoraphobia without history of Panic Disorder include four types of cognitive-behavioral strategies. Describe each one by including the specific goal of the strategy, the rationale for its use, and specific treatment techniques employed in its implementation.

6. In the course of clinical treatment of Agoraphobia, the social worker/psychotherapist must make decisions about which specific cognitive-behavioral treatment strategy to employ and when or when not to refer for psychopharmacological treatment. Based on the evidence provided in the chapter, develop an algorithm that can be used to aid in these decisions, employing the following parameters: severity of avoidance, chronicity of symptoms, previous medication response, situational and interoceptive fears, family involvement with the symptoms, expectations of the client, and motivation for cognitive-behavioral treatment.

7. Psychiatric disorders, including Agoraphobia without history of Panic Disorder, influence and are influenced by the social and environment context in which these disorders occur.

Cite evidence for such an interaction and implications for the treatment of the agoraphobic client.

8. Discuss the objectives of clinical assessment in the process of the psychosocial treatment for Agoraphobia. Then describe the assessment tools that are available to the social worker, including their purpose and usefulness, to achieve those objectives.

9. Discuss the role of the peer-to-peer support group in the recovery process for agoraphobic clients. Include relevant evidence in support of both face-to-face and online support groups.

10. New technologies, including the Internet, have become increasingly relevant within the health care marketplace as a means of sharing information about mental health disorders and available services. Discuss the advantages and disadvantages of their use for agoraphobic clients.

References

American Psychiatric Association. (2000). *Diagnostic and statistical manual of mental disorders* (4th ed., text rev.). Washington, DC: Author.

Amering, M., Bankier, B., Berger, P., Griengle, H., Windhaber, J., & Katchnig, H. (1999). Panic disorder and cigarette smoking behavior. *Comprehensive Psychiatry, 40,* 35–38.

Antony, M. M., & Swinson, R. P. (2000). *Phobic disorders and panic in adults: A guide to assessment and treatment.* Washington, DC: American Psychological Association.

Ballenger, J., Burrows, G. D., DuPont, R. L., Lesser, I. M., Noyes, R., Jr., Becknold, J. C., et al. (1988). Alprazolam in panic disorder and agoraphobia: Results from a multicenter trial. *Archives of General Psychiatry, 45,* 413–422.

Barlow, D. H. (2002). *Anxiety and its disorders.* New York: Guilford Press.

Barlow, D. H., & Cerny, J. A. (1988). *Psychological treatment of panic.* New York: Guilford Press.

Barlow, D. H., & Craske, M. G. (1994). *Mastery of your anxiety and panic: Pt. II. Client workbook.* San Antonio, TX: Psychological Corporation.

Barlow, D. H., Gorman, J. M., Shear, M. K., & Woods, S. W. (2000). A randomized controlled trial of cognitive-behavioral treatment versus imipramine and their combination for panic disorder: Primary

outcome results. *Journal of the American Medical Association, 283,* 2529–2536.

Barlow, D. H., O'Brien, G. T., & Last, C. G. (1984). Couples treatment of agoraphobia. *Behavior Therapy, 15,* 41–58.

Basoglu, M., Marks, I., Kilic, C., Brewin, D., & Swinson, R. (1994). Alprazolam and exposure for panic disorder with agoraphobia: Attribution of improvement to medication predicts subsequent relapse. *British Journal of Psychiatry, 164,* 652–659.

Bekker, M. H. J. (1996). Agoraphobia and gender: A review. *Clinical Psychology Review, 16,* 129–146.

Bentley, K. J., & Walsh, J. (2000). *The social worker and psychotropic medication: Toward effective collaboration with mental health clients, families, and providers.* Florence, KY: Wadsworth Publishing.

Bland, R. C., & Hallam, R. S. (1981). Relationship between response to graded exposure and marital satisfaction in agoraphobics. *Behavior Research and Therapy, 19,* 335–338.

Boyd, J. H. (1986). Use of mental health services for the treatment of panic disorder. *American Journal of Psychiatry, 143*(12), 1569–1574.

Burns, L. E., Thorpe, C. L., & Cavallaro, L. A. (1986). Agoraphobia 8 years after behavioral treatment: A follow-up study with interview, self-report, and behavioral data. *Behavioral Therapy, 17,* 580–591.

Chambless, D. L., Caputo, G. C., Bright, P., & Gallagher, R. (1984). Assessment of "fear of fear" in agoraphobics: The Body Sensations Questionnaire and the Agoraphobic Cognitions Questionnaire. *Journal of Consulting and Clinical Psychology, 52,* 1090–1097.

Chambless, D. L., Caputo, G. C., Jasin, S. E., Gracely, E. J., & Williams, C. (1985). The Mobility Inventory for Agoraphobia. *Behavior Research and Therapy, 23,* 35–44.

Chambless, D. L., & Mason, J. (1986). Sex, sex-role stereotyping, and agoraphobia. *Behavior Research and Therapy, 24,* 231–235.

Cohen, M. E., Monteiro, W., & Marks, I. M. (1984). Two-year follow-up of agoraphobics after exposure and imipramine. *British Journal of Psychiatry, 144,* 276–281.

Craske, M. G., Street, L. L., & Barlow, D. H. (1989). Instructions to focus upon or distract from internal cues during exposure treatment of agoraphobic avoidance. *Behavior Research and Therapy, 27,* 663–672.

Daiuto, A. D., Baucom, D. H., Epstein, N., & Dutton, S. S. (1998). The application of behavioral couples therapy to the assessment and treatment of agoraphobia: Implications of empirical research. *Clinical Psychology Review, 18,* 663–687.

Di Nardo, P., Brown, T. A., & Barlow, D. H. (1994). *Anxiety Disorders Interview Schedule for DSM-IV.* San Antonio, TX: Psychological Corporation.

Eaton, W. W., Kessler, R. C., Wittchen, H.-U., & Magee, W. J. (1994). Panic and panic disorder in the United States. *American Journal of Psychiatry, 151,* 413–420.

Emmelkamp, P. M., & Kuipers, A. C. M. (1979). Agoraphobia: A follow-up study 4 years after treatment. *British Journal of Psychiatry, 128,* 86–89.

Emmelkamp, P. M., Van Dyck, R., Bitter, M., Heins, R., Onstein, E. J., & Eisen, B. (1992). Spouse-aided therapy with agoraphobia. *British Journal of Psychiatry, 160,* 51–56.

Eysenbach, G., Powell, J., Englesakis, M., Rizo, C., & Stern, A. (2004). Health related virtual communities and electronic support group: Systematic review of the effects of online peer to peer interactions. *British Medical Journal, 328,* 1166–1171.

Feigenbaum, W. (1988). Long-term efficacy of ungraded versus graded massed exposure in agoraphobics. In I. Hand & H.-U. Wittchen (Eds.), *Panic and phobias: Treatments and variables affecting course and outcome* (pp 83–88). Berlin, Germany: Springer-Verlag.

Finn, J. (1995). Computer-based self-help groups: A new resource to supplement support groups. *Social Work with Groups, 18,* 109–117.

Finn, J. (1999). An exploration of helping processes in an online self-help group focusing on issues of disability. *Health and Social Work, 24,* 220–231.

First, M. B., Spitzer, R. L., Gibbon, M., & Williams, J. B. (1995). *Structured Clinical Interview for DSM-IV Axis I Disorders (SCID).* New York: New York State Psychiatric Institute, Biometrics Research Department.

Foa, E. B., Blau, J. S., Prout, M., & Latimer, P. (1977). Is horror a necessary component of flooding (implosion)? *Behavior Research and Therapy, 15,* 397–402.

Foa, E. B., Jameson, J. S., Turner, R. S., & Payne, L. L. (1980). Massed versus spaced exposure sessions in the treatment of agoraphobia. *Behavior Research and Therapy, 18,* 333–338.

Garssen, B., de Ruiter, C., & Van Dyck, R. (1992). Breathing retraining: A rational placebo? *Clinical Psychology Review, 12,* 141–153.

Ginsburg, G. S., & Silverman, W. K. (2000). Gender role orientation and fearfulness in children with anxiety disorders. *Journal of Anxiety Disorders, 14,* 57–67.

Goisman, R. M., Warshaw, M. G., Steketee, G. S., Fierman, E. J., Rogers, M. P., Goldenberg, I., et al. (1995). *DSM-IV* and the disappearance of agoraphobia without a history of panic disorder: New data on a controversial diagnosis. *American Journal of Psychiatry, 15,* 1438–1443.

Grilo, C. M., Money, R., Barlow, D. H., Goddard, A. W., Gorman, J. M., Hofmann, S. G., et al. (1998). Pretreatment patient factors predicting attrition from a multicenter randomized controlled treatment study for panic disorder. *Comprehensive Psychiatry, 39,* 323–332.

Hafner, R. J. (1984). The marital repercussions of behavior therapy for agoraphobia. *Psychotherapy, 21,* 530–542.

Hibbert, G. A., & Chan, M. (1989). Respiratory control: Its contribution to the treatment of panic attacks—A controlled study. *British Journal of Psychiatry, 154,* 232–236.

Himle, J., & Hill, E. (1991). Alcohol abuse and the anxiety disorders. *Journal of Anxiety Disorders, 5,* 237–245.

Horwath, E., Lish, J. D., Johnson, J., Hornig, C. D., & Weissman, M. M. (1993). Agoraphobia without panic: Clinical reappraisal of an epidemiologic finding. *American Journal of Psychiatry, 150*(10), 1496–1501.

Horwath, E., Johnson, J., & Hornig, C. D. (1993). Epidemiology of panic disorder in African-Americans. *American Journal of Psychiatry, 150,* 465–469.

Jacobson, E. (1938). *Progressive relaxation.* Chicago: University of Chicago Press.

Jansson, L., Jerremalm, L., & Öst, L.-G. (1986). Follow-up of agoraphobic patients treated with exposure in vivo or applied relaxation. *British Journal of Psychiatry, 149,* 486–490.

Katerndahl, D. A., & Realini, J. P. (1997). Comorbid psychiatric disorders in subjects with panic attacks. *Journal of Nervous and Mental Diseases, 185,* 669–674.

Kessler, R. C., McGonagle, K. A., Zhao, S., Nelson, C. B., Hughes, M., Eshleman, S., et al. (1994). Lifetime and 12-month prevalence of *DSM-III-R* psychiatric disorders in the United States: Results form the National Comorbidity Survey. *Archives of General Psychiatry, 51,* 8–19.

Kurtz, L. F. (1988). Mutual aid for affective disorders: The manic depressive and depressive association. *American Journal of Orthopsychiatry, 58*(1), 152–155.

Kyrouz, K., Humphreys, K., & Loomis, C. (2002). A review of research on the effectiveness of self-help mutual aid groups. In B. J. White & D. J. Madara (Eds.), *American Self-Help Clearinghouse self-help group sourcebook* (7th ed., pp. 1–16). Denville, NJ: American Self-Help Group Clearinghouse.

Magee, W. J., Eaton, W. W., Wittchen, H.-U., Mc-Gonagle, J. A., & Kessler, R. C. (1996). Agoraphobia, simple phobia, and social phobia in the National Comorbidity Survey. *Archives of General Psychiatry, 53,* 159–168.

Marks, I. M. (1978). *Living with fear.* New York: McGraw-Hill.

Marks, I. M., & Gelder, H. G. (1965). A controlled retrospective study of behavior therapy in phobic patients. *British Journal of Psychiatry, 111,* 561–573.

Marshall, W. L. (1985). The effects of variable exposure in flooding therapy. *Behavior Therapy, 16,* 117–135.

Mathews, A. M. (1978). Fear-reduction research and clinical phobias. *Psychological Bulletin, 85,* 390–404.

Mavissakalian, M. R., & Barlow, D. H. (Eds.). (1981). *Phobias: Psychological and pharmacological treatment.* New York: Guilford Press.

McNally, R. J. (1994). *Panic disorder: A critical analysis.* New York: Guilford Press.

Meyer, V., & Gelder, M. G. (1963). Behavior therapy and phobic disorders. *British Journal of Psychiatry, 109,* 19–28.

O'Brian, G. T., & Barlow, D. H. (1984). Agoraphobia. In S. M. Turner (Ed.), *Behavioral treatment of anxiety disorders.* New York: Plenum Press.

Ost, L.-G. (1990). The Agoraphobia Scale: An evaluation of its reliability and validity. *Behavior Research and Therapy, 28,* 323–329.

Paradis, C. M., Hatch, M., & Friedman, S. (1994). Anxiety disorders in African Americans: An update. *Journal of the National Medical Association, 86,* 609–612.

Perron, B. (2002). Online support for caregivers of people with a mental illness. *Psychiatric Rehabilitation Journal, 26,* 70–77.

Peterson, R. A., & Reiss, S. (1993). *Anxiety Sensitivity Index revised test manual.* Worthington, OH: IDS Publishing Corporation.

Pierce, K. A., & Kirkpatrick, D. R. (1992). Do men lie on fear surveys? *Behavior Research and Therapy, 30,* 415–418.

Pinto, R. (1972). A case of movement epilepsy with agoraphobia treated successfully by flooding. *British Journal of Psychiatry, 121,* 287–288.

Raiff, N. R. (1984). Some health related outcomes of self-help participation. In A. Gartner & F. Riessman (Eds.), *The self-help revolution* (pp. 183–193). New York: Human Sciences Press.

Schmidt, N. B., Wollaway-Bickel, K., Trakowski, J., Santiago, H., Storey, J., Koselka, M., et al. (2000). Dismantling cognitive-behavioral treatment for panic disorder: Questioning the utility of breathing retraining. *Journal of Consulting and Clinical Psychology, 68,* 417–424.

Swinson, R. P. (1986). Reply to Kleiner. *Behavior Therapist, 9,* 110–128.

Thyer, B. A., & Himle, J. (1985). Temporal relationship between panic attack onset and phobic avoidance in agoraphobia. *Behavior Research and Therapy, 23,* 607–608.

Thyer, B. A., & Himle, J. (1987). Phobic anxiety and panic anxiety: How do they differ? *Journal of Anxiety Disorders, 1,* 59–67.

Thyer, B. A., Himle, J., Curtis, G. C., Cameron, O. G., & Nesse, R. M. (1985). A comparison of panic disorder and agoraphobia with panic attacks. *Comprehensive Psychiatry, 26,* 208–214.

Thyer, B. A., McNeece, C. A., & Miller, D. F. (1987). Alcohol abuse among alcoholics: A community-based replication. *Alcoholism Treatment Quarterly, 4,* 61–67.

Turgeon, L., Marchand, A., & Dupuis, G. (1998). Clinical features in panic disorder with agoraphobia: A comparison of men and women. *Journal of Anxiety Disorders, 12,* 539–553.

Weinberg, N., Uken, J. S., Schmale, J., & Adamek, M. (1995). Therapeutic factors: Their presence in computer-mediated support group. *Social Work with Groups, 18*(4), 57–69.

Weissman, M. M. (1985). The epidemiology of anxiety disorders: Rates, risks, and familial patterns. In A. H. Tuma & I. D. Maser (Eds.), *Anxiety and the anxiety disorders.* Hillsdale, NJ: Erlbaum.

Weissman, M. M., Leaf, P. I., Blazer, D. G., Boyd, J. H., & Florio, L. (1986). The relationship between panic disorder and agoraphobia: An epidemiologic perspective. *Psychopharmacology Bulletin, 43,* 787–791.

Williams, S. J., & Rappoport, A. (1983). Cognitive treatment in the natural environment for agoraphobics. *Behavior Therapy, 14,* 299–313.

Wittchen, H.-U., Reed, V., & Kessler, R. (1998). The relationship of agoraphobia and panic in a community sample of adolescents and young adults. *Archives of General Psychiatry, 55,* 1017–1024.

Wolpe, J. (1973). *The practice of behavior therapy* (2nd ed.). New York: Pergamon Press.

Zuercher-White, E. (1999). *Therapist protocol for overcoming panic disorder and agoraphobia.* Oakland, CA: New Harbinger.

Obsessive-Compulsive Disorder

Barbara Van Noppen, Joseph A. Himle,
and Gail Steketee

17
Chapter

Learning Objectives

After reading this chapter, the reader will be able to:

- Discuss the prevalence, social and financial costs, importance of social work involvement, and operational definition of Obsessive-Compulsive Disorder (OCD).
- Utilize assessment methods to establish a psychosocial context of the client's OCD symptoms and severity.
- Establish an evidence-based psychosocial treatment plan.
- Identify the rationale and likely efficacy for cognitive-behavioral treatment of OCD.
- Implement evidence-based treatment for OCD.

Overview of the Problem

Prevalence

Obsessive-Compulsive Disorder (OCD), once thought to be a rare illness with a poor prognosis (Nymberg & Van Noppen, 1994), is now recognized as the fourth most common psychiatric disorder in the United States. In the United States a large-scale survey showed a 6-month prevalence of 1.6% and lifetime prevalence of

2.5% (Karno & Golding, 1991). International research has re-vealed that OCD tends to occur at approximately the same rate in various countries despite cultural differences (see Steketee, Van Noppen, Cohen, & Clary, 1998).

Rapoport (1986) reported that 50% of adults with OCD had developed symptoms by age 15, and fewer than 15% of clients experienced symptom onset after age 35 (Rasmussen & Tsuang, 1986). Boys tend to experience an onset of symptoms earlier (ages 14 to 17) and more severely than girls, whose symptoms begin around age 19 (Rasmussen & Eisen, 1990). During childhood, boys are diagnosed with OCD twice as often as girls (Swedo, Rapoport, Leonard, Lenane, & Cheslow, 1989), but in adulthood the diagnosis occurs nearly equally in men and women (Karno, Golding, Sorenson, & Burnham, 1988; Rasmussen & Tsuang, 1986). The course of OCD tends to be chronic, with some fluctuation (Eisen & Steketee, 1997).

There is no correlation between race, socioeconomic status, or religion and OCD in adult populations (Karno & Golding, 1991). No difference in the racial distribution of OCD has been observed in epidemiological research (Myers et al., 1984). However, clients from minority groups rarely present at OCD clinics for treatment, although clinical reports of minority clients are available (e.g., Chambless & Williams, 1995).

Financial and Social Costs

The impact of OCD on clients' lives is often reflected in its tremendous financial and social costs. Impact on functioning and cost of treatment are two important indices of the financial cost associated with OCD. A report derived from a poll of Obsessive Compulsive Foundation members showed that 41% were unable to work due to OCD symptoms, with an average loss of 2 years of wages (Hollander, Rowland, Stein, Broatch, & Himelein, 1995). Lifetime hospital costs were estimated in the $5 billion range and lifetime indirect costs for lost wages at $40 billion (Hollander et al., 1995). In 1990 alone, $2.1 billion was spent on institutional and hospital care, office-based mental health care, medication, and other support costs (DuPont, Rice, Shiraki, & Rowland, 1995). Overall, 25% to 30% of men and women with OCD receive some kind of federal financial assistance (Steketee, 1997). Adults with OCD tend to drop out of college and earn lower salaries (more often under $10,000 and less often over $40,000; Henderson & Pollard, 1988). These figures indicate the profound cost of this illness to society and have implications for health care and family systems.

Obsessive-Compulsive Disorder carries tremendous social costs to clients and families, although these costs are less quantifiable. The obsessions and compulsions experienced by clients can pervade much of their daily behavior and social interaction, leading to drastic interference in social and occupational functioning. Hollander et al. (1995) found that 64% of the OCD sufferers surveyed lowered their career aspirations, and 62% reported difficulty maintaining relationships because of symptoms. Although marriage rates of OCD respondents in epidemiological studies do not differ from national norms, in clinical samples the rates of nonmarriage are much higher (Steketee, 1997).

More than 80% of 225 family members of adults with OCD reported disruption in the personal life of a family member (Cooper, 1996). Seventy-five percent of relatives experienced disrupted family social life, 72% reported a loss of interpersonal relationships, a loss of leisure was noted by 64%, and 62% noted financial problems. Calvocoressi and colleagues (1999) further confirmed the adverse social impact, noting that family accommodation was present for 88% of spouses or parents and correlated significantly with client symptom severity and global functioning, family dysfunction, and relatives' stress. Family accommodation refers to participation in rituals, modification of personal and family routines, facilitating avoidance, and taking on client's responsibilities (Calvocoressi et al., 1995). Some family accommodation may occur because relatives feel responsible for the incapacitation of the person with OCD. Relatives' excessive accommodation to compulsions contradicts exposure-based therapy and may perpetuate and reinforce symptoms and increase relatives' feelings of distress (Steketee, Van Noppen, Lam, & Shapiro, 1998). Family interactions increasingly are being studied in relation to OCD presentation and treatment, an area of much interest to social workers, given their person-in-environment orientation.

Social work practitioners play an important role in the assessment and treatment of OCD. Even with increasing recognition of OCD in the media, many sufferers are unaware that their symptoms represent a formally recognized diagnosis for which efficacious treatment exists. When people with OCD pursue medical treatment for other problems (e.g., dermatitis secondary to excessive washing), their symptoms may not be recognized by medical professionals as OCD. Similarly, OCD sufferers with somatic or hypochondriacal concerns often utilize health care providers to seek excessive reassurance for worries about their physical health. Social workers are likely to encounter clients or family members of clients with OCD as clinical practitioners in a multitude of mental health agencies, medical centers, and private practice settings. As described earlier, OCD impacts relationships within the family and is likely to be a source of stress between family members. Thus, in addition to treating OCD clients, social workers should also focus on family members who can benefit from psychoeducation, emotional support, and guidance for managing the stress associated with having a family member with OCD. Social workers can play a significant role in providing proper diagnosis, assessment, psychoeducation, and treatment of OCD.

Operational Definitions of the Problem

Obsessive-compulsive symptoms have been described in literature (Shakespeare's Lady Macbeth) and in religious writings (Bainton, 1950) throughout history. Clinical and scientific inquiry into OCD began at the turn of the century (Freud, 1909/1925; Janet, 1903; Pavlov, 1960; Schilder, 1938). The fourth edition of the *Diagnostic and Statistical Manual of Mental Disorders* (*DSM;* American Psychiatric Association, 2000) improves on past diagnostic formulations with regard to the clarity of criteria. To ensure proper treatment for OCD, it is critical to make an accurate diagnosis. In general, OCD is characterized by recurrent obsessions or compulsions that provoke distress and interfere with a person's normal routine and social and occupational functioning. Specifically, obsessions are intrusive thoughts, images, or impulses that the person perceives as inappropriate; they cause marked distress and impairment in functioning, and the duration of symptoms is greater than 1 hour per day. Compulsions or rituals are repetitive behaviors or mental acts performed in response to an obsession and purposely aimed at preventing a dreaded consequence or reducing discomfort generated by the obsession. Compulsions are not always overt actions, but can also be covert mental acts, such as praying, reviewing events, counting, and repeating words or phrases, to neutralize anxiety or feared outcomes. In addition, the *DSM* includes a "poor insight type," referring to the lack of recognition that the obsessions and compulsions are unreasonable or excessive for most of the time during the current episode. To meet criteria for OCD, a history of insight at some point during the disorder is required.

The most common obsessions, in descending order, are contamination, pathological doubt, somatic fears, need for symmetry and exactness, and aggressive and sexual fears (Rasmussen & Eisen, 1990). The most common physical compulsions, in descending order, are checking, washing, counting, need to ask for reassurance or confess, ordering, and hoarding (Rasmussen & Eisen, 1990). Examples of mental compulsions are counting, praying, list making, and repeating words or phrases in one's head. Most clients have more than one type of obsession and compulsion.

The distress associated with obsessions stems from cognitive domains of inflated responsibility and overestimation of threat, such as causing harm to others or self. The assumption that having a thought leads to action (thought-action fusion) is very common among clients with OCD. An additional cognitive feature is that thoughts are overly important and that uncertainty is intolerable. Certain compulsions are typically reported in association with specific types of obsessions. For example, worries of being responsible for something bad happening lead to checking rituals, such as repeatedly examining appliances to make sure they are turned off, making sure envelopes are sealed, and excessively seeking reassurance from others. To prevent harm, some clients may use mental rituals, such as counting repeatedly to a "good" number. Clients with contamination fears may take long showers, repeatedly wash their hands, use disinfectants, or avoid contact with objects. Ordering and arranging rituals tend to reduce discomfort about not feeling "just right" or may be used to prevent something bad from happening (magical thinking). Hoarding practices revolve around fears of forgetting, sentimental value, or ideas that ordinary items might be needed in the future (Kyrios, Steketee, Frost, & Oh, 2002).

Determining a precise differential diagnosis of OCD requires close attention to subtle clinical differences among disorders. Generalized Anxiety Disorder and OCD share some characteristics but are quite distinguishable. Obsessions in the form of thoughts, impulses, or images are not simply excessive worries about real-life problems, common to those with Generalized Anxiety Disorder. In addition, the content of the obsessions or compulsions is not restricted to a comorbid Axis I disorder. For example, a depressed person may have guilty ruminations, a person with a substance use disorder may be preoccupied with drugs, but these mental phenomena are not considered obsessions. Another diagnosis from which OCD should be differentiated is Obsessive-Compulsive Personality Disorder (OCPD), a personality syndrome characterized by orderliness, indecisiveness, perfectionism, and rigidity. Clients with OCPD typically have less insight that their behavior is problematic for others, except as it results in interpersonal conflict.

An emerging area of interest is the relationship between OCD and obsessive-compulsive related disorders or OC spectrum disorders. These include eating disorders, trichotillomania, skin picking, hypochondriasis, Body Dysmorphic Disorder (BDD), depersonalization disorder, Tourette's syndrome, sexual addictions and paraphilias, pathological gambling, and impulsive personality disorders. Rather than classifying these disorders categorically, Hollander (1993) proposed that OC spectrum disorders fall along a continuum of the dimensions of compulsivity and impulsivity, with a common inability to resist or delay urges to perform repetitive behaviors. On one end of the spectrum are the compulsive risk-aversive disorders, and at the other end are the impulsive risk-seeking disorders. Despite some similarities, there are distinguishing features between several spectrum disorders and OCD. For example, ruminations in BDD and anorexia are typically ego-syntonic (Steketee, 1993) rather than ego-dystonic. Trichotillomania, skin picking, and other impulse-control disorders such as gambling, shopping, and kleptomania are often referred to as compulsions, but do not necessarily involve obsessive thoughts, a hallmark feature of OCD. Furthermore, the compulsive behavior in spectrum disorders is usually experienced as pleasurable and is not intended to reduce discomfort.

Axis I disorders that commonly appear in conjunction with OCD are anxiety disorders, depression, substance abuse, eating disorders, hypochondriasis, and Schizophrenia. The highest rates of co-occurrence are with specific phobias (Karno et al., 1988), followed by Social Phobia and Panic Disorder (Steketee, Henninger, & Pollard, 2000). The rates of concurrence of minor or major depression with OCD is also high (Steketee, Henninger, et al., 2000). For treatment purposes, it is worth determining if depression is primary or secondary to OCD (Abramowitz, 2004). Clients report that depressive symptoms usually occur following the onset of OCD (Rasmussen & Eisen, 1992) and are often reduced by successful cognitive-behavioral and or pharmacologic treatment of OCD.

The "poor insight type" in *DSM-IV-R* better captures the clinical presentation of a small percentage of OCD clients who display almost delusional or overvalued thinking. In the past, some of these OCD patients may have received the diagnosis of Schizophrenia. This group of clients may have a poorer outcome than those with good insight. Clinically, this is an important diagnostic distinction for social workers to make as it holds relevance for treatment.

Among Axis II diagnoses, the personality disorders most often found in OCD clients are OCPD and Avoidant, Dependent, Histrionic, Passive-Aggressive, and Schizotypal Personality Disorders (Steketee, Henninger, et al., 2000). Interestingly, OCPD, the personality disorder long considered most similar to OCD, does not co-occur more frequently than other personality disorders (Pfohl & Blum, 1991).

Evidence-Based Approaches to Assessment

The assessment phase determines what type of treatment is preferable to clients and most likely to provide a good outcome (Abramowitz & Schwartz, 2003). Consistent with a social work focus on person-in-environment, information is sought about a client's cultural context, including religion and ethnicity, insight, functioning in social and family life, and work and leisure activities. For more detailed reviews of measurement instruments relevant for OCD, refer to Feske and Chambless (2000), Taylor (1998), and Antony, Orsillo, and Roemer (2001).

Structured Clinical Interviews

Diagnostic Interviews

A structured interview tool that measures specific components of OCD is the Anxiety Disorders Interview Schedule (ADIS; Di Nardo, Brown, & Barlow, 1994 [adult version]; Silverman, 1991 [child version]). The ADIS is particularly useful for diagnosing OCD because it permits clinicians to determine the type and severity of presenting obsessions and compulsions, including frequency, persistence, distress, and resistance associated with these symptoms. Included are sections to identify environmental stressors (family, work, finances, and health) and insight into obsessive fears, consistent with new *DSM-IV* criteria for the insight modifier. The ADIS allows diagnosis of other Axis I disorders, such as major depression, dysthymia, psychotic disorders, and substance abuse. The widely used Hamilton Scales for Anxiety and Depression (Hamilton, 1959, 1960), which assess depressed and anxious mood, are included in the ADIS. Finally, this interview contains a historical time line assessment allowing clinicians to date the onset of all current disorders to aid in decision making about the possible interrelationship among comorbid disorders and which to treat first. The value gained from the instrument's breadth of diagnostic inquiry and sensitivity to symptoms of OCD is well worth the 2 to 3 hours required for the interview.

An alternative structured diagnostic interview is the Structured Clinical Interview for *DSM-IV* Axis I Disorders—Patient Version (SCID-I/P; First, Spitzer, Gibbon, & Williams, 1995). Like the ADIS, this instrument determines whether subjects meet the diagnostic criteria for OCD and comorbid conditions. It includes a Global Assessment of Functioning scale that allows the clinician to record the client's level of functioning on a scale from 1 and 100 according to defined anchor points. This interview takes about 2 hours to complete.

Obsessive-Compulsive Disorder Symptom Measures

The Yale-Brown Obsessive Compulsive Scale (YBOCS; Goodman, Price, Rasmussen, Mazure, Delgado, et al., 1989; Goodman, Price, Rasmussen, Mazure, Fleischman, et al., 1989) includes both a symptom checklist and a scale that assesses severity of OCD symptoms. Also available are a children's version (Scahill et al., 1997) and a self-report version (see later discussion). The YBOCS is considered the standard assessment tool for OCD symptom severity and change and has well-established reliability and validity. One of its significant advantages is that it measures severity of OCD, irrespective of the types of obsessions and compulsions the client exhibits. The YBOCS was formulated to determine OCD symptom severity and symptom change during treatment, rather than whether a client qualifies for the diagnosis of OCD. The interviewer first provides definitions of obsessions and compulsions and then administers the symptom checklist, asking clients about 36 different types of obsessions and 23 types of compulsions. The 10-item YBOC Scale then assesses the degree of difficulty regarding time spent, interference, distress, resistance, and control of the client's most common obsessions and compulsions from the checklist. These 5 items are rated on 0 to 4 scales for both obsessions and compulsions.

The following scoring is considered standard: 0 to 7 = Subclinical, 8 to 15 = Mild, 16 to 23 = Moderate, 24 to 31 = Severe, 32 to 40 = Extreme. Most research studies require clients to have a total score of 16 or above (at least 1 hour of symptoms per day) to qualify. Successful outcomes are evident when scores drop below 15, and some studies have achieved average posttreatment scores in the range of 10 to 12 (see Franklin, Abramowitz, Kozak, Levitt, & Foa, in press). A number of revisions and variations of the YBOCS are currently under construction and likely to appear in the literature in the next few years (Steketee & Neziroglu, 2003). A self-report version of the YBOCS is available (see Baer, 1991). Steketee, Frost, and Bogart (1996) determined that the two versions were similar in psychometric properties, although clients tended to rate themselves somewhat lower than did clinicians.

The Maudsley Obsessional Compulsive Inventory (Hodgson & Rachman, 1977), a 30-item true/false questionnaire with five subscales, is another self-report symptom measure. The Padua Inventory is a 60-item instrument that assesses common obsessive-compulsive symptoms (Sanavio, 1988). It has demonstrated good reliability and validity and has also been revised and shortened by several different researchers. The YBOCS remains the instrument of choice at present because it allows greater cross-investigational comparisons.

Family Assessments

The Family Accommodation Scale for OCD, developed by Calvocoressi et al. (1995, 1999), is a 12-item scale administered by clinicians to relatives of OCD clients to assess their accommodating behaviors; it has shown good reliability and validity. Because greater family accommodation is associated with more family dysfunction, family stress, and rejecting attitudes toward the client, family interventions may be needed to address these difficulties (Van Noppen & Steketee, 2003). For example, Grunes, Neziroglu, and McKay (2001) observed that clients whose family members participated in treatment to reduce family stress benefited more from behavior therapy than clients whose family members were not in family treatment.

Assessment of Insight

To assess clients' degree of insight into the rationality of their OCD symptoms, clinicians can use one of two published scales. The Overvalued Ideas Scale (OVIS; Neziroglu, McKay, Yaryura-Tobias, Stevens, & Todaro, 1999) is a 10-item clinician-administered scale with good reliability and validity. The second scale is the Brown Assessment of Beliefs Scale (BABS; Eisen et al., 1998), a 7-item scale developed to assess insight for BDD. As with the OVIS, clinicians ask clients questions about the degree of their belief in their fear and feared consequences if they do not complete rituals. The BABS has shown good to excellent reliability and validity. Clinicians are urged to become familiar with methods for assessing insight because of the growing recognition of insight as a predictor of treatment outcome for OCD and OC spectrum disorders (Neziroglu, McKay, & Yaryura-Tobias, 2000; Neziroglu, Stevens, McKay, & Yaryura-Tobias, 2001).

Self-Report Measures

Personality Assessments

Some personality disorders may interfere with treatment, but these conditions are often difficult to diagnose reliably. Interview measures are quite time-consuming, so we recommend self-report instruments (although they may lead to overdiagnosis). The Personality Diagnostic Questionnaire (Hyler et al., 1988) is a commonly used instrument with adequate reliability and validity (Hyler, Skodol, Kellman, Oldham, & Rosnick, 1990). Another option is the SCID-II (Spitzer, Williams, Gibbon, & First, 1990), in which the patient first completes a questionnaire and the clinician inquires further about personality traits for personality disorders for which patients score at or near the threshold for diagnosis.

Assessment of Beliefs and Interpretations

Cognitive theory postulates that all people hold beliefs about themselves and the world that are derived from their family experience, culture, religion, and personal life experience. A group of expert clinicians have suggested that several types of beliefs are common for clients with OCD (Obsessive Compulsive Cognitions Working Group [OCCWG], 1997). The OCCWG developed an 87-item Obsessional Beliefs Questionnaire (OCCWG, 2001, 2003) that includes subscales for control of thoughts, importance of thoughts, responsibility, intolerance of uncertainty, overestimation of threat, and perfectionism. This instrument demonstrated good reliability and reasonably good validity. The Interpretation of Beliefs Inventory (OCCWG, 2001, 2003) is a 31-item instrument designed to assess immediate interpretations when obsessions occur. Both beliefs and interpretations provide an important basis for designing cognitive therapy.

Observational Measures

One observational instrument for assessing OCD treatment outcomes is the Behavioral Avoidance Test (BAT), which measures observable avoidance behavior and self-reported anxiety levels (Steketee, Chambless, Tran, Worden, & Gillis, 1995). Clients are asked to do a series of up to 7 stepwise tasks that usually produce significant anxiety or rituals. They are rated on whether they did the task, how much anxiety they reported, and whether they engaged in any rituals. A composite BAT score reflects OCD symptom severity. The BAT demonstrated good convergent and divergent validity, as well as sensitivity to the effects of treatment.

Behavioral and cognitive therapies commonly employ self-monitoring or self-recording of obsessions, rituals, distress, and avoidance behaviors as they occur on a daily basis. The distress associated with these features is measured on a subjective units of discomfort scale (SUDS), with ranges from 0 (no discomfort) to 100 (extreme distress). These observational behavioral measures are invaluable for understanding clients' experience of symptoms in real time and for tracking cues that precede symptoms and are important to include in exposure therapy.

Evidence-Based Approaches to Intervention

Individual Behavioral Treatment

Behavioral treatment of OCD involves two main elements: exposure to stimuli that trigger obsessional thoughts and associated anxiety or guilt (e.g., dirty surfaces, items out of order, using a stove, thoughts of harming others), coupled with efforts to prevent accompanying compulsive rituals. This treatment is referred to as exposure and response prevention (ERP) and is rooted in behavioral learning theory. The classic behavioral explanation for the maintenance of obsessive-compulsive behavior is based on Mowrer's two-stage learning theory (see Domjan & Burkhard, 1986). Stage 1 in this paradigm involves classical conditioning, wherein anxiety becomes associated with a specific event or stimulus (such as touching a dirty surface). Stage 2 involves operant conditioning, in which individuals engage in some behavior to neutralize or decrease the conditioned anxiety (e.g., hand washing). Any behavior that successfully reduces the negative emotional state (e.g., hand washing, straightening, checking) is negatively reinforced. Negative reinforcement is thought to maintain obsessive-compulsive behavior, which in turn maintains the conditioned anxiety by preventing natural reduction in anxiety (habituation) associated with prolonged contact with the conditioned stimulus. Over time, the original conditioned stimulus (e.g., blood on a sink) generalizes to other stimuli in the environment (e.g., avoiding doorknobs, shaking hands). Gradually, more avoidant and preventive behavior becomes necessary to reduce the conditioned anxiety.

The ERP treatment involves repetitive and prolonged exposure to the conditioned stimuli, permitting habituation of the conditioned anxiety, while response prevention interrupts the cycle of negative reinforcement that maintains the anxiety and the compulsive behavior. In practice, ERP begins with the generation of a hierarchy of exposure exercises designed to confront feared stimuli. Therapist and client discuss potential encounters with feared and avoided situations and collaboratively develop a list of these, progressing from easier to more challenging exercises. Clients learn to use the SUDS, described earlier, to rate each situation on the hierarchy according to the level of discomfort (0 to 100) it would provoke. After completing the hierarchical list, the client selects a beginning exposure exercise of mild to moderate difficulty, generally at a discomfort level of about 30 to 40 SUDS. For example, a person with contamination concerns might first agree to touch a wall surface in an office, followed by a commonly touched wall surface in the hallway, eventually moving on to a soiled light switch, and finally culminating with handling a challenging public restroom surface. Therapists encourage clients to focus their attention on the feared stimulus during exposure and to continue with the exercise until their anxiety improves. Clients use the SUDS to report their level of anxiety throughout the exposure session. These anxiety ratings help the client and social worker decide when it is time to progress from one exposure exercise to another and when an exposure session can be concluded.

Exposure exercises are often conducted in the presence of the clinician, who models the exercise for the client (Rachman & Hodgson, 1980). However, similar outcomes can be achieved when exposure exercises are given as prescriptive homework assignments without direct therapist involvement during the actual exposures (Emmelkamp, van den Heuvell, Ruphan, & Sanderman, 1989). In addition, clients whose fears include a strong focus on catastrophic outcomes (e.g., dying of AIDS, the house catching fire) can achieve added benefit when these real-life exercises are combined with exposure in imagination (Foa, Steketee, & Grayson, 1985).

Examples of exposure exercises are putting items out of order for persons with ordering or arranging compulsions, throwing away progressively more valued possessions for persons with hoarding compulsions, using a stove for a client with checking concerns, and handling scissors and knives in the presence of others for someone with harming obsessions. Given the wide range of OCD symptoms, the variety of exposure exercises are nearly limitless. All involve prolonged contact with an environmental stimulus that triggers distressing obsessions and an accompanying urge to ritualize.

The second primary feature of ERP, response prevention, involves delaying or blocking rituals altogether once the urge is activated by an exposure exercise. For example, exposure to putting items out of order for a client with ordering rituals would be followed by the response prevention strategy of asking the client not to straighten anything after the exposure. This ritual and avoidance prevention method can be gradual to match the exposure context, or intensive so that rituals are stopped from the outset of treatment. Little research is available to indicate the best method, but most treatments employ a graduated strategy that matches response prevention to the progress on the hierarchy.

The efficacy of individual ERP for adults with OCD is well established (Fals-Stewart & Lucente, 1993; Lindsay, Crino, & Andrews, 1997; Marks et al., 1988; van Balkom & van Dyck, 1998). In each case, ERP proved superior to the control condition in producing clinically significant improvement. Recent meta-analyses have further confirmed that ERP is an efficacious treatment for OCD, with most clients experiencing clinically significant improvements (Abramowitz, Franklin, & Foa, 2003). It is important to note that most of those who receive ERP for their OCD symptoms continue to experience some OCD symptoms posttreatment (Abramowitz, 1998).

Initial evidence also suggests that individual ERP is effective for pediatric OCD (De Haan, Hoogduin, Buitelaar, & Keijsers, 1998; Franklin et al., 1998; Knox, Albano, & Barlow, 1996; March, 1995; Piacentini, Bergman, Jacobs, McCracken, & Kretchman, 2002; Wever & Rey, 1997). One recent study randomly assigned Australian children with OCD to group ERP, individual ERP, or a brief wait-list control (Barrett, Healy-Farrell, & March, 2004). Investigators observed similar positive outcomes for group and individual ERP when each was compared to a wait-list control. Finally, a recent multicenter, randomized trial of CBT, antiobsessive medication (sertraline), and their combination versus a pill placebo control condition firmly established individual ERP as superior to placebo for pediatric OCD (Pediatric OCD Treatment Study [POTS] Team, 2004). The ERP interventions in many of these trials included cognitive therapy enhancements to usual ERP.

Cognitive Interventions

Despite the inherently cognitive nature of obsessions, which are defined as thoughts, images, and impulses, the effects of cognitive therapy (CT) on OCD symptoms were not formally studied until very recently. Cognitive therapy for OCD is based on findings that intrusive thoughts are normal phenomena, experienced by 80% to 90% of ordinary people, and that these normal intrusions are very similar in content to OCD obsessions (e.g., Rachman & de Silva, 1978). Theorists hypothesize that it is the misinterpretation of these intrusions that leads to the development of obsessions; consistent with behavioral theories of OCD, avoidance and rituals prevent the testing and discarding of the erroneous interpretations (Rachman, 1997; Salkovskis & Westbrook, 1989). As identified by expert clinical researchers of OCD (OCCWG, 1997), the types of misinterpretations made fall into the following major categories: overimportance of and need to control thoughts, overestimating the probability and severity of harm, excessive responsibility for harm, and the need for certainty and perfectionism. Some of these beliefs are thought to be specifically associated with OCD pathology (overimportance of thoughts, responsibility), whereas others are common among those with other psychiatric disorders (e.g., perfectionism, overestimation of threat; OCCWG, 1997).

The cognitive therapy developed to treat OCD is based on Aaron T. Beck's cognitive model and derived from methods used to treat other disorders such as depression. One central technique of CT is Socratic dialogue that involves a series of logical questions designed to help the client consider and evaluate the beliefs that support the OCD behavior. The responsibility pie technique is used when clients overestimate their responsibility for causing events (e.g., harming others). Comparisons of original and new estimates almost invariably help clients recognize their overestimation of their own responsibility. Another commonly used CT technique challenges clients' overestimation of harm by having them state the probability of their feared catastrophe (e.g., being fired for making a mistake) and then list all the steps required for this to occur. Invariably, the client's original probability estimate was greatly exaggerated compared to this more rational estimate. Other common strategies for helping clients correct mistaken interpretations and beliefs include metaphors and taking another perspective. Cognitive therapists can ask clients what view or actions others would recommend to them and why.

Several studies have shown the efficacy of this CT method. Van Oppen et al. (1995) determined that 12 sessions of CT were as effective as ERP; nearly 50% of clients who received CT were considered recovered, compared to 28% of those in ERP treatment. However, this study has been criticized for having a less effective ERP treatment than reported in other trials. Cottraux and colleagues (1989) found excellent effects from 20 sessions of CT, which also proved to be as effective as ERP after treatment and at a 1-year follow-up assessment. Both treatments significantly reduced OCD beliefs, and reduction in beliefs was related to improvement in OCD symptoms for *both* therapies. This study suggests that both CT and ERP may lead to change because they alter obsessive beliefs.

An important caveat is that CT does not appear to be as effective when applied in a group format as when delivered as an individual treatment (McLean et al., 2001). Thus, it appears that cognitive treatment should be tailored to each client. Recent studies indicate that cognitive therapy is an effective alternative to ERP, and can readily be combined with ERP methods, probably beginning with CT as a prelude to exposures. Cognitive therapy alone may be especially helpful for those who are reluctant to commit to any anxiety-provoking exposures.

Biological Interventions

Serotonin reuptake inhibitors (SRIs) are now established as the first-line medications for the pharmacological treatment of OCD (March, Frances, Carpenter, & Kahn, 1997). In multiple controlled trials with adults, clomipramine (e.g., Clomipramine Collaborative Study Group, 1991; Mavissakalian, Turner, Michelson, & Jacob, 1985), fluoxetine (e.g., Montgomery et al., 1993; Tollefson et al., 1994), sertraline (e.g., Greist, Chouinard, et al., 1995; Greist, Jefferson, et al., 1995), fluvoxamine (e.g., Goodman, Kozak, Liebowitz, & White, 1996), and paroxetine (Wheadon, Bushnell, & Steiner, 1993) were found to be superior to placebo. Trials with children and adolescents have also found clomipramine (e.g., DeVeaugh-Geiss et al., 1992; Flament et al., 1985), fluoxetine (e.g., Geller et al., 2001; March et al., 1998; Riddle et al., 1992), sertraline (POTS Team, 2004), and fluvoxamine (Riddle et al., 2001) to be superior to placebo and other drugs (Leonard et al., 1989). Meta-analytic results suggest that clomipramine may be superior to other serotonin reuptake inhibiting medicines in reducing OCD symptoms among adults (Ackerman & Greenland, 2002) and children (Geller, Biederman, & Stewart, 2003).

Numerous studies of adults have examined whether combining medication with CBT enhances outcomes over either treatment alone (Cottraux et al., 1989; Foa, Kozak, Steketee, & McCarthy, 1992; Hohagen et al., 1998; Marks et al., 1988; Rachman et al., 1979). Overall, these studies have not shown any added benefit to the combined treatment for adults with OCD (van Balkom & van Dyck, 1998). These studies support the efficacy of SRIs alone or in combination with CBT, but also suggest that OCD can be equally effectively treated without medication. Two recent studies of pediatric OCD showed that combined CBT and medication produced better outcomes than the medication alone (Neziroglu, Yaryura-Tobias, et al., 2000; POTS Team, 2004), and one of these studies found combined treatment superior to CBT alone (POTS Team, 2004).

Psychosurgical procedures, such as deep brain stimulation and gamma knife procedures, have been found to be helpful for persons with severe, treatment-resistant OCD (Baer, Rauch, & Ballantine, 1995; Kim, Chang, & Koo, 2003). These procedures usually result in few adverse effects on cognitive abilities or personality characteristics, yet they can be important methods of last resort for those clients whose severe OCD has not responded to aggressive pharmacotherapy or concentrated behavioral therapy.

Group Interventions

Group interventions for OCD usually involve a combination of psychoeducation, group support, and ERP. Group treatment is usually conducted in a once-weekly format over a 7- to 14-week period with 5 to 10 clinical participants per group and one or two therapists (Himle, Van Etten, & Fisher, 2003). Group sessions usually include some ERP conducted within the group session, in addition to heavy reliance on ERP homework. Many group ERP trials include some amount of family participation (Himle, Van Etten, et al., 2003). Several outcome studies of group ERP for adults with OCD have been completed. In the only controlled trial for adults with OCD, group ERP and individual ERP were both superior to relaxation control, with no significant difference observed between individual and group therapy (Fals-Stewart, Marks, & Shafer, 1993). Himle et al. (2001) reported positive and comparable outcomes with group ERP delivered in 7-week and 12-week formats. Another study found improvement with group ERP including family members, as well as group ERP without family inclusion (Van Noppen, Steketee, McCorkle, & Pato, 1997). Seven uncontrolled studies of group treatment reported significant improvement in OCD symptoms (Enright, 1991; Epsie, 1986; Hand & Tichatzky, 1979; Krone, Himle, & Nesse, 1991; Van Noppen, Pato, Marsland, & Rasmussen, 1998).

Fischer, Himle, and Hanna (1998) were the first to study group CBT for children and adolescents with OCD, and these researchers recently completed a second study of group CBT for adolescents with tic-related versus non-tic-related OCD (Himle, Fischer, et al., 2003). Both studies reported significant improvement in OCD symptoms. Theinemann and colleagues (Theinemann, Martin, Cregger, Thompson, & Dyer-Friedman, 2001) similarly observed significant improvement among 18 adolescents following a 14-week group CBT program. Finally, Barrett and colleagues (2004) recently found similar positive outcomes for children and adolescents.

Family Interventions

Several studies have examined various family characteristics and their relationships to obsessive-compulsive symptoms and treatment outcomes. High levels of expressed emotion, especially high levels of hostile, critical, negative interactions with family members, have been associated with increased symptoms among children (Leonard, Swedo, & Lenane, 1993) and adults (Chambless & Steketee, 1999; Steketee, 1993) with OCD. Clinical impressions suggest that family members who view OCD as an illness rather than a personal fault or malingering strategy are more likely to facilitate positive treatment outcomes (Van Noppen & Steketee, 2003). Family members are also known to adjust their lifestyle to accommodate their loved one's OCD symptoms. Family accommodations often include taking over responsibilities of the person with OCD, such as doing housework, managing home finances, or taking on child care responsibilities (Calvocoressi et al., 1995). Other family accommodations may include participating in rituals such as excessive hand washing and cleaning, providing reassurance, and checking doors, locks, stove, and so on at the request of the family member with OCD (Calvocoressi et al., 1995).

A specific family-based intervention for OCD that directly addresses family accommodation and negative reactions has yet to be developed. However, ERP programs with substantial family involvement have been devised for adults (Van Noppen et al., 1997) and children (Barrett et al., 2004) with OCD. These programs often encourage family members to reduce the amount of criticism and negative communications they direct toward their loved one with OCD. Family members are usually taught a model of OCD wherein symptoms are viewed as resulting from a combination of neurobiological and environmental factors that are not the fault of the person with OCD (Van Noppen & Steketee, 2003). Family members are instructed to disengage from their loved one's OCD symptoms by reducing critical comments and by gradually eliminating accommodating behaviors. Conversely, family members are encouraged to make positive comments when they notice improvement and to provide support when symptoms worsen. For pediatric OCD, interventions to reduce parental guilt and blame are also included in ERP programs that include family involvement (Piacentini et al., 2002).

Empirical support for including family members in ERP, although somewhat limited, suggests enhanced outcomes when family members are involved. Mehta (1990) found improved outcomes for OCD patients given family-based compared to patient-based CBT. Van Noppen and colleagues (1997) found that OCD patients who received group ERP with family participation were more likely to meet criteria for clinically significant improvement at follow-up compared to those who were given group treatment without family involvement. Finally, Grunes et al. (2001) randomly assigned OCD patients to receive either individual ERP coupled with a concurrent psychoeducational group for family members or individual ERP without family group. Those receiving ERP plus family group achieved greater improvements in obsessive-compulsive and depressive symptoms after treatment and at follow-up.

Summary

There are a number of evidence-based approaches to assessing persons meeting the *DSM* criteria for OCD, as well as several well-supported psychosocial and pharmacological forms of treatment. A large proportion of clients receiving these evidence-based treatments are likely to experience substantial clinical and social improvements whose effects are often well-maintained over time. These evidence-based interventions produce improvements considerably superior to those obtained by simply waiting (no treatment), receipt of credible placebo therapies, or experiencing conventional, nonspecific insight-oriented or supportive psychotherapy. Social workers asked to assist individuals who meet the *DSM* criteria for OCD are encouraged to become familiar with these research-based developments and to acquire clinical expertise in their competent provision.

Study Questions

1. Describe the social costs experienced by clients with OCD due to impaired functioning.

2. Provide an operational definition of OCD and differentiate the disorder from generalized anxiety.

3. What are some of the most common evidence-based assessments used by clinicians to diagnose OCD and rate symptom severity? Which are also used to assess OCD in children?

4. Imagine you are ready to begin an exposure and response prevention program for a person with obsessions and compulsions related to dirt, germs, and contamination. Give examples of exposure and response prevention exercises that may be relevant for this client.

5. Can medications and exposure and response prevention therapy be used concurrently to treat OCD? Are outcomes enhanced with this combination?

6. Discuss how cognitive interventions might enhance behavioral treatment.

7. Describe how group and family models have been used for clients with OCD.

References

Abramowitz, J. S. (1998). Does cognitive-behavioral therapy cure obsessive-compulsive disorder? A meta-analytic evaluation of clinical significance. *Behavior Therapy, 29,* 339–355.

Abramowitz, J. S. (2004). Treatment of obsessive-compulsive disorder in patients who have comorbid major depression. *Journal of Clinical Psychology, 60,* 1133–1141.

Abramowitz, J. S., Franklin, M. E., & Foa, E. B. (2003). Exposure prevention and ritual prevention for obsessive-compulsive disorder: Effects of intensive versus twice-weekly sessions. *Journal of Consulting and Clinical Psychology, 71,* 394–398.

Abramowitz, J. S., & Schwartz, S. (2003). Treatments for obsessive-compulsive disorder: Deciding what method for whom.

Brief Treatment and Crisis Intervention, 3(2), 261–273.

Ackerman, D., & Greenland, S. (2002). Multivariate meta-analysis of controlled drug studies for obsessive-compulsive disorder. *Journal of Clinical Psychopharmacology, 22,* 309–317.

American Psychiatric Association. (2000). *Diagnostic and statistical manual of mental disorders* (4th ed., text rev.). Washington, DC: Author.

Antony, M. M., Orsillo, S. M., & Roemer, L. (Eds.). (2001). *Practitioner's guide to empirically based measures of anxiety.* New York: Kluwer Press.

Baer, L. (1991). *Getting control.* New York: Plume.

Baer, L., Rauch, S. L., & Ballantine, T. (1995). Cingulotomy for intractable obsessive-compulsive disorder: Prospective long-term follow-up of 18 patients. *Archives of General Psychiatry, 52,* 384–392.

Bainton, R. H. (1950). *Here I stand: A life of Martin Luther.* New York: New American Library.

Barrett, P., Healy-Farrell, L., & March, J. S. (2004). Cognitive-behavioral family treatment of childhood obsessive-compulsive disorder: A controlled trial. *Journal of the American Academy of Child and Adolescent Psychiatry, 43,* 46–62.

Calvocoressi, L., Lewis, B., Harris, M., Trufan, S. J., Goodman, W. K., McDougle, C. J., et al. (1995). Family accommodation in obsessive-compulsive disorder. *American Journal of Psychiatry, 152,* 441–443.

Calvocoressi, L., Mazure, C., Stanislav, K., Skolnick, J., Fisk, D., Vegso, S., et al. (1999). Reliability and validity of the family accommodation scale for obsessive-compulsive disorder. *Journal of Nervous and Mental Disorders, 187,* 636–642.

Chambless, D. L., & Steketee, G. (1999) Expressed emotion and behavior therapy outcome: A prospective study with obsessive-compulsive and agoraphobic outpatients. *Journal of Consulting and Clinical Psychology, 67,* 658–665.

Chambless, D. L., & Williams, K. E. (1995). A preliminary study of African Americans with agoraphobia: Symptom severity and outcome of treatment with in vivo exposure. *Behavior Therapy, 26,* 501–515.

Clomipramine Collaborative Study Group. (1991). Clomipramine in the treatment of patients with OCD. *Archives of General Psychiatry, 48,* 730–738.

Cooper, M. (1996). Obsessive-compulsive disorder: Effect on family members. *American Journal of Orthopsychiatry, 66,* 296–304.

Cottraux, J., Mollard, E., Bouvard, M., Marks, I., Sluys, M., Nury, A. M., et al. (1989). A controlled study of fluvoxamine and exposure in obsessive-compulsive disorder. *International Journal of Clinical Psychopharmacology, 5,* 17–30.

De Haan, E., Hoogduin, K., Buitelaar, J. K., & Keijsers, G. P. J. (1998). Behavior therapy versus clomipramine in the treatment of obsessive-compulsive disorder in children and adolescents. *Journal of the American Academy of Child and Adolescent Psychiatry, 37,* 1022–1029.

DeVeaugh-Geiss, J., Moroz, G., Biederman, J., Cantwell, D., Fontaine, R., Greist, J. H., et al. (1992). Clomipramine hydrochloride in childhood and adolescent obsessive-compulsive disorder: A multicenter trial. *Journal of the American Academy of Child and Adolescent Psychiatry, 31,* 45–49.

Di Nardo, P. A., Brown, T. A., & Barlow, D. H. (1994). *Anxiety Disorders Interview Schedule for* DSM-IV *(ADIS-IV).* Albany, NY: Graywind.

Domjan, M., & Burkhard, B. (1986). *The principles of learning and behavior* (2nd ed.). Pacific Grove, CA: Brooks/Cole.

DuPont, R. L., Rice, D. P., Shiraki, S., & Rowland, C. R. (1995). Economic costs of obsessive-compulsive disorder. *Medical Interface,* 102–109.

Eisen, J. L., Phillips, K. A., Baer, L., Beer, D. A., Atala, K. D., & Rasmussen, S. A. (1998). The Brown Assessment of Beliefs Scale: Reliability and validity. *American Journal of Psychiatry, 155,* 102–108.

Eisen, J. L., & Steketee, G. (1997). Course of illness of OCD. In L. J. Dickstein, M. B. Riba, & J. M. Oldhan (Vol. Eds.) & M. Pato & G. Steketee (Sec. Eds.), *Annual review of psychiatry: Vol. 16. Obsessive-compulsive disorder across the life cycle* (pp. III-73–III-95). Washington, DC: American Psychiatric Press.

Emmelkamp, P. M., van den Heuvell, C. V. L., Ruphan, M., & Sanderman, R. (1989). Home-based treatment of obsessive-compulsive patients: Intersession interval and therapist involvement. *Behavior Therapy, 27,* 89–93.

Enright, S. J. (1991). Group treatment for obsessive-compulsive disorder: An evaluation. *Behavioral Psychotherapy, 14,* 21–33.

Epsie, C. A. (1986). The group treatment of obsessive compulsive ritualizers: Behavioral management of identified patterns of relapse. *Behavioral Psychotherapy, 14,* 21–33.

Fals-Stewart, W., & Lucente, S. (1993). An MCMI cluster typology of obsessive-compulsives: A measure of personality characteristics and its relationship to treatment participation, compliance, and outcome in behavior therapy. *Journal of Psychiatric Research, 27,* 139–154.

Fals-Stewart, W., Marks, A. P., & Schafer, J. (1993). A comparison of behavioral group therapy and individual behavior therapy in treating obsessive-compulsive disorder. *Journal of Nervous and Mental Disease, 181,* 189–193.

Feske, U., & Chambless, D. L. (2000). A review of assessment measures for obsessive-compulsive disorder. In W. K. Goodman, M. Rudorfer, & J. D. Maser (Eds.), *Obsessive compulsive disorder: Contemporary issues in treatment* (pp. 157–182). Mahwah, NJ: Erlbaum.

First, M. B., Spitzer, R. L., Gibbon, M., & Williams, J. B. W. (1996). *Structured Clinical Interview for* DSM-IV *Axis I Disorders—Patient Edition (SCID-I/P, Version 2.0).* New York: Biometrics Research Department.

Fischer, D. J., Himle, J. A., & Hanna, G. L. (1998). Group behavioral therapy for adolescents with obsessive-compulsive disorder: Preliminary outcomes. *Research on Social Work Practice, 8,* 629–636.

Flament, M. F., Rapoport, J. E., Berg, C. J., Sceery, W., Kilts, C., Mellstrom, B., et al. (1985). Clomipramine treatment of childhood obsessive-compulsive disorder: A double-blind controlled study. *Archives of General Psychiatry, 42,* 977–983.

Foa, E. B., Kozak, M. J., Steketee, G., & McCarthy, P. R. (1992). Treatment of depressive and obsessive-compulsive symptoms in OCD by imipramine and behavior therapy. *British Journal of Clinical Psychology, 31,* 279–292.

Foa, E. B., Steketee, G. S., & Grayson, J. B. (1985). Imaginal and in vivo exposure: A comparison with obsessive-compulsive checkers. *Behavior Therapy, 16,* 292–302.

Franklin, M. E., Abramowitz, J. S., Kozak, M. J., Levitt, J. T., & Foa, E. B. (in press). Effectiveness of exposure and ritual prevention for obsessive compulsive disorder: Randomized versus non-randomized samples. *Journal of Consulting and Clinical Psychology.*

Franklin, M. E., Kozak, M. J., Cashman, L. A., Coles, M. E., Rheingold, A. A., & Foa, E. B. (1998). Cognitive-behavioral treatment of pediatric obsessive-compulsive disorder: An open clinical trial. *Journal of the American Academy of Child and Adolescent Psychiatry, 37,* 412–419.

Freud, S. (1925). Notes upon a case of obsessional neurosis. In *Collected Papers* (Vol. 3, pp. 293–383). London: Hogarth Press. (Original work published 1909)

Geller, D. A., Biederman, J., & Stewart, S. E. (2003). Which SSRI? A meta-analysis of pharmacotherapy trials in pediatric obsessive-compulsive disorder. *American Journal of Psychiatry, 160,* 1919–1928.

Geller, D. A., Hoog, S. L., Heiligenstein, J. H., Ricardi, R. K., Tamura, R., Kluszynski, S., et al. (2001). Fluoxetine pediatric OCD study team: Fluoxetine treatment for obsessive-compulsive disorder in children and adolescents—A placebo-controlled clinical trial. *Journal of the American Academy of Child and Adolescent Psychiatry, 40,* 773–779.

Goodman, W., Kozak, M., Liebowitz, M., & White, K. (1996). Treatment of OCD with fluvoxamine: A multi-center, double-blind, placebo-controlled trial. *International Journal of Clinical Psychopharmacology, 11,* 21–30.

Goodman, W. K., Price, L. H., Rasmussen, S. A., Mazure, C., Delgado, P., Heninger, G. R., et al. (1989). The Yale-Brown Obsessive Compulsive Scale: Pt. II. Validity. *Archives of General Psychiatry, 46,* 1012–1016.

Goodman, W. K., Price, L. H., Rasmussen, S. A., Mazure, C., Fleischman, R. L., Hill, C. L., et al. (1989). The Yale-Brown Obsessive Compulsive Scale: Pt. I. Development, use, and reliability. *Archives of General Psychiatry, 46,* 1006–1011.

Greist, J., Chouinard, G., DuBoff, E., Halaris, A., Kim, S. W., Koran, L., et al. (1995). Double-blind parallel comparison of three dosages of sertraline and placebo in outpatients with obsessive-compulsive disorder. *Archives of General Psychiatry, 52,* 289–295.

Greist, J., Jefferson, J., Kobak, K., Chouinard, G., DuBoff, E., Halaris, A., et al. (1995). A 1-year double-blind placebo-controlled fixed-dose study of sertraline in the treatment of obsessive-compulsive disorder. *International Journal of Clinical Psychopharmacology, 10,* 57–65.

Grunes, M., Neziroglu, F., & McKay, D. (2001). Family involvement in the behavioral treatment of obsessive compulsive disorder: A preliminary investigation. *Behavior Therapy, 32,* 803–820.

Hamilton, M. (1959). The assessment of anxiety states by rating. *British Journal of Medical Psychology, 32,* 50–55.

Hamilton, M. (1960). A rating scale for depression. *Journal of Neurology, Neurosurgery, and Psychiatry, 23,* 56–61.

Hand, I., & Tichatzky, M. (1979). Behavioral group therapy for obsessions and compulsions: First results of a pilot study. In P. Sjoden, D. Bates, & W. S. Dockens (Eds.), *Trends in behavioral therapy* (pp. 269–297). New York: Academic Press.

Henderson, J. G., & Pollard, C. A. (1988). Three types of obsessive compulsive disorder in a community sample. *Journal of Clinical Psychology, 44,* 747–752.

Himle, J. A., Fischer, D. J., Van Etten, M. L., Janeck, A. J., & Hanna, G. L. (2003). Group behavioral therapy for adolescents with tic-related and non-tic-related OCD. *Depression and Anxiety, 17,* 73–78.

Himle, J. A., Rassi, S., Haghighatgou, H., Krone, K. P., Nesse, R. M., & Abelson, J. (2001). Group behavioral therapy of obsessive-compulsive disorder: Seven versus twelve-week outcomes. *Depression and Anxiety, 13,* 161–165.

Himle, J. A., Van Etten, M., & Fischer, D. J. (2003). Cognitive-behavioral group therapy for obsessive-compulsive disorder: A review. *Brief Treatment and Crisis Intervention, 3,* 215–225.

Hodgson, R. I., & Rachman, S. (1977). Obsessional-compulsive complaints. *Behaviour Research and Therapy, 15,* 389–395.

Hohagen, F., Winkelmann, G., Rasche-Rauchle, H., Hand, I., Konig, A., Munchau, N., et al. (1998). Combination of behaviour therapy with fluvoxamine in comparison with behaviour therapy and placebo: Results of a multicentre study. *British Journal of Psychiatry, 173,* 71–78.

Hollander, E. (Ed.). (1993). *Obsessive compulsive related disorders.* Washington, DC: American Psychiatric Press.

Hollander, E., Rowland, C., Stein, D. J., Broatch, J., & Himelein, C. (1995). A pharmacoeconomic and quality of life study of obsessive compulsive disorder [Abstract]. *Psychopharmacology Bulletin, 31,* 526.

Hyler, S. E., Rieder, R. O., Williams, J. B., Spitzer, R. L., Hendler, J., & Lyons, M. (1988). The Personality Diagnostic Questionnaire: Development and preliminary results. *Journal of Personality Disorders, 2,* 229–237.

Hyler, S. E., Skodol, A. E., Kellman, H. D., Oldham, J. M., & Rosnick, L. (1990). Validity of the Personality Diagnostic Questionnaire-Revised: Comparison with two structured interviews. *American Journal of Psychiatry, 147,* 1043–1048.

Janet, P. (1903). *Les Obsessions et la Psychasthenie* (Vol. 1). Paris: Alcan.

Karno, M., & Golding, J. (1991). Obsessive compulsive disorder. In L. N. Robins & D. A. Regier (Eds.), *Psychiatric disorders in America: The Epidemiologic Catchment Area study* (pp. 204–219). London: Free Press.

Karno, M., Golding, J. M., Sorenson, S. B., & Burnham, A. B. (1988). The epidemiology of obsessive-compulsive disorder in five U.S. communities. *Archives of General Psychiatry, 45,* 1094–1099.

Kim, C. H., Chang, J. W., & Koo, M. (2003). Anterior cingulotomy for refractory obsessive-compulsive disorder. *Acta Psychiatrica Scandinavica, 107,* 283–290.

Knox, L. S., Albano, A. M., & Barlow, D. H. (1996). Parental involvement in the treatment of childhood compulsive disorder. *Behavior Therapy, 27,* 93–114.

Krone, K. P., Himle, J. A., & Nesse, R. M. (1991). A standardized behavioral group treatment program for obsessive-compulsive disorder: Preliminary outcomes. *Behaviour Research and Therapy, 29,* 627–631.

Kyrios, M., Steketee, G., Frost, R., & Oh, S. (2002). Cognitions in compulsive hoarding. In R. O. Frost & G. Steketee (Eds.), *Cognitive approaches to obsessions and compulsions: Theory, assessment and treatment* (pp. 269–289). Oxford, England: Elsevier.

Leonard, H. L., Swedo, S. E., & Lenane, M. C. (1993). A 2- to 7-year follow-up study of 54 obsessive-compulsive children and adolescents. *Archives of General Psychiatry, 50*, 429–439.

Leonard, H. L., Swedo, S. E., Rapoport, J. L., Koby, E. V., Lenane, M. C., Cheslow, D. L., et al. (1989). Treatment of obsessive compulsive disorder with clomipramine and desipramine in children and adolescents: A double-blind crossover comparison. *Archives of General Psychiatry, 46*, 1088–1092.

Lindsay, M., Crino, R., & Andrews, G. (1997). Controlled trial of exposure and response prevention in obsessive-compulsive disorder. *British Journal of Psychiatry, 171*, 135–139.

March, J. S. (1995). Cognitive-behavioral psychotherapy for children and adolescents with OCD: A review and recommendations for treatment. *Journal of the American Academy of Child and Adolescent Psychiatry, 34*, 7–18.

March, J. S., Biederman, J., Wolkow, R., Safferman, A., Mardekian, J., Cook, E. H., et al. (1998). Sertraline in children and adolescents with obsessive-compulsive disorder: A multicenter randomized controlled trial. *Journal of the American Medical Association, 280*, 1752–1756.

March, J. S., Frances, A., Carpenter, D., & Kahn, D. (1997). The expert consensus guidelines series: Treatment of obsessive-compulsive disorder. *Journal of Clinical Psychiatry, 58*(4).

Marks, I. M., Lelliott, P., Basoglu, M., Noshirvani, H., Monteiro, W., Cohen, D., et al. (1988). Clomipramine, self-exposure, and therapist-aided exposure for obsessive-compulsive rituals. *British Journal of Psychiatry, 152*, 522–534.

Mavissakalian, M., Turner, S. M., Michelson, L., & Jacob, R. (1985). Tricyclic antidepressants in obsessive-compulsive disorder: Antiobsessional or antidepressant agents? *American Journal of Psychiatry, 142*, 572–576.

McLean, P. D., Whittal, M. L., Thordarson, D., Taylor, S., Söchting, I., Koch, W. J., et al. (2001). Cognitive versus behavior therapy in the group treatment of obsessive-compulsive disorder. *Journal of Consulting and Clinical Psychology, 69*, 205–214.

Mehta, M. (1990). A comparative study of family-based and patient-based behavioral management in obsessive-compulsive disorder. *British Journal of Psychiatry, 157*, 133–135.

Montgomery, S., McIntyre, A., Osterheider, M., Sarteschi, P., Zitterl, W., Zohar, J., et al. (1993). A double-blind, placebo-controlled study of fluoxetine in patients with DSM-III-R OCD. *European Neuropsychopharmacology, 3*, 143–152.

Myers, J. K., Weissman, M. M., Tischler, G. L., Burke, J. D., Kramer, M., & Stoltzman, R. (1984). Six month prevalence of psychiatric disorders in three communities: 1980–1982. *Archives of General Psychiatry, 41*, 952–967.

Neziroglu, F., McKay, D., & Yaryura-Tobias, J. A. (2000). Overlapping and distinctive features of hypochondriasis and obsessive-compulsive disorder. *Journal of Anxiety Disorders, 14*, 603–614.

Neziroglu, F., McKay, D., Yaryura-Tobias, J. A., Stevens, K. P., & Todaro, J. (1999). The Overvalued Ideas Scale: Development, reliability, and validity in obsessive-compulsive disorder. *Behavior Research and Therapy, 37*, 881–902.

Neziroglu, F., Stevens, K., McKay, D., & Yaryura-Tobias, J. A. (2001). Predictive validity of the overvalued ideas scale: Outcome in obsessive-compulsive and body dysmorphic disorders. *Behavior Research and Therapy, 39*, 745–756.

Neziroglu, F., Yaryura-Tobias, J. A., Walz, J., & McKay, D. (2000). The effect of fluvoxamine and behavior therapy on children and adolescents with obsessive-compulsive disorder. *Journal of Child and Adolescent Psychopharmacology, 10*, 295–306.

Nymberg, J., & Van Noppen, B. (1994). Obsessive-compulsive disorder: A concealed diagnosis. *American Family Physician, 49*, 1129–1137.

Obsessive Compulsive Cognitions Working Group. (1997). Cognitive assessment of obsessive-compulsive disorder. *Behaviour Research and Therapy, 35,* 667–681.

Obsessive Compulsive Cognitions Working Group. (2001). Development and initial validation of the Obsessive Beliefs Questionnaire and the Interpretation of Intrusions Inventory. *Behaviour Research and Therapy, 39,* 987–1006.

Obsessive Compulsive Cognitions Working Group. (2003). Psychometric validation of the Obsessive Belief Questionnaire and the Interpretation of Intrusion Inventory: Pt 1. *Behaviour Research and Therapy, 41,* 863–878.

Pavlov, I. P. (1960). Attempt at a physiological interpretation of compulsive neurosis and paranoia. In D. Myshne and S. Belsky (Trans.), *Psychopathology and Psychiatry* (pp. 309–324). Moscow: Foreign Languages Publishing House.

Pediatric OCD Treatment Study Team. (2004). Cognitive-behavior therapy, sertraline, and their combination for children and adolescents with obsessive-compulsive disorder: The Pediatric OCD Treatment Study (POTS) randomized controlled trial. *Journal of the American Medical Association, 292,* 1969–1976.

Pfohl, B., & Blum, N. (1991). Obsessive compulsive personality disorder: A review of available data and recommendations for *DSM-IV. Journal of Personality Disorders, 5,* 363–375.

Piacentini, J., Bergman, R. L., Jacobs, C., McCracken, J. T., & Kretchman, J. (2002). Open trial of cognitive behavior therapy for childhood obsessive-compulsive disorder. *Journal of Anxiety Disorders, 16,* 207–219.

Rachman, S. J. (1997). A cognitive theory of obsessions. *Behaviour Research and Therapy, 35,* 793–802.

Rachman, S. J., Cobb, J., Grey, S., McDonald, B., Mawson, D., Sartory, G., et al. (1979). The behavioral treatment of obsessional-compulsive disorders with and without clomipramine. *Behaviour Research and Therapy, 17,* 467–478.

Rachman, S. J., & de Silva, P. (1978). Abnormal and normal obsessions. *Behaviour Research and Therapy, 16,* 233–248.

Rachman, S. J., & Hodgson, R. J. (1980). *Obsessions and compulsions.* Englewood Cliffs, NJ: Prentice-Hall.

Rapoport, J. L. (1986). Childhood obsessive compulsive disorder. *Journal of Child Psychology and Psychiatry, 19,* 134–144.

Rasmussen, S., & Eisen, J. (1990). Epidemiology and clinical features of obsessive-compulsive disorder. In M. A. Jenike, L. Baer, & W. E. Minichiello (Eds.), *Obsessive-compulsive disorders: Theory and management* (pp. 10–27). Chicago: Year Book Medical.

Rasmussen, S., & Eisen, J. (1992). The epidemiology and differential diagnosis of obsessive-compulsive disorder. *Journal of Clinical Psychiatry, 53,* 4–10.

Rasmussen, S., & Tsuang, M. (1986). *DSM-III* obsessive compulsive disorder: Clinical characteristics and family history. *American Journal of Psychiatry, 143,* 317–322.

Riddle, M. A., Reeve, E. A., Yaryura-Tobias, J. A., Yang, H. M., Claghorn, J. L., Gaffney, G., et al. (2001). Fluvoxamine for children and adolescents with obsessive-compulsive disorder: A randomized, controlled, multicenter trial. *Journal of the American Academy of Child and Adolescent Psychiatry, 31,* 1062–1069.

Riddle, M. A., Scahill, L., King, R. A., Hardin, M. T., Anderson, G. M., Ort, S. I., et al. (1992). Double-blind, crossover trial of fluoxetine and placebo in children and adolescents with obsessive-compulsive disorder. *Journal of the American Academy of Child and Adolescent Psychiatry, 31,* 1062–1069.

Salkovskis, P. M., & Westbrook, D. (1989). Behavior therapy and obsessional ruminations: Can failure be turned into success? *Behaviour Research and Therapy, 27,* 149–160.

Sanavio, E. (1988). Obsessions and compulsions: The Padua Inventory. *Behaviour Research and Therapy, 26,* 169–177.

Scahill, L., Riddle, M. A., McSwiggin-Hardin, M., Ort, S. I., King, R. A., Goodman, W. K., et al. (1997). Children's Yale Brown Obsessive-Compulsive Scale: Reliability and validity. *Journal of the American Academy of Child and Adolescent Psychiatry, 36,* 844–852.

Schilder, P. (1938). The organic background of obsessions and compulsions. *American Journal of Psychiatry, 94,* 1397–1416.

Silverman, W. (1991). *Anxiety Disorders Interview Schedule for children.* Albany, NY: Graywind.

Spitzer, R. L., Williams, J. B. W., Gibbon, M., & First, M. (1990). *Manual for the Structured Clinical Interview for* DSM-III-R *Personality Disorders.* Washington, DC: American Psychiatric Press.

Steketee, G. (1993). Social support and treatment outcome of obsessive compulsive disorder at 9-month follow-up. *Behavioral Psychotherapy, 21,* 81–95.

Steketee, G. (1997). Disability and family burden in obsessive-compulsive disorder. *Canadian Journal of Psychiatry, 42,* 919–928.

Steketee, G., Chambless, D. L., Tran, G. Q., Worden, H., & Gillis, M. M. (1995). Behavioral avoidance test for obsessive compulsive disorder. *Behaviour Research and Therapy, 34,* 73–83.

Steketee, G., Frost, R., & Bogart, K. (1996). The Yale-Brown Obsessive Compulsive Scale: Interview versus self-report. *Behaviour Research and Therapy, 34,* 675–684.

Steketee, G., Frost, R. O., Wincze, J., Greene, K. A. I., & Douglass, H. (2000). Group and individual treatment of compulsive hoarding: A pilot study. *Behavioral and Cognitive Psychotherapy, 28,* 259–268.

Steketee, G., Henninger, N., & Pollard, C. A. (2000). Predicting treatment outcome for OCD: Effects of comorbidity. In W. K. Goodman, M. Rudorfer, & J. D. Maser (Eds.), *Obsessive compulsive disorder: Contemporary issues in treatment* (pp. 257–274). Mahwah, NJ: Erlbaum.

Steketee, G., & Neziroglu, F. (2003). Assessment of obsessive-compulsive disorder and spectrum disorders. *Brief Treatment and Crisis Intervention, 3*(2), 169–186.

Steketee, G., Van Noppen, B., Cohen, I., & Clary, L. (1998). Anxiety disorders. In J. B. W. Williams & K. Ell (Eds.), *Mental health research: Implications for practice* (pp. 118–156). Washington, DC: NASW Press.

Steketee, G., Van Noppen, B., Lam, J., & Shapiro, L. (1998). Expressed emotion in families and the treatment of obsessive-compulsive disorder. *In Session: Psychotherapy in Practice, 4,* 73–91.

Swedo, S., Rapoport, J., Leonard, H., Lenane, M. C., & Cheslow, D. L. (1989). Obsessive compulsive disorder in children and adolescents. *Archives of General Psychiatry, 46,* 335–345.

Taylor, S. (1998). Assessment of obsessive-compulsive disorder. In R. P. Swinson, M. M. Antony, S. Rachman, & M. A. Richter (Eds.), *Obsessive-compulsive disorder: Theory, research, and treatment* (pp. 229–257). New York: Guilford Press.

Theinemann, M., Martin, J., Cregger, B., Thompson, H. B., & Dyer-Friedman, J. (2001). Manual-driven group cognitive-behavioral therapy for adolescents with obsessive-compulsive disorder: A pilot study. *Journal of the American Academy of Child and Adolescent Psychiatry, 40,* 1254–1260.

Tollefson, G. D., Rampey, A. H., Potvin, J. H., Jenike, M. A., Rush, A. J., Dominguez, R. A., et al. (1994). A multicenter investigation of fixed-dose fluoxetine in the treatment of obsessive-compulsive disorder. *Archives of General Psychiatry, 51,* 559–567.

van Balkom, A. J. L. M., & van Dyck, R. (1998). Combination treatments of obsessive-compulsive disorder. In R. P. Swinson, M. M. Antony, S. Rachman, & M. A. Richter (Eds.), *Obsessive-compulsive disorder: Theory, research, and treatment* (pp. 349–366). New York: Guilford Press.

Van Noppen, B. L., Pato, M. T., Marsland, R., & Rasmussen, S. A. (1998). A time-limited behavioral group for treatment of obsessive-compulsive disorder. *Journal of Psychotherapy Practice and Research, 7,* 272–280.

Van Noppen, B. L., & Steketee, G. (2003). Family responses and multifamily behavioral treatment for obsessive-compulsive disorder. *Brief Treatment and Crisis Intervention, 3,* 231–247.

Van Noppen, B. L., Steketee, G., McCorkle, B. H., & Pato, M. (1997). Group and multifamily behavioral treatment for obsessive compulsive disorder: A pilot study. *Journal of Anxiety Disorders, 11,* 431–446.

van Oppen, P., De Haan, E., van Balkom, A. J. L. M., Spinhoven, P., Hoogduin, K.,

& van Dyck, R. (1995). Cognitive therapy and exposure in vivo in the treatment of obsessive-compulsive disorder. *Behaviour Research and Therapy, 33,* 379–390.

Wever, C., & Rey, J. M. (1997). Juvenile OCD. *Australian and New Zealand Journal of Psychiatry, 31,* 105–130.

Wheadon, D., Bushnell, W., & Steiner, M. (1993, December). *A fixed dose comparison of 20, 40, or 60 mg paroxetine to placebo in the treatment of obsessive-compulsive disorder.* Paper presented at the annual meeting of the American College of Neuropsychopharmacology, Honolulu, Hawaii.

SEXUAL DISORDERS

Sexual Desire and Arousal Disorders

Sophia F. Dziegielewski, Barbara F. Turnage, Gary Dick, and Cheryl Resnick-Cortes

18

Chapter

Learning Objectives

After reading this chapter, the reader will be able to:

- Describe what is meant by the term "sexual arousal and desire disorders."
- Describe the estimated prevalence of these disorders.
- Describe and locate evidence-based approaches to assessing clients meeting the *DSM* criteria for sexual arousal and desire disorders.
- Locate and describe evidence-based approaches to the treatment of clients meeting the criteria for sexual arousal and desire disorders.

Operational Definitions of the Problem

As we progress through the human life cycle, each of us develops into a sexual being with certain needs, desires, and expectations. Human sexual behavior is influenced by a complex dynamic interaction among physiological, behavioral, psychosocial, political, and cultural factors (Lipsith, McCann, & Goldmeier, 2003). These needs, desires, and expectations can be highly variable, complicating the definition of sexual problems (Nicolson & Burr, 2003). Sexual response is an outcome of the self's relationship with the self and the self's relations with others. The expression of human sexuality is influenced by previous sexual experiences, internal needs and desires, conflict between socialization and desire, and the relationship with the partner. It consists of cognitive, affective, and physiological components (Rowland, Tai, & Slob, 2003). The lack of access individuals have to information regarding the origins and treatment of sexual problems and social workers' reluctance to discuss human sexuality can further contribute to sexual suffering. Sexual dysfunction can affect the quality of life and self-esteem and lead to depression and anxiety.

The *Diagnostic and Statistical Manual of Mental Disorders* (*DSM*; American Psychiatric Association, 2000, p. 535) defines *sexual dysfunction* as "characterized by a disturbance in the processes that characterize the sexual response cycle or pain associated with sexual intercourse." The *DSM* further defines *desire* as "fantasies about sexual activity and the desire to have sexual activity" (p. 536); defines *excitement* as "a subjective sense of sexual pleasure and accompanying physiological changes" (p. 536); defines *orgasm* as "a peaking of sexual pleasure, with release of sexual tension in rhythmic contraction of the perineal muscles and reproductive organs" (p. 536); and defines *resolution* as "a sense of muscular relaxation and general well-being" (p. 536). H. S. Kaplan (1979) delineates a normal cycle of sexual response as beginning with the desire phase, moving next to the excitement or arousal phase, and culminating in the orgasm phase. When disturbances occur at any point in this cycle, a sexual disorder can result.

The prevalence of sexual disorders is quite common. In a study of 27,500 men and women ranging in age from 40 to 80 from 29 countries, 28% of men and 39% of women reported that they were affected by a sexual dysfunction (Nicolosi et al., 2004). In addition, the National Health and Social Life Survey produced in 1994 found that 43% of women and 31% of men in the United States between the ages of 18 and 59 have some form of sexual dysfunction (Laumann, Paik, & Rosen, 1999). In 2002, the Massachusetts Male Aging Study surveyed 1,709 men ranging in age from 40 to 70 in the greater Boston area and found the prevalence of erectile dysfunction to be 52%, with 9.6% of the sample reporting complete erectile dysfunction (Fazio & Brock, 2004).

Once the definition and diagnostic criteria of what constitutes a sexual desire disorder (i.e., Hypoactive Sexual Desire Disorder and Sexual Aversion Disorder) or a sexual arousal disorder (i.e., Female Sexual Arousal Disorder and Male Erectile Disorder) have been derived, special attention to the application and relevance of these definitions for each individual must be explored. Statistics can be misleading, because consideration needs to be given to what constitutes a sexual desire or arousal problem. Therefore, the problem of assessing *normal* and *abnormal* sexual behavior continues to be complicated. According to Knopf and Seiler (1990), the average couple generally has sexual intercourse two to three times a week; however, this number is questioned in appreciation for individual couples' preferences and needs. Simply stated, the number of times couples have or do not have sexual intercourse is not considered a problem—unless it is deemed so by the participating couple.

The frequency of sexual behavior in a relationship is only one factor to be explored in the determination of a sexual arousal or desire disorder. In the past, the concept of the importance of individual perception in the form of irrational thoughts leading to the inhibition of one's capacity for sexual enjoyment has been questioned. Today, however, many professionals continue to argue just the opposite (Eastman, 1993). It has become clear that an individual's perceptions about sexual desire and arousal can be swayed by a multitude of factors. These factors include personal beliefs, societal attitudes and mores, cultural pressure, parental influence, spiritual and religious teaching, socioeconomic status, and education level (Stuntz, Falk, Hiken, & Carson, 1996). To further complicate understanding, an individual's sexual attitudes and views can and often do change throughout the life cycle. Developmental-related changes in sexual attitudes and views can make certain events problematic that were not considered to be before, and vice versa.

Sexual Desire Disorders

In the *DSM-IV* (American Psychiatric Association, 2000), the sexual desire disorders are divided into two diagnostic types: Hypoactive Sexual Desire Disorder and Sexual Aversion Disorder. Hypoactive Sexual Desire Disorder occurs at the initial (desire) phase of the sexual response cycle. It is identified when "a deficiency or absence of sexual fantasies and desire for sexual activity" exists (p. 539). Leif (1977) termed this condition *inhibited sexual desire,* referring to minimal or no interest in sexual activity. Hypoactive sexual desire can be situational (occurring within a specific context) or global (occurring across situations and partners; Fish, Busby, & Killian, 1994). In addition, hypoactive sexual desire can be primary (lifelong) or secondary (occurring after a normal period of sexual functioning; Salonia et al., 2004).

Sexual Aversion Disorder is defined as "the aversion to and active avoidance of genital sexual contact with a sexual partner" (American Psychiatric Association, 2000, p. 541). Sexual antipathy, which may manifest as anxiety or panic, must be intense enough to cause marked distress or interpersonal dissatisfaction and difficulty and cannot be directly related to another clinical diagnosis. This revulsion can be limited to a particular aspect of sexual conduct, such as vaginal secretions or genital stimulation, or it can be more diverse and include an aversion to such sexual behaviors as kissing and hugging, to the repeated avoidance of sexual relations via coitus (4% and 70%, respectively). Female Arousal Disorder presents in 62% of women seeking sex therapy, whereas the rates for vaginismus and dyspareunia are 12% to 17% and 3% to 5%, respectively (Spector & Carey, 1990). Alexander (1993) found the incidence of decreased libido to be 11% to 48%, with help-seeking behavior occurring more often in women. Further, Alexander stated that 70% of those who seek assistance for sexual disorders present with decreased libido.

Kinzl, Traweger, and Biebl (1995) estimated that nearly 20% of the total U.S. population may experience hypoactive sexual desire disorders. Regardless of specific percentages, several studies indicate that inhibited sexual desire disorders are on the rise, climbing to approximately 40% of those seeking sex therapy and 31% of couples seeking treatment (Fish et al., 1994). The Sex Therapy Clinic of the University of New York at Stony Brook found an increase in reported sexual desire disorders from 32% in 1974 and 1976 to 46% in 1978 and then to 55% in 1981 and 1982 (Trudel, 1991). Although hypoactive sexual disorders appear to be more commonly reported in women, there is a rising incidence of sexual desire disorder among men (Trudel, 1991).

In the area of the sexual arousal disorders, there also appears to be an increasing rate of prevalence. Spector and Carey (1990) estimated the prevalence of inhibited female orgasm to be 5% to 10% of the general population. They also indicated that inhibited female orgasm is the most commonly presented female dysfunction, reported by 18% to 76% of females seeking sex therapy treatment.

In the general population, the prevalence of Male Erectile Disorder is estimated at 4% to 9% of all men, although it is the most common presenting complaint for males. Generally, 36% to 40% of males seeking sex therapy report having this disorder. Fifty percent of these males describe secondary erectile disorder (being able to maintain an erection at some point), whereas only 8% describe primary erectile disorder (never being able to maintain an erection; Spector & Carey, 1990). Estimates of the prevalence rate of Premature Ejaculation were 36% to 38% and inhibited male orgasm 4% to 10%, which makes inhibited male orgasm the least common of the male dysfunctions (Spector & Carey, 1990). In a study of young male drug abusers, 20% reported erectile dysfunction (LePera, Giannotti, Taggi, & Macchia, 2003). The prevalence of Premature Ejaculation for the men in the study was 36%.

Sexual dysfunction is strongly related to the aging process. In a study of 37,742 men ranging in age from 53 to 90, fewer than 2% reported erectile problems occurring before age 40, and only 4% reported that it occurred between ages 40 and 49 (Bacon et al., 2003). After age 50, the prevalence of erectile dysfunction was found to increase with age. Twenty-six percent of the men reported their first problem with erectile dysfunction between age 50 and 59, and 40% between age 60 to 69 (Bacon et al., 2003). In a similar study of 560 aging men and erectile dysfunction, researchers found differences between groups of men in early adulthood, middle adulthood, and late adulthood on several dimensions of erectile functioning (Moore, Straus, Herman, & Donatucci, 2003). Younger men report greater overall rating on their sex life, greater frequency of intercourse, and better overall erectile performance than older men. However, when orgasmic disorders do occur in younger men, they tend to experience more severe psychosocial difficulties than older men. Younger men report greater negative partner reactions to orgasmic disorders, and this factor alone may increase the risk for relationship issues and depression. Erectile dysfunction has been reported in 10% of healthy young males and in more than 30% of males with chronic disease (Moore et al., 2003).

Erectile Dysfunction

One of the leading causes of orgasmic disorders is erectile dysfunction (ED), defined as the inability to achieve or maintain a penile erection sufficient for satisfactory sexual performance (Fazio & Brock, 2004). Erectile dysfunction tends to increase with age and is common in men over 50. There are a number of factors associated with erectile dysfunction, including demographic, medical, behavioral, and psychological variables (Moore et al., 2003). There are a host of medical conditions associated with erectile dysfunction: heart disease, diabetes, obesity, arthritis, and hypertension.

The dynamic model of erectile dysfunction conceptualizes erectile dysfunction as having multiple etiological factors based on medical conditions that affect the psychosocial context in which erectile dysfunction is experienced. This bidirectional model between erectile dysfunction and psychosocial factors is such that psychosocial factors exacerbate erectile dysfunction and erectile dysfunction may increase psychosocial factors (Moore et al., 2003). Whether the etiology of erectile dysfunction is psychological in nature, results from acute or chronic physiological precipitants, or is a combination of relationship factors that coexist with organic causes and psychological factors, they are not mutually exclusive, and it is important for social workers to be able to communicate openly with their clients to assess the severity of erectile dysfunction (Goldstein, 2004).

Evidence-Based Approaches to Assessment

There has been an increase in research into the diagnosis and treatment of sexual dysfunction in the past decade that has resulted in several new instruments designed to diagnose and monitor treatment outcomes (Meston & Derogatis, 2002). These instruments measure several aspects of human sexual dysfunction, including sexual drive, quality of erection, ejaculation, sexual satisfaction, sexual inhibition, sexual excitation, psychological and interpersonal relationship issues resulting from ED, quality of life and ED, and orgasm; all offer valid measures on multiple dimensions of sexual dysfunction. In addition to the use of instruments, a skilled, thorough, clinical interview is critical to any social work assessment. Although not included in the scope of this chapter, the authors recommend Fedoroff's (1991) article as an excellent resource for conducting interviews to assess sexual disorders.

Because many sexual desire disorders present concurrently with arousal and orgasm disorders (Nicolson & Burr, 2003), taking a proper history is essential to the implementation of the best treatment plan. In fact, Segraves and Segraves (1991) reported that of the 475 women they studied with a diagnosis of Hypoactive Sexual Desire Disorder, 41% had at least one other sexual disorder and 18% had sexual disorders in all three phases of the sexual response cycle (desire, arousal, and orgasm). Taking an adequate history ensures that the therapist has endeavored to ascertain all the factors that may have caused, may be related to, and may be maintaining the sexual dysfunction.

As the actual etiology of a sexual disorder may be physiological, psychological, environmental, or situational, a physical exam is critical (Borello-France et al., 2004; Salonia et al., 2004; Zippe et al., 2004). A physical examination should always be the first line of assessment, as many diseases and physical abnormalities produce or exacerbate sexual dysfunction (age, physical health, depression, stress, and hormone insufficiency; medical illnesses such as diabetes, renal failure, endocrine disorders, and neurological disorders; and psychiatric illnesses). A multitude of studies have linked sexual arousability to hormonal determinants (Rosen & Leiblum, 1987). Alexander (1993) indicates that estrogen-androgen replacement in postmenopausal women appears to increase sexual desire, arousal, and drive. Research also has suggested that 50% to 60% of men diagnosed with psychogenic impotence may actually suffer from an organic condition (Conte, 1986). Alexander presented a comprehensive listing of the organic causes of decreased sexual desire. In this review, she delineates both reversible and irreversible organic origins for the pituitary, endocrine, neurological, renal, psychiatric, and pharmacologic determinants.

Some studies have suggested that dysfunctional individuals may experience less of a physiological response during sexual arousal, or are simply less attentive to their own physiological cues than are sexually functional individuals (Barlow, 1986; Borello-France et al., 2004; Hofman et al., 2004; Palace & Gorzalka, 1992). These individuals may, in turn, also have difficulty labeling physiological genital cues relating to their own sexual arousal. However, the results from studies conducted in this area have been conflicting, and it is suggested that more research is required to establish this as a predictor for understanding sexual responses.

During the assessment process, it is important to note the use of substances that can affect sexual behavior, including prescription and nonprescription medications, drugs (certain drugs may interfere with vaginal lubrication), and alcohol (alcohol may result in difficulty gaining an erection; Johnson, Phelps, & Cottler, 2004). It is important that persons with medical problems recognize the effects of some prescription medications on sexual response.

In assessment, the psychological aspects that can affect sexual response should be noted. For example, a type of psychological turning off can actively suppress sexual desire (Read, 1995; Salonia et al., 2004). In such cases, the individual may actively learn to focus on angry, fearful, or distracting associations that result in the physiological inhibition of desire (H. S. Kaplan, 1979). Anxiety, power and control struggles, individual body image, problems with self-esteem, and a history of abuse may also serve to inhibit the sexual response. Postcolostomy and postmastectomy patients have the added complication of the likelihood of body image issues (Jensen, Klee, Thranov, & Groenvold, 2004). The fear of intimacy, inability to form commitment, dependency issues, guilt, and conflicts pertaining to sexual preference and identification can also influence the sexual response cycle (Hofman et al., 2004; Zippe et al., 2004).

In assessing sexual difficulties, it is always important to take environmental and situational issues into account. That is, it is important to examine the nature of the partner relationship and the environmental circumstances. Partner relationship areas that need to be considered include ways of addressing and relating to intimacy, attraction to the partner, communication problems and means of problem solving, sources of marital conflict and discord, family issues and pressure, and the presence of small children, living arrangements, and the sense of security in the relationship. It is frequently useful to gain information regarding both partners' sensitivity to stimulation and responsive body areas (Anderson, 1983). Women displaying inhibited sexual desire are more likely to report greater martial dissatisfaction and refuse sexual invitations from their spouse more often than noninhibited women (Stuart, Hammond, & Pett, 1987). Stuart et al. reported that the inhibited women in their study expressed the view that they experience lower levels of affection and emotional closeness in their marriage. Clearly, the quality and nature of the marital relationship affects most sexual disorders, particularly those of sexual desire.

Parental attitudes and teachings, as well as religious indoctrination, influence lifelong sexuality. Stuart et al. (1987) compared women's perception of parental attitudes toward sex and parental displays of affection and found significant differences between women exhibiting inhibited sexual desire and noninhibited women. The inhibited women rated parental attitudes and teachings and religious indoctrination much more negatively than did the noninhibited women. Closely tied to the parental displays of affection and their attitudes toward sex and the women's attitudes toward parental displays of affection were the failure of parents to appropriately teach sexual education and knowledge (Stuart et al., 1987).

Another environmental and situational factor that needs to be considered in the social work assessment of sexual function is life stress (Johnson et al., 2004). Excessive life stressors frequently result in decreased sexual interest and arousal. It is important to note that environmental and situational factors, although somewhat difficult to isolate and identify clearly, can be extremely amenable to change; therefore, their contribution to intervention success should not be underestimated.

The partners' preferred frequencies of sexual interaction, defined as the frequency of the wish to have sex, should be determined. This is a critical assessment factor, as no criteria for normal sexual desire exist. In fact, when couples are comparable in their levels of desire, disorders may not be identified. Sexual differences are recognized as disorders when one partner's desire differs significantly from the other's. As Stuart et al. (1987, p. 93) stated, "If both partners have a similar level of desire, there is no issue. [However, differences in the couple's] level of [sexual] desire may create a problem."

The social worker must also be careful to assess the client's *desire* for sexual activity along with the *frequency* of sexual activity, as desire and frequency can differ enormously. It is quite conceivable that a person might desire more sexual activity than current circumstances permit (as parents of young children understand all too clearly). In this instance, a low frequency of sexual activity might not reflect a sexual desire disorder. According to Rosen and Leiblum (1987), an individual might experience a strong sexual appetite, manifested in sexual urges, thoughts, and feelings, but fail to initiate or engage in sexual activity because he or she does not have the opportunity to do so. Perhaps a more useful measurement is *sexual fantasy:* "a conscious mental representation which translates itself in more or less imaginary form with hedonic value and is susceptible to produce sexual activity" (Trudel, 1991, p. 265). Trudel also recommended the cognitive evaluation of irrational beliefs, thoughts, and ideas impacting the cognitive-behavioral dimension of sexuality (also see Thyer & Papsdorf, 1981).

In summary, the social worker's assessment of sexual desire and arousal disorders should always include demographic information; identification of the primary and secondary nature of the problem; global versus situational description of the sexual problem; information about the specificity, intensity, and duration of the presenting problem; the antecedent circumstances at the onset of the problem, as well as concurrent factors; a complete sexual history, including desired as well as actual frequency of sexual activity; and the motivation for seeking treatment. Environmental and situational factors should always be explored. Referral for a physical examination by a well-trained physician is also indicated.

Assessment Scales and Methods

In addition to a thorough clinical interview, other self-report assessment techniques include rapid assessment instruments, questionnaires, and behavioral records. Along with these questionnaires, the social worker can also develop a self-designed rating scale that allows the client to report on any aspect of sexual arousal that is of concern. These are often useful, especially if the time of day can be recorded and a space to record circumstances leading up to the sexual activity or the lack thereof is provided. These self-designed rating scales are extremely useful in the assessment of sexual functioning, especially in looking at the contextual factors and the client's own perceptions of the severity of the problem. Indeed, the systematic client-reported tracking of sexual activities is essential for ascertaining whether problems exist and whether clients are benefiting from treatment.

Assessing sexual functioning of women who have been sexually abused is an important concern for social workers working with adult survivors of childhood sexual abuse. Kinzl et al. (1995) designed a 7-item scale to measure sexual dysfunction for their study of sexual dysfunction in women who had been sexually abused as children. Items on their scale include persistent or recurrent deficiency or absence of sexual fantasy and desire for sexual activity in adulthood; aversion to and avoidance of genital sexual contact with a partner; delay in, or absence of, orgasm following normal sexual excitation; genital pain before, during, or after sexual intercourse; and a lack of a subjective sense of sexual excitation (Kinzl et al., 1995).

Understanding the relationship dynamics of couples experiencing sexual difficulties is an important component of a comprehensive assessment. It is useful to inquire about the level of commitment to the relationship, contentment, tension, communication (of both general and sexual needs), enjoyment of sexual activity, frequency of sexual activity, frequency of sexual thoughts, and each partner's own desired frequency of sexual activity, along with the projected partner's desired frequency (Hawton, Catalan, & Fagg, 1991).

The following questionnaires have been tested for their psychometric properties and measure multiple dimensions of sexual dysfunction.

The Sexual Interaction System Scale (Woody, D'Souza, & Crain, 1994) was developed to measure couples' sexual functioning. This instrument explores the nature of the sexual relationship and interactions, sexual satisfaction, and marital adjustment. Their study found strong correlations between marital adjustment, sexual interaction, and sexual satisfaction.

The Sexual Desire Conflict Scale for Women (L. Kaplan & Harder, 1991) is a 33-item scale that measures the subjective discomfort and conflict a woman feels in relation to her sexual arousal and desire. The scale examines the woman's subjective evaluation of her emotional being, as opposed to behavioral factors, such as orgasm. The authors found that women who have been sexually abused display the highest scores. They recommended development of a similar scale for men to delineate male sexual desire conflicts, which the authors suggest could produce the recognition of important gender differences. These instruments are important not only for the assessment of sexual functioning, but they are also important to the development of appropriate interventions.

The 23-item Psychological and Interpersonal Relationships Scales (Swindle, Cameron, Lockhart, & Rosen, 2004) were developed to measure psychological and interpersonal outcomes associated with erectile dysfunction and its treatment. Three domains are conceptualized: sexual self-confidence, spontaneity, and time concerns. The instrument has demonstrative adequate psychometric properties and captures the psychological, behavioral, and relationship factors necessary in assessing the concerns of men with erectile dysfunction.

The Quality of Sexual Life Questionnaire (QVS; Costa et al., 2003) is a 27-item questionnaire designed to assess the quality of life in men with erectile dysfunction. It has three subscales: sexual life, skills, and psychosocial well-being. The QVS detects men with erectile dysfunction as well as the severity of erectile dysfunction. One of the strengths of this instrument is that men are asked about their perceived achievement, their satisfaction, and the importance of each item. For example, on the item asking about the subjects' concerns about the quality of their ejaculation, the questions are: "(a) You think things are going: very badly, fairly badly, neither well nor badly, fairly well, or very well? (b) You are: very dissatisfied, somewhat dissatisfied, indifferent, somewhat satisfied, very satisfied? (c) In your life you consider this to be: unimportant, somewhat unimportant, important, very important?"

The Brief Male Sexual Inventory (O'Leary et al., 2003) is an 11-item questionnaire measuring sexual drive, erectile function, ejaculatory function, sex drive, erections, ejaculations, and overall satisfaction. Inquiring about sexual function within the past 30 days, a sample of questions include: "Over the past 30 days, when you had erections how often were they firm enough to have sexual intercourse (not at all, a few times, fairly often, usually, always)? [and] In the past 30 days, to what extent have you considered a lack of sex drive to be a problem (big problem, medium problem, small problem, very small problem, no problem)?" In the validation of the instrument, there was an age-related decrease in erectile function and sexual functioning in all domains of sexual functioning assessed. Men in their 40s reported erections firm enough for intercourse 97% of the time, whereas 51% of the men in their 80s reported erections firm enough for intercourse.

The Erectile Quality Scale (EQS; Wincze et al., 2004) is a 15-item self-administered questionnaire that measures the most important aspects of erectile quality. Definitions of erectile quality were developed from qualitative interviews in a sample of 93 men with and without erectile dysfunction. Erectile quality was defined in their own words along with their opinions about certain aspects of erectile quality that were important to them. The constructs measured on the EQS, which were the same for both heterosexual and homosexual men were rigidity/hardness, duration, control/confidence, ease of obtaining/speed of onset, sensitivity/sensation, fast recovery, and appearance of penis. This instrument is useful for assessing outcome following treatment for erectile dysfunction.

The Female Sexual Function Index (Rosen et al., 2000) is a 19-item self-report measure of female sexual functioning that provides scores on five domains of sexual functioning: desire, arousal, lubrication, orgasm, satisfaction, and pain (Meston & Degogatis, 2002).

The Golombok-Rust Inventory of Sexual Satisfaction (Kuileter, Vroege, & van Lankveld, 1993) is a 56-item self-report (28 items for males and 28 for females) developed to measure both the quality of a heterosexual relationship and each partner's sexual functioning within the relationship (Meston & Degogatis, 2002). The inventory measures 12 domains of sexual functioning: five for females, five for males, and two common gender domains. The domains measuring female sexuality include anorgasmia, vaginismus, avoidance, nonsensuality, and dissatisfaction.

The Sexual Inhibition (SIS) and Sexual Excitation (SES) Scales I (Janssen, Vorst, Finn, & Bancroft, 2002) is a 45-item instrument designed to measure male sexual inhibition and excitation. The SES factor has 20 items and four subscales. The four subscales measure social interaction with a sexually attractive person, excitation as a result of visual stimuli, ease of arousal when thinking or fantasizing about sex, and excitation as a result of nonspecific stimuli. The SIS factor has 25 items and seven listed subscales: losing one's arousal and erection easily, inhibition due to concern about sexual interactions with a partner, performance concerns, worries and external sources of distraction, fear about the risk of being caught while performing sexual acts, negative consequences of sex, and physical pain, norms, and values (Janssen et al., 2002).

Evidence-Based Approaches to Intervention

Social workers across a variety of practice settings are frequently presented with the sex-related problems of clients. Appropriate interventions and referrals for these clients present obstacles for social work professionals. Empirical research studies on clients with sexual desire or arousal disorders have helped social workers to develop and refine treatment options. (For a comprehensive and excellent review of empirically validated treatment of sexual dysfunction, see Heiman & Meston, 1997). Knowledge of these current methods is essential for social work professionals, particularly in this era of managed care services, when funding for general mental health treatment is often considered only as a last resort (Dziegielewski, 2004).

The process of care model (Goldstein, 2004) provides a set of guidelines for assessment and intervention of Sexual Arousal Disorders. The five-step model consists of (1) identification and recognition of sexual arousal disorder, including concurrent medical and psychological conditions; (2) determining goals based on the individual's and partner's needs; (3) emphasizing communication and education between individual and partner for all phases of assessment, treatment, and follow-up; (4) utilizing a stepwise process for the recognition, assessment, and management of the disorder with regard to the degree of invasiveness in the diagnosis, treatment, and degree of involvement by the therapist; and (5) clear guidelines for follow-up and referral. The use of a thorough medical and psychosexual history, physical exam, and laboratory testing is central to effective treatment of arousal disorder. The assessment must include a detailed medical, sexual, and psychosocial history and, if possible, include the individual's partner early in the treatment (Goldstein, 2004).

Several techniques have been employed to treat sexual dysfunction: sex education, communication training, sexual technique training, systematic desensitization, and sensate focus (Harrison, 1987). Many of the practice strategies employed have been administered on an individual, group, marital, family, and combination basis. With the recent development of sildenafil citrate (Viagra), pharmacologic treatment has become the treatment of choice for men suffering from ED. Research in the use of sildenafil citrate for treatment of women with sexual arousal disorder, including estrogenized and estrogen-deficient women, did not improve physiological sexual response (Basson, McInnes, Smith, Hodgson, & Koppiker, 2002).

Sexual Desire Disorders

Hypoactive Sexual Disorder, or low sexual desire disorder (which includes any type of inhibited sexual desire), is the most common sexual dysfunction. Terms previously used to describe these conditions include "frigidity" and "impotence." Wincze and Carey (1991) warn against using these labels, as they are imprecise and have often been used to describe other sexual dysfunctions. Diagnosis of the conditions that fall under the umbrella of hypoactive sexual disorders can be difficult, because they are often multifaceted. These disorders appear to have a combination of the following aspects: biological (e.g., neuroendocrine), psychological (e.g., cognitive and affective), social (e.g., relationship oriented), and cultural (e.g., religious upbringing; Johnson, Phelps, & Cottler, 2004; Wincze & Carey, 1991). This multifaceted composition also makes it difficult to identify specific treatment techniques.

It is important to determine the influence of life cycle factors, such as age, when assessing sexual arousal disorders. Sexual dysfunction tends to increase with age. In a study of 534 women between the ages 40 and 64, 79% reported being sexually active, and among those who were sexually active, 51% presented with some form of sexual dysfunction. Of these women, 82% were postmenopausal and 23% were on hormone replacement therapy (Castelo-Branco et al., 2003). Risk factors contributing to sexual dysfunction include hysterectomy, age, menopause, erectile disorder, and low education (Castelo-Branco et al., 2003).

Trudel (1991) indicates that Hyposexual Desire Disorder is highly resistant to treatment, and even when positive results are initially obtained, long-term success rates are low. Results have been particularly poor when this disorder is perceived as an exclusively individual symptom (Fish et al., 1994). Hormonal therapy, sex therapy, treatment for depression, increased recognition and perception of pleasurable body sensations, and couples therapy that attends to the diversification of sensual and sexual activity are all meaningful in the treatment of low sexual desire (Trudel, 1991).

There are two primary methods of reasoning that have often been linked to hyposexuality that influence treatment strategy: conscious motivation and unconscious motivation (Knopf & Seiler, 1990). In conscious motivation, individuals are aware of what they are feeling. Here, individuals are believed to make either active or inactive choices as to whether they want to enjoy sex with their chosen partner. In an active choice, individuals may decide not to enjoy sexual acts of expression due to, for example, anger directed at the partner. In an inactive choice, individuals may not be able to identify exactly where the resistance is coming from, only that it exists. In conscious control, some individuals can pinpoint exactly when their desire was lost. However, many of these individuals may be unable to actively control their desire's on-off switch.

In unconscious motivation, individuals seem unaware of what is happening to them, or why. They often do not understand their situation or recognize how it occurred. For these individuals, sexual feelings are often repressed or avoided, and it is not uncommon for their sexual urges to be replaced with depression and anxiety (Barlow, 1986).

Hawton et al. (1991) found that the sexual motivation of the male partner plays a significant role in recovery for women presenting with Hypoactive Desire Disorder. The younger the couple's age and the lower the motivation of the male partner, the poorer the couple's outcome. Sexual arousal disorders can occur in both men and women; however, his type of disorder seems to be diagnosed and treated most commonly in males. Testosterone enhances sexual interest and the frequency of sexual acts in males, therefore it may be necessary for men with Hypoactive Desire Disorder to have their testosterone level checked (Fazio & Brock, 2004).

In a study that addressed sexual dysfunction in either the male or the female partner, Russell (1990) acknowledged the difficulty that couples have in resolving conflicts in expressing emotional and physical intimacy. This study attempted to combine some of the well-known strategies for treating sexual difficulties with a new cognitive approach to treatment in couple's therapy, where self-disclosure is used in conjunction with sensate focus exercises. Here the individual's past, the couple's past, and family history response patterns are examined. Russell expected the combination of these modes of treatment to increase understanding and intimacy for the couple. In her study of 49 couples, 8 couples communicated concerns regarding one member's low sex desire for the other. In the final results, 15 couples who participated clearly reported an increase in emotional and physical intimacy.

Of the research examined in this area, cognitive-behavioral treatment appears to be one of the most effective therapies in treating Hypoactive Desire Disorder. Attention is given to the anticipation of negative consequences tied to sexual experiences. Initially, exercises to help increase comfort during sexual activity are provided, allowing for the exploration of increasing partner attraction, the creation of fantasies and imagery, and the provision of proper sexual education. Of the available treatment options, multimodal treatment has been most effective. Multimodal treatment was effective when it focuses on increasing sensuality, produced insight into the factors that maintained low sexual desire, restructured the cognitions inhibiting sexual desire, and improved the couple's sexual behaviors through the use of traditional sex therapy techniques (Trudel, 1991).

In their study, Fish et al. (1994) highlighted the couple as their focus of treatment. These researchers supported the contention that a structural form of couples therapy would also be effective in treating inhibited sexual desire when the problem was conceptualized in the context of the couple relationship. In this study, inhibited sexual desire was examined in such interactive terms as "Sex serves as a function in relationships, and desire depends on that function and the cues each partner has endowed with sexual meaning" (p. 115).

In summary, working with couples appears to be a viable option for treatment when one or both partners present with Hypoactive Desire Disorder. The prognosis for low sexual desire dysfunctions is poorer than for the excitement and the orgasmic dysfunctions (Friedman & Hogan, 1985). Keeping this in mind, cognitive-behavioral therapy remains a positive treatment modality for dealing with sexual desire disorders. Nevertheless, more research is needed (particularly longitudinal studies) to measure the lasting effects of cognitive-behavioral treatment (Russell, 1990). Not only is exploration of new treatment experiences essential, but the replication of current treatment results is also essential.

The future task of the social work professional in treating clients with sexual desire disorders remains twofold: (1) to measure the effectiveness of new cognitive-behavioral and other treatments and (2) to establish whether these treatments will prove to be effective over time. There does appear to be a shift in emphasis, with the primary emphasis being focused on the second objective—thus highlighting the need for replication of these treatment studies.

Sexual Arousal Disorders

If the assessment indicates erectile dysfunction in the male partner, the first-line treatment or erectile dysfunction is pharmacological treatment with vasoactive agents (Fazio & Brock, 2004). The most common vasoactive drugs for erectile dysfunction are sildenafil citrate (Viagra), vardenafil (Levitra), and tadalafil (Cialis). In the Men's Attitudes to Life Events and Sexuality (MALES) study, of 27,839 men in eight countries, 16% of the men ages 20 to 75 reported erectile dysfunction (Shabbir, Mikhailidis, & Morgan, 2004). Despite the efficacy of these drugs, research has indicated reluctance on the part of men to discuss their erectile dysfunction with a physician, and if they do, they may not follow through in getting their prescriptions filled; if they do fill their prescriptions, many men may discontinue taking sildenafil within the 1st year (Shabbir et al., 2004). The MALES II study examined the treatment-seeking behavior of a subgroup of men reporting erectile dysfunction (2,912 men). Only 58% actively discussed their condition with a physician; 41% discussed treatment with sildenafil, and yet, only 25% of these men filled their prescriptions (Shabbir et al., 2004).

In addition to pharmacological treatment, three behavioral treatments can be helpful for clients suffering from erectile dysfunction: (1) communication technique training (to deal with social and relationship issues), (2) sexual technique training (teaching education and the practice of sexual techniques), and (3) a combination treatment that utilizes both. Kilmann and colleagues (1987) studied 20 couples who were tested to determine the effectiveness of current treatments on secondary erectile dysfunction. To participate in the study, the male partners had to have had successful intercourse approximately 20% of the time, and erectile dysfunction had to have been a problem for the past 5 years. Four couples were assigned to five experimental groups. The first three treatment groups (consisting of eight 2-hour sessions) were all designed to enhance the male's sexual functioning and included a communication education group, which stressed positive communication techniques; a sexual training group, which was designed to enhance positive sexual techniques; and a combination treatment group, which stressed both communication and sexual training. The fourth treatment group, the attention placebo control group, implemented controls to limit the degree of treatment received, thus constituting a less powerful treatment procedure than that given the other groups. In this group, highly structured lectures were provided without any planned applicability or practice time being allotted for individual problem solving. The couples in the no-treatment control group, the fifth group, were pretested and waited 5 weeks for treatment to begin. After the posttest, they were provided with the combination treatment. Several pretest measurement instruments were used, and the results were statistically analyzed.

Each of the treatments for secondary erectile dysfunction was found to be statistically significant when compared to no treatment at all. The small number of couples participating (five groups of four couples each) limits the generalizability of the conclusions. Nevertheless, this study clearly supports the importance of including a structured psychological treatment component in the treatment of sexual dysfunction. It also supports the recommendation by Eastman (1993) that the importance of education, communication, and support should not be underestimated, even when a condition is organically generated.

Goldman and Carroll (1990) highlight the importance of including education when treating secondary erectile dysfunction in older couples. In their study, 20 couples were randomly assigned to two groups; 10 completed an education workshop and 10 were used as controls. The workshop provided a structured educational format that focused on the physiological and psychological changes that occur in the sexual response cycle during aging. Sexual behavior was measured along three dimensions utilizing three standardized scales: (1) the frequency of sexual behavior, (2) sexual satisfaction, and (3) knowledge about and attitudes toward sex. Pretest and posttest scores were reviewed and analyzed. Study results suggest that the couples who attended the workshop had a significant increase in knowledge levels after completion. An increase in sexual behavior was noted for the experimental group, and there was a decline in this behavior for the control group. Overall, the educational workshop was considered a success, with a reported increase in knowledge and positive changes, as well as more realistic attitudes once the etiology related to sexual satisfaction and erectile functioning was identified (Kilmann et al., 1987).

Although the literature has stressed the importance of education in the treatment of erectile difficulty, the addition of play therapy has also been considered. Shaw (1990) focused on this option in treating men who had inhibited ejaculation. The central premise of the inclusion of play therapy is the belief that sexuality should be fun and pleasurable, not performance oriented. However, the reality for many men is that the desire to perform sexually becomes extremely anxiety provoking. In play therapy, performance anxiety is addressed and males are taught to reduce the focus on performance. The focus of the treatment intervention is on helping clients recognize and increase the spontaneous aspects of their personality. In Shaw's study, participants were expected to create and act on fantasies, to participate in sensate focus exercises, and to take part in sexual expression board games. Fifteen males (followed over a 3-year period) were able to successfully ejaculate with their own touch, although they were unable to do so with their partners. Of the 12 men who completed the program, 100% reported relief within 3 to 22 months of the intervention.

Vonk and Thyer (1995) presented one social work case study, evaluated using a single-system research design, of a female college student who had a severe fear of genital penetration, of phobic-like proportions, that prevented her from engaging in coitus. The client's desire for intercourse and capacity for sexual arousal were unimpaired, and the authors construed this problem more as meeting the *DSM* criteria for a specific phobia than for Sexual Aversion Disorder. However, the clinical picture was certainly mixed. In any event, a graduated exposure therapy approach was effective in eliminating this long-standing fear within 2 months.

These studies elucidate the need for both biological and social work therapies for sexual arousal disorders. The behavioral and behavioral-cognitive therapies are among the best supported psychosocial treatments in this regard. More research is needed to determine exactly what types of psychosocial treatments work best and if the results remain consistent over time. This makes the social worker's role as a clinical researcher critical in helping clients.

Combination Approaches

Many researchers express interest in combining strategies for treating the sexual desire and arousal disorders and their resulting sexual difficulties. Russell (1990) compared cognitive marital therapy (CMT), a new couples therapy approach, to previously used interventions. In CMT, self-disclosure between partners is strongly encouraged as a means of increasing understanding and intimacy, thus reducing conflict. Self-disclosure is seen as a means to increase both physical and emotional closeness.

With the 49 couples that Russell (1990) assessed in the clinic, the information gathered consisted of a complete psychosocial history, which included both current and past behaviors and trends. The therapist then made an initial decision regarding the type of sexual disorder each couple was suffering from and devised and discussed an appropriate plan with the couple. Most of the couples in this study chose a combination treatment approach. In this approach, specific concern was devoted to correcting the sexual problem and cognitive marital therapy was chosen to address relationship issues. Sensate focus homework assignments were almost always used, along with factual information to dispel myths about what is normal. Of the 24 couples that completed this year-long longitudinal study, 15 reported an increase in physical and emotional intimacy. Based on the results of the study, Russell reported that sexual dysfunctions cannot be isolated from interpersonal dimensions that ultimately determine the quality of the couple's relationship.

Many current social work and behavioral science researchers concur with the need for the inclusion of a psychosocial component with specific measures to address the marital, social, and personal difficulties an individual may express (Goldman & Carroll, 1990; H. S. Kaplan, 1990; Shaw, 1990). Burte and Araoz (1994), in focusing on cognitive processes and their manipulation as a treatment for sexual dysfunction, attempted to uncover what they termed *negative self-hypnosis.* They define this concept as nonconscious negative statements or defeatist mental images. When using this treatment technique, cognitive interactions between partners are highlighted, along with searching for negative imagery and negative self-talk. When working with couples experiencing sexual dysfunction, Burte and Araoz evaluate the couple's (a) perception of the sexual stimulus, (b) evaluation of the sexual stimulus, (c) physiological arousal, (d) perception of the arousal, (e) assessment of the arousal, (f) sexual behavior, (g) perception of that behavior, and (h) evaluation of the sexual behavior. The studies that were previously discussed centered on faulty perceptions and self-evaluations of arousal. However, *hypnosex therapy,* as Burte and Araoz designated their approach, focuses on altering the cognitive components of these perceptions and evaluations. The couple's awareness of their negative thought patterns is the core of this intervention. Some authors (Bakich, 1995) have advocated the primary use of traditional hypnotherapy techniques in treatment of the sexual desire disorders; however, more research is needed in this area.

In dealing with disease-related sexual dysfunction, Macaluso and Berkman (1984) implemented the use of three groups. The organic causes of dysfunction included diabetes, hypertension, alcoholic neuropathy, and erectile difficulty following prostate surgery. The groups focused on education, attitude change, the use of adaptive sexual techniques, and improved communications. Using pre and postgroup assessment to measure attitude changes, the group approach was found to be effective in educating couples about sexual dysfunction and offering alternative methods of obtaining sexual gratification (Macaluso & Berkman, 1984).

In investigating 65 couples presenting with sexual dysfunction, LoPiccolo, Heiman, and Hogan (1985) found that single-therapist groups show no significant difference from cotherapy groups. Participants assigned to a single male or single female therapist did no better or worse than those assigned to a dual-sex cotherapy team. The authors concluded that sex therapy was effective for both groups of participants.

Sexual Dysfunction among Gay Men

Consideration should be given to the particular needs of gay and bisexual men with sexual dysfunction. Assessment is crucial, and information regarding the use of alcohol and drugs may be pertinent, as well as assessing for organic factors, including chronic diseases such as diabetes, obesity, heart disease, and alcoholism. Fears and concerns relating to HIV and AIDS need to be evaluated, as well as the potential aversion to particular sexual acts (Reece, 1987). Assessment should include exploration of issues related to homophobia and how comfortable each partner is with his sexuality. Areas to be assessed include discussion of unresolved childhood conflicts, sexual orientation guilt, sexual trauma, performance pressures, and lack of insight into relationship needs (Reece, 1988).

As with heterosexual couples, Hypoactive Sexual Desire Disorder can be reframed as partner discrepancy in sexual desire. Desire differences may be a result of disparity in time, place, style, role, or activities preferences (Reece, 1987). Treatment for sexual dysfunction in the gay community involves evaluation of the couple's level of commitment, relationship openness, general sexual education and information, partner cooperation and compromise, couple awareness and increased communication, as well as combating the boredom and routine of sexual relationships (Reece, 1987).

The most frequently related sexual disorder among gay men is secondary erectile dysfunction, yet retarded ejaculation seems to be reported more frequently among homosexual males than it is in heterosexual males (Reece, 1988). Reece hypothesized that inhibited ejaculation may present more often in gay males because they may be more likely to develop rigid patterns in self-stimulation. Such patterns, which include intense rapid stroking of the penis with a tremendous pressure grip and extreme rigid tightening of the abdominal and leg muscles, which may make it difficult for males to orgasm with a partner or under differing circumstances.

It is interesting to note that the development of similar rigid patterns of masturbatory behavior may underlie the problem that many women have in experiencing orgasm during coitus. If masturbatory patterns are set to maximize clitoral stimulation, vaginal coitus may not replicate such stimulation with ease. Further research regarding masturbatory patterns and the orgasm phase of the sexual response cycle with partners is indicated for both gay males and women who present as anorgasmic through coitus.

Summary

Social workers dealing with sexual arousal disorders must develop a comprehensive assessment (including an extensive sexual history), utilize rapid assessment instruments to determine sexual status, be comfortable incorporating sex therapy as an amalgam to individual and couples therapy, and develop a treatment plan with follow-up, all while maintaining a stepwise open communication style that is necessary for the treatment of sexual disorders. The inclusion of pharmacotherapy, along with integrating various forms of sex therapy and cognitive, educational, and behavioral techniques, remains a crucial element in the complete treatment of individuals suffering from any type of sexual difficulty and should not be forgotten or underestimated. In addition to the need for more social work and behavioral science research in the area of sexual dysfunctions, there is the need for research replication. There are many different cognitive and behavioral treatments being conducted on either an individual or a group basis; however, the question of whether the results from these studies will remain consistent across individuals over time needs further exploration.

It is recommended that social workers doing empirical practice in this area, whether as part of an interdisciplinary team or independently, clearly denote that they are social work professionals. In this managed care environment, proving what works is no longer just expected: Positive outcomes are required. Social workers have long been involved in the diagnosis, assessment, and treatment of sexual dysfunctions, and it remains essential to emphasize this continuance.

Study Questions

1. Distinguish between low sexual desire and sexual aversion.
2. Why is a thorough medical examination always indicated in the assessment of a client with a presumptive sexual arousal or desire disorder?
3. Locate and complete one of the self-report assessment scales described in this chapter. Describe why you believe this is or is not a valid assessment instrument.
4. Describe one evidence-based treatment for erectile dysfunction.

References

Alexander, B. (1993). Disorders of sexual desire: Diagnosis and treatment of decreased libido. *American Family Physician, 47,* 832–838.

American Psychiatric Association. (2000). *Diagnostic and statistical manual of mental disorders* (4th ed., text rev.). Washington, DC: Author.

Anderson, B. L. (1983). Primary orgasmic dysfunction: Diagnostic considerations and review of treatment. *Psychological Bulletin, 93,* 105–136.

Bacon, C. G., Mittleman, M. A., Kawachi, I., Glovannucci, E., Glasser, D. B., & Rimm, E. R. (2003). Sexual function in men older than 50 years of age: Results from the health professionals follow-up study. *Annals of Internal Medicine, 139,* 161–168.

Bakich, I. (1995). Hypnosis in the treatment of the sexual desire disorders. *Australian Journal of Clinical and Experimental Hypnosis, 23*(1), 70–77.

Barlow, D. H. (1986). Causes of sexual dysfunction: The role of anxiety and cognitive interference. *Journal of Consulting and Clinical Psychology, 54,* 140–148.

Basson, R., McInnes, R., Smith, M. D., Hodgson, G., & Koppiker, N. (2002). Efficacy and safety of sildenafil citrate in women with sexual dysfunction associated with female sexual arousal disorder. *Journal of Women's Health and Gender-Based Medicine, 11,* 367–377.

Borello-France, D., Leng, W., O'Leary, M., Xavier, M., Erickson, J., Chancellor, M. B., et al. (2004). Bladder and sexual function among women with multiple sclerosis. *Multiple Sclerosis, 10,* 455–461.

Burte, J. M., & Araoz, D. L. (1994). Cognitive hypnotherapy with sexual disorders. *Journal of Cognitive Psychotherapy, 8,* 299–311.

Castelo-Branco, C., Blumel, J. E., Araya, H., Riquelme, R., Castro, G., Haya, J., et al. (2003). Prevalence of sexual dysfunction in a cohort of middle-aged women: Influences of menopause and hormone replacement therapy. *Journal of Obstetrics and Gynecology, 23,* 426–430.

Conte, H. R. (1986). Multivariate assessment of sexual dysfunction. *Journal of Consulting and Clinical Psychology, 54,* 149–157.

Costa, P., Arnould, B., Cour, F., Boyer, P., Marrel, A., Jaudinot, E. O., et al. (2003). Quality of Sexual Life Questionnaire (S): A reliable, sensitive, and reproducible instrument to assess quality of life in subjects with erectile dysfunction. *International Journal of Impotence Research, 15,* 173–184.

Dziegielewski, S. F. (2004). *The changing face of health care social work* (2nd ed.). New York: Springer.

Eastman, P. (1993, May/June). Washington report: Treating erectile dysfunction. *Geriatric Consultant,* 10–13.

Fazio, L., & Brock, G. (2004). Erectile dysfunction: Management update. *Canadian Medical Association, 170*(9), 1429–1436.

Fedoroff, J. P. (1991). Interview techniques to assess sexual disorders. *Families in Society, 72,* 140–145.

424   Sexual Disorders

Fish, L. S., Busby, D., & Killian, K. (1994). Structural couple therapy in the treatment of inhibited sexual drive. *American Journal of Family Therapy, 22,* 113–125.

Friedman, J. M., & Hogan, D. R. (1985). Sexual dysfunction and low sexual desire. In D. H. Barlow (Ed.), *Clinical handbook of psychiatric disorders* (pp. 417–461). New York: Guilford Press.

Goldman, A., & Carroll, J. (1990). Educational intervention as an adjunct to treatment of erectile dysfunction in older couples. *Journal of Sex and Marital Therapy, 16,* 127–141.

Goldstein, I. (2004). Epidemiology of erectile dysfunction. *Sexuality and Disability, 22*(2), 113.

Harrison, D. F. (1987). Clinical research in sexual dysfunctions: Social work contributions. *Journal of Social Service Research, 10*(2/3/4), 105–119.

Hawton, K., Catalan, J., & Fagg, J. (1991). Low sexual desire: Sex therapy results and prognostic factors. *Behavior Research and Therapy, 29,* 217–224.

Heiman, J. R., & Meston, C. M. (1997). Empirically validated treatment for sexual dysfunction. *Annual Review of Sex Research, 8,* 148–195.

Hofman, M., Morrow, G. R., Roscoe, J. A., Hickok, J. T., Mustian, K. M., Moore, D. F., et al. (2004). Cancer patients' expectations of experiencing treatment-related side effects. *Cancer, 100,* 851–857.

Janssen, E., Vorst, H., Finn, P., & Bancroft, J. (2002). The Sexual Inhibition (SIS) and Sexual Excitation (SES) Scales: Pt. I. Measuring sexual inhibition and excitement proneness in men. *Journal of Sex Research, 39,* 114–126.

Jensen, P. T., Klee, M. C., Thranov, I., & Groenvold, M. (2004). Validation of a questionnaire for self-assessment of sexual function and vagnial changes after gynaecological cancer. *Psycho-Oncology, 13,* 8, 577–592.

Johnson, S. D., Phelps, D. L., & Cottler, L. B. (2004, February). The association of sexual dysfunction and substance use among a community epidemiological sample. *Archives of Sexual Behavior, 33,* 55–63.

Kaplan, H. S. (1979). *Disorders of sexual desire.* New York: Simon & Schuster.

Kaplan, H. S. (1990). The combined use of sex therapy and intra-penile injections in the treatment of impotence. *Journal of Sex and Marital Therapy, 16,* 195–207.

Kaplan, L., & Harder, D. W. (1991). The Sexual Desire Conflict Scale for Women: Construction, internal consistency, and two initial validity tests. *Psychological Reports, 68,* 1275–1282.

Kilmann, P. R., Milan, R. J., Boland, J. P., Nankin, H. R., Davidson, E., West, M. O., et al. (1987). Group treatment for secondary erectile dysfunction. *Journal of Sex and Marital Therapy, 13,* 168–180.

Kinzl, J. F., Traweger, C., & Biebl, W. (1995). Sexual dysfunctions: Relationship to childhood sexual abuse and early family experiences in a nonclinical sample. *Child Abuse and Neglect, 19,* 785–792.

Knopf, J., & Seiler, M. (1990). *ISD: Inhibited sexual desire.* New York: Morrow.

Kuileter, M. M., Vroege, J. A., & van Lankveld, J. J. D. M. (1993). *The Golombok Rust Inventory of Sexual Satisfaction* (Nederlandse vertalilng enaapassignnen). Leiden, Holland: Netherlands University Medical Center [Dutch translation and adaptation].

Laumann, E. O., Paik, A., & Rosen, C. (1999). Sexual dysfunction in the United States: Prevalence and predictors. *Journal of the American Medical Association, 281,* 537–545.

Leif, H. (1977). What's new in sex research. *Medical Aspects of Human Sexuality, 7,* 94–95.

LePera, G., Giannotti, C. F., Taggi, F., & Macchia, T. (2003). Prevalence of sexual disorders in those young males who later become drug abusers. *Journal of Sex and Marital Therapy, 29,* 149–156.

Lipsith, J., McCann, D., & Goldmeier, D. (2003). Male psychogenic sexual dysfunction: The role of masturbation. *Sexual and Relationship Therapy, 18,* 447–471.

LoPiccolo, J., Heiman, J. R., & Hogan, D. R. (1985). Effectiveness of single therapists versus cotherapy teams in sex therapy. *Journal of Consulting and Clinical Psychology, 53,* 287–294.

Macaluso, E., & Berkman, A. H. (1984). Sex counseling with groups in a general hospital. *Social Casework, 65,* 19–26.

Meston, C. M., & Derogatis, L. R. (2002). Validated instruments for assessing female sexual function. *Journal of Sex and Marital Therapy, 28,* 155–164.

Moore, T. M., Straus, J. L., Herman, S., & Donatucci, C. F. (2003). Erectile dysfunction in early, middle, and late adulthood: Symptoms patterns and psychosocial correlates. *Journal of Sex and Marital Therapy, 29,* 381–399.

Nicolosi, A., Laumann, E. O., Glasser, D. B., Moreira, E. D., Paik, A., & Gingell, C. (2004). Sexual behavior and sexual dysfunctions after age 40: The global study of sexual attitudes and behaviors. *Urology, 64,* 991–998.

Nicolson, P., & Burr, J. (2003). What is "normal" about women's (hetero)sexual desire and orgasm? A report of an in-depth interview study. *Social Science and Medicine, 57,* 1735–1745.

O'Leary, M. P., Rhodes, T., Girman, C. J., Jacobson, D. J., Roberts, R. O., Lieber, M. M., et al. (2003). Distribution of the Brief Male Sexual Inventory in community men. *International Journal of Impotence Research, 15,* 185–191.

Palace, E. M., & Gorzalka, B. B. (1992). Differential patterns of arousal in sexually functional and dysfunctional women: Physiological and subjective components of sexual response. *Archives of Sexual Behavior, 21,* 135–159.

Read, J. (1995). Female sexual dysfunction. *International Review of Psychiatry, 7,* 175–182.

Reece, R. (1987). Causes and treatment of sexual desire discrepancies in male couples. *Journal of Homosexuality, 14,* 157–172.

Reece, R. (1988). Special issues in the etiologies and treatments of sexual problems among gay men. *Journal of Homosexuality, 15,* 43–57.

Rosen, R., Brown, C., Heiman, J., Leiblum, S., Meston, C., Shabsigh, R., et al. (2000). The Female Sexual Function Index (FSFI): A multidimensional self-report instrument for the assessment of female sexual function. *Journal of Sex and Marital Therapy, 26,* 191–208.

Rosen, R. C., & Leiblum, S. R. (1987). Current approaches to the evaluation of sexual desire disorders. *Journal of Sex Research, 23,* 141–162.

Rowland, D. L., Tai, W. L., & Slob, A. K. (2003). An exploration of emotional response to erotic stimulation in men with premature ejaculation: Effects of treatment with clomipramine. *Journal of Sexual Behavior, 32,* 145–153.

Russell, L. (1990, Summer). Sex and couple therapy: A method of treatment to enhance physical and emotional intimacy. *Journal of Sex and Marital Therapy, 16,* 111–120.

Salonia, A., Munarriz, R. M., Naspro, R., Nappi, R. E., Briganti, A., Chionna, R., et al. (2004). Women's sexual dysfunction: A pathophysiological review. *BJU International, 93,* 8, 1156–1164.

Segraves, R. T., & Segraves, K. B. (1991). Hypoactive sexual desire disorder: Prevalence and comorbidity in 906 subjects. *Journal of Sex and Marital Therapy, 17,* 55–58.

Shabbir, M., Mikhailidis, D. M., & Morgan, R. J. (2004). Erectile dysfunction: An under diagnosed condition associated with multiple risk factors. *Current Medical Research and Opinions, 20,* 603–606.

Shaw, J. (1990). Play therapy with the sexual workhorse: Successful treatment with 12 cases of inhibited ejaculation. *Journal of Sex and Marital Therapy, 16,* 159–164.

Spector, I. P., & Carey, M. P. (1990). Incidence and prevalence of sexual dysfunctions: A critical review of the literature. *Archives of Sexual Behavior, 19,* 389–408.

Stuart, F. M., Hammond, D. C., & Pett, M. A. (1987). Inhibited sexual desire in women. *Archives of Sexual Behavior, 16,* 91–106.

Stuntz, S. S., Falk, A., Hiken, M., & Carson, V. B. (1996). The journey undermined by psychosexual disorders. In V. B. Carson & E. N. Arnold (Eds.), *Mental health nursing: The nurse-patient journey* (pp. 879–895). Philadelphia: Saunders.

Swindle, R. W., Cameron, A. E., Lockhart, D. C., & Rosen, R. C. (2004). The Psychological and Interpersonal Relationship Scales: Assessing psychological and relationship outcomes associated with erectile dysfunction and its treatment. *Archives of Sexual Behavior, 33,* 19–30.

Thyer, B. A., & Papsdorf, J. D. (1981). Relationship between irrationality and sexual arousability. *Psychological Reports, 48,* 834.

Trudel, G. (1991). Review of psychological factors in low sexual desire. *Sexual and Marital Therapy, 6*, 261–272.

Vonk, M. E., & Thyer, B. A. (1995). Exposure therapy in the treatment of vaginal penetration phobia: A case study. *Journal of Behavior Therapy and Experimental Psychiatry, 29*, 359–363.

Wincze, J. P., & Carey, M. P. (1991). *Sexual dysfunction: A guide for assessment and treatment.* New York: Guilford Press.

Wincze, J. P., Rosen, R., Carson, C., Korenman, C. N., Niederberger, C., Sadovsky, R., et al. (2004). Erection Quality Scale: Initial scale development and validation. *Adult Urology, 64*, 351–356.

Woody, J. D., D'Souza, H. J., & Crain, D. D. (1994). Sexual functioning in clinical couples: Discriminant validity of the Sexual Interaction System Scale. *American Journal of Family Therapy, 22*, 291–303.

Zippe, C. D., Raina, R., Shah, A. D., Massanyl, E. C., Agarwal, A., Ulchaker, J., et al. (2004). Female sexual dysfunction after radical cystectomy: A new outcome measure. *Adult Urology, 63*, 1153–1157.

Orgasmic Disorders

Sophia F. Dziegielewski, George Jacinto,
Gary Dick, and Cheryl Resnick-Cortes

19
Chapter

Learning Objectives

After reading this chapter, the reader will be able to:

- Describe the major orgasmic disorders and their estimated prevalence.
- Describe at least two evidence-based methods of assessing clients who meet the *DSM* criteria for Orgasmic Disorder.
- Locate, retrieve, and critique at least two sources of information (e.g., journal articles) describing a presumptively evidence-based intervention for orgasmic disorders.

Overview of the Problem

Human sexuality and in particular sexual problems are often overlooked in the assessment and treatment of individuals and couples, despite the fact that sexual dysfunction can affect quality of life, disrupt intimate relationship, and often lead to depression and anxiety. Despite the lack of interest and attention from mental health professionals, sexual dysfunctions are rather common in the United States. Sexual problems inmen tend to increase with age, especially erection problems. Community samples have found rates of sexual dysfunction ranging from 25% to 63% of women and 10% to 52% of men.

Operational Definitions of the Problem

The *Diagnostic and Statistical Manual of Mental Disorders* (*DSM;* American Psychiatric Association, 2000) lists the following orgasmic disorders: Female Orgasmic Disorder, Male Orgasmic Disorder, and Premature Ejaculation. Orgasmic disorders can affect quality of life and impact an individual's ability to sustain intimate relationships, often leading to depression and anxiety (Heiman, 2002a). This may be particularly true for young adults who experience orgasmic disorders. There are a number of physical and psychological causal factors that are believed to contribute to the diagnosis of the orgasmic disorders in women and men. These factors include side effects of medications such as antidepressants and medications for a number of chronic health conditions, relationship conflict, traumatic experience (e.g., rape), sexual and physical abuse, menopause, surgery, hysterectomy, removal of ovaries, incontinence surgery, pelvic floor problems, and bike riding (FSDInfo, 2004). The focus of this chapter is to explore the treatment implications of the orgasmic disorders for mental health practitioners.

Sexuality is an important domain of human experience to assess both in quality of life studies and in clinical practice, yet mental health therapists have been reluctant to inquire about sexual behaviors, let alone probe further and asked clients about their attitudes and feelings toward their sexual behavior or lack thereof. Human sexual behavior is influenced by a complex dynamic interaction among physiological, behavioral, psychosocial, political, and cultural factors (Lipsith, McCann, & Goldmeier, 2003).

Sexual Development

The growing awareness of one's sexuality is a part of normal human growth and development. Yet sexual development and its expression are generally considered a unique and private affair. As individuals progress through the life cycle and seek to join sexually with a mate, problems can occur. Studies have illustrated that previous sexual experiences that include sexual abuse, sexual behaviors, and parental attitudes toward sex, as well as other environmental factors, greatly impact individuals and can lead to the development of sexual disorders (H. S. Kaplan, 1995; L. Kaplan & Harder, 1991; Kinzl, Traweger, & Biebl, 1995; Stuart, Hammond, & Pett, 1987). Sexual function is important to the quality of life, and yet for a variety of reasons, it is an often neglected area of health care (Rosen, 2003). Because this important aspect of development is often misunderstood, neglected, or abused by society, individuals who suffer from sexual problems may not know how to address them.

According to social learning theory, individuals acquire much of their sexual behavior according to socially acceptable (i.e., reinforced) or unacceptable (i.e., punished) codes of expression (i.e., contingencies). For example, intimate sexual expression is rarely modeled. As a result, the traditional modes of education, such as parental modeling and social influence, are absent in this area. As a result of this privatization of sexuality, children can receive inaccurate, inappropriate, or exploitive information, on which future expectations will be modeled. Also, due to a general attempt to avoid or neglect this phase of human development, there can be gaps in learning how to obtain this information. This can lead to a lack of appropriate channels for obtaining information that is considered to be embarrassing or forbidden. Adult sexuality is an ongoing process of recognizing, accepting, and expressing one's sexuality. As adults go through the life cycle and face developmental changes, these changes affect one's sexuality. Sexuality is affected by such life changes as choosing a mate, the birth of a child, and the aging process, as well as situational factors such as work and illness (Sharpe, 2003).

Culture has a tremendous impact on the expression of sexuality, and even within cultures there are vast differences in sexual norms, values, and expressions of human sexuality. If our culture prohibits honest discourse on human sexuality and health care professionals ignore this aspect of human development, then individuals experiencing difficulties in any aspect of their developing sexuality are at increased risk of other psychosocial problems. This lack of attention to the development of human sexuality can have serious long-term effects that cause adults to struggle with unrealistic expectations, resulting in the lack of proper coping skills to deal with sexual behaviors, which can lead to delay in discussing their concerns about their sexuality with a health care provider (Horton, 1995). For example, men with Premature Ejaculation (PE) report being embarrassed to talk about this problem and believing that no treatment exists (Symonds, Roblin, Hart, & Althof, 2003). Research has shown a time lag of 3 years from the onset of erectile dysfunction (ED) among men and seeking treatment. In a study of men with Premature Ejaculation, 89% tried some form of treatment, regardless of whether they consulted their physician (Symonds et al., 2003). It is important for social workers to explore this aspect of human development, be able to accurately assess the extent of sexual dysfunction, and make evidence-based treatment recommendations.

In our society, it is clear when looking at both males and females that the beliefs and cognitions that an individual holds can impact the individual's sexual performance and ability. The human sexual response, which is dynamic and multidimensional, is influenced by previous sexual experiences, internal needs and desires, conflict between socialization and desire, and the relationship with the partner. It consists of cognitive, affective, and physiological components (Rowland, Tai, & Slob, 2003). Thyer and Papsdorf (1981) found little evidence to support the premise that irrational beliefs inhibit one's capacity for sexual enjoyment; however, many professionals continue to argue the opposite (Eastman, 1993). It is important to explore individuals' thoughts and feelings about their sexual behavior and their needs and desires for human sexual expression.

Defining Sexual Dysfunctions

When an individual believes that he or she has encountered difficulties that cause significant disturbance in the sexual relationship, these problems are often termed *sexual dysfunctions.* In an attempt to understand problems that can develop within the human sexual response cycle, the *DSM-IV-TR* (American Psychiatric Association, 2000, p. 535) lists the essential feature of sexual dysfunction as having a "disturbance in the processes that characterize the sexual response cycle or by pain associated with sexual intercourse."

Further, the *DSM-IV-TR* (American Psychiatric Association, 2000) divides the sexual response cycle into the following phases: *desire phase* (desires and fantasies about sex), *excitement phase* (subjective interpretations and actual physiologic changes), *orgasm phase* (generalized muscular tension and contractions in the sex organs), and *resolution phase* (general sense of relaxation and release of the previously created muscular tension). The female and male orgasmic disorders are sexual difficulty disorders in which orgasm is delayed or absent following a normal excitement phase. Or the opposite reaction occurs, which results in Premature Ejaculation in men (Maxmen & Ward, 1995). It is important to note, however, that for a person to be diagnosed with an orgasmic disorder, the following symptoms must be present: (a) The problem must be persistent and recurrent; (b) it must not occur exclusively in relation to another major clinical diagnosis (such as major depression or an adjustment disorder), and it must not be caused by substance abuse or be related to a general medical condition; and (c) it must cause marked distress or interpersonal difficulty (American Psychiatric Association, 2000).

Prevalence Estimates of Sexual Dysfunction

In a study of 27,500 men and women ranging in age from 40 to 80 from 29 countries, 28% of men and 39% of women reported they were affected by a sexual dysfunction (Nicolosi et al., 2004). Despite the lack of interest and attention from mental health professionals, sexual dysfunctions are rather common in the United

States. Sexual problems in men tend to increase with age, especially erection problems (Heiman, 2002a). The National Health and Social Life Survey produced in 1994 is the only national study using random sampling to study sexual dysfunction (Laumann, Gagnon, Michael, & Michaels, 1994). This study estimated that 43% of women and 31% of men in the United States between the ages of 18 and 59 have some form of sexual dysfunction (Laumann, Paik, & Rosen, 1999). Community samples have found rates of sexual dysfunction ranging from 25% to 63% of women and 10% to 52% of men (Heiman, 2002a). In 2002, the Massachusetts Male Aging Study surveyed 1,709 men ranging in age from 40 to 70 in the greater Boston area and found the prevalence of erectile dysfunction to be 52%, with 9.6% of the sample reporting complete erectile dysfunction (Fazio & Brock, 2004).

It is estimated that 43% of women in the United States have sexual dysfunction (Nicolosi et al., 2006). Sexual disorders are highly prevalent among women and affect women irrespective of education, religious beliefs, socioeconomic status, and age (Meston, 2000). Vaginal lubrication tends to become more of a problem with age and menopause. In a study of 534 healthy women in Chile, researchers found that desire dysfunctions, arousal disorders, and orgasmic disorders increased for women after age 50. Interestingly, the researchers found that the male partner's erectile dysfunction increased the risk of female sexual dysfunction threefold (Castelo-Branco et al., 2003). In a study of sexual dysfunction among 169 individuals with mental illness sampled from outpatient clinics, 42.3% reported sexual problems (Wylie, Steward, Seivewright, Smith, & Walters, 2002).

Prevalence Estimates of Male Orgasmic Disorders

Male Orgasmic Disorder, on the other hand, is uncommon, with only 8.3% of men reporting problems with a lack of orgasm within the past year (Laumann et al., 1994). Premature Ejaculation or rapid ejaculations (RE) is the most widely common male sexual dysfunction (Grenier & Byers, 2001). Ejaculation is an important aspect of male sexuality and has a major impact on men's sexual relationships, sexual self-esteem, and overall quality of life (Chen, Mabjeesh, Matzkin, & Greenstein, 2003). It is estimated that between 22% and 38% of the adult male population suffer from Premature Ejaculation (Laumann et al., 1999) and that 75% of men experienced Premature Ejaculation at some point in their lives (McMahon, 1998). In a study of healthy heterosexual college males, Grenier and Byers (2001) found that 32% of the sample self-reported they had a problem with RE at some time in their life, and of those men, 18% indicated that RE had been a lifelong problem. These rates for RE are similar to the self-reported prevalence rate of 28.5% of men in Laumann et al.'s (1994) study.

Prevalence Estimates of Female Orgasmic Disorders

Orgasmic disorders are common in women. It is estimated that 24% of women have difficulty associated with an orgasm (Laumann et al., 1994). In a study of 3,400 women, 20% reported difficulties with lubrication, 30% reported being uninterested in intercourse, and 20% indicated that sexual relations provided them with minimal pleasure (Meston, 2000). Although it is difficult to calculate the exact prevalence rates of Female Orgasmic Disorder, research indicates that 5% to 10% of American women have dealt with a lifelong inability to achieve orgasm (H. S. Kaplan, 1974; Kinzl et al., 1995; Morokoff & LoPiccolo, 1986; Simons & Carey, 2001). Palace (1995) estimates that 30% of women meet the *DSM-IV-TR* criteria for orgasmic disorder, and 20% of women meet the criteria for sexual desire disorders (about 23.5 million and 15 million women, respectively).

Categories of Orgasmic Disorders

To comprehend the absence of an orgasmic response, it is imperative that the existence and definition of orgasmic response be recognized. Stated simply, *orgasm* is the peak of climax or sexual excitement in sexual activity (McCary, 1973). Physiologically normal men and women are capable of achieving an orgasm. The orgasmic response generally consists of facial grimacing, generalized myotonia, carpopedal spasm, gluteal and abdominal muscle contraction, and rhythmic contractions of the orgasmic platform, which results in vaginal contractions in females and penile swelling and ejaculation in males (Anderson, 1983). Both men and women who experience orgasmic disorders often have a strong sexual drive. For example, in women the capacity to appreciate sexual foreplay, lubricate, and enjoy phallic penetration often shows no impairment (H. S. Kaplan, 1974). One of the primary problems for researchers in understanding the orgasmic response is that it can differ among individuals with regard to intensity, length, duration, and overall pleasure. Further, the response can differ in the same individual from one act of coition to another (McCary, 1973). Variation in male ejaculation can and does occur with a change in intensity and degree, and yet researchers are reluctant to attribute the origins of this variation in ejaculation to either exclusive psychological or physiological sources (Rowland & Koos, 1997).

According to the *DSM* (American Psychiatric Association, 2000, p. 547), this type of sexual dysfunction refers to "the persistent or recurrent delay in, or absence of, orgasm following a normal sexual excitement phase." This problem may be generalized, occurring throughout all of an individual's sexual experiences, or situational, occurring with a specific partner or circumstance. The disorder is also distinguished by whether it is a lifelong or acquired condition, and by whether it is primary or secondary. Generally, Primary Orgasmic Disorder applies to individuals who have never been able to achieve orgasm through any means. Secondary Orgasmic Disorder applies to individuals who have been orgasmic in the past, but for whatever reason are currently anorgasmic.

Secondary Orgasmic Disorder, which is often situational and can take many different forms, may vary in degree (Milan, Kilmann, & Boland, 1988). It can consist of anorgasmia with a specific partner, a complete lack of coital orgasm, vibrator/masturbation-only orgasm, a prior history of orgasm with current decreased frequency, the experience of anorgasmia only in particular contexts, low frequency of orgasm, or recent orgasmic dysfunction with previous orgasmic capability, on all occasions of sexual activity, including masturbation (Heiman & Meston, 1997; McCabe & Delaney, 1992).

Anorgasmia

Anorgasmia, which involves difficulty achieving orgasm, is generally considered to be psychogenic in nature; however, Stuntz, Falk, Hiken, and Carson (1996) warn that the consideration of a physiological factor should not be underestimated. Medical and life circumstances, such as fatigue, acute illness, medication, decreased perineal musculature, or neurological and vascular conditions, can complicate or enhance this difficulty. Psychological factors should also be considered essential in understanding the disorder (Fish, Busby, & Killian, 1994). Situational and environmental factors, such as societal mores as they relate to sexual roles and expectations, family attitudes, sex education or lack of it, and religious beliefs, can all affect the ability to achieve orgasm. Pharmacologically induced Orgasmic Disorder is a new subcategory that has emerged within the past 10 years (Heiman, 2002a). The selective serotonin reuptake inhibitor (SSRI) class of drugs is known to produce side effects that can either delay or prevent orgasm in both men and women. For those men and women who take SSRI medication, it is estimated that 9% to 40% report problems with orgasm. The problem appears to be more prevalent in women (Heiman, 2002b).

In a study of women with sexual arousal and orgasmic disorders, Bechara et al. (2003) reported that the women experienced diminished clitoral vascular responses when compared with women without sexual dysfunction. Data from the 1994 National Health and Social Life Survey reported that of women age 18 through 59, 14% had ongoing problems with lubrication during most sexual activity, 23% complained of a lack of lubrication during intercourse, and 44% reported reoccurring problems with lubrication (Laumann et al., 1994).

Male Orgasmic Disorder is considered rare when compared to the occurrence of Female Orgasmic Disorder. However, in a review of numerous studies in this area, Spector and Carey (1990) reported that occurrence rates among those who present for treatment were similar to those for females, involving approximately 4% to 10% of males. Male prevalence rates in the general population, however, remain much lower. In a review of the literature, Simons and Carey (2001) reported prevalence rates for males who suffer from Male Orgasmic Disorder are approximately 0 to 3%, and from Premature Ejaculation approximately 4% to 5% of the population. This condition remains the least common of the orgasmic disorders in males.

Premature Ejaculation

Men who experience Premature Ejaculation (PE), also referred to as rapid ejaculation (RE), can experience significant stress related to this form of sexual disorder. In this society, males are generally praised for their ability to perform and are chastised when they experience difficulty. Premature Ejaculation can affect a man's self-esteem and his relationships. In an in-depth qualitative study of 28 men with Premature Ejaculation, their major concern was the erosion of their sexual confidence (Symonds et al., 2003). Relationship issues were the second concern mentioned, revealing a reluctance to establish relationships; men in existing relationships reported distress in not being able to satisfy their partner (Symonds et al., 2003). The cause of Premature Ejaculation is considered more psychological than physiological, and rarely can it be attributed to a single cause (Rowland, Tai, & Slob, 2003).

The basic criteria for diagnosing Premature Ejaculation are (a) ejaculation must be persistent or recurrent with minimal sexual stimulation before, during, or shortly after penetration (this ejaculation must also occur before the male desires it); (b) the disturbance must cause marked distress or interpersonal difficulty; and (c) the episodes of Premature Ejaculation must not be related to the direct effects of any substance (American Psychiatric Association, 2000, p. 554). Additionally, when diagnosing Premature Ejaculation, it is important to determine if the problem is lifelong or acquired, generalized or situational, and caused from only psychological factors rather than a combination of factors. Combined factors may include assessing anxiety and/or length of time since the most recent intercourse, fear of intimacy, and whether using various forms of erotica to stimulate and heighten the arousal period is a factor.

A problem noted by Spector and Carey (1990) in examining previous studies in this area is that many times researchers did not clearly define the time period surrounding premature orgasm. Therefore, time periods could vary from seconds after penetration up to 10 minutes.

In a study of 260 men, 70% ejaculated within 7 minutes, 32% in less than 4 minutes, 27% in less than 3 minutes, and

24% in less than 2 minutes. Ejaculating in less than 2 minutes is a common benchmark to measure RE (Grenier & Byers, 2001). Social workers will have to rely on their own judgment as to what constitutes before, on, or shortly after penetration (Symonds et al., 2003). This further complicates the definition by making the range of what could be considered normal unproblematic latency quite broad (O'Donohue, Letourneau, & Geer, 1993). Therefore, in assessing the client, it is important for the social worker to address factors that can affect the duration of the excitement phase, particularly factors that can lead to the occurrence of too quick or unplanned orgasms. Factors that need to be considered include the age of the male, the novelty of the sexual partner or the situation surrounding the encounter, and the frequency of sexual behavior. It is important to note, however, that focusing on just one of the three criteria, such as the time from entry to orgasm, can result in an inaccurate diagnosis.

The five most common measures utilized to diagnose RE are ejaculatory latency (less than 2 minutes after vaginal entry), perceived ejaculatory control (control over first ejaculation during intercourse), concerns over ejaculation (concern that it was sooner than desired), satisfaction with ejaculation control (ability to set the moment of ejaculation), and the percentage of antiportal ejaculation (percentage of intercourse experiences where ejaculation occurred before vaginal entry; Grenier & Byers, 2001). Another factor to consider is that younger and less sexually experienced men are more likely to ejaculate quicker than older men who are more experienced. Additional factors to inquire about include the frequency of intercourse and the time frame since previous intercourse. Increased frequency is associated with increased ejaculatory latency, control, satisfaction, less concern of ejaculating too soon, and self-identification as having an RE problem (Grenier & Byers, 2001).

Evidence-Based Approaches to Assessment

In assessing the orgasmic disorders, as with the other sexual disorders, it is important to note (a) whether the condition is lifelong or acquired (with or without previously normal functioning); (b) whether it is generalized or situational (with a particular partner); (c) if it is conjunct (with or without a partner) or solitary (as in masturbation); and (d) if it is due to psychological, medical, substance use, or combined factors. In clinical assessment, it is suggested that social workers obtain information on such factors as the frequency, intensity, duration, setting, and degree of sexual impairment; the level of subjective distress; and the effects on other areas of functioning (e.g., social, occupational) for each client treated (Maxmen & Ward, 1995).

One of the most important components of assessing sexual dysfunction is to obtain a medical and sexual history (Fazio & Brock, 2004). Proper assessment requires the careful accumulation of data that are likely to affect sexual response. Age; marital status; religious beliefs; whether the couple reside together; socioeconomic status; level of education of both partners; motivation for treatment of both partners; nature of the marital relationship; functional ability of the male partner; levels of anxiety; type of anorgasmia (primary versus secondary); gynecological, physiological, and medical conditions; the presence of psychosis or depression; and drug and alcohol use may all impact an individual's ability to reach orgasm. It is important to distinguish between losses of libido and a sexual disorder. In males, a loss of libido may be attributed to a decrease in testosterone, combined with depression, anxiety, low self-esteem, work-related stress, and relationship problems. These combined factors may interact with one another, contributing to a sexual dysfunction; therefore, it is important to differentiate which came first.

Many medical problems can inhibit orgasmic responses, and Maxmen and Ward (1995) consider failure to address them to be one of the most common reasons for failure of sexual therapy. Erectile dysfunction is strongly related to medical conditions. Predictors of erectile dysfunction include diabetes depression, heart disease, hypertension, and decreased high-density lipoprotein. Medical conditions that can impede assessment and treatment include neurological disorders, such as multiple sclerosis; spinal cord and peripheral nerve damage; endocrine and metabolic disorders; diabetes; and thyroid deficiency.

Drugs (e.g., sedatives and narcotics) and alcohol are also likely to inhibit an orgasmic response. Antidepressant medications and hypertensive medications can potentially suppress the orgasmic response (Heiman, 2002b; Knopf & Seiler, 1990). With the problem of Premature Ejaculation, a link to withdrawal from opioids should also be ruled out (Stuntz et al., 1996). Alcohol may retard orgasmic response in low doses and can inhibit response entirely in higher doses (McCabe & Delaney, 1992). When alcohol abuse is linked to anorgasmia, it is important to assess which came first, the alcohol abuse or the anorgasmia (McCabe & Delaney, 1992). There is a high incidence of alcohol abuse among women who have been sexually abused as children, and these women are also more likely to display sexual disorders (Golden, 1988; Kinzl et al., 1995; Saunders, Villeponteaux, Lipovsky, & Kilpatrick, 1992).

In the assessment process, it is important to establish whether orgasmic dysfunction is primary (individual never has been able to experience orgasm) or secondary (individual formerly was able to reach orgasm). If an individual displays primary orgasmic dysfunction, the therapist must assess whether the individual in fact suffers from orgasmic inhibition or has simply never received sufficient stimulation due to poor sexual technique or poor education of self or partner (H. S. Kaplan, 1979). The importance of a first orgasm cannot be overstated, and therapists should always be asked whether it has occurred, as it is necessary to mark the initial step in deconditioning inhibition. For individuals who are unable to achieve orgasm under situational circumstances, a complete evaluation of anxiety-producing factors during the situations in question may be indicated.

The level of knowledge and education regarding sexuality and sexual behavior should be assessed prior to the implementation of a treatment program. This may include the couple's comprehension regarding male and female anatomy, male and female sexual response, the possible causes of male and female dysfunction, sexual myths and misconceptions, and discussion of masturbation, oral and anal sex, and the variety of intercourse positions (McCabe & Delaney, 1992). Although research results are conflicting, it is assumed that communication skills, marital harmony, sexual anxiety, and performance anxiety may all be important factors in sexual response (McCabe & Delaney, 1992).

Therapeutic consideration of the emotional and cognitive contributing factors to the disruption of the physiological stages of sexual arousal should be given during the assessment phase. In addition, the therapist must differentiate among sexual anxiety, low sexual desire, and the ability of the individual to achieve satisfactory arousal; the functional ability and flexibility of the partner must also be taken into consideration when evaluating an individual's ability to respond sexually (Friedman & Hogan, 1985; Hawton, Catalan, & Fagg, 1991; Trudel, 1991).

Assessment Scales

In addition to self-report measures and partner evaluation measures, several researchers have developed assessment scales to measure sexual drive, sexual arousal, sexual response, sexual satisfaction, erection quality, ejaculation, and orgasmic response. Several psychometric instruments have been developed for diagnosing both male and female sexual disorders. The assessment tools strive to obtain a profile of the sexual functioning of the individuals and the couple, the nature of the marital relationship (levels of marital satisfaction and happiness), levels of sexual anxiety and performance anxieties, and ratings of sexual responsiveness (orgasmic response in relation to masturbation and coitus). Generally, several assessment measures have been used in conjunction with one another. Meston and Derogatis (2002) reviewed five new instruments that met the standards of the Food and Drug Administration Center for Drug Evaluation and Research. These scales demonstrate reliability, validity, and responsiveness, are able to distinguish those with a sexual disorder and those without a disorder, and can detect meaningful differences following treatment.

The Brief Index of Sexual Functioning for Women (BISF-W; Taylor, Rosen, & Leiblum, 1994) is a 22-item self-report that measures female sexual functioning and satisfaction. There are three factors in the BISF-W: interest/desire, sexual activity, and sexual satisfaction. The scale provides an overall composite score for sexual functioning, in addition to scores on seven dimensions of female sexuality: thoughts/desires, arousal, frequency of sexual activity, receptivity/initiation, pleasure/orgasm, relationship satisfaction, and problems affecting sexual functioning (Meston & Derogatis, 2002).

The Changes in Sexual Functioning Questionnaire (CSFQ; Clayton, McGarvey, & Clavet, 1997) is a 35-item structured interview that measures illness- and medication-related changes in sexual functioning. It is also available in a self-report version for both males and females. The CSFQ produces a total score and scores on five domains of sexuality: desire frequency, desire interest, sexual pleasure, sexual arousal, and orgasm (Meston & Derogatis, 2002).

The Derogatis Interview for Sexual Functioning (DISF; Derogatis, 1976) is a 25-item semistructured interview that provides a multidimensional assessment of sexual functioning in both men and women. The DISF measures five domains of sexual functioning: sexual cognition/fantasy, sexual arousal, sexual behavior/experience, orgasm, and sexual drive/relationship (Meston & Derogatis, 2002).

The Female Sexual Function Index (Rosen et al., 2000) is a 19-item self-report measure of female sexual functioning that provides scores on five domains of sexual functioning: desire, arousal, lubrication, orgasm, satisfaction, and pain (Meston & Derogatis, 2002).

The Golombok-Rust Inventory of Sexual Satisfaction (GRISS; Kuileter, Vroege, & van Lankveld, 1993) is a 56-item self-report (28 items for males and 28 for females) developed to measure both the quality of a heterosexual relationship and each partner's sexual functioning within the relationship (Meston & Derogatis, 2002). The GRISS measures 12 domains of sexual functioning: five for females, five for males, and two common gender domains. The domains measuring female sexuality include anorgasmia, vaginismus, avoidance, nonsensuality, and dissatisfaction.

The Sexual Inhibition and Sexual Excitation Scales I (Janssen, Vorst, Finn, & Bancroft, 2002) are 45-item instruments designed to measure male sexual inhibition and excitation. The Sexual Excitation (SES) factor has 20 items and four subscales. The four subscales measure social interaction with a sexually attractive person, excitation as a result of visual stimuli, ease of arousal when thinking or fantasizing about sex, and excitation that is a result of nonspecific stimuli. The Sexual Inhibition (SIS) factor has 25 items and seven subscales: losing one's arousal and erection easily; inhibition due to concern about sexual interactions with a partner; performance concerns; worries and external sources of distraction; fear about the risk of being caught while performing sexual acts; negative consequences of sex; and physical pain, norms, and values (Janssen et al., 2002).

The Brief Male Sexual Inventory (BMSI; O'Leary et al., 2003) is an 11-item instrument designed to measure male sexual functioning. The BMSI measures sexual drive, erectile function, and ejaculatory function, as well as overall satisfaction with sex life.

The Erection Quality Scale (EQS; Wincze et al., 2004) is a 15-item self-report questionnaire designed to assess the quality of penile erections. The EQS is designed to be administered to both homosexual and heterosexual men. Constructs of erection quality were derived from interviews with 93 men and include rigidity/hardness, duration, control/confidence, ease of obtaining/speed of onset, sensitivity/sensation, fast recovery, and appearance of penis.

Additional scales include the Sexual Interaction Inventory, which measures frequency dissatisfaction, pleasure mean, perceptual accuracy, self-acceptance, and mate acceptance (Morokoff & LoPiccolo, 1986). The Sexual History Form rates frequency of sexual intercourse, duration of foreplay, duration of intercourse, frequency of orgasm in masturbation, partner stimulation, intercourse, and stimulation during intercourse, as well as sexual relationship satisfaction and the perceived sexual relationship satisfaction of the partner (Morokoff & LoPiccolo, 1986). The Sexual Interaction System Scale provides a viable measure designed to explore sexual interaction, sexual satisfaction, and overall marital adjustment (Woody, D'Souza & Crain, 1994).

Social work professionals recognize that the experiences, beliefs, and cognitions an individual holds can and do impact sexual performance and ability. In the treatment context, the concepts of desire and arousal are clearly different. *Desire* refers to a mental and emotional state, whereas *arousal* represents a physiological state, manifest in behavior. Distinguishing between the concepts of desire and arousal, much as making the differentiation between the treatments of the sexual arousal and desire disorders, is crucial in the provision of treatment for anorgasmic individuals and for males with Premature Ejaculation.

In summary, the assessment of orgasmic dysfunction requires that the social worker consider the primary versus secondary nature of the problem and take into account psychosocial factors, including prior history of sexual abuse as a child, the nature of the relationship with the partner, the partner's ability to adequately perform sexually, sexual self-esteem, any physiological or medical factors, and the documentation of use of substances or medications.

Special Considerations in Assessment

Heiman (2002a, 2002b) observes that successful treatment of sexual dysfunction, including orgasmic disorders, may require a combination of psychological and physiological interventions. To address only physiologic treatment overlooks the reality that an individual's understanding of human sexuality can be impacted by subjective meanings that may further interfere with sexual functioning. Psychological interventions impact sexual physiology. Heiman further recommends that future research regarding female sexual dysfunction assess the efficacy of psychological and physiological treatments separately and in combination.

It is also important to inquire about substance abuse. In a study of 130 male substance abusers between the ages of 17 and 29, 20% presented with erectile dysfunction and 38% presented with premature orgasm prior to drug usage (LaPera, Giannotti, Taggi, & Macchia, 2003). These findings may indicate that the awareness of a sexual problem in these young men may be a risk factor for drug abuse.

It is also important to inquire about the latency period of ejaculation in men with RE when self-masturbating compared to the latency period during coitus. One of the central features of RE is orgasm with minimal sexual stimulation. Assessment should inquire about whether the orgasm occurs before penetration or upon entry and the latency period after penetration (Atmaca, Kuloglu, Tezcan, & Semercios, 2002).

It is important for clinicians to asses an individual's experiences with masturbation. Masturbation is a normal process of human sexual development that follows three main phases: (1) masturbation, (2) heterosexual/homosexual contact and continued masturbation, and (3) heterosexual/homosexual contact with or without sporadic masturbation (Lipsith et al., 2003). In the assessment it is important to inquire about the details of an individual's masturbatory frequency, fantasies, and technique, as well as feelings and attitudes toward masturbation. In some individuals, despite the availability of heterosexual or, in the case of homosexuals, homosexual contacts, masturbation remains the dominant sexual contact. Understanding the function of masturbation beyond simple sexual gratification, determining whether the masturbation has become compulsive, and determining the impulse to delay masturbation until the individual is in an appropriate location are important to assess. Masturbatory experiences can play a part in Male Orgasmic Disorder (Slosarz, 1992). A conditional learning process may result as positive reinforcement from self-masturbation is associated with ejaculation (Dow, 1981). This masturbatory style may result in the inability to transfer the sexual response to interpersonal relationships (Lipsith et al., 2003). The type of autoerotic sexual orientation reflects the individual's experiences with masturbation as more arousing than the stimulation derived from a partner (Apfelbaum, 1980).

Female sexual dysfunction, including Female Orgasmic Disorder, may be particularly prevalent in women who have experienced sexual abuse or molestation in childhood (Kinzl et al., 1995; Saunders et al., 1992; Stuntz et al., 1996). These negative past psychological experiences will have a direct effect on one's experience of intimate sexual expression in adulthood (Heiman, 2002b). In one report, women who recounted inadequate sex education reported orgasm disorders significantly more often than did either victims of a single incident of sexual abuse or nonvictims. The researchers concluded that "female orgasm requires the ability to be intimate, to confide in a partner, and to become dependent on another person without being afraid of the consequences" (Kinzl et al., 1995, pp. 790–791). Kinzl's work supports the recognition that healthy early family relationships are critical to adult sexual well-being.

Birnbaum (2003) reported that women with Female Orgasmic Disorder perceived heterosexual intercourse as aversive. With regard to heterosexual intercourse, women with the disorder stated that they experienced feelings of (a) immorality or sinfulness; (b) guilt, shame, and anger; (c) derealization; (d) detachment from their partner; and (e) detachment during coitus. Attempting to address these issues by prescribing medication without including psychological intervention will lead to additional frustration for clients.

Evidence-Based Approaches to Intervention

Sex therapy follows a four-phase model of sexual expression: desire, excitement, orgasm, and resolution. Evidence-based interventions are those that are well established, have probable efficacy, and are based on principles of practice, some of which may not meet the criteria for empirically supported treatment (Heiman, 2002b). The well-established treatments use a two-group design to show superiority over another treatment or placebo, or demonstrate equivalency to an established treatment. Well-established studies can also be based on single-subject designs, and usually use treatment manuals. On the other hand, studies with probable efficacy are two or more studies that indicate treatment is more effective than no treatment. Treatment of sexual dysfunction is often a combination of pharmacological and psychoeducational psychotherapy. The focus of medical treatment has primarily been pharmacological treatment, with the use of sildenafil citrate (Viagra) for erectile dysfunction in men, and more recently on Premature Ejaculation in men, and sexual arousal and desire disorders in women (Heiman, 2002b).

Mental health therapists who deal with anorgasmic disorders need to consider psychological aspects of the orgasmic disorder, behavioral aspects, and the causes and associated risk factors (Perelman, 2003). The major treatments for primary orgasmic dysfunction are a combination of (a) sexual education and skills training, (b) Kegel exercises for women, (c) sensate focus and directed masturbation, (d) systematic desensitization, and (e) general behavioral or cognitive-behavioral approaches (Anderson, 1983; McCary, 1973); more recently, pharmacological treatment has been added. In the current literature, most treatments involve a combination approach. Primary anorgasmia in women has primarily been treated with sensate focus, desensitization, and/or directed masturbation (Heiman & Meston, 1997). More recently, secondary anorgasmia has been treated with a combination of psychotherapy and drugs, using sensate focus and a combination of testosterone and diazepam. Testosterone has been associated with increased orgasms in women even after the drug has been discontinued (Heiman & Meston, 1997). For a complete review of empirically validated studies on treatment for sexual dysfunction, the authors recommend Heiman and Meston.

Anorgasmic Disorders

First, addressing sex education and skills training, individuals must have a general knowledge of human sexuality. A basic knowledge of the anatomy and physiology of self and partner is essential. Often, what knowledge the client does have was received sporadically and was not learned in a nonthreatening environment. A good basis of sex education knowledge is needed to assist in further developing skills in the ability to express individual needs and desires, intimacy, affectional touching, reciprocity of sexual needs, and general sexual functioning (O'Donohue et al., 1993).

When dealing with sex education, more has to be provided than simply teaching body awareness. Issues regarding treatment of sexual dysfunction must take into account physiological problems that impact sexual arousal and obstacles to desire that may have emotional causes, such as stress, hidden anger, resentment, intimacy issues, and family-of-origin issues. Most of the treatment modalities address a multiplicity of issues pertaining to anorgasmia; however, their respective ways of addressing the problem of sexual dysfunction can vary. Some treatments concentrate on recognizing and understanding the physiological influences alone (Chambless, Sultan, & Stern, 1984); others view sexual dysfunction as a problem of faulty early sexual development that must be identified and modified (Ravart & Cote, 1992); still other treatments emphasize addressing cognitive-behavioral influences (Palace, 1995); and many treatments use a combination approach that applies physiological, developmental, and emotional components together as they relate to sexual arousal.

Second, one such treatment often utilized with women is the use of Kegel exercises. Arnold Kegel believed that orgasmic difficulty in women is related to poor tone or damage of the vaginal musculature. A treatment he originally designed to address urinary stress incontinence was adapted to increasing female orgasmic response. The type and emphasis of these exercises can vary; however, women are generally taught to control and squeeze the pubococcygeal muscle (Caird, 1988) that surrounds the vagina, urethra, and anus. A simple way to start this exercise process is to instruct the woman to begin to urinate and to stop the urine several times while in midstream. To further measure this phenomenon and its relation to muscle tone, Chambless et al. (1982) and other researchers utilized a perineometer. This instrument was used to measure the response while either fantasizing or imagining sexual fantasies.

Kegel exercises have been used by numerous clinicians and researchers to treat anorgasmic women, with mixed results in regard to their effectiveness. One such study that examined the physiological correlates of pubococcygeal exercise and coital orgasm was conducted by Chambless et al. (1984). No effect related to the completion of Kegel exercises on the rate of orgasm was found. The research in regard to this issue is conflicting, however; others demonstrate a successful link between strengthening the pubococcygeal muscle and effectiveness in the treatment of anorgasmia (Graber & Kline-Graber, 1979).

Third, McCabe and Delaney (1992) describe a number of therapeutic interventions that combine physiological principles with psychoeducational ones, with the success rates of these combined treatment strategies. They found that sex education as a component of sensate focus and directed masturbation, implemented in the pioneering work of Masters and Johnson (1970), continues to be used in conjunction with other modalities. According to H. S. Kaplan (1974), the treatment of orgasmic disorder involves diminishing or extinguishing the involuntary overcontrol of the orgasmic response. This can occur through sensitivity teaching, where the individual learns to recognize erotic sensations associated with orgasm. This can help to inhibit the tendency to feel the need to hold back and to allow the orgasmic response to occur. The individual is then taught how to self-stimulate intensely. If this stimulation brings a concurrent shutting off of response, the individual must simultaneously learn self-distraction.

Sensate focus and directed masturbation techniques can help individuals to become better aware of their own bodily sensations. Senate focus involves relaxation to manage anxious feelings and gradually having the couple move from caresses, to nonsexual touching, and then to sexually touching each other (Heiman & Meston, 1997). Directed masturbation teaches males and females to recognize their own erotic sensations through the use of graduated masturbation exercises. Masturbation is used because (a) it is the sexual practice most likely to result in orgasm, (b) individuals can learn to attend to their own physical sensations and sexual feelings most readily through this means, and (c) it is less anxiety producing, in that partner evaluation is removed (Anderson, 1983).

Generally, the first step in guided masturbation involves visual and tactile total body exploration, learning to accept and identify various parts of one's own sexual anatomy, moving toward increased genital stimulation, with the eventual use of a vibrator (Heiman & Meston, 1997). Visual exploration is highlighted. Fantasy or sexual thinking that stimulates sexual arousal is encouraged. For women, the obvious erogenous zones, such as the clitoris, are identified (LoPiccolo & Stock, 1986). For men, direct massaging of the penis seems most beneficial. The next step generally involves direct instruction in the techniques of masturbation. Because this needs to be a very individualized process, men and women are encouraged to go slowly and to focus on the techniques that bring them the most pleasure.

Sexual fantasy and sexual imagery are highly encouraged. Clients may choose to create their own fantasies or to read sexually oriented magazines or books, or to log into the Internet sites depicting sexual acts that can stimulate erotic thought. For some men and women who are still unable to achieve orgasm and need further assistance, electrical and vibratory stimulation can be introduced. LoPiccolo and Stock (1986) believe that, for women, it is important to begin the use of vibrators and electrical devices only at this late stage in treatment. If introduced earlier, it is believed that orgasm may become more vibrator dependent.

In both males and females, reaching orgasm alone at first, without the partner, is encouraged. Men with RE have a longer ejaculatory latency period with self-masturbation than with coitus (Atmaca et al., 2002). Once this has been accomplished, sensate focus exercises that involve the other partner are added. These exercises focus on the development of mutual caressing, touching, and communication. Once this is accomplished, the convergence of a reciprocal learning process is encouraged. Males are encouraged to follow the instruction of the anorgasmic female partner, helping her to achieve orgasm through direct manipulation of the genital area (LoPiccolo & Stock, 1986). Females are instructed to do the same for anorgasmic males, helping the male to reach orgasm during masturbation while pulling him closer to the vaginal area. It is recommended that combined coital and manual stimulation later be used to achieve orgasm in males (Dekker, 1993). In anorgasmic females, penile-vaginal intercourse should also include direct stimulation of the clitoris. Positions that facilitate this direct stimulation of the clitoris include those with the woman kneeling above her male partner and rear-entry intercourse, where the male can reach around her body and access the clitoris for manual stimulation.

In the treatment of orgasmic dysfunction, a combination approach of sexual education, directed masturbation, and sensate focus exercises is common. Whitehead, Mathews, and Ramage (1987) compared the effectiveness of conjoint therapy based on the work of Masters and Johnson with female-focused intervention designed by Heiman and LoPiccolo (1983). In this work, Whitehead et al. differentiated between the two treatment models. The Heiman and LoPiccolo model (as cited in Whitehead et al., 1987) was primarily a female-focused program that allowed women to learn more about their own needs through a type of directed masturbation that encouraged self-exploration and self-stimulation. This learning was then shared with the partner. In this form of treatment, the problem was identified as existing within the woman, and she was taught how to overcome deficits in sexual response. In this female-focused approach, the achievement of orgasm was a major goal.

In a second treatment group, based on the Masters and Johnson (1970) method, a couples approach was introduced and problems were assumed to reside in the relationship. The couples worked conjointly to improve sexual functioning and address sexual and marital issues, while the overall attainment of orgasm was discouraged. Whitehead et al. (1987) indicate that both forms of treatment showed evidence of being effective in increasing sexual response. However, couples therapy is referred to as the probable model of choice when addressing women who express increased anxiety, poor attitudes regarding masturbation, and problems with primary arousal and orgasm (Whitehead et al., 1987).

To further highlight this type of practice strategy, Morokoff and LoPiccolo (1986) compared minimal therapist contact sessions with a 15-session treatment program. Fourteen couples participated in minimal therapist contact (4 sessions), and 29 couples underwent full therapist contact (15 sessions). In the minimal therapist contact group, the movie *Becoming Orgasmic Together* was used. This movie was shown with supportive interaction and planning on the part of the therapist. In the therapist contact group, specific techniques were also highlighted, including a guided intervention focus on education, information, and systematic progression. A program originally developed by LoPiccolo and Lobitz (as cited in Morokoff & LoPiccolo, 1986) was used, and techniques similar to those described earlier in regard to direct masturbation were introduced.

Overall, both treatment programs were found to be effective in producing orgasm. Unexpectedly, the minimal treatment program produced superior results regarding the attainment of orgasm through masturbation and during coitus (with additional genital stimulation) compared to the full therapist contact group. The authors hypothesize that women in the minimal treatment group may have taken more responsibility for success, a factor that may have increased their motivation. The findings indicate that reduced therapist contact did not decrease effectiveness in the treatment of orgasmic dysfunction. Also, this study supports the use of education, information, feedback, and systematic progress through a program of directed masturbation in treating individuals who experience anorgasmia.

Sensate focus exercises (Masters & Johnson, 1970) and directed masturbation constitute a combined approach linking a sexual skill learning approach designed to alter behavior with educational strategies that modify communication patterns. In this form of directed masturbation, partners engage in nondemand pleasure through a series of graduated tasks ranging from sensual body massage to coitus (McCabe & Delaney, 1992). Couples are treated together, generally by a male-female cotherapy team. Couples are guided through touching techniques and focus on open sharing and communication of feelings and sensations. There is movement from sensual touching to increased genital contact and eventual coitus (Anderson, 1983; Masters & Johnson, 1970). Although sensate focus and directed masturbation are used frequently in treatment, empirical testing of the techniques is still lacking (Anderson, 1983; McCabe & Delaney, 1992).

A fourth technique that has been used repeatedly throughout the years to treat orgasmic dysfunction is systematic desensitization (Anderson, 1983). The use of systematic desensitization brings about positive changes in sexual functioning mainly through reducing sexual anxiety. The underlying premise in systematic desensitization is that sexual anxiety plays a central role in the dysfunction.

It is assumed that the creation of sexual arousal, instead of the usual muscle relaxation, can prevent and help avoid the development of sexual anxiety (Dekker, 1993). In this type of in vivo desensitization, the client is trained to relax the muscles through a sequence of exercises. Anxiety-provoking stimuli are listed in hierarchical order, and the deeply relaxed client slowly confronts each of the anxiety-arousing stimuli until the stimuli fail to generate anxiety (Anderson, 1983). Empirical data relating to systematic desensitization have been mixed, with some studies showing increased orgasmic response and others demonstrating decreased sexual anxiety with increased sexual satisfaction but limited changes in orgasmic response (Anderson, 1983).

In assuming that there is a causal relationship between sexual anxiety and sexual dysfunction, systematic desensitization attempts to decrease levels of anxiety so that increased sexual responsiveness will result.

Last, to further address the treatment of anxiety in anorgasmic individuals, cognitive and cognitive-behavioral techniques have been employed. Palace and Gorzalka (1990) found that preexposure to anxiety-provoking stimuli enhanced both the rate and magnitude of genital arousal in both functional and dysfunctional women.

However, both groups reported less subjective arousal after pre-exposure to anxiety-provoking stimuli. This study lends evidence to the observation that anxiety may enhance sexual physiological arousal without the concomitant cognitive recognition of arousal.

Several studies have been initiated that highlight the treatment of anorgasmic females from a behavioral or a cognitive-behavioral perspective. One of the most popular approaches is Barbach's (1980), which uses behavioral strategies in a group format. This approach has been tested by several researchers and has been found to be a useful technique for treating anorgasmic females (Bogat, Hamernik, & Brooks, 1987). Directive cognitive-behavioral approaches with 16 couples with secondary anorgasmia resulted in an increase from 12% to 30% in orgasm from masturbation and a 12% to 30% increase in orgasm during intercourse (Heiman & Meston, 1997). It employs a supportive and educational group format in which individualized homework sessions are completed. Standardized measures are used and individuals are pretested and posttested throughout the studies. Results support that most of the women tested using this approach not only experience orgasm but seem to accept their own body and their own personal health. Using the coital alignment technique by positioning the male partner's body to provide for direct stimulation produced a 56% increase in orgasm during intercourse (Hurlbert & Apt, 1994).

Another study is that of Wilson and Wilson (1991), who selected 80 female subjects to evaluate two cognitive-behavioral sex therapy formats that were designed to alleviate inhibited female orgasm. Both group and individual sections were employed. Standardized measures were used to gather initial baseline data, and the resulting data were statistically analyzed. In general, the subjects chose individual therapy over group therapy. Women stated that they did not feel comfortable discussing such an intimate problem with a group of strangers.

Premature or Rapid Ejaculation

With the development of new pharmaceuticals for the treatment of erectile dysfunction, there has been a growing awareness of sexual dysfunctions. Many men who were suffering in silence are now more likely to discuss their erectile disorder with a health care professional. In recent years, in addition to traditional methods of treatment for RE, several research studies have tested the efficacy of pharmacological treatment for RE (Abdel-Hamid, 2004; Atmaca et al., 2002; Waldinger, 2003). Premature Ejaculation has also been thought to be brought on by a heightened sensitivity of the glans, and this has led to research on topical anesthetic creams to prolong ejaculation (Henry & Morales, 2003). In a study of 14 men and their partners, Henry and Morales investigated the use of a topical spray to delay ejaculation. Lidocain-prilocaine is an aerosol spray that is sprayed on the glans penis, left on for 10 to 15 minutes, and then wiped off before intercourse. The latency time for ejaculation increased from 1 minute, 23 seconds to 11 minutes, 21 seconds. The use of the aerosol not only delayed ejaculation, but both partners reported an increase in sexual satisfaction.

Another study examined the emotional response of men with RE and the use of clomipramine, a tricyclic antidepressant, in response to erotic stimuli. Clomipramine's side effects result in ejaculatory failure in about 25% of the patients with psychiatric problems, which makes it a drug of choice for RE (Rowland et al., 2003). In a study of 50 men, 37 with RE and 13 having no sexual dysfunction, arousal/sensual emotions decreased under clomipramine, but men with RE showed a higher level of negative emotion such as tense/worry, embarrassment/guilt, anger/annoyed compared to men with no sexual dysfunction. These findings indicate that despite the benefits of drugs to delay ejaculation in RE men, they also could benefit from psychosocial therapy.

In a study of 26 married healthy males ranging in age from 24 to 46, subjects were randomly assigned to two groups in a double-blind design. One group received citalopram, an SSRI, and the other group received a placebo. After 8 weeks of treatment, the men in the group receiving citalopram showed a considerable increase in intravaginal latency, sexual desire, quality of erection, reduced anxiety for RE, satisfaction with the ejaculation, and partner satisfaction compared to the placebo group (Atmaca et al., 2002). The men taking citalopram improved on overall sexual functioning and in latency ejaculation, ranging from a mean of 33 seconds the 1st week to 283 seconds at the 8th week.

Using an escalating approach to treat RE, 138 men were studied to evaluate the efficacy of topical lidocaine, sildenafil, and SSRI for Premature Ejaculation (Chen et al., 2003). Rapid ejaculation was measured on an 8-point scale ranging from never to almost always. To qualify for the study, men with a score of 4 or above (meaning half the time or more they ejaculated prematurely during intercourse) were included in the study. Subjects were also graded in their intravaginal ejaculatory latency time (IVELT; 0 = Longer than 5 minutes, 1 = Between 3 and 5 minutes, 2 = Between 1 and 3 minutes, and 3 = Less than 1 minute). Those scoring with a 2 or higher were admitted into the study. These men were also provided with psychological and behavioral counseling, which included relaxation and sexual stimulation without the demand for erection, ejaculation, or vaginal penetration. The initial treatment implemented was topical lidocaine ointment (5%) applied to the penis 20 minutes before intercourse. Thirty-eight of the subjects reported improvement in RE and IVELT after 3 months of applying the lidocaine. The remaining 100 subjects were switched to the SSRI treatment, and 42% reported improvement in RE and IVELT. The remaining 58 men who were not satisfied with the SSRI treatment were treated with a combination of paraxetine and sildenafil; 97% reported improvement in RE and IVELT (Chen et al., 2003).

Often, treatment for RE utilizes a combination approach such as sensate focus exercises incorporating the use of the squeeze technique discussed by Masters and Johnson (1970). This treatment starts with sensate focus exercises, where the couples are expected to touch each other with no expectation of reaching orgasm. This nondemanding touching should last for several days, and no direct genital penetration is encouraged. Once the female partner has assisted the male in reaching an erection and he reports feeling as though he will ejaculate, the squeeze technique is introduced.

At this stage in the ejaculatory response, the male feels that he cannot control the orgasmic experience, and he can feel the seminal fluid begin to flow. At that moment, the female partner is instructed to stop massaging the penis and to squeeze the glans, below the head of the penis. This means taking her thumb and placing it on the rear side of the shaft (toward the partner's body), opposite the frenulum (directly below the head of the penis); two fingers should be used to apply pressure on the top of the glans. This pressure should be applied for 3 or 4 seconds, or until the male reports that he feels uncomfortable enough to lose the urge to ejaculate. These training sessions should continue for 15 to 20 minutes, alternating between sexual stimulation and squeezing, without ejaculation.

Once control over manually stimulated erections has been achieved (approximately 2 or 3 days later), vaginal penetration is attempted. Generally, the woman assumes the top position so she can control the withdrawal of the penis from the vagina. The female is instructed to insert the penis into her vagina and to move as little as possible. This is to give the male time to think about other things and help distract him from the urge to ejaculate. If the male feels the urge to ejaculate, the female is instructed to withdraw the penis and implement the squeeze technique described earlier. Eventually, thrusting and movement is added to stimulate or maintain the erection. A time span of 15 to 20 minutes is considered desirable for ejaculatory control. Masters and Johnson (1970) caution, however, that in using this technique several considerations should be weighed. First, the female partner, not the male, should be the one to add the pressure to the penis; second, this technique should not be used as a sexual game. If it is overused, the male may become so skilled and insensitive during this process that he becomes able to avoid stimulation even when there is no desire to do so.

LoPiccolo and Stock (1986) believe that there is little evidence for the efficacy of the squeeze technique when used as a solitary method. Further, Kinder and Curtiss (1988) question the use of this isolated technique and urge that before the efficacy of this treatment modality can be measured, more research is needed to compare individuals receiving this technique with a similar control group.

In general, three behavioral treatments are associated with erectile dysfunction: (1) communication technique training (to deal with social and relationship issues), (2) sexual technique training (teaching education and the practice of sexual techniques), and (3) a combination treatment that utilizes both.

Kilmann et al. (1987) studied 20 couples who were tested to determine the effectiveness of current treatments on secondary erectile dysfunction. Three treatment groups (consisting of eight 2-hour sessions) were all designed to enhance the male's sexual functioning and included a communication education group that stressed positive communication techniques; a sexual training group that was designed to enhance positive sexual techniques; and a combination treatment group that stressed both communication and sexual training. The fourth group, referred to as the attention placebo control group, implemented controls to limit the degree of treatment received, thus constituting a less powerful treatment procedure than that given the other groups. In this group, highly structured lectures were provided without any planned applicability or practice time being allotted for individual problem solving. The couples in the no-treatment control group were pretested and waited 5 weeks for treatment to begin. After the posttest, they were provided with the combination treatment.

Several pretest measurement inventories and questionnaires were used, including the Sexual Interaction Inventory, designed by LoPiccolo and Steger (1974); the Marital Adjustment Test, developed by Locke and Wallace (1959); the Sex Anxiety Inventory, developed by Janda and O'Grady (1980); and the Sexual Behavior and Attitudes Questionnaire, developed by Sotile and Kilmann (1978). The results were statistically analyzed; the study supported the view that each of the treatments for secondary erectile dysfunction has statistically significant effectiveness when compared to no treatment at all. This study served to further support the recommendation by Eastman (1993) that the importance of education, communication, and support should not be underestimated, even when a condition is organically generated.

Summary

These studies provide preliminary support for empirically based treatment of orgasmic disorders. In a review of the empirically based literature, it is important to consider both the physical and psychological treatment of these disorders. Many current social work and behavioral science researchers concur with the need for the inclusion of a psychosocial component with specific measures to address the marital, social, and personal difficulties an individual may express (Birnbaum, 2003; Goldman & Carroll, 1990; Heiman, 2002a, 2002b; H. S. Kaplan, 1990; Shaw, 1990). Male Orgasmic Disorder is uncommon, with 8% of men reporting the problem within the past year (Laumann et al., 1994). It is thought that anxiety, stress, and psychological issues may play a role in retarded ejaculation. The importance of the inclusion of cognitive, educational, and behavioral techniques remains a crucial element in the complete treatment of individuals experiencing any type of sexual difficulty, not just the orgasmic disorders. In male orgasmic disorders, clinicians will want to determine the presence and degree of primary autoerotic masturbation, current level of stress, cognitive schemas about the relationship, medical problems, list of medications currently being taken, and the extent to which deep-seated psychological issues are evident.

Empirically based time-limited treatment modalities are at the forefront of social work practice in the current managed care environment (Dziegielewski, 1996, 1997). However, to date, empirical social work practice in the area of sexual dysfunctions, with orgasmic disorders in particular, remains very limited. More research is needed to determine exactly what types of cognitive-behavioral treatments work best and if the results remain consistent over time. This makes the social worker's role as a clinical researcher critical in helping clients.

Several studies have suggested that there is a need for methodological rigor in well-defined outcome studies in almost all topics related to human sexuality (Birnbaum, 2003; Harrison, 1987; Simons & Carey, 2001). Today, this remains a major issue in social work practice, particularly in the area of the treatment of sexual dysfunctions. Contrary to Szasz's (1980, p. 13) assertion that the "so called sexual dysfunctions" (which are psychogenic in nature) are not medical diseases or problems requiring sex therapy, social workers and other behavioral scientists have shown this belief to be outdated—and dangerous. Although the importance of including the psychosocial and psychosexual aspects in understanding sexual dysfunctions is well documented, it is frequently overlooked.

Catalan, Hawton, and Day (1990) strongly suggest that family and relationship issues be addressed in the treatment of sexual dysfunctions prior to the discussion of other issues. The authors of this chapter support this contention, and uphold the view that increasing treatment success requires the consideration of relationship problems through a cognitive-behavioral model. If relationship problems are determined to be critical, a complete social evaluation should be conducted prior to the initiation of physical or biological treatments. A behavioral and cognitive approach to sex therapy is crucial in the treatment of sexual dysfunctions; thus, the roles of the social worker and the behavioral scientist become pivotal as well. With the latest research indicating improvement in Premature Ejaculation in males when using pharmacological treatments, it is important for social workers to keep abreast of these findings, be able to determine the type of RE, and be up to date on the latest medications, so that treatment decisions are based on empirical evidence that is most likely to produce efficacy.

Consistent with the claims made by Heiman and Meston (1997), important issues remain to be examined. Researchers must ascertain which type of treatment technique works best (such as utilizing cognitive or behavioral sex therapy models), and determine how to best utilize the technique chosen (i.e., in a group, family, couples, individual, or combination format). A new need for empirical verification is taking shape, and research replication is imperative. Of the psychological treatments for orgasmic disorder, 57% are for women. We need to conduct studies on male orgasmic disorders. Heiman (2002a) asserts that future research considering the efficacy of separate and combined psychological and physiological treatments for sexual dysfunction may offer the best intervention options. It is yet to be determined whether these treatments and the resultant gains will actually remain consistent over time. What we do know is that further treatment needs to examine both the short- and long-term efficacy of a particular treatment. The psychological and pharmacological treatments may need to be ongoing to arrive at an acceptable maintenance level of sexual functioning.

Study Questions

1. Describe each of the three orgasmic disorders and their estimated prevalence.

2. Explain why clinical social workers need to be familiar with evidence-based approaches to the assessment and treatment of clients with orgasmic disorders.

3. Locate and complete at least one of the self-report assessment instruments described in this chapter. Explain why you believe it is or is not a valid method of assessment.

4. Describe any two evidence-based approaches to treating orgasmic disorders.

References

Abdel-Hamid, I. A. (2004). Phosphodiesterase 5 inhibitors in rapid ejaculation: Potential use and possible mechanisms of action. *Drugs, 64*(1), 13–23.

American Psychiatric Association. (2000). *Diagnostic and statistical manual of mental disorders* (4th ed., text rev.). Washington, DC: Author.

Anderson, B. L. (1983). Primary orgasmic dysfunction: Diagnostic considerations and review of treatment. *Psychological Bulletin, 93,* 105–136.

Apfelbaum, B. (1980). The diagnosis and treatment of retarded ejaculation. In S. R. Leiblum & L. A. Pervin (Eds.), *Principles and practices of sex therapy* (3rd ed., pp. 206–241). New York: Guilford Press.

Atmaca, M., Kuloglu, E. T., Tezcan, B. U., & Semercios, A. (2002). Serum leptin levels in patients with premature ejaculation before and after citalopram treatment. *British Journal of Urology, 91,* 252–254.

Barbach, L. (1980). *Women discover orgasm: A therapist's guide to a new treatment approach.* New York: Macmillan.

Bechara, A., Bertolino, M. V., Casabe, A., Munarriz, R., Goldstein, I., Morin, A., et al. (2003). Duplex Doppler ultrasound assessment of clitoral hemodynamics after topical administration of alprostadil in women with arousal and orgasmic disorders. *Journal of Sex and Marital Therapy, 29,* 1–10.

Birnbaum, G. E. (2003). The meaning of heterosexual intercourse among women with female orgasmic disorder. *Archives of Sexual Behavior, 32,* 61–71.

Bogat, A. G., Hamernik, K., & Brooks, L. A. (1987). The influence of self-efficacy: Expectations on the treatment of preorgasmic women. *Journal of Sex and Marital Therapy, 13,* 128–136.

Caird, W. (1988). The modification of urinary urgency during sexual arousal. *Journal of Sex Research, 24,* 183–187.

Castelo-Branco, C., Blumel, J. E., Araya, H., Riquelme, R., Castro, G., Haya, J., et al. (2003). Prevalence of sexual dysfunction in a cohort of middle-aged women: Influences of menopause and hormone replacement therapy. *Journal of Obstetrics and Gynecology, 23,* 426–430.

Catalan, J., Hawton, K., & Day, A. (1990). Couples referred to a sexual dysfunction clinic: Psychological and physical morbidity. *British Journal of Psychiatry, 156,* 61–67.

Chambless, D. L., Stern, T., Sultan, F. E., Williams, A. J., Goldstein, A. J., Lineberger, M. H., et al. (1982). The pubococcygens and female orgasm: A correlational study with normal subjects. *Archives of Sexual Behavior, 11,* 479–490.

Chambless, D. L., Sultan, F. E., & Stern, T. E. (1984). Effect of pubococcygeal exercise on coital orgasm in women. *Journal of Consulting and Clinical Psychology, 52,* 114–118.

Chen, J., Mabjeesh, N., J., Matzkin, H., & Greenstein, A. (2003). Efficacy of sildenafil as adjuvant therapy to selective serotonin reuptake inhibitor in alleviating premature ejaculation. *Adult Urology, 61,* 197–200.

Clayton, A. H., McGarvey, E. L., & Clavet, G. J. (1997). The Changes in Sexual Functioning Questionnaire (CSFQ): Development, reliability, and validity. *Psychopharmacology Bulletin, 33,* 747–753.

Derogatis, L. R. (1976). The DSFI: A multidimensional measure of sexual functioning. *Journal of Sex and Marital Therapy, 5,* 244–281.

Dekker, J. (1993). Inhibited male orgasm. In W. O'Donohue & J. H. Geer (Eds.), *Handbook of sexual dysfunction: Assessment and treatment* (pp. 279–302). Boston: Allyn & Bacon.

Dow, M. G. T. (1981). Retarded ejaculation as a function of non-aversive conditioning and discrimination: A hypothesis. *Journal of Sex and Marital Therapy, 7,* 49–53.

Dziegielewski, S. F. (1996). Managed care principles: The need for social work in the health care environment. *Crisis Intervention and Time Limited Treatment, 3,* 97–111.

Dziegielewski, S. F. (1997). Time-limited brief therapy: The state of practice. *Crisis Intervention and Time Limited Treatment, 4,* 217–228.

Eastman, P. (1993, May/June). Washington report: Treating erectile dysfunction. *Geriatric Consultant,* 10–13.

Fazio, L., & Brock, G. (2004). Erectile dysfunction: Management update. *Canadian Medical Association, 170*(9), 1429–1436.

Fish, L. S., Busby, D., & Killian, K. (1994). Structural couple therapy in the treatment of inhibited sexual drive. *American Journal of Family Therapy, 22,* 113–125.

Friedman, J. M., & Hogan, D. R. (1985). Sexual dysfunction and low sexual desire. In D. H. Barlow (Ed.), *Clinical handbook of psychiatric disorders* (pp. 417–461). New York: Guilford Press.

FSDInfo. (2004). *Information on female sexual dysfunction.* Retrieved August 29, 2004, from http://www.fsdinfo.org/orgasmic_disorders .html.

Golden, J. (1988). A second look at a case of inhibited sexual desire. *Journal of Sex Research, 25,* 304–306.

Goldman, A., & Carroll, J. (1990). Educational intervention as an adjunct to treatment of erectile dysfunction in older couples. *Journal of Sex and Marital Therapy, 16,* 127–141.

Graber, B., & Kline-Graber, G. (1979). Female orgasm: Role of the pubococcygeus muscle. *Journal of Clinical Psychology, 40,* 348–351.

Greiner, G., & Byers, S. E. (2001). Operationalizing premature or rapid ejaculation. *Journal of Sex Research, 38,* 369–378.

Harrison, D. F. (1987). Clinical research in sexual dysfunctions: Social work contributions. *Journal of Social Service Research, 10*(2/3/4), 105–119.

Hawton, K., Catalan, J., & Fagg, J. (1991). Low sexual desire: Sex therapy results and prognostic factors. *Behavior Research and Therapy, 29,* 217–224.

Heiman, J. R. (2002a). Psychological treatments for female sexual dysfunction: Are they effective and do we need them? *Archives of Sexual Behavior, 31,* 445–450.

Heiman, J. R. (2002b). Sexual dysfunction: Overview of prevalence, etiological factors, and treatments. *Journal of Sex Research, 39,* 73–78.

Heiman, J. R., & LoPiccolo, J. (1983). Clincial outcome of sex therapy. *Archives of General Psychiatry, 40,* 443–449.

Heiman, J. R., & Meston, C. M. (1997). Empirically validated treatment for sexual dysfunction. *Annual Review of Sex Research, 8,* 148–195.

Henry, R., & Morales, A. (2003). Topical lidocaine-prilocaine spray for the treatment of premature ejaculation: A proof of concept study. *International Journal of Impotence Research, 15,* 277–281.

Horton, A. L. (1995). Sex related hot-line calls: Types, interventions, and guidelines. In A. Roberts (Ed.), *Crisis intervention and time limited cognitive treatment* (pp. 290–312). Thousand Oaks, CA: Sage.

Hurlbert, D. F., & Apt, C. (1994). Female sexual desire, response, and behavior. *Behavior Modification, 18,* 488–505.

Janda, L. H., & O'Grady, K. E. (1980). Development of a sex anxiety inventory. *Journal of Consulting and Clinical Psychology, 48,* 169–175.

Janssen, E., Vorst, H., Finn, P., & Bancroft, J. (2002). The Sexual Inhibition (SIS) and Sexual Excitation (SES) Scales: Pt. I. Measuring sexual inhibition and excitation proneness in men. *Journal of Sex Research, 39,* 114–126.

Kaplan, H. S. (1974). *The new sex therapy.* New York: Random House.

Kaplan, H. S. (1979). *Disorders of sexual desire.* New York: Simon & Schuster.

Kaplan, H. S. (1990). The combined use of sex therapy and intra-penile injections in the treatment of impotence. *Journal of Sex and Marital Therapy, 16,* 195–207.

Kaplan, H. S. (1995). *The sexual desire disorders: Dysfunctional regulation and sexual motivation.* New York: Brunner/Mazel.

Kaplan, L., & Harder, D. W. (1991). The sexual desire conflict scale for women: Construction, internal consistency, and two initial validity tests. *Psychological Reports, 68,* 1275–1282.

Kilmann, P. R., Milan, R. J., Boland, J. P., Nankin, H. R., Davidson, E., West, M. O., et al. (1987). Group treatment for secondary erectile dysfunction. *Journal of Sex and Marital Therapy, 13,* 168–180.

Kinder, B. N., & Curtiss, G. (1988). Specific components in the etiology, assessment, and treatment of male sexual dysfunctions: Controlled outcome studies. *Journal of Sex and Marital Therapy, 14,* 40–48.

Kinzl, J. F., Traweger, C., & Biebl, W. (1995). Sexual dysfunctions: Relationship to childhood sexual abuse and early family experiences in a nonclinical sample. *Child Abuse and Neglect, 19,* 785–792.

Knopf, J., & Seiler, M. (1990). *ISD: Inhibited sexual desire.* New York: Morrow.

Kuileter, M. M., Vroege, J. A., & van Lankveld, J. J. D. M. (1993). *The Golombok Rust Inventory of Sexual Satisfaction* (Nederlandse vertalilng enaapassignnen). Leiden, Holland: Netherlands University Medical Center [Dutch translation and adaptation].

LaPera, G., Giannotti, C. F., Taggi, F., & Macchia, T. (2003). Prevalence of sexual disorders in those young males who later become drug abusers. *Journal of Sex and Marital Therapy, 29,* 149–156.

Laumann, E. O., Gagnon, J. H., Michael, R. T., & Michaels, S. (1994). *The social organization of sexuality.* Chicago: University of Chicago Press.

Laumann, E. O., Paik, A., & Rosen, C. (1999). Sexual dysfunction in the United States: Prevalence and predictors. *Journal of the American Medical Association, 281,* 537–545.

Lipsith, J., McCann, D., & Goldmeier, D. (2003). Male psychogenic sexual dysfunction: The role of masturbation. *Sexual and Relationship Therapy, 18,* 447–471.

Locke, H. J., & Wallace, K. M. (1959). Short marital and prediction tests: Their reliability and validity. *Journal of Marriage and Family Living, 21,* 251–255.

LoPiccolo, J., & Steger, J. C. (1974). The Sexual Interaction Inventory: A new instrument for assessment of sexual dysfunction. *Archives of Sexual Behavior, 3,* 585–595.

LoPiccolo, J., & Stock, W. E. (1986). Treatment of sexual dysfunction. *Journal of Consulting and Clinical Psychology, 54,* 158–167.

Masters, W. H., & Johnson, V. D. (1970). *Human sexual inadequacy.* Boston: Little, Brown.

Maxmen, J. S., & Ward, N. G. (1995). *Essential psychopathology and its treatment* (2nd ed.). New York: Norton.

McCabe, M. P., & Delaney, S. M. (1992). An evaluation of therapeutic programs for the treatment of secondary inorgasmia in women. *Archives of Sexual Behavior, 21,* 69–89.

McCary, J. L. (1973). *Human sexuality.* New York: D. Van Nostrand.

McMahon, C. G. (1998). Treatment of premature ejaculation with sertraline hydrochloride: A single-blind placebo controlled crossover study. *Journal of Urology, 159,* 1935–1938.

Meston, C. M. (2000). The psychophysiological assessment of female sexual function. *Journal of Sex Education and Therapy, 25,* 6–15.

Meston, C. M., & Derogatis, L. R. (2002). Validated instruments for assessing female sexual function. *Journal of Sex and Marital Therapy, 28,* 155–164.

Milan, R. J., Kilmann, P., & Boland, J. (1988). Treatment outcome of secondary orgasmic dysfunction: A 2- to 6-year follow-up. *Archives of Sexual Behavior, 17,* 463–480.

Morokoff, P. J., & LoPiccolo, J. (1986). A comparative evaluation of minimal therapist contact and 15 session treatment for female orgasmic dysfunction. *Journal of Consulting and Clinical Psychology, 54,* 294–300.

Nicolosi, A., Laumann, E. O., Glasser, D, B., Brock, G., King, R., & Gingell, C. (2006).

Sexual activity, sexual disorders and associated help-seeking behavior among mature adults in five Anglophone countries from the Global Survey of Sexual Attitudes and Behaviors (GSSAB). *Journal of Sex and Marital Therapy, 32,* 4, 331–342.

Nicolosi, A., Laumann, E. O., Glasser, D. B., Moreira, E. D., Paik, A., & Gingell, C. (2004). Sexual behavior and sexual dysfunctions after age 40: The global study of sexual attitudes and behaviors. *Urology, 64,* 991–998.

O'Donohue, W., Letourneau, E., & Geer, J. H. (1993). Premature ejaculation. In W. O'Donohue & J. H. Geer (Eds.), *Handbook of sexual dysfunctions: Assessment and treatment* (pp. 303–334). Boston: Allyn & Bacon.

O'Leary, M. P., Rhodes, T., Girman, C. J., Jacobson, D. J., Roberts, R. O., Lieber, M. M., et al. (2003). Distribution of the Brief Male Sexual Inventory in community men. *International Journal of Impotence Research, 15,* 185–191.

Palace, E. M. (1995). Modification of dysfunctional patterns of sexual response through autonomic arousal and false physiological feedback. *Journal of Consulting and Clinical Psychology, 63,* 604–615.

Palace, E. M., & Gorzalka, B. B. (1990). The enhancing effects of anxiety on arousal in sexually dysfunctional and functional women. *Journal of Abnormal Psychology, 99,* 403–411.

Perelman, M. A. (2003). Sex coaching for physicians: Combination treatment for patient and partner. *International Journal of Impotence Research, 5,* 67–74.

Ravart, M., & Cote, H. (1992). Sexoanalysis: A new insight-oriented treatment approach for sexual disorders. *Journal of Sex and Marital Therapy, 18,* 128–140.

Rosen, R. (2003). Looking beyond erectile dysfunction: The need for multi-dimensional assessment of sexual dysfunction. *European Urology Supplements, 2*(10), 9.

Rosen, R., Brown, C., Heiman, J., Leiblum, S., Meston, C. M., Shabsigh, R., et al. (2000). The Female Sexual Function Index (FSFI): A multidimensional self-report instrument for the assessment of female sexual function. *Journal of Sex and Marital Therapy, 26,* 191–208.

Rowland, D. L., & Koos, S. A. (1997). Premature ejaculation: Psychophysiological considerations in theory, research, and treatment. *Annual Review of Sex Research, 8*, 224–254.

Rowland, D. L., Tai, W. L., & Slob, A. K. (2003). An exploration of emotional response to erotic stimulation in men with premature ejaculation: Effects of treatment with clomipramine. *Journal of Sexual Behavior, 32*, 145–153.

Saunders, B. E., Villeponteaux, L. A., Lipovsky, J. A., & Kilpatrick, D. G. (1992). Child sexual assault as a risk factor for mental disorders among women: A community survey. *Journal of Interpersonal Violence, 7*, 189–204.

Sharpe, T. H. (2003). Adult sexuality. *Family Journal, 11*, 420.

Shaw, J. (1990). Play therapy with the sexual workhorse: Successful treatment with 12 cases of inhibited ejaculation. *Journal of Sex and Marital Therapy, 16*, 159–164.

Simons, J. S., & Carey, M. P. (2001). Prevalence of sexual dysfunctions: Results from a decade of research. *Archives of Sexual Behavior, 30*, 177–219.

Slosarz, W. (1992). Masturbation fixation and the problems of adaptation to heterosexual partnerships: A few implications. *Journal of Sexual and Marital Therapy, 7*, 275–281.

Sotile, W. M., & Kilmann, P. R. (1978). The effects of group systematic desensitization on orgasmic dysfunction. *Archives of Sexual Behavior, 7*, 477–491.

Spector, I. P., & Carey, M. P. (1990). Incidence and prevalence of sexual dysfunctions: A critical review of the literature. *Archives of Sexual Behavior, 19*, 399–408.

Stuart, F. M., Hammond, D. C., & Pett, M. A. (1987). Inhibited sexual desire in women. *Archives of Sexual Behavior, 16*, 91–106.

Stuntz, S. S., Falk, A., Hiken, M., & Carson, V. B. (1996). The journey undermined by psychosexual disorders. In V. B. Carson & E. N. Arnold (Eds.), *Mental health nursing: The nurse-patient journey* (pp. 879–895). Philadelphia: Saunders.

Symonds, T., Roblin, D., Hart, K., & Althof, S. (2003). How does premature ejaculation impact a man's life? *Journal of Sex and Marital Therapy, 29*, 361–370.

Szasz, T. (1980). *Sex by prescription.* New York: Doubleday.

Taylor, J. F., Rosen, R. C., & Leiblum, S. R. (1994). Self-report assessment of female sexual function: Psychometric evaluation of the Brief Index of Sexual Function for Women. *Archives of Sexual Behavior, 23*, 627–643.

Thyer, B. A., & Papsdorf, J. D. (1981). Relationship between irrationality and sexual arousability. *Psychological Reports, 48*, 834.

Trudel, G. (1991). Review of psychological factors in low sexual desire. *Sexual and Marital Therapy, 6*, 261–272.

Waldinger, M. D. (2003). Towards evidence-based drug treatment research on premature ejaculation: A critical evaluation of the methodology. *International Journal of Impotence Research, 15*, 309–313.

Whitehead, A., Mathews, A., & Ramage, M. (1987). The treatment of sexually unresponsive women: A comparative evaluation. *Behavior Research and Therapy, 25*, 195–205.

Wilson, G. L., & Wilson, L. J. (1991). Treatment acceptability of alternate sex therapies: A comparative analysis. *Journal of Sex and Marital Therapy, 17*, 35–43.

Wincze, J. P., Rosen, R., Carson, C., Korenman, C. N., Niederberger, C., Sadovsky, R., et al. (2004). Erection Quality Scale: Initial scale development and validation. *Adult Urology, 64*, 351–356.

Woody, J. D., D'Souza, H. J., & Crain, D. D. (1994). Sexual functioning in clinical couples: Discriminant validity of the Sexual Interaction Scale. *American Journal of Family Therapy, 22*, 291–303.

Wylie, K. R., Steward, D., Seivewright, N., Smith, D., & Walters, S. (2002). Prevalence of sexual difficulties in three psychiatric outpatient settings: A drug misuse service, an alcohol misuse service, and a general adult psychiatric clinic. *Sexual and Relationship Therapy, 17*, 149–160.

EATING DISORDERS

Anorexia Nervosa, Bulimia Nervosa, and Binge Eating Disorder

Laura L. Myers

20
Chapter

Learning Objectives

After reading this chapter, the reader will be able to:

- Understand the operational definitions of Bulimia Nervosa, Anorexia Nervosa, Atypical Eating Disorder, and Binge Eating Disorder.

- Distinguish between the eating disorders based on the criteria currently defined in the *DSM*.

- Discuss the various assessment methods that are currently used to assess eating disorders.

- Discuss the various treatment methods that are used to treat eating disorders.

Overview of the Problem

Given that social workers are the largest discipline providing mental health care in the United States (Weissman et al., 2006), it is crucial that we be familiar with evidence-based methods to assess and treat clients with eating disorders. In part this is due to the widespread prevalence and seriousness of these conditions. Apart from clinical services, social workers have contributed in a variety of ways toward an understanding of clients with eating disorders. To date, such contributions have taken a variety of forms, including conceptual and theoretical analyses (e.g.,

Chassler, 1997; Wilson, 2004), studies in the descriptive psycho-pathology or etiology of these conditions (e.g., Chan & Ma, 2004; Ma & Chan, 2004; Thiels & Garthe, 2000), investigations into assessment methods useful for clients with eating disorders (e.g., Guest, 2000), case studies (e.g., O'Halloran, 2005), the development of recommended intervention practices (e.g., Kindy & Patterson, 1980; Myers, 1996; Shekter-Wolfson, Woodside, & Lackstrom, 1997; Weiss, Wolchik, & Katzman, 1994; Wempner, 1984), as well as some general overviews of the subject (e.g., McKay, 1984; Myers, 1998; von Bulow, 1991).

It is especially worth recognizing the exemplary writings of social worker Richard B. Stuart in the area of eating disorders. His landmark and widely cited article, *Behavioral Control of Overeating* (Stuart, 1967), followed by his best-selling popular books *Slim Chance in a Fat World: Behavioral Control of Obesity* (Stuart & Davis, 1972) and *Act Thin, Stay Thin* (Stuart, 1978), proved to be tremendously influential. Indeed the nationally known Weight Watchers program incorporated many of his ideas and practices into its system, a legacy that remains today. However, despite these illustrations, it is also fair to say that social workers as a whole have not been active contributors to the emerging field of evidence-based practice for clients with eating disorders. Given the close contact and intimate involvement social workers have in providing health care services to clients with anorexia, bulimia, or obesity, this chapter presents an overview of existing evidence-based practice in this area, in the hope that readers will be stimulated to not only keep abreast and adopt such practices but also become more active participants in the design and conduct of empirical research.

Operational Definitions of the Problem

Many people suffer from eating disorders in our society. Some people starve themselves, some participate in bouts of extreme overeating, some eat and immediately attempt to purge the food through vomiting, laxatives, fasting, or excessive exercise, and others vacillate between all three of these dysfunctional eating patterns. A majority of people with eating disorders are secretive about their eating behaviors and avoid discussing them with friends, family members, or professionals. Because social workers work in a variety of community agencies, such as schools, churches, and counseling centers, they are in a unique position to identify and help individuals who suffer from these serious disorders.

Bulimia Nervosa

The distinctive core psychopathology for both Bulimia Nervosa (BN) and Anorexia Nervosa (AN) is a person's constant concern and evaluation of his or her shape and weight. Whereas most people assess themselves on a variety of domains (i.e., academics, sports, relationships, work, parenting skills), people with eating disorders judge their self-worth almost exclusively, and in extreme cases, exclusively, on their shape and weight (Fairburn & Harrison, 2003).

The current criteria for BN, as defined in the *Diagnostic and Statistical Manual of Mental Disorders* (*DSM*; American Psychiatric Association, 2000, p. 549), include (a) recurrent episodes of binge eating; (b) recurrent inappropriate compensatory behavior to prevent weight gain, such as self-induced vomiting, misuse of laxatives, diuretics, enemas, or other medications, fasting, or excessive exercise; (c) occurrence, on average, at least twice a week for 3 months; (d) self-evaluation unduly influenced by body shape and weight; and (e) occurrence not exclusively during episodes of Anorexia Nervosa. There are two subtypes of BN: the purging type and the nonpurging type. The purging type uses self-induced vomiting or the abuse of laxatives or diuretics to control weight gain, and the nonpurging type uses fasting and excessive exercise to compensate for binge eating (Herrin & Matsumoto, 2002).

Defining the terms used in the criteria for BN has prompted numerous debates, including the presence and frequency of binging, the size of the binge, the presence and frequency of purging activity, and the presence of distorted body image. Binging is defined in the criteria for BN as being characterized by both of the following: (a) eating, within any 2-hour period, an amount of food that is definitely larger than most people would eat during a similar period of time and under similar circumstances; and (b) a sense of lack of control over eating during the episode, such as feeling that one cannot stop eating or control what or how much one is eating (American Psychiatric Association, 2000, p. 594).

Schlundt and Johnson (1990, p. 4), believing that the classification of food intake as a binge is subjective and differs from client to client, define a binge as "the ingestion of any food substance or quantity that violates the individual's idea of dieting and thereby increases anxiety regarding weight gain." They argue that for different clients, a binge may involve the consumption of thousands of calories, a normal-size meal, or even a single doughnut. In response to this argument, two types of binges have now been classified. The objective binge meets the *DSM* definition given earlier. A subjective binge is a binge during which the client eats a normal or even a small amount of food, but feels the loss of control characteristic of a binge (Fairburn, 1995).

Anorexia Nervosa

One could argue that the main difference between clients with AN and clients with BN is how successful the client has been in his or her goal of weight loss, as part of the criteria for AN is weight loss of 15% of total body weight. Indeed, clients with BN sometimes describe themselves as failed anorexics. Some perceive the difference as a matter of severity, with clients with AN having a more severe body image disturbance, therefore continuing to feel overweight even at extremely low weights (Fairburn & Harrison, 2003).

The current criteria for AN, as defined by the *DSM* include (a) refusal to maintain body weight at or above a minimally normal weight for age and height (weight loss leading to maintenance of body weight less than 85% of that expected, or failure to make expected weight gain during a period of growth, leading to body weight less than 85% of that expected); (b) intense fear of gaining weight or becoming fat, even though underweight; (c) disturbance in the way in which one's body weight or shape is experienced, undue influence of body weight or shape on self-evaluation, or denial of the seriousness of the current low body weight; and (d) in postmenarcheal females, absence of at least three consecutive menstrual cycles. If the client meets the criteria for both BN and AN, only the diagnosis for AN is made. The distinguishing factors between BN and AN are the presence of significant weight loss and the absence of menstrual cycles in the criteria for AN.

There are two subtypes of AN. A person with the restricting type attempts to lose weight by reducing his or her intake of calories, exercising excessively following food intake, and frequent fasting. A person with the purging type also restricts food intake, but usually as a result of the starvation participates in periods of binge eating and purging. The purging may involve self-induced vomiting or the abuse of laxatives, diuretics, or enemas. Sometimes purging is used after only small amounts of food are eaten (Herrin & Matsumoto, 2002).

Atypical Eating Disorder

A third eating disorder defined in the *DSM* called Eating Disorder Not Otherwise Specified, also referred to as Atypical Eating Disorder (AED). This is a category for eating disorders that are considered severe enough to warrant a diagnosis, but that do not meet the specific criteria for either AN or BN. For example, the client may not quite meet the weight loss requirement of AN or may still be menstruating. Or the client may meet all the criteria for BN, except the binging and purging behaviors have not occurred with the required frequency or duration. Atypical Eating Disorder can be as severe and as long-lasting as BN and AN and should not be overlooked by clinicians and counselors simply because the criteria for BN and AN are not met.

Binge Eating Disorder

Binge Eating Disorder (BED) is an eating disorder included in the *DSM* (American Psychiatric Association, 2000, pp. 785–787) as a diagnosis warranting further study, but which did not yet justify including as a new formal diagnostic category. Z. Cooper and Fairburn (2003) explain that the diagnosis of BED is still somewhat controversial, and the criteria have still not been agreed on by professionals. Binge Eating Disorder is defined in the *DSM* as: (a) recurrent episodes of binge eating (defined in discussion of BN); (b) binge eating episodes associated with three (or more) of the following: (1) eating much more rapidly than normal, (2) eating until feeling uncomfortably full, (3) eating large amounts of food when not feeling physically hungry, (4) eating alone because of being embarrassed by how much one is eating, and (5) feeling disgusted with oneself, depressed, or very guilty after overeating; (c) marked distress regarding binge eating; (d) occurrence, on average, at least 2 days a week for 6 months; and (e) occurrence not associated with the regular use of inappropriate compensatory behavior (e.g., purging, fasting, obsessive exercise) and not exclusively during the course of AN or BN (American Psychiatric Association, 2000, p. 731).

The distinguishing factor between BN and BED is the absence of compensatory purging in BED. However, there is some controversy in trying to distinguish between BED and the nonpurging BN. Drawing the line to determine which clients with nonpurging BN should be diagnosed with BN and which should be diagnosed with BED has become a research question for many professionals working with eating disorders. The question has led to a change in the criteria for nonpurging BN that some researchers feel has resulted in almost eliminating the diagnosis of nonpurging BN. Z. Cooper and Fairburn (2003) argue that this is a disservice to the field and offer revised diagnostic criteria for BED and nonpurging BN so that clients can be more accurately diagnosed.

Prevalence

The prevalence of eating disorders is difficult to ascertain, as people who suffer from these disorders are usually secretive until the physical and medical consequences make it impossible for them to hide their problem. Indeed, clients with eating disorders who lose a great deal of weight are often envied by friends and family members for their great self-control. Therefore, unless the psychological or physical symptoms become extreme, many eating disorders remain undiagnosed.

Prevalence rates of BN offered by researchers vary significantly from study to study, depending on the age and race of the sample and the criteria used. Fairburn and Harrison (2003) estimate that 1% to 2% of females age 16 to 35 have BN, with 29 females and 1 male per 100,000 population. They estimate the prevalence of AN in adolescent women at 0.7%, with 19 females and 2 males per 100,000 people.

There are no clear prevalence estimates for AED; however, there has been research regarding the distribution of eating disorders. Fairburn and Harrison (2003) report that AED is the most common diagnostic category among the three *DSM*-defined eating disorders, with AED comprising approximately half of the cases of diagnosed eating disorders. The estimates are made more difficult as research suggests that clients with AN, BN, and AED tend to migrate between the three disorders.

In an effort to ascertain the prevalence of BED, one study (Smith, Marcus, Lewis, Fitzgibbon, & Schreiner, 1998) evaluated almost 4,000 men and women and found an overall prevalence rate of 1.5%, finding BED more prevalent than BN. Yanovski (1999) estimated a prevalence of 2% in community samples. Striegel-Moore and Franko (2003) suggest that BED is more common than BN, and the population with BED is also more diverse than the population with BN. Men and women are more evenly affected by BED, and African American women seem to have increased risk of BED. The age group affected by BED is also broader, with people ages 20 to 50 being at increased risk.

Other research considers the association between BED and obesity. Fairburn (1995, p. 25) writes, "It is a common misconception that *all* people with BED are overweight. Community studies indicate that only about half are overweight (defined as having a body mass index of 27 or more)." Yanovski (1999) found 25% of severely obese individuals to have BED. Smith et al. (1998) found the prevalence rates of BED among overweight individuals (2.9%) to be almost double that of the overall sample (1.5%).

Prognosis

Like most eating disorders, BN usually starts with dieting. In about 25% of the cases of BN, the criteria for AN are met for a period of time before developing into BN. Extreme food restriction and the resulting weight loss are interrupted by repeated binge eating episodes (Sullivan, Bulik, Carter, Gendall, & Joyce, 1996). On average, people who seek help for BN have suffered with the disorder for 5 years. Approximately 30% to 50% of those diagnosed with BN still have a serious eating disorder 5 to 10 years later, although in many cases it evolves into an Atypical Eating Disorder (Fairburn, Cooper, Doll, Norman, & O'Connor, 2000).

The average age of onset for AN is slightly earlier than for BN. The onset of AN most often occurs during the midteen years and usually begins with dieting, which then develops into extreme and unhealthy food restriction. Some people with AN grow out of the disorder naturally as they mature through adolescence. Others get entrenched in their compulsions toward weight loss and require intensive treatment to overcome the disorder. In 10% to 20% of clients with AN, the disorder proves to be intractable (Steinhausen, 2002). The mortality rate among people with AN is 12 times the normal rate, usually resulting from starvation, suicide, or extremely low potassium levels (Herrin & Matsumoto, 2002). Hall and Ostroff (1998) estimate that 10% of people who suffer with AN die as a result of complications of the disorder.

Findings regarding the prognosis of BED are mixed. Fairburn et al. (2000) suggest that the disorder tends to remit spontaneously, with only 18% of the individuals studied having any form of eating disorder at the end of a 5-year study. Other studies (Agras, 1999; Crow, 2002) found that 38% of BED patients still met the criteria for the disorder at 1-year follow-up, and an additional 55% of the sample met the criteria for other eating disorders. Thus only a small portion of the sample had fully recovered, suggesting that BED does not simply remit over time. One study (Spurrell, Wilfley, Tanofsky, & Brownell, 1997) found that the average age of individuals with BED who sought treatment was 45, and many had experienced the onset of symptoms 20 years earlier.

Evidence-Based Approaches to Assessment

A variety of assessment methods have been developed for use in the diagnosis, treatment, and treatment evaluation of eating disorders. Assessments usually include a structured interview, self-report measurement instruments, assessment of body image distortion, observation methods to directly measure the amount and type of food involved in the binge and purge behaviors, and a complete physical examination to discover possible medical complications.

Structured Clinical Interviews

The Eating Disorder Examination (EDE; Fairburn & Cooper, 1993), currently in its 12th edition, is a structured clinical interview that allows the clinician to gather behavioral and psychological information pertaining to eating disorders. The authors, both leading experts in the field of eating disorders, designed this instrument because they felt the interview format would provide more detailed and accurate information for the diagnosis of an eating disorder than the self-report questionnaires. Because of its reported high reliability and validity, the EDE is a very effective instrument not only for clinical use but also for use in treatment outcome studies. Three different types of assessment data are gathered through the EDE: (1) Frequency or severity ratings on individual items indicate the presence of key behavioral and attitudinal aspects of eating disorders; (2) four subscales (Restraint, Eating Concern, Shape Concern, and Weight Concern) assess key aspects of the eating disorder diagnosis; and (3) a global score measures the overall severity of the eating disorder psychopathology.

A coding sheet and detailed instruments for coding are provided by the authors. It takes approximately 30 to 60 minutes to complete the interview. A majority of items on the EDE use a scale of 0 to 6 on which either frequency or severity is rated, and guidelines for making the ratings are given for each individual question. A code of 8 is used when it is impossible to decide on a rating but the symptom should not be excluded, and a code of 9 is used when the behavior is not applicable to the client. The interviewer is instructed to use the less severe of two ratings when it is difficult to choose between the two (Fairburn & Cooper, 1993). In addition to the structured interview, Fairburn and Beglin (1994) derived a self-report EDE-Questionnaire from the EDE that generates the same four subscales.

Self-Report Questionnaires

The Eating Disorder Inventory (EDI; Garner, Olmsted, & Polivy, 1983) is a self-report questionnaire useful in determining the severity level of an eating disorder as well as differentiating the subtypes of AN and BN. It has also been widely used as an outcome measure in treatment research. The EDI includes 64 items, three subscales pertaining to eating disordered behaviors (Drive for Thinness, Bulimia, and Body Dissatisfaction), and five subscales pertaining to the more general psychological characteristics of clients with eating disorders (Ineffectiveness, Perfectionism, Interpersonal Distrust, Interoceptive Awareness, and Maturity Fears). A revised edition, the Eating Disorder Inventory 2 (Garner, 1991) added 27 more items forming three additional subscales (Asceticism, Impulse Regulation, and Social Insecurity). Most of the research on psychometric properties of the instrument has been completed using the first version. Each question is scored on a 6-point scale from always to never, and the EDI can be completed in about 20 minutes. Copies of the instrument can be obtained from Psychological Assessment Resources, Inc., P.O. Box 998, Odessa, FL 33556 (800) 331-TEST.

The Eating Attitudes Test (Garner, Olmsted, Bohr, & Garfinkel, 1982) is a self-rating scale that was designed to evaluate the attitudes and behaviors associated with AN. It has 26 items, each scored on a 6-point Likert scale (1 = Never to 6 = Always), with higher scores indicating the presence of AN symptoms. The scale includes three subscales: Dieting (an avoidance of fattening foods and a preoccupation with being thinner); Bulimia and Food Preoccupation (recurrent thoughts about food and bulimic behaviors); and Oral Control (self-control of eating and perceived pressure from others to gain weight). The test and instant scoring are available online at www.eatingdisorderinfo.org (select "Is there a problem?").

The Bulimia Test-Revised (Thelen, Farmer, Wonderlich, & Smith, 1991) is a 28-item self-report questionnaire measuring the presence of BN symptoms, the severity of the symptoms, and treatment outcome. Each multiple-choice question has five responses unique to each question, and takes approximately 10 minutes to complete. The instrument is fully described in Thelen et al. (1991) and has been reprinted in Williamson, Anderson, Jackman, and Jackson (1995).

The Body Shape Questionnaire (P. J. Cooper, Taylor, Cooper, & Fairburn, 1987) is a self-report questionnaire consisting of 34 questions that measure client concerns about body shape, particularly the concept of "feeling fat." The questions are answered on a 6-point Likert scale (1 = Never to 6 = Always).

The Setting Conditions for Anorexia Scale (SCANS) was developed by Slade and Dewey (1986) in an effort to identify individuals who are at high risk for developing AN or BN. The SCANS is divided into five scales: (1) Dissatisfaction and Loss of Control, (2) Social and Personal Anxiety, (3) Perfectionism, (4) Adolescent Problems, and (5) Need for Weight Control. It includes 40 items answered on a 5-point scale anchored by different responses depending on the nature of the question (i.e., 1= Very often to 5 = Never, or 1 = Very satisfied to 5 = Very dissatisfied). The instrument takes 10 to 20 minutes to complete and less than 10 minutes to score. Butler, Newton, and Slade (1988) have developed a computerized version of the SCANS. Through the use of the SCANS and the significant research that has been completed in identifying risk factors for developing eating disorders, it seems there is a great potential for preventive work in the area of eating disorders.

Computerized Assessment Methods

A computerized system, the Body Image Testing System (Schlundt & Bell, 1993), was developed to measure the client's perception of his or her body. Clients adjust the onscreen profile of a body until the shape matches their own self-image. A variety of assessment tasks can be constructed using this system, including selecting one's own body shape and selecting one's ideal body shape.

The Self-Monitoring Analysis System (SMAS; Schlundt, 1989) is a computer database designed to manage and analyze food intake data. The Vanderbilt Food Diary is a one-page form that allows the client to specify all food eaten, along with other data items, including the time, whether it was a meal or a snack, the place, other people involved, and the client's feelings. The data are then entered into the SMAS database, where the nutritional composition of the food is analyzed, including protein, carbohydrates, and fats. Compliance between the dietary plan and the actual food intake is summarized. The program also looks at meal frequency and timing and can analyze variables that reflect the individual's self-perception of his or her eating behavior. A variety of reports can be produced using this system.

While there are problems with self-monitoring procedures, such as difficulty in verifying the accuracy of the data and the client's failure to comply with the self-monitoring procedures, Schlundt (1995) argues that with carefully designed forms and properly trained and motivated clients, accurate data can be gathered. He further suggests that such data be supplemented by data collected through direct observation.

Observational Methods

Standardized test meals have been used for assessment and research purposes (Rosen, 1988). Clients are asked to consume as much of a standardized meal as they feel comfortable eating. Three different meals are used: (1) a full-course dinner, (2) a spaghetti dinner, and (3) candy. The amount of food eaten at each meal is measured, as well as the client's ratings of fear, anxiety, and urge to vomit. Clients with BN are instructed not to vomit for at least 1.5 hours after eating the test meal. In most cases, the clinician stays with the client throughout the process, measuring cognitions and affects.

Evidence-Based Approaches to Treating Bulimia Nervosa

Cognitive-Behavioral Treatment

Research has found that cognitive-behavioral therapy (CBT) focusing on the specific eating behaviors and the distorted thinking is the most effective treatment for clients with BN. Current CBT therapies are based on a treatment manual originally developed by Fairburn, Marcus, and Wilson (1993). Components include self-monitoring, reducing environmental cues to binge, meal planning, introducing forbidden foods, problem-solving skills, relaxation training, nutrition education, and cognitive restructuring. Treatment usually involves 20 individual sessions stretching over 5 to 6 months, with 30% to 50% of the clients making a complete and lasting recovery (Fairburn & Harrison, 2003). Research suggests that these programs "produce substantial improvements in both eating behavior (including, in episodes of overeating, a reduction in the use of other methods of weight control and in the level of dietary restraint), as well as an improvement in attitude about body shape and weight" (Kennedy & Garfinkel, 1992, p. 311).

The three main goals of CBT are (1) establishing a regular eating pattern, (2) evaluating and changing beliefs about shape and weight, and (3) relapse prevention. These goals are what define the three phases of CBT for BN. In Phase 1, the therapist helps the client establish an eating pattern that includes three meals and two snacks per day. This phase usually lasts 6 weeks and 8 sessions (2 sessions the first 2 weeks, weekly thereafter). Clients monitor their eating patterns by recording what they eat throughout each day, when, where, whether the episode constitutes a binge, and when purging occurs. Eating on a regular schedule helps counteract binging and thus reduces purging behaviors.

Phase 2 begins after the client has established a fairly regular eating pattern, and binging and purging are usually significantly reduced. Increasing the types of food that are eaten is a goal of this phase. The client creates, then moves through, four lists of food, ranging from least threatening to most threatening. Another goal of this phase is to help clients change their beliefs that have contributed to body dissatisfaction, dieting, and eating disorder behaviors. A third goal of this phase is to improve problem-solving skills. Some clients use binging and purging to cope with difficult and unpleasant situations.

Problem-solving techniques are used to help clients learn alternative ways of coping with stressful situations. The final phase of CBT, Phase 3, is focused on relapse prevention. Clients learn to identify warning signs and develop strategies to use in case of relapse (Spangler, 1999). Research has shown CBT to be as or more effective in treating BN than supportive psychotherapy, focal psychotherapy, exposure with response prevention, behavior therapy, or treatment with antidepressants (Fairburn et al., 1993).

Advanced Cognitive-Behavioral Therapy Research

Despite the clear research finding that CBT can help many clients with BN, Mussell et al. (2000) found that few psychologists are actually providing this therapy for their patients with BN. Based on this finding, several areas of research have surfaced. A recent study (Chen et al., 2003) compared group and individual CBT. The group CBT was adapted from the manual for individual CBT written by Fairburn et al. (1993). Group sessions lasted 90 minutes, were closed, and began with only six patients per group. Both individual and group CBT were effective in reducing the BN symptoms, and the improvements were maintained at 6-month follow-up. This suggests that group CBT may be a cost-effective alternative to individual CBT for clients with BN (Chen et al., 2003).

Self-help manuals using CBT have also been developed by the leading professionals in the eating disorders field (P. J. Cooper, 1995; Fairburn, 1995; Schmidt & Treasure, 1993) and have been offered as a treatment to be completed unassisted or guided by a therapist. Outcome research has been very promising, and self-help manuals may prove to be another cost-effective and readily available alternative to the standard individual CBT (Bailer et al., 2004; Birchall & Palmer, 2002).

One group of researchers (Bara-Carril et al., 2004) is investigating the use of CD-ROM-based self-help CBT for clients with BN. The outcome showed significant reduction in binging and purging behaviors at posttreatment and follow-up. Another study (Bakke, Mitchell, Wonderlich, & Erickson, 2001) considered the use of telemedicine to treat clients with BN in a rural setting. A telecommunication link was used to treat two women with BN using individual CBT, and both were abstaining from binging and purging behaviors at 1-month follow-up.

Interpersonal Psychotherapy

Interpersonal psychotherapy (IPT) does not directly address eating disorder symptoms, but focuses instead on helping clients identify and resolve interpersonal problems (Fairburn, 1997). Research (Agras, Walsh, Fairburn, Wilson, & Kraemer, 2000; Fairburn et al., 1991) has shown that IPT can be as effective as CBT in treating clients with BN, although the effects are delayed and sometimes fail to emerge until the follow-up assessment.

Nutrition Therapy

Nutrition education is a vital component of most CBT models. The purpose of nutrition education and management is "to educate eating-disordered patients about basic principles of good nutrition, and to help them use this information in planning healthy and appropriate patterns of food intake" (Schlundt & Johnson, 1990, p. 321). One research study suggests that nutritional counseling may be effective as a sole form of treatment for clients with BN who show little evidence of other underlying psychopathology (O'Connor, Touyz, & Beaumont, 1987). A survey of 117 dietitians identified the need for more outcome research on nutrition therapy and on the effectiveness of prevention programs for clients with eating disorders (Whisenant & Smith, 1995).

The American Dietetic Association (ADA; 1994, p. 902) stated its position that "nutrition education and nutrition intervention be integrated into the team treatment of patients with anorexia nervosa, bulimia nervosa, and binge eating during assessment and treatment phases of outpatient and/or inpatient therapy." Assessment involves measuring various aspects of the patient's eating and dieting history and his or her current nutritional status. The treatment as defined by the ADA includes two phases: the education phase and the experimental phase. There are five major objectives during the education phase: (1) Collect relevant information, including a comprehensive history of weight changes, eating and exercise patterns, and purging behaviors; (2) establish a collaborative relationship between the client and the registered dietitian that will enable the client to talk about food fears and develop realistic goals for weight and behavior change; (3) define and discuss relevant principles and concepts of food, nutrition, and weight regulation, as it has been found that understanding why and how the body responds to starvation, binge eating, purging, and restriction is typically necessary before the client will risk making behavioral changes; (4) present examples of hunger patterns, typical food intake patterns, and the total caloric intake of a person who has recovered from an eating disorder, helping the client understand what recovery means; and (5) educate the family members to increase their understanding of the eating disorder and their support of the client (pp. 902–903).

During the experimental phase, the client is encouraged to make changes in eating and dieting behaviors. The primary objectives are to (a) separate food and weight-related behaviors from feelings and psychological issues; (b) change eating behaviors in an incremental fashion until food intake patterns are normalized, emphasizing that changes must be gradual and setbacks are normal; (c) slowly increase or decrease weight; (d) learn to maintain a weight that is healthful without the use of abnormal food or weight-related behaviors; and (e) learn to be comfortable in social eating situations (ADA, 1994, pp. 903–904).

Pharmacological Treatment

The outcome research on pharmacological treatment of clients with BN has shown mixed results. Antidepressant drugs result in a quick decline in the frequency of binging and purging behavior, but dropout rate is high, the effect is not generally sustained, and the improvement is not as great as that obtained with CBT (Wilson & Fairburn, 2002). Combining antidepressant drugs with CBT provided few consistent benefits over CBT alone (Fairburn & Harrison, 2003). Most clinicians agree, however, that a subgroup of clients with BN are vulnerable to depression and may require treatment with antidepressants for concurrent major depression (Kennedy & Garfinkel, 1992). One clinician-researcher (Mitchell, 1990, p. 89) recommends the following:

> *Prescribe antidepressants as part of the initial treatment for patients who give a clear history of an affective disorder, in particular if*

there is evidence that the affective disorder preceded the onset of the eating disorder, for patients who remain depressed despite improvement in their eating symptoms, and for those patients who show only a partial response or a lack of response to a psychotherapy intervention, whether or not they are depressed.

Evidence-Based Approaches to Treating Anorexia Nervosa

The treatment of AN has been the subject of surprisingly little research. Because outcome research in this area is inconsistent, Lappalainen and Tuomisto (1999, p. 174) stress, "The importance of an individual analysis should not be underestimated. Understanding the functions of 'anorectic behavior' is a challenge, because it is a result of a multifaceted interaction between inherited and learned behaviors affected by a cultural context." Of course, one of the problems with all eating disorders is that as long as clients are successful in controlling their shape and weight, they often do not consider the behavior a problem and will not seek help. Unlike BN, however, because of the severe weight loss, parents, teachers, and others close to clients suffering with AN often recognize the problem regardless of whether the client seeks help.

Behavior Therapy

The first step in the treatment of AN is generally to restore the client's weight. Behavior therapy has been used successfully during this early phase of treatment. Reversing the effects of malnutrition usually results in a significant improvement in the client's overall state. This step may have to be completed in a hospital, especially if there are indications of suicide risk, severe and rapid weight loss, or medical complications, such as edema, severe electrolyte imbalance, hypoglycemia, or infection (Fairburn & Harrison, 2003). Most of the behavior therapy programs involve "establishing a contract with the patient in which reinforcers are provided contingent on attainment of weight goals or on appropriate eating behavior" (Solanto, Jacobson, Hellers, Golden, & Hertz, 1994, p. 989). Usually a weight gain goal is set, and reinforcers are offered to clients when these goals are reached. Reinforcers may include recreation or amusement activities, telephone use, wearing one's own clothes, visitation, freedom to move about the hospital grounds, and similar privileges. Okamoto et al. (2002) found liquid nutrition was more effective than regular meals at achieving weight gain as the clients viewed the liquid as medication and were less anxious about the caloric intake.

Behavioral Family Therapy

Another important component of the treatment of AN involves clients' distorted thinking regarding their weight and shape, their disordered eating habits, and their overall psychosocial functioning. Behavioral family therapy (BFT) has been helpful with younger adolescent clients with AN (Lock & le Grange, 2001; Russell, Szmukler, Dare, & Eisler, 1987) and is probably the most widely used treatment for clients with AN (Robin, Gilroy, & Baker, 1998). A treatment manual for using BFT with AN has now been developed (Lock, le Grange, Agras, & Dare, 2001). The main focus of this treatment is the "empowerment of the parents in order to succeed in refeeding their starving adolescent offspring" (le Grange, Lock, & Dymek, 2003, p. 243). It is only after the disordered eating behaviors are under control that the parents can return the control of eating behaviors back to the adolescent.

In a recent controlled study, Ball and Mitchell (2004) found that BFT and CBT both resulted in significant improvements for clients with AN on measures of eating attitudes and behaviors, self-esteem, depression, and state anxiety. Treatment involved 25 1-hour sessions over a 12-month period. The BFT in this study was based on behavioral interventions described by Robin and Foster (1989) and emphasized normalizing eating behaviors, nutrition counseling, and relapse prevention. Of the total sample, 60% had good outcomes, defined as weight within 10% of average body weight and regular menstrual cycles. There were no significant differences between the outcomes for CBT and those for BFT. These findings are modest, however, in that a majority of the clients did not fully recover from eating disorder symptoms, and the more severely disordered patients required hospitalization during the treatment (Ball & Mitchell, 2004).

Cognitive-Behavioral Treatment

There has been very little research on CBT for clients with AN (Wilson, 1999; Wilson, Vitousek, & Loeb, 2000), and outcomes are inconsistent. Cognitive-behavioral therapy for AN is based on models developed by Garner and Bemis (1985) and Freeman (1995). The main goals of this therapy are to increase knowledge about the eating disorder, enhance motivation for change, teach behavioral techniques to help the client eliminate disordered eating behaviors, teach cognitive skills that help clients challenge their dysfunctional thoughts regarding food, weight, and size, and to offer support and understanding as they attempt to overcome their eating problems (Leung, Waller, & Thomas, 1999).

Freeman (2002) has recently published a self-help book for AN based on CBT treatment methods. The first part of the book includes a description of the disorder, how AN affects people both mentally and physically, how it overlaps with and differs from other eating disorders, what causes it, and what is known of the treatment of AN. The second part of the book includes a self-assessment in which readers examine their motivation for change and the potential stumbling blocks they may encounter. It then moves through a series of steps to help the client change eating patterns, deal with body image issues, and improve interpersonal relationships.

Pharmacological Treatment

Zhu and Walsh (2002, p. 228) point out that in the current treatment of AN, "although pharmacotherapy is a frequent adjunct intervention, there is scant evidence for its effectiveness." Researchers have long considered the use of antipsychotic medications to reduce obsessional thinking, compulsivity, and anxiety, but outcomes have been mixed (Bosanac, Burrows, & Norman, 2003). Kaye et al. (2001) found the drug fluoxetine helpful in preventing weight loss among clients with AN after they were discharged from the hospital.

Evidence-Based Approaches to Treating Binge Eating Disorders

Wilson and Fairburn (2000, p. 351) point out that "research on the treatment of BED is at an early stage." Some of the shortcomings of this early research include weak assessment measures, insufficient controls, short follow-up periods, and samples made up almost exclusively of clients who also meet the criteria for obesity. Yanovski (2003, p. S119) states, "Our challenge in the future is to understand better the ways in which BED and obesity co-exist, and to find treatment strategies that will relieve the distress and dysfunction due to this disordered eating while enhancing appropriate weight loss or preventing future weight gain."

Cognitive-Behavioral Treatment

Cognitive-behavioral therapy for BED has been adapted from the much studied treatment protocol used with BN (described earlier), although a group format is generally used with BED (Wilson & Fairburn, 2000). Studies show that CBT leads to a decrease in binge eating behaviors, but does not cause weight loss (de Zwaan, 2001). Another study (Agras, Telch, Arnow, Eldredge, & Marnell, 1997) combined CBT and weight loss treatment and found that abstinence from binge eating was associated with sustained weight loss at 1-year follow-up. A study by Wilfley (1999) found that 59% of clients with BED participating in a group format CBT were still free of binge eating behaviors at 1-year follow-up. Self-help forms of CBT (P. J. Cooper, 1995; Fairburn, 1995) are aimed at helping all people who suffer from binge eating, and remission rates are similar to those found in studies using CBT and IPT (Carter & Fairburn, 1998; Loeb, Wilson, Gilbert, & Labouvie, 2000).

Interpersonal Psychotherapy

Treatment for BED using IPT has been adapted from the therapy used to treat BN (Wilson & Fairburn, 2000). Interpersonal psychotherapy is also generally administered in a group format. In one study (Wilfley, 1999), 64% of clients with BED showed a cessation of binge eating at 1-year follow-up. Like CBT, this approach does not produce weight loss.

Behavioral Weight Loss Treatment

Although CBT and IPT have been used successfully with clients with BED, they do not promote weight loss, although in some cases weight loss does occur. The more traditional behavioral weight loss treatment (BWLT) uses increased dietary restriction to reach its primary goal of weight loss and also results in a reduction in binge eating (Wilson & Fairburn, 2000). Behavioral weight loss treatment is designed to alter eating behaviors, reduce the disorganized quality of eating, and produce more regular eating patterns, including moderate caloric restriction (Wilfley, Wilson, & Agras, 2003).

In addition to weight-loss, another strength of BWLT over CBT and IPT is that it is more widely available than either of these therapies (Wilfley et al., 2003; Wilson & Fairburn, 2000). A limitation is that interventions involving BWLT have consistently resulted in weight regain at follow-up (Jeffery et al., 2000). Although BWLT has been effective in reducing binge eating in obese patients, Nauta, Hospers, and Jansen (2001) found that at 6- and 12-month follow-ups, CBT was superior to BWLT in terms of the continued remittance of binge eating behaviors. Cognitive-behavioral therapy was also more effective in reducing concerns about shape, weight, and eating. However, because BWLT produces greater weight loss and is more available as it does not require the same professional training and expertise, additional research should consider the long-term effects of this treatment method. Wilson and Fairburn conclude that self-help CBT is their treatment of choice for BED clients who are not obese, and BWLT is the treatment of choice for obese BED clients.

Pharmacological Treatment

There has been very little research on the use of drugs in the treatment of BED (Wilson & Fairburn, 2000). Antidepressant medication (tricyclics and selective serotonin reuptake inhibitors) and appetite suppressants (d-fenfluramine) have had modest effects on binge eating behaviors, but there is rapid relapse in clients when they discontinue the drug treatment. There is also a high placebo response rate. Wilson and Fairburn suggest that it would be reasonable to combine psychological treatment with the use of antidepressant drugs for those BED clients who have significant depressive symptoms.

Evidence-Based Approaches to Treating Atypical Eating Disorders

As symptoms of AED vary from client to client, research on treatment tends never to look exclusively at a sample with AED. Instead, research on clients with BN will sometimes distinguish between clients who meet the full criteria for BN and those who fail to meet some criteria and are thus categorized as AED. Likewise, research on AN will sometimes include a portion of the sample who are diagnosed with AED as they fail to meet all criteria of AN. Therefore, to gain even an elementary understanding of treatment of this possibly large group of clients, one must look at the outcome research that has been completed on the other eating disorders, including AN, BN, and BED.

Summary

Eating disorders are a vast problem in our society. Many people live with disordered eating patterns throughout their lives. Social workers are in a position to help many individuals with eating disorders who may or may not present for treatment for their eating problems. It is imperative that social workers be familiar with the most effective ways to treat eating disorders. In some situations (i.e., self-help manuals), the social worker can help guide clients through treatment that can help reduce or even eliminate their eating problems. Where more specialized treatments are needed, including hospitalization in extreme cases, social workers should be familiar with the resources that are available in their local area. Treatment of eating disorders does help many suffering from these disorders, but more research is needed to develop effective treatments that are cost-effective and are available to the people who need them.

Study Questions

1. What symptoms can help the clinician differentiate between BN and AN?

2. What symptoms can help the clinician differentiate between BN and BED?

3. Describe two eating disorders that would be classified as an Eating Disorder Not Otherwise Specified or AED.

4. Which eating disorder is probably the least common?

5. Based on prognosis information, which eating disorder do you think is generally the most serious? Why?

6. What assessment instruments might you choose to assess a client who has entered a counseling center with a potentially serious eating disorder?

7. How is cognitive-behavioral therapy used to treat eating disorders?

8. What is the advantage of using behavioral weight loss treatment over cognitive-behavioral therapy in the treatment of BED?

9. How does interpersonal psychotherapy compare with cognitive-behavioral therapy in the treatment of eating disorders?

10. How have drugs been used to treat eating disorders?

References

Agras, W. S. (1999, November). *Diagnostic significance of binge eating disorder.* Paper presented at the annual meeting of the Eating Disorders Research Society, San Diego, CA.

Agras, W. S., Telch, C. F., Arnow, B., Eldredge, K., & Marnell, M. (1997). One-year follow-up of cognitive-behavioral therapy for obese individuals with binge eating disorder. *Journal of Consulting and Clinical Psychology, 65,* 343–347.

Agras, W. S., Walsh, B. T., Fairburn, C. G., Wilson, G. T., & Kraemer, H. C. (2000). A multicenter comparison of cognitive-behavioral therapy and interpersonal therapy for bulimia nervosa. *Archives of General Psychiatry, 57,* 459–466.

American Dietetic Association. (1994). Position of the American Dietetic Association: Nutrition intervention in the treatment of anorexia nervosa, bulimia nervosa, and binge eating. *Journal of the American Dietetic Association, 94,* 902–907.

American Psychiatric Association. (2000). *Diagnostic and statistical manual of mental disorders* (4th ed., text rev.). Washington, DC: Author.

Bailer, U., de Zwaan, M., Leisch, F., Strnad, A., Lennkh-Wolfsberg, C., El-Giamal, N., et al. (2004). Guided self-help versus cognitive-behavioral group therapy in the treatment of bulimia nervosa. *International Journal of Eating Disorders, 35,* 522–537.

Bakke, B., Mitchell, J., Wonderlich, S., & Erickson, R. (2001). Administering cognitive-behavioral therapy for bulimia nervosa via telemedicine in rural settings. *International Journal of Eating Disorders, 30,* 454–457.

Ball, J., & Mitchell, P. (2004). A randomized controlled study of cognitive behavior therapy and behavioral family therapy for anorexia nervosa patients. *Eating Disorders, 12,* 303–314.

Bara-Carril, N., Williams, C. J., Pombo-Carril, M. G., Reid, Y., Murray, K., Aubin, S., et al. (2004). A preliminary investigation into the feasibility and efficacy of a CD-ROM based cognitive-behavioural self-help intervention for bulimia nervosa. *International Journal of Eating Disorders, 35,* 538–548.

Birchall, H., & Palmer, R. L. (2002). Doing it by the book: What place for guided self-help for bulimic disorders? *European Eating Disorders Review, 10,* 379–385.

Bosanac, P., Burrows, G., & Norman, T. (2003). Olanzapine in anorexia nervosa. *Australian and New Zealand Journal of Psychiatry, 37,* 494.

Butler, N., Newton, T., & Slade, P. D. (1988). Validation of a computerized version of the SCANS questionnaire. *International Journal of Eating Disorders, 8,* 239–241.

Carter, J. C., & Fairburn, C. G. (1998). Cognitive-behavioral self-help for binge eating disorder: A controlled effectiveness study. *Journal of Consulting and Clinical Psychology, 66,* 616–623.

Chan, Z. C. Y., & Ma, J. L. C. (2004). Aetiology of anorexia nervosa in Hong Kong: A social work qualitative inquiry. *Child and Family Social Work, 9,* 177–186.

Chassler, L. (1997). Understanding anorexia nervosa and bulimia nervosa from an attachment perspective. *Clinical Social Work Journal, 25,* 407–423.

Chen, E., Touyz, S. W., Beumont, P. J. V., Fairburn, C. G., Griffiths, R., Butow, P., et al. (2003). Comparison of group and individual cognitive-behavioral therapy for patients with bulimia nervosa. *International Journal of Eating Disorders, 33,* 241–254.

Cooper, P. J. (1995). *Bulimia nervosa and binge eating: A guide to recovery.* London: Robinson.

Cooper, P. J., Taylor, M. J., Cooper, Z., & Fairburn, C. G. (1987). The development and validation of the Body Shape Questionnaire. *International Journal of Eating Disorders, 6,* 485–494.

Cooper, Z., & Fairburn, C. G. (2003). Refining the definition of binge eating disorder and nonpurging bulimia nervosa. *International Journal of Eating Disorders, 34,* S89–S95.

Crow, S. J. (2002, November). *Does binge eating disorder exist?* Paper presented at the annual meeting of the Eating Disorder Research Society, Charleston, SC.

de Zwaan, M. (2001). Binge eating disorder and obesity. *International Journal of Obesity and Related Metabolic Disorder, 25*(Suppl.), S51–S55.

Fairburn, C. G. (1995). *Overcoming binge eating.* New York: Guilford Press.

Fairburn, C. G. (1997). Interpersonal psychotherapy for bulimia nervosa. In D. M. Garner & P. E. Garfinkel (Eds.), *Handbook of treatment for eating disorders* (pp. 278–294). New York: Guilford Press.

Fairburn, C. G., & Beglin, S. J. (1994). Assessment of eating disorders. *International Journal of Eating Disorders, 16,* 363–370.

Fairburn, C. G., & Cooper, P. J. (1993). The eating disorder examination. In C. G. Fairburn & G. T. Wilson (Eds.), *Binge eating: Nature, assessment, and treatment* (12th ed., pp. 317–360). New York: Guilford Press.

Fairburn, C. G., Cooper, Z., Doll, H. A., Norman, P., & O'Connor, M. (2000). The natural course of bulimia nervosa and binge eating disorder in young women. *Archives of General Psychiatry, 57,* 659–665.

Fairburn, C. G., & Harrison, P. J. (2003). Eating disorders. *Lancet, 361,* 407–416.

Fairburn, C. G., Jones, R., Peveler, R. C., Carr, S. J., Solomon, R. A., O'Connor, M. E., et al. (1991). Three psychological treatments for bulimia nervosa. *Archives of General Psychiatry, 48,* 463–469.

Fairburn, C. G., Marcus, M. D., & Wilson, G. T. (1993). Cognitive-behavioral therapy for binge eating and bulimia nervosa: A comprehensive treatment manual. In C. G. Fairburn & G. T. Wilson (Eds.), *Binge eating: Nature, assessment, and treatment* (pp. 361–404). New York: Guilford Press.

Freeman, C. G. (1995). Cognitive therapy. In C. Szmulker, C. Dare, & J. Treasure (Eds.), *Handbook of eating disorders: Theory, treatment, and research* (pp. 309–332). Chichester, England: Wiley.

Freeman, C. G. (2002). *Overcoming anorexia nervosa: A self-help guide using cognitive behavioral techniques.* London: Robinson.

Garner, D. M. (1991). *Eating Disorder Inventory 2 manual.* Odessa, FL: Psychological Assessment Resources.

Garner, D. M., & Bemis, K. M. (1985). Cognitive behavior therapy for anorexia nervosa. In D. M. Garner & P. Garfinkel (Eds.), *Handbook of psychotherapy for anorexia nervosa and bulimia* (107–146). New York: Guilford Press.

Garner, D. M., Olmsted, M. P., Bohr, Y., & Garfinkel, P. E. (1982). The Eating Attitudes Test: Psychometric features and clinical correlates. *Psychological Medicine, 12,* 871–878.

Garner, D. M., Olmsted, M. P., & Polivy, J. (1983). Development and validation of a multi-dimensional eating disorder inventory for anorexia and bulimia. *International Journal of Eating Disorders, 2,* 15–34.

Guest, T. (2000). Using the Eating Disorders Examination in the assessment of bulimia and anorexia: Issues of reliability and validity. *Social Work in Health Care, 31*(4), 71–83.

Hall, L., & Ostroff, M. (1998). *Anorexia nervosa: A guide to recovery.* Carlsbad, CA: Gurze Books.

Herrin, M., & Matsumoto, N. (2002). *The parent's guide to childhood eating disorders.* New York: Henry Holt.

Jeffery, R. W., Drewnowski, A., Epstein, L. H., Stunkard, A., Wilson, G. T., Wing, R., et al. (2000). Long-term maintenance of weight loss: Current status. *Health Psychology, 19*(Suppl.), 5–16.

Kaye, W. H., Nagata, T., Weltzin, T. E., Hsu, L. K. G., Sokol, M. S., McConaha, C., et al. (2001). Double-blind placebo-controlled administration of fluoxetine in restricting and restricting-purging type anorexia nervosa. *Biological Psychiatry, 49,* 644–652.

Kennedy, S. H., & Garfinkel, P. E. (1992). Advances in diagnosis and treatment of anorexia nervosa and bulimia nervosa. *Canadian Journal of Psychiatry, 37,* 309–315.

Kindy, P., & Patterson, P. M. (1980). Behavioral-cognitive therapy in a group for the prevention of obesity. In Rose, S. D. (Ed.), *A casebook in group therapy: A behavioral-cognitive approach* (pp. 114–151). Englewood Cliffs, NJ: Prentice Hall.

Lappalainen, R., & Tuomisto, M. T. (1999). Functional analysis of anorexia nervosa: Some applications to clinical practice. *Scandinavian Journal of Behavior Therapy, 28,* 167–175.

le Grange, D., Lock, J., & Dymek, M. (2003). Family-based therapy for adolescents with bulimia nervosa. *American Journal of Psychotherapy, 57,* 237–251.

Leung, N., Waller, G., & Thomas, G. (1999). Group cognitive-behavioral therapy for anorexia nervosa: A case for treatment? *European Eating Disorders Review, 7,* 351–361.

Lock, J., & le Grange, D. (2001). Can family-based treatment of anorexia nervosa be manualized? *Journal of Psychotherapy Practice and Research, 10,* 253–261.

Lock, J., le Grange, D., Agras, W. S., & Dare, C. (2001). *Treatment manual for anorexia nervosa: A family-based approach.* New York: Guilford Press.

Loeb, K. L., Wilson, G. T., Gilbert, J. S., & Labouvie, E. (2000). Guided and unguided self-help for binge eating. *Behavior Research and Therapy, 38,* 259–272.

Ma, J. L. C., & Chan, Z. C. Y. (2004). The different meanings of food in Chinese patients suffering from anorexia nervosa: Implications for clinical social work practice. *Social Work in Mental Health, 2,* 47–70.

Mackay, L. (1984). Eating disorders: Anorexia nervosa and obesity. In F. J. Turner (Ed.), *Adult Psychopathology.* New York: Free Press.

Mitchell, J. E. (1990). *Bulimia nervosa.* Minneapolis: University of Minnesota Press.

Mussell, M. P., Crosby, R. D., Crow, S. J., Knopke, A. J., Peterson, C. B., Wonderlich, S. A., et al. (2000). Utilization of empirically supported psychotherapy treatment for individuals with eating disorders: A survey of psychologists. *International Journal of Eating Disorders, 27,* 230–237.

Myers, L. L. (1996). Bulimia nervosa: What social workers need to know. *Journal of Applied Social Sciences, 20,* 63–75.

Myers, L. L. (1998). Bulimia nervosa. In B. A. Thyer & J. S. Wodarski (Eds.), *Handbook of empirical social work practice: Mental disorders* (pp. 439–450). New York: Wiley.

Nauta, H., Hospers, H., & Jansen, A. (2001). One-year follow-up effects of two obesity treatments on psychological well-being and weight. *British Journal of Health Psychology, 6,* 271–284.

O'Connor, M. A., Touyz, S. W., & Beaumont, P. J. V. (1987). Nutritional management and dietary counseling in bulimia: Some preliminary observations. *International Journal of Eating Disorders, 7,* 657–662.

O'Halloran, M. S. (2005). Emily: From "I'm nothing special" to "I don't need anorexia anymore." In C. W. LeCroy (Ed.), *Case studies in child, adolescent, and family treatment* (pp. 38–50). Belmont, CA: Brooks/Cole.

Okamoto, A., Yamashita, T., Nagoshi, Y., Masui, Y., Wada, Y., Kashima, A., et al. (2002). A behavior therapy program combined with liquid nutrition designed for anorexia nervosa. *Psychiatry and Clinical Neurosciences, 56,* 515–520.

Robin, A. L., Gilroy, A., & Baker, A. (1998). Treatment of eating disorders in children and adolescents. *Clinical Psychology Review, 18,* 421–446.

Robin, A. L., & Foster, S. L. (1989). *Negotiating parent-adolescent conflict: A behavioral-family systems approach.* New York: Guilford.

Rosen, J. C. (1988). Test meals in the assessment of bulimia. In M. Hersen & A. S. Bellack (Eds.), *Dictionary of behavioral assessment* (pp. 473–474). New York: Pergamon Press.

Russell, G. F. M., Szmukler, G. I., Dare, C., & Eisler, I. (1987). An evaluation of family therapy in anorexia nervosa and bulimia nervosa. *Archives of General Psychiatry, 44,* 1047–1056.

Schlundt, D. G. (1989). Computerized behavioral assessment of eating behavior in bulimia: The self-monitoring analysis system. In W. G. Johnson (Ed.), *Advances in eating disorders: Pt. 2. Bulimia* (pp. 1–23). New York: JAI Press.

Schlundt, D. G. (1995). Assessment of specific eating behaviors and eating style. In D. B. Allison (Ed.), *Handbook of assessment methods for eating behaviors and weight-related problems: Measures, theory, and research* (pp. 241–302). Thousand Oaks, CA: Sage.

Schlundt, D. G., & Bell, C. D. (1993). The Body Image Testing System: A microcomputer program for the assessment of body image. *Journal of Behavioral Assessment and Psychopathology, 15,* 267–285.

Schlundt, D. G., & Johnson, W. G. (1990). *Eating disorders: Assessment and treatment.* Boston: Allyn & Bacon.

Schmidt, U., & Treasure, J. (1993). *Getting better bit(e) by bit(e).* London: Erlbaum.

Shekter-Wolfson, L. F., Woodside, D. B., & Lackstrom, J. (1997). Social work treatment of anorexia and bulimia: Guidelines for practice. *Research on Social Work Practice, 7,* 5–31.

Slade, P. D., & Dewey, M. E. (1986). Development and preliminary validation of the SCANS: A screening instrument for identifying individuals at risk of developing anorexia and bulimia nervosa. *International Journal of Eating Disorders, 5,* 517–538.

Smith, D. E., Marcus, M. D., Lewis, C. E., Fitzgibbon, M., & Schreiner, P. (1998). Prevalence of binge eating disorder, obesity, and depression in a biracial cohort of young adults. *Annals of Behavioral Medicine, 20,* 227–232.

Solanto, M. V., Jacobson, M. S., Hellers, L., Golden, N., & Hertz, S. (1994). Rate of weight gain of inpatients with anorexia nervosa under two behavioral contracts. *Pediatrics, 93,* 989–991.

Spangler, D. L. (1999). Cognitive-behavioral therapy for bulimia nervosa: An illustration. *Psychotherapy in Practice, 55*(6), 699–713.

Spurrell, E. B., Wilfley, D. E., Tanofsky, M. B., & Brownell, K. D. (1997). Age of onset for binge eating: Are there different pathways to binge eating? *International Journal of Eating Disorders, 21,* 55–65.

Steinhausen, H.-C. (2002). The outcome of anorexia nervosa in the 20th century. *American Journal of Psychiatry, 159,* 1284–1293.

Striegel-Moore, R. H., & Franko, D. L. (2003). Epidemiology of binge eating disorder. *International Journal of Eating Disorders, 34,* S19–S29.

Stuart, R. B. (1967). Behavioral control of overeating. *Behaviour Research and Therapy, 5,* 357–365.

Stuart, R. B. (1978). *Act thin, stay thin.* New York: Norton.

Stuart, R. B., & Davis, B (1972). *Slim chance in a fat world: Behavioral control of obesity.* Champaign, IL: Research Press.

Sullivan, P. F., Bulik, C. M., Carter, F. A., Gendall, K. A., & Joyce, P. R. (1996). The significance of a prior history of anorexia in bulimia nervosa. *International Journal of Eating Disorders, 20,* 253–261.

Thelen, M. H., Farmer, J., Wonderlich, S., & Smith, M. (1991). A revision of the Bulimia Test: The BULIT-R. *Psychological Assessment, 3,* 119–124.

Thiels, C., & Garthe, R. (2000). Prevalence of eating disorders in students. *Nervenarzt, 71,* 552–558. (Original work German)

von Bulow, B. (1991). Eating problems. In A. Gitterman (Ed.), *Handbook of social work practice with vulnerable populations* (pp. 205–233). New York: Columbia University Press.

Weiss, L., Wolchik, S., & Katzman, M. (1994). A treatment program for adolescent bulimics and binge eaters. In C. W. LeCroy (Ed.), *Handbook of child and adolescent treatment manuals* (pp. 278–306). New York: Lexington Books.

Weissman, M. M., Verdeli, H., Gameroff, M. J., Bledsoe, S. E., Betts, K., Mufson, L., et al. (2006). National survey of psychotherapy training in psychiatry, psychology, and social work. *Archives of General Psychiatry, 63,* 925–934.

Wempner, M. P. (1984). The role of social work in a model self-help organization. *Psychiatric Clinics of North America, 7,* 395–404.

Whisenant, S. L., & Smith, B. A. (1995). Eating disorders: Current nutrition therapy and perceived needs in dietetics education and research. *Journal of the American Dietetics Association, 95,* 1109–1112.

Wilfley, D. E. (1999, September). *Group CBT and group ITP in the treatment of BED: A controlled comparison.* Paper presented at the Annual meeting of the Eating Disorders Research Society, San Diego, CA.

Wilfley, D. E., Wilson, G. T., & Agras, W. S. (2003). The clinical significance of binge eating disorder. *International Journal of Eating Disorders, 34,* S96–S106.

Williamson, D. A., Anderson, D. A., Jackman, L. P., & Jackson, S. R. (1995). Assessment of eating disordered thoughts, feelings, and behaviors. In D. B. Allison (Ed.), *Handbook of assessment methods for eating behaviors and weight-related problems: Measures, theory, and research* (pp. 347–386). Thousand Oaks, CA: Sage.

Wilson, G. T. (1999). Cognitive behavior therapy for eating disorders: Progress and problems. *Behavior Research and Therapy, 37*(Suppl. 1), S79–S95.

Wilson, G. T., & Fairburn, C. G. (2000). The treatment of binge eating disorder. *European Eating Disorders Review, 8,* 351–354.

Wilson, G. T., & Fairburn, C. G. (2002). Treatment for eating disorders. In P. E. Nathan & J. M. Gorman (Eds.), *A guide to treatments that work* (2nd ed., pp. 559–592). New York: Oxford University Press.

Wilson, G. T., Vitousek, K. M., & Loeb, K. L. (2000). Stepped-care treatment for eating disorders. *Journal of Consulting and Clinical Psychology, 68,* 564–572.

Wilson, J. (2004). Beyond psychiatry: How social workers conceptualise women and self-starvation. *Australian Social Work, 57,* 150–160.

Yanovski, S. Z. (1999). Diagnosis and prevalence of eating disorders in obesity. In B. Guy-Grand & G. Ailhaud (Eds.), *Progress in obesity research* (pp. 229–236). London: Libby.

Yanovski, S. Z. (2003). Binge eating disorder and obesity in 2003: Could treating an eating disorder have a positive effect on the obesity epidemic? *International Journal of Eating Disorders, 34,* S117–S120.

Zhu, A. J., & Walsh, B. T. (2002). Pharmacologic treatment of eating disorders. *Canadian Journal of Psychiatry, 47,* 227–234.

PART VIII

PERSONALITY DISORDERS

Antisocial Personality Disorder

Carolyn Hilarski

21
Chapter

Learning Objectives

After reading this chapter, the reader will be able to:

- Describe the psychopathic construct as a current clinical taxonomy of Antisocial Personality Disorder (ASPD).
- Describe the definition and diagnosis of ASPD.
- Describe the prevalence, risk factors, and costs of ASPD.
- Locate and describe evidence-based assessment measures useful in evaluating persons with presumptive ASPD.
- Locate and describe evidence-based interventions found useful in helping persons with presumptive ASPD.

Overview of the Problem

Asocial behaviors have been described throughout history in biblical, medieval, and classical narratives (Arrigo & Shipley, 2001). Yet, effective assessment and treatment remains illusive due to the recurrent differences of opinion over the definition and conceptualization of the natural constructs relating to the condition (Lilienfeld & Andrews, 1996).

Antisocial Personality Disorder, as defined in the twenty-first century, actually began its evolution in the very early 1800s, when it was suggested that abusive behaviors occurred as a result of illness rather than evil forces (Werlinder, 1978). To illustrate,

Philippe Pinel (1745–1826) and Benjamin Rush (1745–1813), in the early nineteenth century, described seemingly rational individuals who engaged in impulsive and self-destructive behaviors as suffering from "mania without delirium" (later termed "moral imbecility" and "morally defective," in that order; Arrigo & Shipley, 2001). The cause of these disorders was thought to be a disease or some kind of birth defect (Black & Larson, 1999).

Koch (1889), suggested that "psychopathic inferiority" was a more meaningful descriptor for the term moral insanity described by James Prichard, a British physician, in 1835 (Ozarin, 2001). Prichard (see Prichard, 1835), professed that an individual suffering with moral insanity maintained a keen intellect but lacked, as a result of a disease of the *will*, the ability to empathize or morally self-govern. Koch on the other hand, believed that the etiology for psychopathic inferiority was a combination of genetic predisposition and learned behavior, which shaped the dysfunctional temperament (Arrigo & Shipley, 2001).

Nevertheless, the term moral insanity came to include an array of clinical conditions, such as Schizophrenia, mania, hypomania, obsessive states, personality disorders, and organic brain damage, and remained unopposed for many years (Werlinder, 1978). Indeed, it was used as a legal defense for the accused assassin of President Garfield in 1881 (Ozarin, 2001). Yet, this varied mix of mental health states had one seemingly common thread: dysfunctional impulse control residing in clearly confused reality.

In the early twentieth century, Kraepelin (1907/1981), inspired by Koch's work and those before him, laid the foundation for future theorists to understand *psychopathy* in its current form, as a personality disorder. Kraepelin proposed that the syndrome "psychopathic inferiority," which included several different subtypes: the unstable, the liars and swindlers, the quarrelsome, the excitable, the impulsive, and the eccentrics (Cleckley, 1988). This psychiatrist and others (e.g., Patridge, 1930) struggled with the challenge of understanding and describing this seemingly deceptive disorder, yet continued to confound its diagnostic validity (Cleckley, 1988).

"Constitutional psychopathic state" was considered a less subjective descriptor for moral insanity, according to the American Medical Psychological Association in 1917, and this categorization remained in debate for many years. "Psychopathic personality" was proposed in 1934 and included the subtypes pathological sexuality and emotionality and asocial or amoral trends (Cleckley, 1988).

In 1952, the *Diagnostic and Statistical Manual of Mental Disorders* (*DSM;* American Psychiatric Association, 1952) pronounced that "sociopathic personality disturbance" would replace psychopathic personality. Sociopathic personality included the subtypes antisocial reaction, dissocial reaction, sexual deviation, and addiction.

In 1968, the second edition of the *DSM* (American Psychiatric Association, 1968) considered ASPD a more empirical and less confusing nomenclature than earlier classifications, and that taxonomy remains today (Ozarin, 2001).

So, after 200 years of transformation, how is this continually evolving disorder currently defined?

Operational Definitions of the Problem

Antisocial Personality Disorder, also known as psychopathy or sociopathy, is a chronic pattern of behaviors that violate and disregard the rights of others. It is characterized as a disturbance in relating to self, others, and the environment (Hare, 1996).

Personality disorders are generally defined as having fixed *characteristics* and *behavior* patterns that influence and may precede or live comorbidly with other mental health issues (Dogan, Onder, Dogan, & Akyuz, 2004). Individuals with ASPD use primitive coping mechanisms that are largely action-oriented and expressive of the individual's inability to regulate impulses and relate successfully with others. Antisocial behaviors include burglary, violent crimes, drug use, heavy drinking, drunk or reckless driving, sexual promiscuity or risky sex behavior, divorce separation or unstable sexual relationships, spouse or partner abuse, child abuse or neglect, unemployment or an unstable employment history, debts, dependence on welfare benefits, heavy gambling or smoking, repeated lying, and conning. Personality characteristics are impulsiveness, selfishness, callousness, egocentricity, low frustration tolerance, high aggressiveness, lack of planning, empathy, remorse, and guilt (Farrington, 2003). The individual may also possess an inflated and arrogant self-appraisal and glib superficial charm (American Psychiatric Association, 1994).

Diagnostic and Statistical Manual of Mental Disorders IV Criteria

Antisocial Personality Disorder diagnostic criteria have a history of proven reliability when compared to other personality disorders (Mellsop, Varghese, Joshua, & Hicks, 1982). The *DSM-IV* (American Psychiatric Association, 1994) states that to diagnose ASPD (301.7) there must be an inflexible and persistent history, since age 15, of at least three of the following circumstances: arrests, deceitfulness, physical fights or assaults, disregard for safety of self or others, and irresponsibility (chronic unemployment and not honoring financial obligations) that causes significant functional impairment or distress. Additionally, the individual must be age 18 or older, report a history of Conduct Disorder prior to age 15, and presenting behaviors must not be the outcome of a schizophrenic, substance abuse, or manic episode (American Psychiatric Association, 1994).

Personality disorders maintain their own Axis coding (Axis II) separate from the major mental disorders, which lie on Axis I in the *DSM-IV* multiaxial scale. The 11 personality disorders described in the 4th edition of the *DSM* are organized into three groups based on comparable characteristics. Antisocial Personality Disorder is found in Cluster B, along with Borderline, Histrionic, and Narcissistic Personality Disorders. The overlapping traits among these four disorders are a propensity for crisis and impulsivity (American Psychiatric Association, 1994).

Prevalence

The prevalence of ASPD in the world population is 3% in males and 1% in females (Pitchford, 2001). Hare's (1996) findings suggest that this figure is low. In the prisons, ASPD involves more than three-quarters of the population (Hare, 1998). The lifetime prevalence in the United States was found to be 7.3% for males and 1% for females (Robins & Price, 1991) and, for youth, 15% across the United Kingdom, New Zealand, and the United States (Fergusson, Swain-Campbell, & Horwood, 2004).

Men are 5 times more likely than women to be diagnosed with ASPD. This disparity may be due, in part, to females presenting with fewer overt violent behaviors, in addition to professional expectation bias (Widiger & Spitzer, 1991). The symptoms most often appear in middle or late childhood (Millon, 1981) and have intrapersonal implications. Antisocial behaviors that appear before school age are considered permanent and irreversible (Martens, 2000). The likelihood of being diagnosed with ASPD decreases with age for both genders (Bland, Newman, & Orn, 1997).

Cost

The costs of ASPD include poor and unstable interpersonal relations, deficient occupational functioning, and an increased risk of involvement in criminal activity and subsequent incarceration (Hare, 1998; Moran, 1999).

The victims' cost is immeasurable. The financial costs are staggering. Annually, approximately $1 billion is spent on Canadian corrections not including policing and court provisions. One of every 10 corrections dollars is spent on rehabilitative programming (Johnson & Becker, 1997).

Implications for Social Work

Individuals suffering with ASPD are responsible for a significant portion of the aggressive and violent crimes committed each year.

Further, they are very likely to repeat these crimes (Woodworth & Porter, 2002). Of particular concern is the harmful social cost of ASPD, which begins early and is most often evident, in some form, throughout the life span.

Antisocial Personality Disorder is recognized as a mental condition that is not fully understood in terms of other mental health conditions. The multifaceted character of this syndrome complicates the assessment and treatment process. Identifying antisocial personality traits and assessing the likelihood of recidivism and violence with a reasonable degree of accuracy is the ever-present challenge for professionals. Yet, as violent crime remains pervasive, social policy considerations are pressing the need for effective assessment and treatment. It is vital to recognize the reliable and accessible instruments available to assist with this process and to understand the appropriate interventions to ameliorate the suffering by all concerned.

Evidence-Based Approaches to Assessment

There are several ways to measure ASPD. One suggestion is to use a two-stage process (Farrington, 2003), beginning with a brief symptom screen, for example, the Psychopathy Checklist: Screening Version (PCL: SV; Hart, Cox, & Hare, 1995), and ending with an intensive interview, if clinical relevance is found (Farrington, 2003). Another proposal is to use an evaluation that does not require a trained interviewer, for example, the Diagnostic Interview Schedule (Helzer, Spitznagel, & McEvoy, 1987). This model also includes a semistructured interview with family members (Standardized Assessment of Personality; Pilgrim & Mann, 1990), a rating scale for associated professional staff (PCL-R; Hare, 1991), and a consumer self-report questionnaire (Psychopathic Personality Inventory; Lilienfield & Andrews, 1996) to complete the evaluation package (Farrington, 2003). Essential issues are the prevalence and significance of the antisocial symptoms at different developmental stages: What was the age of onset, the persistence of symptoms after onset, and desistance or discontinuous episodes (if applicable)?

The following are empirical tools and techniques used for obtaining needed diagnostic data.

Self-Report Methods

It is common for antisocial individuals to exaggerate or underestimate thoughts or behaviors to manipulate external circumstances. Validity scales can be helpful to correct this circumstance, but few antisocial self-report measures include such scales (Sandoval, Hancock, Poythress, Edens, & Lilienfeld, 2000).

Lilienfeld and Andrews (1996) developed the Psychopathic Personality Inventory (PPI), a self-report instrument intended to overcome this validity issue. The authors purposely avoided questions pertaining to criminal behavior and composed queries, meant to identify ASPD personality characteristics, with a normative approach.

The PPI provides a general index of ASPD character traits expressed in eight subscales: Machiavellian Egocentric measures narcissistic and ruthless attitudes in interpersonal functioning; Social Potency assesses perceived ability to influence and manipulate others; Cold-heartedness determines callousness, guiltlessness, and lack of sentimentality; Carefree Nonplanfulness calculates indifference in planning one's actions; Fearlessness appraises the absence of anticipatory anxiety concerning harm and the willingness to participate in risky activities; Blame Externalization considers the tendency to blame others for problems and to rationalize misbehavior; Impulse Nonconformity evaluates the lack of concern regarding social rules; and Stress Immunity weighs the absence of marked reaction to anxiety-provoking events (Lilienfeld & Andrews, 1996).

The PPI also contains three validity scales: Deviant Responding contains10 items meant to detect malingering and random responding with questions that do not relate to any understood form of psychopathology; Unlikely Virtues includes 14 items intended to measure social desirability; and Variable Response Inconsistency contains 40 pairs of items proposed to identify careless or inconsistent responding (Lilienfeld & Andrews, 1996).

Semistructured Assessment

Hare (1998) developed the Psychopathy Checklist-Revised (PCL-R), a rating scale to identify ASPD/Psychopathy with Cleckley's (1988) profile in mind—in other words, evaluating personality characteristics in addition to antisocial behaviors. The PCL-R is a 20-item rating scale that must be completed by a trained professional and is based on a semistructured interview and very detailed historical information. The interview may take 2 to 3 hours, and institutional files are required for collateral support. The scale measures such traits as glibness or superficial charm, lack of remorse or guilt, shallow affect, marital relationships, and impulsivity, in addition to the fundamental constructs of ASPD: child and adolescent behavioral issues (Hare, Hart, & Harpur, 1991). The rater is provided with a description and specific behaviors consistent with each trait or behavior as well as instructions on how to gauge the extent to which a certain person expresses each trait or performs each behavior. Each item is scored on a 3-point scale: 0 = Does not apply; 1 = Somewhat applies; and 2 = Applies. The suggested cutoff score is 30 out of a possible 40 points (Hare, 1991). The interrater reliabilities of .88 to .92 are good (Schroeder, Schroeder, & Hare, 1983), and the behavioral aspects correlate strongly with the *DSM-IV* diagnostic criteria (Hare, 1991). The instrument is shown to be valid and reliable among adult and juvenile male institutionalized or forensic populations (Forth, Hart, & Hare, 1990), with a potential for false-negative estimations when the scores range between 27 and 33 (Meloy & Gacono, 1995). Its use outside of these milieus is not well established (Arrigo & Shipley, 2001).

Multidimensional Structured Interview

The Diagnostic Interview Schedule (DIS-IV; Helzer et al., 1987) is a widely used comprehensive tool based on *DSM-IV* and intended to diagnose a range of syndromes, including personality disorders. It was originally designed for trained clinicians, but revisions and continued research are proving that is can be useful in service settings where untrained nonprofessionals evaluate mental health issues with adults, though a children's version is also available (Shaffer, Fisher, Lucas, Dulcan, & Schwab-Stone, 2000). The DIS-IV has been translated into 30 languages (Cao, McFarlane, & Klimidis, 2003; Ortega et al., 2003), including American Sign Language (Steinberg, Lipton, Eckhardt, Goldstein, & Sullivan, 1998; Vernon & Miller, 2001). A considerable disadvantage to the paper-and-pencil interview version is that it takes almost 2 hours to complete. A computerized version, the Quick Diagnostic Interview Schedule (Bucholz, Marion, Shayka, Marcus, & Robins, 1996) is available and useful for evaluation of antisocial populations (Draine & Solomon, 2001). In this computer edition, the assessment can remain a structured interview, with the interviewer entering the data, or the consumer may enter as a self-report (Barry & Fleming, 1990).

Evidence-Based Approaches to Intervention

Treatment Prognosis

Antisocial Personality Disorder is difficult to treat, and effective treatment is generally unknown (Salekin, Ziegler, Larrea, Anthony, & Bennett, 2003). Assorted methodological issues such as self-reports regarding treatment progress, lack of control groups or nonequivalent groups, no follow-up data, faulty selection criteria, and lack of theoretical framework distort results and confuse rational explanation for varied outcomes (Serin & Brown, 1997). Moreover, personality disorders are often overlooked and

devalued as influencing variables to presenting mental health issues and treatment (McGlashan et al., 2000), thus reducing the
energy that might be spent in searching for successful treatment
modalities.

Interestingly, time-honored intervention programs have no
established empirical effectiveness (D'Silva, Duggan, & McCarthy,
2004). It appears that ASPD individuals respond poorly and leave
treatment earlier than individuals who do not have this diagnosis
(Kunz et al., 2004; Losel, 1998). The cause is thought to derive
from the ASPD person's worldview, which says, "The *world* is
messed up, not me" (Skeem, Monahan, & Mulvey, 2002). This is a
provocative attitude for mental health practice where the focus is
on personal change. The suggestion of scheme modification is
puzzling for an individual satisfied with the self. Moreover, the
therapeutic alliance is based on trust and mutual respect—quite a
challenge when the ASPD individual regards intimacy as a failing
(Martens, 2000).

The characteristics of personality disorders are considered
lasting (Kunz et al., 2004). Thus, treatment should focus on individual change and risk management (Blackburn, 1993; Quinsey &
Walker, 1992). Risk is supervised through self-regulation techniques in addition to avoidance of perilous situations and dangerous cues (Newman, Schmitt, & Voss, 1997; Pithers, 1995). This
model has been successfully used with sex offenders (Marques,
Day, Nelson, & West, 1994), substance abusers (Graham, Annis,
Brett, & Venesoen, 1996), and sexual psychopaths, but it needs further replication to determine the specific model characteristics that
improve prevention efforts.

Individuals with ASPD are notoriously noncompliant with
treatment. Research suggests that these individuals operate under
specific methods of interpersonal interaction and information
processing that, if addressed when negotiating treatment goals,
might increase cooperation (Serin & Brown, 1997).

The following are currently investigated treatment models
for ASPD.

Pharmacological Treatments

There appears to be some form of genetic marker that predisposes
ASPD, because children adopted as infants with antisocial fathers
showed antisocial tendencies at a much higher rate than average
(Dinwiddie, 1994; Hicks, Krueger, Iacono, McGue, & Patrick,
2004; Langbehn & Cadoret, 2001). Biological theorists suggest that
ASPD behavior is caused by limbic system dysfunction or low serotonin levels (Anthenelli, Maxwell, Geracioti, & Hauger, 2001). At
present, it is not clear if biological issues are the cause or effect of
ASPD. Nonetheless, antidepressants, lithium, benzodiazepines,
stimulants, and anticonvulsants are common forms of medication

used with personality disorders *as a complement to psychological treatment*. However, medication effectiveness takes time; consequently, client cooperation must be maintained. There is no specific antiaggression medication; thus, using a sedative-type medication is sometimes helpful and necessary during a crisis (Ward, 2004).

Individual Therapies

Whether a person is treatable is determined by his or her level of motivation and attitude toward the therapeutic structure and process (Berry, Duggan, & Larkin, 1999). Certain authors suggest that ASPD individuals are resistant to change, abhor authority, view the patient role as contemptible, and generally consider therapy a waste of time and therapist's objectives to deceive, threaten, or use (Maxmen & Ward, 1995). As a result of this and therapists' personal countertransference issues, individual psychotherapy is not recommended for treating ASPD (Goaln, 2004). However, if this is unavoidable, it is important to keep in mind that behavioral therapy that includes *a balance* of limit setting and confrontation is quite useful. This is important to remember, as Murphy and Baxter (1997) reviewed confrontation as an intervention with violent offenders and found that professional disapproval and hostile confrontation concerning client defenses (e.g., rationalization) are often not helpful. Empathy was deemed more successful (Murphy & Baxter, 1997).

Other useful methods include a *here-and-now stance* focused on the client's behavior and taking responsibility while therapist and collaterals remain attentive to manipulation tactics and avoid rescuing behavior. Strategies such as pacing and leading recommend that the therapist empathize with the experiences of the individual (pacing), then offer a leading suggestion for a new way to think or act (Gilligan, 1987). This process respects the client's perception of the experience, yet rejects the negative behavior by discussing an alternative way to understand and behave in relation to the circumstance (Saunders, 1982). The goal of therapy is not necessarily a cure but is restorative in nature (Messina, Wish, Hoffman, & Nemes, 2002).

Group Therapies

Group therapy seems promising with ASPD individuals (Kunz et al., 2004). Membership in a therapeutic or self-help group is recommended over one-on-one therapy. The social nature of the group setting provides an opportunity to examine family and social network struggles. The diverse nature of group composition offers complex group member interaction that supports increased understanding of self and other relationship fundamentals. Moreover, groups can provide a nurturing environment and may help to reparent group members (Shine & Hobson, 2000). In some instances, self-help groups have been more useful than prison or psychiatric hospitalization. Group formation is critical, however. It is recommended that groups meant to help ASPD folks be primarily homogeneous and structured, with two leaders to reduce manipulative and disruptive behavior (Seto & Barbaree, 1999).

Community Prevention and Intervention Models

Community-oriented programs offer up to 80 hours of treatment. Their focus is to enhance self-control, interpersonal problem solving, social perspective taking, critical reasoning, and the values that govern behavior.

Cognitive-behavioral methods that combine social skills and problem-solving training appear to be somewhat effective in mixed groups, when using recidivism as the outcome variable. To illustrate, a review showed an average of 10% to 15% reduction in reconvictions in matched comparison groups (Vennard, Hedderman, & Sugg, 1997). Although cognitive-behavioral training (CBT) varies across professions and agencies, the prominent mode of delivery is brief and focused. An example of a community CBT program currently under evaluation is the Reasoning and Rehabilitation Program (R&R; Ross, Fabiano, & Ewles, 1988; Van Voorhis, Spruance, Ritchey, Listwan, & Seabrook, 2004). This model is meant to enhance self-control, interpersonal problem solving, social perspective taking, critical reasoning, and understanding of the values that govern behavior; it is used in both prison and community populations. A matched control study showed that medium-risk offenders exposed to R&R treatment had a 14% reduction in reconvictions when compared to controls over a 2-year period (Friendship, Blud, Erikson, & Travers, 2002).

A variant of cognitive behavioral therapy, dialectical behavior therapy (Linehan, 1993), in a modified format, has been modestly successful with forensic ASPD populations. This version focuses on suicidal and homicidal issues, behaviors that interfere with treatment, and therapist motivation and willingness to treat (McCann, Ball, & Ivanoff, 2000; Newhill & Mulvey, 2002).

Programs meant to modify violent behavior are varied and cognitive and behavioral in theory. Problem solving (McMurran, Egan, Blair, & Richardson, 2001) and violence risk (Wong, 2000) interventions are two examples; however, they need further evaluation.

Family Therapies

Developmental theorists suggest that ASPD has a genetic or family etiology (Robins, 1966). Therefore, prevention efforts that focus on family system dysfunction are important for reducing the consequences of ASPD (Salekin et al., 2003). One example of this is a family development program employed by Syracuse University. The model implemented a specialized child care curriculum for uneducated single mothers living in poverty (significant risk factors for ASPD). The mothers received health care, parenting training, mental health counseling, education, day care, and employment help along with 2 years of home visits. The outcome of this intervention showed that the short-term costs far outweighed the long-term consequences of not providing the program. The treated families' children demonstrated a significant reduction in crime when compared to the control families (Methvin, 1997).

Indeed, poor parenting skills have been linked to children with antisocial behavior; conversely, children with parents who set boundaries and are responsive are less at risk (Reti et al., 2002). Thus, type of parenting is both an important risk and protective factor and a primary target for preventive intervention regarding adolescent antisocial behavior (a precursor to ASPD). Promoting resiliency in antisocial youth by presenting an ecological, community-based prevention program that includes youths, educators, and school environments is vital to reducing further escalation to chronic antisocial activity. This can be accomplished by working with families to improve parenting and family communication skills, in addition to working with schools, community agencies, and community leaders to achieve the *multilevel preventive intervention* that is necessary for success in resiliency-building efforts (Henggeler, Melton, Brondino, Scherer, & Hanley, 1997).

In multisystemic therapy (MST), problem behaviors are conceptualized as being associated with individual characteristics, family, friends, and community. This approach is designed to intervene in all ecological systems, with goals that attempt to promote positive relational interactions, improve family management skills, and develop greater social competencies (Curtis, Ronan, & Borduin, 2004).

The MST program is based on developmental theory (Bronfenbrenner, 1979). This approach emphasizes the character and dynamics of interaction over time with the family during early childhood and within environments (such as the family or school). It shares with some risk factor theories a concern with early developmental deficits or predisposing factors. It differs, however, from risk factor theories in its heavy concentration on characteristics of the family and school environments that directly reinforce undesirable patterns of affect, belief, and behavior. It also concentrates on environmental reinforcement of the development of positive motivation, educational potential, and prosocial behavior. The developmental approach has a wide target base to support long-term environmental and institutional change.

Multisystemic therapy is comprehensive, flexible, and individualized for targeting the many complex issues (e.g., concerning work, school, family, institutions) of antisocial adolescents and adults (Henggeler et al., 1997). Its goal is to promote positive behaviors within the individual's natural environments (home, work, and neighborhood) through intensive treatment (24 hours a day and 7 days a week for a period of at least 4 months), which helps to reduce barriers (e.g., family dysfunction and mental illness) to treatment. It involves intensive assessment, acquiring information from multiple systems (Borduin, 1999), and it has proven successful in African American and White (male and female) populations of diverse age groups and socioeconomic status (Borduin et al., 1995) . The family is respected as a vital resource for stabilization and recovery (even when chaos reigns). Its multisystem focus naturally incorporates the many systems (e.g., substance abuse treatment, psychological treatment, AA, medications) that the individual might need for recovery. Staff are highly trained, supervised professionals who are held accountable for intervention outcomes. A recent meta-analysis of the effectiveness of MST in treating antisocial youth and their families showed a significant reduction in offending behavior and increase in family functioning when compared to youth receiving an alternative treatment (Curtis et al., 2004). Finally, this intervention is cost-effective as it reduces out-of-home placements (Randall, Swenson, & Henggeler, 1999).

Summary

Antisocial Personality Disorder is an intrinsic condition that has a poor treatment prognosis and no universally recognized treatment protocol. This is thought to be the result of ill-defined diagnostic parameters and a lack of research interest. In spite of this, it is vital that professionals understand the potential problems of individual therapy with this population and arm themselves with community resources to support a comprehensive multisystemic model of treatment. As environment appears to be a significant risk factor for ASPD, early prevention efforts are essential and cost-effective.

Study Questions

1. Discuss the most effective treatments for individuals diagnosed with Antisocial Personality Disorder.
2. Discuss the intervention you might choose for an individual still in his or her teens.

3. Discuss the positive and negative issues of engaging in individual therapy with ASPD consumers.

4. What evaluative model would you use to aid in a diagnosis of ASPD? Explain your choice.

5. What are the diagnostic parameters for ASPD?

6. Discuss the issues that have hindered established assessment and intervention methods for ASPD.

7. Discuss the usefulness of family intervention and prevention efforts regarding antisocial behavior.

8. Explain the theory that supports the family intervention model.

References

American Psychiatric Association. (1952). *Diagnostic and statistical manual of mental disorders*. Washington, DC: Author.

American Psychiatric Association. (1968). *Diagnostic and statistical manual of mental disorders* (2nd ed.). Washington, DC: Author.

American Psychiatric Association. (1994). *Diagnostic and statistical manual of mental disorders* (4th ed.). Washington, DC: Author.

Anthenelli, R. M., Maxwell, R. A., Geracioti, T. D., Jr., & Hauger, R. (2001). Stress hormone dysregulation at rest and after serotonergic stimulation among alcohol-dependent men with extended abstinence and controls. *Alcoholism Clinical and Experimental Research, 25,* 692–703.

Arrigo, B. A., & Shipley, S. (2001). The confusion over psychopathy: Historical considerations. *International Journal of Offender Therapy and Comparative Criminology, 45,* 325–344.

Barry, K. L., & Fleming, M. F. (1990). Computerized administration of alcoholism screening tests in a primary care setting. *Journal of the American Board of Family Practice, 3,* 93–98.

Berry, A., Duggan, C., & Larkin, E. (1999). The treatability of psychopathic disorder: How clinicians decide. *Journal of Forensic Psychiatry, 10,* 710–719.

Black, D. W., & Larson, C. L. (1999). *Bad boys, bad men.* New York: Oxford University Press.

Blackburn, R. (1993). Clinical programs with psychopaths. In K. Howells & C. R. Hollin (Eds.), *Clinical approaches to the mentally disordered offender* (pp. 179–208). New York: Spectrum.

Bland, R. C., Newman, S. C., & Orn, H. (1997). Age and remission of psychiatric disorders. *Canadian Journal of Psychiatry, 52,* 916–924.

Borduin, C. M. (1999). Multisystemic treatment of criminality and violence in adolescents. *Journal of the American Academy of Child and Adolescent Psychiatry, 38*(3), 242–249.

Borduin, C. M., Mann, B. J., Cone, L. T., Henggeler, S. W., Fucci, B. R., Blaske, D. M., et al. (1995). Multisystemic treatment of serious juvenile offenders: Long-term prevention of criminality and violence. *Journal of Consulting and Clinical Psychology, 63,* 569–578.

Bronfenbrenner, U. (1979). *The ecology of human development: Experiments by nature and design.* Cambridge, Ma: Harvard University Press.

Bucholz, K. K., Marion, S. L., Shayka, J. J., Marcus, S. C., & Robins, L. N. (1996). A short computer interview for obtaining psychiatric diagnoses. *Psychiatric Services, 47,* 293–297.

Cao, H., McFarlane, A. C., & Klimidis, S. (2003). Prevalence of psychiatric disorder following the 1988 Yun Nan (China) earthquake: The first 5-month period. *Social Psychiatry and Psychiatric Epidemiology, 38,* 204–212.

Cleckley, H. M. (1988). *The mask of sanity* (5th ed.). St. Louis, MO: Mosby.

Curtis, N. M., Ronan, K. R., & Borduin, C. M. (2004). Multisystemic treatment: A meta-analysis of outcome studies. *Journal of Family Psychology, 18,* 411–419.

Dinwiddie, S. H. (1994). Psychiatric genetics and forensic psychiatry: A review. *Bulletin of the American Academy of Psychiatry and the Law, 22,* 327–342.

Dogan, O., Onder, Z., Dogan, S., & Akyuz, G. (2004). Distribution of symptoms of conduct disorder and antisocial personality disorder in Turkey. *Psychopathology, 37,* 285–289.

Draine, J., & Solomon, P. (2001). Threats of incarceration in a psychiatric probation and parole service. *American Journal of Orthopsychiatry, 71,* 262–267.

D'Silva, K., Duggan, C., & McCarthy, L. (2004). Does treatment really make psychopaths worse? A review of the evidence. *Journal of Personality Disorders, 18,* 163–177.

Farrington, D. P. (2003). Advancing knowledge about the early prevention of adult antisocial behavior. In D. P. Farrington & J. W. Coid (Eds.), *Early prevention of adult antisocial behavior* (pp. 1–31). New York: Cambridge University Press.

Fergusson, D., Swain-Campbell, N., & Horwood, J. (2004). How does childhood economic disadvantage lead to crime? *Journal of Child Psychology and Psychiatry and Allied Disciplines, 45,* 956–966.

Forth, A. E., Hart, S. D., & Hare, R. D. (1990). Assessment of psychopathy in male young offenders. *Psychological Assessment: A Journal of Consulting and Clinical Psychology, 2,* 342–344.

Friendship, C., Blud, L., Erikson, M., Travers, R., & Thornton, D. (2003). Cognitive behavioral treatment for imprisoned offenders: An evaluation of HM Prison Service's cognitive skills programmes. *Legal and Criminological Psychology, 8*(1), 103–114.

Gilligan, S. (1987). *Therapeutic trances.* New York: Brunner/Mazel.

Goaln, S. (2004). Transference-countertransference: Where the (political) action is. *Journal of Psychotherapy Integration, 14,* 371–396.

Graham, K., Annis, H. M., Brett, P. J., & Venesoen, P. (1996). A controlled field trial of group versus individual cognitive-behavioral training for relapse prevention. *Addiction, 91,* 1127–1139.

Hare, R. D. (1991). *Hare Psychopathy Checklist-Revised (PCL-R).* Toronto, Ontario, Canada: Multi-Health Systems.

Hare, R. D. (1996). Psychopathy and antisocial personality disorder: A case of diagnostic confusion. *Psychiatric Times, 13,* 39–40.

Hare, R. D. (1998). The PCL-R assessment of psychopathy: Some issues and concerns. *Legal and Criminological Psychology, 3,* 101–122.

Hare, R. D., Hart, S. D., & Harpur, T. J. (1991). Psychopathy and the *DSM-IV* criteria for antisocial personality disorder. *Journal of Abnormal Child Psychology, 100,* 391–398.

Hart, S. D., Cox, D. N., & Hare, R. D. (1995). *Manual for the Psychopathy Checklist: Screening Version (PCL: SV).* Toronto, Ontario, Canada: Multi-Health Systems.

Helzer, J. E., Spitznagel, E. L., & McEvoy, L. (1987). The predictive validity of lay diagnostic interview schedule diagnoses in the general population: A comparison with physician examiners. *Archives of General Psychiatry, 44,* 1069–1077.

Henggeler, S. W., Melton, G. B., Brondino, M. J., Scherer, D. G., & Hanley, J. H. (1997). Multisystemic therapy with violent and chronic juvenile offenders and their families: The role of treatment fidelity in successful dissemination. *Journal of Consulting and Clinical Psychology, 65,* 821–833.

Hicks, B. M., Krueger, R. F., Iacono, W. G., McGue, M., & Patrick, C. J. (2004). Family transmission and heritability of externalizing disorders: A twin-family study. *Archives of General Psychiatry, 61,* 922–928.

Johnson, B. R., & Becker, J. V. (1997). Natural born killers? The development of the sexually sadistic serial killer. *Journal of the American Academy of Psychiatry and Law, 25,* 335–348.

Koch, J. L. (1889). *Kurzgefaßter leitfaden der psychiatrie* (2nd ed.). Ravensburg, Germany: Dom'schen Buchhandlung.

Kraepelin, E. (1907). *Clinical psychiatry: A textbook for students and physicians.* London: Macmillan.

Kunz, M., Yates, K. F., Czobor, P., Rabinowitz, S., Lindenmayer, J. P., & Volavka, J. (2004). Course of patients with histories of aggression and crime after discharge from a cognitive-behavioral program. *Psychiatric Services, 55,* 654–659.

Langbehn, D. R., & Cadoret, R. J. (2001). The adult antisocial syndrome with and without antecedent conduct disorder: Comparisons from an adoption study. *Comprehensive Psychiatry, 42,* 272–282.

Lilienfeld, S. O., & Andrews, B. P. (1996). Development and preliminary validation of a self-report measure of psychopathic personality traits in noncriminal populations. *Journal of Personality Assessment, 66,* 488–524.

Linehan, M. M. (1993). *Skills training manual for treating borderline personality disorder.* New York: Guilford Press.

Losel, F. (1998). Treatment and management of psychopaths. In D. J. Cooke (Ed.), *Psychopathy: Theory, research, and implications for society* (pp. 303–354). Dordrecht, The Netherlands: Kluwer Academic.

Marques, J. K., Day, D. M., Nelson, C., & West, M. A. (1994). Effects of cognitive behavioral treatment on sex offender recidivism: Preliminary results of a longitudinal study. *Criminal Justice and Behavior, 21,* 28–54.

Martens, W. H. (2000). Antisocial and psychopathic personality disorders: Causes, course, and remission—A review article. *International Journal of Offender Therapy and Comparative Criminology, 44,* 406–430.

Maxmen, J. S., & Ward, N. G. (1995). *Essential psychopathology and its treatment* (2nd ed.). New York: Norton.

McCann, R. A., Ball, E. M., & Ivanoff, A. (2000). DBT with an inpatient forensic population: The CMHIP forensic model. *Cognitive and Behavioral Practice, 7,* 447–456.

McGlashan, T. H., Grilo, C. M., Skodol, A. E., Gunderson, J. G., Shea, M. T., Morey, L. C., et al. (2000). The Collaborative Longitudinal Personality Disorders Study: Baseline Axis I/II and II/II diagnostic co-occurrence. *Acta Psychiatrica Scandinavica, 102,* 256–264.

McMurran, M., Egan, V., Blair, M., & Richardson, C. (2001). The relationship between social problem-solving and personality in mentally disordered offenders. *Personality and Individual Differences, 30,* 517–524.

Mellsop, G., Varghese, F., Joshua, S., & Hicks, A. (1982). The reliability of Axis II of *DSM-III. American Journal of Psychiatry, 139,* 1360–1361.

Meloy, J. R., & Gacono, C. B. (1995). Assessing the psychopathic personality. In J. N. Butcher (Ed.), *Clinical personality assessment* (pp. 410–422). New York: Oxford University Press.

Messina, N. P., Wish, E. D., Hoffman, J. A., & Nemes, S. (2002). Antisocial personality disorder and TC treatment outcomes. *American Journal of Drug and Alcohol Abuse, 28,* 197–212.

Methvin, E. (1997). Mugged by reality: Nine lessons we've learned about the epidemic. *Policy Review, 84,* 28–32.

Millon, T. (1981). *Disorders of personality:* DSM-III *Axis II.* New York: Wiley.

Moran, P. (1999). *Antisocial personality disorder: An epidemiological perspective.* London: Gaskell.

Murphy, C., & Baxter, V. (1997). Motivating batterers to change in the treatment context. *Journal of Interpersonal Violence, 12,* 607–619.

Newhill, C. E., & Mulvey, E. P. (2002). Emotional dysregulation: The key to a treatment approach for violent mentally ill individuals. *Clinical Social Work Journal, 30,* 157–171.

Newman, J. P., Schmitt, W. A., & Voss, W. D. (1997). The impact of motivationally neutral cues on psychopathic individuals: Assessing the generality of the response modulation hypothesis. *Journal of Abnormal Psychology, 106,* 563–575.

Ortega, A. N., McQuaid, E. L., Canino, G., Ramirez, R., Fritz, G. K., & Klein, R. B. (2003). Association of psychiatric disorders and different indicators of asthma in island Puerto Rican children. *Social Psychiatry and Psychiatric Epidemiology, 38,* 220–226.

Ozarin, L. (2001). Moral insanity: A brief history. *Psychiatric News, 36*(10), 21.

Patridge, G. D. (1930). Current conceptions of psychopathic personality. *American Journal of Psychiatry, 10,* 5399–5401.

Pilgrim, J., & Mann, A. (1990). Use of the ICD-10 version of the Standardized Assessment of Personality to determine the prevalence of personality disorder in psychiatric in-patients. *Psychological Medicine, 20*(4), 985–992.

Pitchford, I. (2001). The origins of violence: Is psychopathy an adaptation? *Human Nature Review, 1,* 28–36.

Pithers, W. (1995). Relapse prevention: A method for enhancing behavioral self management and external supervision with the sexual aggressor. In B. Schwartz & H. Cellini (Eds.), *The sex offender: Correction, treatment, and legal practice* (pp. 20/22–20/31). Kingston, NJ: Civic Research Institute.

Prichard, J. C. (1835). *A treatise on insanity and other disorders affecting the mind.* London: Sherwood, Gilbert, and Piper.

Quinsey, L., & Walker, W. D. (1992). Dealing with dangerousness: Community risk management strategies with violent offenders. In D. V. Peters, R. J. McMahon, & V. L. Quinsey (Eds.), *Aggression and violence throughout the lifespan* (pp. 244–262). Newbury Park, CA: Sage.

Randall J., Swenson, C. C., & Henggeler, S. W. (1999, December). Neighborhood solutions for neighborhood problems: An empirically based violence prevention collaboration. *Health Education Behavior, 26*(6), 806–820.

Reti, I. M., Samuels, J. F., Eaton, W. W., Bienvenu, O. J., III, Costa, P. T., Jr., & Nestadt, G. (2002). Adult antisocial personality traits are associated with experiences of low parental care and maternal overprotection. *Acta Psychiatrica Scandinavica, 106,* 126–133.

Robins, L. N. (1966). *Deviant children grown up: A sociological and psychiatric study of sociopathic personality.* Baltimore: Williams & Wilkins.

Robins, L. N., & Price, R. K. (1991). Adult disorders predicted by childhood conduct problems: Results from the NIMH Epidemiologic Catchment Area project. *Psychiatry, 54,* 116–132.

Ross, R. R., Fabiano, E. A., & Ewles, C. D. (1988). Reasoning and rehabilitation. *International Journal of Offender Therapy and Comparative Criminology, 32,* 29–35.

Salekin, R. T., Ziegler, T. A., Larrea, M. A., Anthony, V. L., & Bennett, A. D. (2003). Predicting dangerousness with two Millon Adolescent Clinical Inventory Psychopathy Scales: The importance of egocentric and callous traits. *Journal of Personality Assessment, 80*(2), 154–163.

Sandoval, A. M., Hancock, D., Poythress, N., Edens, J. F., & Lilienfeld, S. (2000). Construct validity of the Psychopathic Personality Inventory in a correctional sample. *Journal of Personality Assessment, 74,* 262–281.

Saunders, D. (1982). Counseling the violent husband. In P. Keller & L. Ritt (Eds.), *Innovations in clinical practice: Vol. 1. A source book* (pp. 16–29). Sarasota, FL: Professional Resource Exchange.

Schroeder, M., Schroeder, K., & Hare, R. (1983). Generalizability of a checklist for the assessment of psychopathy. *Journal of Consulting and Clinical Psychology, 51,* 511–516.

Serin, R. C., & Brown, S. L. (1997). Treatment programs for offenders with violent histories: A national survey. *Forum on Corrections Research, 9,* 35–38.

Seto, M., & Barbaree, H. E. (1999). Psychopathy, treatment behavior, and sex offender recidivism. *Journal of Interpersonal Violence, 14,* 1235–1248.

Shaffer, D., Fisher, P., Lucas, C. P., Dulcan, M. K., & Schwab-Stone, M. E. (2000). NIMH Diagnostic Interview Schedule for Children Version IV (NIMH DISC-IV): Description, differences from previous versions, and reliability of some common diagnoses. *Journal of the American Academy of Child and Adolescent Psychiatry, 39,* 28–38.

Shine, J., & Hobson, J. (2000). Institutional behavior and time in treatment among psychopaths admitted to a prison-based therapeutic community. *Medicine, Science and the Law, 40,* 327–335.

Skeem, J. L., Monahan, J., & Mulvey, E. P. (2002). Psychopathy, treatment involvement, and subsequent violence among civil psychiatric patients. *Law and Human Behavior, 26,* 577–603.

Steinberg, A. G., Lipton, D. S., Eckhardt, E. A., Goldstein, M., & Sullivan, V. J. (1998). The Diagnostic Interview Schedule for deaf patients on interactive video: A preliminary investigation. *American Journal of Psychiatry, 155,* 1603–1604.

Van Voorhis, P., Spruance, L. M., Ritchey, P. N., Listwan, S. J., & Seabrook, R. (2004). The Georgia Cognitive Skills Experiment: A replication of reasoning and rehabilitation. *Criminal Justice and Behavior, 31,* 282–305.

Vennard, J., Hedderman, C., & Sugg, D. (1997). *Changing offenders' attitudes and behavior: What works?* London: HMSO.

Vernon, M., & Miller, K. (2001). Interpreting in mental health settings: Issues and concerns. *American Annals of the Deaf, 146*(5), 429–434.

Ward, R. K. (2004). Assessment and management of personality disorders. *American Family Physician, 70,* 1505–1512.

Werlinder, H. (1978). *Psychopathy: A history of the concepts—Analysis of the origin and development of family concepts in psychopathology.* Uppsala, Sweden: Almqvist & Wiksell.

Widiger, T. A., & Spitzer, R. L. (1991). Sex bias in the diagnosis of personality disorders: Conceptual and methodological issues. *Clinical Psychology Review, 11,* 1–22.

Wong, S. (2000). Psychopathic offenders. In S. Hodgins & R. Muller-Isberner (Eds.), *Violence, crime and mentally disordered offenders: Concepts and methods for effective treatment* (pp. 87–112). Chichester, England: Wiley.

Woodworth, M., & Porter, S. (2002). In cold blood: Characteristics of criminal homicides as a function of psychopathy. *Journal of Abnormal Psychology, 111,* 436–445.

Borderline Personality Disorder

André Ivanoff, Jennifer Manuel,
and Henry Schmidt III

22

Chapter

Learning Objectives

After reading this chapter, the reader will be able to:

- Explain the biosocial basis for the development of Borderline Personality Disorder.

- Explain behavioral dysfunctions across domains associated with Borderline Personality Disorder.

- Identify clinically useful means of assessing Borderline Personality Disorder and measuring clinically relevant indicators of change.

- Identify the modes and functions of evidence-based approaches to treating Borderline Personality Disorder.

- Identify important supervisory and collaborative needs in implementing evidence-based treatment for Borderline Personality Disorder.

Overview of the Problem

Borderline Personality Disorder (BPD) is a serious public health problem, affecting approximately 2% of the general population, 10% of all mental health outpatients, and 20% of psychiatric inpatients (American Psychiatric Association, 2000). Of these groups, somewhere between 70% and 77% are women (Widiger & Frances, 1989). Rates of self-injury and attempted suicide range from 69% to 80% (Frances, Fyer, & Clarkin, 1986).

Suicide rates among individuals suffering from BPD range from 5% to 10%, on par with rates of suicide among those with Schizophrenia and Major Affective Disorder (Frances et al., 1986; Perry, 1993; Stone, 1990).

Individuals diagnosed with BPD are high users of health, mental health, and social services, particularly the highest cost emergency, crisis, and acute medical and supportive services. Due to the interpersonal difficulties afflicting many individuals with BPD, efforts to obtain needed services and assistance often result in frustration, anger, depression, and failure. Due to their impulsivity, poor problem solving, and interpersonally chaotic lifestyles, these individuals are often found among the multiproblem clients seen in social service and forensic settings for committing interpersonal violence, child abuse, or sexual abuse, as well as in more traditional health and mental health settings, from outpatient to acute to long-term inpatient care. Traditional outpatient psychotherapy has been largely ineffective at addressing the behavioral dysfunctions of BPD, often leaving relatively untrained line staff and caseworkers to deal with the multiple psychosocial and environmental problems this disorder occasions.

Unfortunately, the term *borderline* has become exceptionally popular among care providers (mental health and beyond) as a pejorative term used to describe difficult-to-manage clients who tend to make clinicians feel incompetent. "Splitting," "manipulative," and "attention seeking" are a few of the common interpretations used to label the behavior of these clients, often without assessment. Three cardinal characteristics of this disorder—client anger, threats of suicide, and suicidal behaviors—are identified by therapists as the most challenging professional stressors (Hellman, Morrison, & Abramowitz, 1986), so it is no surprise that individuals who suffer from BPD are regarded as among the most challenging to treat. Many clinicians choose to avoid working with BPD clients when possible; others stipulate they will work with them only in the absence of suicidal behavior (which effectively eliminates many as clients). Although we recommend best practices, there is no single method of intervention demonstrated effective at reducing all domains of dysfunction. Practitioners who are members of a team rather than lone practitioners (National Institute for Mental Health in England, 2003) and those able to behaviorally specify, analyze, and target individual client dysfunctional behavior for intervention may have an easier time tailoring treatment to the needs of the client suffering from BPD.

Operational Definitions of the Problem

Borderline Personality Disorder is a severe Axis II personality disorder characterized by a debilitating set of pervasive dysfunctions.

Individuals suffering from BPD experience intense and labile negative emotions or affective instability, generally characterized by an inability to regulate negative internal emotional states. Individuals attempting to cope with these states often engage in impulsive and maladaptive behaviors, including self-injury and suicidal behaviors, alcohol and substance abuse, and eating binges. Self-injurious and suicidal behaviors have been described as the behavioral specialty of BPD clients (Gunderson, 1984), requiring direct focus in treatment (Linehan, 1993a). This emotional and behavioral dysregulation results in unstable and chaotic interpersonal relationships. Themes of BPD beliefs include dependency; helplessness; distrust; emotional control; fears of rejection, abandonment, or losing emotional control; and extreme attention-seeking behavior (A. T. Beck & Beck, 1991; Butler, Brown, Beck, & Grisham, 2002). Cognitive rigidity is common, and there is a tendency to engage in dichotomous, that is, all-or-nothing thinking. Dysfunctional beliefs as measured by the Personality Belief Questionnaire (A. T. Beck & Beck, 1991) discriminate individuals diagnosed with BPD from those with other personality disorders.

Borderline Personality Disorder remains a controversial and complex diagnosis. Diagnosis is more complex than for most Axis I disorders and many Axis II disorders. The *Diagnostic and Statistical Manual of Mental Disorders* (*DSM-IV;* American Psychiatric Association, 2000) identifies nine criteria illustrating the characteristics listed earlier; five are necessary for diagnosis, four for "probably diagnostic." J. S. Beck (1996) cites an unnamed study in which only 40% of patients diagnosed with BPD actually met *DSM* criteria for the disorder, illustrating the difficulty of obtaining reliable diagnoses. The *International Classification of Diseases 10* (World Health Organization, 1992) identifies two subtypes for Emotionally Unstable Personality Disorder: borderline type and impulsive type. The borderline type is largely consistent with *DSM-IV* criteria. The heterogeneity among individuals meeting criteria for BPD (i.e., two individuals meeting criteria may present very differently) is a recognized problem in assessment and in treatment (Binks et al., 2006).

Another controversy is diagnosing personality disorders in adolescents, which we advise against for two reasons: First, patterns of behavior cannot be established over extended periods of time for youth experiencing regular developmental changes; second, developmentally appropriate conflicts and dilemmas may be mistaken for characteristics linked to BPD. We are not wedded to psychiatric diagnosis as a driver for treatment, although we do believe there is an identifiable set of behaviors that characterize individuals called *borderline personality disordered.* While there are not treatments that have been empirically demonstrated to cure the disorder, treatments focusing on behavioral dysfunctions linked to diagnostic criteria (e.g., suicidal behavior) have proven

Table 22.1 **Characteristics and Behaviors Associated with Borderline Personality Disorder**

1. Affective dysregulation	A. Affective lability
	B. Problems with anger
2. Interpersonal dysregulation	A. Chaotic relationships
	B. Fears of abandonment
3. Self-dysregulation	A. Identity disturbance, difficulties with sense of self
	B. Sense of emptiness
4. Behavioral dysregulation	A. Parasuicidal behavior threats
	B. Impulsive behavior
5. Cognitive dysregulation	A. Dissociative responses, paranoid ideation

successful. Table 22.1 reorganizes BPD diagnostic criteria by behavioral dysfunction (Linehan, 1993a).

Evidence-Based Approaches to Assessment

Several features associated with BPD have undergone substantial empirical investigation. These include self-injurious and suicidal behaviors, cognitive deficits, psychotic symptoms, neurological dysfunctions, substance abuse and chemical dependency, and sexual and physical abuse. Consistent with a biosocial theory of understanding human behavior, findings suggest that BPD impacts all functional domains: cognitive, behavioral, affective, and interpersonal.

Borderline Personality Disorder is frequently comorbid with Axis I disorders, commonly Mood and Anxiety Disorders (Friedman, Shear, & Frances, 1987; Fyer, Frances, Sullivan, Hurt, & Clarkin, 1988) and Psychoactive Substance Abuse Disorders (Craig, 1988; Inman, Bascue, & Skoloda, 1985; Nace, Saxon, & Shore, 1983). Millon (1985) suggests that this overlap occurs because BPD increases vulnerability to Axis I conditions. Co-occurrence with other personality disorders is also significant (Pfohl, Coryell, Zimmerman, & Stangl, 1986; J. H. Skodol, Rosnick, Kellman, Oldham, & Hyler, 1988). Considerable overlap has been found with Avoidant, Histrionic, Dependent, and Paranoid Personality Disorders.

Self-Report Methods

Several self-report inventories, personality scales, and structured interviews show good potential as clinical screening measures, but most require further development and validation prior to meeting standards for research use. Among self-report instruments for assessing personality disorder, the Personality Diagnostic Questionnaire-Revised (PDQ-R; Hyler et al., 1989) is a brief, true-false questionnaire based on *DSM-III-R* criteria for personality disorders, including BPD. The PDQ-R format is such that all questions for any single disorder appear on one page. The Millon Clinical Multiaxial Inventory III (Millon, Davis, & Millon, 1997) is another brief, true-false instrument that takes about 25 minutes to complete and generates three scales: Personality, Severe Personality Patterns, and Clinical Syndromes. Although there are a number of other self-report inventories available, many are not appropriate for use in smaller clinical settings; unfortunately, those strongest psychometrically tend to be infeasible outside settings with large data collection capacity.

Specific to BPD, the McLean Screening Instrument for BPD (Zanarini et al., 2003a) is a 10-item yes-no measure. Initial data suggest it has both adequate sensitivity and specificity.

Interview instruments, some of which are available in computer-assisted interview format, include the Diagnostic Interview for Borderline Personality Disorders-Revised (DIB-R; Zanarini, Gunderson, Frankenburg, & Chauncey, 1989), a semi-structured interview using both psychodynamic and *DSM-IV* criteria; the Personality Disorders Examination (Loranger, 1996), a general personality disorder interview; and the Structured Clinical Interview for *DSM-IV* criteria (First et al., 1995).

Among clinician-administered scales, the Structured Interview for *DSM* Personality Disorders (SIDP-IVP; Pfohl, Polum, & Zimmerman, 1995) addresses personality traits from the perspective of the affected individual. A range of behaviors are included rather than relying on a single symptom endorsement, and the SIDP-IVP allows for more natural conversational flow. The use of a collateral informant is also possible (Pfohl et al., 1995). The semistructured nature of some of these interviews may require probing to clarify client responses; most require some knowledge of *DSM* Axis I and II criteria and administration training prior to use. The Zanarini Rating Scale for Borderline Personality Disorder (ZAN-BPD; Zanarini et al., 2003b) is the first clinician-administered scale for the assessment of change in *DSM-IV* BPD. Each of the nine criteria for BPD were adapted to reflect a 1-week time frame and are rated on a 5-point scale from 0 to 4, yielding a total score of 0 to 36. Good convergent validity was found between the ZAN-BPD and the DIB-R and relevant scales of the SCL-90, and preliminary study suggests that the ZAN-BPD measures change in a clinically meaningful way (Zanarini et al., 2003b).

Behavioral Assessment

Both initial and ongoing assessments serve multiple functions. When entering treatment, individuals are distressed and want their lives to change (whether due to internal or external impetus) and are also generally aware that they are entrenched in their current patterns and view change as difficult and even frightening. The conduct of assessment strongly affects whether an individual returns to treatment. Considering how to engage and motivate clients to participate in treatment is important beginning with initial contact, and even more so with involuntary clients (Schmidt & Ivanoff, in press). The validation, understanding, and level of clinician involvement demonstrated contribute to a client's early commitment. Clinicians should regard themselves as clinical scientists and ward off the impulse to assume; each clinical hypothesis should be tested and the results used to derive subsequent or alternative hypotheses for further testing.

Given the rates of self-injurious and suicidal behaviors among clients who suffer from BPD, assessing the immediate risk of these behaviors is critical. Although long-term and statistical risk factors are important background information, they do not inform *current* risk assessment. During initial assessment, a thorough history of all prior self-injurious and suicidal behaviors is obtained, including details about the environment and social contingencies. An understanding of the specific variables precipitating and following such events is critical in treatment planning and crisis management.

The chain analysis (e.g., Linehan, 1993a) is a step-by-step primary assessment tool used both initially and throughout treat-

Table 22.2 Instructions for Conducting the Chain Analysis

1. Describe the specific problem behavior targeted in the treatment plan. Detail exactly what the client did, said, thought, and felt, including the intensity of the feelings.

2. Identify the specific precipitating event that began the chain. Start with environmental events; for example, "Why did *the problem* occur yesterday rather than the day before?"

3. Identify factors such as physical illness, poor sleeping, drug or alcohol abuse, or intense emotions that heightened the client's vulnerability to the problem chain at this time.

4. Describe the moment-by-moment chain of events. Examine thoughts, feelings, and actions, and determine whether there were any possible alternatives to these.

5. Identify the consequences of the problem behavior.

6. Generate alternative solutions; for example, what skills might the client have used to avoid the problem behavior as a solution?

7. Identify a prevention strategy to reduce future vulnerability to this problem chain.

8. Repair the significant consequences of the problem behavior.

Figure 22.1

**Condensed
Chain
Analysis**

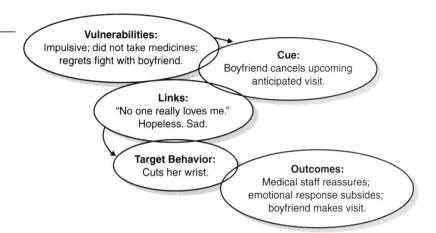

Vulnerabilities:
Impulsive; did not take medicines; regrets fight with boyfriend.

Cue:
Boyfriend cancels upcoming anticipated visit.

Links:
"No one really loves me."
Hopeless. Sad.

Target Behavior:
Cuts her wrist.

Outcomes:
Medical staff reassures; emotional response subsides; boyfriend makes visit.

ment to examine incidents of target behavior. The analysis answers the questions "Why did this behavior occur at this time, in this context, and what problem did it solve for the client?" The analysis includes a blow-by-blow narrative explanation of the events leading up to and following a target behavior. Table 22.2 lists the steps in a chain analysis. Figure 22.1 illustrates the components of the chain analysis.

Another assessment function is monitoring the client's progress in treatment. It is the clinician's responsibility to remain mindful of treatment goals and to ensure that treatment activities attend to identified specific targets. We recommend the use of daily diary cards, which include general and individually tailored targets such as self-harm, suicidal urges, and illicit drug use. These cards are reviewed at the beginning of each individual session and help determine session priorities.

Evidence-Based Approaches to Intervention

Psychopharmacological Treatments

In his 2005 review of BPD treatments, Paris notes that the evidence for the effectiveness of pharmacotherapy to treat BPD is far less than the evidence for psychotherapy effectiveness. No drug produces clinical remission; reduced impulsivity is the most significant effect (Paris, 2005). There have been eight randomized controlled trials using medications to treat symptoms of BPD. These trials investigate treatment of one of three BPD symptom clusters: impulsivity, including self-injurious and suicidal behaviors; psychotic-schizotypal symptoms; or affective instability.

Low-dose neuroleptics such as haloperidol, olanzapine, and risperadol are often used to reduce impulsivity associated with BPD; data from three trials support this use (Bogenschutz

& Nurnberg, 2004; Zanarini & Frankenburg, 2001; Zanarini, Frankenburg, & Parachini, 2004). However, the side effects of neuroleptics argue against their long-term effective use (Paris, 2005). Zanarini (2004) suggests that they provoke obesity, a major quality-of-life issue in this population.

Mood stabilizers, such as toprimate, valporate, and lamotrigine, have also been subjected to clinical trials, with equivocal results. Interestingly, their effect on symptoms of BPD appears to have more to do with reducing aggression, anger, and impulsivity than with mood stabilization itself (Frankenburg & Zanarini, 2002; Kavoussi & Coccaro, 1998; Tritt et al., 2005). Paris (2005) suggests that the affect dysregulation present in BPD may be different than that in Bipolar Disorders, where these drugs are regarded as effective mood stabilizers. Drugs such as lithium, with no data supporting efficacy, and carbamazepine, which may reduce impulsivity, are not recommended due to their dangerous overdose potential (Paris, 2005). Selective serotonin reuptake inhibitors (SSRIs), such as fluoxetine, are widely used to treat depressive symptoms associated with BPD, although they do not appear effective to the extent they are in Axis I depression. SSRIs may also reduce anger and impulsive symptoms (Coccaro & Kavoussi, 1997; Markowitz, 1995) and in high, difficult-to-tolerate doses, reduce self-mutilation (Markowitz, 1995).

Prescribing practitioners treating individuals suffering from BPD may engage in polypharmacy, prescribing more than one drug, even if the added drug is likely to have the same effect (and possibly, the same side effects) as the first. This practice is not evidence-based and increases the likelihood of side effects. Unfortunately, current American Psychiatric Association guidelines for treating BPD encourage this practice (Paris, 2005). The nonspecific effects of psychopharmacology with this population suggest that more research is needed prior to recommending such strategies.

Individual Therapies

For the purpose of this chapter, an independent review of all psychosocial treatment studies for BPD was conducted by the second author. To our delight, a review conducted under the Corcoran Collaboration was completed shortly thereafter (Binks et al., 2006) and corroborates our findings. Only seven randomized controlled trials were found, described as of "moderate" quality with lost data due to "unclear reporting" (Binks et al., 2006). One additional controlled trial was found since Binks et al. completed their review (Davidson et al., in press). Whereas we have included quasi-experimental and evaluation designs in our review (see Table 22.3), Binks et al. did not, further excluding 51 uncontrolled studies.

Table 22.3 Evidence-Based Treatments for BPD: Controlled and Uncontrolled Studies

Treatments	Study Design	Sample	Main Outcomes	Reference
DBT Treatments				
DBT (*n* = 24) versus mental health TAU (*n* = 22)	RCT 1-year follow-up	BPD diagnosis Female	Fewer incidences of parasuicide, less medically severe parasuicides, more likely to stay in individual treatment, fewer inpatient hospitalization days.	Linehan et al. (1991) Linehan, Heard, et al. (1993) Linehan et al. (1994)
DBT (*n* = 12) versus TAU (*n* = 16)	RCT 1-year follow-up	BPD diagnosis and drug dependence Female	Greater reductions in illicit drug use, improvements in social and global adjustment, and increased treatment retention.	Linehan et al. (1999)
DBT (*n* = 52) versus community treatment by suicide and BPD experts (*n* = 51)	RCT 1-year follow-up	BPD diagnosis Female	Reductions in suicide attempts, suicidality, medical risk, emergency and inpatient treatment, and expressive anger.	Linehan, Comtois, et al. (2002)
DBT (*n* = 31) compared to mental health TAU (*n* = 33)	RCT 1-year follow-up	BPD and drug dependence Female	Reductions in frequency of suicide attempts, self mutilation, and self-damaging impulsivity, and increased treatment retention.	Verheul et al. (2003) van den Bosch et al. (2002)
DBT (*n* = 40) versus wait list control plus outpatient usual care (*n* = 20)	RCT 1-month follow-up	BPD Female	Significant changes in DBT group on 10 psychopathological variables and reductions in self-injurious behavior.	Bohus et al. (2004)
DBT (*n* = 12) versus client-centered therapy (*n* = 12)	RCT 1-year follow-up	BPD diagnosis	Reductions in parasuicide (suicide attempts and self injury), impulsiveness, anger, depression, and use of inpatient treatment, and greater global adjustment.	Turner (2000)
DBT (*n* = 10) versus VA mental health TAU (*n* = 10)	RCT 6-month follow-up	BPD diagnosis Female	Reductions in suicide attempts, self injury, suicide ideation, hopelessness, depression, anger expression.	Koons et al. (1998, 2001)

(continued)

511

Table 22.3 continued

Treatments	Study Design	Sample	Main Outcomes	Reference
DBT inpatient (*n* = 8) versus TAU (*n* = 9)	Quasi-experimental design 6-month follow-up	BPD forensic patients Male	Reductions in violence-related incidents, self report measures of hostility, cognitive anger, disposition to anger, outward expression of anger, anger experience.	Evershed et al. (2003)
DBT in inpatient setting (*n* = 10) No comparison group	Uncontrolled 6-month follow-up	Female patients with BPD	Reductions in deliberate self-harm and dissociative experiences; improvements in survival and coping beliefs, depression, suicidal ideation, and impulsiveness.	Low et al. (2001)
DBT evaluation (*n* = 24) No comparison group	Uncontrolled 1-month follow-up	BPD female subjects in an inpatient setting	Decrease in number of parasuicidal acts; improvements in depression, dissociation, anxiety, global stress.	Bohus et al. (2000)
Adapted DBT Treatments				
DBT + LAAM (*n* = 11) for substance abusers (specifically for opiate use) versus comprehensive validation therapy with 12-Step + LAAM (*n* = 12)	RCT 1-year follow-up	Females with BPD diagnosis and comorbid opiate use	Both treatments reduced opiate use and maintained reduction at 4 months. DBT showed greater reduction in opiate use at 12 months. Combined CVT and 12-Step was effective treatment retention. Both groups reduced overall psychopathology.	Linehan, Dimeff, et al. (2002)
Manual assisted cognitive therapy, a brief form of cognitive therapy combined with DBT techniques (*n* = 18) versus TAU (*n* = 16)	RCT 6-month follow-up	Females with episode of self harm, personality disturbance, past parasuicide	Reductions in suicide attempts, depressive symptoms, and costs of care.	Evans et al. (1999)
Adapted DBT (*n* = 29) for adolescents, which included a shortened time frame for treatment, focused on core issues of adolescent development, and implemented multifamily skills training groups core versus TAU (*n* = 82)	Quasi-experimental design Pre-post	Suicidal adolescents with borderline features	Fewer psychiatric hospitalizations and suicide attempts during treatment, higher treatment completion rate.	Rathus & Miller (2002)

Table 22.3 **continued**

Treatments	Study Design	Sample	Main Outcomes	Reference
Adapted DBT for inpatient setting and incorporated limited DBT skills training No comparison group	Uncontrolled Pre-post	General inpatient unit; patients with diagnosis of personality disorder	More likely to believe that skills training would help them manage their lives post hospitalization; engaged in more parasuicidal behaviors.	Springer et al. (1996)
Shortened (6 months) DBT ($n = 15$) versus TAU ($n = 15$)	Uncontrolled 6-month follow-up	Female patients with BPD diagnosis and enrolled in DBT and matched with patients receiving TAU in community	Baseline mean number of suicide attempts did not differ between groups. Assessments of Beck Hopelessness Scale, Hamilton Depression, Beck Depression, and GAS did not decline. However, self-rated suicide ideation reduced significantly in DBT as did suicidal urges and urges to self mutilate. Actual self-mutilation decreased.	Stanley et al. (1998)
Adapted DBT for substance users, addressing relapse, i.e., "dialectical abstinence;" teaching new and modified skills relevant to substance abusers; and emphasizing maintenance of abstinence ($N = 3$) No comparison group	Uncontrolled 12-month follow-up	Women who met criteria for methamphetamine dependence and BPD	Drug use decreased over time; neither subject attempted suicide at 12-month follow-up; one participant continued to engage in self-mutilation until week 40; increase in global adjustment evident in both subjects, but no changes in global social adjustment; state anger decreased in both subjects and depression decreased considerably in one subject at 12 months. One patient dropped out of treatment.	Dimeff et al. (2000)
Adapted DBT (evaluation only) for inpatient setting; incorporated psychodynamic focus ($N = 130$) No comparison group	Uncontrolled Pre-post	Mostly female on inpatient personality disorders unit	Mean monthly parasuicide rate decreased.	Barley et al. (1993)

(continued)

513

Table 22.3 continued

Treatments	Study Design	Sample	Main Outcomes	Reference
Family Connections (evaluation only): mix of psychoeducational materials, family functioning, and some skills adapted from individual DBT (*n* = 44) No comparison group	Uncontrolled 6-month follow-up	BPD family members: 39 parents (27 mothers, 12 fathers), 4 spouses/partners, 1 sibling	From pre to posttreatment, levels of burden and grief decreased and mastery increased. At 6 months, levels of burden continued to decrease by average 5.78 points. Changes in mastery and grief stayed the same. No changes in depression or perceived burden at posttreatment or 6 months.	Hoffman (2005)

Other Cognitive/Psychodynamic Treatments

Treatments	Study Design	Sample	Main Outcomes	Reference
Cognitive behavior therapy plus treatment as usual (*n* = 52) versus treatment as usual (*n* = 54)	RCT 2-year follow-up	BPD diagnosis	For both treatment groups, there was sustained improvement in suicidal and self-harm behaviors, affective distress, and dysfunctional thoughts, with evidence of improvement with the addition of CBT in areas of symptom distress, anxiety, and number of suicidal acts at the 2-year follow-up. Significant reduction in suicidal acts over 2 years in favor of CBT plus TAU, compared to TAU only.	Davidson et al. (in press)
Psychoanalytic partial hospitalization (*n* = 19) versus TAU (*n* = 19)	RCT 18-month follow-up	BPD diagnosis	Reductions in self-mutilation, suicide attempts, use of inpatient services, anxiety, and depression, and improvements in social and global adjustment.	Bateman & Fonagy (1999, 2001)
Psychotherapy based on conversational model (*n* = 30) versus treatment as usual (*n* = 30)	Uncontrolled 5-year follow-up [Original TAU group unavailable, thus tx sample compared to 150 consecutive BPD patients upon admission at clinic]	Patients with BPD received treatment; subsequently compared to patients on waiting list who received TAU	40% no longer met *DSM-III* criteria; reduction in hospitalizations; results indicate that if untreated borderline patient were followed up after 5 years, there is a 79% likelihood of self-harming behaviors; whereas 5 years after having received psychotherapeutic therapy results in a 6% likelihood of self-harming behaviors.	Stevenson et al. (2004)

Table 22.3   continued

Treatments	Study Design	Sample	Main Outcomes	Reference
Schema therapy (evaluation only), which is based on a cognitive-integrative model targeting the therapeutic relationship through patient's emotions and bonding issues ($N = 6$) No comparison group	A-B single case design 12-month follow-up	Patients with BPD diagnosis	Five of the six patients improved in general symptomatic and interpersonal distress 12–16 months posttreatment. Three of the six patients did not meet diagnostic criteria for BPD post treatment. No one attempted suicide or engaged in self-harm behaviors. GAF score increased from 58 to 62, a relatively large improvement.	Nordahl & Nysaeter (2005)
Cognitive analytic therapy ($N = 5$) No comparison group	Single subject design 9-month follow-up	Patients with BPD diagnosis	Positive reductions in BPD severity; Clinically significant changes across measures of dissociation, symptomatic distress, interpersonal adjustment, personality fragmentation.	Wildgoose et al. (2001)
Cognitive therapy ($N = 12$) No comparison group	Single subject design Pre-post	Patients with BPD diagnosis	Improvement in target problems, including self-harming behaviors and symptom distress.	Davidson & Tyrer (1996)

Psychodynamic and Psychoanalytic Therapies

Although psychodynamic and psychoanalytic therapists have long been interested in treating BPD and include many prolific authors on the subject, studies of psychodynamic psychotherapy with BPD clients suggest most drop out within a few months, making it impossible to accurately measure outcomes (Gunderson et al., 1989; A. E. Skodol, Buckley, & Charles, 1983). Bateman and Fonagy (1999, 2001) conducted a controlled trial of "psychoanalytically oriented partial hospitalization"; treatment included a weekly individual psychoanalytic session and three weekly psychoanalytically oriented group sessions. Weekly community meetings and expressive groups, that is, psychodrama, and a monthly medication group, were also included. Results included reductions in self-mutilation, suicide attempts, inpatient hospitalization, anxiety, and depression. Social and global adjustment also improved.

A randomized controlled trial of transference-focused psychotherapy, an adaptation of psychoanalysis focused on correcting patient distortions of the therapist and significant others, is also currently under way (Clarkin, Levy, Lenzenweger, & Kernberg, 2004), although there are no results at present.

Cognitive Therapy

The borderline study of cognitive therapy (BOSCOT) trial compared cognitive-behavioral therapy (CBT; Davidson, 2000) plus National Health Service treatment as usual (TAU) to TAU only in Glasgow, Scotland. The 1-year treatment offered approximately 27 tightly conducted CBT sessions (participants attended 16 on average). Significant differences were found in favor of CBT plus TAU on suicidal acts, inpatient hospitalization, and emergency contacts. At 2-year follow-up there was still a significant difference in the number of suicidal acts between treatment conditions.

Dialectical Behavior Therapy

Seven controlled trials measured the application of dialectical behavior therapy (DBT), a cognitive-behavioral treatment originally designed to treat chronically suicidal women (Linehan, 1993a, 1993b). To date, DBT has the largest body of evidence supporting its use treating BPD and is the only treatment to have its effects replicated. Dialectical behavior therapy is effective at reducing self-harm and suicidal behaviors, the frequency and number of days of inpatient hospitalization, anger, and hopelessness. Dialectical behavior therapy improves treatment retention and global and social adjustment (Koons et al., 1998, 2001; Linehan, Armstrong, Suarez, Allmon, & Heard, 1991; Linehan, Dimeff, et al., 2002; Verheul et al., 2003). These results were also true in DBT adapted for use (Linehan & Dimeff, 1995) with drug-using clients with BPD (Linehan et al., 1999).

Core elements of DBT (Linehan, 1989) include (a) a biosocial framework used to explain the development of BPD as a transaction between individual biologic vulnerabilities and environmental invalidation; (b) a developmental framework of stages of treatment; (c) a target hierarchy, prioritized within each stage; (d) a set of comprehensive functions that must be addressed in treatment and the treatment modes used to accomplish this (see Table 22.4); and (d) delineated sets of dialectical, acceptance, and change strategies (Robins, Schmidt, & Linehan, 2004). Based in behavioral and cognitive-behavioral principles of treatment, DBT differs from standard cognitive-behavioral treatments in three significant ways: (1) the use of a dialectical philosophical framework; (2) the use of Zen principles in a treatment based on Western behavioral change principles (Heard & Linehan, 2005); and (3) therapist acceptance strategies of validation, reciprocal

Table 22.4　**Summary of DBT Treatment Modes and Functions**

Mode of Treatment	Function of this Mode	Frequency	Duration of Each Content
Pretreatment/commit-ment sessions	Orient clients to DBT and establish commitment to DBT agreements	Annual (2–3 meetings)	30–60 minutes
Individual therapy	Enhance clients' motivation for treatment and treatment goals and strengthen skills	Weekly	60 minutes
Group skills training	Enhance clients' capabilities via skills acquisition and strengthening	Twice weekly	90 minutes
Phone consultation	Assist clients' to generalize skills to daily life and in crises	As needed	10–20 minutes
Case management	Assist clients to acquire, strengthen, and generalize life skills such as managing money, finding housing, or applying for jobs	As needed	30 minutes (unless longer in vivo practice)
Medication management*	Enhance clients' capabilities and motivation by reducing psychiatric symptoms; also provide assistance with medical and health issues	1–3 months (as needed)	30 minutes
Consultation team meeting	Enhance therapists' capabilities and motivation to adhere to DBT and to prevent burnout	Weekly	75 minutes consultation 45 minutes didactic training

*In DBT-S and Community Mental Health Settings.

communication, and direct environmental intervention, balanced with the change strategies of problem solving, irreverent communication style, and coaching clients in how to deal with their environments (Robins et al., 2004).

Dialectical behavior therapy was developed as an outpatient model consisting of several simultaneous treatment modes: individual treatment, group skills training, telephone consultation, case management, and consultation team meetings. These modes carry out the functions listed in Table 22.4. Dialectical behavior therapy has been successfully extended to both inpatient and residential programs.

Marital/Couple/Family Therapies

There are currently no evidence-based treatments for BPD that are marital- or family-based, although investigators such as Fruzzetti and Levensky (2000) have examined the use of DBT for interpersonal violence in couples. Hoffman and colleagues (Hoffman, 2005; Hoffman, Fruzzetti, & Swenson, 1999) have extended DBT skills groups to family members of BPD clients, who attend separate groups addressing family functioning and psychoeducation about BPD and the associated grief and burden it places on families. These groups also teach DBT skills so that significant others can assist in skills coaching.

Summary

Borderline Personality Disorder is a debilitating set of pervasive dysregulations, affecting individuals, their families and loved ones, the mental health practitioners charged with providing care, and the emergency health care delivery system. The suffering associated with this disorder is enormous, as are the costs. Unlike other personality disorders, however, primary BPD symptoms, notably self-injury and suicidal behaviors, can be effectively treated with psychosocial interventions. Although more than one treatment shows promise, DBT currently has the most supporting data and is the only treatment that has been successfully replicated. Compassionate, based on the person-in-situation perspective, and highly consistent with the principles of evidence-based assessment and treatment, it is currently our best choice for treating individuals afflicted with BPD.

Study Questions

1. What are the primary dysfunctions associated with Borderline Personality Disorder, and how do these present themselves in client behavior?

2. Why is Borderline Personality Disorder considered a public health problem?

3. When we talk about effective treatment of Borderline Personality Disorder, what exactly are we changing?

4. How is a behavioral chain analysis used in assessment?

5. What is the purpose of a diary card, and how does this contribute to evidence-based assessment?

6. Why is it important for nonprescribing practitioners to understand issues surrounding the psychopharmacology of Borderline Personality Disorder?

7. Looking across all the studies reviewed, what types of outcomes (positive changes) occur most often?

References

American Psychiatric Association. (2000). *Diagnostic and statistical manual of mental disorders* (4th ed., text rev.). Washington, DC: Author.

Barley, W. D., Buie, S. E., & Peterson, E. W. (1993). Development of an in-patient cognitive-behavioral treatment program for borderline personality disorder. *Journal of Personality Disorders, 7,* 232–240.

Bateman, A., & Fonagy, P. (1999). Effectiveness of partial hospitalization in the treatment of borderline personality disorder: A randomized controlled trial. *American Journal of Psychiatry, 156,* 1563–1569.

Bateman, A., & Fonagy, P. (2001). Treatment of borderline personality disorder with psychoanalytically oriented partial hospitalization: An 18-month follow-up. *American Journal of Psychiatry, 158,* 36–42.

Beck, A. T., & Beck, J. S. (1991). *Personality Belief Questionnaire.* Unpublished assessment instrument. Bala Cynwyd, PA: Beck Institute for Cognitive Therapy and Research.

Beck, J. S. (1996). Cognitive therapy of personality disorders. In P. A. Salkovskis (Ed.), *Frontiers of cognitive therapy* (pp. 165–181). New York: Guilford Press.

Binks, C. A., Fenton, M., McCarthy, L., Lee, T., Adams, C. E., & Duggan, C. (2006). Psychological therapies for people with borderline personality disorder. *Cochrane Database of Systematic Reviews* (Issue 1, Art. No. CD005652, DOI: 10.1002/14651858.CD005652).

Bogenschutz, M. P., & Nurnberg, H. G. (2004). Olanzapine versus placebo in the treatment of borderline personality disorder. *Journal of Clinical Psychiatry, 65,* 104–109.

Bohus, M., Haaf, B., Simms, T., Limberger, M. F., Schmal, C., Unckel, C., et al. (2004). Effectiveness of inpatient dialectical behavior therapy for borderline personality disorder: A controlled trial. *Behavior Research and Therapy, 42,* 487–499.

Bohus, M., Haaf, B., Stiglmayr, C., Pohl, U., Boehme, R., & Linehan, M. (2000). Evaluation of inpatient dialectical behavior therapy for borderline personality disorder: A prospective study. *Behavior Research and Therapy, 38,* 875–887.

Butler, A. C., Brown, G. K., Beck, A. T., & Grisham, J. R. (2002). Dysfunctional beliefs in borderline personality disorder. *Behavior Research and Therapy, 40,* 1231–1240.

Clarkin, J. F., Levy, K. N., Lenzenweger, M. F., & Kernberg, O. F. (2004). The Personality Disorders Institute/Borderline Personality Disorder Research Foundation randomized control trial for borderline personality disorder: Rationale, methods, and patient characteristics. *Journal of Personality Disorders, 18,* 52–72.

Coccaro, E. F., & Kavoussi, R. J. (1997). Fluoxetine and impulsive aggressive behavior in personality-disordered subjects. *Archives of General Psychiatry, 54,* 1081–1088.

Craig, R. J. (1988). A psychometric study of the prevalence of *DSM-III* personality disorders among treated opiate addicts. *International Journal of the Addictions, 23,* 115–124.

Davidson, K., Norrie, J., Tyrer, P., Gumley, A., Tata, P., Murray, H., et al. (in press). The effectiveness of cognitive behavior therapy for borderline personality disorder: Results from the BOSCOT trial. *Journal of Personality Disorders.*

Davidson, K., & Tyrer, P. (1996). Cognitive therapy for antisocial and borderline personality disorders: Single case study series. *British Journal of Clinical Psychology, 35,* 413–429.

Davidson, K. M. (2000). *Cognitive therapy for personality disorders: A guide for clinicians.* London: Arnold Hodder.

Dimeff, L., Rizvi, S. L., Brown, M., & Linehan, M. M. (2000). Dialectical behavior therapy for substance abuse: A pilot application to methamphetamine-dependent wome with borderline personality disorder. *Cognitive and Behavioral Practice, 7,* 457–468.

Evans, K., Tyrer, P., Catalan, J., Schmidt, U., Davidson, K., Dent, J., et al. (1999). Manual-assisted cognitive-behavior therapy (MACT): A randomized controlled trial of a brief intervention with bibliotherapy in the treatment of recurrent deliberate self-harm. *Psychological Medicine, 29,* 19–25.

Evershed, S., Tennant, A., Boomer, D., Rees, A., Barkham, M., & Watson, A. (2003).

Practice-based outcomes of dialectical behavior therapy (DBT) targeting anger and violence, with male forensic patients: A pragmatic and non-contemporaneous comparison. *Criminal Behavior and Mental Health, 13,* 198–213.

First, M. B., Spitzer, R. L., Gibbon, M., Williams, J. B. W., Davies, M., Borus, J., et al. (1995). The Structured Clinical Interview for *DSM-III-R* Personality Disorders (SCID-II): Pt. II. Multi-site test-retest reliability study. *Journal of Personality Disorders, 9,* 92–104.

Frances, A. J., Fyer, M. R., & Clarkin, J. F. (1986). Personality and suicide. *Annals of the New York Academy of Sciences, 487,* 281A.

Frankenburg, F. R., & Zanarini, M. C. (2002). Divalproex sodium treatment of women with borderline personality disorder and bipolar II disorder: A double-blind, placebo controlled pilot study. *Journal of Clinical Psychiatry, 63,* 442–446.

Friedman, C. J., Shear, M. C., & Frances, A. J. (1987). *DSM-III* personality disorders in panic patients. *Journal of Personality Disorders, 1,* 132–135.

Fruzzetti, A. E., & Levensky, E. R. (2000). Dialectical behavior therapy for domestic violence: Rationale and procedures. *Cognitive and Behavioral Practice, 7,* 435–447.

Fyer, M. R., Frances, A. J., Sullivan, T., Hurt, S. W., & Clarkin, J. (1988). Comorbidity of borderline personality disorder. *Archives of General Psychiatry, 45,* 348–352.

Gunderson, J. G. (1984). *Borderline personality disorder.* Washington, DC: American Psychiatric Press.

Gunderson, J. G., Frank, A. F., Ronningstam, E. F., Wahter, S., Lynch, V. J., & Wolf, P. J. (1989). Early discontinuance of borderline patients from psychotherapy. *Journal of Nervous and Mental Diseases, 177,* 38–42.

Heard, H. L., & Linehan, M. M. (2005). Integrative therapy for borderline personality disorder. In J. C. Norcross & M. R. Goldfried (Eds.), *Handbook of psychotherapy integration* (pp. 299–320). New York: Oxford University Press.

Hellman, I. D., Morrison, T. L., & Abramowitz, S. I. (1986). The stresses of psychotherapeutic work: A replication and extension. *Psychological Medicine, 42,* 197–205.

Hoffman, P. D. (2005). Family connections: A program for relatives of persons with borderline personality disorder. *Family Process, 44,* 217–225.

Hoffman, P. D., Fruzzetti, A., & Swenson, C. (1999). Dialectical behavior therapy: Family skills training. *Family Process, 38,* 399–414.

Hyler, S., Reider, R., Williams, J., Spitzer, R. L., Lyons, M., & Hendler, J. (1989). A comparison of clinical and self-report diagnoses of *DSM-III* personality disorders in 552 patients. *Comprehensive Psychiatry, 30,* 170–178.

Inman, D. J., Bascue, L. O., & Skoloda, T. (1985). Identification of borderline personality disorders among substance abuse inpatients. *Journal of Substance Abuse Treatment, 2,* 229–232.

Kavoussi, R. J., & Coccaro, E. F. (1998). Divalproex sodium for impulsive aggressive behavior in patients with personality disorder. *Journal of Clinical Psychiatry, 59,* 676–680.

Koons, C. R., Robins, C. J., Bishop, G. K., Morse, J. Q., Tweed, J. L., Lynch, T. R., et al. (1998, November). *Efficacy of dialectical behavior therapy with borderline women veterans: A randomized controlled trial.* Paper presented at the meeting of the Association for the Advancement of Behavior Therapy, Washington, DC.

Koons, C. R., Robins, C. J., Tweed, J. L., Lynch, T. R., Gonzalez, A. M., Morse, J. Q., et al. (2001). Efficacy of dialectical behavior therapy in women veterans with borderline personality disorder. *Behavior Therapy, 32,* 371–390.

Linehan, M. M. (1989). Cognitive and behavior therapy for borderline personality disorder. In A. Tasman, R. E. Hales, & A. J. Frances (Eds.), *Review of psychiatry* (Vol. 8, pp. 84–102). Washington, DC: American Psychiatric Press.

Linehan, M. M. (1993a). *Cognitive behavioral therapy of borderline personality disorder.* New York: Guilford Press.

Linehan, M. M. (1993b). *Skills training manual for treating borderline personality disorder.* New York: Guilford Press.

Linehan, M. M., Armstrong, H. E., Suarez, A., Allmon, D., & Heard, H. L. (1991). Cognitive-behavioral treatment of chronically parasuicidal borderline patients. *Archives of General Psychiatry, 48,* 1060–1064.

Linehan, M. M., Comtois, K., Brown, M., Reynolds, S., Welch, S., Sayrs, J. H. R., et al. (2002, November). *Dialectical behavior therapy versus nonbehavioral treatment-by-experts in the community.* Symposium conducted at the 36th annual Association for Advancement of Behavior Therapy Convention, Reno, NV.

Linehan, M. M., & Dimeff, L. A. (1995). *Extension of standard dialectical behavior therapy to treatment of substance abusers with borderline personality disorder.* Unpublished manual, University of Washington, Seattle.

Linehan, M. M., Dimeff, L. A., Reynolds, S. K., Comtois, K. A., Welch, S., Heagerty, P., et al. (2002). Dialectical behavior therapy versus comprehensive validation plus 12-step for the treatment of opioid dependent women meeting criteria for borderline personality disorder. *Drug and Alcohol Dependence, 67,* 13–26.

Linehan, M. M., Heard, H. L., & Armstrong, H. E. (1993). Naturalistic follow-up of a behavioral treatment for chronically parasuicidal borderline patients. *Archives of General Psychiatry, 50,* 971–974.

Linehan, M. M., Schmidt, H., Dimeff, L. A., Craft, J. C., Kanter, J., & Comtois, K. A. (1999). Dialectical behavior therapy for patients with borderline personality disorder and drug-dependence. *American Journal on Addictions, 8,* 279–292.

Linehan, M. M., Tutek, D. A., Heard, H. L., & Armstrong, H. E. (1994). Interpersonal outcome of cognitive behavioral treatment for chronically suicidal borderline patients. *American Journal of Psychiatry, 151,* 1771–1776.

Loranger, A. (1996). *Manual for the International Personality Disorder Examination.* White Plains, NY: New York Hospital, Cornell Medical Center.

Low, G., Jones, D., Duggan, C., Power, M., & MacLeod, A. (2001). The treatment of deliberate self-harm in borderline personality disorder using dialectical behavior therapy: A pilot study in a high security hospital. *Behavioral and Cognitive Psychotherapy, 29,* 85–92.

Markowitz, P. (1995). Pharmacotherapy of impulsivity, aggression and related disorders. In D. Stein & E. Hollander (Eds.), *Impulsive aggression and disorders of impulse control* (pp. 263–287). Sussex, England: Wiley.

Millon, T. (1985). Depression and personality. In E. Beckman & W. Leber (Eds.), *Depression, treatment, assessment, and research.* Homewood, IL: Dow Jones-Irwin.

Millon, T., Davis, R. D., & Millon, C. (1997). *Millon Clinical Multiaxial Inventory III (MCM-III) manual* (2nd ed.). Minneapolis, MN: National Computer Systems.

Nace, E. P., Saxon, J. J., & Shore, N. (1983). A comparison of borderline and non-borderline alcoholic patients. *Archives of General Psychiatry, 50,* 157–158.

National Institute for Mental Health in England. (2003). *Personality disorder: No longer a diagnosis of exclusion.* London: Author, HMSO.

Nordahl, H. M., & Nysaeter, T. E. (2005). Schema therapy for patients with borderline personality disorder: A single case series. *Journal of Behavior Therapy and Experimental Psychiatry, 36,* 254–264.

Paris, J. (2005). Recent advances in the treatment of borderline personality disorder. *Canadian Journal of Psychiatry, 50,* 435–441.

Perry, J. C. (1993). Longitudinal studies of personality disorders. *Journal of Personality Disorders, 7,* 63–85.

Pfohl, B., Coryell, W., Zimmerman, M., & Stangl, D. (1986). *DSM-III* personality disorders: Diagnostic overlap and internal consistency of individual *DSM-III* criteria. *Comprehensive Psychiatry, 27,* 21–34.

Pfohl, B., Polum, N., & Zimmerman, M. (1995). *The Structured Interview for* DSM-IV *Personality Disorders.* Iowa City: University of Iowa.

Rathus, J. H., & Miller, A. L. (2002). Dialectical behavior therapy adapted for suicidal adolescents. *Suicide and Life-Threatening Behavior, 32,* 146–157.

Robins, C., Schmidt, H., III, & Linehan, M. M. (2004). Dialectical behavior therapy: Synthesizing radical acceptance with skillful means. In S. C. Hayes, V. M. Follette, & M. M. Linehan (Eds.), *Mindfulness and acceptance: Expanding the cognitive-behavioral tradition* (pp. 30–44). New York: Guilford Press.

Schmidt, H., III, & Ivanoff, A. (in press). Behavioral prescriptions for treating self-injurious behavior in correctional settings. In M. Piasecki & O. Thienhaus (Eds.), *Handbook of forensic psychiatry.* Washington, DC: Civic Research Press.

Skodol, A. E., Buckley, P., & Charles, E. (1983). Is there a characteristic pattern to the treatment history of clinic outpatients with borderline personality? *Journal of Nervous and Mental Diseases, 171,* 405–410.

Skodol, J. H., Rosnick, L., Kellman, D., Oldham, J., & Hyler, S. (1988). Validating structure of *DSM-III-R* personality disorder assessments with longitudinal data. *American Journal of Psychiatry, 145,* 1297–1299.

Springer, T., Lohr, N. E., Buchtel, H. A., & Silk, K. R. (1996). A preliminary report of short-term cognitive-behavioral group therapy for in-patients with personality disorders. *Journal of Psychotherapy Practice and Research, 5,* 57–71.

Stanley, B., Ivanoff, A., Brodsky, B., & Oppenheim, S. (1998, November). *Comparison of DBT and "treatment as usual" in suicidal and self-mutilating behavior.* Paper presented at the meeting of the Association for the Advancement of Behavior Therapy Convention, Washington, DC.

Stevenson, J., Meares, R., & D'Angelo, R. (2004). Five-year outcome of outpatient psychotherapy with borderline patients. *Psychological Medicine, 35,* 79–87.

Stone, M. H. (1990). *The fate of borderline patients: Successful outcome and psychiatric practice.* New York: Guilford Press.

Tritt, K., Nickel, C., Lahmann, C., Leiberich, P. K., Rother, W. K., Lowe, T. H., et al. (2005). Lamotrigine treatment of aggression in female borderline patients: A randomized, double-blind, placebo-controlled study. *Journal of Psychopharmacology, 19,* 287–291.

Turner, R. M. (2000). Naturalistic evaluation of dialectical behavior therapy-oriented treatment for borderline personality disorder. *Cognitive Behavioral Practice, 7,* 413–419.

van den Bosch, L. M. C., Verheul, R., Schippers, G. M., & van den Brink, W. (2002). Dialectical behavior therapy of borderline patients with and without substance use problems: Implementation and long-term effects. *Addictive Behaviors, 27,* 911–923.

Verheul, R., van den Bosch, L. M. C., Koeter, M. W. J., De Ridder, M. A. J., Stijnen, T., & van den Brink, W. (2003). Dialectical behavior therapy for women with borderline personality disorder. *British Journal of Psychiatry, 182,* 135–140.

Widiger, T. A., & Frances, A. J. (1989). Epidemiology, diagnosis, and comorbidity of borderline personality disorder. In A. Tasman, R. E. Hales, & A. J. Frances (Eds.), *American Psychiatry Press review of psychiatry* (pp. 163–194). Washington, DC: American Psychiatric Press.

Wildgoose, A., Clarke, S., & Waller, G. (2001). Treating personality fragmentation and dissociation in borderline personality disorder: A pilot study of the impact of cognitive analytic therapy. *British Journal of Medical Psychology, 74,* 47–55.

World Health Organization. (1992). *International classification of diseases—10th revision* (ICD-10). Geneva, Switzerland: Author.

Zanarini, M. C. (2004, July). *Obesity and drug treatment of BPD.* Paper presented at the NIMH International Think Tank for the More Effective Treatment of Borderline Personality Disorder, Lincthinum, MD.

Zanarini, M. C., & Frankenburg, F. R. (2001). Olanzapine treatment of female borderline personality disorder patients: A double-blind, placebo-controlled pilot study. *Journal of Clinical Psychiatry, 62,* 849–854.

Zanarini, M. C., Frankenburg, F. R., & Parachini, E. A. (2004). A preliminary, randomized trial of fluoxetine, olanzapine, and the olanzapine-fluoxetine combination in women with borderline personality disorder. *Journal of Clinical Psychiatry, 65,* 903–907.

Zanarini, M. C., Gunderson, J. G., Frankenburg, F. R., & Chauncey, A. B. (1989). The revised Diagnostic Interview for Borderlines: Discriminating BPD from other Axis II disorders. *Journal of Personality Disorders, 3,* 10–18.

Zanarini, M. C., Vujanovic, A. B., Parachini, E. A., Boulanger, J. L., Frankenburg, F. R., & Hennen, J. (2003a). A screening measure for BPD: The McLean Screening Instrument for Borderline Personality Disorder (MSI-BPD). *Journal of Personality Disorders, 17*, 568–573.

Zanarini, M. C., Vujanovic, A. B., Parachini, E. A., Boulanger, J. L., Frankenburg, F. R., & Hennen, J. (2003b). Zanarini Rating Scale for Borderline Personality Disorder (ZAN-BPD): A continuous measure of *DSM-IV* borderline psychopathology. *Journal of Personality Disorders, 17*, 233–242.

CONCLUSIONS

The Role for Social Workers in the Managed Health Care System: A Model for Evidence-Based Practice

Kimberly J. Long, Lindsay Homesley,
and John S. Wodarski

Learning Objectives

After reading this chapter, the reader will be able to:

- Discuss the growing influence the managed health care industry is having on traditional models of social work practice.
- Discuss the congruence (and conflicts) existing between managed care and the evidence-based practice movement.
- Articulate the influence of social work-client characteristics on the outcomes of treatment.
- Identify the value of cost-benefit and cost-effectiveness studies to the practice of clinical social work.

Overview of the Problem

Much like other helping fields, the social work industry is rapidly changing from one of preferred helping strategies to that of evidence-based helping strategies based on the demands of managed health care companies, which for the past 15 to 25 years has insisted that health care providers use scientific models (evidence-based models) to provide the most effective, cost-efficient interventions possible. Or, according to McNeece and Thyer (2004, p. 8), the simplest definition is "treatment based on the best available science." Evidence-based practice has been

527

defined by the Institute of Medicine (2005, p. 1) as "the integra-tion of best research evidence with clinical expertise and client values." Because of the enormous power held by the managed health care system, the mental health care delivery system has undergone massive changes (Cohen, 2003) in how services are provided. According to the Institute of Medicine, the rules for health care are undergoing changes that support evidence-based practices. Some of the changes that affect mental health care providers as well as medical health care providers are reflected in the new rules about the decision-making process; other rules are reflected in quality of care and client autonomy levels. Although this is a clinically oriented definition, it is important to note that most of the elements of evidence-based practice can be modified to encompass many aspects of community, administrative, and so-cial policy practices (McNeece & Thyer, 2004).

Evidence-based social work practice is performed by utilizing the best available scientifically supported evidence as the basis for formulating interventions for individual clients, families, groups, and communities (DeAngelis, 2005; Gray & Gray, 2002). Because of power shifts, continuing budget cuts, and increased costs, de-livery systems are changing. Health care and mental health care are evolving into a more succinct delivery system, becoming more and more integrated (Wodarski, 2000).

This chapter identifies and discusses what evidence-based practice is and how social work is grappling with and helping to shape the concepts of evidence-based practice (DeAngelis, 2005) within the managed care community. The chapter also examines the variables affecting positive outcomes of psychosocial interven-tions, such as statistically supported evidence for best worker characteristics for affecting behavioral change (Wodarski, 2000). Among the characteristics explored are knowledge base, skills base, and the ability to utilize various techniques that will facili-tate behavioral change. Intervention components, such as length of treatment, worker characteristics, behavior acquisition proce-dures, technology used for treatment, levels of intervention and cost versus benefits, are also discussed.

Managed Health Care

Managed health care, according to Shapiro (1995, p. 441), is "any kind of health care services which are paid for, all or in one part, by a third party, including any government entity and for which the locus of any part of clinical decision-making is other than be-tween the practitioner and the client or patient." According to Davis (2005), managed health care has been a strong performer in the utilization of money-saving services for third-party pay sources, such as government health plans and private, individual insurance companies. Wodarski (2000) claims that it is largely political and economic forces that are instrumental in the changes that are reshaping the way health and mental health care are delivered. Managed health care is the delivery system that reflects the paradigm shift that involves the restructuring of health care in terms of effectiveness, cost, and integration (Cummings, 1995; Strosahl, 1994, 1995).

At its inception, managed health care attempted to regulate the escalating costs of care by insisting on tried and true treatments as opposed to those still in the experimental stages. This scientific methodology quickly began to include mental health care services as well. This forced compliance has benefited health, mental health, and educational fields, although there are possibilities of ethical drawbacks in evidence-based social work. According to Levant (2005), managed health care defined evidence-based practice for mental health practitioners for Medicare/Medicaid clients and patients by dictating what treatments are acceptable and what types of evidence are privileged. Therefore, social workers should define evidence-based practice in social work, or it will be defined by the managed health care system for us. It is important to consider how multiple designs should be integrated into a definition of evidence-based practice. Evidence-based practice should also explain the application and appropriate role of clinical expertise in all aspects of practice, including the consideration and investigation of various streams of information currently pouring into the field of mental health and the integration of this information into the pool of clinical expertise. Finally, Levant (2005) states that health care providers should articulate the role of patient values in making decisions about intervention and treatment; that is, our definition should include a consideration of the role of client diversity and situational diversity in clinical practice.

Because evidence-based treatment is supported by statistical empirical research, they will, in general, be the most effective treatments available. Managed health care dictates that formal mental health diagnoses be provided and then grants the (mental) health care worker an allotted amount of time to deliver treatment. Treatment options are based on current evidence-based treatment plans for current mental health. Therefore, social work is changing from a subjective care delivery system to that of an objective delivery system that uses evidence-based practice models from which to deliver services.

Psychosocial Treatment Configuration

According to Wodarski (2000), the role of the evidence-based social worker is to determine the center from which to devise evidence-based practice. Some of the determinants for a strong evidence-based practice are "worker and client characteristics, components of treatment, the type of context, level of intervention and relapse-prevention procedures" (p. 110). Cohen (2003) suggests that the majority of interventions that are distinguished in comparative outcome studies are based on behavioral or cognitive-behavioral theories. These theories tend to be collaborative, goal- and present-oriented, behavior-specific, symptom-directive, educational, and aimed toward the resolution of symptoms in a brief period of time.

Worker and Client Characteristics

Constantino, Castonguay, and Schut (2002) write that the patient-therapist relationship has become one of the most frequently identified—and studied—influential factors in determining the outcomes of mental health treatment. The therapeutic alliance, which reflects patient-therapist collaborative engagement in the therapy process in the context of attachment based on affiliation (Horvath & Bedi, 2002), is a consistent predictor of patient improvement across a variety of psychotherapies and clinical problems (Constantino et al., 2002). Because of this phenomenon, it is imperative that the clinical social worker understand that worker variables, as well as client perceptions, and factors such as social class, race and ethnicity, religion, age, sex, and verbal skills (Harrison, Wodarski, & Thyer, 1992; Wodarski, 1997) have been associated with the formation of the therapeutic alliance. Wodarski (2000) suggests that one practice generalization is that client-worker differences should be minimal. It is imperativ for clients to feel as though their social worker understands their situation. Data regarding group work demonstrate this contingency beautifully. Wituk, Shepeard, Slavich, Warren, and Meissen (2000) discuss the prevalence of positive group involvement and the overall opportunities of support, learning opportunities, and development of self-esteem that occur because the group members are each in various stages of healing from a particular problem. The group members trust one another because each knows where the other is coming from. Another demonstration of the importance of client-worker similarities is the settlement movement. Workers in settlement houses, which served diverse populations in their own environments, lived among the people they served. Despite language barriers, lack of resources, and discrimination, the settlement movement was a success (Harrison, Wodarski, & Thyer, 1992). These same concepts are important to understanding the client-worker relationship: Clients respond better to workers who are, overall, more like themselves, and when similarities exist there is a higher probability of the client remaining in treatment and achieving behavioral change.

Professionals versus Paraprofessionals

It is important to realize that the original "social workers" (friendly visitors) were not professionals. They were women helping other women and children. The settlement houses were not staffed by professional social workers. Very often, social helping occurs within friendships, religious organizations, and communities as well as through professional counselors, social workers, and therapists. Findings from earlier studies that evaluated services offered by professionals and paraprofessionals often showed no statistically significant differences between services offered (Durlak, 1979; Emrick, Lassen, & Edwards, 1997; Strupp & Hadley, 1978). The reason paraprofessionals fare as well as professionals is because of their similarities to their clients; that is, the paraprofessional is similar to the client in ways that he or she deems important. This phenomenon is demonstrated in a study conducted by De Jong and Emmelkamp (2000). Paraprofessionals were trained by professionals to conduct stress management workshops. The investigators concluded that there was no statistical evidence that the workshops conducted by the paraprofessionals were less successful than those conducted by the professionals. Additional findings demonstrated that the workshops conducted by the paraprofessionals showed a greater decrease in the targeted behavior. These findings, however, but were not considered relevant because there were no other statistically significant differences in training, presentation, or testing of participants. In other words, because only one part of the testing was found to have statistical significance when none of the others displayed any, the data cannot be considered relevant because of the lack of internal validity.

Worker Characteristics

Professionally trained social workers should exhibit characteristics of genuineness, warmth, empathy, and understanding, which are considered the foundation of social work practice. Although the relationship between the acquisition of these attributes and professional education remains unclear, research does demonstrate that one third of social work graduates do not possess an adequate level of these qualities (Wodarski, Feit, & Green, 1995).

A number of researchers have studied worker characteristics and their relationship to the therapeutic outcome. That social workers and other mental health care providers should possess or utilize certain characteristics has been substantiated in repeated studies (Wodarski, 2000). Demonstrated effective characteristics should provide the focus for the training of workers. Shealy (1995) describes these characteristics:

- *Fit.* The client and worker mesh well on similarity levels.
- *Acceptance/unconditional positive regard.*

- *Empathy.*
- *Encouragement of autonomy.* The worker must encourage the client's independence.
- *Responsibility.* The worker and client must both demonstrate an obligation to success.
- *Ability to relate.* The worker must demonstrate that he or she can connect with the client through understanding and awareness. This is related to the fit between client and worker.
- *Providing intervention as intended.*
- *Exploration of client expectations.* The worker should be willing to discuss and explore the client's expectations as opposed to imposing his or her personal expectations on the client.
- *Unafraid of confrontation or emotional stimulation.*
- *Directness.* The worker should be direct in speech and mannerisms.
- *Sets limits.* The worker should have the ability to set and maintain limits and boundaries.
- *Persistent advocates for client.* The worker should always be an advocate for his or her client as well as for disenfranchised persons in society.
- *Nurturing.* The worker must be nurturing and caring, but not controlling.

Treatment Components

Length of Therapy

There have been a substantial number of evidence-based studies that have had an impact on the traditional therapeutic practice. Changes resulting from these studies have been numerous and profound. One such change is related to the length of intervention. According to Cohen (2003), brief therapy now appears to be the preferred mode of intervention, and longer, time-consuming psychotherapy is reserved for private-pay clientele, except in very specific circumstances.

The shift in intervention modality has also resulted in changes in mental health care providers' expectations. Clinical social workers and other health care providers are attempting to align themselves with the goals and preferred modes of treatment of the clients' insurance providers. Austad (1996) states that mental health care providers are now embracing more focused, goal-directed, and short-term approaches in treatment delivery. This new stance is also in line with the desires of managed health care providers.

Current trends indicate that the optimal number of visits for outpatients is between 8 and 16 and the maximum number of visits is not more than 20 (Wodarski, 2000). The number of days reserved for inpatient intervention delivery is between 10 and 30. Various researchers indicate that brief interventions have a consistent outcome advantage over long-term interventions (Giles, Prial, & Neims, 1993). Others provide a rationale for the development of a short-term model of therapy. Managed health care will support payment of evidence-based interventions that are short in duration because evidence supports this modality (Wodarski, 2000).

Behavior Acquisition

Helping clients to learn new behaviors to overcome problems is a second major focus of study (Wodarski & Wodarski, 1993). It is believed that changing attitudes or motivation first will lead to behavioral change. Taylor, Peplau, and Sears (2003) argue that changing attitudes will motivate behavioral changes. This concept is also demonstrated by the paradigm of cognitive dissonance. Cognitive dissonance occurs when individuals are presented with conflicting ideas about a certain thought or behavior. They then have to either accept the thought as truth, and therefore change their own concept, or ignore the concept as truth and cling to their own false perceptions. Other evidence-based research indicates that teaching clients problem-solving skills and behaviors that equip them to influence their internal and external behaviors will increase their social functioning (Wodarski, 2000).

Behaviors are believed to be developed through structured therapeutic interventions in which intervention procedures follow a pattern to develop and maintain homeostasis within positive social contexts. The development of behaviors will occur within the intervention process through mutually agreed upon goals between worker and client, methods of carrying out the goals, and termination responsibilities of both client and worker, as well as the rights and responsibilities of both the worker and client.

Evidence-Based Approaches to Intervention

Evidence-based practice allows the social work practitioner to make practice decisions utilizing a variety of sources of scientifically supported evidence. When these data are utilized in conjunction with the skills of the worker and the client's preferences, intervention becomes more than a preference for certain models; intervention becomes a credible and logical point of behavior modification and healing (McNeece & Thyer, 2004).

Most of the progress in evidence-based practice comes from experience-derived guidelines that suggest the favorable ingredients and circumstances for successful treatment adoption efforts. According to Thyer and Wodarski (1998), the development of psychosocial treatments has been shown through scientific tests to be genuinely helpful in the treatment process. There are several factors that facilitate the transfer of knowledge and technology derived from evidence-based research, including direct personal contact and collaboration between researchers and clinicians and shared beliefs about basic principles of change and the value of combining the evidence-based treatment model with an existing service program (Backer, David, & Soucy, 1995). It is through this collaboration that research evolves into practice; that is, after research has been shown to be valid and relevant through repeated studies, it can be translated into practice models that mental health care providers can utilize for client treatment strategies.

Evidence-based treatment interventions often consist of behavioral or cognitive-behavioral approaches to solving interpersonal problems (Wodarski, 2000). However, all forms of evidence are not being equal. There is a clear hierarchy of research methods that are deemed more or less acceptable as methods for providing credible answers to research questions. The following methods are, in rough order from most to least acceptable, the best methods of evidence-based research (Kahn, Riet, Popay, Nixon, & Kleijnen, 2001; McNeece & Thyer, 2004):

- Systematic reviews/meta-analyses
- Randomized controlled trials
- Quasi-experimental studies
- Case-control and cohort studies
- Preexperimental group studies
- Single case experimental designs
- Epidemiological research
- Surveys
- Qualitative studies

It has become increasingly evident that, within the human service field, certain psychosocial interventions are effective for particular problems and not for others. Take, for example, multidimensional family therapy. This treatment has been shown to be highly successful for treating adolescent substance abuse, but has not been tested for success in treating adolescent depression. The key issue is validity and reliability of results over repeated studies. When examining evidence-based intervention strategies, it is important to examine the statistical evidence and testing criteria for each.

There are several means whereby one can view and pursue the integration of research and practice in social work. Likewise, evidence-based practice can be conceptualized and used in a variety of ways. Social workers who engage in evidence-based practice will:

- Utilize research maximally.
- Systematically monitor and collect data from the interventions they practice.
- Show evidence supporting the level of effectiveness of interventions.
- Be specific and concrete when discussing problems, interventions, and outcomes.
- Use research methods when defining problems, formulating questions for practice, assessing data, and evaluating effectiveness of interventions.
- View research and practice as equal parts of the problem-solving process.

In sum, the social worker utilizes research as a tool for practice while ensuring that the tool accomplishes the job that it is intended to do.

Evidence-Based Approaches to Treatment

Adults and children treated through mental health centers, psychiatric hospitals, public welfare agencies, hospitals, and other treatment contexts are reaping the benefits of data from studies of evidence-based interventions. Evidence-based studies continue to provide a multitude of opportunities to utilize knowledge for the betterment of society as a whole. All life stages, from infancy through the later years, can benefit from interventions directed at assisting clients in developing coping skills and special skills for specific situations, as well as helping clients develop and maintain healthy behaviors that will carry them throughout the remainder of their lives.

For example, children of birth parents and foster parents can be helped when parents are taught to manage child behaviors through appropriate behavioral management skills and coping techniques supported by evidence, such as contingency contracts, stimulus control, and time-out procedures to help with the development of social skills children need for effective adult functioning (Wodarski, 2000). In the family context, help is often needed in the development of positive interactional skills, communication skills, effective problem solving, and goal-setting skills.

School-age children benefit academically through the utilization of evidence-based research. Certain techniques have been demonstrated to be significant for teaching children to learn to read, write, and do arithmetic. Techniques used for reducing delinquent behavior and absenteeism have been instated by school administrative bodies. Likewise, techniques to help children with interpersonal skills training have been instituted and have achieved positive results in school systems across the country (Wodarski, 2000).

In the juvenile court system, evidence-based interventions are helping to reduce deviant behaviors and increase pro-social behaviors. This is accomplished through the use of contracting and teaching significant adults to provide positive reinforcement for desired behaviors as well as providing programs that train children in those behavioral skills that will allow them to experience satisfaction and gain desired reinforcements through socially acceptable means (Wodarski & Wodarski, 1993).

In relation to adult behavioral deficiencies, interventions developed within a cognitive-behavioral paradigm have proven effective in increasing the probability of behavioral change and in the maintenance of change.

Implementation of Change Strategy: Level of Intervention

Historically, social work has emphasized the one-on-one relationship with clients to accomplish needed change (Wodarski, 2000). With the ever-increasing role of managed care in the profession, this individual practice technique is being challenged in regard to the best and most cost-effective method of treatment (Cohen, 2003). Individual, or solo, private practice may be in jeopardy due to the increasing pressure from managed care companies to switch from individual to group practice (Cohen, 2003). The main challenge to individual treatment comes from the conclusion of numerous research studies indicating that group and individual interventions are equivalent in their effectiveness (Kivlighan & Kivlighan, 2004). Because group therapy is less expensive and more time-efficient than individual practice, managed care companies are urging and sometimes mandating that professionals adopt group therapy.

Numerous other advantages have been attributed to group as compared to individual therapy. In groups, clients can test and observe behaviors in a realistic yet safe environment while receiving immediate feedback from others (Wodarski, 2000). Also, many role models are available in the group setting, providing a more powerful means for changing behaviors in clients (Wodarski, 2000).

Although it has been proven that group and individual therapy provide relatively similar outcome results, there is a need for research to demonstrate whether these treatments reach outcomes through similar or different processes (Kivlighan & Kivlighan, 2004). Some of the differences being questioned are therapeutic factors, therapist approach and style, and the cognitive activity of the therapist (Kivlighan & Kivlighan, 2004). More research is needed to determine the impact of these characteristics on outcome measures and to what degree these processes take place in individual and group therapy. Also, more research is needed to determine what populations and problems are most benefited by the two types of treatment (Wodarski, 2000).

Macrolevel Intervention

Evidence-based research pertains not only to individual and group therapies, but is increasingly expanding to involve the scientific measure of effectiveness for macro and community practice. Although relatively new and requiring a tremendous amount of research yet to be done, preliminary research evidence underscores the importance of *multilevel interventions* (Glasgow & Vogt, 1999; Wodarski, 2000). The environment exerts a huge influence on individuals, and persons living in an environment that reinforces negative behaviors will have difficulty changing those behaviors and maintaining positive ones (Wodarski, 2000). Effecting positive change will require the social worker to promote institutional, policy, and community interventions (Wodarski, 2000). Also, it requires the evaluation of the various types of multilevel interventions to determine which type is most beneficial for different populations and issues (Glasgow & Vogt, 1999).

Glasgow and Vogt (1999) state that progress in the areas of public health and community practice have been hurt by the lack of a well-designed evaluation of these programs and their effectiveness. They conclude, "Multilevel interventions that incorporate policy, environmental, and individual components should be evaluated with measurements suited to their settings, goals, and purpose" (p. 1322). In general, macropractice is less concerned than is clinical practice with the role of scientific and research knowledge, but with the social work push toward evidence-based practice this is destined to change (McNeece & Thyer, 2004).

Relapse Prevention

Relapse prevention and maintenance of behavior are becoming increasingly important, due mainly to the large amount of research showing that relapse is frequent and behaviors are difficult to maintain (Wodarski, 2000). An example of nonmaintenance in behavior is supported in a 5-year follow-up study done on antisocial children who had participated in a year-long behavior modification program (Wodarski, 2000). The results indicated that very few of the positive changes that occurred during the program had been maintained in the individuals (Wodarski, 2000). Relapse prevention is defined by Witkiewitz and Marlatt (2004, p. 224) as "a cognitive-behavioral approach with the goal of identifying and preventing high-risk situations for relapse." Witkiewitz and Marlatt also state that it is very common for a person attempting to change a behavior to experience lapses, which often lead to relapse or an inability to maintain a behavior. For a relapse prevention program to be successful, clinicians need to be aware that its maintenance is a complicated and dynamic process (Witkiewitz & Marlatt, 2004). The focus of change should not be limited to the individual, but should include many aspects of life. Clinicians must be able to gather information through an in-depth assessment that covers the individual's background, self-efficacy, coping strategies, and personality (Witkiewitz & Marlatt, 2004). Information should be assessed about the individual's social and emotional support because it has been empirically supported that low levels of external support are predictive of relapse episodes (Witkiewitz & Marlatt, 2004). This supports Wodarski's (2000) claim that maintenance of behaviors can be improved if change is focused on macrolevels as well as on the individual.

An example of a successful relapse prevention program that encompasses change in many areas of life comes from an interdisciplinary substance abuse program with prison inmates (Tayar, 2004). The inmates were taught coping and social skills, assertive communication, identified values, interests, and strengths, and social support development (Tayar, 2004). More scientific research is needed on the specific outcome measures of this program, but all participants involved reported satisfaction and personal growth from this relapse prevention method (Tayar, 2004).

Research is still needed on relapse and relapse prevention in social work. Two suggestions for future research are the refinement of measurement devices for individuals and the development of clearer data strategies for measuring behavioral change and outcome measures (Witkiewitz & Marlatt, 2004). The more social workers know about relapse prevention, the better prepared they will be to help individuals deal with this common and multifaceted issue.

Analysis of Social Work Practice: Economic Perspective

Cost Analysis

Funding will always be of concern to the social work and mental health fields. Due to managed care, cost analysis of programs and treatments is gaining importance and is increasingly mandated for maintaining funding for services (Cohen, 2003). A top priority of managed care is to provide the best quality care at a lower cost than a fee-for-service option (Cohen, 2003). One way to achieve this is by finding the most cost-saving and time-efficient methods of treatment by monitoring and evaluating services (Cohen, 2003). Programs and practitioners increasingly are required to provide performance indicators and outcome measurements that help provide clear descriptions of treatments, identify most successful treatments, and enhance the credibility of practitioners (Cohen, 2003). Not only does program evaluation help third-party payers, but it is helpful for clients as it allows them to have concrete evidence of the effectiveness of the treatment provided (Cohen, 2003). Cost analysis in program evaluation provides a scientific, empirically based way to establish accountability, which is a major theme in the mental health field (Cohen, 2003). Accountability is defined in two ways; the need for social workers to be able to prove that what they provide for clients is effective and that the methods used for achieving these goals are accomplished through the most cost-effective means possible (Wodarski, 2000). Only through the accountability provided by testing various methods of treatment can changes be made to programs and treatments in a cost-effective manner (Wodarski, 2000).

Cost Benefits

Cost-benefit analysis is a common method, originally used in the economic and business fields, to make decisions regarding which programs need modification or termination (Wodarski, 2000). It provides a means for identifying program outcomes and costs and comparing which produces the greatest, most cost-efficient results (Wodarski, 2000). The main purpose is to establish funding priorities (Wodarski, 2000). An important empirically supported cost-benefit analysis finding is that clinical social workers provide results in nonmedical practice equivalent to clinical psychologists and psychiatrists (Cohen, 2003). Moreover, clinical social workers are a less expensive source of service compared to psychologists or psychiatrists, and therefore are often deemed more cost-efficient (Cohen, 2003). Many managed care organizations are seeing clinical social workers as the better choice for service providers and are hiring more of them due to this empirically supported data (Cohen, 2003). In the simplest terms, the cost for managed care companies is less when hiring clinical social workers, while the benefit is the same for the clients.

Cost Effectiveness

Cost effectiveness is another aspect of project evaluation. This approach does not focus on establishing program priorities, but instead aims to develop and implement the most beneficial program alternatives to meet already identified goals (Wodarski, 2000). Outcomes are not measured solely in dollars, but also according to other nontangible benefits, such as recidivism rates or number of elderly persons remaining in their homes (Wodarski, 2000). Prevention initiatives are an example of programs that are gaining cost-effective validity and popularity. While the high cost of therapeutic and rehabilitative services is becoming a national concern among citizens and public officials, prevention programs have been scientifically supported as especially successful in reducing negative behavior acquisition, especially among youth facing such problems as teen pregnancy, substance abuse, and youth violence (Nation et al., 2003). Prevention programs can be extremely useful if designed and implemented carefully, but to maximize effectiveness and to help ensure maintenance of desired behaviors in the participants, the environment of the participants must be included and manipulated (Nation et al., 2003). This further supports the need for multilevel interventions and macrolevel involvement to advocate for policy and community change. The January 2006 issue of the journal *Research on Social Work Practice* is devoted entirely to the topic of cost-benefit analyses in social work and is an especially valuable resource for learning more about this important topic.

Evaluation Summary

Program evaluation encompasses many aspects of practice, including cost analysis, cost benefits, and cost effectiveness. Efforts in program evaluation must look beyond individual outcome measures and personal satisfaction ratings to include an overall evaluation of a specific program or of the entire agency, without which administrators will find it difficult to rationalize treatments, programs, and services (Wodarski, 2000). Program evaluation is also beneficial to the clients receiving services. If an agency is constantly monitoring services and outcomes and making appropriate changes where they are needed, the client will be receiving the most up-to-date, empirically supported treatments that will provide for improved outcome measures (Huffman et al., 2002). Huffman et al. state, "A successful evaluation process is relevant to the needs of the user and yields results that can be used to improve the assessed activities and practices" (p. 194).

Profiling the Clinical Social Worker

Social workers must be able to access and understand the available empirically based research. They must possess the scientific knowledge and conceptual understanding of human behavior and how it relates to the research (Wodarski, 2000). Further, unless they possess the ability to take the acquired knowledge and apply it to individual or macrolevel practice, the research findings are useless. A helpful tool available to practitioners interested in acquiring information regarding evidence-based interventions is the Cochrane Electronic Library (Gibbs & Gambrill, 2002). The Cochrane and Campbell Collaborations are international efforts involving researchers and practitioners who endeavor to prepare, maintain, and promote the accessibility of systematic reviews (see www.cochrane.org and www.campbell.org). Such technological advances have made the availability and accessibility of evidence-based research findings easier for anyone interested in learning about the latest data in the helping professions.

The mental health field is experiencing dramatic changes due to the influence of managed care and evidence-based practice. The president of the American Psychological Association has urged all practitioners to join in the effort to embrace and participate in the evidence-based practice initiative (Levant, 2005). Levant further states that the challenge of defining evidence-based practice will not go away if practitioners do not participate; instead, others outside the field, such as lawyers and insurance companies, will define it for us. It is the clients that will suffer the most if we as professionals do not take on the challenge and responsibility of evidence-based practice.

Study Questions

1. How has managed care influenced contemporary social work practice?
2. What have some studies shown regarding the equivalence of care from professionals and paraprofessionals? Why to you think this finding occurs?

3. Locate the Strupp and Hadley (1978) study cited in this chapter. Summarize what they did and what they found. What implications does this have for the necessity of advanced graduate-level training in traditional psychotherapy?

4. Describe two worker characteristics that have been shown to positively affect the outcomes of therapy.

5. What is relapse prevention and why is it an important aspect of care?

6. How can cost-effectiveness and cost-benefit studies contribute to evidence-based social work practice?

References

Austad, C. (1996). Can psychotherapy be conducted effectively in managed care settings? In A. Lazarus (Ed.), *Controversies in managed mental health care* (pp. 229–254). Washington, DC: American Psychiatric Press.

Backer, T., David, S., & Soucy, G. (Eds.). (1995). *Reviewing the behavioral science knowledge base on technology transfer* (NIDA Research Monograph 155, pp. 1–10). Rockville, MD: U.S. Department of Health and Human Services, Public Health Service, National Institute of Health.

Cohen, J. (2003). Managed care and the evolving role of the clinical social worker in mental health. *Social Work, 48,* 34–43.

Constantino, M. J., Castonguay, L. G., & Schut, A. J. (2002). The working alliance: A flagship for the scientist-practitioner model in psychotherapy. In G. S. Tryon (Ed.), *Counseling based on process research: Applying what we know* (pp. 81–131). Boston: Allyn & Bacon.

Cummings, N. (1995). Impact of managed care on employment and training: A primer for survival. *Professional Psychology: Research and Practice, 26,* 10–15.

Davis, M. (2005). HMO stocks are on shaky ground [Electronic version]. *The Street.* Retrieved March 10, 2005, from www.thestreet.com/pf/stocks/melissadavid/10207291.html.

DeAngelis, T. (2005). Shaping evidence-based practice. *Monitor on Psychology,* 26–31.

de Jong, G., & Emmelkamp, P. (2000). Implementing a stress management training:

Comparative trainer effectiveness. *Journal of Occupational Health Psychology, 5,* 309–320.

Durlak, J. A. (1979). Comparative effectiveness of paraprofessional helpers. *Psychological Bulletin, 86,* 86–92.

Emrick, C. D., Lassen, C. L., & Edwards, M. T. (1977). Nonprofessional peers as therapeutic agents. In A. S. Gurman & A. M. Razin (Eds.), *Effective psychotherapy* (pp. 120–161). New York: Pegman Press.

Gibbs, L., & Gambrill, E. (2002). Evidence-based practice: Counterarguments to objections. *Research on Social Work Practice, 12,* 452–476.

Giles, T. R., Prial, E. M., & Neims, D. M. (1993). Evaluating psychotherapies: A comparison of effectiveness (Special series: Evaluation in treatment methods in psychiatry: 3). *International Journal of Mental Health, 22,* 43–65.

Glasgow, R. E., & Vogt, M. T. (1999). Evaluating the public health impact of health promotion interventions: The re-aim framework. *American Journal of Public Health, 89,* 1322–1328.

Gray, G., & Gray, L. (2002). Evidence-based medicine: Applications in dietetic applications. *Journal of the Dietetic Association, 9,* 1263–1272.

Harrison, D., Wodarski, J., & Thyer, B. (1992). *Cultural diversity in social work practice.* Springfield, IL: Charles Thomas.

Horvath, A. O., & Bedi, R. P. (2002). The alliance. In J. C. Norcross (Ed.), *Psychotherapy relationships that work: Therapists' contributions and responsiveness to patients* (pp. 37–69). New York: Oxford University Press.

Huffman, L., Koopman, C., Blasey, C., Botcheva, L., Hill, E. K., Marks, A., et al. (2002). A program evaluation strategy in a community-based behavioral health and education services agency for children and families. *Journal of Applied Behavioral Science, 38,* 191–215.

Institute of Medicine. (2005). *Crossing the quality chasm: A new health system for the 21st century.* Retrieved April 10, 2005, from http://www.iom.edu/report.asp?id=5432.

Kahn, K., Riet, G., Popay, J., Nixon, J., & Kleijnen, J. (2001, March). Study quality assessment. In K. Kahn, G. Riet, J. Glanoille, A. Sowden, & J. Kleijnen (Eds.), *Undertaking systematic reviews of research on effectiveness: CRD's guidance for those carrying out or commissioning reviews* (CRD Report No. 4, 2nd ed., Sec. 2.5, pp. 1–20). York, England: University of York.

Kivlighan, M. D., & Kivlighan, C. M. (2004). Counselor intentions in individual and group therapy. *American Psychological Association, 51,* 347–353.

Levant, R. (2005). Evidence based practice in psychology. *Monitor on Psychology.* Retrieved April 2005, from http://www.apa.org/monitor/feb05/pc.html.

McNeece, C., & Thyer, B. (2004). Evidence based practice in social work. *Journal of Evidence-Based Social Work, 1,* 7–23.

Nation, M., Crusto, C., Wandersman, A., Kumpfer, K. L., Seybolt, D., Morrissey-Kane, E., et al. (2003). What works in prevention. *American Psychologist, 58,* 449–456.

Shapiro, J. (1995). The downside of managed mental health care. *Clinical Social Work Journal, 23,* 441–451.

Shealy, C. (1995). From Boys Town to Oliver Twist: Separating fact from fiction in welfare placement of children and youth. *American Psychologist, 50,* 565–580.

Strosahl, K. (1994). Entering the new frontier of managed mental health care: Gold mines and land mines. *Cognitive and Behavioral Practice, 1,* 5–23.

Strosahl, K. (1995). Behavior therapy 2000: A perilous journey. *Behavior Therapist, 18,* 130–133.

Strupp, H. H., & Hadley, S. W. (1978). Specific versus nonspecific factors in psychotherapy: A controlled study of outcome. *Archives of General Psychiatry, 36,* 1125–1136.

Tayar, G. S. (2004). Description of a substance abuse relapse prevention program conducted by occupational therapy and psychology graduate students in a U.S. women's prison. *British Journal of Occupational Therapy, 67,* 159–166.

Taylor, E., Peplau, L., & Sears, D. (2003). *Social psychology* (11th ed.). Trenton, NJ: Prentice-Hall.

Thyer, B., & Wodarski, J. (1998). First principles of empirical research practice. In B. Thyer & J. Wodarski (Eds.), *Handbook of empirical social work practice: Vol. 1. Mental disorders* (pp. 1–21). Hoboken, NJ: Wiley.

Witkiewitz, K., & Marlatt, G. A. (2004). Relapse prevention for alcohol and drug problems. *American Psychologist, 59,* 224–235.

Wituk, S., Shepherd, M., Slavich, S., Warren, M., & Meissen, G. (2000). Topography of self-help groups: An empirical analysis. *Social Work, 45,* 157–164.

Wodarski, J. (1997). Procedures for the maintenance and generalization of achieved behavioral change. *Journal of Sociology and Social Welfare, 7,* 298–311.

Wodarski, J. (2000). The role for social workers in the managed health care system: A model for empirically based psycho-social intervention. *Crisis Intervention, 6,* 109–139.

Wodarski, J., Feit, M., & Green, R. (1995). Graduate social work education: A review of two decades of empirical research and considerations for the future. *Social Service Review, 69,* 108–130.

Wodarski, J., & Wodarski, L. (1993). *Curriculum and practical aspects of implementation: Preventive health services for adolescents.* Lanham, MD: University Press of America.

Author Index

Aarons, G. A., 100
Aasland, O. G., 164
Abbeduto, L., 46
Abbott, A., 235
Abbott, P. J., 242
Abbott, R., 127
Abby, S. L., 98
Abdel-Hamid, I. A., 447
Abelson, J., 391
Aben, I., 315
Abikoff, H., 100, 120
Abolt, T., 120
Abramowitz, J. S., 382, 384, 388
Abramowitz, S. I., 504
Abrams, D. A., 170
Abrams, D. B., 166, 214
Achenbach, T., 80, 102, 103, 120
Acierno, R., 194
Ackerman, D., 390
Adamek, M., 370
Adams, C., 43, 505, 510
Adams, P., 64
Addis, M. E., 345
Adler, D. A., 310
Agarwal, A., 408, 409
Agras, W. S., 465, 470, 473, 474, 475
Agrawal, S., 174
Ahearn, W. H., 60
Ahmed, N., 315
Akerele, E., 194
Akiskal, H. S., 312, 323
Akmal, M., 139, 140
Akyuz, G., 487
Albano, A. M., 388
Aldor, R., 110
Alessi, J., 214
Alessi, N., 315
Alexander, B., 406, 408
Alexander, D., 188, 190, 191
Alexander, J., 125
Alexopoulos, G. S., 298
Allen, J. P., 161, 163, 166, 167
Allen, R. L., 108
Allmon, D., 511, 516
Altamura, A. C., 294
Alterman, A., 205, 211, 212, 217, 234
Althof, S., 429, 434, 435
Amador, X. F., 253
Aman, K., 122
Aman, M. G., 63

Amass, L., 242
Amering, M., 355
Ammerman, R. T., 18
Amundsen, A., 170
Anastasiades, P., 343
Anders, T. F., 55
Andersen, J., 257
Anderson, B. L., 409, 432, 442, 444, 446
Anderson, D. A., 467
Anderson, G. M., 390
Anderson, J. E., 139, 140
Anderson, L. T., 64
Anderson, R. L., 312
Anderson, S. R., 62
Anderson-Butcher, D., 44
Andersson, G., 345
Andreasen, N. C., 254, 255, 258
Andrews, B. P., 485, 489, 490
Andrews, D. W., 105
Andrews, G., 388
Andrews, J. A., 295
Angold, A., 99, 100, 118, 119
Angst, J., 309
Angus, J. W. S., 262
Anker, A., 213
Annis, H. M., 162, 165, 170, 212, 492
Ansberry, C., 36
Ansello, E. F., 47
Anthenelli, R. M., 492
Anthony, A., 55
Anthony, J. C., 202
Anthony, V. L., 491, 495
Anthony, W. A., 272, 278
Anton, R. F., 166, 169
Antonuccio, D., 299
Antony, M. M., 335, 355, 356, 360, 363, 364, 365, 367, 368, 383
Apfelbaum, B., 441
Appel, P. W., 208
Applegate, B., 104, 118
Apt, C., 447
Araoz, D. L., 420
Araya, H., 415, 431
Arbiter, E. A., 139
Arbuthnot, J., 125
Areán, P., 296, 297, 298, 300
Arend, R., 117
Arkava, M. I., 2
Armano, V. L., 65
Armstrong, H. E., 511, 516

545